ALSO BY DAVID E. SANGER

The Inheritance

Confront and Conceal

The Perfect Weapon

NEW COLD WARS

NEW COLD WARS

CHINA'S RISE, RUSSIA'S INVASION, AND AMERICA'S STRUGGLE TO DEFEND THE WEST

DAVID E. SANGER

WITH MARY K. BROOKS

CROWN
NEW YORK

Copyright © 2024 by David E. Sanger

Published in the United States by Crown, an imprint of the Crown Publishing Group,
a division of Penguin Random House LLC, New York.

CROWN and the Crown colophon are registered trademarks of
Penguin Random House LLC.

Library of Congress Cataloging-in-Publication Data

Names: Sanger, David E., author. | Brooks, Mary K., author.
Title: New cold wars: China's rise, Russia's invasion, and America's struggle to defend the
West / David E. Sanger, with Mary K. Brooks.
Description: First edition. | New York: Crown, [2024] | Includes bibliographical
references and index.
Identifiers: LCCN 2023056051 (print) | LCCN 2023056052 (ebook) |
ISBN 9780593443590 (hardback: acid-free paper) | ISBN 9780593443606 (ebook)
Subjects: LCSH: Putin, Vladimir Vladimirovich, 1952– | Strategic rivalries (World
politics) | Cold War. | Xi, Jinping. | China—Foreign relations—United States—21st
century. | United States—Foreign relations—China—21st century. | Russia
(Federation)—Politics and government—1991– | Russian Invasion of Ukraine, 2022. |
Russia (Federation)—Foreign relations—United States. | United States—Foreign
relations—Russia (Federation)
Classification: LCC JZ5595 .S336 2024 (print) | LCC JZ5595 (ebook) |
DDC 320.9—dc23/eng/20240118
LC record available at lccn.loc.gov/2023056051
LC ebook record available at lccn.loc.gov/2023056052

Printed in the United States of America on acid-free paper

crownpublishing.com

2 4 6 8 9 7 5 3 1

First Edition

Editor: Kevin Doughten | Associate editor: Amy Li | Production editor: Evan Camfield |
Production manager: Richard Elman | Managing editors: Allison Fox and Sally Franklin |
Copyeditor: Martin Schneider | Proofreaders: Melissa Churchill, Jill Falzoi, Jolanta
Benal | Indexer: Ina Gravitz | Publicist: Stacey Stein | Marketer: Kimberly Lew

For Sherill,
who brings love and wisdom to every journey in our lives together,
and in memory of
Joan, Ken, and Ellin

XI JINPING: "There are changes happening, the likes of which we haven't seen for 100 years. Let's drive those changes together."

VLADIMIR PUTIN: "I agree."

—At the Kremlin, March 22, 2023

CONTENTS

NEW COLD WARS

THE MOTHER LODE

The great democracies triumphed, and so were able to resume the follies which had so nearly cost them their life.

Winston Churchill, *Triumph and Tragedy* (1953)

THE RUSSIANS WERE getting ready to roll.

That was the stark warning contained in a top-secret set of briefings circulating among a tight group of White House, Pentagon, State Department, and intelligence officials in the third week of October 2021. Its contents were shocking, but not a surprise to anyone who had listened carefully over the previous summer, when Russian president Vladimir V. Putin argued that Ukraine was not an independent nation, but rather an integral part of the old Russian empire. Seven years after he had annexed the Crimean Peninsula and launched a low-level war in Ukraine's south and east, Putin, along with his closest aides, was fine-tuning a plan to seize the entire country.

This was the kind of naked aggression, from a nuclear-armed power, that wasn't supposed to happen three decades after the collapse of the Soviet Union. When he was first presented with the evidence, President Joe Biden told one of his aides that it beggared belief, even for Putin. Yet the intelligence report was comprehensive: a massive compilation of electronic intercepts, skillful cyber penetration of Russia's networks, and reports from a small number of informants nurtured along by the CIA, who, after a long drought, had once again tapped into the upper reaches of the Kremlin. It was, as one key administration official described the analysis to me, the "mother lode" of intelligence on Putin's planning.

Barely four months earlier, Putin had sat opposite Biden in a mansion on the shore of Lake Geneva in a tense diplomatic session that was primarily about halting Russian ransomware attacks on American pipelines, hospitals, and other critical infrastructure. Ukraine had been discussed, Biden and Putin both said after the session, albeit briefly. When Biden raised the topic, Putin complained anew that the Ukrainians were failing to obey the terms of an accord that had been negotiated, with the help of the West, after Crimea. That agreement did nothing to end the slow, grinding conflict that was playing out in the Donbas region. But Putin gave no indication that his patience had run out or that he was preparing a far larger attack.

Some aides were left wondering whether Putin had used the meeting to take the measure of Biden's mindset and concluded that the new president was so focused on other issues—America's domestic political struggles, made so vivid on January 6 of that year; competing with China; the imminent withdrawal from Afghanistan—that he had no bandwidth for engaging in another foreign conflict. Biden, he may well have concluded, had no stomach for mounting a serious, costly effort to stop Russia from taking what Putin believed, to his core, was rightfully Russia's territory.

"He emerged from COVID thinking he was Peter the Great," one of Biden's top advisors later told me. And like Tsar Peter, Putin planned to restore Russia to its former glory.

As the "mother lode" was passed around the White House Situation Room, Biden and his aides debated whether they should confront Putin directly. Clearly, Putin had the intent to invade. Among those deep in the details of the intelligence was Jake Sullivan, the Minnesota wunderkind whose meteoric rise to national prominence began during the 2008 elections, when he advised Hillary Rodham Clinton in the primaries and then Barack Obama in the general. At forty-two, he had emerged as Biden's last-minute choice for national security advisor. "I didn't believe this was an absolutely hopeless situation," Sullivan recalled later, walking me through his feelings when he first saw the evidence. He remembered thinking, "Okay, this is the plan now. Can we try to design some strategy, knocking them off the plan?"

Ordinarily, it would be too great a risk to confront the Russians with evidence that U.S. officials were so plugged into their top leadership that the White House knew what Putin was planning. It might tip off Putin to the traitor—or traitors—in his midst or to the electronic and cyber intercepts that were diverting Russian military plans straight to American intelligence agencies. But there were so many sources in the mother lode—signals intelligence, satellite images, the handful of human spies with access to Moscow's leadership—that it would be difficult for the Russians to identify any single breach.

So Biden decided to send an emissary, armed with a letter from the American president, to warn the Russian leader of the danger he faced if he tried to topple Volodymyr Zelensky's government and occupy the country. Several candidates for the job were discussed, but only one made sense: William J. "Bill" Burns, the former career diplomat, tapped by Biden to run the CIA. Burns was a natural for the task: He had served as the American ambassador to Russia in the heady days when Putin was taking power and Russia seemed neutered. Among Biden's inner circle, Burns knew Putin best. ("That's where I got most of my white hair, I think," he liked to quip.) And Biden, a president who values old relationships above all else, trusted Burns deeply.

Burns's objective was clear: Engage Putin in a conversation, tell him that the United States knew exactly what he was planning, and try to slow or derail his final decision. It was the kind of frank discussion that always went over better in a face-to-face conversation. But it wasn't until Burns landed in Moscow aboard an unmarked CIA plane, the letter securely in his portfolio, that he learned that the Russian leader—famously reclusive since the COVID pandemic had begun, a year and a half earlier—was in isolation in his Sochi dacha. The Russians offered Burns a phone call with the president, something Burns could have done from his office back in Langley. He agreed to conveying his message by phone. He hadn't come all this way to miss the chance to speak with Putin directly.

So over a secure line in a Soviet-era government office in Moscow, Burns laid out his case to Putin that an invasion would be a horrific mistake, one that would cost Putin, and Russia, dearly. The Russian leader offered little reaction, as usual. If he was upset, or surprised, that the United States was onto his plans, he showed no sign. Nor did he alter his plan. Putin, Burns told me later, felt "almost an entitlement to control Ukraine, and control Ukraine's choices as well."

By December 2021, American spy satellites had begun to detect Russian forces moving into place, exactly along the lines the intelligence had warned. A few short weeks later, you didn't need a billion-dollar spy satellite to realize what was happening. Daily images pouring in from Maxar and Planet Labs and other commercial satellite firms all told the same story: Rows of Russian tanks were massing less than a hundred miles from Kyiv, just inside Belarus, a nation run by one of Putin's most loyal lackeys. Estimates suggested that some 60 percent of Russia's land-based fighting forces were already deployed along Ukraine's borders, some massing in attack formations. Medical units were spotted carrying blood for transfusions—something almost never seen when troops are conducting routine exercises. Eager to complicate Putin's preparations, the administration released a bit of the evidence every few days or quietly guided reporters to commercial satellite photos or social media posts that captured, often in more granular detail, actions that had the United States' early-warning systems sounding the alarm.

By February 2022, there was no doubt in the minds of America's top national security officials that Putin was preparing to redraw the borders of Europe by force. From the intelligence they were viewing, it would happen something like this:

First, a mad dash from the north down to Kyiv, in the hopes of taking over the capital city and capturing or killing Zelensky within the first few days of action.

Then an amphibious landing in Odessa, the critical port where so much of Ukraine's grain and other goods are shipped across the Black Sea to feed much of the world. Russian forces would then take over the coast, cutting off Ukraine's access to the sea and linking the Crimean Peninsula overland to Russian territory.

And to finish the country off, a Russian drive across the industrial east and south—where Russian and Ukrainian forces had conducted a low-level war since 2014, when Putin seized the Crimean Peninsula and held a sham referendum to declare it a Russian province once again—and then a sweep back to the west.

If anything still remained of the old Ukrainian government, Biden was told, it would operate only in exile, as a rump state retreating west toward the Carpathian Mountains. Quietly, the United States had already outfitted Zelensky with secure communications equipment so that he could keep talking with Biden over systems that would complicate Russia's effort to track him down and kill him.

But in the best traditions of the worst days of the old Cold War, the Russians declared this series of American-orchestrated leaks to be fake news. When General Mark Milley, the gruff, Princeton-educated chairman of the Joint Chiefs of Staff, called his Russian counterpart, Valery Gerasimov, he got a straight-up denial that invasion was imminent. It's just military exercises, Gerasimov told Milley. "I don't bitch you out when you line up troops and do exercises on the Mexican border," Milley later recalled Gerasimov telling him, in essence. Milley pushed back: "Well, we don't put *150,000* troops on the Mexican border."

Meanwhile, Antony J. Blinken, Biden's secretary of state and his closest confidant on global issues, conducted a similarly dead-end conversation with the infuriating Sergey Lavrov, the longtime Russian foreign minister. Lavrov was in high dudgeon about the American warnings of an imminent invasion: It was all Western disinformation, he insisted, the latest effort to spur what he called "Russophobia."

Blinken, who had served as Biden's chief national security advisor when Biden was a senator and again when he was vice president, suspected that Lavrov was out of the loop—that if Putin was planning a war, he wouldn't bother to tell his own foreign minister. But it was such a bizarre performance that, at a session in Geneva, Blinken pulled aside the Russian diplomat to ask him—quietly, out of the earshot of reporters—why he was denying what was clear to anyone with eyes. Did he even believe what he was saying? Lavrov—who began his diplomatic career when Blinken was still a teenager living in Paris—stared at him, then turned and walked away.

FOR THEIR PART, the Europeans were in denial, too, unable to imagine that part of their continent could soon be in flames, with Ukrainian populations massing in the subway stations to avoid bombardment. In mid-February, Western leaders gathered in Germany for the Munich Security Conference, the annual event of the Atlantic establishment that had gained a reputation as the meeting place of Western world leaders, diplomats, and CEOs. The meeting was often a bellwether for trans-atlantic anxieties, and when I arrived the night before the conference opened, it was clear that stress levels were sky-high.

Still, European foreign and defense ministers adamantly insisted to me that an invasion would not happen. Putin was putting on a show to scare the world, I was told. He wouldn't be so stupid as to threaten his own economic interests, most significantly, the imminent opening of the Nord Stream 2 pipeline that would pump gas directly from Russia to Western Europe, routing around Ukraine. Putin's goal, one German leader told me, was to make the continent more dependent on Russian gas—and on his whims—than ever. He wouldn't threaten that plan to settle old scores.

When I caught up with Blinken over breakfast toward the end of the conference, the rationalizations were clearly driving him crazy. "This is going to happen," he told me of the invasion. "I can't give you an exact day, but it is just days away." Yet no matter how many satellite photographs he laid on the table for his counterparts, he said, many of Europe's leaders saw only what they wanted to see.

The Ukrainians appeared to be in denial, too. When Zelensky arrived in Munich—just for a few hours, and in a plane leased by the Pentagon, which the Biden administration was betting the Russians would not shoot down—he insisted in public that he didn't believe an invasion was imminent. But there were indications he didn't believe his own message.

At the security conference that Saturday afternoon, Zelensky took the stage to press his case, as people stuffed into the crowded auditorium to hear the Ukrainian leader, wondering if it was the last time they would see him alive. They were struck by his anger.

"What are you waiting for?" he demanded, urging the leaders there to act immediately rather than wait to see if Putin would really pull the trigger. "We don't need your sanctions" after the Ukrainian economy has collapsed, he said, and after "part of our country will be occupied." But perhaps because he was in Munich—a city synonymous with Neville Chamberlain's failed effort to appease Hitler more than eighty years before—Zelensky also warned his "partners and friends to not agree about anything behind our back" with Putin.

"We're not panicking," Zelensky insisted, before heading back to Kyiv, on an indirect route that avoided sending him over Russian airspace.

It didn't sound that way.

JUST TWO WEEKS before the Munich conference Putin had emerged from isolation for what became his biggest gamble yet. He flew to the site of the Winter Olympics in Beijing, ostensibly to take in the opening ceremony. His real purpose, however: to make a show of his relationship with China's president, Xi Jinping.

For years, Putin had courted Xi, and vice versa. While both leaders were reclusive during the pandemic, they kept talking to each other, and each, in his own way, cemented his authority and became vocally more nationalistic. Now Putin needed Xi to demonstrate to the world that he and his fellow autocrat could combine their power and influence. For all their differences—and there were many—they had one common purpose: to stand up to the United States, frustrate its ambitions, and speed along what they viewed as its inevitable decline.

It was a remarkable pre-Olympics show. As the athletes prepared to compete, Putin and Xi signed a lengthy statement attesting a common interest in opposing the West's attempts at global influence, vowing there would be "no limits" to their partnership, and calling on all countries to have respect for the sovereignty and territorial integrity of other states. It wasn't exactly an alliance. But it was almost exactly the kind of arrangement Henry Kissinger had tried to head off in the 1970s, when he urged President Richard Nixon to initiate diplomatic discussions with China in an effort to avoid opening a second front in the Cold War.

Of course, in the 1970s, China was an agrarian nation, a tiny player in economic terms, a nonplayer in global technologies still shattered by the traumas of the Cultural Revolution. The Soviet Union was the senior partner whenever they crossed paths. Now the balance was reversed: China was the leading power and Russia the dependent one.

There is some dispute about exactly what Putin said to Xi about his plans for Ukraine. Some U.S. national security and intelligence officials believe Putin simply assured Xi there would be no invasion during the

Olympics, which would distract from China's big moment on the world stage. Senior U.S. intelligence officials later concluded that Putin described to Xi plans for a limited military operation—one that might take some eastern regions but would be quick and easy.

If so, Putin lied. Except for the part about waiting for the Olympics to end.

FOR THOSE IN MUNICH, the forces massing to invade Europe carried echoes of 1938. But some five thousand miles away, at the Microsoft headquarters in Redmond, Washington, the warning signs looked more like June 2017.

That was the month, just five years before, when Russian hackers targeted the Ukrainian economy with an innovative cyberattack awkwardly called "NotPetya." The fallout was devastating: The attack crippled small businesses and large, making it all but impossible for them to conduct simple credit card sales in stores. Worse, the malware spread quickly beyond Ukraine's borders and flattened Western firms in the region like FedEx and Maersk, costing them hundreds of millions of dollars. The world was reminded that Russia knew how to kneecap a country without firing a shot.

So at both the Microsoft campus and at the White House, the assumption was that the Russians would replicate the NotPetya attack in the first hours of any invasion of Ukraine. "This is what we think the first wave attack will look like," said Tom Burt, Microsoft's chief of trust and safety, one Saturday night in January 2022, just weeks before the war began.

Burt, an intense executive with equal passion for hunting down hackers and piloting his racecar at breakneck speed on racetracks across the country, had been on high alert for Russian cyber activity for months. He was convinced that the first shot in this new conflict would be digital. "A cyberattack first, the land attack next" was his prediction. The Russians' goal, he said, would be to prevent Ukrainian leaders from communicating with each other or their own people in the opening salvos of the war.

Burt called me on that January evening to describe the latest Russian activity in cyberspace that his team had found: in this case, a type of wiper malware they dubbed "Whispergate," so named because the Russians seemed to be hinting at more to come. Whispergate had a limited number of targets—both civilian infrastructure and government entities—but it didn't initially cause any significant damage. Burt's team responded quickly by warning the White House and devising a security fix nearly simultaneously. After eight long years of incessant Russian cyberattacks—including on their election system in 2014 and their power grid in 2015 and 2016—the Ukrainians mostly just sighed and brought their systems back online as soon as they could. But to Microsoft, the attack helped firm up their suspicions.

"It was pretty clear the Russians were preparing for something," recalled Justin Warner, one of Microsoft's security engineers and a former Air Force cyber operations officer. For months now, Warner and his colleagues had been focused almost entirely on how to defend against attacks from Russia as part of a hundred-person team that Microsoft had quietly set up as geopolitical tensions ratcheted higher. Meanwhile, senior executives at Microsoft were quietly trying to convince Ukraine to move its data into the cloud and off of servers inside Ukraine that would be sitting ducks when the Russians attacked.

Warner suspected that the January incident was exploratory, a scouting expedition designed to test Russia's ability to paralyze Ukraine's government and military communications. And the assumption—right or wrong—was that the real cyberattack, whenever it came, would be a prelude to an invasion.

At midday on February 23, 2022, Microsoft began to see evidence of another incident, and Warner got the call he was waiting for.

"It was a little after 1 p.m. Eastern time on the twenty-third," he recalled a few months later. One of his colleagues, another Microsoft analyst, was on the line, and "he basically just said, 'I think we have another incident going down in Ukraine.'"

Whatever was "going down" was clearly worse than what they had seen in January. This malware, while different in the details from the previous incident, shared several key indicators. And it had clearly been activated at scale, hitting government agencies, financial institutions, and the energy sector. It was spidering out from high-level servers called "domain controllers" to the computer networks that kept Ukraine going.

This looked like it might be "the big one"—but the team wasn't yet sure, so they brought in Ramin Nafisi, Warner's teammate and a malware expert and former defense contractor whose specialty was reverse-engineering suspect computer code.

"It was my job to disassemble it, piece by piece, to understand what the actual destructive capability of the malware was," Nafisi later told me.

It didn't take him long. The evidence screamed out from the five monitors in his home office in Maryland. The program was a "wiper code," so named because it was designed to wipe a hard drive clean, making computers useless. And in the code, he could see a list of the malware's Ukrainian targets: mostly government systems, a lot of them.

"It was pretty obvious within minutes," Nafisi said, "what the target was and what they were trying to achieve." Soon, they had Tom Burt on the line.

AT 3:43 P.M. on Wednesday, February 23, 2022—four days after my breakfast with Blinken in Munich and just hours before tanks would roll across the border, headed for Kyiv—Burt composed an urgent warning to the White House.

"We have learned of and are investigating a significant destructive attack," he wrote to Anne Neuberger, President Biden's deputy national security advisor for cyber and emerging technologies. He went on to provide the details: Several of Ukraine's government ministries were under attack.

Already, Burt wrote, 150 or so Ukrainian digital systems had been hit, across ten different organizations. And the count kept climbing.

Neuberger had been the National Security Council's point person for dealing with several major Russian ransomware attacks on the United States in the administration's first year, including the shutdown of the Colonial Pipeline, which provided nearly half the gasoline and diesel fuel for the East Coast. Starting in the fall of 2021, she began shuttling back and forth to the headquarters of the North Atlantic Treaty Organization (NATO) in Brussels with the warning that it was possible that a cyber winter was approaching, encouraging them to brace themselves so that a devastating Russian attack didn't take out their networks—or those of NATO itself. "There's muscle memory for what to do with a traditional attack," she often told me in the days leading up to the outbreak of fighting. "There isn't any for cyberattacks."

In a series of quick conversations on February 23, Neuberger connected Burt to her counterparts abroad—starting with Serhii Demediuk, the deputy secretary of Ukraine's National Security and Defense Council, and Mircea Geoană, the deputy NATO secretary general. The Ukrainians needed to move fast, Neuberger thought, but the Europeans also needed to be prepared if the attack spread beyond Ukraine, hitting NATO and non-NATO allies.

"I was very concerned," Neuberger told me later. "I had NotPetya on my mind," she said, fearing that an attack aimed at Ukraine could spread like wildfire across Europe. The damage could have run into the billions of dollars. But NotPetya had hit at a time of peace. If this attack spread at a moment of open warfare, it could bring NATO directly into the war—exactly what Biden had ordered his staff to avoid.

Neuberger brought Burt's report to Sullivan, the national security advisor, at his nightly meeting to assess the risk of imminent conflict. For more than a week, Sullivan had been operating on an "any day now" basis for the start of the conflict. The problem, he recalled, was that there were so very many indicators of the coming violence—troops in attack formations, orders coming down the line, flight patterns that preceded the launch of cruise missiles—that it was hard to pinpoint the actual day that the Russians might kick off hostilities.

Still, Sullivan said, Burt's warning was important. "Microsoft," he told me, "could see things we could not."

IN FACT, THOSE hours before the war began demonstrated how radically different this new era was from wars past—and from the Cold War. The physical war for Ukraine might be contained to the country's borders. But the worry that cold February day was that the digital war could spread much more quickly and change the dynamic, turning a war against Ukraine into a war against NATO.

As it turned out, the concern was misplaced, or at least premature. The Russians had prepared neither a cyberattack nor a physical attack beyond Ukraine other than taking out a European satellite system that the Ukrainians used for some of their government communications. It seemed that Putin was being careful.

But it was clear in Sullivan's office that night, as the participants mulled Microsoft's findings, that a new era had dawned. "There was this assumption in the past," Neuberger told me later, "that governments had access to perfect information. But today it's reversed. Companies have all the insight."

Two other things had changed, she said. Those same tech companies had the ability to defend national networks, independently, from thousands of miles away, in ways the U.S. government could not. Furthermore, when Burt reached out to Neuberger—and when Google and others turned to the U.S. government as well—it wasn't simply to notify the authorities. It was to coordinate the rollout of protections and defenses, starting with moving the operations of the Ukraine government to the cloud so that Russia could not take out the government by bombing Ukraine's servers. In short, in the effort to keep the country running—even if Kyiv was a smoking ruin—companies were now the front line of support.

Yet in the heat of that moment, it wasn't clear that even the best cyber defenses would matter. From Sullivan's office that night, it looked like the Russians held every advantage: From three sides they were ready to roll across the country and into Kyiv. Their force looked overwhelming. Their goal was not only to isolate Ukraine's leadership; it was to kill its leaders—in three days, if all went smoothly. The only question was: How long could Zelensky and his government hold on?

BY THE NEXT MORNING, Europe was at war again. Microsoft's warning had been prescient: The wiper code was indeed a prelude to the Russian tanks.

But as the days and weeks wore on, almost nothing unfolded as expected. The acclaimed Russian military failed to take Kyiv. Putin and American intelligence agencies alike had wildly overestimated the capabilities of Russian troops and wildly underestimated the fighting spirit of the Ukrainian people. Putin's commanders proved plodding and unimaginative—how else could you explain the forty-mile traffic jam of armored vehicles and tanks frozen in place on the road between

Belarus and Kyiv? The world watched as Russia's once-vaunted forces became sitting ducks for Ukrainian attacks on fuel tanks at the two ends of the convoys. Twitter was soon awash in photos of Russian troops whose bodies were ejected from their own tanks after the Ukrainians succeeded in their aim of setting off the explosive rounds stored under the Russians' very seats.

Within months, the Russians began a humiliating retreat, headed back to Ukraine's industrial south and east. They shelled cities mercilessly along the way, and dug into their positions, only to be routed from some of them months later in a renewed Ukrainian counterattack.

This turn of events wasn't what Putin expected. It wasn't what anyone expected. But then again, everything about this war, and the era it demarcated, seemed at once familiar and surprising.

There is never a clear line between the old world and the new, between traditional conflicts and modern ones. Ukraine was a particular blur. General Milley saw, as the first months of the war unfolded, thousands of Ukrainians and Russians digging in, seeking safety in long trenches meant to survive brutal artillery fire. As it wore on, the threat that Russia might use a nuclear weapon against its non-nuclear-armed foe surfaced and resurfaced every few months, altering critical decisions in Washington over how to arm Ukraine and what restrictions to place on how those arms could be employed. And within a year, hordes of drones, some guided by artificial intelligence, were identifying targets on the battlefield or had been turned into weapons themselves, hovering over Russian trenches in search of targets.

"Trench warfare!" Milley exclaimed to me one day about six months into the war, shaking his head. "For a while we thought this would be a cyber war. Then we thought it was looking like an old-fashioned, World War II tank war. And then," he said, pausing, "there are days when I thought they are fighting fucking World War I."

In his colorful way, Milley had put his finger on one of the most unsettling features of the new geopolitical era: It is part 1914, part 1941, and part 2022.

All at once.

THE SHAPE OF THE
NEW COLD WARS

THIS IS A book about a global shock that took Washington by surprise: the revival of superpower conflict.

In Washington, London, and Berlin, many government officials today insist that they had seen all this coming. If so, neither the United States nor its Western allies acted as if they had. For more than thirty years—from the fall of the Berlin Wall until the invasion of Ukraine—there was a sense of certainty that the greatest byproduct of America's undeniable victory in the Cold War was something like a permanent era of peace among the world's nuclear superpowers.

Even before the fall of the Berlin Wall, much less the collapse of the USSR, there were declarations that we were in a new world—one in which democracy had won out, permanently. "What we may be witnessing," American political scientist Francis Fukuyama famously wrote in 1989, "is not just the end of the cold war, or a passing of a particular period of postwar history, but the end of history as such: that is, the end point of mankind's ideological evolution and the universalisation of western liberal democracy as the final form of human government."

Fukuyama had his doubters at the time, of course. But over the past fifteen years, the warning signs that this optimism was deeply misplaced have only accelerated: the invasion of Georgia and then Crimea; cyber-attacks launched from Moscow and Beijing; Putin's move into Syria and his effort to influence an American presidential election and destabilize the country; Xi's determination to use the Belt and Road Initiative and Huawei and other national champions to wire Europe, Africa, and Latin

America with Chinese-made 5G networks to spread Beijing's influence. But America was distracted—by two misbegotten wars in the Middle East that cost thousands of American lives and trillions of dollars and blurred our focus on bigger strategic threats. Then came a deadly pandemic followed by the internal upheavals epitomized by the effort to overturn a legitimate election. It was hard to focus on America's role in the world when we were consumed by the attendant images of a democracy that had lost its bearings.

We were also convinced that, for all the shock, trauma, and disorder of the twenty-first century, the world would sort itself out in the way we had long anticipated. Key to that was the almost universally held assumption that Russia and China—a fast-declining power and a fast-rising one—would integrate themselves into the West in their own ways. Each, it was argued, had an overwhelming national interest in keeping its products, profits, and financial interactions flowing, even with geopolitical adversaries. Economics would ultimately trump nationalism and territorial ambition.

So while it might be true that Vladimir Putin wanted to reconstitute Peter the Great's Russian empire, the thinking went, in the end he would value his oil and gas revenues more than imperial expansion. And in China, the same logic ran, Xi Jinping would follow his immediate predecessors, Jiang Zemin and Hu Jintao, by focusing on the urgent issue of keeping China's astounding domestic growth from falling back to earth. He would not take the risk, the intelligence assessments concluded, of immediate challenges to the United States' global predominance. As I traveled the world with five U.S. presidents—Clinton, Bush, Obama, Trump, and Biden—I heard variations of this argument from their lips and those of their closest advisors, though uttered, as the years passed, with diminishing levels of conviction.

There were shocks to the system, of course. Putin's cyberattacks on the West and his invasions of neighboring countries. Xi's consolidation of power in Beijing, his interest in extending China's military reach to the South China Sea, and his efforts to wire up the world with Chinese-made technologies, sometimes freely chosen by China's customers, though often not. But for years nothing shook the dominant view that when Xi was faced with a choice between taking control of Hong Kong and Taiwan and preserving the flow of revenue, technology, and ideas that China needed to make the next great leap forward, he would inevitably choose the latter.

It is only in the past few years that this faith in the power of globalization has come to be regarded as a fantasy era of early-twenty-first-century American foreign policy. It was a bipartisan assumption that the post–Cold War age would last indefinitely and that for all of America's internal divisions and outside challenges—and despite China's aggressive rise and Russia's violent disruptions—American power would remain fundamentally unchallenged.

Each one of those presidents believed that the strength of America's economy, its technology, or the U.S. president's own persuasive power could bend history in Washington's direction.

I was with Bill Clinton at Beijing University in 1998 when he told students that the internet would undercut the Communist Party by exposing young Chinese to democratic ideals and the corruption of the Chinese system and lay the groundwork for democratic rejuvenation.

George W. Bush was certain, at least for a while, that he could join forces with Putin in a common war against terrorism and that over time he could lure the former KGB officer into joining the European Union—and maybe even NATO.

Barack Obama deeply distrusted Putin but was oddly reluctant to call him out for cyberattacks on the White House, the Pentagon, and the State Department, and, ultimately, for directly seeking to influence America's election outcome in 2016. And when Putin annexed Crimea, Obama made it clear that while the United States disapproved, he wasn't going to risk war over a remote spit of land that for hundreds of years had been part of the Russian empire.

Donald Trump wanted a deal with China so badly that he chastised his secretary of state for harshly criticizing the "Chinese Communist Party" for the spread of COVID-19—until it became clear to Trump, early in the pandemic, that it was politically more useful to vilify the originators of what he came to call "the China virus." And to the end of his term—even after the full invasion of Ukraine—Trump could not stop expressing admiration for Putin's strength, the only thing that seemed to impress him.

Each president claimed he had achieved meaningful progress toward integrating America's adversaries into a world order Washington had created and nurtured for seventy-five years. Clinton brought China into the World Trade Organization. Bush made Beijing and Moscow uneasy partners in counterterrorism. Obama struck an arms control treaty with Putin and a climate change agreement with Xi. Obama boasted that Russia and China joined the West in negotiating the 2015 nuclear deal with Iran and were episodically helpful in reining in North Korea. Trump finally struck a modest trade deal with Xi in 2020. Each new bond was trumpeted as a major win, as a sign the world's most powerful nations were rowing together.

They were not.

"I think it's fair to say that just about every assumption across different administrations was wrong," one of Biden's closest advisors told me. "The internet would bring political liberty. Trade would liberalize the regime" while creating high-skill jobs for Americans. The list went on. A lot of it was just wishful thinking.

Much of the rest was oversold, part of what became known as the "Washington Consensus" that globalization was, on balance, the pathway to economic growth and political stability, despite the evidence that middle-class workers, not tech entrepreneurs, were its primary victims. Or that economic interdependence was no guarantee that countries would restrain their instincts to take power or land or disrespect human rights.

"I was as guilty as anyone else," the advisor concluded.

Eventually, we reached the point at which the cognitive dissonance—between the future we expected and the reality we confronted—was too big to ignore.

WHEN PRESIDENT BIDEN'S team took office in January 2021, American power seemed at a nadir: COVID-19 had the country on lockdown, the previous president was trying to cling to power, China seemed ascendent, NATO had lost its way, and the Russians paid little price for their panoply of disruptions.

It was clear that Biden faced a challenge parallel to the one that confronted Harry Truman, the president who dropped the atomic bomb and then confronted the first cold war: how to prepare the country for what looked increasingly like an emerging, protracted era of superpower confrontation.

But what would this look like?

The easy temptation was to fit this new landscape into a familiar paradigm. In Washington and beyond, the phrase "New Cold War" began to be bandied about—as if history were directly repeating itself. Which it never does exactly. In early 2021, the phrase almost exclusively referred to America's relationship with China; Russia was still an afterthought, a sort of superpower emeritus that would barely attract attention save for the fact that it still possessed six thousand nuclear weapons.

The Biden administration, still finding its footing in its first year, immediately pushed back on the Cold War characterization. That race, they said, concerned who would be the first in space, who could build more intercontinental ballistic missiles, who could amass a larger, more deadly arsenal. Today, Biden and his aides pointed out, China was a far broader potential strategic adversary than the Soviet Union ever was. It was a technological threat, a military threat, and an economic rival all in one—while, confoundingly, remaining a critical trading partner. Eager to squash the historical analogy, Biden told the United Nations in his first appearance there as president that "we are not seeking a new Cold War or a world divided into rigid blocs."

But it was Biden himself who gave this confrontation an ideological edge, a sense that a struggle was under way from which only one victor could emerge. He argued that the world was facing an "inflection point," a term he used again and again in the months that followed. "This is a battle between the utility of democracies in the twenty-first century and autocracies," he said in his first press conference. "We've got to prove democracy works."

He singled out Xi, saying he was "a smart, smart guy" who shared with Putin a belief that "autocracy is the wave of the future and democracy can't function" in the complexities of the modern world.

The timing couldn't have been more awkward. The world had just watched rioters tear through the U.S. Capitol Building to try to overturn the outcome of a presidential election—effectively, to stage a coup. The Chinese broadcast to their own people images of the worst moments of the attack, making the unsubtle point that the road to democracy was littered with chaos, destruction, and death. The Russians broadcast the same images outside of Russia, to show the world that the hypocritical Americans should be lecturing no one—least of all, them—about true democratic rule.

Still, in making this argument, there were more than a few political benefits for Biden. Some contended that it had less to do with calling out autocrats like Putin and Xi than affirming America's democracy in one of its darkest hours. For those who predicted Biden would be a caretaker president—a bridge between the traumas of the Trump era and a brighter future—Biden's words suggested a larger mission at stake.

The dichotomy rankled American allies with authoritarian tendencies, from Saudi Arabia to Singapore, and by the third year of his presidency, Biden rarely repeated it. But at home the democracy vs. autocracy construct cleared the way for him to capitalize on fears of Beijing and direct hundreds of billions of dollars to technology, research, and domestic infrastructure.

The administration began with optimistic diplomatic bromides— "We'll cooperate wherever we can; we'll contest where we must"—and a conviction that the only way to stay competitive with China was to rebuild American capacity at home while starving Chinese industry of the Western technologies it most coveted. New export controls were implemented to buy time, depriving China of the specialized equipment it needed to make the most advanced computer chips, including the high-end chips that have a clear use for artificial intelligence as well as in China's stealth bombers, its hypersonic missiles, and its omnipresent surveillance equipment. Gina Raimondo, Biden's commerce secretary, who was put in charge of blocking the most advanced exports, put it simply: "We are trying to choke their military capacity." No wonder the Chinese called it a containment policy.

Biden made no apology that his devotion of federal funds to rebuilding America's ability to produce chips was classic industrial policy—the use of taxpayer dollars and government programs to influence the private sector with the aim of reviving America's technological edge. In 2022, he pushed Congress to approve $52 billion for chipmakers in an effort to give them time to restore a lead America had once held—and then squandered. It would take the better part of a decade, his aides agreed, to make it succeed.

Most Republicans went along, because it was easy to sell an anti-China policy back in their home districts—especially if you left out the words "industrial policy." To many Americans, and certainly to China's leader, the U.S. plans resembled a classic containment strategy, a concept imported straight from the old Cold War. Then, the idea of "containment" meant preventing other countries from becoming communist; now it meant starving American competitors of key technologies in order to maintain an edge in AI and nuclear weapons, in space and cyberspace.

The technology race today runs far deeper than the one that defined the old Cold War. Back then, America had never been dependent on its chief adversary for either the technology it needed to keep the United States running or the supply chains that kept America fed, clothed, and connected. Those chains now linked American consumers directly to the whim of Chinese leaders. Apple's iPhone—a device millions of Americans depend on for everything from their financial lives to their medical histories to the apps that open their front doors—has been assembled in China since its invention, and the company's efforts to diversify its sources of manufacturing have made a difference only around the margins. "If you gave us five years," one senior Apple executive told me, "I think we'd be lucky to move 10 or 15 percent of production out of China."

What worried many in Washington, in fact, was that China's success no longer depended on stealing Western technologies, like the design for the F-35 fighter. (The Chinese version closely resembles the American one.) Slowly, then quickly, Chinese engineers began beating their American counterparts to market with innovations that seemed to understand the mindset of American consumers better than Americans did. TikTok, the addictive app that 150 million Americans put on their phones—first for the dance videos, then for the memes, and finally for news—was the first piece of Chinese software to go viral across the United States. No American firm seemed capable of displacing it. Its ubiquity raised concerns about whether the Chinese government could use it to track the habits and tastes of American citizens—and then influence the next election. Panicked, governments across the United States started banning the app from state-owned phones. But officials knew they could not wrest it from the hands of a third of the country.

. . .

THEN CAME THE invasion of Ukraine.

Suddenly there wasn't much debate about whether the United States was in a new Cold War. With Russia, at least, it seemed obvious. The crisis in Ukraine posed a classic, direct challenge to the West—whether it would defend an emerging, if corruption-ridden, democracy against Putin's efforts to restore Russia to what he regarded as its greatest era of glory: the first quarter of the eighteenth century, when the Russian Empire coalesced.

But there was more to it. If Putin succeeded in Ukraine, there was no telling where he might reach next. And because war changes the nature of power relationships, Washington soon began to worry that the conflict could prove an accelerant for China and Russia to join forces in facing off against the United States. The war was regional; the stakes were global.

When the effort to expose and undercut Putin's plan in Ukraine failed to prevent war, Biden faced an immediate choice. Ukraine was not a NATO member; the United States had no treaty obligation to defend its territory. He could have stayed out of it—as Putin expected he would—denouncing the violation of sovereignty and imposing some sanctions, exactly as Obama had done in response to the annexation of Crimea in 2014. For Biden, arming the Ukrainians, feeding them intelligence, helping them strategize about how to kill Russians faster—basically throwing everything into the effort except American troops—was an option, not an inevitability.

Biden's instinct, he made clear to his staff, was that if the United States abandoned Ukraine, everything he was saying about the struggle between democracy and autocracy would ring hollow. But taking action to stop a superpower from rolling over another state's borders carried real risks, including nuclear escalation. So Biden laid out two goals, in tension with each other: Do everything you can to help Ukraine, and don't get sucked into World War III.

For the first year of the war, Biden's strategy proved an unexpected success, and, improbably, American power was resurgent as well. Russia's military failures exposed a system so rotten that it could not produce fresh ammunition or defeat a far smaller, if remarkably innovative, opponent. Biden's ability to rally allies revived NATO and reversed perceptions of who had the upper hand between Washington and Moscow. It also likely unnerved many in Beijing.

China's prospects also seemed dimmer. For the first time in decades, its population was shrinking. Its insistence on relying on its own technology led Xi to reject the idea of importing COVID-19 vaccines that worked—worsening the country's own suffering. Suddenly a country that had known nothing but growth for decades was fighting deflation and youth unemployment so worrisome that Beijing eventually discontinued publishing the statistics. Yes, China remained the one power with the technology, economic strength, and military capability to challenge the United States over the long term—the reason that many feared the Ukraine war was a distraction from the real contest. But for the short term Xi Jinping found himself facing down protests that were likely to grow more intense if he could not restore the era of atypical growth that fueled China's rise.

All of this was an important reminder that America's adversaries were not ten feet tall. They had weaknesses, just as the United States does, though ours are often on more vivid display. The question was whether China and Russia had both peaked and were now facing years of decline or slow growth—and what they might do on the way down.

IF THIS IS an era of new Cold Wars—two under way simultaneously—it is a more complex and dangerous era than we have faced in nearly a century. Almost everything about how we think about the next few decades—how we defend ourselves, how we nurture international alliances, how we spend money at a time when the national debt has soared to over $30 trillion—is up for contentious debate, at home and around the world. In Washington, it is no longer a safe assumption that the United States views its role as being the indispensable nation; a major swath of the Republican Party, which throughout the Cold War advertised itself as the defender of democracy and individual freedom around the world, has abandoned that view. And while just a few years ago it was commonplace to say that we could not solve climate change or manage pandemics without the close cooperation of the world's most powerful nations, now even floods, droughts, wildfires, and new viruses cannot bring together leading nations that are undermining each other every day. Nor can the fight against terrorism: In the years after the September 11 attacks, the major powers came together in something akin to a common cause. When Hamas killed 1,200 Israelis, triggering a new crisis in the Middle East, there was no semblance of unity.

Clearly, the "peace dividend" that dominated Washington rhetoric after the end of the Cold War—taking the money spent on the military and moving it to projects at home—is long gone. (Thanks to Afghanistan and Iraq, the dividend never paid out.) The money we hoped to spend on improving the climate, or education, or ending income inequality will get sucked into bolstering our forces in Europe, even as we "pivot" to concentrate more firepower in the Pacific. But the effects go beyond federal budgets. One of the many risks ahead is that innovation may well be more focused on the military dimensions of space and cyberspace, on autonomous weapons rather than autonomous cars. We all have a lot to lose.

"The post–Cold War era is definitively over," Biden's national security strategy declared in late 2022, as the Ukraine war devolved into a stalemate, "and a competition is underway between the major powers to shape what comes next."

Yet the strategy never specified what comes next; what "victory" might look like in this competition is murkier than ever. The old Cold War had a beginning, a long middle, and a surprise ending. If we are looking for this one to follow the same pattern—to end with the collapse of our opponents and a clear victory for the West—we are likely to be disappointed. And there is no guarantee that these cold wars will stay cold.

This is the story of how we misjudged what would happen after the last Cold War ended. But it is also the story of trying to discern "what comes next" at a moment of maximum peril.

PART ONE

DREAMING OF ONE WORLD

CHAPTER 1

FLOATING PAST THE HERMITAGE

Who lost Russia? It's an old argument, and it misses the point. Russia was never ours to lose.

Bill Burns, director of the CIA, March 8, 2019

I**T WAS A** perfect "White Night" on the Neva River in late May 2002. The sun barely set, and Vladimir Putin's romance with the United States—and the West—seemed at its zenith. The shock of the September 11 attacks, just eight months before, had not worn off. America was at war in Afghanistan, and George W. Bush was still struggling to define—in his own mind, and the world's—what a "war against terror" would look like.

Bush had gone to Moscow to seek the help of Putin. As midnight neared, Putin and his wife at the time, Lyudmila Verbitskaya, were floating down the Neva River in St. Petersburg on a luxury yacht, headed toward the Hermitage, the vast collection of the Tsar's treasures built on the site of Peter the Great's Winter Palace.

Their guests that evening were Bush and his wife, Laura, and a gaggle of Bush's aides. Condoleezza Rice, Bush's national security advisor and later his secretary of state, was along, too. The sounds of traditional Russian music and laughter from their yacht wafted across the river as they cruised past the city's spectacular waterfront, bathed in orange hues, and ate dinner on the deck.

The menu included black caviar with chopped eggs, foie gras, and filet of beef—elegantly served during the dinner cruise by a brooding man in a dark suit. That night aboard the *New Island* yacht, we only knew he was Putin's favorite caterer. Only years later did I learn that the man was Yevgeny Prigozhin, a former convict turned restaurateur. He would, of course, go on to become a central player in much that would go wrong between Moscow and Washington, from trying to manipulate the United States' 2016 election to recruiting prison inmates to fight in Ukraine for the private army he had founded—an army that he briefly tried to turn against Putin's own regime. But that night, he was just Putin's chef.

Just a few hours before, the Putins and the Bushes had been at the Mariinsky Theatre, watching a performance of *The Nutcracker*—not the lighthearted version typically served up around the holidays, but a much darker story. The set, the costumes, and the production were all done by a former Soviet dissident who had fled to America during the Cold War and returned after the collapse of the Soviet Union.

The presidential visit, of course, was as choreographed as *The Nutcracker.* The storyline of the evening was that the Cold War was over, never to return. Like the Neva itself, Russia was flowing toward Europe, soon to be seamlessly intermingled in its waters.

Putin seized on that perception to show he was the man to run the project—helping Bush fight terrorism and guiding Russia toward international markets. On this evening, Putin played the gracious host, chatting with Laura Bush and joking with the American president.

Earlier in the day, the two leaders had signed an arms control treaty—not much of one, but a significant achievement since Bush had just abandoned the Anti-Ballistic Missile Treaty, fearing it was getting in the way of his effort to defend America against a North Korean attack. Putin's willingness to negotiate a new treaty, with modest cuts in each side's nuclear arsenal, seemed to indicate that the two countries could still work together in limiting the fearsome weapons. The day was marked less by discussion of eliminating warheads than by their mutual agreement that terror was the biggest threat. There was vague talk of cutting arsenals even further.

The two men then headed to a vast lecture hall at St. Petersburg State

University, where Russian students were invited to ask them anything—another stage-managed signal that a new era had dawned.

On stage, Bush and Putin's seeming ease with each other was stunning to anyone who had witnessed the stiff meetings between U.S. and Soviet leaders during the Cold War. The two cracked jokes at each other's expense and seemed overly familiar, referring to each other as "George" and "Vladimir." The students asked not a single question about the arms control treaty, which to them may have seemed a remnant of a lost age. But they were deeply interested in Russia's integration with Europe—and their prospects of studying and working abroad and, ultimately, finding lucrative employment back in Russia.

The sense of the evening, of the whole trip, was not simply that the Cold War was over but that with effort it could almost be erased from history. Bush's visit—one of some two dozen with Putin during his presidency, ranging from the inner sanctums of the Kremlin to Bush's ranch in Crawford, Texas—would come to seem emblematic not only of a lost age but of a lost last chance. Those visits, the performance, their walk by the burial place of the tsars in Saints Peter and Paul Cathedral, were all part of an elaborate, consciously designed effort by both countries to convince each other and the rest of the world that Russia was coming into the West, and being embraced in return.

In background briefings, officials made clear they had even figured out the progression: Russia would join the World Trade Organization, just as China had done. Then, perhaps, the European Union. And maybe—just maybe—NATO itself, the organization that had been created to contain, and ultimately crush, the Soviet Union. There remained plenty of brewing disputes, many of them concerning the Western drift of the former Soviet states. But the idea that Russia might follow them into NATO didn't, at that moment, sound insane.

Long after, Russians complained it was all a hoax, a vast shell game by the United States to keep Russia neutered. In their telling, America never intended to let Moscow into the club. It was just dangling enticements to tame the country into submission. The Russians suspected, in fact some said later that they knew, that in private American officials preferred to think of Russia as a vanquished former superpower. A common wisecrack was that it was "Italy, but with nuclear weapons."

The Russians did not find such jokes particularly amusing. Even during that 2002 visit, one could sense the tension running just beneath the surface—even if few acknowledged it publicly. And for their part, as my *New York Times* colleague Michael Wines wrote early that week, the United States was not a particularly gracious winner. "American officials are not trying to spare Russian sensibilities," he wrote. Wines quoted one of Russia's top America experts, Anatoly I. Utkin: "For five centuries Russia never paid tribute to anybody. Now for the first time we became a minor partner. You are boss; we are partner."

Years later, it would become nearly accepted wisdom in Washington that the Vladimir Putin of 2002 was playing out the early scenes of a drama of his own making, darker than *The Nutcracker*'s fantasies. But an alternative explanation considered that perhaps, back then, he was a different Putin—one who thought he could execute his agenda without overt confrontation. Or perhaps a bit of both versions was true—that he just wanted to extract what he could from the West until Russia was stronger.

EIGHT MONTHS BEFORE that sparkling night on the Neva River, Bush and Putin had found common ground following the September 11 attacks. Putin had been the first to call Bush—an act of goodwill that Bush brought up often. As the Pentagon and the World Trade Center towers burned, the Russian leader agreed to keep nuclear alert readiness levels to a minimum. It was the kind of thing responsible leaders do to make sure that military moves are not misread and do not lead to accidental escalation. But it was also a signal that, in the minds of the two men who oversaw more than 90 percent of the world's nuclear weapons, there was not even a whiff of superpower involvement in the attacks.

"For one brief moment the thought flashed through my head: *The Cold War really is over*," Condoleezza Rice told me years later.

That declaration meant something coming from Rice. Long before she was George W. Bush's right hand on foreign policy, Rice was known as one of the U.S. government's most prominent young Russia experts. Her PhD dissertation, submitted at the age of twenty-six, focused on the military and politics of Czechoslovakia. She had studied Russian at Moscow State University. Her faculty mentor at the University of Denver, Josef Korbel, was the father of Madeleine Albright. Then she worked for Bush's father and for Brent Scowcroft, the man many considered the model national security advisor.

By the time Bush took office in 2001, he already relied on Rice for everything from advice to admonishment. So it was no surprise she was along that night on the river, as advisor and occasional translator. When we talked about it almost exactly twenty years after that night on the river, she spoke of the trip—and the era—almost sentimentally.

In retrospect, she characterized Bush's approach of the early 2000s as an effort to pull Putin—and by extension, the battered Russian state—closer to Washington by finding convergences in American and Russian interests and pursuing "strategic cooperation." The obvious convergence for both leaders was the response to the 9/11 attacks.

"Putin really thought he had found a new concept for strategic relations between the United States and Russia: terrorism," Rice said, with the benefit of two decades of perspective. As America dealt with the fallout of 9/11, hunting down Bin Laden, and ramping up its Global War on Terror, Russia was hurting, too—having suffered a series of brutal terrorist attacks, including a deadly string of Moscow apartment bombings in 1999. Later, in 2002, some eight hundred Russians were taken hostage in a Chechen attack on a Moscow theater—a siege that ended in the deaths of nearly all the attackers and more than a hundred hostages, the vast majority of whom died from the gas deployed by the police in their counterattack. Bush offered condolences and support, as Putin had done for him after 9/11.

For a little while, the concept of terrorism as a unifying cause seemed like it could work. In the early years of the administration, it seemed that relations between the United States and Russia had never been better. "Moscow likened the anti-terror cooperation to the anti-Hitler coalition in World War II," noted Angela Stent, the former national intelligence officer for Russia and a Putin biographer. "The common enemy was Islamic fundamentalism and together the two great powers would defeat it."

In the wake of 9/11, Russia shared logistical information that enabled U.S. forces to navigate Afghan mountain caves in their search for Osama Bin Laden. Soon the two countries expanded their cooperation, working together to promote peacebuilding in the central Caucasus.

The two countries developed something that Stephen Hadley, President Bush's deputy national security advisor, described to me as "The Checklist," in which cabinet secretaries from the Bush administration would work with their equivalents at the Kremlin on joint projects. "They would write quarterly reports on their progress, jointly addressed to the two presidents," noted Hadley. "It's unheard of."

The content of the projects was fungible. The whole point of the exercise was to give Washington and Moscow a joint sense of mission. And for a while, the plan seemed to be working. From her West Wing office, Rice told me that she believed the United States was experiencing the best simultaneous relationship with the Chinese and Russians in its history. In retrospect, she was probably right.

But as the years wore on, the bonhomie began to fade. The terrorism concept worked, but only if it wasn't examined too carefully or for too long. Bush thought he was doing Putin a favor by cleaning up Afghanistan, a country the Soviet Union had invaded and then, in a humiliation that would portend others to come, retreated from. Putin thought he was entering into an equal partnership with the United States that would restore Russia to the global superpower status it had enjoyed before the collapse of the Soviet Union.

Yet it soon became clear that everyone had a different definition of who was a terrorist and what to do about them. Bush's problem was al-Qaeda and its ilk, but for Putin, terrorism was about the Chechens—a Muslim ethnic group from the Caucasus Mountains. The Russians, like the Chinese, wanted to designate their most disfavored minorities as "terrorists," thereby opening the door to dealing with them however harshly the regime desired.

Then came the Iraq War. Putin had vehemently opposed the unilateral invasion and rejected outright the concept that by ousting Saddam Hussein the West would be ridding the world of a safe harbor for terrorists. But Putin was often careful to avoid blaming Bush directly for the failures in Iraq, even as he made clear that he disagreed wholeheartedly with the invasion. It was Putin's bet that if he joined with the Americans' antiterrorism efforts, the West would look the other way on some of Russia's human rights issues.

That was where things began to unravel. Bush made it clear he disapproved of the Chechen conflict, and his administration went so far as to meet with what they viewed as the "moderate" Chechen separatist leadership, a fact that was later twisted into the oft-repeated claim, including by Putin, that the United States was arming and training Chechen terrorists. Counterterrorism, it was becoming clear, could never be the bridge that Putin and Bush had once hoped for.

But few in the West—and likely not even the Russians—imagined how fast the relationship would sour. Except, maybe, for Paul Kolbe.

IN THE EARLY 2000s, Kolbe was the Moscow station chief for the CIA. A native Michigander with the affect of a midwestern businessman, Kolbe was known as one of the intelligence community's most savvy Russia-watchers. From early on he thought that Putin would steer the country in ways America would soon find problematic.

"In retrospect, there was a real naïve expectation that Russia was going to go the same way as Poland, as the Baltics," Kolbe told me, two decades later. "And that they were on this inevitable march to capitalist democracy. I think we fooled ourselves about the nature of Russia."

The Russians knew exactly who Kolbe was. While his business card suggested he was a diplomat, he was one of the "declared" spies that both governments acknowledged. His job was to manage the agency's liaison relationship with the Russian security services—moving around Moscow, from restaurants to parties, as a known quantity in the genteel, day-to-day game of spycraft—while also running a staff of covert operatives engaged in stealing the Kremlin's most carefully guarded secrets.

In the old days of the Cold War, spies had operated by the "Moscow Rules," de facto operating guidelines for conducting oneself in a Soviet environment. These were later popularized by spy novels that offered guidance like "Assume nothing" and "Do not look back; you are never alone." By the time Kolbe arrived, new Moscow Rules had been added, but they looked a little different—especially around the winter holidays.

"We were hosting a holiday party for FSB contacts in the Pushkin café," recalled Kolbe, referring to the Russian Federal Security Service, the successor to the feared Soviet KGB. "Had the whole place rented out. It was a liaison party, so we brought in the U.S. declared officers, the U.S. Special Services, the FBI. This would have been in 2004.

"It was deep in the night, you know, human wreckage scattered around the place. And I'm standing talking with one of the senior liaison officers, this FSB general. He puts his arm around me, and he goes, 'Oh, Mr. Kolbe'—and he's standing there with his, like, aide-de-camp—and he says, 'Oh, Mr. Kolbe, I'm FSB, you're CIA. We used to be enemies, but the Cold War is over. Now we're friends and allies.' And he's sort of grinning and teetering.

"And the young officer standing with him looks up at him—and he's boring his eyes into him, just glaring—and he says, 'General, that's why my generation *hates* your generation. Because you lost the Cold War, and we're going to win it back.' And it was just awkward. The general goes beet red, and I just sort of snapped back and it was this absolute crystallizing sort of moment that the Russia that we expect, that generational change and exposure to the West is all going to make for something that looks more like Western Europe than what Russia really is—this is not where Russia is going."

It struck Kolbe hard because this wasn't his first exposure to Russia. He'd been there a decade before, in the mid-1990s, during the wild period of privatization, with the Russian economy in free fall. Money had poured into the hands of oligarchs. The military was in chaos. Organized crime was rampant. Red Army soldiers in uniform were begging outside the Pizza Hut—one of many American companies to flood into the successor states just before the USSR dissolved. The American embassy was getting so many walk-ins—unsolicited visits from Russians who wanted to spy for the West, or defect there—that it had to make a new rule: No one under the rank of colonel was worth their time. But that window, Kolbe recalled, closed quickly.

"IT WOULD BE simplistic to say there was one moment where the relationship was great before, and after it wasn't," argued Mary Elise Sarotte, a history professor whose experience studying abroad in West Berlin in 1989, as the collapse of East Germany was under way, sparked a lifetime of research on the Cold War and six major books. "But I do tend to see the nineties as formative. In the year 1999, a lot of things happened that caused irreparable damage to the new Washington/Moscow relationship."

First among these was the expansion of NATO, whose creation in 1949 was primarily designed to curb Soviet adventurism in the post–World War II era. NATO's expansion had never been a given. In 1990, after the fall of the Berlin Wall but before the end of the USSR, Secretary of State James A. Baker posed a hypothetical question to Mikhail Gorbachev, the Soviet premier: What if, he suggested, the Soviets were to retreat militarily from the occupied eastern half of Germany in exchange for the promise that NATO would not expand farther east, toward the remains of Russian territory?

Of course, that speculative conversation was before the USSR dissolved in 1991. In the throes of the postwar unipolar order that followed, Americans realized they could reunite Germany *and* expand NATO—and that the Russians would be in no position to stop them.

Whether or not the West broke a promise to refrain from expansion has been the source of argument and revisionism for the better part of three decades. The Americans argued that nothing had been promised in Baker's meeting with Gorbachev. No guarantees had been put into writing, and the discussion itself had also been left unresolved. But long after the fact, Gorbachev—and later Putin—claimed that the Russians had been tricked by the deceitful West.

Whether the West was being deceitful, opportunistic, or merely disorganized would be debated for years. In the post–Cold War period, with its mix of hope, mistrust, optimism, and suspicion, things moved quickly. Ideas flitted into existence and vanished. And even the Western allies could not agree on whether expanding NATO was the right decision.

George Kennan, the famed Cold War diplomat, believed the West would come to regret NATO expansionism: "[It] would be the most fateful error of American policy in the entire post-cold-war era," he wrote in the late 1990s. "Such a decision may be expected to inflame the nationalistic, anti-Western and militaristic tendencies in Russian opinion; to have an adverse effect on the development of Russian democracy; to restore the atmosphere of the cold war to East-West relations, and to impel Russian foreign policy in directions decidedly not to our liking."

Of course, there were many arguments in favor of NATO expansion: the promise of bolstering democracy in the fledgling republics, the hope of uniting Europe enough to prevent another horrible world war. And so, with his second term coming to an end and eager to leave a legacy that would bury memories of his impeachment, Bill Clinton had no intention of closing NATO's doors to the newly minted European democracies. On March 12, 1999, Poland, the Czech Republic, and Hungary became full members of the alliance. And, by happenstance of timing, two weeks later, NATO took direct military action, launching an aerial bombing over Kosovo, an action that had not been authorized by the UN Security Council.

To the Western allies, this was all about protecting minorities facing extinction, in this case an Albanian secessionist faction that was being hunted down and summarily executed by those answering to the president of the Serbian republic, Slobodan Milošević.

To the Russians, and particularly to Putin, then on the verge of becoming prime minister, the war was about the destruction of an ally and the height of America's arrogant unipolar moment that was driven in part by America's technological dominance and in part by its insistence that, as the winner of the Cold War, it could mandate how world markets operated, which technological standards would dominate, and which norms the globe would follow. But what seemed to send the Russians over the edge was the image of American B-2 bombers lifting into the air from a military base in Missouri at midday, flying an 11,000-mile, thirty-two-hour mission to drop laser-guided weapons over Belgrade, and getting back in time for dinner the next evening—all of which underscored the reach of American power. The Russians responded by flying a ragtag force into Kosovo; the Chinese declared they had developed their own neutron bomb. Each seemed an effort to declare that neither country would sit idly by while the United States flexed its muscles.

In 2022, Sarotte was blunt about the way Russians interpreted NATO's involvement in Kosovo. It "seemed to convince not just the Russian elite but the broad mass of the Russian public that the point of enlarging NATO was to kill Slavs. . . . We in the West didn't really understand how widespread that perception was. American diplomats in Russia at the time sent back flashing red alarms: warnings, emails, texts saying, 'Whoa, this is really not playing well here.' This isn't to say there was no hope afterwards. But you start to have a profound distrust, irreparable damage."

Few of those seeds of distrust—real, imagined, or manufactured—were widely debated in the United States at the time, except among a tiny group of experts. The establishment view in Washington and most of Western Europe was that the West had expanded NATO responsibly, even soberly. Prior to the expansion in 1999, Clinton had taken pains to enmesh the Russians further into NATO with the signing of the "Founding Act," designed to guide cooperation and security between NATO and Russia. And before expanding again in 2004—including the three Baltic states of Estonia, Latvia, and Lithuania that to Putin were still as good as Russian territory—Russia had been invited to the 2002 Rome Summit, in which the participants declared that "we are today opening a new page in our relations, aimed at enhancing our ability to work together in areas of common interest and to stand together against common threats and risks to our security." They also established a "NATO-Russia Council" to further enmesh Russia into the strategic mission of NATO, up to the point of including them in military exercises.

What the Russians really thought about NATO expansion at the time remained unclear—perhaps intentionally so. In 2004, Foreign Minister Lavrov, then as later an unreliable barometer of the Russian government's thinking, warned that the West was making a dangerous mistake in expanding NATO, one that could not help but increase Russian fears and paranoia. Not surprisingly, his caution was undercut, on that same day, by the Kremlin itself, which claimed that "Russia has no concerns about the expansion of NATO from the standpoint of ensuring security."

Russia, under Putin, may have still harbored some hope of being accepted as a coequal into the new world order. When Bill Burns showed up in Moscow to serve as ambassador in 2005, he was preempted in his attempt to greet Putin by the man himself: "You Americans need to listen more," Putin demanded abruptly. "You can't have everything your way anymore. We can have effective relations, but not just on your terms."

"The constant theme in this era," said Sarotte, "was that Russia wanted to be on eye level with the Americans. Russia wanted to come into NATO as a peer—and obviously that kept not happening. Instead Russia had to watch not only as former Warsaw Pact members but also former Soviet states got ahead of Russia in line. For the West, this made sense, since those countries were working hard to become democracies and yearned for membership. But for Moscow, it became increasingly grating."

Other grievances piled up. Iraq was one of them. But far more existential were the Color Revolutions—the democratic uprisings that swept across the fringes of the Russian empire in the early 2000s. Putin, Condoleezza Rice recalled, had "a real sense that they were coming his way." And Ukraine was the epicenter of the contagion. Its Orange Revolution—three months of protests starting in late November 2004 to reject an election rigged on behalf of the Russia-favored candidate, and later president, Victor Yanukovich—hit close to home. Putin publicly vowed to protect Russia from the "tragic consequences" of "the wave of so-called color revolutions."

Meanwhile, Russia's old neighbors were growing increasingly nervous. "It was in the 2002–2003 period," recalled Heather Conley, a midlevel State Department official in charge of Central Europe, "that we started to hear from the Baltic states and select Central Europeans that they were seeing troubling Russian behavior—internally and externally—that was cumulatively growing into a threat. It had them worried." Mostly, it was little things, or so it seemed at the time: periodic incursions into Baltic airspace, growing economic influence, reciprocal expulsions of diplomats accused of spying, bigger-than-usual military exercises. "But we sort of patted them on the head and said, 'You've been through a great trauma, but the Cold War is over, you will be in NATO, and this is a different Russia.'" There was a tendency, she said, to view these threats as noise and nuisance.

So there was no single obvious rupture in the relationship between the United States and Russia in those years, but rather a pattern of intermittent backsliding, ebbs and flows, moments of confrontation and moments of relative cooperation.

And clearly, much of this story wasn't about Russia. It was about Putin.

FIONA HILL, WHO EMERGED first in Washington as one of the most perceptive biographers of the Russian leader, then as Donald Trump's ignored Russia expert, and later as a damning witness in the hearings over his first impeachment, argued in an addendum to the 2015 book she co-authored, *Mr. Putin: Operative in the Kremlin,* that Russia's interests are "tightly fused with, and now largely inseparable from, [Putin's] own . . . interests."

Putin was, in Hill's analysis, an angry, grievance-ridden bundle of contradictions, a talented strategic thinker with a ready mind for contingency planning who was able to pivot quickly based on an adversary's reaction to his actions. His problem was that he didn't understand the West—and saw the world through the shadows of his KGB experience.

"Putin," she wrote, "falls back on his (and Russia's) age-old threat perceptions. He looks for, and finds, plots and conspiracies. The plots he finds are consistent with his logic. They make sense in terms of his frame of reference—as seen through his filters of the Cold War, the KGB, his time in Dresden, and the prevailing political views of conservative and patriotic Russia circles."

In fact, Putin would rely on those very circles—most particularly, the security services and the KGB, which were some of the only functioning institutions—to consolidate his power throughout the 1990s. By 1991, he embarked on his political career—serving in various administration roles in St. Petersburg and moving to Moscow after his mentor, St. Petersburg mayor Anatoly Sobchak, lost his reelection campaign, which Putin had been leading. Once in Moscow, Putin's rise was positively meteoric. In 1996, he joined Boris Yeltsin's presidential staff and achieved the highest rank in civilian service. In 1997, he earned his PhD in economics (notably, accused of having plagiarized large sections of his dissertation). After serving briefly as the head of the FSB and secretary for the Security Council of Russia, he was appointed prime minister by an aging, beleaguered Yeltsin in 1999.

Years later, it was a quick and easy line for commentators to say that Putin's goal all along was to reconstitute the USSR. But the truth is that Putin was dismissive (to the point of anger) of the Soviet-era leaders. By allowing the Soviet republics to flourish, each with its own distinctive culture, he argued, they sowed the seeds of splitting away from Moscow. In one of his sharper public comments, on the anniversary of Lenin's death, Putin called Lenin's dream of a global communist revolution "an atomic bomb under the building that is called Russia which later exploded."

Putin was the opposite of a communist fanatic. He was a royalist. He didn't keep a bust of Lenin in his office; he kept one of Peter the Great. To his mind, communism was responsible for Russia's loss of its greatest expanse: its empire from the days of the tsars. Communism had left him, as a young lieutenant colonel, hurriedly burning papers in a KGB command post in Dresden as the Wall fell and nonviolent protesters overran the East German police headquarters next door. He and his colleagues, he recounted later, burned documents "night and day" until "the furnace burst." Moscow, then under the hand of Mikhail Gorbachev, said nothing as the Wall fell. It appeared that Putin never forgave Gorbachev for that silence.

Rice argued that if Putin had an ideological bent, it was in the direction of Russian exceptionalism. He mixed in a show of horror and contempt for Western decadence and decline—though it was never clear how much of that mindset was sincere belief and how much convenient caricature. What was clear is that in Putin's mind there was only one man who could save Russian civilization: Putin himself.

Each American president who has dealt with Putin has seemed to sense his perceived call of destiny—even if they failed to internalize its implications. Perhaps because presidents convince themselves that the solution to many problems lies in developing a leader-to-leader relationship, they were convinced they could talk him into what they saw as the rational decision, such as joining the West for the good of the Russian economy.

Clinton barely had a chance: Putin was just taking office in the last year of his term. Bush believed that the key to bridging the gap between the United States and Russia was a personal relationship with Putin, so he kept reaching out, hoping that he could uncover Putin's "soul," which he once said he'd glimpsed in an early face-to-face meeting.

It wasn't until the later years of his presidency that Bush started privately confiding to advisors and fellow leaders his concern that Putin didn't seem to understand the whole democracy thing. "I think Putin is not a democrat anymore," he reportedly told Slovenia's prime minister in 2006. "He's a tsar. I think we've lost him." (Of course, in hindsight, it's not clear that anyone had ever "had" him.)

The debate over whether Putin was a pliable nationalist or a man on a mission to restore Russian greatness at any cost should have been resolved just a few months later, in the spring of 2007. It was then, in a speech at the Munich Security Conference that got far too little attention at the time, that Putin laid his cards on the table.

The conference's conversation that year was dominated by the unfolding disaster in Iraq and by America's effort to extract itself from a war that was looking a lot more complicated than it had when the United States invaded four years before. Putin, however, was consumed by his own rising anger at American, and NATO, arrogance. A series of recent events—not only the Iraq invasion, but also U.S. support for the color revolutions, and the steady expansion of NATO—reinforced his certainty that the Americans would condescend to him, even appease him, but never truly count him as an equal. At Munich, the Russian delegation was treated as an afterthought, he and his colleagues complained, a once-great power being patted on the head and told that it had a bright future, as long as it played by Western rules. If Western leaders listened, it was only because Russia still had a nuclear arsenal.

As Putin strode into the hotel's great hall, dressed in a black suit and black striped tie, to face the allies he had spent a career in the KGB trying to defeat, he was determined to deliver a message: We're not going quietly.

"Only two decades ago the world was ideologically and economically divided and it was the huge strategic potential of two superpowers that ensured global security." Now, he said, that balance had been destroyed. America was determined to be a hyperpower, to lead in a unipolar world with no competitors and no limits on its power. "Today we are witnessing an almost uncontained hyper use of force—military force—in international relations, a force that is plunging the world into an abyss of permanent conflicts. . . . One state and, of course, first and foremost the United States, has overstepped its national borders in every way.

"And of course this is extremely dangerous. It results in the fact that no one feels safe. I want to emphasize this—no one feels safe!"

The room turned quiet—this wasn't the kind of speech that was on the agenda. What had happened to all the happy talk of joining the European Union and NATO?

Putin concluded his speech by pointing to his more paranoid fears. "NATO has put its frontline forces on our borders." The Russians, he argued, were playing by the rules and fulfilling their treaty obligations. It was the Americans, the hypocrites who talked about "norms" all the time, who were firing when ready. He referred to the supposed American promises to refrain from moving NATO east. If the United States was going to violate its own assurances, he said, "We have the right to ask: Against whom is this expansion intended?"

It wasn't an unreasonable question, but it was one that no one in the room really wanted to tackle. The pat description given by diplomats at the time was that NATO's expansion wasn't directed at anyone; it was a way to allow nations once captive to the Soviet Bloc to choose their own alliances. To decide, freely, with whom they wanted to associate. To support liberty and freedom and prevent democratic backsliding. Of course, that was the high-minded, easy-to-justify element of the goal. But there was no question that enlargement was also a kind of insurance policy to assure permanent Russian containment.

The audience gave Putin a round of polite applause and then retreated to a series of private what-was-that-all-about conversations. But as David Ignatius of *The Washington Post* noted years later, at the time the speech "didn't make much of an impression" beyond the room where it was given. "Putin's Russia seemed too feeble to worry about," he wrote.

Still, the Bush administration could not let the diatribe go unanswered. A day later, Bob Gates, the American defense secretary and former CIA chief, tried to deal with Putin's complaints with disarming humor. "I guess old spies have a habit of blunt speaking," he said, referring to himself and Putin. He pushed back on the Russian's complaints, taking them up one by one. Then Gates delivered his final judgment: "One Cold War was quite enough."

Bush was rattled enough by Putin's speech to dispatch Hadley, the national security advisor, on a quiet trip to Moscow to sit down with Putin and determine where his head was. Hadley flew to Moscow and was escorted into a room at the Kremlin, where Putin received him. "He had himself at a desk on a dais, and I was about six feet below him," Hadley told me, a reminder that he was "a staff person talking to the president of Russia." Putin was armed with a stack of cards, Hadley recalled, "each one of which had a separate grievance against the United States, against the West, and he went through them one by one." Hadley tried to respond to each one, but—lower both physically and in rank—he was at a distinct disadvantage. After seventy-five minutes, Putin stepped down and said, "Thanks for coming. I'll see you anytime you come to Russia."

Looking back on the era, Hadley recalled to me later, "We thought that with the end of the Cold War there was an opportunity to bring Russia permanently into the West," and Putin repeatedly told Bush that he was on board with the strategy. "That's what I want to do," Putin said. Then he added: "But there are dark forces in Russia. And it's important that they not be awakened. So you need to let me do it in my own time."

This was, of course, classic Putin disinformation. His interest in joining the West was episodic at best and nonexistent after he saw the American support for the color revolutions in Georgia, Ukraine, and Kyrgyzstan. "We thought those were good things—people trying to insist on accountable governments that would be prosperous and stable, good neighbors for Russia," Hadley recalled. "Putin didn't see it that way. He thought these uprisings were CIA front operations to install anti-Russian governments on his border, and they were a dress rehearsal for destabilizing Russia."

IN RETROSPECT, it's easy to look back and say that the West was naïve about Putin. After all, he repeatedly told the world where he was headed and the logic under which he was operating. And clearly the United States either dismissed those warnings or heard only the parts it wanted to hear.

Yet it was a reasonable assumption in the Bush era—as well as for several years into the Obama administration—that Putin was not irredeemable. Almost everyone clung to the theory that over time, he was going to increasingly value his relationship with Europe, the hefty dividends from oil sales, and the status that came with being a nuclear power. All that, the theory went, would tamp down his instincts to reconstruct an empire.

The more mystifying aspect is how the West reacted—or underreacted—to actual acts of aggression, the precursors to the Ukraine invasion. In 2008, in Bucharest, Bush pushed the Western Europeans hard to set Georgia and Ukraine on the path to becoming full-fledged NATO members. Ultimately, neither one even received a road map for entering the alliance—called, in diplo-speak, a "membership application plan," naturally shortened to "MAP." Instead, they were issued a consolation prize: an artfully vague statement promising them eventual membership. Bush and the prime minister of Britain, Gordon Brown, were delighted. "We didn't give them MAPs," Bush recalled Brown crowing at the end of the summit, "but we may have just made them members!"

It was a terrible compromise that combined the worst of both options by exposing the two countries to Russian anger while providing them none of the protection that comes with actual NATO membership. Putin was furious. "Ukraine is not even a state!" he allegedly raged at Bush. "What is Ukraine? Part of its territory is Eastern Europe, and part—and a significant one—was donated by us!" he said, in an apparent reference to 1954 when Nikita Khrushchev handed over the Crimean Peninsula to Ukraine, then part of the Soviet Union. (From the earliest days of the dissolution of the USSR, Russian leaders had been trying to claw the peninsula back—partly because Sevastopol, a major Russian naval base, was headquartered there. In 1997, Ukraine granted Russia a twenty-year lease to the base.)

In the weeks and months after the conference, a pattern of regionalized Russian aggression began to build. The first strike was digital: a wave of cyberattacks in the spring of 2007 that kneecapped the Estonian government. Then, in August 2008, Putin turned his glare on Georgia. This time he escalated exponentially—invading the country to claim disputed territory in South Ossetia—with techniques that were not surprising to anyone who had seen the brutality unleashed in Chechnya nearly a decade before. The Russians, claiming that the democratically elected Georgian government was a nest of terrorists, joined with separatists to battle the Georgian armed forces. Ultimately, nearly two hundred thousand were displaced, several hundred killed, and both Georgian and Russian forces accused of war crimes. The war lasted only five days, but it redrew Georgia's boundaries and gave the world a glimpse of the future.

For this war, Putin paid almost no price. The Bush administration debated the use of force to slow the Russian advance—perhaps through air strikes—but quickly took that option off the table. A number of ongoing initiatives or negotiations, including military cooperation and the potential for Russian accession to the WTO, were temporarily placed in jeopardy or on hold.

And the United States and other countries continued to buy oil from the Russians. In fact, they bought more than ever. By the U.S. Energy Department's own statistics, American imports of Russian oil moved from 170 million barrels a year in 2008 to 205 million in 2009 and 223 million in 2010.

As the Bush administration prepared to leave the White House in early 2009, they prepared a series of briefings for the incoming administration of Barack Obama. Recently declassified, the papers warned the new president that the Russian government was undertaking destabilizing activities across the board: threatening Eastern European states, increasing Western Europe's dependence on Russian gas, and undercutting the rule of law at home. Despite seven years of outreach, Bush did not seem to have appealed to Putin's better angels. And, outgoing officials warned, Ukraine was a particular target: "Russia attempts to challenge the territorial integrity of Ukraine, particularly in Crimea, which is 59 percent ethnically Russian and is home to the Russian Navy's Black Sea Fleet, must be prevented."

THE INVASION OF Georgia shook more than a few U.S. politicians—or at least the ones whose first thought, on hearing the word "Georgia," was not about the electoral map of Cobb County. Perhaps the one most energized was Barack Obama's choice as a running mate: Joe Biden.

Obama had served briefly on the Senate's Committee on Foreign Relations, but he had an acute sense that most of America's overseas adventures had been disastrous. Iraq was the "dumb war," he said, Afghanistan the "necessary" one. And he wasn't looking for America to flex its muscles in new corners of the world, especially those he didn't think were at the heart of America's strategic interests. Georgia and Ukraine fit that description—places that, as Obama often said, the Russians care about more than we do.

Biden, in contrast, had run that same Committee on Foreign Relations, and he had a different view. He didn't want American troops at risk—in fact, he wanted to get out of Afghanistan faster than Obama did. But he was also nearly two decades older than Obama, very much a product of the Cold War—and he believed, like Blinken, that if America did not fill power vacuums, someone else would. So it was Biden, not Obama, who got on an airplane to Georgia in the midst of its crisis. "He came back and said we needed to give them a billion dollars in aid," recalled Michael McFaul, the Montana-born political scientist whom Obama had pulled in from Stanford, first as a foreign policy advisor on his campaign, then as his Russia expert at the White House, and later as ambassador to Moscow.

McFaul spent the heat of the 2008 campaign fearful that John McCain, the hawkish Vietnam vet who had secured the Republican nomination, would outflank Obama on the issue of Putin's aggression and make the Democrats look soft on Russia. "We were just worried about looking weak compared to McCain and all that," he said. Of course, this is exactly why Joe Biden was on the ticket, to give some Washington experience and foreign policy heft, given that the presidential nominee had been in the Illinois State Senate just a few years before. "Biden was put out front as being, you know, the guy who knows Georgia, the guy who knows the region."

After Obama's win in November, the informal division of labor continued. Obama was in charge of handling the Russians, Biden the surrounding states. In their first year in office, Biden visited Georgia and Ukraine. Obama took on the two big nuclear counterparts and went to Beijing and Moscow, including his first meeting with Putin. The strained smiles were evident to all. Obama treaded carefully, trying to be diplomatic without sounding naïve.

"I'm aware of not only the extraordinary work that you've done on behalf of the Russian people," Obama said over breakfast with Putin at the Russian leader's country dacha. "We think there's an excellent opportunity to put U.S.-Russian relations on a much stronger footing."

Obama wasn't willing to go much further than to offer token support for the Georgians. He had more urgent agenda items and needed help from Moscow for many of them. He wanted to negotiate the New START treaty to ensure there were new limits on the American and Russian nuclear arsenals. He wanted to stop Iran from putting together the fuel and technology to make a nuclear weapon—and needed help from the Russians, who had built Iran's only major nuclear power reactor. And he wanted to go kill Osama Bin Laden, a mission that required expanding American access to supply lines that did not run through Pakistan, emphasized McFaul, who moved into the White House as the chief Russia policymaker. "To make any of those happen, the Americans needed the Russians to play ball."

The result, McFaul said, was that "there was just no appetite" for bolstering Georgia. "We debated it when we got into office in January. What are we going to do on Georgia?" he recalled, paraphrasing the debate. "So they asked, 'Well, what did the guys before us do, these "tough guys"? Send them weapons?' No. So why are we sending them weapons, seven months after? Did they sanction any Russians? No, they didn't sanction a single person."

Obama was hoping for a "reset" with Russia, even though the relationship had gotten off to a bad start. When Hillary Clinton, Obama's secretary of state, took her first trip to Moscow to meet Lavrov, she was armed with a giant red button—the kind you might buy in an office supply store—with the word "reset" printed on it. Or at least Clinton's people thought that was what it said. Unfortunately, the Russian term was a mistranslation: It read, roughly, "overcharge." The two diplomats gamely pressed the button for the cameras anyway.

For a while at least, "reset" seemed like a working strategy—in part because Obama got to deal with Dmitry Medvedev, the Putin lackey who took over the presidency between 2008 and 2012. Medvedev's term in office was a giant sham; he was there to avoid having Putin violate presidential term limits. Putin resumed his post as prime minister—the role he had previously held under Yeltsin—but everyone knew where the real power lay.

Hill recalled that Medvedev—at least at the time—was "a warmer, fuzzier person to deal with. Kind of the kinder, gentler version of Vladimir Putin. Same issues he was concerned with, pushing Russian interests, but a very different style and approach."

But the Eastern European countries weren't comforted. "Our region is one part of the world that Americans have largely stopped worrying about," said an open letter to the Obama administration, signed by nearly two dozen regional leaders, including Lech Walesa and Václav Havel. "Indeed, at times we have the impression that U.S. policy was so successful that many American officials have now concluded that our region is fixed once and for all. . . . That view is premature," they warned. "Russia is back as a revisionist power pursuing a 19th-century agenda with 21st-century tactics and methods." It was published in mid-2009— and would prove entirely prophetic.

Still, Obama and his senior aides focused on the progress that they could make with Moscow during that era. There was cooperation on terrorism, on climate change, and—for a while—on the Middle East. In 2010, presidents Obama and Medvedev signed New START, bringing each country down to 1,550 deployed nuclear weapons, with strengthened inspections to make sure neither side cheated. Russia even helped with negotiating what would eventually become the 2015 Iran deal, and had voted with Washington on a United Nations resolution to sanction Tehran. Obama was "able to actually achieve some stability and predictability in what was usually a rather contentious and difficult relationship to manage," Hill later said.

But stability is different than progress.

In private, Obama administration officials were willing to admit that relations with the Russians, even under Medvedev, weren't improving as much as they had hoped. Even getting to yes on the modest New START treaty was "very, very hard," in the words of one official. And when McFaul and Blinken floated the idea of creating a bilateral commission to further cooperation in areas of mutual interest—chaired on the U.S. side by Biden and on the Russian side by Putin, at the time the prime minister—the Russians immediately shot it down. "We were all enthusiastic about it," recalled McFaul, "but Putin said 'I'm not interested in that,' because he didn't see Vice President Biden as his equal."

Putin, it was clear, was increasingly mistrustful of American intentions. Russia hadn't stood in the way when the United States pushed for a cease-fire and no-fly zone in 2011 in Libya. But when this "humanitarian" intervention ended in regime change—the killing of Col. Muammar Qaddafi, the country's longtime dictator—Putin became enraged at what he viewed as a thinly disguised imperialist mission.

Then, in 2011, Putin declared that he was going to seek the presidency again. Medvedev, of course, had no choice but to get out of the way. McFaul, recalling the era, shook his head. "When Putin announced that he was running for reelection in September 2011—that's when I told the president, 'Look, all bets are off. There's no more reset.'"

Obama's reply, he recalled, was along the lines of " 'Yeah, we had a good run and got a lot of things done. This guy is going to be harder. We got to play the long game, right?' That's a phrase that Obama would use with us. 'We've got to see what we can do,' but that to me was the end of cooperation with these guys."

It was near the end of the line for the Russian political opposition too. Later that year, tens of thousands took to the streets—rallied by opposition leaders who quickly became famous not only within Russia but around the world—to protest the fraud-filled 2011 parliamentary elections. The two who captured the most attention were Boris Nemtsov, a longtime outspoken Putin critic, and Alexei Navalny, who electrified crowds by calling Putin a crook and a thief and urging people to "keep taking to the streets until we regain that which belongs to us." Putin's own election was scheduled for March 2012, and Navalny kept repeating that the Russian people held the power to force the regime to "change peacefully."

Putin was well practiced in dealing with street protesters. But he bristled when Secretary of State Hillary Clinton joined the chorus of those who declared that the parliamentary elections had been fixed. "We have serious concerns about the conduct of the election," Clinton said in a December statement from the State Department that called for an investigation into the results. (Later, American intelligence analysts would identify this statement as the moment when Putin's burning hatred for Clinton hardened, which contributed to the launch of the hacking and disinformation operations that went after her 2016 presidential campaign.)

By American diplomatic standards, hers was boilerplate language. To Putin, it was evidence that the next U.S. target for regime change might be Moscow. Conveniently, he accused Russian opposition activists of being puppets of the U.S. State Department. "We will have to think about strengthening the law and holding more responsible those who carry out the task of a foreign government to influence internal political processes," he threatened.

Unsurprisingly, in March 2012 Putin won the presidential vote with a resounding 65 percent. The protests were crushed, opposition leaders were targeted, and laws were changed to impose a heavy penalty on activists. Nemtsov was assassinated just three years later, presumably at the orders of the FSB, on a bridge in Moscow near the Kremlin. Navalny began his cycle in and out of prison, survived a poisoning attempt, and returned to Moscow, where he was forced to endure a show trial. In August 2023, nineteen years were added to his already draconian sentence in a high-security prison. Six months later, he was announced dead.

Little of this narrative permeated the American consciousness. In 2012, after Mitt Romney, the Republican presidential nominee, identified Russia as the U.S.'s number one geopolitical foe during the presidential campaign, Obama mocked him. "The 1980s are now calling to ask for their foreign policy back," he laughed during a debate, "because the Cold War's been over for twenty years."

Romney was wrong that Russia was America's top geopolitical foe. Like many politicians of that era, he didn't understand the fundamentally different kind of challenge that was emerging in China. But he was right that the United States was consistently underreacting to Putin's escalating gambits. As Condoleezza Rice put it to me in 2022, "Fighting for territory, thinking in ethnic terms, using resources to wage war. I thought we had moved beyond that."

She added: "This wasn't supposed to happen. We thought the linearity of human progress should have left all of this behind."

CHAPTER 2

THE LOST DECADES

By joining the WTO, China is not simply agreeing to import more of our products; it is agreeing to import one of democracy's most cherished values: economic freedom. The more China liberalizes its economy, the more fully it will liberate the potential of its people—their initiative, their imagination, their remarkable spirit of enterprise. And when individuals have the power, not just to dream but to realize their dreams, they will demand a greater say.

President Bill Clinton, March 2000

Americans have often thought that they could alter another country to their liking, and then felt frustrated when things turned out otherwise.

Wang Jisi, president, Institute of International and Strategic Studies, Peking University, Summer 2018

WHEN ROBERT RUBIN, Bill Clinton's secretary of the treasury, took off from Andrews Air Force Base for China in an aging Air Force plane in 1997, it was the first time the former investment banker had traveled to the Middle Kingdom.

In that era, China was still considered an "emerging market," and usually found itself in American headlines more for its post–Tiananmen Square struggle with human rights than for its economic prowess. "When I was at Goldman," Rubin told me mid-flight, referring to his twenty-six years at Goldman Sachs, the investment bank where he started in the 1970s and ended up as co-chairman, "there weren't enough commercial transactions in China to even justify a trip."

Rubin's lack of experience dealing with the mainland wasn't unusual. For the first two decades after Nixon's diplomatic opening in 1972, China's market was still too small—and its practices too protectionist—for Wall Street's biggest financial institutions to notice. Even as Rubin prepared to step foot in the People's Republic for the first time, five years into the Clinton administration, China's gross domestic product was only $961 billion, compared to the United States' nearly $32 trillion. Per capita, that came out to about $782, putting China very much in the category of developing countries.

What fixated American officials was how fast China was growing. Its year-over-year GDP growth in the early 1990s averaged around 11 percent, and even in the midst of the 1997 Asian financial crisis it still hovered close to 8 percent. And even though China was still a bit player on the economic scene, on international security it was clearly poised to become a powerhouse.* It maintained the world's largest standing army, a small but effective nuclear arsenal, and a permanent seat—with veto rights—on the UN Security Council. It was clear the United States was going to have to figure out a way to talk to China at a depth and with a sophistication that had been missing in the glow of reopening relations. "We can properly be faulted," Rubin told me at the time, "for vastly underinvesting in our relationships with Chinese officials up and down the line." Part of Rubin's mission on this trip was to rectify that lapse, in hopes of drawing China's economy closer to the West.

Looking back in 2023 on his time in the Clinton administration, what stood out to Rubin most was his relationship with Vice Premier Zhu Rongji. Zhu emerged as the driving force in the Chinese Communist Party's increasing embrace of market economics. There was nothing in his history to suggest such capitalist zeal: He joined the Communist Party in 1949, the year Mao Zedong proclaimed the creation of the People's Republic, and rose quickly over the next decade before being purged twice—partly because of his family's pre-revolution wealth and partly for his own open criticism of Mao's economic policies.

* China replaced Taiwan on the UN Security Council in 1971.

But as the country looked to new leadership following Mao's death in 1976, Zhu resumed his public career, moving quickly from dean of the economics school at Tsinghua University, to mayor of the boomtown of Shanghai, to head of the People's Bank of China. By the 1990s Zhu was aggressively making the case that as the Chinese market opened and Western-style laws and regulation began to take hold, Americans would want—would *need*—to get in on the ground floor. Infamous for his hard-charging and often inflexible nature, Zhu was a relentless reformer. Quickly, he also became known as a skilled America-handler, the rare Chinese official with fluency not only in English but also in the language of investment bankers and tech entrepreneurs.

Zhu was "an enormously impressive man," Rubin recalled with some nostalgia. He and Zhu had grown close because of Zhu's single-minded determination to move China from a state-run economy dominated by overstaffed and inefficient state-owned firms to a market economy more in line with the West. The two made an odd couple: the communist preaching capitalism-with-Chinese-characteristics and the former Goldman banker trying to coax China into adopting Western rules. Zhu talked of market reforms and capital flows so easily that Rubin joked with him that if it weren't for America's constitutional restrictions "what he ought to do was leave China and come to the United States and run for president."

"I did think at the time that with Zhu Rongji there, they were changing. . . . I don't think I ever thought they would *be* a market-based economy," Rubin told me, perhaps with the benefit of hindsight. "I thought they were heading towards being *more* of a market-based economy."

Rubin's trip, carefully choreographed by the Treasury Department to encourage China's still-rare experiments with the private sector, became something of a model for the next quarter century, as a steady parade of American leaders—secretaries of state, commerce, and energy, trade representatives, and the chief executives of Apple, Boeing, and Exxon—made pilgrimages to Beijing and echoed his message. They visited factories, encouraged American investment, and warned China that if it wanted to attract Western investors, it had to learn how to play by Western rules. And they reaffirmed their belief that China would continue to open up and liberalize—though they complained, of course, that it was happening too slowly and without the needed protections for intellectual property and the rule of law. But it was happening.

The belief underpinning these visits—and virtually every element of American policy toward China—was that it would be economic and diplomatic malpractice not to entice the country toward the West. Wrapping Beijing into the Western-led economic world would change everything, it was assumed. Increased exposure to Western norms and legal systems would seep into Chinese society. Newly acquired wealth would embolden China's population to seek more capitalist reforms and, ultimately, political reforms. Meanwhile, the expansion of the internet would put China on a slow train to freer expression and some form of democracy. "China," Bill Clinton famously quipped in 2000, "has been trying to crack down on the Internet. Good luck! That's sort of like trying to nail Jell-O to the wall."

Often left unstated was the final goal: The more deeply that China and the West became intertwined, the less chance there would be for conflict because both sides would have too much to lose. China would hardly become America, of course. But it might come to look like Europe, at least economically—with lots of regulation, a predilection for supporting national companies, and more than a touch of protectionism.

That narrative fit Washington's global agenda so perfectly that few questioned the underlying logic. And so Washington—willfully—began to see every bit of progress in China through this lens and every setback as a brief deviation from Beijing's inevitable destiny. Over the next two decades Washington assumed China's economic interests would overwhelm its other national objectives. For years, until they could no longer ignore what was occurring in plain sight, Republican and Democratic presidents publicly played down the mounting evidence that China had territorial ambitions that stretched throughout the Pacific, that its use of cyber tools to steal both industrial and state secrets was designed to serve a broader national agenda, and that its growing economic power would foster a commensurate desire for political influence—as it did for every other rising power across history. Some of this misreading was encouraged by the Chinese leadership, who talked about the need to "hide one's strength and bide one's time," but few asked many questions about what would happen when China moved to the next phase.

Only when China's power plays grew impossible to ignore—when it used its repressive technology to crack down on Hong Kong, found an excuse to expand its threats against Taiwan, claimed exclusive rights to vast parts of the South China Sea, and adopted a strategy of becoming less dependent on foreign technologies while increasing foreigners' dependence on Chinese technology—did the United States react, and then, perhaps, overreact. By the 2020s, with the COVID-19 pandemic and the accusations that China accidentally or deliberately let the virus leap from a lab, many in the United States moved from distrusting Beijing to detesting it.

It was a remarkable shift. In a quarter century, Americans went from viewing China as an economic opportunity and diplomatic partner to wondering if our technology and political competition placed us on an eventual course toward war.

ALMOST AS SOON as Rubin returned to Washington, China stepped up its long-running campaign to join the most important economic club on the globe: the newly created World Trade Organization. But to qualify for membership—and to reap the ensuing economic benefits— China would first have to convince other nations that it was prepared to radically transform the closed, state-dominated economy that was Mao's enduring legacy. And this meant Chinese leaders had to travel the world forging bilateral deals with existing WTO members, concluding with the United States, the largest economy on earth and the one best positioned to extract concessions from Beijing.

By 1999, the thankless task of negotiating this complex, politically risky trade deal between the United States and China fell to a wiry, acerbic forty-nine-year-old lawyer, Charlene Barshefsky. The child of Polish and Russian Jewish immigrants on the north side of Chicago, she rose to become United States Trade Representative during Clinton's second term. Dogged and quick-witted, Barshefsky was a master of improvisation in the service of a deal: She once dragged the male head of President Clinton's national economic council into a ladies' room in Beijing to call the president from the one place they could avoid Chinese listening devices and American journalists.

Barshefsky knew that the politics of getting China into the WTO were nearly as complicated in Washington as they were in Beijing. In Washington, union officials—the core of Clinton's Democratic base—had spent the 1980s and '90s fighting Japanese auto imports and now feared that China's WTO membership would further open the floodgates. It was a familiar battle for Clinton, who had pushed through NAFTA—the North Atlantic Free Trade Agreement—with more Republican votes than Democratic ones. Freer trade would bring pain, Clinton knew, but he also believed that it would launch China on a path of westernization as inevitable as it was desirable. "Membership in the WTO," he said, "will not create a free society in China overnight or guarantee that China will play by global rules. But over time, I believe it will move China faster and further in the right direction, and certainly will do that more than rejection would."

In Beijing the Communist Party feared the social implications of opening its economy, but with a slightly different twist: China wanted—needed—a wave of foreign investment right at the moment it was emerging as one of the most critical manufacturing hubs in the world. But party officials worried that opening China's market to the West would eviscerate their state-owned industries, leaving millions unemployed and threatening political stability. Opening the Chinese market to Western telecommunications, banking, insurance, and other financial services firms would bring in unpredictable foreign influences—and reduce China's levers on its own economy.

It fell to Barshefsky, operating out of the small Winder Building near the White House where Abraham Lincoln used to drop by for updates on Civil War battles, to work both sides, trying to negotiate a deal that each capital could live with.

On the Chinese side, Zhu Rongji, who believed it was possible to open China's markets without unraveling its political system, led the charge. (When the Americans called him "China's Gorbachev" during an early visit to the United States, he snapped, "I'm China's Zhu Rongji!") With his technical acumen, finely tuned understanding of American business culture, and relentless commitment to crushing rampant corruption, he was Washington's idealized vision of the Chinese leader of the future. "He had extraordinary intellectual power," Barshefsky recalled, "and was dogged, determined, and had a vision on the economic side, I'm not talking about politics, far more compatible with the West."

Zhu was adept at playing American power games—sometimes to the shock of his interlocutors—and he wanted a quick deal. So when he realized in the spring of 1999 that President Clinton was slow-walking the negotiations because of opposition on Capitol Hill, Zhu took to the road. In a five-day tour, he visited Denver, Chicago, New York, and Boston to persuade American business leaders who wanted to enter the Chinese market to put the hard sell on their own president. It was a re-markable scene: a Communist Party leader in the den of American cap-italism, whipping votes. It worked—the administration was flooded with angry emails and phone calls from top executives.

"Zhu basically went to the country," Robert Hormats, the vice chair-man of Goldman Sachs International, which handled many of China's bond offerings, told me at the time. "City by city, he said, 'Look what's in this for you.' It was remarkable. I've never seen a foreign leader, much less a Chinese leader, pull this off."

But just three weeks after Zhu returned to China, the negotiations came to an abrupt halt after a U.S.-led NATO air campaign in Yugosla-via accidentally struck the Chinese embassy in Belgrade, killing three journalists. Suddenly memories of the darker Cold War days were re-vived: Beijing, insisting that the attack had been intentional, cut mili-tary visits, port calls, and communications with the United States. It took months of phone calls and a personal meeting between Clinton and Jiang Zemin to get negotiations back on track.

By November 1999, Barshefsky had been shuttling back and forth to Beijing for months, trying to finalize a deal. But as happens in all trade negotiations, the toughest issues had been kicked down the road. After three days of little progress in the Chinese capital, Barshefsky was ready to head home. "We weren't making much progress, and I thought the longer our delegation stayed, the weaker the United States looked." So she and her delegation sent their luggage to the airport and dropped by the Chinese trade ministry the next morning to declare that if they wanted to talk further, "they knew our phone number."

Barshefsky's Chinese counterparts seemed stunned—and asked her to stay just a little longer. They quickly summoned Zhu Rongji to the ministry. "He's never been here before," Barshefsky recalled them saying. Once Zhu arrived, she said, "We just went through the list and came out with an agreement. They were determined to get it done—or I should say, *he* was determined to get it done."

Soon a landmark agreement was announced. The United States and China would permanently normalize trade relations—and the United States would support China's WTO bid. Barshefsky gave the credit to Zhu: "I don't think I knew another leader like him," she told me in 2023, "because he took it upon himself to modernize the Chinese economy, even in the absence of strong political backing."

In the years after, China grew at an unbelievable rate. By 2007, per capita GDP had nearly tripled to $2,694; by 2017, it had tripled again, to $8,817. But Zhu was hardly hailed as a hero when he retired in 2003—the domestic financial and economic reforms he championed within China shocked the economy. Chinese families poured their savings into a booming stock market, then were wiped out by the predictable crash. There were looming fears of a Japanese-style banking crisis. Millions were lifted out of poverty—while others lost their jobs as state-owned enterprises were gutted. The suddenly wealthy class of private entrepreneurs driving BMWs and Mercedes around the streets of Beijing and Shanghai underscored the wildly unequal distribution of gains.

Yet just two decades later it seems almost impossible to imagine that a Chinese premier would be given the kind of power that Zhu exercised. And by the 2020s, Zhu's whole philosophy—that China's future lay in nurturing an innovative private sector, largely free of the rigid control over state-owned industries—had been reversed, a possibility few American officials had even contemplated given China's trajectory under Deng and immediately after.

"I think that along the way, there was perhaps a misjudging of China's changing intentions," Barshefsky told me later, "and therefore, a failure to take action to block or sanction imports, when action could have appropriately been taken," she said.

The next four American presidents, she said, gradually edged toward a different focus: "to keep the peace, to improve relations—without thinking through what more recent actions, particularly under Xi's leadership, portended for China's direction and its insatiable desire to dominate."

. . .

"I'M TRYING TO figure out if your question is a trick question."

George W. Bush, just days away from being sworn in as the forty-third president, narrowed his eyes, giving me a look that paired bemusement with suspicion. My colleague Frank Bruni and I had gone to Bush's ranch house in Crawford, Texas, for a ritual of *New York Times* journalism: a long interview with the man about to assume the presidency. Bush, disarmingly informal as he padded around his house with his small black terrier, Barney, offered to brew us some coffee.

The "trick question" that Bush was half-complaining about wasn't intended as a trick at all: As his presidency approached, was Bush more worried about a strong China or a weak one?

"That's an interesting question," he said, seeming to stall for time while he figured out an answer. "Well, internally weak is going to mean that there is uncertainty and instability in the government. . . . To me, particularly as China develops as a military power, a chaotic China would be something that should cause great concern to people in the region and to us."

It wasn't the most decisive response for a man who had blasted Clinton during the campaign for being soft on China, going so far as to call the country a "strategic competitor" with the United States. On one issue, Bush did agree with his predecessor. "Look," he told me, "I completely agree with the concept that trade equates to freedom. Once the Internet is in place, I mean, it is going to be a powerful conduit for change." But he admitted that relying on trade alone to open the political system was not a viable strategy.

Setting aside the fact that trade in no way equates directly to political freedom—the United States trades a lot with Saudi Arabia—Clinton's approach *did* fall well short of a strategy. But that afternoon in Crawford, Bush seemed uncertain how to diagnose our relationship with China, much less fix it.

"I view China as a great nation," he told us as we headed out for a hike down to a waterfall on his ranch. "It is a nation that is going to require my administration to spend a lot of time on explaining that competitors can find areas of agreement and be firm in our resolution when it comes to weapons of mass destruction and consistent in our support of freedom and democracy." That was the easy fallback stuff of politicians who had not yet grappled with the realities of dealing with

Beijing—an assurance that, somehow, the United States would balance its economic interests with its commitments to human rights and national security.

Just over a year later, Bush showed up in Beijing for a state visit. As he also did the same year in St. Petersburg, Russia, he met with local students. At Tsinghua University he reassured the crowd that there was plenty of room at the top for both superpowers. "China," he said, "is on a rising path, and America welcomes the emergence of a strong and peaceful and prosperous China."

What's more, he argued, democracy was about to sweep across the land. "Change is coming," he said. "China is already having secret ballot and competitive elections at the local level. Nearly twenty years ago, a great Chinese leader, Deng Xiaoping, said this—I want you to hear his words. He said that China would eventually expand democratic elections all the way to the national level. I look forward to that day."*

Then it was the students' turn to ask questions. Clearly, they had been carefully selected by the Chinese government. Rather than asking about getting visas to study in the United States or scientific cooperation between the two nations, they drilled Bush on his stance on Taiwan, asked about rising crime levels in the United States, and worried that the United States had "a lot of misunderstandings about China."

They weren't wrong. By the time Bush returned to China in November 2005, enmeshed in wars going poorly in both Afghanistan and Iraq, it was clear that all the progress on democracy he had predicted was dead in the water.

President Hu Jintao made it clear he had no intention of giving in to American pressure on human rights, driving the point home by sending police out to put dissidents under house arrest—and cutting off their telephones—in the hours before Bush arrived. Administration officials denounced the move but went ahead with the meetings. At the Great Hall of the People, Bush and Hu, looking for something to celebrate, told reporters they were taking extraordinary steps to curb the piracy of movies and software. Clearly their message wasn't traveling far: I walked

---

* In fact, it's not clear that Deng said that. While Deng did frequently offer commentary on how Chinese-style democracy should be expanded and overseen by the Chinese people, it is likely that Deng and Bush had very different interpretations of what that commitment looked like in practice.

out of the Great Hall that day, strolled to a market a few blocks away, and bought up a handful of DVDs of current movies.

More disappointments would follow in short order. China skillfully employed its commitment to Bush's "war on terror" to justify its crackdown on the Uyghurs and other minorities. In January 2007 Beijing shot off what may be one of the most irresponsible anti-satellite tests in modern times, aiming a ground-based ballistic missile at a failing Chinese weather satellite that weighed nearly a ton. The test was a success—a warning to the Pentagon—but the satellite shattered into three thousand "trackable objects"—pieces of debris the size of a golf ball that the International Space Station and other spacecraft dodge to this day. "It was extremely irresponsible," Bush's national security advisor, Stephen Hadley, complained to me at the time.*

It wasn't just satellites that China was blowing up. Over the next few years it gained influence on, and sometimes control over, obscure rule-making and standards-setting bodies that govern everything from global food distribution to the internet. China was entirely within its rights to do so. But it was brilliant bureaucratic jujitsu: Rather than be constrained by Western rules, the Chinese government was learning how to rewrite them.

And to Bush's frustration, China pursued a strategy of pegging its currency to the dollar at a clearly undervalued level to make its exports cheaper. That helped cement its hold over critical supply chains—as Americans would discover in 2020, when they started looking for medical masks in bulk. While some Chinese markets opened, China's trade surplus with the United States surged in the Bush years—far beyond the Japanese surpluses that were viewed as such a crisis in the 1980s.

But the far larger problem arose from China's accelerating theft of

---

* China is one of four countries to have tested anti-satellite missile capabilities, including the United States itself. Washington's complaints were twofold: The debris created by the test would be a danger to other satellites for years, and China was militarizing space. The first complaint was legitimate, but the second was not: The United States was the first country to successfully test an ASAT system. And in February 2008, the Navy shot down what the U.S. government called a nonfunctioning satellite just before it entered space. The Americans argued that the debris would deorbit within a few days; the Russians argued that it was cover to conduct a new missile test. See "U.S. Shoots Down Toxic Satellite," *The Daily Telegraph*, February 21, 2008, web.archive.org/web/20081222024953/http://www.news .com.au/dailytelegraph/story/0%2C22049%2C23251796-5001028%2C00.html.

Western technology, a systematized, frequently government-commanded campaign to acquire intellectual property and know-how in any way that worked. Sometimes that meant entering a joint venture with a company, then stealing the inventions and manufacturing processes of its partners. One of the most famous campaigns began in 2010 when China's largest airplane manufacturer collaborated with GE Aviation to produce a new jet engine for the Chinese market. Within a few years the Chinese manufacturer had penetrated the company's suppliers, had stolen their designs, and was busy making component parts without them.

Increasingly, China relied on a sweeping array of cyber exploitation campaigns to siphon key commercial and national security data to Beijing. Nothing was off-limits: Reams of details on American naval warship capabilities and nuclear test data were collected side by side with the trade secrets of General Motors, DuPont Chemical, and Boeing. In one of the worst instances, Chinese hackers broke into the defense contractor Lockheed Martin and stole the plans for the Pentagon's cutting-edge new joint strike fighter, the F-35. The Chinese air force decided to test-fly the plane just as Robert Gates, the American defense secretary under Bush and Obama, was visiting the country.

Suddenly the volume of complaints from American companies began to rise. They protested that they were being ripped off. But as Condoleezza Rice, Bush's secretary of state, noted to me, they hadn't exactly been naïve innocents going into China unaware of the risks of losing their valuable intellectual property. "Lots of companies saw the writing on the wall," Rice said, and entered the market anyway because "it was a good economic deal." Claiming victimhood was "a narrative excuse to benefit CEOs."

Bush's answer to the avalanche of disputes with China was to launch a "Strategic Economic Dialogue" in which top officials from both nations met at the cabinet level to hammer out differences. But the conversations seemed endless, and there was little progress before the 2008–2009 financial crisis hit—and after that, all bets were off.

At one meeting in the midst of the crisis, the head of the Chinese delegation confronted Bush's treasury secretary, Hank Paulson, another former Goldman executive, and warned him that the Chinese weren't so sure they were content to remain deferential in the relationship. "You were my teacher," he told Paulson, "but now here I am in my teacher's domain, and look at your system, Hank. We aren't sure we should be learning from you anymore."

By the time Obama was elected, there was a sense that eight years of dealing with China had left behind more suspicions than wins. The American people, Bush's national security officials wrote in the hand-off memorandum to the incoming administration, were deeply suspicious of China's emergence. "The debate over whether China will be a strategic adversary 15 or 20 years from now will continue. Adversarial views on the U.S. side can feed those on the Chinese side who are equally certain that we will never allow China its 'rightful' place in the world."

Today Bush administration officials are adamant that they made the right decisions at the time, based on the information they had. "If we had not tried to bring China into the international system," Hadley later said to me, "we'd be having a debate right now about who lost China. And some people would be arguing that 'it was you aggressive, Cold War, Bush administration types who forced China into an adversarial relationship with the United States.'"

ON A COLD Tuesday night in Washington in February 2012, Vice President Joe Biden invited Xi Jinping into his library at the Naval Observatory, his official residence in Washington. The two men—along with much of the president's cabinet—had just had dinner, part of an elaborate meet-the-Americans tour for Xi in the months before he ascended to China's presidency.

Biden's job was to serve as Xi's guide and confidant, with the hope of taking the measure of the Chinese leader's interests, instincts, and goals. As Biden recounted later, they talked in the library about every detail of American politics, with Xi quizzing him about the personalities and motivations of individual members of Congress.

It would be a busy week for Xi. The next day he traveled to Muscatine, Iowa, to visit the farm family who had hosted him more than a quarter century before, when he was part of an official delegation examining pig farming. "That trip to the United States was the first trip I made to this country," Xi said, recalling how he had stayed in a room normally occupied by the couple's son. "You were the first group of Americans that I came into contact with," he told his host family. "My impression of the country came from you. To me, you are America."

Xi used his return to Muscatine to portray himself as a different kind of Chinese leader, humble and open, as interested in getting to know ordinary Americans as he was in getting to know Biden. But he left no doubt that he—like China itself—had risen in the world's ranks. His interests had moved from pig farming to geopolitical power plays. As political myth-making went, it was pretty masterful.

Biden went along. "You and I have spent a substantial amount of time together, and that's fairly rare in modern diplomacy," he told Xi in Los Angeles a few days later. Biden, by his own estimate, had spent some twenty hours in the previous six months conversing with Xi directly—both in the United States that February and in Beijing and Chengdu the summer before. Those long, private, frank conversations, Biden would say, were the highlight of his trip.

"I think Xi's own good personality traits were there then," one of Obama's top diplomats told me later. "I remember President Obama commenting at the time—and Biden did, too, as vice president—that so many senior Chinese leaders are kind of a slave to their talking points and reading things. He was much more self-assured about that."

Officials believed—or at least hoped—that Xi was seeking a closer relationship to help sustain the two countries through the inevitable moments of friction. They noted that Xi and his family had been exposed to the worst excesses of an isolated, paranoid China during the Cultural Revolution. His father was exiled to a remote Chinese province during a Communist Party purge. Now he peppered his speeches with American cultural phrases, and he'd even sent his daughter to Harvard—under an assumed name, of course.

It was easy to make the mistake of presuming that because Xi seemed fascinated by America, he was gradually becoming Americanized. To those who were watching closely, though, the visits contained hints that the rising China that Xi imagined would not slot itself deferentially into the U.S.-led order.

Elizabeth Economy, an academic and economist who years later would help navigate the Biden administration's technology competition with Beijing, noted at the time that the balance of power between the two countries was changing. "Usually it's the United States that has the laundry list of issues that we want China to take action on," she said in 2011. Now, China had its own list and its own red lines. "Really, the big trouble," she said, was that "we have issues that we want to discuss that the Chinese simply have no interest in discussing." As a consequence, the achievements in the U.S.-China relationship of the previous five or ten years were "unfortunately somewhat negligible."

To the nation's intelligence agencies, Xi's agenda remained a mystery. The assessments that spilled out of CIA headquarters before he took office suggested that Xi would likely focus on managing domestic concerns, bolstering China's competitiveness, and avoiding the trap of going head-to-head with the United States and other potential adversaries.

It was an impression that the Chinese government was going out of its way to cultivate—most notably in a pair of articles by Dai Bingguo, one of Hu Jintao's top foreign policy officials, that appeared in Western European newspapers. In them, Dai vowed that his country would "unswervingly pursue the path of peaceful development" and hew to the "win-win strategy of opening up." He assured skeptical Westerners that this was "neither simply an act of expediency nor a perfunctory gesture to soothe foreigners. . . . We hope that the world welcomes rather than worrying about China's peaceful development and supports rather than doing anything to obstruct it."

Xi was peddling the same reassurances. What the Chinese people wanted, he said in his first public speech as party chairman in late 2012, was "better education, more stable jobs, more satisfactory income, more reliable social security, medical services with higher standards, more comfortable living conditions, and a more beautiful environment." It would be his government's job to fight corruption, eliminate the gap between ordinary Chinese and the party elite, and ensure that China's new wealth benefited all its people.

THAT, AT LEAST, was the public line. His private speeches, delivered at the time behind closed doors to party leaders and only revealed later, suggested otherwise. Even as Xi and Biden were traveling through the Chinese and American heartlands, China's counterintelligence units were completing a two-year effort to dismantle the CIA's spying operations in

China. They hunted down nearly two dozen of the agency's sources, executing some of them—including one whom my *Times* colleagues reported had been "shot in front of his colleagues in the courtyard of a government building" to send a message to others who might have thought about being useful to the Americans. It was both a human tragedy and a huge setback for the CIA, forcing the agency to spend years rebuilding its assets in China and setting off a hunt inside the agency to determine whether an insider had betrayed the spies.

The dismantling of the human intelligence network was kept secret in both Beijing and Washington, not surprisingly, until word of the damage it did leaked out years later. But vivid evidence of China's growing military and intelligence ambitions played out on the front pages, a litany of seemingly unrelated but increasingly aggressive actions, each one touching off a debate about what, exactly, Xi and his new government were trying to achieve.

Some of the most violent steps were clearly aimed at consolidating Xi's domestic control—starting with a growing crackdown against Uyghur Muslims in the northwestern province of Xinjiang and the rapid introduction of new national security restrictions designed to crush the once-vibrant democracy movement in Hong Kong, followed by a humbling of the Chinese tech entrepreneurs whose wealth had become a challenge to state power.

Some of Xi's efforts were clearly designed to extend Chinese influence regionally. By 2014, American satellites over the South China Sea revealed Chinese ships dredging sand and pouring concrete over reefs to create "reclaimed" islands where previously none had existed. Meanwhile, Chinese fleets moved in on shoals controlled by the Philippines. It was clear that this was a first foray. Back home, new missile emplacements facing Taiwan appeared on the eastern coast, and China's first aircraft carrier—rebuilt from a hulking leftover of the Soviet fleet—was commissioned, followed by new submarines. Americans denounced the buildup; the Chinese pointed out it was exactly what the United States did in the years between World War I and World War II.

Subtler efforts were aimed well beyond China's shores—most notably, the 2013 announcement of the Belt and Road Initiative: a state-subsidized effort to bring countries from Africa to the Pacific Islands into China's orbit by building their ports, hospitals, schools, and stadiums. It was often a package deal, one that threw in 5G networks built by Huawei and other Chinese manufacturers, giving Beijing control over a nation's communications. At first the Obama administration dismissed Belt and Road as "a silly combination of existing programs, nothing more," Barshefsky recalled. Then, realizing it was part of a larger plan, the United States belatedly raced to catch up. But the American plans came with human rights requirements and demands for financial transparency. Autocrats were happy to stick with China's aid program.

One after another, these stories made their way into the press, a drip-drip-drip of revelations that led to a cycle of denials from Beijing. But rarely were they woven together into a broader tapestry of Chinese goals. Inside the Obama White House there were constant debates about whether to call out Chinese actions—and, if so, whether the attacks should be ascribed to Xi's increasingly overt efforts to displace the United States.

Obama's first response—the "pivot to Asia" that his administration talked about frequently in its first years—seemed insufficient. It was heavily focused on shifting America's military presence, but rebalancing proved harder than it looked given American commitments in the Middle East, the new demands of countering ISIS, and, increasingly, the need to rotate troops through Eastern Europe to deter adventurism by Putin. There were nascent efforts to strengthen American partnerships with China's neighbors. But those struggled from the starting blocks amid doubts about the seriousness of the U.S. commitment.

What increasingly attracted the attention of the CIA, the NSA, and the FBI, though, was what Chinese operatives were doing in the United States. They presented a confusing picture that took years to piece together.

Some of the activity was happening in the American heartland. Officials watched with suspicion as China bought up parcels of American farmland and the Chinese telecommunications giant Huawei offered remarkably cheap bids to build the 3G and 4G networks of rural telecom carriers located around the country's nuclear missile silos. But much of it was taking place on a national scale. When the FBI discovered a Chinese police ring in 2015 operating secretly in the United States to target "fugitives"—often Chinese dissidents—the Obama administration quietly told Beijing it had to shut down the illicit "police stations." After Unit 61398, a hacking operation run by the People's Liberation Army, was caught in a broad campaign of stealing corporate secrets for the benefit of Chinese companies, the Chinese military officers who led the effort were indicted in the United States. (They have never stood trial.) And in 2015, the Ministry of State Security was discovered to be the mastermind behind the theft of the digital security clearance files of 22 million federal employees and their families—part of a broader campaign by China to understand every detail and vulnerability of the American elite. For many in the national security apparatus, it seemed like a breaking point. After all, what the Chinese had stolen was their personal information, down to medical and financial histories, and details about children and past relationships.

"There was this sense of feeling violated that really pissed people off," one former senior administration official told me. He acknowledged that countries spy on each other all the time—but in this instance, it felt like the Chinese had crossed a line. It dramatically, he said, decreased the Obama administration's willingness to assume that Beijing was acting in good faith.

Obama told his aides that he was without effective tools to rein in Xi's excesses. Sanctions were largely useless; the Chinese were masters of evading them. Indictments had mostly symbolic impact. In most of the hacking cases, Obama and his aides chose not to name the Chinese as the offender, for fear that publicly revealing the evidence would only lead to vociferous Chinese denials and make it impossible to talk with the Beijing leadership. So they handled each crisis one by one, avoiding public accusations and trying not to trigger a new Cold War.

Finally, though, Obama had had enough. He decided he had to confront Xi directly. It happened during Xi's 2015 state visit to the United States, which the Chinese wanted to make sure went flawlessly. As part of a carefully negotiated deal, Xi promised cooperation in hunting down cyber threats—as if their source were a mystery—and assured Obama, in a Rose Garden appearance, that "China does not intend to pursue militarization" of the reclaimed islands in the South China Sea.

The cyber action slowed, but only for a few months. When the cyberattacks resumed, they were executed with more stealth, leading officials to conclude that the temporary hiatus was part of Xi's effort to reassert control. And by the following spring, aircraft hangars appeared on those islands in the South China Sea, eventually housing fighter jets.

BY THE SUMMER of 2015—around the time that Donald Trump was descending on his golden escalator at Trump Tower to run for the presidency—a clutch of senior Obama administration officials was trying to figure out how to deal with a China that was not turning in the way America had hoped.

"Everybody really started getting frustrated," recalled one senior administration official working on trade policy. There was then a broad recognition that Xi was "not only an economic nationalist, but he's also engaged in kind of nefarious conduct." The question was what to do about it.

Secretary Penny Pritzker and her team at the Department of Commerce were struck by a Chinese plan called "Made in China 2025." Released in May 2015, it outlined in no uncertain terms Beijing's determination to lead the world in the development and manufacture of critical technologies—semiconductors and long-range batteries for electric vehicles, biotechnology and robotics, quantum computing and artificial intelligence. The list went on, buried in layers of description about China's commitment to green technology and a "fair and competitive market environment." By 2025, they aimed for 70 percent self-sufficiency. By 2049, according to the plan, China's goal was to dominate.

At first, the initiative was dismissed in Washington as more or less another five-year plan. China published "a whole bunch of these—I don't want to call them bullshit documents—but they put out a lot of stuff that's a lot of talk and not always a lot of action," the senior official later recalled. But then American officials started learning about the billions in funding that China was setting aside to juice these critical industries. "All of a sudden the Chinese are putting up this $250 billion fund, and there was this sort of collective, like, 'Oh shit, this is serious.'"

Then came China's buying spree in Silicon Valley, which included efforts to snap up small, highly innovative firms like Lattice Semiconductor, a maker of low-power chips critical to communications. That transaction was ultimately shot down in 2017 by a secretive U.S. government committee that reviews foreign efforts to invest in the country, but it was becoming clear that this was part of a broader, coordinated strategy that American officials didn't have the right tools to deal with.

Bruce Andrews, then the deputy secretary at the Department of Commerce under Pritzker, was jarred by the juxtaposition of a pair of meetings in the same week in November 2015. The first was with steel companies and workers who felt devastated by the influx of cheap, subsidized Chinese-made steel, which was flooding world markets. The steelmakers wanted the U.S. government to step in more aggressively, but Obama's options for coercing China on trade issues were limited: They'd already filed complaints with the WTO, launched Commerce Department investigations, and offered some domestic subsidies. So by the time Andrews met with the steelworkers, there were "really no tools that the U.S. government had left in the toolbox," he recalled, "other than tariffs, which, you know, the administration didn't see as a viable option."*

Just a few days later, he met with the board of the Semiconductor Industry Association—the trade lobbying group for the companies that were supposed to represent America's leading edge. They came to see Andrews to discuss "Made in China 2025," or at least the part that most worried them, China's plans to subsidize semiconductor manufacturing, in a clear bid to knock out U.S. suppliers.

Andrews feared that the semiconductor industry was headed down the same path that the steel companies had been treading for two decades—and the Silicon Valley executives seemed to anticipate that, too. "I could see the palpable sense of fear in the eyes of these very overconfident business leaders about what this fund was going to do to American industry and American competitors," he recalled.

The CEOs were chiefly worried about their long-term competitiveness. But the security implications were obvious: A China that dominated the creation and production of semiconductors—the foundational technology at the core of every computer, car, refrigerator, or fighter

---

* Eventually they would, slapping a new tariff on certain steel products in early 2016. Abigail Stevenson, "Obama Just Changed the Game for Steel," CNBC, April 12, 2016.

jet—would exercise untenable influence over the global supply chain. Given China's growing hostility, that wasn't a world the United States wanted to see.

At the end of the day, Andrews went into Secretary Pritzker's office and reported on his twin meetings. "The semiconductor guys are petrified of what the Chinese are about to do," he warned. "And we don't want to be, in ten years, having a meeting like I had to have with the steel companies and the union on Monday."

But Andrews and Pritzker were out of time. It was already early 2016, and the clock on their final year was ticking. While Andrews and a growing group in the Pentagon and the intelligence agencies were focused on the risks of losing the semiconductor industry, the country—and the nation's political candidates—were not. Congress was not about to vote on a national industrial policy in an election year. The best Andrews and Pritzker could hope for was to start coming up with a plan to hand over to the woman they were certain would become the next American president: Hillary Clinton. So they proceeded—quietly. And they began to float, along with some senators on Capitol Hill, the idea of a new federal fund for domestic semiconductor investment.

"Let me be clear," Pritzker said in a speech in Washington a week before the election. "We will not allow any nation to dominate this industry and impede innovation through unfair trade practices and massive, non-market-based state intervention."

At the last meeting of the NSC on this topic, chaired by Deputy National Security Advisor Avril Haines, Andrews remembered thinking, "God, if only we had six more months to close some of the loopholes and deal with these things." But they had only ten more days.

IN EARLY FEBRUARY 2016, just a few months after the Commerce Department began awakening to the threat of "Made in China 2025," Ashton B. "Ash" Carter took the podium in front of a crowd at the Economic Club of Washington, D.C., located two blocks north of the White House. He was the first sitting defense secretary, he noted, to speak to what was essentially a business group—and that was the point.

Carter—a physicist by training who had dealt with everything from North Korea's nuclear program to refitting personnel carriers to protect troops against mines—wasn't one to mince words. The United States was back in "great power competition," he told the crowd of executives, and this time that meant squaring off against both Russia and China. "Today's security environment is dramatically different than the one we've been engaged in for the last twenty-five years, and it requires new ways of thinking and new ways of acting."

Carter's comments that morning were intended to signal that future conflicts would look dramatically different from Iraq and Afghanistan. But the United States, he argued, wasn't changing as fast as the strategic challenges it faced. His was perhaps the sharpest public analysis by any top Obama administration official of the challenges facing American power.

But just a few months later, Carter and other defense officials stopped talking about "great power competition." It soon became clear why: A classified directive from the White House to the Pentagon instructed officials to stop using that language, especially about China. Obama administration officials insisted that the relationship between the two countries was far too complex to be boiled down to such a simple phrase. It was dangerous and reductive. And it also pissed off the Chinese diplomats.

The Pentagon complied. Carter fumed. Then one day that September, testifying at a congressional hearing, he was asked point-blank whether the United States was in the midst of renewed great power competition. Neither he nor the chairman of the Joint Chiefs of Staff, Joseph Dunford, could contain himself.

"We are, Senator," said Dunford.

"We are," said Carter. "Absolutely right."

XI JINPING'S MANY surprises—his rapid moves to challenge the United States, to reverse China's openings, to concentrate power in the hands of one leader, Mao-style, instead of the pattern of collective leadership that had emerged over the previous three decades—raise fundamental questions about what the United States government missed. Did the intelligence services misunderstand China's real ambitions? Did business leaders fool themselves, convinced that China wanted profits more than global power? Or, despite all the hours spent talking with him, did American officials simply misread Xi?

There are several theories, and they say as much about America's preconceptions about China's national interests as they do about China.

Biden's leading advisors argue that China has always had a master plan to displace the United States as the top power and to remake the world in its own image, and that for decades Beijing was simply biding its time. "Since the end of the Cold War, China has pursued a grand strategy to displace American order, first at the regional and now at the global level," Rush Doshi, an academic who became the director for China and Taiwan for the National Security Council, wrote before going to the White House.

Doshi may be right, but a second theory argues that even in the absence of a secret plan, an eventual collision of great powers was baked into China's rise. That is the essence of the "Thucydides Trap," a phrase made popular by Graham Allison of Harvard. The trap is named for the titanic clash between Sparta and Athens—the rising power versus the status quo power—during the Peloponnesian War. Under that theory the United States' own seeming weaknesses, starting with the 2008 financial crisis, then Obama's unwillingness to draw red lines or call out affronts, then the isolationism and chaos of the Trump years, emboldened Beijing to make its move. In short, China was doing to the United States what the United States had done, more than a century ago, to Britain. It was the natural order of things. And rather than alleviate that fear, China fed it. "There is no such thing as the so-called Thucydides Trap in the world," Xi insisted in 2015, "but should major countries time and again make the mistakes of strategic miscalculation, they might create such traps for themselves."

The third theory is that Xi himself has hijacked China's "peaceful rise," convinced that the only way for the country to survive in a world of chaos and upheaval is to centralize power again, even at the cost of the openings that made China rich. As he turned seventy, with only a decade or so to leave a mark as notable as Mao's, he was determined to establish China's preeminence. In other words, Xi was at least an accelerator, if not the very architect, of China's confrontation with the West.

Insofar as any of these theories are correct, it would suggest that Washington suffered a tremendous intelligence failure.

But it is also possible that China's path was simply unknowable until Xi's actions made it obvious, said Avril Haines, who after her time in the

Obama administration resurfaced as Biden's director of national intelligence, the first woman to ever hold the nation's top intelligence job. Haines had one of the most unusual backgrounds of any Biden appointee: A New York City native, she took a year off after high school to study judo in Japan, graduated with a bachelor's degree in physics from the University of Chicago, learned how to fly—and crash—small planes, and owned a bookstore-café in Baltimore. Her government career began when she earned a law degree and worked for the Senate Foreign Relations Committee during Biden's tenure as chairman. Later, as Obama's deputy director of the CIA, she was thrown into some of the hardest and most morally fraught issues of the day, and drew criticism for her role in redacting a Senate report that described the agency's checkered history of torture and in codifying America's drone-strike program. But she also gained a reputation as one of the most thoughtful insiders on what works and doesn't work in the sprawling intelligence community, and launched a minor war against overclassification.

When we spoke one evening from the intelligence director's spacious headquarters in Virginia, she recalled to me the uncertainty in late 2016, as Obama's team packed up, about whether the United States was on a collision course with Xi. "We talked about Xi as 'increasingly aggressive,'" she said, "That was the line, precisely. So I don't think we misjudged him so much as we were waiting to see how he evolved, and we weren't confident in predicting what would happen."

Bill Burns was similarly reflective. "I'm not a fatalist in the sense that I think Xi had kind of a fully formed worldview and persona when he became president a decade ago," he told me.

But Xi did harbor "a more expansive view of China's role in the world as well. And the pace of those ambitions and the sharpness of his willingness to butt heads with us was something that evolved over time.

"So, yeah, I mean did anybody foresee in 2013 that we'd have as increasingly an adversarial relationship as we do now? Probably not."

CHAPTER 3

PUTIN'S SEVEN-YEAR ITCH

FICTIONAL GERMAN CHANCELLOR ANGELA MERKEL: Hello! My congratulations. We decided to [accept] your country [in]to the European Union.

FICTIONAL UKRAINIAN PRESIDENT VASYL PETROVYCH HOLOBORODKO (GLEEFUL): Oh! Fuck! Oh—I'm sorry—wow! Woo! Oh, you know, I am so happy. Yes, oh, thank you very much. All of the Ukrainians, and all of our country, we've been waiting for this so much time.

MERKEL: Ukrainians? . . . Oh, I'm so sorry. That's a mistake. I was calling Montenegro.

HOLOBORODKO: Fuck. M-m-montenegro. Oh, I see. Yeah, my . . . my congratulations. Yes . . . to Montenegro. Bye-bye. . . . [ends call] FUCK!

> A 2017 scene from the popular Ukrainian sitcom *Servant of the People,*
> in which a humble, ethical everyman—played by then-actor Volodymyr
> Zelensky—is catapulted into the Ukrainian presidency

BY THE TIME that Ukrainian comedian Volodymyr Zelensky created and starred in the TV show *Servant of the People*—a political satire mocking both his own government and the West that aired starting in late 2015—his country was engaged in a constant low-grade war with Russia.

A little less than two years earlier, "little green men" had descended on the Crimean Peninsula—just over ten thousand square miles of highly desirable real estate poking into the northern shores of the Black Sea. Everyone was certain they were Russian soldiers or mercenaries out of uniform—though Putin denied it, of course. Later he would maintain that if they did happen to be Russians, they were patriots who had gone there of their own volition. But when they raised a Russian flag in the Crimean parliament building, he wasted no time happily annexing the whole peninsula.

Within weeks, the little green men were showing up in the east of the country—Ukraine's poorer and heavily Russian-speaking industrial heartland, sometimes called the Donbas. They kindled a low-grade war that would simmer for the next eight years, at a cost of roughly fourteen thousand lives, and to the detriment of the Ukrainian (and, to a far lesser degree, the Russian) economy.

In those years Zelensky was still a made-for-TV president, not a real one, and his main goal when he talked about Russia or Putin was to get a laugh. The show's characters, Zelensky included, spoke mainly in Russian—not Ukrainian. It was a sort of *Mr. Smith Goes to Washington,* if that 1939 classic were moved to Kyiv and Jimmy Stewart constantly said "fuck."

Years later, it would be jarring to watch reruns of *Servant of the People.* The lighthearted way that Ukraine's aspirations to join the European Union were handled in retrospect seems tragic. There was also little discussion of Putin himself—and no outrage that he had just annexed Crimea. It was such a glaring omission that critics of Zelensky's fledgling real-world presidential campaign warned, while the show was still running, that the actor was "dangerously pro-Russian."

Yet there was little appetite, particularly beyond Ukraine, for making Putin pay a heavy price for the invasion. The United States was in no mood to tangle with Putin over a piece of territory that had changed hands—and governments—several times over the previous few centuries. The Germans had made clear that they did not want to endanger their gas supplies or their broader relationship with Moscow. The rest of Europe was divided, and there was considerable wariness over Ukraine's well-deserved reputation for corruption. Now that Putin held Crimea, the Europeans argued, he wouldn't go beyond the Russian-speaking part of the Donbas—Ukraine was too big to swallow, and a full invasion was too risky for Russia's economic future.

The argument assumed that Putin was driven by the same economic logic that was guiding European leaders: in short, projecting European and American thinking onto an authoritarian regime that Bill Burns argued was sustained largely by "high energy prices and wounded pride." And it ignored when he had signaled his intention, at Munich in 2007 and after.

There was one more miscalculation in the mix, and it was Putin's. He got away with taking a piece of Ukraine in 2014. Why couldn't he get away with taking all of it in 2022?

VLADIMIR PUTIN'S ROAD to the full-scale invasion of Ukraine was not a straight line. But once the invasion was a reality, the most introspective of American officials looked back at the signals they had missed as the relationship between Russia and the West began to come apart. Most concluded that the United States had made a series of bad assumptions about how far Putin would pursue his ambitions. In retrospect, they blamed themselves—and the Europeans—for not pushing back faster and harder against the episodic acceleration of Putin's aggressions, particularly the annexation of Crimea.

And these officials became increasingly self-reflective—and self-critical—about how a series of Western distractions, missteps, and unrealistic expectations left Putin with the mistaken impression that the price he would pay for his land grabs would be manageable—and probably brief. It was like a seven-year itch, one senior British official told me: Every seven to eight years Putin ended up trying to seize or otherwise bring to heel another part of the old Russian empire. Chechnya in 1999–2000, Georgia in 2008, Crimea in 2014, and then all of Ukraine in 2022.

In the United States, the low-grade war in Ukraine spanned three presidential administrations—from Obama's second term in 2014 through Donald Trump's bizarre four years and the beginning of Joe Biden's first term. At times, Washington was obsessed with Putin—particularly in the months before and just after the 2016 election. In those days, Putin was frequently described as a brilliant strategist and tactician whose hacking and disinformation operations were exploiting the fault lines in American democracy from the inside. At other moments, Russia was brushed to the side: a third-rate power that was in decline, its nuclear arsenal its only remaining claim to superpower status. Sure, it was a disruptor, but it was no existential threat like China. The Pentagon's priority, said one of Trump's short-term acting defense secretaries, Patrick Shanahan, had to be "China, China, China." In November 2020, an anonymous Biden campaign official modestly amended the formulation to "China. China. China. Russia."

But while Russia cycled into and out of the American consciousness, there was one constant theme in Washington: the battle over whether a corrupt, unruly Ukraine would be lured into the West or fall back into Putin's grasp.

"WHERE THE HELL is this guy?!" a frustrated Vice President Joe Biden demanded of his aides on the morning of February 22, 2014. He'd been trying, repeatedly, to get Ukraine's deeply corrupt and increasingly unpopular president Victor Yanukovich to pick up on the other end of the secure line. But there was nothing. No one seemed to know where he was. Finally, it became clear that, after months of fearing for his life and enduring protests against his corrupt ways and his desire to draw Ukraine closer to Moscow, Yanukovich had fled the country for exile in Russia.

For months before Yanukovich headed to exile, Biden had worked the phones, trying to put his personal touch on the crisis unfolding on the other side of the world—one that had reignited in 2013, when Yanukovich turned his back on an association agreement between Europe and Ukraine in favor of closer ties with Moscow. In some ways, it was a decision that seemed to turn more on Yanukovich's own interests than on a true desire to steer Ukraine back toward Russia.* He had asked the Europeans for $160 billion to stabilize Ukraine's shaky finances, enact reforms, and cushion the economy from the expected Russian blowback. Instead, the Europeans offered him just under $1 billion with

---

* "We will pursue integration with Europe," Yanukovich reportedly told members of his party who warned him over the summer that the move would irritate the Russians. While Yanukovich was undeniably Moscow's candidate—Putin had backed his presidential candidacy back in 2009, and Yanukovich had vowed to improve relations with the Kremlin—he was irritated by the condescending manner with which the Russians treated him. Elizabeth Piper, "Special Report: Why Ukraine Spurned the EU and Embraced Russia," Reuters, December 19, 2013.

vague assurances of more to follow. Worse—in Yanukovich's eyes—a series of anticorruption requirements threatened to end his presidency and undercut his lavish lifestyle. (Yanukovich, born poor in an eastern Ukrainian mining town, had somehow acquired a 345-acre estate north of Kyiv, complete with a zoo, luxury yacht, car collection, and golf course, all tucked behind a sixteen-foot-high fence.) By mid-December, Yanukovich agreed to a very different economic deal with Russia, one that offered Ukraine gas subsidies and $15 billion. It wasn't the $160 billion he'd asked for, but it was fifteen times more than the Europeans had offered.

"Yanukovich was always trying to flirt with us *and* be loyal to Putin," recalled Michael McFaul, the outspoken Stanford academic who was serving as Obama's ambassador to Russia. "And it all came to a head over the accession agreement. The Russians offered him more money, and they won that round."

McFaul went to see Igor Shuvalov, the first deputy prime minister of Russia, and told him, "Congratulations, you beat us this time."

Shuvalov's reply was matter-of-fact, McFaul recalled. "I think he said, 'We planned to pay eight billion and we ended up paying fifteen billion. So it's expensive. But Mike, we're demonstrating to you we care more about Ukraine than you do.' And that's lingered with me ever since."

In fact Putin had been arguing for years that Ukraine was not only integral to Russia, it *was* Russia. As one Kremlin official later insisted to Bill Burns and Jake Sullivan, "You Americans don't understand that Ukraine is not a real country. Some parts are really central Europe, and some are really Russian, and very little is actually Ukrainian. Don't kid yourselves." And when it came to the question of who had the best claim on the Crimean Peninsula, it wasn't just the radical nationalists: "Even liberal Russians think Crimea is a part of Russia," a top former American government official admitted to me privately.

Ukraine, of course, was an internationally recognized and independent state with a seat at the United Nations. But the links between the two countries certainly were complex: Millions of Ukrainians had Russian relatives, and both Russian and Ukrainian were widely spoken in Ukraine. The country's famously fertile wheat fields had sustained both tsarist Russia and the Soviet Union—at least, until Joseph Stalin's policies created a horrific famine in Ukraine, the Holodomor, that killed roughly 10 percent of the population.

Fifteen billion dollars of Russia's money might have been enough to buy off Yanukovich, but for many Ukrainians no amount would be enough to dampen their resolve to move closer to Europe. They took to the streets in record numbers starting in November 2013, first in the tens of thousands and then in the hundreds of thousands. In Kyiv, the heart of the protests, a semipermanent camp was established in the central square, the Maidan, complete with barricades, self-organized groups of "defenders," soup kitchens, and performance stages. "The country realized that we're getting back to the Soviet Union, and then people got united, people got on the streets," recalled Dmytro Shymkiv, then the CEO of Microsoft Ukraine and later the head of Ukraine's digital strategy.

Polling at the time indicated that the country was split. About half the country supported the protesters and closer ties with the EU, while half did not. Many of the protesters were younger liberal reformers from western Ukraine; some were right-wing ultranationalists.

Then things took a deadly turn. There had been a series of clashes between protesters—armed and unarmed—and government security forces. But as the protests endured, the violence grew more pronounced, culminating in February 2014. "I was in Maidan when they tried to storm," Shymkiv said grimly, recalling how a friend had brought him a bulletproof vest. "It becomes really serious, when people get killed." Ultimately, over a hundred people died—mostly protesters, but police as well.

This was the maelstrom into which Biden had been dropped. Since the start of the protests, he had spoken directly to Yanukovich at least nine times—the last call just a few days before he fled—in an effort to persuade him to pull back government troops and stop the violence that had engulfed the heart of Kyiv. It was classic Biden: He inserted himself into a complex dispute half a world away, convinced that his long experience in diplomacy and personal touch could make a difference. Like a hostage negotiator, Biden was trying to build a rapport with Yanukovich even as he tried to talk him down, to convince him to take a deal that the European Union—along with the Russians—had brokered to guarantee elections by the end of 2014 and end the crisis. Under that plan, Yanukovich would have stayed in power in the interim.

When they'd ended their last conversation, Biden wasn't sure what Yanukovich would do.

On February 21, both Yanukovich and the protesters took the deal. But on February 22, the day Biden was trying to reach him, the parliament had decided to impeach Yanukovich—and he fled the country. The West said he ran away. Yanukovich called it a coup plotted in Washington and Europe. The Russian foreign minister, Sergey Lavrov, accused the West of seeking to create a "sphere of influence" in Ukraine—part of a plot to draw Ukraine away from Russia and, eventually, put NATO's arms on Russia's borders. Taking advantage of the power vacuum, Putin moved against Crimea, occupying its strategic sites—its airports and ports— within days of Yanukovich's escape.

Ukraine was melting down. So was the U.S.-Russia relationship. In Moscow, McFaul was increasingly convinced he'd reached the end of his usefulness to his boss, Obama, with whom he had a long and close relationship. From the moment of his arrival, McFaul was viewed with suspicion and outright hostility by the very Russian officials with whom he was supposed to be building relationships. They had read his books on democracy-promotion and human rights and followed his first few years serving on the National Security Council. They believed that he had come to Russia to help foment revolution against Putin, McFaul recalled.

The harassment began quickly. While he expected he would be trailed by intelligence operatives—he was, after all, the American ambassador—he wasn't prepared for them to show up at his kids' soccer games. There were online disinformation campaigns denouncing him, demonstrations outside the embassy and the ambassador's residence, and more than a few death threats. "In Putin's Russia, there's no good work to be done by an ambassador in Moscow," he told me ruefully. So he resigned, packed up, and flew home to Palo Alto.

For President Obama, the urgent question was how to respond to Russia's move into Crimea. It was a clear violation of Ukraine's sovereignty. Biden and Victoria "Toria" Nuland, the Russia hawk who was serving as Obama's assistant secretary of state for European and Eurasian affairs, were pressing him to act. Biden himself was eager to make Moscow "pay in blood and money," as my colleagues Glenn Thrush and Ken Vogel later reported.

Obama resisted the effort. *Don't* get me into a war with Russia, he warned his aides repeatedly. That, first and foremost, was his goal. Such a war would not only be a new conflict with potentially unimaginable consequences for the United States—it's a different calculus taking on a nuclear-armed state—it would, Obama believed, become a fundamentally losing battle. Obama told his aides that Russia would always care more about the Ukrainians than Americans would. Intervention, in Obama's view, would have been a violation of the guiding principle of foreign policy that he once boiled down for reporters on Air Force One into one pithy phrase: "Don't do stupid shit."

The fate of Crimea, Obama determined, was important but hardly a core U.S. security interest. In public, he sought to downplay both the geopolitical significance and the impact that U.S. involvement would have. "The fact is that Ukraine, which is a non-NATO country, is going to be vulnerable to military domination by Russia no matter what we do," he later said.

In Belgium, less than a week after the annexation, Obama had already made up his mind. "This is not another Cold War that we're entering into," he said. "Unlike the Soviet Union, Russia leads no bloc of nations, no global ideology."

Yet he acknowledged that something had changed in the unspoken rules of the post–Cold War world. "Russia's leadership is challenging truths that only a few weeks ago seemed self-evident—that in the 21st century, the borders of Europe cannot be redrawn with force, that international law matters, that people and nations can make their own decisions about their future."

John Kerry, the secretary of state, was more blunt: "You just don't in the twenty-first century behave in nineteenth-century fashion by invading another country on completely trumped-up pretext," he protested.

Of course, Putin believed the Americans had done exactly that in Iraq in 2003. He himself had already done it in Georgia in 2008.

The worry was that Putin wouldn't stop there.

IN THE END, Washington's response to the Russian incursion into Crimea was typically tepid. Obama spun out a handful of executive orders sanctioning individuals and organizations for their roles in Ukrainian corruption or the Russian annexation. The U.S. military conducted exercises with European allies and shored up its presence on the continent. There was nothing that would ruin Putin's day.

Mild as the American moves seemed, the Europeans did even less. What they were mostly interested in, they were quick to emphasize, was the opportunity to stabilize the situation and allow cooler heads to prevail. So they hit pause on ongoing trade and visa discussions and launched several rounds of meetings to hammer out a diplomatic solution that moved among different European capitals—Brussels, Madrid, Paris, Geneva—to utterly no effect. Catherine Ashton, the European Union foreign policy chief, later recalled that at one "shambolic" meeting in early March 2014, as the invasion of Crimea was under way, everyone looked around the room, and "it became obvious that the Ukrainians, Russians and Americans weren't there. They were somewhere else, making our own meeting pretty pointless. It was at some dark level actually funny."

Symbolism ruled the day. Soon after the annexation, Obama and his European allies voted to kick Russia out of the G8, the largely economic group that had invited Moscow to join in 1997 as proof that the major powers were serious about making Russia a full partner in the Western-led international order. Now, as quickly as the Russians had been woven in, they were expelled.

By May 2014, the newly elected Ukrainian president, Petro Poroshenko, took office despite a last-minute cyber and influence operation mounted by the Russians to make it appear that he had been defeated. He signed the original association deal with the Europeans, triggering a raft of reforms and funding. And he managed to reverse the Yanukovich-era neutrality law that blocked Ukraine from joining NATO—a move that the Kremlin ominously condemned as "unfriendly."

Then Russian forces took a step that forced Europe to respond—and revealed Putin's recklessness. On July 17, 2014, a Malaysia Airlines passenger jet carrying nearly three hundred civilians was shot down over southern Ukraine. It quickly became clear that it had been taken down with a Russian-designed missile by pro-Russian rebels in Ukraine, who later claimed they had mistaken it for military aircraft. Ultimately, Dutch investigators found that the weapons transfer to the rebels had likely been authorized by Putin himself.

In the days that followed, their hand forced by the incident, Europeans issued their own list of modest sanctions, but their main hope was still negotiation. And that meant peace talks—ones that would have to start with an immediate bilateral cease-fire between the rebels and Poroshenko's new government. Named after the capital city of Minsk, Belarus, where the negotiations were opened in 2014, the resulting accord quickly fell apart after multiple violations by both parties to the conflict. In the meantime, the West was dutifully insisting that it would never recognize Crimea as Russian territory. NATO nations began shipping military aid to Ukraine—but only the nonlethal kind. Helmets. Body armor. Radar. Medical kits. Food.

For much of his political career, Joe Biden had played the role of the hard-liner when it came to Russia. He had pushed for NATO expansion, despite Putin's protests. So it wasn't a surprise when he sided with the relatively small group of Obama aides seeking a harder line and real weapons for the Ukrainians. At the same time, he was careful not to be caught publicly disagreeing with Obama, recalled Toria Nuland.

Biden used his weekly lunches with Obama to press for the kind of lethal aid that might make a difference in the war for the Donbas. "Biden was the pit bull for defensive weapons," Nuland told me. "He especially wanted Javelins sent," she said, referring to the powerful American anti-tank missiles that Obama declined to ship, for fear they would be provocative.*

Blinken concurred. Biden was "very forward-leaning," he said, weighing each word, "in terms of our support for Ukraine."

Part of this drive stemmed from the deep ties Biden had built with people in the region, stretching back decades. It was why he led the American support for anticorruption reforms in Ukraine—including his support, now infamous, in accordance with established U.S. policy at the time, for firing the corrupt chief Ukrainian prosecutor.

What tainted Biden's initiative were the activities of his troubled younger son, Hunter Biden, a lawyer and lobbyist with a long record of addiction problems and poor judgment. Hunter appeared to accept hundreds of thousands of dollars—starting in 2014—to sit on the board

---

* The counterargument was that American weapons often fall in the wrong hands— especially in corrupt lands—and the Javelins were just as likely to make their way to the pro-Russian forces.

of the Ukrainian energy company Burisma that was also under investigation for corruption. But when Obama aides broached the potential conflict of interest with Biden during their first presidential campaign, he lit into them—the blind spot Biden has often had when issues touch his family—and told them to back off. Biden maintained that his son was an independent adult and that there was no crossover between their work.

Later, Biden's aides would cite his early work in Ukraine to make the case that he was always a Russia hawk—and that his support for Kyiv was the product of years of scar tissue as he tried to aid a country that often undercut its own interests. But Biden was the vice president, and as in so many other things, he wasn't going to get his way unless he became president.

WHEN ANGELA MERKEL met with Obama in the Oval Office in February 2015 to discuss the course of U.S. and European support for Ukraine, she had an axe to grind.

Just three days before her visit, Toria Nuland, Senator John McCain, and Philip Breedlove, then head of U.S. military forces in Europe, held an Americans-only briefing in Germany about the need to better arm and aid Ukraine. They made it clear that they believed that the Europeans, and particularly the Germans, were making a mess of things: dragging their feet, being played by the Russians to buy time, and not learning from past mistakes. "History shows us that dictators will always take more if they are only allowed," McCain declared, with the I-don't-care-who-I-offend bluntness that always made him the favorite of Washington's press corps. Supplying Javelins, he would argue, was the best way to stop the Russian incursions.

The Germans, complained another American attendee, were "defeatists"—particularly their defense minister, Ursula von der Leyen. Merkel's back-channel diplomatic dialogue with Putin was dismissed as "Merkel's Moscow stuff." The Europeans' overall efforts were "Moscow bullshit."

The conversation was intended to be strictly off-the-record—and strictly among the Americans. But a German journalist had slipped into the room, and so the meeting made headlines a few days later in the largest newspaper in Germany, the center-right tabloid *Bild* ("'Cold Feet,' 'Bullshit,' 'Fear': What U.S. Politicians REALLY Think About the Germans in the Ukraine Crisis").

Merkel, predictably irate, reamed Obama out when she got to the Oval Office in February 2015. Obama pushed back. Well, he told Merkel, you already tried negotiating. You got the Minsk Protocol. And look how that turned out—the Russians had flagrantly ignored it and conquered more territory in a major offensive that destroyed surrounding cities and towns in eastern Ukraine and resulted in the deaths of some three hundred Ukrainian soldiers.

So, he asked Merkel, what's your next move?

Three days later, the Europeans negotiated a second cease-fire agreement, called Minsk II. That failed just as quickly.

A FEW MONTHS LATER, Merkel and a smattering of her European allies made a decision that, in retrospect, ranks among the most short-sighted and damaging European geopolitical moves since the end of World War II. At the very moment that the world was still debating how to punish Putin for his Crimean land grab, Chancellor Merkel and a small group of allies chose to reward him.

In June 2015, Royal Dutch Shell and a handful of other Western European oil and gas producers announced a new agreement with the Russian energy giant Gazprom, a new $10 billion–plus pipeline project called Nord Stream 2 that would run nearly eight hundred miles from Russia to Germany along the bottom of the Baltic Sea. It would parallel Nord Stream 1, the pipeline that had been supplying Europe's biggest economy with much-needed energy since 2011. The billions Russia would reap in revenues every year would dwarf the cost of the sanctions it had endured since the Crimea land grab.

The first pipeline had been relatively uncontroversial when it was pitched in the late 1990s. Germany was bursting with demand for more energy, and what it could obtain from Russia through the aging network of pipelines running across Ukraine was simply insufficient. At the time, it also seemed like a bright idea to become less dependent on the Middle East. Putin sold the idea of Nord Stream 1 as a win for Russia's integration with its democratic neighbors. Shortly after coming to office for the first time, he stood before the German Bundestag and said he aspired for his country to be modeled after nations like Germany. "Democratic rights and freedoms," he said, were the "key goal of Russia's domestic policy." He spoke in German, a language he learned fluently when he was a KGB spy in Dresden. And he received a standing ovation. "Putin captured us," said Norbert Röttgen, a Bundestag member and former head of its foreign affairs committee. "The voice was quite soft, in German, a voice that tempts you to believe what is said to you."

By 2011, gas was beginning to flow, and Nord Stream 1's success made it easier for Merkel and other German politicians to kill off Germany's nuclear power industry. Merkel had been unnerved by the 2011 Fukushima nuclear accident in Japan, but the slow shutdown of the reactors, combined with a booming economy, put her and her party on the hunt for new energy sources.

But back in Washington, Nord Stream 2 was a lot more problematic than its predecessor. While the first pipeline had seemed a clean geopolitical win, even if it made Europe marginally more dependent on Russia, the second pipeline set off alarms. Already with Nord Stream 1, more than 50 percent of German natural gas imports was coming from Russian energy sources—and thus subject to Putin's control. Nord Stream 2 would only increase that dependency.

Not surprisingly, Ukraine immediately objected, realizing that one of Putin's goals was to route more gas around Ukraine, depriving the country of the transit fees it was accustomed to receiving for Russian gas imported by Europe through the old Soviet-era pipelines. But a new pipeline would do more than deprive Ukraine of up to $3 billion a year; it would also deprive it of the potential power that comes from the ability to shut off exports from Russia in the event of a confrontation—or a war—with Moscow. "Nord Stream 2 is a political bribe for loyalty to Russia, imposing an economic and energy blockade on Ukraine, which will hurt us greatly," President Poroshenko warned the Germans. Röttgen concurred. "Nord Stream 2, from the start and by conception, was constructed as a political weapon by Russia against Ukraine," he told me years later.

In Washington, Benjamin L. Schmitt, a physicist by training who found himself handed the Nord Stream 2 problem in his first few weeks at the State Department, quickly came to the conclusion that the Kremlin was deliberately fostering more German reliance on Russian energy supplies and infrastructure. At the upper reaches of the State Department, this was also a political issue: Russia was getting rewarded for invading its neighbor and biting off a piece of its territory.

Nonetheless, Germany continued to argue that this was purely an *economic* deal, not a political or security issue. German diplomats repeatedly made the case that even during the tense days of the Cold War, Russia kept gas flowing to Europe. Angela Merkel herself led the way with this argument. "Russia in principle has shown itself as a reliable supplier of natural gas in the past," she said in 2015, as many in the Obama White House winced. Merkel's argument later came to seem either self-interested or unimaginably naïve, most likely both. But behind her comments was an enormous lobbying machine—led by her predecessor, Gerhard Schröder, who in his last days as chancellor in 2005 had signed off on the approval for Nord Stream 1. A few weeks later, he resurfaced on the company's board, with extravagant remuneration.

"Why should we have been distrustful? It always worked," Schröder later said. "They need oil and gas to pay for their budget. And we need oil and gas to heat and to keep the economy going."

As Nord Stream 2's approval rolled ahead, Putin continued to show his true stripes. He had invaded part of Ukraine. He was weaponizing energy. His past manipulations of the Ukrainian election were looking like a practice run for a bigger project: the 2016 U.S. election. At this moment Merkel and her party fell back on a Cold War analogy that no longer applied. She and her allies noted that pipeline projects were initiated and built during the Cold War era—creating robust, if somewhat inefficient, networks that kept the gas flowing.

It was a faulty assumption. At the State Department, Schmitt and others presented German diplomats with several recent examples to the contrary, in which Putin had deployed energy exports for political gain. They presented analysis emphasizing the risks of overdependence on a single Russian supply route and warned that it posed a direct security threat to Ukraine. None of it stuck.

Robin Quinville, a European security expert whose thirty-year career in the State Department culminated as acting chargé d'affaires at the U.S. Embassy in Berlin, recalled hearing the same talking points. "I wanted to say, 'People! Are we *in* the Cold War? Because it doesn't look like that to me.'" In the Cold War, she said, it was easier to deal with Moscow. The Russians needed hard currency from the West and relied on that income. Now, they were actually less dependent—and far more willing to mess with the West.

TODAY WHAT MOST stands out about the 2014 invasion of Crimea isn't just the audacity of the invasion; it's the West's failure to grapple with the new reality. It was almost as if the United States and its NATO allies were collectively flying on autopilot, assuming that small course corrections would safely land the plane. That was clear from the modest European sanctions that would never change Russian behavior, the Javelin anti-tank missiles that Obama never sent. And when the Russian economy continued to grow, steadily, few wanted to declare that the American "deterrent" to further Russian action wasn't, in fact, a deterrent at all. Instead, geopolitical momentum won out over good sense. "We underreacted," said Eric Rosenbach, who served as Defense Secretary Ash Carter's chief of staff at the Pentagon in those days. "You can see that in Obama's refusal to send the Ukrainians even the most defensive weapons."

Hindsight is perfect, of course. Sending Ukraine the weapons that it needed when it needed them could well have cemented in Putin's mind that the United States was committed to Ukraine's defense—and that broader moves to take the country eight years later could be far riskier than taking Crimea. It is one of those questions of alternative history that no one will ever be able to answer.

But there is reason to be cautious about leaping to the conclusion that sending some Javelins, or even a far more aggressive program of defensive aid, would have kept Putin from calculating that he could get away with seizing the whole country in 2022. One of the characteristics of the post–Cold War era—particularly after the United States exhausted itself in Afghanistan and Iraq—was that Washington had far less ability to shape other countries' actions than Americans like to believe: what Herbert Raymond "H. R." McMaster, who would serve as Trump's second national security advisor, wonderfully termed "strategic narcissism." "It's the tendency to define the world only in relation to us, and to assume that what we do or what we don't do is decisive toward achieving the desired outcome," he told me.

MCMASTER WAS CERTAINLY correct on one level. It quickly became clear that no level of sanctions, no diplomatic pressure, would have dislodged Putin from Crimea in 2014. And it's equally clear that the world had neither the will nor the means to support a military move to restore the status quo. Obama himself made that explicit. "With time, so long as we remain united, the Russian people will recognize that they cannot achieve the security, prosperity, and the status that they seek through brute force," he told an audience in Brussels in March 2014. "Nor will Russia be dislodged from Crimea or deterred from further escalation by military force."

Obama's last line was a clear acknowledgment that unless Europe grew a spine and unless the United States got some considerably more powerful tools, no one should expect Putin to be deterred. But even if Russia could not be stopped, clearly the decision to go ahead with Nord Stream 2 sent a message to Putin: Invade, wait a year, and all will be forgotten. Business will return to normal. Europe's decision—especially Germany's—was a green light for Putin to regroup and try again to bite off a chunk of Ukraine when conditions looked ripe.

Perhaps the greater sin was that the United States failed to update its own perception about who Putin was and where he was headed. We somehow convinced ourselves that his adventurism would be limited to seizing Crimea, and that while he might seek to disrupt the West, he did not have the power to remake the European order. The United States was stuck in oldthink: that Putin would rail about restoring Russia as a power that Peter the Great would have envied but would not act on his words. The United States assumed it was largely hot air, that at most he would try to pick off a few Russian-speaking enclaves surrounding his borders. In short, the United States misunderstood Putin's changed risk calculus—and thus failed to take the right steps, at home and abroad, to brace for a bigger crisis.

It was as if there were "two different Putins," Christoph Heusgen, the longtime German national security advisor to Merkel, told me later. One was the Putin who spoke at the German Bundestag in 2001, full of aspirations to cooperate because it would be good for the Russian economy. But that Putin melted away, replaced by the second Putin, a dictator more consumed by restoring the old Russian empire and addressing old grievances.

Clearly this would be a challenge for the next president. Toward the last months of Obama's time in office, as Putin grew increasingly bold—including interfering in the 2016 U.S. presidential election—the Obama administration began circulating drafts of a new, top-secret Russia strategy. It was late in the administration, everyone knew, but the concept was to leave a well-thought-out, tougher approach for Hillary Clinton, who at that moment just about everyone in the White House assumed would be the next president.

The process immediately bogged down. There were essentially two strategy drafts, one referring to Russia as a declining competitor, the other calling it a looming, increasingly potent threat to the United States. Secretary of State John Kerry lined up with the first version, though some on his staff, including Toria Nuland, thought that was the wrong approach and urged the far tougher description. The Pentagon also favored the second view, citing Putin's threats, the Russian nuclear modernization, and of course the fear that the Crimea invasion was an opening move.

The bitter debate sputtered to a conclusion, but in the end it didn't make any difference: Trump wasn't about to pick up a Russia strategy designed by Obama.

CHAPTER 4

AMERICA FIRST

It was a godsend that we didn't have a fast-moving crisis. I mean, COVID is a pretty big crisis, I acknowledge, but had it been a Cold War–style nuclear crisis . . . I don't even want to think what would have happened.

John Bolton, former national security advisor to Donald Trump, January 2022

ON FEBRUARY 20, 2017, exactly a month into Trump's presidency, H. R. McMaster was walking down Walnut Street in Philadelphia, preparing to give a talk about a U.S. Army study that concluded that the United States risked falling behind Russia's rapidly advancing next-generation warfare capabilities.

McMaster, a three-star Army general, hadn't written the study himself, but it had been his brainchild. The speed with which Putin's military took Crimea in 2014 showed stunning audacity, technological expertise, and creativity. Now he was determined that the United States Army had to figure out how the Russians had modernized their forces so quickly—and what the Army needed to do to stay ahead.

McMaster, who had made his reputation in part on his willingness to challenge authority, made no secret of his belief that the United States was underestimating Russia's capabilities and its willingness to use its forces. "It had been very much on my mind," he recalled, "that we were behind in great power competition based on fundamentally flawed assumptions about the post–Cold War world."

"A revisionist Russia is increasing its military capabilities and threatening U.S. allies and partners across Eurasia and the Middle East," the report concluded. "It is likely that a perceived reduction in the United States' comparative military advantages emboldens Russian actions."

For more than a year McMaster had been making the case that while the United States was distracted in Afghanistan and Iraq, Putin's generals had figured how to counter the U.S. military. They had taken great pains—and spent billions—to modernize a force still mired in its humble Soviet origins. He wasn't alone: Among Pentagon planners in 2017, this was the accepted wisdom.

On Walnut Street that February morning, McMaster's cellphone rang. It was President Trump, calling to offer him the role of his national security advisor. Just months before, Trump had passed over McMaster for the role—privately saying that he looked like a "beer salesman"— and chose instead the retired, embittered Lt. General Michael Flynn, who had been forced out of his post running the Defense Intelligence Agency during the Obama administration.

As McMaster and the whole world knew by the time his phone rang on Walnut Street, Flynn had self-immolated barely three weeks into his tenure after lying to the FBI about his earlier contacts with the Russian ambassador to the United States. Suddenly Trump was operating without anyone at the helm of his National Security Council, the organization that runs the vast foreign policy, defense, and intelligence apparatus of the United States. And suddenly the "beer salesman" didn't seem like such a bad choice.

In retrospect, McMaster and a handful of his deputies brought Trump something he desperately needed, and that he never took the time to absorb or understand: the beginnings of an enduring strategy to deal with a new age of superpower conflict. Often it was hard to find, under the barrage of Trump bluster and declarations of toughness. But many of the measures that were dismissed by Trump's critics at the time as hawkish or ad hoc or fearmongering would end up repackaged and carried into the Biden years. That reflected Washington's hardening assessment, a sense that unless America got aggressive, it would be rolled over. Yet for McMaster and his staff, it was hardly a smooth path, and it was Trump himself who usually got in the way of explaining the strategy to the world. When McMaster arrived in the West Wing, he had one major goal: to reverse what he believed was a decades-long trend of failing to understand the real threats that faced the United States. The American bureaucracy hadn't gotten the memo, he figured, that the era of counter-terrorism was not yet over—but that a new era of great power competition had already arrived.

As he settled into his corner office overlooking the White House's driveway, McMaster knew he had the perfect vehicle to kickstart his vision. One of his first big tasks was to write the new administration's national security strategy, the document that is supposed to set the tone for the next four years of a president's term. For the past fifteen years, this succession of strategies has been more or less predictable. Terrorism was the number one threat since 9/11, North Korea and Iran the nuclear disruptors. There were usually brief warnings about nontraditional threats—cyber, climate change, and migration.

McMaster's version, when it came out in December of Trump's first year in office, looked different:

> Following the remarkable victory of free nations in the Cold War, America emerged as the lone superpower with enormous advantages and momentum in the world. Success, however, bred complacency. A belief emerged, among many, that American power would be unchallenged and self-sustaining. The United States began to drift. We experienced a crisis of confidence and surrendered our advantages in key areas. As we took our political, economic, and military advantages for granted, other actors steadily implemented their long-term plans to challenge America and to advance agendas opposed to the United States, our allies, and our partners.

The magnitude of the change was easily overlooked, dropped as the strategy was a few days before the winter holiday break, amid the episodic threats by members of Congress to shut down the government over a dispute about raising the debt ceiling.

Yet the change was largely lost on the president whose name was on the strategy. He had been briefed on the high points, and when he announced its release, he slammed his predecessors and promised that his administration was committed to putting "America first." But he seemed to miss the titanic collision between great powers that his own strategy saw coming; he referred only once to "rival powers" that "seek to challenge American influence, values, and wealth." Then, in his usual way, he promised to "build a great partnership" with Russia and China. Those were still the days when Trump talked endlessly about the great trade deal he would negotiate with China and asked, in his rote way, variations on the question, "What's wrong with being friends with Russia?"

Before the 2016 election, when I had interviewed then-candidate Trump for *The New York Times* in an effort to learn more about his foreign policy views, Trump had not been shy about his notion that the United States was getting taken advantage of by other countries. "NATO," he told Maggie Haberman and me, was "obsolete." Instead, he argued, "we should be looking at terror," not Russia, "because terror today is the big threat."

Russia's invasion of Ukraine and forced seizure of Crimea had been two years earlier, in 2014, but he didn't seem to think it merited any American action. "One of the things that I hated seeing is Ukraine," he said. "Now I'm all for Ukraine, I have friends that live in Ukraine, but it didn't seem to me, when the Ukrainian problem arose, you know, not so long ago, and we were, and Russia was getting very confrontational, it didn't seem to me like anyone else cared other than us." Ukraine, he seemed to be saying, was on the other side of the ocean, so it must be someone else's problem. It was a classic isolationist argument, and his own national security strategy largely rejected it—arguing for standing up to aggressors. Trump's aides would roll their eyes at his numerous inconsistencies—while maintaining that the strategy was still his at its core.

As for McMaster, he argued that it was more important to pay attention to what Trump did, not what he said. "We imposed more sanctions on Russia in the first four months of the Trump administration than the entire eight years of the Obama administration," he insisted. What was more, he said, Trump sold Javelin anti-tank missiles to Ukraine when Obama had not. (That was true but oversold: the 210 missiles sent in 2018 had to remain boxed in storage facilities far from the front line to serve as a symbolic "strategic deterrent.")

"Of course," he admitted, "the audio didn't match the video" when it came to Trump. But that, to McMaster, was because Trump—like

Obama and like Bush before him—believed that he could break through with Putin on a personal level.

"Don't," he recalled warning his boss, "fall into the same trap." He tried to illustrate for Trump the threat that Putin posed in the clearest possible way: "I would bring him charts that would show the pattern of Russian aggression, going back to at least 2003," McMaster recalled, including everything from the poisoning of Russian dissident Sergei Skripal and his daughter in 2018 to cyberattacks and the shadow war that continued in Ukraine. "I had a timeline and insets with pictures on what they did." Trump ignored all those warnings and fell into the same trap anyway—most egregiously in Helsinki in July 2018, when he embarrassingly agreed with Putin's contention that Russia had not involved itself at all in the 2016 election.

McMaster's tenure lasted just over one year. Trump found him condescending. "Look at this guy, he's so serious!" Trump once complained during one of McMaster's briefings. It didn't help that McMaster committed the deadly sin of believing in Russian election interference—a fact that Trump categorically refused to admit, fearing it would call into question his narrow victory.

McMaster was expelled from the West Wing long before it became clear that Putin was aiming for the rest of Ukraine. But McMaster was convinced, he told me, that it was coming. "There are some things in life that are black swans," he told me after the invasion, quoting a friend of his. "But there are some things that are pink flamingos. And this was a pink flamingo."

IF MCMASTER HAD the strong views of a general with an attitude, his successor, John Bolton, was an ideologue who believed he himself should be president. Long before he became the third of Trump's four national security advisors, Bolton enjoyed his role as the party's foreign policy enfant terrible. He had once declared that were the United Nations Secretariat Building in New York to lose ten stories, "it wouldn't make a bit of difference." As the undersecretary of state for arms control and international security under George W. Bush, he pressed for intervention in Iraq and derailed efforts to control biological and chemical weapons, warning that such accords would undercut U.S.

sovereignty. To his supporters, he was a realist; to his critics, he was abrasive and deeply undiplomatic, which is probably why Bush made him UN ambassador. War and aggression, his critics argued, were often his policies of first resort.

Trump loved that Bolton knew how to sound tough when he appeared on Fox, especially when discussing North Korea and Iran. It apparently didn't matter to Trump that Bolton's worldview directly clashed with his own episodic America-first anti-interventionism: While Bolton had applauded the ousting of Saddam Hussein in Iraq as a fabulous example of regime change at work, Trump called the American invasion "the single worst decision ever made."

Everyone who knew both Trump and Bolton just stood back, waiting for the inevitable implosion of their relationship.

Trump's foreign policy thinking, Bolton wrote in his book, "was like an archipelago of dots, leaving the rest of us to discern—or create—policy." To Bolton, that opened the way to impose his own philosophy. He centralized authority in his office, ensuring that competing power centers—like Tom Bossert, the homeland security advisor—were quickly fired, or their positions dissolved entirely. When he developed new policies, he deliberately brought them to be signed by Trump when the president was watching television in the small dining room off the Oval Office. He knew the president didn't read much of what was put before him—especially if it competed with TV time.

When Bolton entered the White House, one of his top goals was to transform the way America dealt with the breadth of the China problem—its coercive use of trade deals around the world and its challenge to America in space, in cyberspace, and in the Pacific. After railing for decades that politicians and policymakers were getting China wrong, Bolton saw this as his moment to get tough on Beijing across the board. "I had huge ideas about how to change China policy," Bolton recalled, but what he quickly discovered was that he was working for a president whose interest in China started and ended with trade deficits and who would not sit still for discussion of much else.

"Every day," Bolton recalled, Trump was hearing "how big the Chinese economy is. And he's looking at the trade deficit—which is about the only thing in economic policy he really understands. He misunderstands it, but he thinks he understands it because it's a balance sheet. We have a trade deficit: bad. They have a trade surplus: good for them. I mean, you would think this eighteenth-century mercantilist idea would have been dispelled when he went to the University of Pennsylvania, but that's what he focused on."

By the spring of 2018, just as Bolton was settling into office, a tit-for-tat trade war broke out between the United States and China; it had been sparked by the Trump administration's tariffs on solar panels and washing machines, and later by ones on steel and aluminum, consumer technologies, and more. Not surprisingly, they were quickly matched by Chinese tariffs on American automobiles, chemicals, and soybeans. The tariff war escalated, with Trump insisting that it was the Chinese who were paying the economic penalties he was imposing; actually, it was American consumers.

Trump welcomed the fight, certain that the pain would drive the Chinese to a major trade deal, which he could declare he had forced them into. Sure, a trade war might hurt Republicans in the upcoming midterm elections—which was why he'd rushed through a series of financial bailouts to farmers across the country, at a cost of billions of dollars to American taxpayers. But it was exactly the type of wheeling and dealing he believed was his trademark.

What followed was a series of back-and-forth missions between Chinese and American economic officials in search of Trump's elusive deal. Yet meeting after meeting ended inconclusively. Much of the problem was that Trump's own top economic advisors were deeply divided on the direction of trade with China and, embarrassingly, bickered with each other in front of their Chinese counterparts.

At one extreme was Peter Navarro, the hardline director of the White House Office of Trade and Manufacturing Policy. On the other was Treasury Secretary Steve Mnuchin, a closet globalist in an administration that professed to hate globalists who was trying to make good on Trump's desire for a deal, without offending his friends from Hollywood and Wall Street who were making a fortune dealing with China. As one of Trump's top national security officials told me later, instead of the Americans debating with the Chinese, "it was basically them arguing with each other on their side of the table."

For months the Chinese negotiators exacerbated splits in Trump's economic team, delaying the negotiation of a "Phase One" trade deal until the very end of 2019—one that ostensibly committed China to open its markets to more American firms; to increase farm, manufacturing, and energy purchases by $200 billion; and to protect American technology. With his usual hyperbole, Trump called it "a momentous step—one that has never been taken before with China toward a future of fair and reciprocal trade." He also promised a follow-on deal. "Together," he said, "we are righting the wrongs of the past."

The deal was signed just weeks before the COVID pandemic hit, undercutting an agreement that seemed bound to fall apart anyway. In the end, several studies suggested, China didn't buy any of those additional exports. The follow-on agreement, which was supposed to handle more complex issues, from cybersecurity to data transfers and cloud computing, never happened.

TRUMP'S PREOCCUPATION WITH trade was reassuring to Beijing. As long as Trump's team was bickering about how to narrow the American trade deficit in goods—the U.S. surplus in the sale of software and services to China didn't seem to register with the president—the Chinese felt free to move ahead with the rest of their agenda: gaining technological and military dominance.

The Trump White House did not ignore these issues—they just had a hard time sustaining the president's interest in them. "We were strapped to the vicissitudes of trade talks as the proxy issue for the entire relationship with China," said Matt Pottinger, who ran the Asia operations of the National Security Council before becoming Trump's deputy national security advisor. "And so we were riding that dolphin into the water and back out again."

Pottinger was a rarity in the Trump White House. A close student of Chinese politics, he spoke fluent Mandarin and had spent years reporting on the country for Reuters and then *The Wall Street Journal.* He joined the Marines after 9/11, serving one tour in Iraq and two in Afghanistan—experiences that made him acutely aware of the limits of American power. Inside the Trump White House, he was among the first to raise the alarm about COVID when it was still primarily a Chinese phenomenon. Trump famously mocked him for wearing a mask early in the pandemic.

Pottinger was a steady presence in an administration marked by constant turmoil and turnover, one of a small group inside the White House who thought there were far more serious worries about China than what showed up in the trade numbers. When he came into the job in 2017, Pottinger was dismayed—but not entirely surprised—to discover that almost no one in the U.S. government had a complete picture of China's actions or intentions. The Pentagon was counting planes in the South China Sea and missiles along the coast; the U.S. Trade Representative, Robert Lighthizer, was logging new limits on American companies operating in China and trying to leverage tariffs on a wide range of Chinese products to punish Beijing for the country's rampant IP theft and coerced transfers; the Department of Homeland Security was watching out for Chinese cyberattacks on critical infrastructure; and a Treasury-led government-wide committee was raising red flags about Chinese investment in Silicon Valley. But almost no one was synthesizing these trends to glean the larger picture.

Pottinger's office quickly became known as the place where the puzzle pieces of China's actions were collected and interpreted. And the pieces were many. When Trump came to office in 2017, satellite photographs were already circulating showing new runways, fighter jets, and missile emplacements on remote Chinese islands in the South China Sea—the place that Xi had promised, during a 2015 visit to the White House, never to militarize. Reports from the Middle East and Southeast Asia detailed new Chinese efforts to build ports that seemed likely to have military uses. Even more concerning were indications that NATO countries—notably Italy—were preparing to sign on with Chinese telecommunications manufacturers to build the latest generation of cellular networks, with no apparent concern about the potential security implications.

In the middle of Trump's term, a giant Chinese electrical transformer—weighing half a million pounds—arrived by cargo ship at the Port of Houston, ultimately bound for a Colorado utility company. Tipped off by suspicions that it might have been tinkered with, the government seized it and shipped it to the Sandia National Laboratories in Albuquerque for examination. While the government classified the results, enough details leaked out to make it clear the United States suspected the transformer had a hidden digital back door that could be accessed from China—one of the first glimpses of the lengths to which Beijing would go to gain access to the U.S. power grid, presumably in case its conflict over Taiwan ever turned ugly.

Meanwhile, America's ability to pierce Xi's inner circle was limited. The CIA was still rebuilding from the intelligence calamity resulting from China's systematic dismantling of American spy operations in the country.

But Pottinger's biggest concern was that many in the bureaucracy were still operating under an outdated vision of China, one that dated back to the pre–Xi Jinping era, when an embrace of economic and diplomatic engagement was the guiding philosophy. "That would have been defensible in 2003," he said, but it was "grossly out of date by 2017." It left him "kind of stunned" to see that the big events of Xi's first several years in office—the theft of the security clearance files on 20 million Americans, the coercive trade practices, even the increasing crackdown on Hong Kong, all in violation of China's promises—were often dismissed as the growing pains of a rising power rather than a concerted effort to challenge the United States for primacy around the world.

Pottinger found that many of the China experts the United States relied on continued to believe that China was "happy to draft in the wake of the United States"—and to fall in line behind the American-designed rules-based order—in the service of continued economic growth. Among those who thought China's leaders would be driven primarily by their economic interests was Trump himself, which is why he thought he could count on billions of dollars in tariffs on Chinese goods to punish Beijing, restore a balance of trade in America's favor, and presumably to pressure Xi to change his behavior.

It wasn't until two years into his time in office that Pottinger finally got the evidence he had been seeking that Xi was on a very different path. And it came out of Xi's own mouth.

In January 2013, less than two months before becoming president, Xi gave a major address to the party leaders who were still trying to figure out where he would take the country. But the address was kept secret. In 2019, China declassified the speech—an interesting move in itself—and published it, still in its original Chinese, in internal Communist Party journals. "I was electrified by it," Pottinger told me. "I mean, it's painful reading, but it was a Rosetta Stone to Xi Jinping. . . . Xi had laid it all out, saying essentially that we are in a zero-sum struggle to the finish with the United States."

While recent Chinese leaders had been masters of pragmatism— reaching back to the days when "to get rich is glorious" was an acceptable slogan—Xi revealed himself to be an ideologue, one who cast himself as Mao's intellectual successor, while liberally quoting Deng Xiaoping and including a snippet of Mao's poetry.

In the speech, Xi predicted that it was "inevitable that the superiority of our socialist system will be increasingly apparent. . . . Capitalism is bound to die out and socialism is bound to win. This is an inevitable trend in social and historical development."

But, Xi warned his party's top leadership, they had to brace themselves for an extended battle. "The road is tortuous," he said. "We must diligently prepare for a long period of cooperation and of conflict between these two social systems." The important thing to do for the moment, he said, was to focus on "laying the foundation for a future where we will win the initiative and have the dominant position."

To most Americans these words might have simply sounded jingoistic, and even deeply boring. Reading opaque Communist Party documents, China experts sometimes quip, is comparable to "swallowing sawdust by the bucketful." But for Pottinger, there was only one way to interpret Xi's speech: as a declaration of China's determination to displace the United States, peacefully if it could, but using whatever tools were necessary. He saw the speech as confirmation that Xi had a unifying theory that had guided China's behavior for the previous six years. And it explained why Xi had at times sounded conciliatory toward the Americans: "I think what Xi was testing was whether or not he could lull or flatter the United States into continued complacency and ignorance about China's ultimate goals," Pottinger told me. "It was clear that we didn't have our arms around the full breadth of the problem, but every time a new clue emerged, it was deeply disturbing."

Not everyone agreed with Pottinger that Xi's 2013 speech was a clear turning point. But many China scholars, even Democrats who agreed with Trump on almost nothing, came to roughly the same conclusion that Pottinger did, around the same time—including Rush Doshi, the Harvard scholar who would later serve as the China director on Biden's

National Security Council. "After the Cold War," Doshi wrote in his 2018 dissertation, later published online, "China sought to 'blunt' American power and subsequently to 'build' a constraining regional order." Consequently, the U.S. strategy "must be to prevent or delay Chinese hegemony through measures short of war. Washington needs to learn from China's grand strategy and adopt its own strategy for peace-time competition with Beijing."

Taken together, Pottinger and Doshi—among others—came to define the new Washington consensus on China and its intentions.

Yet Trump, for all his tough talk, did little in response. Pottinger and his small team at the NSC developed what he called a plan to counter Chinese economic aggression—a "blueprint" for bolstering America's manufacturing base, ensuring the United States had access to semiconductors, and preventing China from dominating in 5G, among other steps. But the plan was immediately classified—meaning that it was impossible to use it to develop a consensus. And at every step along the way, Trump and his obsessions stood in the way of executing a government-wide response.

"YOU DON'T SAY no to the president," said Randall Stephenson, then the chief executive of AT&T, about the day in the spring of 2019 that Donald Trump called him out of the blue. Trump, frequently channel surfing, had seen Stephenson being interviewed on a talk show about the complications of dealing with Chinese companies, like Huawei and ZTE, inside American telecommunications networks. Trump wanted him to come by the White House, he said, to talk about it.

Stephenson is a lanky Oklahoman with a dry sense of humor and a passion for fly-fishing, golf, and advanced technology. He had spent the bulk of his career in the telephone business, which made it all the more remarkable that he became the architect of AT&T's moves to diversify the company into new arenas, buying up DirecTV and Time Warner, the parent of HBO, CNN, and one of the world's most valuable movie archives. Along the way he became an expert in China's moves into the world of telecommunications, but when he showed up at the Oval Office with an AT&T colleague for his hour-long meeting, it wasn't exactly as advertised. He was in for The Trump Show.

The bizarre nature of what followed was symbolic of the chaos of the Trump era. Trump burned up the first forty-five minutes of the session by riffing on how men got into trouble—it was all about women and private planes, he claimed. Then he went into a long diatribe about Stormy Daniels, the former porn star who claimed she had had an affair with him. It was "all part of the same stand-up comedy act," Stephenson later recalled to me, and "we were left with fifteen minutes to talk about Chinese infrastructure."

Trump seemed fixated on the question of whether the Chinese, by moving their equipment into Western markets, could listen in on phone calls or read emails—the "back door" problem that intelligence agencies often briefed Trump about. Stephenson was less concerned: If Xi Jinping's goal was simply to intercept conversations or emails, he didn't really need to own the network. China's hacking teams had proven quite successful even before the days of 5G.

Stephenson tried to explain the bigger risks. If Huawei or ZTE, two of China's telecommunications giants, were in the spine of the American system, that could give Beijing "a very elegant path to shutting down networks" and crippling the U.S. communications grid. The biggest risk was a global one: China was already having success selling heavily subsidized Huawei equipment in Europe, Africa, and Latin America. If China did the same in the United States, "you would have guaranteed a 5G monopoly infrastructure" around the world, giving Chinese leaders far more options in a time of conflict to attack critical infrastructure.

As Stephenson unfolded the complexity of the challenge, he could see that the president's mind was elsewhere. "This is really boring," Trump finally said. Just then his daughter Ivanka appeared at the door of the Oval Office and came in to join the meeting. Not certain of her security clearances, Stephenson and his colleague edited what they were saying to the president. The session soon ended.

The moment encapsulated the fundamental problem with how Trump dealt with China. On the one hand, his administration grasped the emerging threat. With an enthusiasm rarely seen in the Obama administration, they used many of the levers of power available to them to respond: sanctions, investigations of unfair trading practices, export bans, "naming and shaming," and criminal indictments of hackers and thieves of intellectual property. They used existing rules—and created some new ones—to block new categories of Chinese investments into the United States.

Yet it wasn't enough. Trump's aides understood the problem, and identified ways to push back in specific arenas. But they never had a holistic strategy for countering the problem. Tackling China's efforts to achieve economic and technical dominance would have required something much bigger than the bits and pieces that Trump's officials generally offered. Trump himself would often derail their best efforts. When Xi complained in 2018 about export restrictions against ZTE—imposed after the company violated U.S. sanctions in Iran—Trump agreed to reverse course. When prodemocracy demonstrators took to the streets of Hong Kong the following year in response to a shocking crackdown on a city once known for its freedoms, Trump promised Xi not to raise the issue so as not to jeopardize trade talks. When Canadian officials arrested Meng Wanzhou, a top executive of Huawei and the daughter of its founder, on charges brought by the U.S. Department of Justice—on the very night that Xi and Trump met for dinner at a G-20 summit in Argentina—Trump publicly said that he "would certainly intervene" to drop the charges if he got "the largest trade deal ever made." Quickly, Beijing retaliated, arresting two Canadian nationals—Michael Spavor and Michael Kovrig—and charging them with espionage.

The Trump whiplash on China played out in private meetings with foreign officials too. When the late prime minister Shinzo Abe would raise concerns about Chinese military action in the Pacific, one Japanese official told me, Trump would often wave it away and talk about pending trade deals with Beijing. So Abe learned how to manage Trump: He would come to meetings with him armed with almost cartoonlike charts, showing how the United States and Japan were working together to sell gas or other products in Asia. Sometimes they would bring the same chart to the next meeting, because Trump didn't recall seeing it previously.

Nowhere was dysfunction more visible than in the effort to keep Chinese telecommunications technologies—particularly Huawei—out of American networks. For one thing, banning Huawei—or ZTE, DJI (the Chinese drone maker), or TikTok—in an open society guided by the rule of law was a lot harder than it was for China to ban Google or Amazon. In the Huawei case, the U.S. government failed to offer any hard evidence that China had used the company to manipulate or cripple foreign networks. (When pressed, officials hinted that the classified record was more damning, but that didn't help either their political or their legal arguments.) They fell back on citing new national security laws in China that required all companies—Huawei included—to comply with any request from local law enforcement or national authorities. But even then, the administration couldn't identify any viable alternatives to Huawei. It talked about creating a true Western competitor in 5G but never did so.

AND ALL THE WHILE, the instructions from the top were conflicting and often demoralizing. "Even for staff on a given day, it wasn't clear whether we were departing in some fundamental way from the strategy Trump had approved," Pottinger recalled, or "whether it was simply this wild sine wave, this corkscrew sort of journey." In January 2020, Undersecretary of State Keith Krach, whom Trump had appointed to run America's economic diplomacy, hosted three dozen top CEOs, mostly from the tech industry, at his four-story white mansion on "Billionaires' Row" in San Francisco. Krach was no stranger to this group; before his stint at the State Department, he had been the CEO and chairman of DocuSign, the company that had turned electronic signatures into a multi-billion-dollar enterprise.

When the group assembled, Krach had been in the State Department for only six months, one of the series of Trump appointees from the business world who had been sent in to change the culture of the State Department. For some, like Trump's first secretary of state, Rex Tillerson, the ExxonMobil CEO and chairman, it didn't seem to sink in that America's diplomatic corps should run differently from a for-profit oil company. But to his credit, Krach was trying to do his job with a bit more subtlety, bringing in a dozen Silicon Valley strategists to integrate with senior Foreign Service officers and introduce some fresh ideas for dealing with the growing economic challenge posed by China.

Krach knew one part of the dynamic that had led to paralysis on China policy: For decades, while intelligence officials sounded the alarm on economic or surveillance threats from China, the nation's biggest businesses had lobbied to keep markets open and profits rolling in. Now

Krach believed that the sentiment among business executives was finally turning. The continued theft of intellectual property and forced technology transfer, the Chinese requirements on keeping corporate data inside China, the harassment of some expatriate executives and the jailing of a few—these were all souring the atmosphere. So that evening, Krach had a goal in mind: to convince any holdouts in the group—those tech CEOs who still believed that investing in China and tapping its market potential was their future—that the deck was stacked against them. If business executives got on the same page and agreed to put security and their collective long-term competitiveness over the juicy lure of short-term gain, Beijing would lose its most powerful pro-China lobby in the United States. And what better way to convince a tech executive than by hearing directly from their peers? "I had them go around the room," Krach recalled of that evening, "and tell their China horror stories. And you could see lightbulbs go off." The executives, he said, could be divided into roughly three groups. "There was a group that wasn't doing business there anymore because they had been burned," he told me. "Then there was the cha-ching-ing group"—they were counting their profits and uninterested in anything else. But "the biggest group were the ones in the middle who were saying, 'I thought I was the only one getting the shaft from Chinese authorities. I need to learn more.'"

At the end of the night, Krach told me, he laid it out for the executives: "We all believe in the free market. But when somebody doesn't play by the rules, the market is no longer free," he said. "If I can buy your companies but you can't buy mine . . . I get access to your data but you get none of mine . . . and if I don't have to obey the law or I am the law: I am going to beat you every time." The only solution, he argued, was to band together—U.S. government and private sector alike—to protect themselves. Over the next year, Krach and other members of the administration spun out a series of new initiatives that—though no one could have known it at the time—would become the core of Biden's approach to China a year later.

First on the list was Taiwan Semiconductor Manufacturing Company's announcement that it would invest $12 billion to build an advanced chip factory in Arizona. The company said the move was about building trust because some of its biggest customers were located in the

United States—Apple, Nvidia, and others. But there was undeniably an element of arm-twisting of the Taiwanese giant by American officials. "They're probably the most important foreign company to the United States' economic security and national security," Krach later said. "So it was critical for us to convince them to onshore. . . . We figured if we could get TSMC to onshore the rest would follow."

Then there was a program to maintain "clean networks"—an effort to block a range of Chinese-made technologies from the digital systems of American allies. It centered on a diplomatic approach to bringing allies together around a single strategy, a vast improvement over Secretary of State Mike Pompeo's disastrous first efforts, which involved threatening allies with a cutoff of U.S. intelligence if they struck deals with companies like Huawei.

The third element of Krach's plan was a far more severe crackdown on Huawei itself. The Chinese company had easily circumvented the Trump administration's first, ill-executed efforts to choke off the computer chips that the company needed to produce cellphones and network equipment. Huawei was able to buy almost all of what it needed from other countries. By the end of the administration, the Trump team had gotten smarter, expanding an obscure Commerce Department rule to require that any microelectronic component based on U.S. technology could be subject to American export controls—even if it was manufactured abroad and never entered the United States. This became a powerful tool in the American arsenal, and over the next few years it devastated Huawei's revenues.

Trump's aides even began discussing with senators a more ambitious bill designed to catalyze American investment in scientific research and chip making at home, an idea that would grow slowly over the next few years before being signed into law as a $52 billion investment in 2022.

These strategies took three years to brew inside the Trump administration, and by the time Pottinger, Krach, and others rolled them out, the administration was in the midst of a reelection campaign—and a pandemic. Trump himself barely mentioned them on the campaign trail, and clearly many around him were concerned about being tarred with creating "industrial policy"—government intervention in the free market, an approach Republicans instinctively opposed.

The ironic result was that a handful of Trump's aides laid the foundation for one of the signature efforts of the Biden administration. (Biden adopted much the same approach on two other major Trump-era initiatives: the Abraham Accords in the Middle East and Operation Warp Speed, the effort to develop COVID vaccines.) In 2022, Kurt Campbell, Biden's Asia coordinator, personally credited Krach's efforts for creating a foundation for Biden's team to build on. The initiatives Krach and his team introduced during their final year in office "have been followed on in this administration," Campbell said, "and, in many respects, that's the highest tribute."

Soon, though, these Trump-to-Biden-era efforts snowballed into a movement that scared economists and business leaders alike: "decoupling." Starting around 2020, the word began to appear everywhere, from front-page headlines to the titles of academic conferences. It suggested that just as the United States and China had woven their economies together for decades—creating an interdependent, symbiotic economic beast that the historian Niall Ferguson and the economist Moritz Schularick had dubbed "Chimerica"—the strands could somehow be separated again. The idea took hold in both countries. That is what "Made in China 2025" was all about, and it lay at the root of every tariff imposed on Chinese firms and every call for "reshoring" American manufacturers who had abandoned the U.S. decades ago.

When one pressed Chinese and American leaders in off-the-record events, they all acknowledged that total decoupling was almost impossible to imagine. Yes, both countries were now suddenly celebrating what they could make at home and warning against dependence on their chief military rival and technological competitor. Yet even as American companies began to pull their industrial manufacturing out of China, and as Washington hobbled Huawei, banned China Telecom, and tried to regulate TikTok, they knew that they could not afford to divorce. Apple was not going to find the workforce to make the iPhone back in America—at least not affordably. Walmart was not going to fill its stores with non-Chinese goods; consumers would rebel. Americans might tell pollsters that they viewed Beijing as their country's number one threat, but they weren't going to give up their shopping habits. Still, a new era had dawned—and perhaps not entirely for the better. Both countries remained interlinked. But increasingly both signaled they would think about national security first—and all those "win-win" deals second. Or, as my colleague Tom Friedman put it: "Love it or hate it, the U.S.-China partnership forged between 1979 and 2019 delivered a lot of prosperity to a lot of people and a lot of relative peace to the world—and, baby, we will miss it when it's gone."

THE VERY DAY that Volodymyr Zelensky won the presidency of Ukraine—April 21, 2019—on a platform of fighting corruption and finding a way to negotiate an end to the long-simmering war in the Donbas with Vladimir Putin, Donald Trump called to congratulate him. He also promised Zelensky a visit to the White House.

It was a good opening to what would become a disastrous relationship—one that would lead to an impeachment and arguably help pave the way for Russia's invasion.

The White House meeting—had it happened—would have been a big deal for Ukraine and Zelensky, a true showing of American backing for the government. It was necessary because in the eyes of many in Washington, Zelensky was a joke. His sole qualification for the job was his work as a comedian, and if he had a governing ideology, no one could quite figure it out. His party was named "Servant of the People"—the title of his TV show—and Ukrainians liked the irreverent character he played, a fictional Ukrainian president. Now he had leveraged that image to defeat the incumbent president, Petro Poroshenko, with over 70 percent of the vote.* Life had imitated art, and much of the world was worried. Zelensky was such a novice that it was unclear how he could take on a Machiavellian figure on the level of Putin. And no one could quite understand how Zelensky would wind down the war with Russia without losing any territory, as he'd promised.

What Zelensky presumably did not know was that Trump's view of Ukraine was essentially identical to Putin's: The country shouldn't exist. "Trump made it very clear that he thought, you know, that Ukraine, and

---

* Poroshenko had tried to position himself as the pro-Ukraine candidate and Zelensky as the Russian speaker from the east who couldn't be relied upon to oppose Putin. But by 2019, the pro-Putin faction in Ukraine was small indeed—and the claim that Zelensky would focus on appeasing the Russians was not compelling.

certainly Crimea, must be part of Russia," Fiona Hill, the White House director for Russia and Ukraine, told me in 2021. "He really could not get his head around the idea that Ukraine was an independent state."

In fact, Trump had two obsessions about Ukraine. The first, which he started pushing in April 2017, was that it was the Ukrainian government and not Putin's Russia that had sought to manipulate the 2016 American presidential campaign—and that there was proof on a computer server belonging to the Democratic National Committee. The problem, he claimed, was that the FBI was being kept from investigating the server, which he alleged had been spirited out of the United States and taken to Ukraine by Crowdstrike, which he called a shady Ukrainian cybersecurity company.

It was a conspiracy theory that Putin himself had promoted a few months before. The DNC server remained in the basement of the DNC headquarters on Capitol Hill. Crowdstrike was an American cybersecurity company, and one of its founders, Dmitri Alperovitch, had been born in Russia, not Ukraine. It was Alperovitch, among others, who had investigated the hack of the DNC server and traced it back to Russian actors. American intelligence agencies had concluded in 2017 that Russia, and Russia alone, was to blame—and the Republican-controlled Senate committee had agreed.

But nothing could shake Trump's conviction that it was all Ukraine's fault. Ukraine, he said, "tried to take me down in 2016." It was "a terrible place, all corrupt, terrible people."

As the 2020 reelection campaign approached, what Trump cared about even more—his second Ukraine obsession—was extracting from the Ukrainian government anything he could elicit to take down his then-presumed opponent, Joe Biden. And on that issue, the unseemly connections between Biden's son Hunter and the Burisma energy firm provided an ideal pretext. Seeking influence and a connection to the West, Burisma put Hunter on its board of directors, even though his qualifications for that post were as thin as Zelensky's qualifications for the presidency. Hunter reciprocated by putting his father on the phone, presumably to show off his access, even though there is no evidence that Biden ever talked business or changed policies.

By July 2019, no formal invitation to the White House had been proffered, and Zelensky's aides were starting to sense that something had gone wrong. Worse yet, something or someone was holding up hundreds of millions of dollars of military and diplomatic aid that Congress had designated for Ukraine. Quietly, the Ukrainians were trying to figure out how to unblock it all—and so they asked for a direct call between Zelensky and Trump.

The call was finally scheduled for July 25, over the objections of John Bolton, who told his staff he feared it would end up being "a disaster" because Trump would not stick to his talking points and would demand that Zelensky help him impugn Biden.

Bolton was right. In the call, President Trump made it clear to Zelensky that the United States' support for Ukraine was contingent on Zelensky's willingness to launch two politically motivated investigations: one based on the discredited theory that it was Ukraine, not Russia, that had interfered in the 2016 election and a second that could implicate Joe Biden in some kind of corruption with Burisma.

Following the call, Zelensky's administration quietly tried to negotiate their way out of what they realized was a trap. Zelensky said he was willing to launch an investigation into any accusations of general corruption, but he refused to say that it was focused on Biden or Burisma. Their staffs went back and forth until the inevitable happened: a media leak about Trump's moves to withhold hundreds of millions of dollars in military aid that would help the Ukrainians to defend themselves.

All this, of course, led to Trump's first impeachment. Zelensky found himself caught in the midst of a pitched partisan battle in the United States—exactly where he did not want to be. In the impeachment hearings and the trial that followed, it was clear that Trump had sought to extort a foreign leader for his own reelection purposes. In a verdict that was entirely predictable, the Republican-controlled Senate acquitted Trump on what was a purely party-line vote in February 2020; among Republicans, only Senator Mitt Romney of Utah crossed party lines to vote to convict Trump of abuse of his presidential power.

The message to America was that the new era of hyperpartisanship was here to stay. The message Putin took away from the affair was that Americans didn't really care about Ukraine.

· · ·

IN THE TRUMP YEARS, America's capability to shape the world shrank. Allies were regularly insulted and unsurprisingly had no interest in signing up to Washington's initiatives. Adversaries thrived. Putin exulted in an American president who believed Russian propaganda over American intelligence findings. China expanded its reach in every domain, delighted that America was wrapped up in contested elections, two impeachments, and an attempted insurrection.

But Trump's advisors, or at least a subset of them, recognized Putin's ambitions, indicted his hackers, sanctioned Russian oligarchs, and pressed the president to throw Russian diplomats out of the United States after the Skripal poisoning. They mounted effective campaigns to combat Russia's hackers, disrupting their efforts to meddle in the 2018 midterm elections and the 2020 presidential election. But they had to do much of this behind Trump's back. As one senior official said to me when *The New York Times* was about to reveal one such operation, "we try not to trouble the president with too many details" about what the United States was doing to counter Russia. In short, they acted as if they had a Russian stooge—a "useful idiot"—presiding over the United States government.

Similarly, it was the Trump administration that identified China as having a long-term plan to displace the United States as the world's dominant power. "The Trump administration deserves disproportionate credit for saying, 'Whoa, China is the biggest threat to us,'" Sue Gordon, a top career intelligence official who had no love for Trump, told me in 2022.

The trouble, of course, was execution. Some of Trump's aides insist that they ran out of time—and that the COVID pandemic made it worse. That part is undeniable: As the world shut down, citizens panicked, and basic supplies ran short, shaping the long-term balance of power between the United States and China looked less urgent. But the president's own ego, his inability to focus on strategy, and his habit of undercutting policy for his own personal gain also stymied the efforts. Ultimately, it would take a new administration, and a new strategy, to rechart America's course in a world of great power rivalry.

PART TWO

THE ARC OF HISTORY

CHAPTER 5

INHERITING THE WRECKAGE

There are countries around the world that would say, "I want my country to run like Germany, or Japan, or Canada." There's no one around the world that looks at the United States and says, "I wish my political system would run like that."

Ian Bremmer, geopolitical consultant, July 2021

"**I HAVE SOMETHING** extremely sensitive."

That was the cryptic message that Kevin Mandia, CEO of one of the country's most renowned cybersecurity firms, FireEye, delivered in a late-November 2020 call to Anne Neuberger at the National Security Agency.*

It got her immediate attention. Neuberger was the grandchild of Holocaust survivors. She grew up in a Hasidic Jewish community in Brooklyn, and had barely imagined life outside of New York when, in her twenties, as a mother of two small children, she changed direction and won a prestigious White House fellowship. She soon ended up at the National Security Agency, where she rocketed up through the ranks in a male-dominated intelligence bureaucracy known for more than a little bit of sexism. Among her first tasks was a classified program to counter Chinese plans to compromise the firmware running the U.S. govern-

---

* At the time of the incident, Mandia's security company, Mandiant, was a subsidiary of FireEye. Mandiant then split from FireEye and was acquired by Google in 2022.

ment's computer systems, followed by a high-profile damage-control effort to seal up the holes in the NSA's system that had allowed Edward
Snowden to reveal some of the agency's greatest secrets. She then turned
to helping rebuild the hacking capabilities aimed at foreign networks,
and later ran the small group tasked with defending American election
systems in the wake of the 2016 Russian interference.

It was during those operations that she grew to know Mandia, a
former Air Force intelligence officer who made his mark tracking Chinese, Russian, Iranian, and other hackers. Mandia, she knew, had a nose
for emerging trouble and didn't panic easily. When he called, it was usually with an urgent problem.

It was Mandia and his team that in 2013 warned the public of Unit
61398, the Chinese hacking team that had raided much of corporate
America. When the North Koreans attacked Sony Pictures Entertainment in a failed effort to kill off the release of *The Interview,* a madcap
tale of two reporters hired by the CIA to assassinate Kim Jong Un, it was
Mandia who was called in to restore order. Over the years, Mandia had
also quietly been called in to work for U.S. government clients, including intelligence agencies, because he could see into networks they could
not. Congressional restrictions dating back to the 1970s barred U.S.
intelligence agencies from operating inside the United States. In the
cyber age, that made the U.S. cyber defensive agencies more reliant than
ever on private-sector firms like Mandia's to raise the alarm.

Now, Mandia told Neuberger, his team—many of whom used to
work in the intelligence world—had discovered a problem so big they
needed to meet in person at the agency. He would be alone, he said. But
time was of the essence.

Neuberger and her staff had, of course, spent the year almost entirely
focused on the 2020 presidential election. After the debacle of 2016,
they had quietly gone to extraordinary lengths to make sure that there
was no repeat of the Russian digital break-in at the Democratic National
Committee, nor of the massive disinformation campaign mounted at
Putin's behest. In the end, the agency was not only surveilling the Russians (and the Chinese, the Iranians, and the North Koreans) but lock-
ing up the computers of some of Russia's ransomware gangs, disrupting
them so they had no time to contemplate interfering in the election.

In his cryptic call, Mandia made it clear that whatever he had tripped on was not about the election, but was perhaps even more worrisome. "He made it sound pretty urgent," Neuberger told me. She set up a meeting for late in the day on Tuesday, November 24, two days before Thanksgiving.

Mandia arrived alone at the NSA's headquarters near Baltimore/ Washington International Airport. Neuberger invited two NSA specialists to join her at the long conference room in her office. Mandia was blunt. "Someone stole our tools," he told Neuberger. These weren't hammers and saws he had in mind but rather "red-teaming tools"—the company's most closely guarded instruments that allowed Mandia and his team to act as if they were the bad guys breaking into networks, seeking vulnerabilities for clients who paid handsomely for the unpleasant simulation.

The very fact that someone could attack one of America's leading cybersecurity firms and walk off with some of their crown jewels was striking. And almost immediately, Mandia suspected he knew the culprit: "I took one look at this and in thirty minutes I knew who did it," he told me shortly after the discovery. "It had to be the Russians."

His hunch was soon confirmed by America's intelligence agencies. The highly sophisticated intelligence operation that stole the red team's tools bore all the hallmarks of the SVR, one of Russia's most advanced intelligence services. It was the SVR that had pulled off some of the operations around the 2016 election. And now, Mandia and Neuberger were coming to realize, it had a new goal: penetrating a vast swath of the federal government and corporate America.

In retrospect, Neuberger would view that realization as the first indication that the newly elected Biden administration was on a collision course with Vladimir Putin.

IT TOOK MANDIA and his experts several weeks to figure out that they had been robbed—and several more days to find out how.

The first hint that something had gone very wrong was an especially understated subject line on a meeting invite distributed by his staff one November morning. "It just said 'security brief,' " Mandia later recalled. "About five minutes into it, I started getting pattern recognition. . . . I knew my Friday was ruined."

An alert analyst had noticed something slightly off inside the cyber-security company's systems. It was disarmingly simple: It appeared that a FireEye sales representative had registered a second mobile phone to an account on the company's network—a phone that could receive a multifactor authentication alert confirming that they were logging into the company's networks, just as a bank might text you a code before al-lowing you into your online bank account. But when a security techni-cian checked with the sales rep, it turned out that the second phone wasn't the employee's. Whoever had registered it was an impostor.

This set off all the warning bells. Someone had gotten deeply enough into FireEye's networks that they were able to register their own phone—and acquire for themselves all the privileges of a bona fide Fire-Eye employee. They'd parlayed those privileges into high-level access that enabled them to steal the red-teaming tools and to poke around for other interesting nuggets on the system.

It was less clear how the hackers had pulled it off. Following days of round-the-clock investigations into their company's systems, Mandia's investigators had come up with nothing. "We were still sitting there going, 'So how did they break into FireEye?' And I remember on a Monday, talking to some folks, saying, 'It's got to be the SolarWinds server.'" At that point, it seemed to Mandia, there was simply nothing else it could have been.

The problem was, Mandia did not want to be right about this. Be-cause if it was the SolarWinds server, then all hell was about to break loose.

For years, SolarWinds had marketed itself to clients across the gov-ernment and the Fortune 500 as the leading provider of "network man-agement software"—basically, a way for a company's IT team to track what was happening on different corporate systems at the same time. It could, for example, help an electric utility catch an unexpected surge in air conditioning demand on a hot day. SolarWinds was part of the little-seen ecosystem of internet infrastructure—one of the companies that provide technology so foundational to the modern digital world that most people don't even think about it.

But some eighteen thousand clients used the SolarWinds product that Mandia suspected was compromised, from the Treasury Depart-ment and Cisco Systems to the Department of Homeland Security—

including the nation's cybersecurity defenders—and *The New York Times*. It was that combination of invisibility and ubiquity that made invading the software so appealing to the Russians.

The hackers' strategy was simple, but their technique was masterful. Rather than target each individual customer, the Russian hackers spent months figuring out how they could break into SolarWinds' software, drop in some malicious code, and rely on the company to do its dirty work for them: disseminating the malware to its clients in future rounds of software updates. So they did exactly that—an effort that was facilitated by the company's exceptionally poor level of cybersecurity.

From there, hackers could pick and choose which victims presented the most compelling targets for the Kremlin's intelligence-gathering needs.

FireEye took a little heat, at first, for losing its tools. But they were just among the first to figure out they had been robbed. It turned out the other victims—including the federal government—didn't have a clue.

IT TOOK A few weeks—and some return visits to the NSA—before Mandia and Neuberger pieced all of this together. But over time it became increasingly clear that the Kremlin's cyber spies had succeeded in burrowing deep inside the federal government's systems. The question resounding inside the NSA was whether the Russians were just using their access to spy or were positioning themselves to take over those systems, with the prospect of causing far more havoc. "I've always thought it was a huge, huge amount of effort to put into something that was just an espionage campaign," said Angus King, the Maine senator and political independent who had co-chaired Congress's Cyberspace Solarium Commission, an effort to overhaul both America's cyber offense and defense. "I thought we weren't anywhere close to the bottom of it."

After the first warning in November, Neuberger created a small task force to try to understand the damage—a quiet operation amid the acrimony, lies, and chaos caused by Trump's refusal to concede the 2020 election. What they found went straight into President Trump's Daily Brief—and ultimately to Joe Biden himself, as the president-elect overcame Trump's resistance to giving him access to current intelligence updates.

For the new team, it was an immediate reminder that Putin wasn't going to wait for the new president to get settled. They would have to hit the ground running. "It really woke people up," remembered Toria Nuland, who was about to come back into government as the top policy official for the State Department. "I think it crystallized minds . . . that we were going to have to be pretty strong right back if we wanted to get Putin's attention."

Perhaps no one was more aware of the depth of the problem than Biden himself. Yes, he had clearly slowed down compared to the days when he was a backslapping, always-on member of the U.S. Senate. And he was no technologist. But frequently forgotten was Biden's presence in the Situation Room alongside Barack Obama as the United States accelerated its secret cyber program against the Iranians, dubbed Operation Olympic Games, using computer code to sabotage Iran's nuclear centrifuges, which spun at supersonic speeds to make nuclear fuel.

For the vice president, then in his midsixties, Olympic Games was a seminal event that shaped his view of what the world would look like in coming years. With Olympic Games—the U.S.-and-Israeli-led cyber-attack against Iran's fledgling nuclear program—Biden had been immersed in the details of what was at the time the most sophisticated cyberattack in history, one he even participated in designing. That experience meant he knew better than many government officials of the potential of using cyberweapons to dismantle the infrastructure of an adversary country. When a reporter asked the president-elect in December 2020 whether he could trust the government systems he was about to inherit, Biden sounded exasperated. "Of course I can't," he snapped. "I don't know what the state of them is. They're clearly not safe right now."

Yet at the White House, the Trump administration was spending its final weeks in office pretending nothing of significance was happening. Trump knew the SolarWinds hack was the work of the Russians, of course—every intelligence briefing on the subject made that clear. Yet because of his long-running unwillingness to confront Putin or his singular focus on denying Biden the election he clearly had won, or some other factor we can only guess at, Trump was doing nothing about it. He blew up at his briefers one day, claiming they had no way of knowing that Putin was behind the SolarWinds hack. Then he tweeted out that maybe it was the Chinese. "The Cyber Hack is far greater in the Fake News Media than in actuality," he tweeted. "I have been fully briefed and everything is well under control."

"We couldn't fucking believe it," one top intelligence official told me shortly after Trump had left office. "He just didn't want to hear the truth."

That left Biden to respond, even though as president-elect he had no authority—yet—to retaliate. He held a public event to highlight the attack. "Enough's enough," he said. "In an age when so much of our lives are conducted online, cyberattacks must be treated as a serious threat by our leadership at the highest levels. We can't let this go unanswered. That means making clear and publicly who is responsible for the attack, and taking meaningful steps to hold them to account."

Biden laid the blame squarely at Trump's feet. "This assault happened on Donald Trump's watch when he wasn't watching. . . . It is still his responsibility as president to defend American interests for the next four weeks, but rest assured that even if he does not take it seriously, I will."

But Biden's message was washed away in the next news cycle, overtaken by a far more visually arresting threat to the United States government: an armed attack on the Capitol. There was only so much the people of the United States—or the country's media apparatus—could focus on at one time.

JANUARY 6 WAS an embarrassment for the United States and a stain on the country's democratic ideals. For America's adversaries, the confrontation provided iconic imagery of what they were eager to advertise as the demise of democracy.

Certainly, there was no shortage of evidence to make that case. There was Jacob Chansley, the face-painted "QAnon shaman," brandishing his spear-tipped flagpole and bullhorn in the Capitol rotunda. There was the mob chasing Eugene Goodman, the police officer who savvily led protesters up a staircase and, meaningfully, *away* from the Senate chamber. There was the shooting of Ashli Babbitt, the Air Force veteran killed while climbing through a broken door that led to the Speaker's Lobby.

A single day provided a year's worth of memes—rioters climbing the walls of the Capitol or sitting with their feet up in the ransacked office of the Democratic speaker of the House, Nancy Pelosi.

From Moscow to Beijing, mock solemnity masked the all-too-obvious schadenfreude. A senior member of Russia's parliament declared that for the United States, "the holiday of democracy is over. This is sadly a new low, I say this without a shadow of malice. America is no longer plotting a course and has thus lost all rights to set one, let alone impose it on others."

The Global Times—China's English-language propaganda sheet that can be counted on to turn any adverse event in the United States into an object lesson on the evils and inconsistencies of democracy—compared the storming of the Capitol to the Hong Kong prodemocracy protests of 2019. It all played to the Russian and Chinese narrative that American democracy is not a viable governing system; it is chaos.

Tellingly, though, American intelligence officials quickly noticed that the Russians and the Chinese exploited the moment differently. The Russians took the imagery of the mayhem and broadcast it around the world in an effort to undercut the American brand and heighten American embarrassment. In contrast, the Chinese broadcast the imagery mostly at home, in an effort to undercut the lectures from American presidents during visits to Beijing. The implication was clear: The American model would undo all the progress that China had made over decades to modernize its economy, elevate its populace from poverty, and unify its people ideologically.

This opportunism was blatant. But clearly there was more than a kernel of truth in the accusations streamed by authoritarians around the world. As Chris Coons, the Delaware senator and close friend of Biden's, told me not long after order had been restored, the damage to American democracy—and to democracy's brand—would be enduring: "That we had an armed, angry mob overrun our Capitol and stop the certification of the election, even for a few hours, was, to me, a shocking development that had a huge impact on how the world sees us—and how we see ourselves."

But January 6 was also a shock to the Europeans and key Asian allies. For several weeks after the announcement of the election results, they reveled in the thought that the days of Trump were over—that when he was gone, the threats to withdraw from NATO or pull troops out of South Korea and Japan would also disappear. They thought Biden was a known quantity and instinctual alliance-builder who would be happy to set the clock back to the Obama era.

They had it partially right. Biden was, above all, an institutionalist, a creature of the U.S. Senate and the vice presidency. He trusted that the system could be made to work. But he also knew that the world increasingly saw America as a broken vessel and wondered whether it could ever be trusted again. Yes, the allies knew Biden—or they thought they did. But they also wondered whether his election marked a true return to the America they had known or whether, in a few years, they would view his presidency as a blip in time, an interregnum of normalcy sandwiched between Trump and something Trump-like. They wondered whether Biden was capable of steering the United States back to the middle lanes.

If it was unclear that Biden could change the country's direction, it was because Trump was more a symptom of what was happening to America than the cause. It was easy to attribute "America First" and the country's seeming lack of faith in science, its political dysfunction and gridlock, to one man. And the Europeans did that plenty. But deep down, they knew that Trump had been a product of many forces, from American anger about trade, about jobs displaced by technology, about the increasingly glaring evidence of economic disparity—and also by legacies of isolationism and racism and distrust of government agencies and most media. Joe Biden's election didn't change any of that.

Add to that brew the recognition—long bandied about but now discussed with increasing urgency—that America was no longer the sole hyperpower. Clearly, China had caught up. Clearly, Russia was seeking to disrupt, even if it was a declining power. Biden was unlikely to change these fundamental dynamics. And it was entirely possible that the American tendency to panic and cling to a strongman's promises to restore the country to an earlier, halcyon time would not go away simply because Joe Biden was taking office as the un-Trump.

Coons and others made the case that Biden could, in fact, change that dynamic—that he could prove to be a more revolutionary president than predicted. And Coons argued that the first step in that direction would be to admit the errors of the previous few years. "The United

States has always been strongest when we have been most open about who we are, our failings as well as our strengths," he told me early in Biden's term. It would all depend on "how we look back at this pandemic and how we look forward to climate change and how we are accountable for episodes of racial violence and inequality in our own country."

Allies remained deeply uncertain whether the United States could ever again be counted on in a crisis. Yes, Biden sold himself as the engager, the anti-Trump. Blinken would repeat his favorite line—"the world doesn't organize itself"—to make it clear that if America decided it didn't want the role, Beijing would happily take it over. The implication was that Biden would restore America's traditional role as NATO's spine and Asia's ultimate protector. But there were elements in Washington—powerful ones, on both sides of the aisle—who questioned whether that was still the United States' responsibility.

As some of Biden's aides admitted to me when the tape recorders were off, there was the risk that Biden's extensive foreign policy experience might actually work against him. The world he felt comfortable managing—relying on his old relationships, backslapping his way through G7 summits—had changed dramatically, not just in the four years his party had been out of power but in the decades since the Cold War ended. There was a sense in many world capitals that the era when superpowers could throw around their weight—the behavior that had fostered colonialism, proxy wars, technological and financial supremacy—was ending. Something else, something multipolar, would replace it. But no one quite knew what.

And so, as Trump raged through the last days of his presidency and Biden's scheduled inauguration, some fundamental questions remained: Could a seventy-eight-year-old politician who was a product of the old Cold War become a transformational president who could push the country into a new era? And could he do that while still beset by the COVID-19 pandemic, the rocky economy, and the uniquely looming threat of his predecessor?

Kevin McCarthy, who would briefly emerge as Biden's bête noire in the House of Representatives, was dismissive of Biden's chances. "He's yesterday, we're the future," he told colleagues just weeks before the Capitol was stormed. "He's bringing everybody back from the past. He's misreading this election. People are going to be bored with him."

.   .   .

RON KLAIN, BIDEN'S new chief of staff, had served in the White House more than half a dozen times—he told me he lost count at some point—before the 2020 election. So as the inauguration approached, he didn't exactly need a tour guide around the West Wing. What he didn't know, he said, was where the land mines were: the non-obvious, perhaps classified, problems that a new president could step into on the first day in office.

So he tried to set up conversations with Mark Meadows, the bombastic former congressman who had served as Trump's last chief of staff. This was Transition 101. In ordinary times, the outgoing team was supposed to put together detailed materials to hand off to the incoming team. There should have been piles of briefing books on everything from ongoing plans to get the COVID-19 vaccine into millions of arms to the military blueprints to disarm North Korea in the event of a crisis. There should have been briefings on the future of education budgets and readouts about the plan to draw down troops in Afghanistan. With elections over, politics are supposed to be set aside by the outgoing and incoming White House teams: That is how a smooth transfer of power happens. And Trump's team should have known what that looked like, because the Obama-to-Trump transition even came with war-game simulations—including how to handle the at-the-time unimaginable eventuality of an unexpected flu that came from China and paralyzed the United States.

Needless to say, this was no ordinary transition. Not only had the president refused to concede he lost the election, he didn't want to give the impression that he was leaving. So the "landing teams" of incoming officials—this time renamed to avoid leaving the look of a Normandy-style invasion—were being blocked at the Pentagon and the Office of Management and Budget. It was a lot of "radio silence, certainly at the more senior levels," Klain recalled. And as the weeks went on and January 20 grew closer, it was starting to become a major problem.

Klain and his aides first pressed the issue quietly, making the case that after even the most bitter of elections—Bush versus Gore, for example—responsible adults made sure the incoming team was well briefed. When that argument fell on deaf ears, the Biden team leaked details, hoping to embarrass the Trump administration into doing the right thing. That effort also failed. When Klain called Meadows directly, he got nowhere. "We talked on the phone, and he was perfectly pleasant," Klain told me later. "I'd say, 'Hey, we need to get people into the Pentagon,' and Meadows would say, 'I'm on it. I'm on it.' Then nothing would happen."

When the Trump team did share plans, they were partial at best—even on the most urgent issue of the day: distributing the COVID vaccine. "Everything I thought was bad was worse than we could have believed," Klain told me later, after Biden took office and he discovered the worst of the damage.

It became clear that no one working for Trump wanted to be caught planning for a transition that the sitting president insisted was not happening. It got worse after January 6. Disgusted, Trump's most reliable White House aides disappeared, some because of late-onset outrage, some because 1600 Pennsylvania Avenue had become an eighteen-acre super-spreader site, and some because they feared that sticking with Trump a day longer would kill their prospects on the job market.

Even so, Meadows remained unavailable to Klain. Finally, Meadows made an appointment for a face-to-face meeting. Come meet me in the Situation Room, he told Klain, on the morning of the inauguration. Trump was leaving that morning for Florida, refusing to attend Biden's swearing-in: the first president to willingly reject attending the ceremony since Andrew Johnson declined to make time for Ulysses S. Grant's ceremony more than a century and a half before. (Woodrow Wilson also skipped the inauguration of Warren G. Harding, but for reasons of illness.)

It made sense to Klain. Trump would be gone, so there would be no repercussions. But when Klain showed up for the long-deferred meeting, Meadows informed him that he had no time. Trump had signed a last-minute pardon—as it later turned out, for the ex-husband of Jeanine Pirro, a Fox News personality and longtime Trump supporter. Pirro's husband had landed in prison for tax evasion over a decade earlier—and Meadows had to get the signed document to the Justice Department before noon so that it could be properly enrolled along with Trump's other last-minute pardons. "So there was no real meeting," Klain said.

He shrugged. The new administration was on its own. They shouldn't have expected anything else.

But Klain didn't have much time to sit around. Biden's inauguration was about to begin.

TYPICALLY, INAUGURATION DAY in Washington, D.C., is a festive affair. Crowds descend upon the National Mall by the hundreds of thousands, packing the area between the Lincoln Memorial and the Capitol Building. Those lucky—or important—enough to be invited attend elaborate balls thrown throughout the city—nine to mark Bush's second inauguration, ten for Obama's first, three for Trump's sole event. It's a chance to celebrate, just for a moment, the promise of the coming four years—before the challenges begin to mount.

This one looked like none that had gone before—not even when Lincoln was inaugurated in the last days of the Civil War. In the wake of January 6, the White House was at the epicenter of a locked-down D.C. A maze of metal barricades topped by barbed wire snaked through the downtown streets. Some twenty thousand members of the National Guard were sleeping in the hallways of the Capitol, in scattered hotels, or on the floors of government buildings. The city was on a hair trigger.

So instead of watching from the steps of the Capitol Building, Klain left his meeting with Meadows and headed to join other senior colleagues—including Jake Sullivan, Lisa Monaco, and Liz Sherwood-Randall—in the White House Situation Room, the secure space from which presidents from John F. Kennedy on have monitored terrorist assassinations and convened to respond to national tragedies. On this day, screens around the room streamed in feeds from command centers representing a variety of law enforcement agencies: FBI, DHS, and more. No one was taking any chances.

"At 12:01 P.M. on January 20 of 2021," recalled Jake Sullivan, the president's newly appointed national security advisor, "I was actually sitting in the Situation Room. Not out on the Mall, not watching the president's speech but rather watching the secure monitors.

"I was in an N95 mask," he said, "and it was a vivid reminder of what we were inheriting, the challenge of the pandemic, the challenge of a contested election by the previous president who refused to accept his defeat. And all of this was playing out for the whole world to see."

Klain joined him. Minute by minute, as Inauguration Day progressed with blue skies and no sign of the armed white supremacists that QAnon had promised, Klain and Sullivan started to relax. The streets were quiet.

Biden's speech was written to be intimate, personal, and hopeful—the balm, he hoped, for weeks of trauma and conflict. Because it was Biden, parts sounded more like a fireside chat than soaring rhetoric. And like most inaugural speeches, it was deliberately focused on domestic issues—though Biden made it clear that America's diminished status could only be restored by ending the damage at home and replacing the "America First" swagger with a dose of post-COVID humility.

Yet there was no escaping the reality of what Biden was inheriting. The scope of that damage could be seen from the West Front of the Capitol. The city was empty. There were more uniforms than suits. And missing were the hundreds of thousands who usually flock to the lawns below the Capitol to witness the peaceful transfer of power—a ritual of American democracy that Biden was determined must look normal, even boring, to the millions tuning in.

As long as the camera shots were tight, it did look that way: the new president and vice president, the large family Bible, the chief justice, the former presidents.

But the oddities of the day could not be ignored. Neither could the prospect of Trump's second impeachment trial, the tens of millions of Republicans around the country who would adamantly refuse to acknowledge Biden's victory even after his inauguration, or the cold reality that the United States was still trapped in the midst of a pandemic that had killed more Americans than World War II, Korea, Vietnam, Iraq, and Afghanistan *combined*—and that would, inevitably, kill tens of thousands more.

SOMETHING NOTABLE WAS missing from Biden's speech: a sense that America, even in shell shock over what was happening at home, had to prepare to survive in a very different world. For while Biden did not face a single international crisis—no Vietnam or Iraq—he knew he would confront a series of interlocking crises in which the boundary between domestic and international was meaningless.

He listed a few: the pandemic, of course, and "joblessness and hopelessness," a crisis of racial justice, and another of climate. He talked of the collapse of faith in democracy itself. "America has been tested, and we have come out stronger for it," he insisted, promising to "repair our alliances and engage with the world once again."

But he avoided addressing some of the most important challenges—quite deliberately, it seemed, because they did not fit with his tone of hope and restoration. He never mentioned China, the country that posed the longest-term challenge to American preeminence. He didn't talk about a disruptive Russia threatening its neighbors. He didn't talk, as Kennedy had from the same place exactly sixty years before, about the fear of a new nuclear arms race or the possibility—which seemed remote even then—that Moscow and Beijing would team up to take on the United States. He never mentioned the new challenge represented by SolarWinds: that nations seeking to undercut the United States would manipulate its computer networks or exploit its social media.

At that moment, a return to Cold War thinking, to a hardening of borders, to containment, seemed the furthest thing from Americans' minds.

Yet it was right around the corner.

CHAPTER 6

THE END OF THE FEVER DREAM

The United States is in the midst of the most consequential rethinking of its foreign policy since the end of the Cold War. Although Washington remains bitterly divided on most issues, there is a growing consensus that the era of engagement with China has come to an unceremonious close. The debate now is over what comes next.

Jake Sullivan and Kurt Campbell, *Foreign Affairs,* August 2019

EVEN BY THE standards of China's new breed of "wolf warrior" diplomats—known for their deliberately brusque demeanor, their certainty of America's decline, and their conviction that Beijing would emerge as the world's leading superpower—the first in-person encounter between Chinese diplomats and the Biden administration was particularly nasty.

The meeting took place in what passes for a ballroom in the Hotel Captain Cook in Anchorage, a place better known to salmon fishermen as their last stop in civilization before flying out to the Alaskan wilderness. The locale was chosen quite deliberately. Jake Sullivan and the newly minted secretary of state, Antony Blinken, wanted to ensure that the first meeting happened on American soil. Perhaps more important, they wanted to make sure that their first meeting with the Chinese happened after getting together with American allies in the region to plot a strategy. So Blinken arrived in Alaska fresh from a visit to Japan and South Korea.

On his way, he had foreshadowed his opening lines in South Korea, saying "we are clear-eyed about Beijing's consistent failure to uphold its commitments" and speaking of "how Beijing's aggressive and authoritarian behavior are challenging the stability, security, and prosperity of the Indo-Pacific region." The message was clear: China's days of dividing America from its closest partners in the Pacific were over.

But on that March day at the Captain Cook, the Chinese had an agenda of their own: to make it plain, especially to those back in China who were watching on television, that they had no intention of enduring any lectures from the Americans. So when Yang Jiechi, the nation's top diplomat, settled in across from the American officials at the long table, he was ready with a broadside of his own.

"Chinese-style democracy," he said through a translator, was clearly superior to America's—just look at what had happened at Washington's own vaunted Capitol just a few weeks earlier. And Blinken and Sullivan must surely know, he said, that America was a bundle of quivering contradictions, something the Chinese had often talked about in their own press but had rarely flung in the faces of U.S. officials. Clearly, they weren't holding back anymore. "We believe that it is important for the United States to change its own image and to stop advancing its own democracy in the rest of the world," Yang said. "Many people within the United States actually have little confidence in the democracy of the United States."

Blinken and Sullivan weren't surprised that the Chinese were on the attack while the cameras were rolling. They were just taken aback by the length and ferocity of the exchange. It seemed out of character for Yang, a normally soft-spoken diplomat whom Americans knew well from his time as ambassador to the United States starting in 2001, when he was close to the Bush family. Any blast from him, the experienced America hand, had without question been carefully tailored to fit a new, more confrontational era.

"They wanted everyone to know," one American participant told me, "that China wasn't going to 'eat its bitterness.'"

By all accounts, the meeting proceeded significantly more smoothly once the press had departed the ballroom. Yet no one who witnessed the public clash could fail to see a new China—one that used radically different language and took far more provocative actions than it had only a half a dozen years before, when Xi was planning his first state visit to the United States. On that occasion, Xi was "almost pathological about wanting the trip to go perfectly," with no hint of discord between Washington and Beijing, as one American official associated with the pre-visit negotiations remembered.

Now, just two months into Biden's presidency, it was strikingly clear that Biden was operating in a changed geopolitical environment. Xi's diplomats had returned, but this time they were ready to spar, to threaten, to mock. It is always easier to be blunter at a working meeting of government officials than a state visit, where pomp and circumstance matter as much as the substance. But it was also a clear message from the Chinese that they no longer needed the approval of the United States, much less to play by American-created rules.

Less clear was where the Chinese hoped to go from there. Was the battle of words solely about posturing for audiences at home, or was it instead a sign of a relationship spiraling down?

The Americans were quick to play down the divisive rhetoric of the encounter and eager to show they had a handle on the situation. Blinken and Sullivan insisted the session was better than it sounded. "It's no surprise," Blinken said afterward, that "we got a defensive response. But we were also able to have a very candid conversation over these many hours on an expansive agenda," he maintained, citing an array of places where U.S. and Chinese interests aligned, like non-proliferation in North Korea and Iran.

On Chinese state television just a few days later, Yang, the returning hero of the meeting in Beijing, was much sharper. "There are major disputes between us. China will firmly defend national sovereignty, security and development interests, and China's development and growing strength are unstoppable."

Not long after the session, Biden offered a less-than-tactful assessment of what he was facing. Xi "doesn't have a democratic—with a small 'd'—bone in his body," he warned, repeating a line from the campaign trail in the East Room of the White House. "He's one of the guys, like Putin, who thinks that autocracy is the wave of the future and democracy can't function in an ever-complex world.

"I made it clear to him again what I've told him in person on several occasions: that we're not looking for confrontation, although we know there will be steep, steep competition." A few moments later Biden declared, "I predict to you, your children or grandchildren are going to be doing their doctoral thesis on the issue of who succeeded: autocracy or democracy? Because that is what is at stake."

Something else was increasingly evident: The drive in Washington and Beijing to build critical technologies at home had turned into a vicious, reinforcing cycle. As Xi declared that China's goal was to dominate those technologies and force the rest of the world to buy them from China, Biden became more determined to bring that manufacturing home. It turned into a contest of national will—and of the capital to back it up.

For all the divides in Washington, on this one issue almost everyone agreed: A bipartisan consensus had sprung into being that China's "peaceful rise" had been a fever dream. The old mantras that trade equaled freedom or that WTO entry would change the way China operates had been tossed aside. The debate now turned on how to respond to a China that was far more than a traditional competitor, one that had made the leap to "revisionist power" and "adversary," led by a man with a secret plan to displace the United States.

"THE UNITED STATES does need to get tough with China," Biden wrote early in his campaign in 2020, trying to shake off Trump's critique that "#BeijingBiden" was soft on China. "If China has its way, it will keep robbing the United States and American companies of their technology and intellectual property. It will also keep using subsidies to give its state-owned enterprises an unfair advantage—and a leg up on dominating the technologies and industries of the future."

It was the kind of thing you might expect a candidate for president to say—especially a Democrat who knew that his constituency was convinced that China was stealing American jobs and ideas. But it would have been reasonable to suspect that once in office Biden would set the posturing aside. The conventional wisdom held that Biden would try for a "reset" with China. At the least, he would score some early wins by removing some of the sanctions that Trump had imposed on China, many of which seemed purely punitive, rather than linked to national security. After all, it was consumers and businesses in both countries, not the Chinese leadership, who were paying the price.

There was another good reason to believe that Biden would shift back to the middle: because he usually did. This was what he'd done for decades: as a senator and then later as vice president. Biden was a card-carrying member of the "engagement" camp who embraced the adage that the more the United States immersed China in Western institutions and Western rules, the more Beijing would be willing to play by those same rules.

Biden didn't just buy the argument. For decades, he peddled it. "Bringing China into the global trading regime continues a process of careful engagement designed to encourage China's development as a productive, responsible member of the world community," he'd argued on the Senate floor in 2000, in the midst of a debate on whether to permanently normalize America's trade relationship with China. He clung to this position for at least another decade. "I remain convinced that a successful China can make our country more prosperous, not less," he wrote in a 2011 *New York Times* opinion piece titled "China's Rise Isn't Our Demise." "As trade and investment bind us together, we have a stake in each other's success."

At the time, that was still the mainstream position, and it had a compelling logic. As Obama himself said, the United States could not contain China even if it wanted to; the only option was to engage. The engagement strategy came with its own canned toast at U.S.-China meetings: "The United States," Obama would often say, "welcomes the continuing rise of a China that is peaceful, stable, prosperous, and a responsible player in global affairs."

Yet by the time Obama left office, many of his aides were beginning to regard that line as empty rhetoric—and the policy of "engagement" as even emptier.

"I DON'T THINK there has ever been a foreign policy so fully accepted and carefully defended than the idea of engagement with China." So said Kurt Campbell, the man Biden had appointed to be his policy coordinator for the Indo-Pacific, and to make real his new approach to Asia.

He was referring, of course, to the overwhelming orthodoxy in Washington that had reigned for decades: that if one just wrapped China in Western institutions and offered the lure of American technology and Western market access, Chinese leaders would see the wisdom of joining the U.S.-designed system and not challenge it. Every national security advisor from Kissinger on down, he said, "thought that the careful management of the U.S.-China relationship was almost a mystical thing that must be sustained." Campbell had little time for mysticism. He had spent years thinking about how to organize other allies, especially those in Asia, to counter the Chinese, if not openly confront them.

Campbell was the ultimate Washington Asia hand: part of the small group of foreign policy professionals who grew up in the 1980s persuaded that the world's center of power was shifting to the east. In the years since, he had been just about everywhere: an officer in the Navy, on the staff of the Joint Chiefs, a skilled bureaucratic infighter at the Departments of Treasury, Defense, and State. And he helped found one of Washington's most successful new think tanks, the Center for a New American Security, where many of the young foreign policy experts who would later populate the Obama and Biden White Houses got their start. Now, he had finally reached the pinnacle of policymaking, serving as Biden's Asia chief, with the opportunity to reengineer how the U.S. and its allies deal with Beijing at the very moment that the two seemed to be spiraling toward confrontation, if not outright war.

Campbell had been sitting at the far end of the table in the ballroom of the Hotel Captain Cook when Blinken and Sullivan met with their Chinese counterparts in Anchorage. He hadn't said much that day—at least not in the public portion of the remarks—but Campbell was undoubtedly the bull in the China policy shop. To many, including Biden himself, he was a visionary, ready to dispense with forty years of failed policy in which the U.S. underinvested in its alliances in the Pacific and deluded itself into thinking that, with the right incentives, China would change its behavior. To others—including some State Department diplomats who felt rolled over—Campbell was domineering and overly certain in his view, and skilled at narrating a history of U.S.-China relations designed to lead listeners to the hawkish policies he'd been advocating for years. Campbell was among a select group of the foreign policy elite at the forefront of recognizing that the main battleground with China was going to be over technology and economics, not traditional military power. For a decade he had made the case that the United States could not go it alone—that American allies and partnerships were the country's competitive advantage. China had a lot of capabilities, he argued. It didn't have a lot of friends.

Those conclusions had underpinned his central role in articulating the Obama administration's strategy of moving the ballast of American foreign policy away from the Middle East and toward Asia—the region that Campbell was certain was the key to the future of American jobs, exports, commercial opportunities, and defense challenges. ("The Pivot" was quickly rebranded "The Rebalance" after the Europeans complained that when you pivot you turn your back on someone else.)

"In the last fifteen or so years, we have been so principally engaged in dramas playing out in the Middle East and South Asia," he said in 2012, when American forces were still engaged in Iraq and Afghanistan, "that I think many nations question whether the United States would have the wit and wisdom to recognize the importance of Asia."

For all its talk about rebalancing, the strategy was never fully executed in the Obama years, but the seeds were planted for Campbell's long-term project: Reinvigorate the long-neglected alliances around Asia, but attempt to do so in a way that doesn't make the Chinese feel that their power is being contained.

Campbell left the State Department after Obama's first term and plunged into creating a successful consulting business, aimed at getting into Asian markets. But he was doing more than monetizing his expertise: He now had considerably more freedom to challenge the premise that what he called "Capital E" engagement with China still made sense as a guiding concept of American foreign policy. And gradually—in speeches, in articles, in seminar rooms in Cambridge and Aspen—he argued that the meager results from that form of engagement could no longer be ignored. Washington, he said, had to shake itself of the naïve presumption that China would mellow. It should be obvious to the world, Campbell said, that Beijing would not accept Western-written rules regulating trade, or the internet, or the peaceful resolution of territorial disputes. It would create its own operating system in its own image.

"The greatest challenge that we will face as a country, from any nation that we've ever dealt with—the Soviet Union or Iraq, Afghanistan, you name it—will come from China," he told the Democratic National Convention as it tried to put together a platform for Hillary Clinton's campaign. "And that will be at every level. It will be militarily, but it will also be about setting the rules for how commerce, trade, and economic affairs will be regulated in the twenty-first century."

Campbell, Jake Sullivan, and other key Democrats were clearly planning for a significant change in direction as soon as Clinton took her predestined place as Obama's successor. Then the unthinkable happened, interrupting their plan. Four years of exile ensued. But the Trump years left many of the exiles with time to write. And in 2019, Campbell and Sullivan published what became the manifesto for ditching engagement for engagement's sake.

It appeared in *Foreign Affairs*—the nearly-century-old magazine where George Kennan had elaborated the rationale for containing the Soviet Union in an article published anonymously in 1947 and derived from his famous secret State Department cable, "The Long Telegram."

The Sullivan-Campbell essay was clearly fashioned to follow Kennan's model. "The United States is in the midst of the most consequential rethinking of its foreign policy since the end of the Cold War," they wrote. "Although Washington remains bitterly divided on most issues, there is a growing consensus that the era of engagement with China has come to an unceremonious close. The debate now is over what comes next."

"The basic mistake of engagement," Sullivan and Campbell wrote, "was to assume that it could bring about fundamental changes to China's political system, economy, and foreign policy." Taking a shot at Trump's approach, they added: "Washington risks making a similar mistake today, by assuming that competition can succeed in transforming China where engagement failed—this time forcing capitulation or even collapse." They insisted their new strategy did not add up to a call for containment—mostly because containment wouldn't work anyway. The idea, Campbell and Sullivan wrote, was to aim for "a steady state of clear-eyed coexistence on terms favorable to U.S. interests and values."

This was the opposite of an academic exercise. McMaster and Pottinger had established the basis for a dramatic shift during the Trump years, even if the president himself could not articulate the new strategy. But the Democrats were revising their thoughts, too. Suddenly the trail of essays in *Foreign Affairs* and other journals became the basis for the new team's policy. America was making a fundamental shift: This was a rare moment when the mainstream foreign policy orthodoxy simply collapsed. In fact, the U.S. intelligence community's assessment of why Beijing didn't try to interfere in the 2020 presidential election was that the country's leadership believed there was "no prospect for a pro-China administration regardless of the election outcome."

The surprise was that Biden himself, the ultimate traditionalist and institutionalist, was willing to dispense with the approach to countering China that had dominated his entire political career. On other issues— the future of NATO or America's involvement in Afghanistan or support for Israel—Biden had long-held beliefs that only seemed to harden during his presidency. China was different. As one of his aides noted to me, he had not spent as much time throughout his career thinking through the conundrum of how to confront a country with which the U.S. was so interdependent.

Then came the transition. "It was really when everyone sat down with the intelligence and saw all of its vectors—the technology, Taiwan, the territorial ambitions, the influence campaigns from Latin America to Europe," one of his senior aides told me later. "It was pretty shocking to Biden."

When it came to China, Campbell, unsurprisingly, had an orderly schema that divided the Washington establishment into five camps. "The first of the schools of thought—and the most prestigious—was the engagement school," Campbell told me. "That's Kissinger, Scowcroft, Berger," referring to a series of prominent national security advisors of past decades. "Just go down the list," he said. It included "everyone who was anyone in American foreign policy."

This was where Biden had resided for the majority of his career. It was also the box where a significant number of Biden administration officials outside the White House quietly admitted—though never on the record—that they still fit. "I'm a huge fan of engagement," one cabinet secretary told me. "What is lost in sitting across the table from someone and talking?" In fact, Biden had never turned down an opportunity to talk to the Chinese. But the fact that members of the cabinet still didn't understand how Biden's top aides defined the failures of the past era of engagement, and differentiated it from diplomatic efforts to resolve specific disputes, was testament to how badly the new approach had been communicated, even internally.

The second school, the one Campbell put himself in, was an "allies-first" model. It focused on building relationships with the allies surrounding China, figuring that the only way to get China's attention and change its behavior was to make it realize that its micro- and macro-aggressions were driving its neighbors into a camp of resistors. This didn't mean, Campbell emphasized, that America couldn't talk to the Chinese. The third group, he said, was the "small school and the ideologically extreme school—until recently." It held "that China is the enemy and that we have to get ready and gear up." That view, he said, was now the one held by most Republicans—certainly those in Trump's orbit—as well as a notable tally of Democrats. A subset of this group, which was gaining in numbers, thought an armed confrontation was inevitable and that America needed to prepare.

The fourth school, he said, wanted to pursue the old approach of focusing on one regional issue at a time, hoping to win China's cooperation without sparking broader confrontation. That mindset worked in the past when it came to rebuilding Cambodia in the 1990s or defanging North Korea's nuclear program in the 2000s or negotiating with Iran in 2015. China helped with all of those efforts, but it was doing so with decreasing frequency and enthusiasm.

And the fifth group is what Campbell called the globalist school: those who urged the world to move beyond great power politics and focus on the existential transnational issues like climate change and pandemic prevention. In other words, ignore the traditional great power competition and focus on areas of possible cooperation.

The breakdown was classic Campbell: a geostrategic lesson delivered with certitude that only one approach made sense—his own—and that everyone, policymakers and journalists alike, fit more or less cleanly into one of his boxes. When pressed, Campbell himself would admit the world wasn't that neat. Some of his colleagues chuckled at the precision of his boxes. But as a rough approximation of the many conflicted camps in Washington dictating how to deal with America's most powerful full-spectrum rival, it wasn't a bad organizing principle.

Biden wasn't the only one taken aback by the intelligence briefings that he received about China during the transition. So were many of the returnees from the Obama administration, who had been out of the intelligence stream for four years and saw how much had changed—

almost all of it pointing toward a comprehensive plan by Xi's government to challenge American interests across the globe. "When we left in 2017, China was largely still a regional player," one of those officials told me. "When we came back, it was global." There was an intelligence-gathering base in Cuba, ninety miles from the shores of Florida, where China was improving its ability to collect data on the United States—less worrisome in the cyber age than it was back when the Russians were building bases in the runup to the Cuban Missile Crisis, but worrisome nonetheless. Strange surveillance balloons were showing up around Hawaii and other key strategic areas—a cheap, innovative way to tap into American communications and learn details that couldn't be obtained by satellite. There were silos appearing on Chinese territory, signs of a potential expansion of its nuclear program, and evidence of preparations for a nuclear test, the first in decades, at the old testing ground at Lop Nor.

Those were the traditional technologies, of course. The truly concerning list involved new capabilities: a hypersonic missile program that no one could quite figure out but that was clearly designed to evade all existing missile defenses. New cyber teams had surveyed the world's networks and found entirely new entry points with stealthy code that was particularly hard to detect. The Biden administration ran into one of those Chinese groups, called "Hafnium," in its first few weeks. Hafnium installed back-door access on tens of thousands of corporate computer systems, many of them run by defense contractors. It was, as one official put it to me in those first weeks of the new administration, "a sort of welcome note."

The list of Chinese advances—and the worry about how artificial intelligence and quantum computing might fit into the mix—was so long that soon after Bill Burns settled into the CIA in March, he concluded that the world's premier spy agency needed to restructure itself to reflect their scope and importance. His first major step was to create a new "China Mission Center," a place to bring together the full scope of intelligence on Chinese actions—be they political, technological, or military. "Part of it is just to signal the priority that we attached—the U.S. government is going to attach for decades to come—to competition with China," Burns told me. "It's the only single-country mission center that we have now, and that was quite deliberate."

Among the first challenges for the new Mission Center was to grapple with the paradoxes of Xi himself. Clearly, he had upended China's national priorities, putting the security of the state—and his role atop it—ahead of economic growth. American intelligence analysts were reporting that the Communist Party was carefully designing the hagiography around Xi as the indispensable leader for life. A Chinese document circulating among the Biden national security staff declared Xi the "core navigator and helmsman," a phrase not used since the era of Mao Zedong.

While everyone was struck by the obvious similarities with the Mao era—the cult of personality, the elimination of potential competitors for power—there were also important differences. China's new contest with the West wasn't about ideology; it was chiefly a technological battle for supremacy and for the global influence that comes with spreading Chinese telecommunications networks and aid around the world.

Also new since Mao's time: the seeming certainty among Chinese leaders that the United States was in accelerating decline and that, with the right focus, the right control over the Chinese populace, the right technology, and the right influence campaigns, it would be possible to displace the United States as the world's number one power. Xi said as much in 2021. The United States, he declared just as Biden was getting settled in, was "the biggest threat to [China's] development and security." But in the long term, he said, "the East is rising and the West is declining."

AS BIDEN ENTERED OFFICE, it seemed clear to his team that the first urgent task was to convince the Chinese that the United States wasn't about to cede the region to them. Biden held the first conversation of his presidency with President Xi Jinping on February 10—three weeks after his inauguration, two weeks after his first call with Vladimir Putin, and days after his calls with most other major world leaders. By waiting so long, he was making a point. The United States was returning to a deliberative, strategy-based foreign policy. There would be no ad-hoc pronouncements, midnight Twitter rants, or half-effective export bans. Sure, Biden liked to brag about how well he knew Xi, but Xi shouldn't expect that their relationship—even if Biden overstated it—would win out over national interests.

The White House's readout of the call was almost a ritual incantation of boilerplate foreign policy goals. Biden "affirmed his priorities of protecting the American people's security, prosperity, health, and way of life, and preserving a free and open Indo-Pacific."

The Chinese take was more interesting. Xinhua News, China's official state news agency, seemed to imply that the United States was repenting for the Trump years. "Some Washington politicians, who remain stuck in the Cold-War mentality, saw in China a grave threat to the United States," it wrote in February. "They even tried to decouple the two countries and advocate for a new Cold War. . . . With the inauguration of the Biden administration, returning the China-U.S. relationship to the right track has become a common aspiration of the international community."

If the Chinese believed that, they had misread Biden as badly as America had misread Xi.

OVER THE NEXT YEAR, from the Old Executive Office Building, Biden's team began to execute a three-part squeeze on Beijing—a play few expected when he came to office. The first move was to win back alienated allies, many of whom were still smarting from the Trump years and skeptical of once again putting themselves out on a limb for the mercurial Americans.

It wasn't an easy sell. China's influence—and its ability to retaliate against perceived slights—was so great that even those who despised Chinese dominance were hesitant to describe it as a threat to world order. More than a few allies reminded the Americans that Washington hadn't exactly made the best decisions for the region when it was the controlling colonial power over the Philippines at the turn of the twentieth century or when it was the world's unipower at the dawn of the twenty-first. They rolled their eyes at the thought of another "pivot."

To build consensus and a rationale for change, Campbell set up what he later termed a "listening tour," going country to country to hear out the fears surrounding China's behavior. The list was long. Publicly, the Australians complained about economic coercion and retaliation. India detailed skirmishes on its border with China. The Philippines and Taiwan worried about the militarization of the South China Sea: Satellite photographs made clear that the islands that Xi promised would never be militarized were now air bases for fighter jets, visible wingtip-to-wingtip on the "reclaimed" islands. Even the Germans—who were mostly interested in selling luxury BMWs and Mercedes in the Chinese market—had begun thinking about China as a strategic problem.

The second tactic was to rebuild at home. To Biden, that meant deep investment in America and the reinvigoration of its domestic economy. Biden said that his vision of competition and survival was very different from Trump's "America First." It certainly didn't include the go-it-alone approach, isolationism, or the air of xenophobia that had permeated Trump's term. But Biden's approach shared with Trump's a conviction that the only way to counter China was by building up capabilities in the United States that had gone fallow. Both men seemed fine with tariffs. (While Trump visited coal mines, though, Biden spent his time attending groundbreaking ceremonies for semiconductor plants.)

Part of Biden's strategy turned on old-fashioned industrial policy. He started with a nascent plan to bring back America's ability to survive on its own supply chains—making our own chips, extracting our own strategic minerals for batteries, building communications systems that didn't rely on Chinese parts. Essentially, he was attempting to undo thirty years of manufacturing globalization; alternatively interpreted, he was matching the Chinese at their own game of consolidating production at home. Biden and his aides were still allergic to publicly referring to this as "decoupling," given that that was an obvious impossibility, so they picked up on the European phrase that sounded more defensive— "derisking"—and made the point that this was about diversifying supply chains rather than severing them completely. It worked better in some industries than others.

The administration's third tactic was the most novel: an effort to cut China off from the American technologies it was using to fuel its military and intelligence services. In the Trump years, the Department of Justice had begun to aggressively investigate Chinese researchers and students in the United States, looking for signs that they were exploiting the openness of American universities to funnel technology to China. The Biden approach was more targeted: His Commerce Department began to draw up lists of products that would no longer be exported to Beijing—and to limit sensitive technologies, especially in communications, that China would be permitted to sell in the United States. To Biden and his aides, this recalibration was long overdue. The Chinese saw it differently: Xi would later label it "containment, encirclement, and suppression."

In retrospect, one of the most interesting elements of Washington's new view of China is that it largely reflected Xi's view of America: In both capitals, the other side began to look more like a security threat and less like a lucrative market. So after decades of celebrating a "flat world," where an iPhone could be designed in California, built in China, and sold in Germany, no one wanted to be dependent on long supply lines—or one another.

WITH A NEW variant of the coronavirus settling in Washington in late 2021, China's new ambassador to the United States, Qin Gang, sat down for dinner with about two dozen journalists and China hands.

The setting—an opulent home in the Kalorama neighborhood of the city, less than two miles from the White House—seemed like something out of a novel, a parody of how the rest of the country imagines elite Washingtonians entertain themselves. Multi-million-dollar homes lined the streets, many of them dating from the early 1900s. Barack and Michelle Obama lived directly across the street from the house where the dinner was held, meaning that dog walkers and joggers had to divert elsewhere because the Secret Service had blocked off the area with barriers that lift from the road. The neighborhood oozed exclusivity.

"I guess all Americans would like to live like this," Qin said drolly, a drink in his hand, as the group gathered, one at a time, after virus-testing on the front porch. "I know all Chinese would."

The guest of honor that night was, despite his protestations, the ultimate Chinese "wolf warrior." Hand-selected by President Xi himself, Qin arrived in the summer of 2021 to an American capital city that was increasingly wary not only of his message but of his boss's long-term goals—and increasingly willing to do something about it.

Under normal circumstances, one might expect a newly arrived ambassador to strike the most conciliatory chord possible. Perhaps he would stress the longtime bonds between the United States and China, two nations intertwined technologically and economically that shared—at least when it came to climate change and restraining North Korea—national interests. Yet Qin had been sent to Washington with a different mission. The wolf-warrior talk was well rehearsed and well delivered. His first few months in America, Qin said, had convinced him that the United States was "very complicated."

"There are many things that I don't understand," Qin said, without ever specifically mentioning the divisions that were engulfing the United States both before and after January 6 or the vitriol the insurrection had unleashed. He said that he had "asked some wise people"—all of them Americans—"and they said, 'We don't understand either, we are confused.'" It was a well-constructed way to reach his next point. In America, he discovered, "China is everywhere," and "in the United States everyone talks about China.

"But many of them don't understand China," he argued, picking up speed. "They don't even speak the Chinese language. They don't know the history, the culture, and the people of China. But everybody appears like a China expert. And everybody appears that they know China much more than I do."

There was a smattering of knowing laughter. It was clear where Qin was going: If Americans wanted to complain about fake news, they should start at home, he argued, with the major media portrayals of the country's greatest geostrategic rival. There were "lies, disinformation" about China that were "spreading every day." He continued, "China is being treated like a kid, being scolded by his or her parents every day. 'You are wrong. You need to do this. You shouldn't do that.'"

A great example, he pointed out, was this "battle between democracy and authoritarianism" that Biden had spun up. China was inherently a democracy, Qin said, one that was in its own way more fulsome than the American model. Its "whole-process democracy" should be understood to be just as true as anything Washington or Lincoln could have aspired to.

Then he brought his point home. He and his fellow diplomats were no longer going to sit quietly and smile as they faced "unfriendly words and actions" and interference in China's "internal affairs"—code words for China's treatment of the Uyghurs in Xinjiang or threats toward Taiwan. "So, as a Chinese national, let alone a Chinese diplomat, he or she has to rise up to say 'no,'" Qin said, keeping his tone flat. It was time, he told the crowd, "to argue, to fight back."

The room went silent. People stopped eating.

"We are not fighting, but we are fighting back. So if I can use more precise language to describe the Chinese diplomats, I'd use this one: They're not wolf warriors. . . . Maybe they're dancing with wolves."

Having delivered his soliloquy, Qin took questions. I asked him whether he feared we were descending into another cold war—one very different from the kind that I grew up witnessing as a college student in the United States and that he had also witnessed as a college student in China.

He barely paused. The difference, he said, was the interdependency between the two countries—far different from the much more self-contained economies of the United States and the USSR decades before. And anyway, he said, Xi didn't want a cold war at all. If a cold war were brewing, he said, it was brewing here in America. "We want peaceful coexistence with the United States." But the constant "China-bashing every day" posed the risk of creating just what America said it didn't want.

Then came the message he was clearly waiting to deliver: "I think that if people really want to make a cold war against China, I can say that China won't be the loser."

CHAPTER 7

A DANGEROUS DANCE

The Biden administration has been clear that the United States desires a relationship with Russia that is stable and predictable.

White House Statement, April 15, 2021

THE GAS LINES were stretching down the block.

This wasn't supposed to be happening, not while everything was starting to fall into place for Joe Biden's first few months in office. As the summer of 2021 approached, the pandemic's grip was lifting, and all over the country masks were coming off. The stock market was hovering near a remarkable high. About a third of the country was fully vaccinated—and in some states upward of 60 percent had received at least one shot. In Washington and around the country, people could spend whole weekends without looking at their Twitter feeds, awaiting the latest eruption from the White House residence.

And despite the most divisive presidential election in memory—an insurrection, a sitting president who denied reality, a continuing effort to somehow cast the forty-sixth president as illegitimate—Biden's approval rating still hovered around 60 percent. That was mostly a reflection of a fleeting national sense that he embodied the kind of boring, no-drama competence that the country had once taken for granted.

But every president's fear is that the approval ratings are ephemeral, that they last just as long as nothing goes wrong. And things always go wrong.

Now, out of nowhere, a strange pipeline shutdown, the result of a ransomware attack, threatened to upend the message of smooth recovery. Before Colonial Pipeline was hit by a ransomware group, few Americans had ever heard of it. Privately held, intensely secretive, the Colonial Pipeline Company operated the network that carried 45 percent of the East Coast's gasoline, diesel, and jet fuel from the Texas Gulf Coast all the way to New York Harbor. It was a slow journey: two weeks from the time the petroleum flowed out of the refinery and up to Linden, New Jersey, moving at five miles an hour. Like most critical infrastructure, the pipeline network was invisible as long as it was working.

When it stopped working, though, everyone noticed. And that is what happened on Friday, May 7. In the early morning hours, a Colonial employee discovered a digital ransom note on one of the company's systems. Its message was brief: We have encrypted your data. If you want it unlocked, it will cost you millions—payable in Bitcoin.

The ransomware attack was aimed at Colonial's business computers—the systems that keep track of billing and how much oil is flowing through the pipeline. While the hackers hadn't gotten into the actual operation of the pipeline, they didn't need to. Without the business-side computers, Colonial wouldn't know where its gas and jet fuel were or how much to bill its customers. Potentially worse, Colonial feared that the malicious code might interfere with the operational systems as well, increasing the likelihood of an accident or sabotage of the pipeline itself. So the company turned off the pipeline entirely—all 5,500 miles of it.

The next morning, a Saturday, Biden got a call at his Delaware home from his national security advisor, Jake Sullivan. The FBI, Biden was later told, had attributed the hack to a Russian-based gang that called itself DarkSide. But as far as anyone could tell, this was not something ordered up by Vladimir Putin—it was launched by cyber criminals looking for a quick payout. Still, Biden would have immediately understood the political peril. Nothing would puncture the air of COVID recovery, of economic optimism, more swiftly than seeing panicked buyers lining up for gas, live on cable television.

In fact, within hours Americans were seeing just that—as consumers rushed out to fill their car tanks, then gas cans, and then, despite the risks, plastic bags. Suddenly the White House Situation Room was filled with aides trying to come up with alternatives to get gas moving across the country. Could it be trucked up I-95 or put on barges or railroad cars? Should the National Guard be called out to get gas flowing?

All these things could be done, the experts told Liz Sherwood-Randall, Biden's homeland security advisor, and Brian Deese, head of the National Economic Council. But it would take time—time that the confidential assessment circulating on their desks issued by the Energy Department and the Department of Homeland Security suggested they did not have. In three to five days, chemical plants would cease to operate, and mass transit would begin grinding to a stop. Buses needed diesel. Airplanes would be grounded.

Biden vented to one aide that this was the kind of little incident that, mishandled, could turn a successful presidency into Jimmy Carter's stressful single term. The problem was that there was very little the federal government could do to force Colonial Pipeline to cooperate with it. It could not compel other companies to take the security precautions Colonial had neglected to invest in or make Colonial say whether they'd paid the multi-million-dollar ransom directly to the criminals, even as White House officials coordinated with private security firms to retrieve as much of Colonial's data as they could. Meanwhile, the various centers of power in the U.S. government were struggling to get on the same page, especially over whether Colonial should pay the ransom.

Sure, paying it was giving in to extortion. But the country could not afford to lose a key source of energy powering the East Coast for much longer.

A week later, Colonial's chief executive, Joseph Blount, admitted the truth: He'd authorized the company to pay the ransom within hours of the attack. The trouble was that the decryption tool DarkSide provided in exchange for the Bitcoin worked too slowly to get the network back online fast enough. Eventually, Colonial pieced together an old backup system to get its fuel flowing again.

"I will admit that I wasn't comfortable seeing money go out the door to people like this," Blount later claimed in an interview about his decision to pay the $4.4 million ransom. Shrewdly, he cast it as an act of patriotism rather than one of self-preservation: "It was the right thing to do for the country."

Even if Blount was right in this individual case, he was disastrously wrong in the larger picture. Each ransom paid to criminal groups provided an incentive for the next ransomware attack. (The federal government was able, eventually, to claw some of the payment back, using a new and untested set of legal powers to find—and empty—the cryptocurrency wallets where the ransom was being held.) But the company's incompetent reaction—and its refusal to communicate clearly about what had happened or its decision to pay the ransom—pointed to far bigger vulnerabilities that infuriated the White House, particularly Anne Neuberger.

Neuberger found it ridiculous that the cybersecurity practices of the private companies that run the vast majority of America's pipelines—gas, petroleum, jet fuel, water supplies—received so little scrutiny from the U.S. government. She moved to patch that hole quickly, working with other executive agencies to regulate the pipelines. Then she moved on to other sectors, searching for the authority to mandate minimum cybersecurity rules for hospitals and airports and the electric power grid, all of which were big targets.

"This has been a wakeup call about how actors anywhere in the world can affect us right here at home," Biden's young transportation secretary, Pete Buttigieg, later told CNBC. He was right: While America was awash in hacks of computer networks, this one had a different political salience. It laid bare how vulnerable we were to a small group of hackers hanging out, in this case, on suspected Russian territory.

"It's all fun and games when we are stealing each other's money," Sue Gordon, the former deputy director of national intelligence, said as the government was scrambling to get the gas flowing again. "When we are messing with a society's ability to operate, we can't tolerate it."

Biden had come to much the same conclusion. Even as Colonial Pipeline was struggling to bring its systems back online and get fuel flowing, he told his advisors to think about how to use the incident as leverage to force Putin to crack down on the near-constant stream of ransomware attacks on the United States. While there was no evidence Putin had had anything to do with the disruption, his government harbored DarkSide and other ransomware gangs: tolerating their attacks as long as they were focused on the West and not on Russia or its immediate neighbors and, occasionally, tapping their expertise for the government's own ends.

Sullivan later passed on to me Biden's final determination on the matter: "Ultimately, even though the Russian government itself is not responsible for the direct hack, the Russian government is responsible for crimes of this kind that are emanating from their territory, and I'm going to hold them responsible to do something about it."

IN A SERIES of Situation Room meetings during his first hundred days in office, Biden and his top advisors had agreed on one thing: The only way to get Putin's attention—and limit his provocations—was with a hard push back.

That was a sharp departure from what had happened in the Obama administration, where the first instinct was usually to avoid confrontation. "Every time we ignored Putin in Obama's time," said one senior official who had worked on Russia issues during a 2014 series of hacks into the State Department, the White House, and the Joint Chiefs, "we came to regret it."

It fell to Biden to hold Putin accountable, retroactively, for his actions going back to the 2016 election. The question, of course, was how: Everyone agreed that a repeat of Hillary Clinton's experience in the early days of the Obama administration, a "reset" that immediately veered off course, was undesirable. "I have lived through a number of 'resets,'" said Avril Haines, Biden's director of national intelligence, with a faint smile. "By the end of the Obama administration, we knew we were already in a different place with Russia. And coming into the Biden administration, we had more caution and less optimism."

By that point, she recalled, "We saw a Russia in decline. And to us, the question from the beginning was how to manage the decline, as they already were becoming more destabilizing and dangerous. And that was front and center."

But that left open the question of how to focus Biden's approach to Putin, with whom he had clashed on everything from human rights issues to the 2014 invasion of Ukraine. To Biden, the ransomware scourge was a far more potent threat than others first understood, as the Colonial case had driven home. Even if its roots were simple criminal extortion, the incident demonstrated Russia's ability to shut down commerce and travel inside the United States. And stopping it would be the new administration's first signal to Putin that the United States would indeed push back on incremental aggression from Moscow.

But to respond appropriately, Biden needed some new tools. Previous playbooks—diplomatic expulsions, targeted sanctions packages, and "naming and shaming" the culprits—had not accomplished much. Sullivan asked the Treasury to come up with more effective sanctions, and the National Security Agency was authorized to seek what Sullivan called "innovative" actions to strike back at Putin's hacking infrastructure. "We have to break the cycle," Sullivan told me.

The question was how to do it. Biden's team quickly discovered, to the surprise of no one, that their options were limited. More sanctions invited more evasion—and more opportunities for retaliation and escalation.

Fortunately, Biden had brought on some of the Russia hawks who for years had been pushing for a harder line. Chief among them was Toria Nuland, who was adamant from the beginning of the administration that it was well past time for the United States to get more aggressive about dealing with Putin.

What this meant, she said, was "stop waiting for [the Russians] to move and then react. Try to create the environment in which we want to live," she told me in late 2021. Yes, there was lots of room to work with Russia on issues like climate change and nonproliferation and Iran—all areas where Putin had cooperated before. But Nuland believed that Putin respected only a show of strength, and that meant "being absolutely firm in strengthening our deterrent and the deterrent of our allies against malign influence and aggressive behavior by Russia."

In retrospect, while the public's attention was fixated on the Colonial Pipeline cyberattack that was unfolding in public, satellite imagery showed another crisis brewing, and this one was far more worrisome.

IT WAS LATE March 2021, recalled Jake Sullivan, when "we began to see indications of a massive Russian military buildup around Ukraine: the movement of thousands of troops, of tanks, of personnel carriers— armored personnel carriers—and of other sophisticated, advanced weaponry."

No one was quite sure how to read the situation. Putin clearly knew that American satellites would pick up the armored personnel carriers, the missile launchers, and the tent encampments. Troop numbers were increasing every week. None of the buildup was designed to be subtle.

Naturally, the Kremlin pled innocence. Russia, said Putin's spokesman and confidante, Dmitry Peskov, was just protecting itself from Ukrainian instability: "The Kremlin has fears that a civil war could resume in Ukraine," he told the *Associated Press* on April 9. "And if a civil war, a full-scale military action, resumes near our borders, that would threaten the Russian Federation's security."

It was the thinnest pretext imaginable. It was true that violence in the eastern part of Ukraine was escalating. Over the previous seven years, international diplomats had negotiated cease-fires and political agreements about the future of disputed territory in Crimea and to the east. But nothing lasted. Breakdowns led to low-grade battles, and by the spring of 2021, casualty counts were rising again. The Ukrainians accused the Russians of escalating. The Russians, claiming that the government in Kyiv was starting "a new war" in the Donbas, insisted they had the right to move troops within their own borders.

By mid-April 2021, Putin had massed roughly one hundred thousand Russian troops just a few miles from the Ukrainian border, and the Russian Defense Ministry announced that it would be conducting four thousand small military "exercises." They claimed that this was to test their force readiness, but the message was clear: Mess with Russia, and you'll run the risk that more than just Crimea will be claimed as Russian territory. Even if Putin didn't attack, the buildup of troops on the border was a gun to Zelensky's head: an implicit threat and a point of ongoing leverage.

Finding itself low on options, Biden's team conducted a burst of diplomacy. Blinken assured Ukraine's foreign minister, Dmytro Kuleba, that the United States was fully committed to Ukraine's territorial integrity. General Mark Milley called his Ukrainian counterpart—and then his Russian counterpart—to drive the point home. And Lloyd Austin, the newly appointed defense secretary, told the Ukrainians they would not be left alone to fend off the Russians. The United States would continue to fund training and send weapons, he said, referencing a $125 million defensive package the administration had announced the month before.

But the Russian buildup was a huge blow to Zelensky. During his campaign for Ukraine's presidency, he had promised to end the war in Donbas and build a relationship with Putin and Russia. After taking office, he had even sat down in December 2019 with Putin, Angela Merkel, and Emmanuel Macron in Paris to restart the peace talks that had stalled for the better part of three years. It was the first time that the two leaders had ever met face to face; according to a biography published in 2022, Zelensky was "noticeably nervous." He was such a rookie at the basics of diplomacy that he accidentally moved to sit down in Putin's seat at the table and inadvertently showed journalists some of his talking points. Later, Putin had to remind Zelensky that they shouldn't start in on the meat of the negotiation until the photographers had left the room.

Ultimately, Putin agreed to an exchange of prisoners and a recommitment to a cease-fire—which seemed, at first glance, a success for a political neophyte like Zelensky. Their next meeting was scheduled for March 2020, but it was canceled because of the outbreak of the COVID-19 pandemic. The talks never restarted.

While Zelensky was talking to Putin, he was also reviving Ukraine's effort to get into NATO, a move that was bound to play to Putin's insecurities. The idea had gained support soon after Putin annexed Crimea, though NATO remained reluctant—largely because it was unclear whether Ukraine was on a democratic path. But by 2017, Ukraine's parliament had declared that joining NATO was a foreign policy priority, and a year later, Ukrainian soldiers were regularly training with NATO forces. By 2020, Zelensky had signed off on his first national security strategy, and it called for eventual NATO membership.

Despite all this, few in Europe believed it would be a short process, and some were blunter than others. "Ukraine will definitely not be able to become a member of the EU in the next twenty to twenty-five years, and not of NATO either," European Commission president Jean-Claude Juncker said in 2016.

Still, Ukraine pressed forward. Starting in the late spring—right around the time that Russian troop numbers on the border spiked and the previous year's cease-fire was clearly collapsing in the east—Zelensky began an increasingly public campaign to catalyze new diplomatic breakthroughs. "NATO is the only way to end the war in Donbass," he tweeted in early April 2021, arguing that the resumption of the 2008 understanding that would place Ukraine on a pathway to membership would "be a real signal for Russia." By mid-April, he'd issued a public call for Putin to meet him in the Donbas to discuss peace. "Ukraine and Russia, despite their common past, look to the future differently," he said. "We are we. You are you. But this is not necessarily a problem, it is an opportunity. At the very least—an opportunity, before it's too late, to stop the deadly mathematics of future military losses."

Putin wasn't interested. Ukraine wasn't a real country, he'd long held, and therefore Zelensky wasn't a real president.

But Putin could not ignore the new American president. On April 13, 2021, Biden called Putin directly, warning him of the severe consequences if he tried to invade an independent state. In the bland language of White House readouts, Biden "emphasized the United States' unwavering commitment to Ukraine's sovereignty and territorial integrity." But Biden's main purpose for the call wasn't to talk about Ukraine—it was to tell Putin that the sanctions were coming, as punishment for a series of digital incursions, including SolarWinds and the 2016 election interference.

A few days after the call, Biden announced the sanctions. Ten Russian diplomats (some of them known spies) were expelled; about three dozen individuals who had sought to interfere in the 2020 elections or been involved in aggression against Ukraine were sanctioned; six Russian cyber companies who worked with Russian intelligence services were "designated"—meaning that U.S. firms could no longer conduct business with them. Most important, American financial institutions could no longer buy newly issued Russian debt. That last one sounded pretty tough—but Russia doesn't issue much debt, and American financial institutions held only about 7 percent of ruble-denominated debt.

While the list was lengthy, it hardly seemed the kind of sharp retaliation that Biden had talked about so stridently during the transition. Biden's own wording suggested he wanted to avoid an escalatory cycle. "I was clear with President Putin that we could have gone further, but I chose not to do so. I chose to be proportionate," Biden said in the East Room of the White House. "The United States is not looking to kick off a cycle of escalation and conflict with Russia. We want a stable, predictable relationship."

"Stable and predictable" were exactly what Putin desperately needed to avoid. His power, he knew, came from the perception that he was a mix of irrationality and instability—that he could lash out, that he could strike back at the United States through the back doors of Solar-Winds or over the border in Ukraine. Just days after Biden announced the sanctions, Putin celebrated his ability to take on the United States by means other than traditional military strikes. Russia's response will be "asymmetrical," "quick," and "tough" if it is forced to defend its interests, Putin said in late April, in an annual press conference that was always filled with bravado. He cast himself as the victim and warned against pushing Russia around. "The organizers of any provocations threatening the fundamental interests of our security will regret their deeds more than they have regretted anything in a long time," Putin told members of parliament. "I hope no one gets the idea to cross the so-called red line with Russia—and we will be the ones to decide where it runs in every concrete case."

Just a few days after Putin delivered this broadside, Sergei Shoigu, his defense minister, announced that troops would begin to pull back from the border with Ukraine. Not entirely, of course—they left their armored personnel carriers behind, a reminder that it wouldn't take much to return and go over the border.

The mystery was why he pulled back. "I think this was a dress rehearsal," Radek Sikorski, a former Polish foreign minister and now a member of the European Parliament, said a few days later. He pointed out that Putin had done this before past attacks.

Nuland told me in late 2021 that she believed that Putin had not anticipated how quickly the United States would call him out for the troop buildup—or how firmly European and Asian partners would back Biden up. "I think at that point the Russians were surprised at how quickly—now that we were actually talking to our allies again—we were able to pull together a more united response," she said. Still, she reflected, "It doesn't mean that it's positive in terms of going forward."

Biden and Putin were engaging in a dangerous dance. This time, escalation was avoided. But that was no guarantee for how the next incident would play out. And it seemed certain there would be a next one.

. . .

THE PRESIDENT'S MOTORCADE blasted out of the parking lot of the InterContinental Geneve at exactly 1:10 P.M. on June 16—nearly five months into Biden's presidency and over a month after the Colonial Pipeline hack. Biden and his aides had waited—motors running, Swiss police revving their motorcycle engines—until they were certain that Putin was already inside the aging mansion on the side of the lake opposite the city's downtown. Putin, they knew, was always playing mind games—and he had previously kept several American presidents and secretaries of state cooling their heels, a power play to show that the world awaited Russia's leader, not the other way around. This time, though, the White House had made it clear: Putin would arrive first at a summit that Biden had proposed, or the American president wouldn't be coming.

Now, certain there would be no embarrassing wait, Biden's motorcade raced down the hill toward the lake, screaming sirens announcing his arrival at the quiet villa.

While it is traditional that new American presidents meet their Russian—and, before that, Soviet—counterparts early in their presidency, this was different. Colonial Pipeline drove home that Putin had a new weapon of mass disruption. And Biden decided that was the place to draw the line. Even if he used the summit opportunity to raise all the other irritants in the relationship—including Russia's newest threats to Ukraine—the focus was on the criminal use of cyber, what Nuland called "the wolf closest to the sled."

The session was designed to be brief. That was in stark contrast to the summit meetings of the Cold War. In 1955 Eisenhower traveled to Geneva to meet Nikita Khrushchev in the hopes of defusing growing tensions. Reagan had likewise traveled to Geneva in 1985 to seek an end to nuclear competition with Mikhail Gorbachev. Those meetings stretched out over many days and many meals in an effort to show that even superpower rivals could be civilized and work toward some common goals. Not this one.

Back in the United States Biden was already being criticized by Republicans who said he shouldn't be meeting with Putin at all. (They seemed to have a memory lapse about Trump's meetings, including his unctuous encounter in Helsinki, where Trump publicly endorsed Putin's contention that Russia had nothing to do with the 2016 election interference.) Biden may not have been the biggest fan of Putin—a man whom he'd rather undiplomatically called a "killer" just a few months before—but the new American president saw no other choice. In his view, when dealing with authoritarian states, it was personal relationships between leaders—more than formal negotiations or links between institutions—that ultimately made the difference and got things done. In this belief, of course, Biden's approach wasn't dissimilar from Trump's. The difference was that Trump thought leader-to-leader agreements were sufficient, while Biden knew they were just a necessary starting point.

"Biden thinks about foreign policy through relationships," reflected Avril Haines. What's more, she said, "Biden recognized how important it was for Putin to feel respected. To be treated as an equal and to be perceived as a great leader." He didn't want to lose easy points for not treating people with respect. Biden believed that berating Putin in public wouldn't work anyway. "The standard answer is if you want to deter Russia, talk to Putin privately," Haines concluded.

Yet even as the two presidents settled into the library of the mansion—surrounded by books and an old globe—Biden had confided to aides that his expectations for achieving any kind of breakthrough with Putin were negligible. At best, he thought, Putin might promise the brief arrest of some hackers, maybe stage a show trial of one or two of them.

When the obstreperous reporters were finally cleared from the room—a mild skirmish had broken out between Russians and Americans jockeying for a better view of the two leaders—the two men settled in. Biden said that while all nations spy on each other—hardly news to the former KGB officer he was meeting—cyberattacks on critical infrastructure were of a fundamentally different nature. And they were no longer just a criminal issue, he said. They were a direct national security threat, and he planned to treat them as such.

Biden handed Putin a list of what he considered off-limits: the sixteen sectors that the United States Department of Homeland Security designates as "critical infrastructure." These, he warned Putin, were America's red lines. He should know that if he crossed them—if he messed with the infrastructure that held the country together, as the ransomware actors had done with Colonial Pipeline, followed in the weeks after by an attack that disrupted one-fifth of the United States' meat-processing capacity—the price would be high. He was not specific.

Biden's problem, of course, was that many countries had crossed several of the sixteen red lines before, including Russia, Iran, and North Korea. These actors had put malicious code in the American electric grid. They had interfered with the financial markets and, famously, a major movie studio. They had frozen schools and universities and hospitals with ransomware campaigns. They had launched influence operations targeting the integrity of the electoral process. Biden had to convince Putin that there was a new sheriff in town—and that the price of these attacks going forward would be far more severe. He would not make excuses for Putin's actions, as Trump had. He would not hesitate to name the Russians as the bad actors, as Obama had.

The meeting ended early. Having said their pieces, the two men, despite having flown around the globe to get together, did not even bother with the ritual walk in the garden or a shared lunch. Each retreated to give his separate press conference. Putin knew that back in Moscow the details of the meeting meant little; the important thing was that Biden still viewed Russia as a major player, a force to be reckoned with. He announced that it was the United States, not Russia, that was the biggest cyber threat in the world. When it came to explaining what his troops were doing on Ukraine's doorstep, he had a ready answer. "We're holding these exercises in our territory, just like the United States does with regards to many drills. But we do not hold our exercises by deploying military equipment close to the U.S. border. Unfortunately that's what the American partners are doing with regards to our border."

Biden was under pressure to show that he had gotten through to Putin in establishing some new boundaries, particularly as the only concrete outcome of the summit was the creation of two high-level joint working groups on cyber and arms control.

"I did what I came to do," he told reporters in a press conference a few hours after Putin spoke. "We, in fact, made it clear that we were not going to continue to allow this to go on."

I asked him whether he worried that the two countries were now on the verge of escalating into a new, digital version of the Cold War.

"I think that the last thing [Putin] wants now is a Cold War," Biden told me, pointing out that the Russian leader shared several thousands of miles of border with China, which was "hell-bent" on becoming the most important and powerful nation in the world. There would be no

Obama-era reset, Biden said, but it was clear that Russia didn't want two enemies at once. He said he'd told Putin that " 'it's clearly not in any-body's interest—your country's or mine—for us to be in a situation where we're in a new Cold War.' And I truly believe he thinks that—he understands that."

JUST TWO AND A HALF weeks after the Geneva summit came the mo-ment of truth: A Russian-speaking ransomware group called REvil that used similar techniques to those of DarkSide struck. This time the group had gained access to a software company named Kaseya that served, indirectly, thousands of small businesses around the world. The damage from this REvil attack was limited, in part because Kaseya was able to get hold of a decryption key and shared it widely. But REvil was clearly emboldened—it was now responsible for a quarter of all the ransom-ware attacks emanating from Russian soil toward the West.

At the White House it was immediately clear that this was the mo-ment to see if Putin would deliver. From the Situation Room, Biden discussed his options with General Paul Nakasone, the director of the NSA and the head of United States Cyber Command, who had already prepared a series of possible actions to go after REvil. There was no ques-tion, Nakasone told Biden, that the United States could dismantle the group's infrastructure. It just couldn't dismantle it for good. It was the nature of cyberweapons that they can be reconstituted on servers any-where in the world.

But Biden wanted to try, once again, to get Putin to do this dirty work himself. So in early July, he called Putin again, reminding him of the conversation they had had the previous month—and the American threat to act. "I made it very clear to him," Biden said at a press confer-ence, "that the United States expects, when a ransomware operation is coming from his soil, even though it's not sponsored by the state, we expect him to act, and we give him enough information to act on who that is." Putin had a limited amount of time to move, or, Biden sug-gested, he would take care of the problem himself.

Four days after Biden's phone call to Putin, REvil went dark. The cause was unknown: The gang might have shut itself down, given the spotlight on its operations, or someone might have taken it offline. Months later, they came back but were promptly shut back down by American cyber-warriors in coordination with international partners.

Behind the scenes, Biden's team was hoping for more. At the White House, it had fallen to Neuberger to lead the U.S. side of the new cyber working group—an effort to get the Russian authorities to stop turning a blind eye and hold criminal ransomware actors on their territory personally responsible. Biden's team wasn't interested in extraditing the hackers to the United States. The idea, recalled Neuberger, was, "You take care of it. It's your criminal." But the broader importance was this: The United States and Russia could disagree, vehemently, and still find a way to work together on areas of common interest.

Months later, Russian authorities arrested a string of cyber criminals operating out of Russia, including several of REvil's former members— responding, they said, to information provided by the United States. The timing seemed deliberate, right as the United States and Russia were squaring off over Russia's mounting threats to Ukraine. "I don't speak for the Kremlin's motives," noted a senior White House advisor at the time. "In our mind, this is not related to what's happening with Russia and Ukraine." The question was this: As the relationship spiraled back down, could any collaboration last?

IN RETROSPECT IT seems strange that the Geneva meeting—Biden's single in-person opportunity to get through to Putin personally—was mainly about the threat of ransomware, rather than the more apocalyptic issues of nuclear arms control or Putin's clear belief that Ukraine was not a legitimate country. Later, aides reported that Ukraine and Russia's accusations about encirclement by an expanded NATO were all discussed but were not the focus.

Not surprisingly, there was second-guessing—even within Biden's own team—about whether the Geneva summit was a missed opportunity or even a mistake. By focusing on ransomware rather than the fate of Ukraine, some of his aides wondered, Biden might have left Putin with the impression that he was so inwardly focused on events inside America's borders that the Russian leader felt emboldened. That Biden had already laid out a plan to exit Afghanistan in April—as the Soviets had done three decades before—may have contributed to Putin's conclusion.

But to Haines, the answer was simple: The United States needed to confront a practical, immediate threat to America's interests that Putin could resolve—if he chose to. "It's hard to imagine framing the Geneva summit about anything other than ransomware," Haines reflected later. "With Putin, we can talk about common interests—of which controlling ransomware is one—and of course he will use it to his advantage, but we could still imagine something useful might come from it." On Ukraine, Biden and Putin would just be repeating old talking points.

But, she admitted, there was nothing in their analysis—or imagination—that suggested Putin was readying himself to launch the biggest land war in Europe since World War II. "There was a real concern before the Geneva summit," Haines later told me, that the Russians might use their military to force Ukraine to concede parts of the Donbas, near the Russian border. "At that time, the most significant and aggressive move we could imagine was an incursion into eastern Ukraine."

Just four months later, new evidence emerged that would force Haines and her colleagues in the nation's intelligence agencies to reverse that conclusion.

CHAPTER 8

THE MELTDOWN

Whatever happens in Afghanistan, if there is a significant deterioration in security, that could well happen. We've discussed this before. I don't think it's going to be something that happens from a Friday to a Monday. So I wouldn't necessarily equate the departure of our forces in July, August, or by early September with some kind of immediate deterioration in the situation.

Secretary of State Antony J. Blinken, testifying to Congress, June 7, 2021

IN THE EARLY morning hours of Thursday, August 12, 2021, Jake Sullivan was woken up by a phone call to his townhouse in Washington's West End. On the other end of the line was the chairman of the Joint Chiefs of Staff, Mark Milley, whose gruff demeanor and blunt public pronouncements episodically amused and frustrated Sullivan. Go to the secure room in your house, Milley told him, and call me back on that line.

Sullivan had little doubt as to the chairman's reason for calling. For days now, Sullivan and the president's other top aides had been spending most of their days in the Situation Room trying to get their heads around why the security situation in Afghanistan was unraveling so quickly. In a few weeks, the last American troops were scheduled to withdraw from the country, after nearly two decades of war. The question, increasingly, was whether the American military and other foreign citizens would actually be able to leave before the Taliban pressed in on the capital city of Kabul.

Sullivan and other members of Biden's team were starting to fear the worst. Every few days, images poured into the Situation Room of the Taliban taking one provincial capital after another. Afghan troops, stunned by the sudden absence of the American troops they had trained beside for years and bitter that their government paychecks were disappearing, were melting away, laying down arms and blending back into the civilian population. There were rumors that the Taliban was assembling a retribution list with the names of soldiers who stayed loyal to the American-backed government as well as the staffers, fixers, translators, and cooks who had helped the Americans for the previous two decades. Everything was going wrong, with almost unbelievable speed.

Publicly, Biden was doing his best to project an aura of confidence in the Afghan army—forces the United States had spent billions training, on the premise that they could prepare them to operate on their own in the defense of the democratically elected president, Ashraf Ghani. It was the responsibility of the Afghans to fight for Afghanistan, Biden said throughout the first months of his presidency, to stand up for their own government. The United States had prepared them as well as they possibly could, he maintained, so keeping Americans in the country another six months or another year wouldn't make a difference. If the Afghans couldn't make it on their own now, they never would.

Quietly, his generals—including Defense Secretary Lloyd Austin, General Milley, and the head of Central Command, General Kenneth F. McKenzie Jr.—had been warning him that the opposite was likely true. In early 2021, they came to the White House to make the case that a full withdrawal of American troops would be disastrous. With just a few more years—and a minimal U.S. force able to provide intelligence and advice to the Afghan government, they contended—the Afghan force could better hold its own. But without a modest American presence, Austin and the generals told Biden, a Taliban takeover looked increasingly like a matter of time. It was an analysis the intelligence community agreed with. A Taliban victory in Afghanistan might take a year or maybe eighteen months, Biden was told that summer, but if the Americans retreated, it looked increasingly inevitable.

"We've seen this movie before," said Austin, in an attempt to win over the president. It was a reference to the chaotic American retreat from Saigon in 1975, which left behind so many who had helped the United States and the South Vietnamese government.

The problem was that Biden had also heard it all before. It was the same litany of arguments for continuing the war that he'd heard as a senator during the Bush administration and later, as Obama's vice president. And so, in April, he'd taken his case straight to the American people.

"I'm now the fourth United States president to preside over American troop presence in Afghanistan: two Republicans, two Democrats. I will not pass this responsibility on to a fifth," Biden said in a speech announcing the full withdrawal of American troops within the next six months. He was speaking from the same room in the White House complex where, twenty years previously, George W. Bush had announced the opening strikes of the Afghanistan war. "When will it be the right moment to leave? One more year, two more years, ten more years? Ten, twenty, thirty billion dollars more above the trillion we've already spent? . . .

"It's time to end America's longest war. It's time for American troops to come home."

It wasn't an unpopular decision, at least at the time. Afghanistan had long receded from newspaper headlines. But what followed over the next six months was the first major foreign policy test for the Biden administration's national security team. The allies were watching to see how Biden put into practice his promise to reengage with them. Vladimir Putin and Xi Jinping were taking the measure of Biden's resolve. Asian countries were seeing whether Biden would carry through on the promise, made from Day One in office, to end two decades of fixation on the Middle East and refocus on the more complex challenge of China.

"Our true strategic competitors—China and Russia—would love nothing more than the United States to continue to funnel billions of dollars in resources and attention into stabilizing Afghanistan indefinitely," Biden said that August.

But as events on the ground unraveled and the fragile American-backed Afghan government imploded, the optics were the opposite of what Biden sought. Rather than a principled, competent withdrawal that demonstrated American resolve, it looked to the rest of the world like a hasty, deadly retreat. Not surprisingly, adversaries abroad used the moment opportunistically to make their point that the United States was a pitiful, declining power and a deeply unreliable ally.

THE WARNING SIGNS on Afghanistan had been flashing red for so long that most Americans had stopped paying attention. Bush's decision to invade Iraq bled military resources from the fight against al-Qaeda and the Taliban—though Bush and his aides denied it. Slowly, the Taliban began retaking territory. Yet it wasn't until 2006 that most Americans began to understand how bogged down the United States had become. While the CIA's paramilitary units and the U.S. military had brought down the Taliban government with ease, they were astoundingly bad at nation-building—that is, creating the right balance of economic success, central governance, and social stability needed to sustain the country.

When Obama came into office, he was determined to make a quick exit from Iraq, but he viewed Afghanistan as different. That was the "good war," he said in 2007. The fight against al-Qaeda, he said in 2008, would be "the top priority that it should be."

Obama's pick for vice president, then-Senator Joe Biden, had long soured on the war and had changed his mind on the strategic and moral value of keeping troops there. Amid the passions that followed the 9/11 attack, he had voted alongside ninety-seven other senators in 2001 to authorize an invasion intended to hunt down Osama Bin Laden. But within a few years, it was evident to him and to many of his colleagues that Bush's follow-on effort to turn Afghanistan into a model democracy was doomed. Ultimately Biden came to believe that there was no country in the world that could unify Afghanistan. "The British tried," he told me one evening when he was vice president. "How'd that work out?"

Then, suddenly, Biden found himself in the Situation Room amid Obama's bottom-up review of the American strategy for Afghanistan and Pakistan. General Stanley McChrystal, the Afghanistan commander, sent the group a plan for a decade-long commitment to reconstruct the country at an additional cost of about $50 billion a year. After weeks of arguments in which Biden pressed for a fairly rapid pullout, Obama went in a different direction, embracing a rapid but brief "surge" of American troops into the country. Once they made Afghanistan stable and secure, the task of defending the country would be turned over to Afghan troops.

Biden was appalled. He was convinced that the Pentagon was trying to "box in" Obama and suspected that it was behind the leaks of stories claiming that without a surge of troops, the mission in Afghanistan would fail. Biden, Obama later recounted, put his face "a few inches from mine and stage-whispered, 'Don't let them jam you.'"

Biden wasn't alone in that view. The U.S. ambassador to Afghanistan, Karl Eikenberry, who had commanded troops there before retiring from the military, thought surging forces into Afghanistan might work in the short term but would fail in the long run. The key to a successful counterinsurgency strategy, he said, required strong partners on the ground. And the flaw in Obama's plan was that the Afghan military was not up to the job. "We overestimate the ability of Afghan security forces to take over," he warned in a diplomatic cable. Worse, the democratically elected president, Hamid Karzai, he argued, was "not an adequate strategic partner." Eikenberry's cables leaked in November 2009—an embarrassing breach just before Obama was scheduled to announce his plans in a speech at West Point. From then on, Eikenberry was sidelined.

Six months later came the next embarrassment. A *Rolling Stone* article profiling McChrystal was filled with quotes from his aides disparaging Obama's team—Biden in particular—for its failure to understand the need for the American mission. Taking responsibility for what his team of advisors said, McChrystal resigned.

Obama's surge went ahead—and so did the quick drawdown soon after. At the peak of the American presence in 2011, there were roughly one hundred thousand troops in the country; by the time Obama left office, six years later, that number had plummeted to just above eight thousand.

Trump came to office declaring he would be the president who got America out. He had vehemently opposed the war, for nearly as long as Biden. "Why are we continuing to train these Afghanis [*sic*] who then shoot our soldiers in the back? Afghanistan is a complete waste. Time to come home!" he tweeted in 2012, three years before he ran for office. When I interviewed Trump during the campaign, though, he had no strategic plan for accomplishing the task. He simply said that he would strike a great deal. He didn't seem very interested in the details.

What emerged during Trump's single term was a prolonged negotiation with the Taliban. Over the course of a year and a half and some nine rounds of talks, a team led by Zalmay Khalilzad, the perennial American negotiator and lifelong diplomat who was himself born and raised in Afghanistan, met with representatives of the Taliban to hammer out what a political "solution" might look like. By the middle of 2019, the rough outlines of an agreement were in place. Ultimately, Mike Pompeo, Trump's secretary of state, showed up to witness the signing of the agreement on February 29, 2020, in Doha, Qatar, looking deeply uncomfortable, hands grimly folded, next to the Taliban commander, Mullah Abdul Ghani Baradar. If any other administration had signed such an agreement, Trump and Pompeo would instantly have described it as a sellout of American interests. "Trump just wanted to get out of Afghanistan and he really didn't care what the consequences would be," one of his national security aides told me.

The deal itself included a guarantee that the Americans would exit by May 2021—so long as the Taliban avoided killing U.S. soldiers in the interim. And it required the Taliban's promise—entirely unenforceable, of course—that the country would never again be a safe haven for terrorists.

The negotiation had excluded the Afghan government: a classic case of the United States and its allies, in the name of diplomatic expediency, negotiating away the fate of another country. President Ghani publicly criticized that, as well as the part where the Americans had committed him to swapping five thousand Taliban prisoners for a fifth as many Afghan soldiers. Negotiations between the Afghan government and the Taliban to decide the shape of a post-American withdrawal government were delayed and ultimately stalled out.

Trump hailed the deal as a victory. "The other side is tired of war," he said from the press room the day he announced the new deal. "Everybody is tired of war." (This was true.) Everyone was happy with the deal, he insisted—including the Afghans. (This was not true.)

Trump spun a vision of a world where the Taliban would side with the West and spend its time killing al-Qaeda and ISIS-K, never mentioning how much effort it was putting into bringing down Ghani's government. The Afghan Security Forces who were still Taliban targets weren't mentioned at all.

"I really believe," Trump said, "the Taliban wants to do something to show that we're not all wasting time. If bad things happen, we'll go back." The rest of Trump's news conference focused on what was then, in February 2020, a little-known illness called COVID-19.

BY THE TIME Biden took over in early 2021, he was in about the worst possible position in Afghanistan. America was about to run up against the May withdrawal deadline in Trump's treaty, and the Taliban was the strongest it had been in twenty years. If Biden reversed the drawdown, the Taliban would almost certainly target Americans again, saying they had violated the terms of the agreement between the two governments. That would require Biden to send in more troops to protect those already there—sucking troops back into the country just as he was trying to get the last ones out.

Biden was well aware that just about every intelligence analyst, regional expert, and military general on his staff believed that Afghanistan wouldn't be able to stand on its own for long. In January 2021 the Pentagon's special inspector general for Afghanistan issued a classified report with a warning to the new president: When the Americans left, the Afghan air force would collapse. It wasn't an issue of flying the planes: He noted that without American contractors to service and maintain the equipment, the Afghan air force simply couldn't stay in the sky very long.

In February, a congressionally mandated working group published a study arguing that keeping several thousand troops in the country while continuing negotiations was critical to the peace process. Otherwise, the Taliban would feel no pressure to fulfill its part of the bargain; it would just wait the Americans out.

Waiting them out was, of course, exactly what the Taliban had in mind. Although the three-hundred-thousand-strong Afghan army seemed formidable on paper, the truly effective troops numbered about twenty-two thousand. Those were the Afghan "commandos," who were already overextended fighting across the country. The rest of the army—its numbers bloated by "ghost soldiers," its effectiveness undercut by desertions, lack of training, and a deep unwillingness to fight—could not defend the country without foreign soldiers to back them up.

So it was no surprise that Secretary Austin and a parade of other Pentagon officials urged Biden—despite his instincts—to keep a small contingent of soldiers in the country: something on the order of 2,500 to 4,500 individuals. But by March 2021, officials confided, they had the sense that they weren't getting anywhere, that Biden had made up his mind.

Indeed he had. His three predecessors in the Oval Office had each promised victory, even if each defined it differently. That vision became emptier and emptier with each administration. Now he just wanted to avoid the fate of the British, who retreated from Afghanistan in 1842 after suffering 4,500 killed, amid massacres that preceded the invention of the roadside bomb.

Biden told Austin and Milley in April that he was ordering them to bring the troops home—in an orderly way, by September 11—twenty years after the event that precipitated the war and a few months after the deadline laid out in the Trump agreement with the Taliban. Still, Biden and his team argued in those days, this wouldn't be a disaster. They would have time. Time for an orderly withdrawal, time to evacuate everyone who had supported the two-decade-long American experiment in Afghanistan. There was no sense from the intelligence briefings that the "Taliban were on the march," one of Biden's senior advisors said in the late spring—an assessment that proved short-lived at best.

Within weeks the Taliban in May launched a new offensive across the south and central part of the country. The Taliban move proved so successful that the U.S. embassy quickly sensed that, whatever time the small contingent of American forces had left, it was running out faster than any of their predictions. On May 15, the embassy warned American civilians to "make plans to leave Afghanistan as soon as possible."

But Biden's team stopped short of a rapid, full-scale evacuation of Afghans who might be targeted by the Taliban. Though refugee and activist groups begged and pleaded for quick visas—rather than the cumbersome procedure Congress had established—Ghani had asked

Biden not to begin evacuations. That would send a signal, he argued, that Americans had lost faith in his government. The State Department compromised by reforming and speeding up the process for acquiring the "special" visas for Afghans who might be vulnerable because of their work with the Americans.

The one group that wasn't staying around was the U.S. military. Its leaders might have disagreed with Biden, but when faced with a direct order they executed it at high speed. Their biggest fear was that American troops would be increasingly vulnerable to attack during the months-long withdrawal—what the Pentagon calls "retrograde operations"—and particularly as troops were required to depart on a strict schedule to meet the administration's timeline. What this meant, an anonymous defense official told *Politico,* was that "speed equals safety."

So the Pentagon devised a plan: Get out a lot faster than the Taliban was expecting. And it started with the biggest symbol of the twenty-year-long American presence in Afghanistan—Bagram Airfield—which since the American invasion had been popping with takeoffs, landings, renditions, training sessions, and tours for visiting VIPs, Biden included.

On the morning of July 2, the Afghan commander of Bagram woke to discover that the entire base had been abandoned by the Americans. He had not been told what date the Americans were planning to leave, and now they were gone. The Afghan soldiers on patrol outside the base had not been told. Instead, the Americans had packed up and left overnight—cutting the electricity barely twenty minutes after they'd departed. Bagram went dark, and the looters rushed in.

Left behind were 3.5 million items, all the detritus of twenty years of American presence: prepackaged meals and bottles of water, small weapons and old laptops, ammunition, door handles, even complete armored vehicles. Some were intended as a parting gift to the Afghan troops. Others were just too inconvenient, or too insignificant, to take along, like the fleet of civilian cars, many of them left behind without the keys. "In one night, they lost all the goodwill of twenty years by leaving the way they did," one Afghan soldier told the Associated Press.

Later that morning, at the White House, I asked Biden what the withdrawal from Bagram portended. If the Taliban continued making progress and Kabul was threatened, would the United States still be in position to come to President Ghani's aid?

Biden, ready for Independence Day celebrations and much more eager to talk about the robust job numbers that the government had just published, wasn't thrilled. "I want to talk about happy things, man," he said partway through my question.

It would all be good, he insisted, even without the giant air base to mount operations. "We have worked out an over-the-horizon capacity," he insisted, referring to the ability of U.S. forces to launch attacks from beyond a country's borders and sweep in. But, he added, "the Afghans are going to have to be able to do it themselves with the Air Force they have, which we're helping them maintain."

A few days later, the questioning grew even sharper. A reporter asked Biden if the United States might face the kind of chaotic, devastating retreat from Kabul that it had when Saigon fell in April 1975. Biden was quick to dismiss the comparison. "The Taliban is not the North Vietnamese army," he said. "They're not—they're not remotely comparable in terms of capability. There's going to be no circumstance where you see people being lifted off the roof of a embassy in the—of the United States from Afghanistan. It is not at all comparable." (As it turned out, the analogy was apt. Or, as Ian Bremmer put it: "My God, not only were people pulled out of the embassy, we were pulling people off of the tarmac in Kabul Airport.")

Still, the incoming warnings from the military, intelligence community, and diplomatic staff were growing increasingly bleak. In mid-July, a secret diplomatic cable led by two dissenting American diplomats in Kabul—and co-signed by two dozen colleagues—warned that if the central government collapsed, the non-American embassy staff and others who had helped the Americans—all the translators, military support staff, and their families—would be left in danger. The State Department, they warned, needed to prepare for the possibility of an imminent evacuation. But when the dissent cable landed back at the State Department, it seemed unduly pessimistic—or so leadership later claimed. The department sped up processing of the special visas that Afghans with ties to the Americans were eligible for—a program that had been horrifically backlogged for years—but only pushed through a few thousand over the summer of 2021. Another couple of thousand people—including some still in the visa pipeline—were evacuated in the same time period. But despite warnings, almost none of the infrastructure, personnel, or training that would be critical for a possible mass evacuation had been put into place.

On August 3, a classified U.S. intelligence assessment warned that district capitals across Afghanistan were falling so quickly that the central government could collapse in a matter of "days or weeks." It was not the most likely outcome, but it was increasingly plausible, warned the assessment. Yet as late as Wednesday, August 11—just hours before Sullivan's early morning wake-up call—Biden was told in a Situation Room meeting that while outer provinces were falling quickly, there was still hope the situation could stabilize. This assessment rested on a key assumption: that the Afghan army units around Kabul, which included some of the best of the forces, would remain disciplined.

As a precaution, Biden agreed at the end of the meeting to a "prepare to deploy" order to American forces in the region, in case their help was needed with the evacuation efforts. He had little choice: The United States and its coalition partners still had thousands of diplomats, staff, contractors, soldiers, weapons, and aircraft stuck in the capital. Pulling them out rapidly would be no easy task. And with Bagram closed, they had only one way out: Hamid Karzai International Airport (as it was then known). It would be the single checkpoint. If the Taliban seized it, there would be no fast way out.

In no world did Biden want to send in more troops just weeks after pulling them out. That would be a messy last resort—it would risk Taliban attacks on American soldiers and civilians as it played out minute by minute on TV and online. But the alternative, he knew, was probably far worse.

When the August 11 Situation Room meeting broke up, the national security staff tried to get some sleep. That lasted only until Milley called Sullivan in the early morning hours. Sullivan later told me that as he hurried downstairs to the secure room in his house to call Milley back, he knew that the situation on the ground must have deteriorated fast.

The chairman, Sullivan recalled, informed him that "the Taliban had taken a city called Ghazni, which is on the highway approach to Kabul." Ghazni, a provincial capital, was only ninety miles away. "To have a city that close to Kabul in Taliban hands meant that a lightning strike on the capital could unfold very, very quickly, and we knew we had to move."

Early that morning, Biden's national security leadership gathered in the White House Situation Room. The assessment they heard there from Avril Haines was even more dire than what they'd received just hours before. Kabul's security situation had changed dramatically overnight, she warned. And it was devolving so fast that she could no longer guarantee they could offer any advance warning to the president about when the capital would fall. In other words, she said, the collapse could very well happen in the midst of an evacuation, leaving Americans in the crossfire. "The intelligence community's conclusion that they could no longer give any kind of specific warning for when Kabul would fall weighed heavily on us," Sullivan told me. "That came that Thursday, that's when they laid that out."

Unanimously, the meeting attendees recommended that Biden deploy the thousands of troops he'd put on high alert the previous night: a Marine Corps unit—part of the 5th Marine Expeditionary Brigade—based in the Gulf and the 82nd Airborne, part of America's Contingency Force.

Suddenly, Biden was doing the opposite of what he wanted: sending more troops into Afghanistan.

WHEN MAJOR GENERAL Chris Donahue, the fifty-two-year-old commander of the 82nd Airborne Division, touched down at Hamid Karzai International Airport just three days later, on August 16, he found absolute chaos.

Lean and fast-talking, Donahue had a reputation for being both direct and humble, a rare combination, and was known around Fort Bragg, North Carolina—his home base for many years—simply as "C.D." Over his decades in the U.S. Army, he had been deployed to nearly every continent: He'd begun his service as a rifle platoon leader in South Korea in the early 1990s, spent time in Panama, and parachuted into Europe and North Africa. But where he really made his career, like so many of his generation, was in the extended American wars in the Middle East after 9/11—and in the military's rapid transformation into a force dedicated to counterterrorism and counterinsurgency. As a member of Delta Force, the Army's most elite unit, he had served in just about every major operation in Iraq, Afghanistan, and Syria.

Over his thirty-plus years in the military, Donahue had gained a well-deserved reputation for being entirely unflappable—so much so that he was nicknamed "Flatliner" early in his career. "We do not heavy-breathe in this division," he said of the 82nd in May 2021, just months before he arrived in Kabul. "Whatever you ask us to do, we can handle it." He would need every bit of that composure, he knew, as he landed in the chaos of the ongoing emergency evacuation.

"So we show up, and people are rushing the aircraft," Donahue later recalled. "It had been a fairly okay situation," he said, referring to the relative calm on the ground in Afghanistan when he and his soldiers had departed from Fort Bragg. But now "the situation was completely changing."

As Donahue stepped off the flight that Monday morning, he took in the sight of thousands of Kabul's civilian residents who had already made it inside the high walls of the airport, desperate for a ticket out. Young men were racing after planes as they sped down the runway. Three of them died as a C17 cargo plane they'd managed to cling to took off. Families with young children were sitting on the scorching tarmac without food or water, and thousands more were waiting outside the gates. A contingent of young Marines was already busy processing personal documents to determine who qualified for a life-saving ticket out of the country—forced to play God by deciding who got to leave and who had to stay behind at the mercy of the Taliban.

Up until the day before Donahue arrived, Blinken and the State Department had responded to the unfolding crisis in Afghanistan by trying to negotiate the creation of a unity government between the Taliban and the existing regime—a last-ditch idea to avoid a battle for control of the capital. But it was obvious to everyone that for a coalition government to come together, the Afghan-born, U.S.-educated President Ghani was going to have to go.

Intellectual and technocratic, Ghani had come to power in 2014 amid high hopes that he would restore some economic competency to a country that for some decades had floundered. On paper, he looked like the Americans' ideal candidate: incorruptible, regimented, visionary, and a leading theorist on how to build democratic stability from violence. In practice, he was difficult to get along with, inflexible, egotistical, paranoid, and often deeply unpopular. He micromanaged the military, compulsively rotating its leadership and trying to center authority on himself. When we talked in a videoconference in early 2021, he seemed largely uninterested in the Taliban's advances—he was talking about budgets and reconstruction plans and education, with little reference to the growing existential threat to his own rule.

Of course, much of what was unfolding in 2021 had little to do with Ghani. The Taliban, viewing him as an American puppet, refused to negotiate with any Afghan government that he was a part of. That was why the February 2020 agreement had been negotiated between the United States and the Taliban. To reach an accord, Ghani was sidelined— and, he argued, completely blindsided.

In a June 2021 private meeting with President Biden at the White House two months after the announcement that the United States was leaving, Ghani railed about the risks of the rapid withdrawal of U.S. troops and the even more rapid diminishment of air strikes and maintenance support during combat with the Taliban. It was a betrayal and an insult, he told Biden. The least the American president could do, he insisted, was to avoid publicly ramping up the evacuation of potentially vulnerable Afghans. That, he said, would only trigger a panic and indicate to the Taliban and the rest of the world that Biden's administration had no faith in Ghani's government.

As the Taliban ran roughshod over the country in mid-August and the situation grew more dire, Blinken had increasingly intense—and frustrating—conversations with Ghani. It would likely become necessary, Blinken warned him, for him to step out of the way so that the Americans could send a team of government officials to Doha, restart the follow-on negotiation to what Trump brought about, and create a new power-sharing agreement. It wouldn't be pretty, Blinken warned. The new government would inevitably be dominated by the Taliban— the same Taliban that had harbored Osama Bin Laden and made clear it would reimpose Sharia law across the land. The best anyone could hope for was that at least a few officials in the present government would remain in office. It might be the only way, Blinken thought, "to avoid bloodshed, to try to put Afghanistan on some kind of reasonable foundation going forward."

In the first part of August, Ghani refused even to discuss the possibility. He was the duly elected president of the country, and he wasn't going anywhere. He claimed he warned the Americans that chaos would break out—a consequence of the abrupt withdrawal of troops.

But on the afternoon of August 14, with the Taliban virtually at the gates of the city, Blinken called Ghani again. To the relief of the exhausted Blinken, Ghani agreed to send a new negotiating team empowered to create a coalition government with the Taliban. And Blinken recalled Ghani saying, "If the Taliban doesn't agree and engage in good faith, then I will stay and fight to the death."

"That was Saturday," Blinken told me somberly, recalling the moment from the wood-paneled seventh floor of the State Department. "He fled the country the next day, on Sunday."

To many Afghans, it was an unforgivable defection. But to Ghani's mind, he had been betrayed, most of all by the Americans. There is some evidence that he didn't believe that the United States would actually withdraw its forces—at least not so rapidly. "My life work has been destroyed," he said publicly, some months later. "My values have been trampled on and I have been made a scapegoat."

Within hours of his departure, the Arg—the nineteenth-century presidential palace at the heart of Kabul, fortified over recent years by concrete walls and razor wire—was overrun by the Taliban, as factions jostled to gain as much control as possible in advance of the full U.S. withdrawal.

Overnight, everything had changed.

BY MONDAY, AUGUST 16, with Ghani gone and Donahue and the 82nd Airborne trying to manage the chaos at the airport, Kabul's civilian population was in a panic. It had not lived under the Taliban since the American invasion in 2001. While millions stayed at home, thousands—including translators, contractors, and military personnel, many of whom had spent years waiting for immigration papers to be processed—fled to the international airport, their only option for escape.

The Biden administration's plans from early in the year had discussed the possibility that the Taliban would sweep through the capital—but they did not imagine an Afghan collapse that was so rapid that American forces could not hold the airport long enough to stage the evacuation. So there was no infrastructure set up outside the airport walls to help constrain the thousands of civilians pressed up to the gates. There wasn't enough food or water for the American soldiers on duty, let alone the Afghans waiting for days in the hot sun.

Donahue, following the procedures that had been drilled into him and his troops, started with the simplest thing: evaluating the security perimeter of the airport. What he discovered surprised even him. The entire southern half of the airfield was controlled by the Taliban. The threat to the aircraft evacuating thousands—embassy personnel and the Afghans and their families who made it through—was obvious. "We had to push the Taliban out," Donahue later told me. "Without getting into a gunfight with them. . . . We just physically went and said, 'Get out,'" he recalled, matter-of-factly. "Like, that first hour, we're just pushing people out" and off the runway.

Then Donahue, along with his aide, his driver, and a squadron of paratroopers, went into the international terminal on the other side of the runway. "And we bump into the Taliban. They're cleaning up glass. And I go up on the roof, and there's Taliban snipers on the roof." Their weapons were pointed at the American side. Through his cultural aide, Donahue threatened them, and they left.

It seemed touch-and-go. But Donahue was well aware that the Taliban had its own reasons to avoid picking a fight: The American soldiers were doing what the Taliban wanted—namely, getting everyone the hell out. Donahue quickly concluded that the Taliban was likely every bit as astounded by its own success as everyone in Washington was. It had no interest in slowing the Americans' evacuation timeline by attacking. The Taliban, Donahue told me later, "would have loaded the planes for us."

But the Taliban also made it clear that it wanted the civilian American presence and the embassy to remain in Kabul—because that, it understood, was the only way to ensure that international aid would keep flowing into the country. (Of course, with the Taliban taking over the country, it was unimaginable that Biden and Blinken would let embassy personnel stay.)

A week after Donahue arrived, with the security situation still deteriorating, CIA Director Burns was dispatched to talk to the Taliban leadership. His chief interlocutor was Mullah Abdul Ghani Baradar—one of the original four co-founders of the Taliban and the representative with whom Trump's administration had signed the May 2020 agreement that launched the American withdrawal. The meeting at the old civilian terminal at the Kabul airport was, Burns recalled, more than a little tense. Just getting the two men together was a challenge for both sides, one aide recalled; there was an argument over whether they would meet alone or do so with their security details present.

In the end, Burns recalled, "we had both of our security detachments outside kind of eyeing each other very warily. Remembering very well the few weeks before they could have been locked in a firefight with one another as well."

Part of the message that Burns had been dispatched to deliver was a warning: Don't interfere with the American-led evacuation, and don't let terror groups—whether ISIS or al-Qaeda or something new—use Afghanistan as a base. The terror groups had Burns's analysts particularly worried. American intelligence officials were increasingly worried that ISIS—now a battered and broken wannabe caliphate—was planning something big to take advantage of the chaos. Whatever that something was, the intelligence suggested it was aimed squarely at the airport. A terror attack on the airport was the nightmare scenario, one that, as Burns recalled, "we were all trying to avoid, which helped explain the sense of urgency not only with which the U.S. military was conducting the evacuation and all of us intelligence officers and diplomats who were trying to support that, but also the sense of urgency we all felt about the threats that we could see coming in about potential ISIS attacks."

Frustrated by the chaos around the airport, as Burns perceived it, Baradar worried that the United States would use it as an excuse to delay their departure. But, Burns admitted, the Taliban was also worried about the threat posed by ISIS. The Taliban, the CIA chief quickly concluded, was "beginning to realize that the challenge of governance in Afghanistan was going to be at least as complicated as the challenge of running an insurgency."

Burns left, fairly confident that Baradar "understood the message that I was delivering."

But no sooner had he returned to the United States than his worst fear came true. Just before 1 p.m. local time on August 26, the Pentagon received an intelligence warning that an ISIS attack would be launched that day—likely within the hour. In preparation, stretchers and emergency vehicles were set up to accommodate a mass casualty event. For the rest of the afternoon, nothing happened. The Marines continued to process evacuees. But at approximately 6 P.M. in Kabul, an Islamic State militant named Abdul Rahman al-Logari, who had escaped from prison during the chaos of the Taliban takeover, loaded himself up with twenty-five pounds of explosives, wrapped in ball bearings and other shrapnel, and detonated it in the packed crowds outside Abbey Gate.

It was just before 10 A.M. in Washington, and Burns was gathering alongside other top national security officials in the White House Situation Room in anticipation of a meeting with President Biden. General McKenzie, beaming in over a video link, shared that he had "just gotten handed a report about an attack at Abbey Gate at Kabul International Airport," Burns recalled. "The president came into the room shortly thereafter, and at that point General McKenzie informed him of the attack and also the fact that there had been at least several American military casualties, fatalities in the attack. That number grew over the course of the meeting as well.

"I remember the president just paused for at least thirty seconds or so and put his head down because he was absorbing the sadness of the moment and the sense of loss as well."

More than 150 civilians and 13 American troops were killed, and hundreds more were injured. Over the next few days, the U.S. military launched two air strikes against targets they believed might be planning additional attacks on the ground while U.S. soldiers continued to process the evacuations. One of the strikes hit a car with three suspected ISIS collaborators. The second hit a suspected terrorist who was driving around the city in what the Pentagon thought was an effort to gather materials for an attack. They had it completely wrong. Their "terrorist" was an aid worker gathering water and other supplies for his family and neighbors. But before anyone could figure that out, a drone strike was unleashed, killing the aid worker, two other adults, and seven children. For days, General Milley and the Pentagon insisted it was a "righteous strike" against a terrorist target—even though, seconds after the missile was shot but before it hit the target, the CIA warned the Department of Defense that children had been present.

"It is a pretty good encapsulation of the entire twenty-year war," one U.S. official told CNN. A week later, when colleagues at the visual investigations unit of *The New York Times* demonstrated that the military had killed the wrong man, the Pentagon relented.

On August 30, 2021, the last U.S. military transport flight departed from Kabul's international airport. Aboard it was the acting U.S. ambassador to Afghanistan, Ross Wilson. The final person to board—and the last American combat soldier to leave Afghanistan—was Commander Chris Donahue.

IN THE AFTERMATH of the Kabul debacle, the White House was quick to blame everyone but itself.

First, officials said, it was the Afghan government's own fault. The United States and its allies spent billions training an Afghan force in America's own image, but in the end that force appeared unwilling to fight for its own country.

It was Trump's fault for signing a bad deal that was unenforceable and precipitating the rapid pullout. This was their best case—the Trump deal was in fact terribly thought out—but by July 2021 the Biden White House owned the problem and was warned multiple times that the security situation was spiraling. Thousands of Afghan civilians who had supported the Americans over the decades were left behind, subjected to reprisal killings by the Taliban and ongoing attacks from Islamic State terrorists.

It was Ghani's fault for blocking the withdrawal of vulnerable civilians, for fear it would show an absence of American confidence in the elected Afghan government. The fact was that the process of getting the paperwork through to enable those who had helped the United States get out was so arduous—as designed by Congress—that speeding it up for a large-scale evacuation might have violated the law. But the last chaotic week showed it was possible.

It was also a failure of the intelligence community, which assessed in early 2021 that "Taliban advances would accelerate across large portions of Afghanistan *after* a complete U.S. military withdrawal and potentially lead to the Taliban's capturing Kabul within a year or two." But as the spring wore on, the CIA assessments in particular turned pessimistic about the challenges of holding the Taliban at bay. The Pentagon, officials told me, was significantly more optimistic for far longer.

It wasn't until summer that everyone discovered just how wrong they had been.

Or, as Bill Burns later put it to me, "As President Biden said, none of us expected things to unfold as fast as they did in July and August."

When historians look back at the ugly end of the American experience in Afghanistan, they may well conclude that Biden's instincts to get out when he did were right—at least from a strategic perspective. Keeping a small American military force inside the country wasn't going to accomplish any of America's stated military and political objectives. It wasn't going to slow down the Taliban. It wasn't going to build a stable democracy. At home, Biden was likely also betting that after it fell off the front pages, Americans wouldn't spend much more time thinking about Afghanistan—nor punish him electorally.

But as the government's own special inspector general concluded, the execution of the withdrawal was miserable.* The administration ignored multiple warnings from the State Department personnel on the ground and from the Afghans themselves. They set themselves up for failure. So although Biden was correct in saying that they had pulled off the greatest emergency airlift in history, the fact is that America's abandonment of thousands of Afghans who had aided the United States was the larger disaster. And that failure, though mounded upon the mistakes of previous presidents, was largely of the administration's own making.

Biden's team—which prided itself on experience and an ability to see around corners—misread the situation and moved far too slowly. The consequences went beyond the tragic loss of thirteen American soldiers

---

* When the Pentagon watchdog—whose responsibility it has been since 2008 to evaluate and oversee the aid, arms, and support flowing into Afghanistan—published its final report on how the U.S. withdrawal went so wrong, so fast, it found two things. First, a number of short-term factors destabilized the Afghan government and security forces, precipitating a devastating yet inevitable reversal of all the gains in the country over the previous twenty years. These, the watchdog found, were mostly associated with the commitment, made by Trump and sustained by Biden, to rapidly pull out American forces and contractors. Afghan soldiers, who'd trained and served alongside the Americans for years, were blindsided and lost faith. Ghani's mismanagement of the military further weakened it. And, of course, the Taliban took advantage at every turn. Second, and more foundationally, they found that the United States had profoundly misread, despite twenty years of effort, what it would take to build a strong, self-sustaining, and centralized military force in Afghanistan. Short-term solutions—like relying on U.S. weapons procurement processes or subbing in U.S. fighters—prevented the Afghan forces from learning. Corruption undercut the best of intentions. And an effective internal police force was never created.

at Abbey Gate, the hundreds of dead and wounded Afghan civilians, and even beyond the tens of thousands more vulnerable Afghans left behind in the country to this day. It reminded the world that superpowers have limits. America was relearning the lesson that it had failed to learn so many times before: that invading a nation is easier than building one. The United States had entered Afghanistan at the height of its unipolar moment, confident in its ability to invest enough time, energy, money, and blood to utterly transform a country a world away. It had talked about making Afghanistan a model democracy. And it had utterly failed.

Biden appeared to have decided that he could live with criticism if the withdrawal allowed the U.S. to refocus on strategic interests that were, to his mind, more vital than Afghanistan or the Middle East. But it is doubtful that the rest of the world saw the chaos as a manifestation of American strength.

And so the mullahs in Tehran, and the Chinese generals fulfilling Xi's orders to prepare for a conflict in Taiwan, and Putin's apparatchiks, all had good reason to believe that Biden, and the United States, with its famously short attention span, had no stomach for the kind of international entanglements that had dominated the American Century.

CHAPTER 9

A "SPUTNIK" MOMENT

The relationship between China and the United States is today totally dysfunctional. . . . There are areas where a serious negotiation is needed—in trade and technology—if you want to avoid that the world becomes separated in two economies, in two sets of rules, two internets. . . . Unfortunately today we only have confrontation.

António Guterres, UN secretary general, September 2021

IN THE EARLY morning hours of July 27, 2021, General John Hyten, the vice chairman of the Joint Chiefs of Staff, received an urgent, if perplexing, call in his office in the outermost ring of the Pentagon.

On the other end of the line was a watch officer from the National Military Command Center. From the center, located deep underneath the Pentagon, civilian analysts and military operators monitored potential threat activity around the world on a 24/7 basis—anything that might require a military response. One of their most important streams of data came from the constellation of "early warning" satellites, which were constantly on the lookout for the flash of a rocket igniting on a launchpad or an anomalous heat signature indicating a missile flying through the atmosphere.

The watch officer told Hyten that the satellites had recorded a launch out of China. There was nothing unusual about that—the People's Liberation Army's rocket force tested intercontinental ballistic missiles on a regular cadence. But it was immediately clear that something about this particular test wasn't routine at all. For starters, it appeared that the missile was flying in the wrong direction.

"I would get notified of all the missile launches," recalled Hyten, who had run the United States Strategic Command—the force in charge of the nation's nuclear arsenal—before being promoted to the Joint Chiefs by Trump. "If it was a big enough deal, I would get woken up in the middle of the night with a call. But this time it was in the middle of the day. And the only reason they called me was because the missile went backwards."

Missiles usually get fired from west to east, moving with the rotation of the earth, which requires less effort, energy, and fuel than going in the opposite direction. This projectile, however, seemed on an arc to circumnavigate the globe by flying west. Why would China shoot something off in the opposite direction?

"Well, what is it?" Hyten told me he asked the watch officer on the line.

"No idea," the officer admitted.

Quickly enough, a few things became clear to American analysts. The missile had soared high above the continental United States. And at some point during its trip, it had released a "hypersonic glide vehicle," a highly maneuverable warhead that could fly more than five times the speed of sound in a seemingly erratic, shifting path. In some ways, it was more like a stunt plane at an airshow, and it flew much closer to the ground than traditional missiles. The glide vehicle appeared designed to carry a nuclear payload, if needed—though it could also do plenty of damage as an unstoppable conventional weapon. And then the Pentagon lost track of it, Hyten was told.

That was the part that left so many at the Pentagon worried. "Our systems are built to track ballistic attacks" from intercontinental ballistic missiles following a highly predictable arc, Hyten told me. The glide vehicles used "a technology and a trajectory our systems are not built to track." It was like the difference between following the paths of a long fly ball to the outfield and of a buzzing mosquito. Meanwhile, America's traditional long-range fixed missile defenses—based in California and Alaska—peered west. Those defenses are directionally configured to track and intercept missiles launched by rogue nations like

North Korea—again, on a predictable trajectory—and can only handle a limited number of incoming missiles at a time.*

Three years before the Chinese test, General Hyten had testified before Congress that there was no existing U.S. defense that could block a hypersonic weapon—not just because of its speed but also due to its ability to operate within Earth's atmosphere and to change its altitude and direction unpredictably while flying much closer to the Earth's surface than comparable conventional weapons. For years now, China—and Russia—had been showing off hypersonic systems. Now it was clear they were progressing—more rapidly than many planners had anticipated.

Not surprisingly, the news of the test sent the Pentagon and the intelligence community scrambling. Predictably, their first instinct was to classify the whole set of conclusions. "We have no idea how they did this," one source later admitted to Demetri Sevastopulo of the *Financial Times,* who was the first to break the news of the launch in October 2021, three months after it took place.

The whole test hadn't been a complete success, it turned out—the glide vehicle, unarmed, had struck several miles off its goal. Still, Hyten said, it was "close enough," and his boss, Mark Milley, came out swinging.

"It has all of our attention," Milley said publicly. It was "very close" to a Sputnik moment, he added, recalling the 1957 launch of a Soviet satellite that jolted Washington because it seemed to represent evidence that the United States had fallen behind in the space race.

When I asked Milley later what he meant, he explained: "Because it's a new capability that travels at speeds that there is no known defense— that there's nothing I know of that can acquire, track, engage, and kill a weapon traveling at hypersonic speeds."

Once public, the news of the test quickly reverberated across Washington, D.C.—and so did the confusion. Everyone in the defense community was convinced that this was A Big Deal. But they differed on why. Some, like Milley, agreed it was the speed of the missile. Others said it was its maneuverability. But most were astonished that China— a country that not so long ago was regularly accused of stealing and copy-

---

* Even then, the successful interception rate remains far lower than first hoped when the United States entered a new era of missile defense decades ago.

ing American weapons systems like the F-35 fighter—had managed to leap ahead with a technology that the United States had so far failed to master. And it was clear that the real utility of the weapon for the Chinese might not be a strategic strike on the American homeland but instead a precision strike against our most critical—and vulnerable—weapons platforms, like the big, lumbering aircraft carriers that in a crisis would be slowly steaming toward Taiwan. The real purpose, one senior Pentagon official told me, might be to dissuade the U.S. Navy from coming too close.

Senator Angus King of Maine, who sits on the Senate Intelligence Committee, said his takeaway was that the United States was potentially four to five years behind the Chinese in developing a similar capability. "The significance," he said, "was that it scared the hell out of everybody."

When it came to China, the hypersonic tests were hardly the only "Sputnik" moment for the new administration. There was the steady buildup of new nuclear missile silos in China's desert, discovered at the very end of Trump's term, which had continued to grow in number. There was the September 2020 test of a mysterious Chinese "space plane" that stayed in orbit for months and appeared able to release an object while orbiting. There was the improved Chinese "intelligence base" in Cuba that some officials believed Beijing wanted to turn into a military facility ninety miles from Miami.

Particularly worrisome, the head of Space Command warned publicly in mid-2021, was a new type of robotic satellite technology with a giant "grappling arm" of sorts that could seize and move an entire satellite. (Viewed one way, that was a responsible way of cleaning up space junk; viewed another, it was a sign of what China could do to disable America's own satellites.)

In Washington, each of these developments fed the narrative of an ambitious China, preparing to displace the United States in old military domains and new ones. Beijing's narrative was quite different: Xi, who also had the title of chairman of the Central Military Commission, was worried that his military was underreacting to the spread of American influence in the Pacific. "The 'laws of the jungle' of international competition have not changed," he said in 2014.

Yet none of these tests by the Chinese were overtly aggressive—and certainly not in violation of any treaties. In fact, with the exception of the hypersonic flight, a technology the United States had experimented with and failed to master before giving up—these were capabilities the United States either possessed or had also tested. Few in the United States complained at the time about the impression that these American tests would leave on the rest of the world. But of course, we don't question our own intentions, while ascribing the worst to adversaries.

The larger shock was that China had emerged, suddenly, with weapons that clearly ran circles around the fixed antimissile defenses the United States had spent nearly $70 billion developing by 2018. And they fueled the fear in Washington that the era of American preeminence in space was ending—if it wasn't over already.

THE DAY THAT the Soviet Union launched Sputnik 1—the world's first artificial satellite—in 1957, it barely merited a mention on the front page of the Soviet daily, *Pravda*. A short column under the heading "Tass Report" relayed the bare statistics of the launch: "In the course of the last years in the Soviet Union scientific research and experimental construction work on the creation of artificial satellites of the Earth has been going on." It was hardly the crowing of a major victory—nor was it particularly secret. The launch had been long planned and wasn't classified.

What seemingly bored *Pravda*, though, electrified the public and politicians in the United States, who feared the country was falling behind its Soviet adversary. It quickly became an issue in the 1960 presidential campaign, when Senator John F. Kennedy blamed President Dwight D. Eisenhower—and, by extension, Kennedy's opponent, Vice President Richard M. Nixon—for "losing the satellite-missile race with the Soviet Union."

This event sparked cries of the infamous "missile gap" bolstered by government charts warning that the Soviet missiles were superior in number and quality. The missile gap turned out to be pure fiction, as the Kennedy administration itself was forced to concede once in office, but by then the facts didn't matter: The American shock over the Soviet achievement triggered the space race, catalyzed the creation of NASA, and ultimately led to the fulfillment of Kennedy's goal to land a human on the moon by the end of the decade.

The moment, as it turned out, had bigger political implications than technological ones. "*Sputnik* shocked a seemingly complacent society, secure in their new suburbs, vast highways, color televisions, and the highest peacetime budget in history," the space historian Asif Siddiqi said. "Launched on the same night that *Leave It to Beaver* premiered, *Sputnik* awoke a nation."

More than six decades later, as word of China's hypersonic weapons test emerged, similar rhetoric was ringing around Capitol Hill. Washington had been working on hypersonic technology ever since the Truman administration had spirited away Nazi scientist Wernher von Braun, one of the developers of the Germans' V-2 rocket, to jumpstart America's hypersonic program in the wake of World War II.* Von Braun enjoyed a long and prestigious science career, with officials willfully ignoring his Nazi past—and, beginning in the 1960s, the United States grew to enjoy a commanding lead in the field.

But then, recalled Mark Lewis, a top aerospace engineer whose government career includes a stint as the chief scientist for the Air Force and who was also the Pentagon's lead for R&D in the final year of the Trump administration, "we took our foot off the gas."

In his years in government and academia, Lewis had a front-row seat to America's habit of investing in critical science programs and then pulling the plug—sometimes because they simply didn't work, sometimes because there was no political constituency, often because they got caught in budget fights. America's investment in its hypersonic weapons program epitomized that trend. "How is it," Lewis asked me, "that in a field the United States basically invented, we wake up one day and it looks like Russia and China are already deploying systems, and we're still in the research and development phase?"

The truth is that the squandering of an advantage happens all the time. As new technologies emerge, as research efforts succeed or fail, governments make choices. Legacy systems—aircraft carriers, fighter jets, tanks—are deliberately manufactured in key congressional districts around the country so that the argument over whether a weapons system is needed gets subsumed by the question of whether it produces jobs.

---

* The world's very first working hypersonic weapon, the V-2 rocket, was built with concentration-camp forced labor and deployed to devastating effect over the city of London in 1944, but it achieved hypersonic speeds only on its descent.

Add to that the technical challenge: Hypersonic weapons aren't exactly the easiest technology to master. At speeds of Mach 5 and above—roughly equivalent to a mile a second—within Earth's atmosphere, the physical challenges faced by a weapons system increase as it is exposed to extreme heat. (This is why, in *Top Gun: Maverick,* Tom Cruise's titular pilot couldn't have physically ejected at Mach 10. As one interviewee colorfully phrased it to me, he would have been "squashed like a fly swatted by a chainmail glove.") There were also many in the U.S. military who argued that the Pentagon could rely on other weapons already in its arsenal to achieve some of the same effects—without the expense or difficulty.

But even as the United States was easing up, the Chinese were doubling down. The People's Liberation Army, General Hyten said toward the end of his term as vice chairman, had conducted "hundreds" of tests between 2016 and 2021. In that same period, the United States, Hyten offered as a point of comparison, had conducted nine.

By 2018, the Chinese payoff was already becoming apparent. In August, they claimed to have successfully tested the Xingkong-2 "Waverider"—a hypersonic cruise missile capable of moving forward on its own shockwaves. (The U.S. Air Force had been developing a similar concept called the X-51 but allowed the program to die out in 2013.) In 2019, China claimed it had added the "Dongfeng-17" to its arsenal—a hypersonic glide vehicle, similar to what was ultimately part of the "Sputnik moment" test—mounted on a rocket so powerful that it was dubbed the "aircraft-carrier killer." Also debuting in 2019 was the WZ-8: an uncrewed spy plane with the potential to carry a nuclear warhead.

China wasn't the only adversary claiming these achievements. Vladimir Putin, generally more inclined to dramatics and hype than Xi Jinping, was attempting to convince the world that he had mastered the same technologies—and then some. In March 2018, during his rough equivalent of the State of the Union Address, Putin stood before a giant screen with animated images of a new class of what were dubbed his "superweapons." There was the "Avangard"—a revamped Soviet-era ballistic rocket with the Russian version of the hypersonic glide vehicle mounted on top—and the "Kinzhal," a shorter-range, air-launched hypersonic missile. Inside the White House, one of the Russian weapons that got the most attention was the Poseidon: an unmanned, nuclear-armed submarine designed to be undetectable.

There was reason to believe that Putin's presentation was part truth, part propaganda, and part rebranding. Clearly, not all of his missiles worked: In 2019, a year after Putin's bravado-filled presentation, a small nuclear reactor that appeared to be the power source for a new Russian cruise missile exploded. Seven Russians died, and Putin's aides did everything they could to cover up the accident. That didn't mean the end of the project, but it suggested that Putin was running into troubles.

But neither the Russian nor the Chinese developments, Lewis told me later, should be considered "amazingly innovative." Instead, he said, "everything we've ever seen come out of either of those countries are things that we've already thought about." But while the United States might still have the edge in innovation, that doesn't translate into fully developed and field-tested weapons in our arsenals.

By the time of the 2021 test, it was clear that America had lost its leading edge in hypersonic development. The question was by how much—and how much it directly impacted U.S. security. But there wasn't agreement in Washington on the nature of the threat, or how far behind in capabilities the United States truly was, or why America needed to match—or overmatch—every major foreign offensive capability. Plenty of people argued that the focus on developing offensive hypersonic capabilities in the United States was an expensive gimmick and that it would be a better use of resources and money to double down on hypersonic defenses. While the Pentagon asked Congress for $4.7 billion in 2023 for offensive hypersonic weapons, it sought only a twentieth of that amount for defenses. Still, nothing in that offensive budget line included the funding to actually start building and fielding the weapons, what is called a "program of record" in DOD-speak.

The alarmist view of the Chinese and Russian buildup was that America needed a crash program to match the progress being made by its adversaries. That was the essence of Milley's comparison to Sputnik: that this is a race we have to win, no matter the cost. But while that might have been possible in 1960, Sputnik moments looked different in the 2020s. There were so many technologies that the United States was competing for advantage in—hypersonics and space weapons, semiconductors and artificial intelligence, cyberdefenses and biodefenses—that you could have a Sputnik moment just about every month. And Washington simply wasn't prepared to sort out the vital from the merely important, and the technologies that America must have from those it could survive without.

THE PARTY INVITATION was promising. Hundreds of Washingtonians, from Biden administration officials to members of Congress, the military, and the press, were invited to the French Embassy on September 17, 2021, to join the country's naval chief in a celebration of the Battle of the Virginia Capes. "Service dress or cocktail attire," if you please.

The battle in question had taken place some 240 years before— when France helped the Colonies finish off the British to end the American Revolution. But the glittering party at the embassy—where fine champagnes flowed and the pastry chef was second to none—never happened.

Two days beforehand, Philippe Étienne, the highly connected French ambassador to the United States, awoke in his Kalorama mansion to front-page news that the United States and Britain were about to sign a deal to build nuclear submarines with Australia. After months of secret negotiations with the new Biden team, the Australians had made a critical strategic choice. China might be their biggest customer for raw materials, but the United States and its allies were the key to its security. The submarines would be the visible manifestation of a much deeper alliance: sophisticated, stealthy technology that could patrol from the South Pacific to the Chinese coast and pop up undetected.

The benefits were obvious. If the Australian submarines actually got built—using secret technology developed over five decades by the Americans and British to run deep and silent—Biden would leave a tangible, hard-power symbol of his pushback against China's territorial ambitions in Asia. Australia would be the first country to share in a propulsion technology program that the United States and Britain had kept to themselves since 1958.

The deal, dubbed "AUKUS," wasn't limited to submarines. A less-discussed pillar of the agreement included joint work on undersea autonomous vehicles, quantum computing, and the hypersonic delivery vehicles that China appeared to be making such progress in—and was estimated to be, in some measures, significantly ahead of the West in developing.

But as the negotiators moved between Canberra, Washington, and London in secrecy throughout the first half of 2021, they quickly concluded that Australia would first need to ditch a preexisting $60 billion agreement with France, which was under contract to supply Australia with a dozen comparatively noisy attack submarines over the next fifteen years. Those were based on an aging propulsion technology that would be limited in range, easy for the Chinese to find, and obsolete by the time the first submarines were put in the water. And not a single one had yet been delivered.

The problem was that, in a severe case of diplomatic avoidance, no one wanted to tell the French that they were being cast aside. Biden himself never mentioned it to President Macron when the two met a few months earlier for a chummy seaside chat in Cornwall on the British coast.

So when the news broke in September, the French, who basked in their description as America's oldest ally, were outraged. Jean-Yves Le Drian, the French foreign minister, called the move a "knife in the back." The chief of the French navy flew home, fuming, and an email went out pointedly telling invitees the party was off. The French recalled Étienne to Paris for several days. It took a public Biden apology to Macron the next month—"What we did was clumsy. It was not done with a lot of grace"—to begin to patch things up.

Diplomatic spats come and go; parties are rescheduled. But France's $60 billion contract, and its pride, were collateral damage in the brutal calculus involved in shifting America's focus to Asia. What the whole incident made clear was that in the struggle with China, there was a pecking order—and some nations, by dint of their technological prowess or geographical presence, were more critical than others.

"As much as the pivot has been described as pivoting to Asia without pivoting away from someplace else, that is just not possible," Richard Fontaine, who runs the Center for a New American Security, told me. "Military resources are finite. Doing more in one area means doing less in others."

. . .

THE DEAL WITH Australia mostly hit the headlines for the blowup with France, but Biden was beginning to bring about real change in the Pacific. Not even two weeks after the submarine announcement, Biden welcomed the prime ministers of Australia, India, and Japan to the White House for a meeting of the Quadrilateral Security Dialogue, dubbed the "Quad," that had re-formed in earnest in 2017 to counter the rising concerns about China in the region. It wasn't as formal as NATO or even the G20. Instead, it had been Biden who thought to turn the little-known grouping into a high-level leaders' summit with real teeth. Originally, Biden's aides told me, Prime Minister Narendra Modi had been the most difficult to persuade to join—he was hesitant to appear to be taking the West's side—yet within a year or so, he had become the most enthusiastic member. In fact, the Quad was a key part of what Blinken called the "new geometry" of geopolitics: figuring out ways to ally with more countries on issues of common interest.

Blinken's geometry had one main purpose: to box out China, and prevent it from attracting old American allies, or wavering Pacific nations, into its camp. The Americans called it bridge-building, and argued that it would bring both prosperity and deterrence to the Indo-Pacific. Not surprisingly, the Chinese saw it very differently. "The U.S. is hysterically polarizing its alliance system," the *Global Times,* Beijing's mouthpiece, declared. "Washington is losing its mind." Hyperbole aside, there was already a settling suspicion in both capitals that the United States and China were sinking into a "new cold war."

The White House hated the phrase, and it seized every opportunity to push back on it. It wasn't anything like the Cold War, Kurt Campbell had argued earlier that summer. During the Cold War, the Soviet Union was primarily a military threat. But China was emerging as a far broader potential strategic adversary: a technological threat, a military threat, an economic rival. The comparison, Campbell said, "obscures more than it illuminates" and is "in no way helpful, fundamentally, to some of the challenges presented by China."

In many respects, Campbell had a good point. Every so often over the past three decades, someone or other had used the "cold war" phraseology to describe the challenge du jour. Sometimes it made sense. Sometimes—like when George W. Bush used it in a 2002 conversation with reporters in the Oval Office to refer to America's fight with al-Qaeda—it didn't.

It was also true that the current standoff between the United States and China was fundamentally different at its core: The deep links between the two economies—the mutual dependencies on technology, trade, and information that leaps the Pacific in milliseconds on American- and Chinese-dominated networks—never existed in the old Cold War. The Berlin Wall not only delineated a sharp line between spheres of influence, freedom, and authoritarian control, it stopped most communications and trade. By contrast, in 2021, China was the largest supplier of goods to the United States and the third-largest consumer of its exports, after Canada and Mexico. That was a huge difference from the Cold War era, when, beyond caviar and vodka, the United States had no real interest in Soviet exports.

Perhaps worst of all, comparisons to the Cold War invited the danger of becoming a self-fulfilling prophecy: They encouraged the idea of a conflict with a definitive end and a unilateral victory for only one side. In an effort to diagnose the current moment, Hal Brands and John Lewis Gaddis wrote in the autumn of 2021 that "it's no longer debatable that the United States and China, tacit allies during the last half of the last Cold War, are entering their own new cold war: Chinese President Xi Jinping has declared it, and a rare bipartisan consensus in the United States has accepted the challenge."

Or as Joseph Nye, the Harvard strategist and the creator of the concept of "soft power" put it: "The fact that the Cold War metaphor is counterproductive as a strategy does not rule out a new Cold War. We may get there by accident."

THROUGHOUT 2021, as Biden was consumed by the withdrawal from Afghanistan, commercial satellite images began showing fields of what appeared to be new nuclear missile silos, freshly dug in the barren desert, some twelve hundred miles west of Beijing.

Of all the military developments in China that American officials had worried about over the previous few years—cruise missiles and satellite killers and threatening sorties around Taiwan—new nuclear weapons had not ranked among them. Mao Zedong had always taken a moral-high-ground pride in designing China's "minimum deterrent" strategy, which held that a few hundred nuclear weapons was all Beijing needed to deter an attack from larger powers. While the United States had briefly considered attacking China's nuclear test facilities in 1964 (perhaps with Soviet help), in the end it decided to learn to live with the Chinese Bomb. After all, even by the double standards of the West's nuclear calculus—in which Western powers with nuclear weapons are fine and everyone else a mortal threat—it seemed hard to complain about a few hundred Chinese nuclear weapons when the United States and Russia both maintained deployed arsenals five times larger, not including thousands more weapons that Washington and Moscow kept in storage.

But now, it seemed apparent, Chinese leaders had changed their minds. Xi was declaring that China must "establish a strong system of strategic deterrence." And satellite images from near the cities of Yumen and Hami showed that Xi was now ready to throw Mao's "minimum deterrent" strategy out the window.

No one was quite sure why. Maybe this had always been Xi's long-term plan, or maybe it was accelerated by Trump's insistence, in the last months of his presidency, that any renewed arms control treaty with Russia, for the first time, must include China as well. (The Chinese refused to play along.) Perhaps Xi was concerned that American missile defenses might improve, and he would need a larger force to overwhelm them. He may have been worried about India, whose own arsenal had been modernized.

Yet to produce that many weapons, China's leaders knew they also had to produce their own nuclear fuel. So they set upon a plan to build just that—starting with a new nuclear reactor, called a fast-breeder, which can produce the plutonium needed for hundreds of new atomic weapons. The fuel for the reactor, conveniently, came from Russia.

When Pentagon officials and intelligence analysts looked at this broad expansion of China's nuclear capabilities, they came to a few intriguing conclusions. First, the 230 silos under construction were built to be discovered, just like the hangers for military jets on the manufactured Chinese islands in the South China Sea. They existed to send a message. Second, they were just a start, part of a larger plan to match the American "triad" of land-launched, air-launched, and sea-launched weapons.

The Pentagon estimated that by 2030 China would have an arsenal of 1,000 strategic nuclear weapons. By 2035, they would move up to 1,500, essentially matching the Russians and Americans.* "The silo construction at Yumen and Hami constitutes the most significant expansion of the Chinese nuclear arsenal ever," wrote Matt Korda, a researcher from the Federation of American Scientists who first identified much of the earlier silo construction, and his colleague Hans M. Kristensen.

For a while, experts debated whether the Chinese would even fill all those silos—they might be establishing an elaborate shell game in which some were filled and others were empty. "Just because you build the silos doesn't mean you have to fill them all with missiles," said Vipin Narang, a Massachusetts Institute of Technology professor who specializes in nuclear strategy and who later joined the Biden administration. "They can move them around."

But the more that American officials dug into the construction sites, the more curious they became about them. One was sixty miles or so from one of the "re-education camps" where China detains Uyghurs, among other minority groups that have been the subject of brutal crackdown. Another was near one of the military bases where the People's Liberation Army was installing lasers designed to blind the optical sensors on American spy satellites.

No one knew what China planned to do with their revived nuclear complex, and it seemed possible no one would know for many years. But it was clear that even if the United States was descending into a very different kind of Cold War competition than the last, the era when Americans could regard nuclear competition as some artifact of the past was over. As Jake Sullivan, Biden's national security advisor, said later, the "cracks in our post–Cold War nuclear foundation are substantial." And fixing them would require America to update its old concepts of deterrence.

It was complicated enough during the Cold War era to defend against one major nuclear power. The message of the new silos was that now the United States would, for the first time in its history, have to think about defending in the future against two major nuclear powers

---

* They didn't indicate how they got to those estimates, and those numbers do not include short-range "tactical" nuclear weapons being deployed opposite Taiwan.

with arsenals roughly the size of Washington's—and be prepared for the possibility that they might decide to work together. General Milley, who got blunter and blunter as his term as chairman of the Joint Chiefs of Staff wore on, told Congress, "We are probably not going to be able to do anything to stop, slow down, disrupt, interdict, or destroy the Chinese nuclear development program that they have projected out over the next ten to twenty years."

He was right. The United States could not stop China's entry into the nuclear club in 1964, just as it could not stop it from becoming a nuclear-weapons peer to the United States and Russia six decades later.

In 2021 Biden, Milley, and the new White House national security team discovered that America's nuclear holiday was over. A new class of weapons would force a rethinking of American nuclear strategy. They were plunging into a new era that was far more complicated than the Cold War had ever been. The dynamic among three nuclear powers, they knew, was substantially more complicated than that between two. When the old Cold War standoff involved just the United States and the Soviet Union, the dark logic of mutually assured destruction prevented the worst; even at the most acrimonious moments of mutual hostility, no American or Soviet leader wanted to start down the road to a nuclear conflict if it risked the destruction of both nations. That was the essence of the famous Ronald Reagan and Mikhail Gorbachev declaration that "a nuclear war cannot be won and must never be fought," a line that the Biden administration encouraged all five of the declared nuclear weapons states to reaffirm about a year after he took office.

Yet with a third player in the mix, Biden and his advisors knew that the old rules of deterrence were about to go out the window. If China became a full-fledged nuclear power unrestrained by treaties or traditions, it would create conditions for all kinds of new nuclear instability, as the Pentagon itself soon noted when it published a new defense strategy.

There was every possibility of a slow burn to a new arms race. But in 2021 no one was thinking that one of the major nuclear powers might actually threaten to use its arsenal against a small neighbor that had no nuclear weapons of its own. It increasingly seemed that that was merely a failure of imagination.

CHAPTER 10

BLOWING SMOKE

I would never underestimate, in dealing with President Putin over the last couple of decades, his risk appetite with regard to Ukraine.

Bill Burns, director of the CIA, December 2021

IF THERE WAS one member of the Biden administration Vladimir Putin seemed to hate to her core, it was probably Victoria Nuland. Putin suspected her of plotting against Russian ambitions for the better part of twenty years.

While Putin was rising from the KGB to his first political posts in St. Petersburg in the 1990s, Nuland was already a young Foreign Service officer in Moscow, covering internal Russian politics for the U.S. embassy there. Over the next few decades, she pressed repeatedly for a more open and democratic Russia that would be a better partner for the United States—including during her time as the American ambassador to NATO, where she made the case for the Europeans and Russians to work together on missile defense systems aimed at Iran. In 2014, a call from Nuland to Geoffrey Pyatt, then the American ambassador to Kyiv, was secretly recorded by Russian intelligence and then released publicly in order to undercut her. It went viral for her most famous line, "Fuck the EU," as she pithily rejected the idea of waiting for the European Union to decide to help break the Ukraine impasse. No one knew for sure whether Putin was directly involved in the decision to make her call public, but it was widely assumed that he enjoyed embarrassing her.

In 2021, Nuland was back, serving in the Biden administration as the State Department's number three official. The symbolism of putting the government's chief Russia hawk in the job overseeing relations with Moscow was lost on no one. She was hardly the only American diplomat working the Russians in the summer of 2021, and the first encounters with the Russians after the Geneva summit seemed somewhat promising. Wendy Sherman, the experienced deputy secretary of state, had opened up what Washington called "strategic stability talks" that summer, setting up a series of working groups with the Russians that were supposed to explore longer-range questions. One explored what it would take to craft a new arms control agreement that would limit the size of American and Russian nuclear arsenals after the expiration of the New START treaty in February 2026. Another was supposed to think about how new technologies and the sudden expansion of China's nuclear arsenal might affect nuclear decision-making. Meanwhile, Anne Neuberger was holding a parallel set of talks about cracking down on ransomware actors.

In early October, it was Nuland's turn. She traveled to Moscow with Eric Green, Biden's senior director for Russia at the National Security Council, to see if there was anything of substance to build upon following the Geneva summit, particularly on the issue of resurrecting a peace deal between Russia and Ukraine. During the Geneva summit in June, Nuland recalled, Putin had rebuffed Biden's request for Putin to rejoin the much-maligned 2015 Minsk peace agreement negotiated by the Europeans. "You have all the influence in Ukraine," Nuland recalled Putin saying. "The European Union is feckless, and Minsk doesn't work." Putin claimed he had "tried" with Zelensky but hadn't gotten far.

Now, as Biden looked around for opportunities to restart the peace process in eastern Ukraine, it made the most sense to dispatch Nuland—not only for her fluency in Russian and blunt manner of speaking but also for her expertise at running a series of below-the-radar negotiations between Moscow and Kyiv during the Obama administration.

Nuland was the first to admit her transatlantic trip that fall was a failure. "I was trying to test if they were serious about recommitting to Minsk, and truly getting back to the 'stable and predictable' relationship," she said, "but I came back thinking it was a lot of razzamatazz."

First on her Moscow dance card that October was Sergei Ryabkov—the Russian deputy foreign minister, a preferred interlocutor for many American diplomats, partly because of his fluent English and his straightforward personality and partly because he wasn't his much-derided boss, Sergey Lavrov. But this time, Ryabkov completely iced her out, much to her disappointment. "I had known Ryabkov forever," said Nuland, "and this time he was very formal, very cold. And he had the deputy defense minister with him—a real refrigerator. It was useless."

Then she met with Dmitry Kozak—the deputy chief of staff for the Kremlin, dubbed the "Cheshire Cat" for his broad, completely unreadable smile. That session went even worse. "He was smoking cigarettes in my face," she recalled, mimicking how Kozak would take drags during the meeting. "I told him if he kept smoking it was going to ruin his beauty." He didn't let up.

Nuland left Moscow empty-handed but with no immediate sense of foreboding. As she landed back in Washington, D.C., she still had hope that the Biden administration, then barely nine months old, could achieve a working relationship with the Russians. Maybe not stable all the time. Maybe not predictable. But workable.

"But then they briefed us on the invasion plan," she recalled grimly.

BETWEEN THE GENEVA summit and Nuland's trip, during the protracted COVID summer of 2021, Vladimir Putin established a predicate for taking over all of Ukraine: a nearly seven-thousand-word manifesto entitled "On the Historical Unity of Russians and Ukrainians." At the time, no one was quite sure what it meant: To some, it looked like more venting from the Russian leader, but to others, it seemed like a road map for Putin's eventual move toward full-scale war with Ukraine.

In the article, published on the Kremlin's website in July, Putin expounded at length on an argument he had been making frequently during the previous seven years of undeclared war over Crimea and the Donbas: Ukraine was not an independent state. It existed solely due to historical injustices perpetrated during the Soviet era. Ukrainians and Russians were "a single whole"—and both were suffering from their prolonged separation by national borders. Putin chronicled his interpretation of twelve hundred years of Slavic history, winding the clock all the way back to the ninth century A.D. and the formation of "Kievan Rus"—the ancient empire to which both Russians and Ukrainians claim they are the natural successor state—to make the claim that the ongoing conflict in eastern Ukraine constituted "fratricide."

Today, Putin railed, the Ukrainian wannabe state was run by Nazis, who were forcing ethnic Russians "not only to deny their roots, generations of their ancestors, but also to believe that Russia is their enemy." It was a deadly path, he warned. "It would not be an exaggeration to say that the path of forced assimilation, the formation of an ethnically pure Ukrainian state, aggressive towards Russia, is comparable in its consequences to the use of weapons of mass destruction against us."

Ukraine didn't "need Donbas," Putin wrote, adding that the region could never accept Kyiv's mastery anyway. Still, he concluded, hedging a bit: "Russia has never been and will never be 'anti-Ukraine.' And what Ukraine will be—it is up to its citizens to decide."

The article was a reminder that in Putin's mind, reestablishing control over Ukraine was as central as regaining Taiwan was for China's leaders. "It has been said that, for Russia, losing Ukraine was like the United States losing Texas or California," wrote Condoleezza Rice back in 2011. "But that doesn't begin to capture it; it would be like losing the original thirteen colonies."

Biden's advisors knew that reacting publicly to Putin's rant wouldn't accomplish anything, other than to fuel more attention. Russian forces had retreated from Ukraine's borders back in April—and even if they had left much of their heavy equipment behind, leaving everyone distinctly uneasy, there was no evidence of imminent action.

That was the quiet message to Volodymyr Zelensky when he finally made it to Washington on September 1, 2021, after two years of waiting to visit the White House. There was no way he could step foot in the city amid the first impeachment of President Trump, which had hinged on evidence that Trump was holding up much-needed military aid to Ukraine in order to get Zelensky's government to dig up—indeed, make up—dirt about Biden and his son Hunter. Then came the pandemic.

Now Trump was gone and Zelensky finally made his long-awaited pilgrimage to the Oval Office. He had never met Biden before, but he wanted more than a photo op sitting next to the president in front of the fireplace. He wanted NATO membership—or, at least, a close partner-ship. He wanted the United States to help revive the potential for a new political settlement in the Donbas. And he wanted more defensive lethal weapons, starting with Javelin anti-tank missiles. It was, he acknowl-edged publicly, "a very big agenda for our relations, maybe not for this meeting, which is too short to answer all the questions."

In Washington, visits like Zelensky's are usually choreographed to make sure the visiting leader leaves with something to boast about back home—and this was no exception. Biden announced another $60 mil-lion in aid to Ukraine—including the Javelin anti-tank missiles that Ukraine had long sought. And he verbally backed Zelensky: "In the 21st century, nations cannot be allowed to redraw borders by force. Rus-sia violated this ground rule in Ukraine," a joint statement from the two men declared, adding that "the United States does not and will never recognize Russia's purported annexation of Crimea."

But it seemed that Zelensky was worried about something deeper than continued skirmishing in the east. A week after he left Washington, he was asked whether full-scale war with Moscow was possible. He said he thought it was—but that it would end in disaster. "All-out war would be the biggest blunder on Russia's part," he was quoted in *The Indepen-dent.* "It's a spooky scenario but unfortunately it isn't unlikely. The dan-ger is reaching a point of no return."

There is no evidence Zelensky had any special knowledge of what was coming, but around this same time, intelligence specialists at the Pentagon who answered to the chairman of the Joint Chiefs of Staff were examining a new exercise that the Russians had just launched. And they began to see something very ominous.

GENERAL MARK MILLEY entered the U.S. Army at a time when the brass focused more on countering terrorism and rogue states than superpow-ers. A special forces operative, he had started in Georgia, serving tours in Somalia, Panama, Egypt, Haiti, South Korea, Afghanistan, and Iraq, among others.

When we spoke toward the end of his tenure, it was from the dining room in Quarters Six—the designated residence of the chairman of the Joint Chiefs that sits atop a bluff on the Virginia side of the Potomac, in the middle of a secluded block of perfectly preserved Victorians built at the end of the Spanish-American War.

The very fact that Milley was still living there as President Joe Biden was beginning to rethink how to confront China and Russia was something of a miracle. Milley had been appointed the most senior military official in the country by Donald Trump, who had been entranced by Milley's central-casting top-brass looks along with his chest full of medals. But Milley had no appetite for bullshit, and so the two men were bound for conflict. Trump turned on him, as he did with most of his senior commanders, in 2020—angry that Milley had publicly apologized for following Trump across Lafayette Square during the protests over George Floyd's murder in Minneapolis.

Trump openly talked about firing him. In the last days of the Trump administration, *The Washington Post*'s Bob Woodward and Robert Costa later reported, Milley was on the phone to the Chinese, trying to calm them down in the wake of January 6. They wanted to know if the United States government was stable—or if American democracy was about to collapse. Eventually, Trump got on his helicopter and left Washington. Milley remained at Quarters Six.

To Biden's team, Milley was a grumpy hero of sorts, a strange mix of tough-talking Boston and scholarly Princeton, with a tendency to pontificate at length during Situation Room meetings. At sixty-four, he was old enough to be the father of many of Biden's national security aides. While he was often the in-house pessimist—you can't be in the Army for four decades without seeing a lot of things go wrong—he was in judgment, if not demeanor, quite well attuned to the vibe of the Biden national security team.

Milley was a student of history, maybe to a fault, and was entirely capable of offering up half-hour lectures at the dining table about Thucydides or how the slow pace of reloading muskets changed the nature of the American Revolution. But he was also a highly experienced consumer of American intelligence, which is why he paid attention when a handful of Joint Staff intelligence officers showed up in his Pentagon office in September 2021 with a topographical map of Ukraine and a startling analysis of what was going on along its border with Russia.

The officers, all from the Defense Department's intelligence directorate, within the Defense Intelligence Agency, had been tracking a planned military exercise that was being conducted by Russian and Belarusian soldiers just beyond the borders of Ukraine. The exercise itself wasn't so unusual; the Russians had held similar demonstrations of power in the post–World War II era. But this one looked different.

"They showed me the pattern analysis and all that, and we went through it in excruciating, micro, tactical detail," Milley told me later. Milley was increasingly of the mind that the troop movements were no exercise.

The first problem, he said, was simply "mass." There were far too many people for a training exercise. The Russians said there would be two hundred thousand participants; even if that number wasn't fully accurate, it still looked *very* big. As he told me later, "One of the things at this level we always look at is things like logistics, medical, blood supplies, hospitals, that kind of thing. And then, the more ammunition, the more it's going to be real."

Looking at the pieces in front of him, Milley's staff quickly suspected a full invasion might be in the offing. Milley himself wasn't "absolutely convinced" by what he saw, he told me later. But, he said, "these are probabilities. We're dealing with probabilities and confidence levels. Something more likely than not."

He found the maneuvers worrisome enough to take the analysis to Secretary of Defense Lloyd Austin, CIA Director Burns, and Director of National Intelligence Avril Haines. They and the other heads of America's spy agencies were watching the Russian buildup, relying on their own sources and generating their own analysis. It was, they agreed, deeply troublesome.

But from September into early October, there was no agreement on the broader implications of what they were seeing. Putin, many of the analysts thought, certainly had the *capability* to take the entire country. But did he have the *intent*? Occupying the country would be a nightmare, thought many of those who knew Ukraine best. The resistance put up by the Ukrainians would turn into a bloody melee, many of the analysts predicted. "They should look at what happened to us in Iraq," one said to me that fall.

And there was always the possibility that the troop movements were part of a giant bluff—what they called "coercive diplomacy," undertaken to exact concessions. While the intelligence agencies could tap into conversations among the Russian military and political leadership, understanding the true intent of the buildup meant crawling into Putin's brain—territory off-limits even to America's best spies.

When Toria Nuland departed for Russia in the second week of October, analysts were still split on Putin's intentions. But by the third week of October, several Biden officials agreed, the accumulating evidence had become overwhelming. It all added up to the "mother lode" of intelligence, as one of the officials briefed around that time described it: Putin, they increasingly believed, finally thought the stars were aligning for him. He was getting ready to pull the trigger.

WHEN JAKE SULLIVAN was first briefed about the growing pattern of intelligence that suggested Putin was seriously contemplating a major military invasion of Ukraine, he wasn't sure he believed what he was reading. The analysis from Milley's colonels had been fed into the river of data flowing from the borders of Ukraine and from Moscow. It was combined with information from other intelligence agencies, including the NSA's most sensitive signals intercepts from Russian troops and officials, who were remarkably sloppy about their phone calls. There were intercepted texts. There was information from the CIA's fragile network of human spies. And of course there was "overhead," the satellite imagery of troop movements. It all painted a picture of a Russian military once again on the move.

Even today, officials remain cagey when talking about the steady accumulation of intelligence that emerged from mid-September through the fall. They were particularly circumspect, understandably, about how much of the "mother lode" contained revelations snatched from the inner circle around Putin: the key to understanding his intent. But the fact of the information deriving from a vast array of sources provided some reassurance inside the intelligence community that it was unlikely they were being fed deliberate disinformation—or leaping to a worst-case conclusion.

What emerged was an intelligence picture rich in detail about every dimension of Russian plans to move into Ukraine—not just into territories in the south and east but the entire country. Intercepted conversations and other intelligence indicated that Moscow would call up 100 to 150 Russian battalions—tens of thousands of troops—to post on the Ukrainian border. There was chatter about a squeeze move on the capital, Kyiv. And there was, in the words of one leader, "a fairly precise plan" for toppling the Zelensky government and "installing a sort of puppet Russian government."

Once the invasion was a fait accompli, the intelligence indicated that the Russians were discussing another force that they planned to keep in reserve: some hundred thousand troops—all akin to National Guard troops—that would be sent in after Kyiv fell to form an occupying force. Its role would be to control the newly conquered territories, hunt down and eliminate dissenters, and control every aspect of daily life. This struck White House officials as a critical piece of evidence. As one top-ranking NSC official put it to me, "You don't make a new military force just for an exercise."

Given the urgency of the issue, Sullivan immediately arranged for a full briefing for Biden. But it took Sullivan some time to wrap his own mind around the idea that Putin would risk Russia's oil and gas exports— and his standing in the world—in a vain effort to turn his long-winded article about Russia and Ukraine's shared future into an active battle plan. Sure, Putin would talk about the need to expand Russia and rebuild its rightful empire, but who would risk the first full-scale land war in Europe in nearly eight decades to satisfy their ego?

The intelligence officials who briefed him, Sullivan later told me, displayed no doubt in their analysis. "The minute they started seeing indicators in October, they're absolutely done," he said. "I probably took, I don't know, another week." It wasn't that he didn't believe it, he told me. "I was just trying to exclude every other possibility."

It didn't take long to come up with a new strategy, part of which would play out in secret, part in public. Stopping Putin was a long shot, and Biden's team knew it. But even if the plan to deter Putin didn't work, the hope was that there would be other benefits, most importantly a united West that had time to figure out its response.

. . .

THE FIRST EFFORT to derail the invasion—the secret one that had begun by deploying Bill Burns to Moscow in the opening days of November—focused on warning Putin that the cost of the invasion would be far higher than the Russian president thought.

Burns had prepared for the conversation by asking for everything his analysts could work up on how Putin's thinking about Ukraine had evolved in the dozen or so years since the CIA chief had departed from his job as ambassador to Moscow. The conclusions were no surprise. During COVID, Burns became convinced, Putin had become even more isolated than usual. His circle of advisors had shrunk. "I think he kind of stewed on this over the last couple of years," Burns told me, "and just became convinced that this was the moment."

When Burns was finally connected to Putin by phone from Moscow, the former KGB agent was typically hard to read and impassive to a fault. There were no rants from the Russian leader about American plots to destabilize him or wild theories about America putting nuclear or biological weapons near Russia's borders. "I found President Putin in the hour or so I spoke with him to be quite measured," Burns told me a few weeks after the encounter, when I saw him in his seventh-floor office at the CIA, "but unapologetic about Russian concerns about Ukraine, most of which are very familiar."

Putin had assembled, he recalled, a list of grievances about Ukraine that cast Russia—and Putin himself—as the victim. "He was almost convincing himself," Burns told me later. Putin was making the argument that he had "really no alternative here. 'Americans are trying to keep us down.'" Burns's job was to make it clear that an invasion of Ukraine would be catastrophic for Russia—and that the United States and its allies would push back, hard. "I conveyed not only that serious concern but also, on the president's behalf, a message of serious consequences that would flow from a Russian decision to renew military aggression against Ukraine." That included, he said, "taking high-impact economic steps that we had refrained from taking in the past," steps that would undercut Russia's ability to emerge from the COVID downturn.

Burns wasn't sure he got through to Putin, who, he feared, was likely discounting the odds that he would truly be made to pay a price for an invasion. "He thought that the West in general, not just the United States but the Europeans, were risk-averse and distracted."

As the conversation ended, Burns departed with low expectations. He composed a long memo to Biden and his advisors—highly classified but described by one who read it as "almost lyrical"—dissecting how decades of grievances and frustrated ambitions had brought Putin to this moment and how dismissive Putin seemed of the idea that the West would mount a serious, sustained defense of Ukraine.

"I left with the impression that President Putin hadn't, at that point in early November of 2021, yet made up his mind about what he was going to do in Ukraine, but he was tempted to resort to a use of force," Burns told me. "He certainly wanted to put the Russian military and security services in a position where if he made a decision to use force they could act quickly."

SENDING THE CIA director to Moscow to confront Putin directly was intended to rattle the Russian leader and make him think twice. But Biden and his team were well aware that it wasn't likely, by itself, to derail an invasion. So what came next was a full-court press to warn the European allies—and the Ukrainians themselves—of what Russia was planning, in an effort to muster the kind of united resolve that might make Putin reconsider. At the very least, it would allow NATO to start making plans and give the Ukrainians time to prepare.

At the COP26 climate summit in Glasgow—held while Burns was in Moscow, talking to Putin directly—Blinken sat President Zelensky down on the sidelines to lay out the details for him. Avril Haines, Bill Burns, and Mark Milley took the message to NATO. Kurt Campbell even took the evidence to the Chinese, urging them to weigh in with Putin.

But soon, Sullivan and Blinken began reporting back, with no small astonishment in their voices, that most of the leaders and officials they briefed—Zelensky included—simply did not believe the American analysis that Putin was getting ready to invade. European leaders drew comparisons to the torqued intelligence around Iraq in 2003. Others suggested that Putin was engaged in a bluff to improve his negotiating position.

What exacerbated the situation, they said, was that Putin clearly wasn't telling some of his own officials what he was planning. The result was that just about every time that the Americans warned the Europeans, the Europeans would ask their Russian contacts, who would in turn give flat—often sincere—denials. "You know, it was kind of a lonely position at the time," Burns said afterward, "because other than the Brits, most every other intelligence service thought this was all about him trying to build pressure and that he was then going to extract something and back down."

So back in the United States, Biden officials began a very public effort to expose Putin's plans before he could execute them—to get ahead of the torrent of lies, disinformation, and accusations that they knew, from bitter experience, would be cooked up to justify the invasion.

The effort began, Sullivan recalled, with a conversation with Jon Finer, his chief deputy. A former *Washington Post* foreign correspondent, Finer had left journalism and shot up through the ranks of the State Department during the Obama administration. The analogy that came to Sullivan's mind as he sought to characterize the moment they were facing did not exactly come out of the pages of *Foreign Affairs* magazine. "You know that scene in *Austin Powers,* where there's the steamroller on the far side of the room?" Sullivan recalled saying to Finer. "And there's a guy who's standing there, and they zoom in on the steamroller, and then they show the guy, and the guy's like 'Noooo!' like he's about to get run over by the steamroller. And then they zoom out, and the steamroller is, like, a hundred yards away, and moving, like, an inch an hour. But he's just standing there, frozen, like, 'Noooo!'

"I said to Finer, 'This is us.' Like, we're watching this unfold. And I don't want to be that guy who's just standing there, shouting. We've got to *do* something."

Sullivan's desire not to be flattened by the slow-motion steamroller had its roots in what had happened during the Obama administration in 2014. When Putin first moved to annex Crimea, there had been little warning, and Sullivan knew that the slow reaction hurt the allies and assured that Putin's move would be a fait accompli. "We had been caught flat-footed in Crimea," he said, "and that came at some cost to our ability to mobilize an effective response" and "to shape the information narrative about who was responsible, what exactly had happened, why it had happened."

Sullivan was determined not to let that happen again. And to his mind, there was only one real way to accomplish the goal: Tell the world, in advance, exactly what Russia was planning by making public the American intelligence findings. The evidence to him was clear. It spoke for itself. It was just a matter of getting it into the public eye.

Even if the revelations failed to deter Putin, Sullivan figured there were three things to be gained. "First," he recalled, it "denies Russia pretext. They are doing this by choice. It's not because it's a provocation. Second, it denies Russian surprise. And third, it gives us the time to aggressively work over our allies and partners on a swift and united response—in advance—that we put together. And so the backbone of that entire effort was publicly narrating the plan for it, the plan for war."

What Sullivan was proposing to do was to take a super-classified set of details and, after sanitizing it to hide sources and methods, package it in such a way that it could first be shared privately with allies but also with America's fiercest opponents, including China. They knew the information would immediately be funneled to the Kremlin. And then, afterward, they would try to get it splashed on the front pages and home pages of the world's most influential news organizations.

AMERICA'S EIGHTEEN INTELLIGENCE agencies—and their allied counterparts around the world—have an aversion to publicity that has only gotten worse in the wake of a series of embarrassing and highly unauthorized disclosures over the past fifteen years. First came Wikileaks, in 2010, disclosing thousands of State Department cables sent from diplomats around the world to their leadership, along with a smattering of military communications and videos from Iraq. Then came Edward Snowden, who in 2013 revealed scores of highly secret NSA projects, which Snowden said he was convinced violated the privacy rights of Americans. In truth, the most interesting parts of the Snowden leaks described intelligence operations against China and other targets, the kind of surveillance that American officials publicly decry when it is done to us. Then came the 2017 leak of some of the tools used to design offensive cyberweapons. It wasn't long before those leaked tools got put to use by the North Koreans and the Russians against the West.

So when the word began to circulate that Biden, pressed by Sullivan and Blinken, had decided to make public the findings about Putin's plans, it shocked some of the intelligence operatives and analysts who had spent years trying to lock down America's secrets. They came to work each day trying to steal Russia's secrets, analyze them, and funnel the best of their conclusions into the "Presidential Daily Brief." For many of them, getting their work into the PDB, as it's called, is the reporter's equivalent of breaking a front-page story. But the whole idea that those secrets would now appear deliberately on those front pages seemed anathema. Why tell Putin how plugged in you are to his military's every move—and risk blowing future access?

"I think that's a culture that we have here in our agency, that we protect our secrets," General Paul Nakasone, the director of the National Security Agency, said when I visited him at the new operations center he opened about ten months into the war. "I know that there was tension here." Still, Nakasone said, there wasn't nearly as much backlash as some individuals who worked closely with the NSA—and to some extent, the CIA—had feared. What's more, the experience brought about a shift, Nakasone told me later, in how the intelligence community now views its own role in national defense.

For decades intelligence collectors thought they had one job: Steal or gather secrets and hand them off to the president or other officials to give them an advantage. Secrecy was baked into the cake. Now they were being told that secretly collected information might be most useful if it is made public. It was a huge shift.

"What," Nakasone asked me rhetorically, "are the cultural implications of a place like NSA releasing information like that? You can imagine that there are people who have spent their livelihood collecting this information." This was the first time they were being asked—actually, ordered—to release it publicly.

Ultimately, the debate that broke out behind closed doors in Washington in the late fall of 2021 was not whether the Biden administration should share the information—once the president weighed in, that was decided—but how. Clearly the Russians would quickly figure out that the United States and its "Five Eyes" allies—the English-speaking victors of World War II—were plugged into their military communications. The goal was to figure out how to release enough details to convince the global public of Putin's intentions without revealing so much that intelligence sources dried up or were exposed.

By the last months of 2021, Sullivan and his aides had come up with a plan for a series of "authorized" leaks. They realized that trying to release the information without a centralized declassification process wasn't feasible—there were too many ideas for what information should be declassified, and the intelligence community needed to understand what information the policy community wanted to release to ensure the protection of sources and methods. Eventually, the White House settled into a rhythm: The National Security Council, led by the senior director for intelligence, Maher Bitar, would draft a script of what the administration wanted to share. Then they would send that message to Avril Haines's team at the Office of the Director of National Intelligence, which would shoulder the responsibility for coordinating with the rest of the intelligence community to confirm what could be shared and what was simply too dangerous to reveal. Then they'd send a revised version of the script back to the NSC. Often, it was possible to share information by "downgrading" the level of classification, or "sanitizing" the information by stripping out any details that could point back to a source.

Their process may have been unique, but the Biden White House was hardly the first presidential administration to use the technique in a general way—authorized leaking goes back to George Washington. Recent history, however, had turned journalists, myself included, into skeptics. Reporters had all been burned before, to greater or lesser degrees, when George W. Bush was building a case for going to war in Iraq. Too much was taken on faith by too many. And the lesson that emerged from the Bush experience was that it was easy to cherry-pick evidence, declassify intelligence that served your purpose, and keep counternarratives secret.

So this time, as the administration made their rounds of authorized leaks, several news organizations pushed back. Reminding the Biden officials of the Iraq experience, I and others told them we were not going to publish claims merely on their say-so.* Soon I found myself in after-hours phone conversations with a series of top intelligence officials, as they tried to make me and others comfortable with how they had reached their findings. "Look, we're not the Bush administration, and we're not making this up," one of Biden's top aides said to me with some exasperation one evening. "They were trying to invade a country; we're trying to prevent an invasion." It was a reasonable argument. But if we took the government's conclusions and threw them into print without doing our own due diligence, I said, we would be failing at our basic journalistic responsibility.

Eventually the administration and the press found a middle ground. When the intelligence dealt with something easily confirmable—say, Russian troop positions on the border—they suggested geo-coordinates and the media confirmed them with publicly available commercial satellite imagery. In other cases, we were referred to NATO allies, some of whom had developed separate intelligence themselves. And of course reporters used social media to track what Russian soldiers, massed along the Ukrainian border, were saying in their down time. But other elements of the leaks were trickier: How exactly was the press supposed to confirm what inner members of Putin's circle were relaying to each other in private conversations? And what about the British allegation that the Russians had already identified Ukrainians-in-exile who would be placed into top government jobs as soon as the Russians won, to form a government that would bend to Moscow's commands?

The first release of "downgraded" information happened in December, with a leak to *The Washington Post* with evidence that the Russians were beginning to build up 175,000 troops and planning to surround Ukraine on three sides. The accompanying map displayed commercial satellite imagery of troop formations and weapons pegged to their locations in Russia and Belarus.

This was one in a series that would emerge across different media outlets. Another in January warned of a false flag attack by the Russian Army that would target their own proxy forces in eastern Ukraine—and then pin it on the Ukrainians. And in early February, there was, as Sul-

---

* *The New York Times*, for example, did not publish the details of the "Steele Dossier" about Donald Trump, because we could not verify the conclusions.

livan later recalled it, a "fairly colorful plan" to stage a video displaying corpses to make the case that Zelensky and his "Nazi" regime were slaughtering defenseless ethnically Russian civilians.

On that one, Sullivan admitted, "We had a debate about that level of specificity . . . because the minute we said it, they [the Russians] weren't going to do it" anymore. The alternative—saying nothing—was no better, of course. The lie would be beamed around the world, and the image of the corpses, however fictional, would stick. The American countercharge, that the Russians had made it all up, would never catch up with the original lie. Sullivan feared that the United States would find itself chasing these stories with barely heard denials, the way it did in 2016, during the presidential election campaign—when Sullivan was working for candidate Hillary Clinton.

It was a vexing choice. Say something and the operation will be scratched, making it look like your intelligence was wrong. Don't say something and pay the price. It was the political equivalent of the "Heisenberg Uncertainty Principle," Sullivan mused, a reference to the scientific paradox that you can never truly measure both the position and velocity of an atomic particle, because the process of measuring one attribute changes the other.

As the early weeks of 2022 passed, the debate between those who believed the American and British intelligence interpretation and those who didn't only hardened. President Zelensky, frustrated, told the Americans to stop fomenting panic, a position that later looked ridiculous. Biden officials later said that they believed that Foreign Minister Lavrov, who was regularly appearing in front of cameras accusing the United States of making up a story, was never even told about Putin's true intentions. But the military chief, Sergei Shoigu, clearly would have to know, along with Valery Gerasimov, the Russian equivalent to the chairman of the Joint Chiefs. Alexander Bortnikov, the head of the Russian intelligence service, would almost certainly be read in.

So the Americans began calling them. It quickly became an exercise in futility. Gerasimov, Milley said, lied about the invasion plans. "Of course he knew. He was the general planning it," Milley told me without any hesitation. "I even said, 'This is gonna be the largest conflict on the European continent since World War II. This is not necessary. Don't do this. This is stupid.' I think I said words to the effect of, 'You're gonna get in in fourteen days, but you're not gonna get out for fourteen years, and you're gonna have body bags streaming back to Moscow the entire time.'"

ON DECEMBER 17, Putin issued eight public demands to NATO and the United States that were so drastic that it was immediately obvious that Washington and its European partners could never agree to them. When the demands landed at the State Department, Blinken and the two diplomats who dealt most directly with the Russians—Wendy Sherman and Toria Nuland—took a few hours to read and digest them. Most of them were "nonstarters," Nuland later told me. (That omits a few of her more colorful adjectives.)

The demands—phrased by the Russians, rather generously, as "security guarantees"—made clear that if the West wanted to avoid the biggest conflict in Europe since the end of World War II, they had to roll back the clock nearly twenty-five years, to 1997. Putin was demanding in non-negotiable terms that NATO pull back any Western-supplied arms, all NATO forces, and all nuclear weapons from former Soviet states that were now NATO members.* The West had to promise that Ukraine and Georgia would never join the NATO alliance. And they had to recognize a sphere of influence for Russia in the region— something along the lines of the 1823 Monroe Doctrine, in which the United States claimed a separate sphere of influence over the Americas.

A few days later, Putin doubled down, threatening "retaliatory military-technical measures" if the United States did not agree to the whole list. And when a British reporter asked Putin in a rare open press conference whether he would promise to not invade Ukraine, the Russian president was adamant: "It was the United States that came with its missiles to our home, to the doorstep of our home. And you demand from me some guarantees. You should give us guarantees. You! And right away, right now."

Putin did take a moment to soften his remarks, saying the United States had displayed somewhat of a "positive reaction" by agreeing to

---

* There were no nuclear weapons based in those states, American officials told me, but Putin didn't believe that.

hold direct talks in Geneva in early January. He seemed to be opening the door to diplomacy—but, he made it clear, he would only talk to the Americans, not the Ukrainians. It had the faint whiff of a century ago, of the conferences that concluded World War I and II, when great powers decided the fates of lesser ones.

But with war on the horizon, there was little choice but to engage. A few weeks later Sherman met in Geneva with her Russian counterpart, Ryabkov. Then Blinken met with Lavrov. The NATO-Russia Council, the body founded at the 2002 Rome Summit as a conciliatory measure to make Russia feel more involved in NATO decisions in Eastern Europe, convened. And when French president Emmanuel Macron suggested that Putin and Biden meet directly, Biden said he was willing—but only if the Russians promised not to invade.

There didn't seem to be much cause for optimism. The Russians complained that the Americans weren't taking their security demands seriously. The Americans feared, as Burns had warned, that Putin didn't believe how strongly the West would retaliate if Russia invaded Ukraine.

Biden himself sent some mixed messages. "I think what you're going to see is that Russia will be held accountable if it invades," he told us at a White House press conference. Then he stepped in it: "And it depends on what it does. It's one thing if it's a minor incursion and then we end up having a fight about what to do and not do." Suddenly Washington was debating what constituted a "minor incursion" and what was cause for war.

On one issue, though, Biden was consistent. When asked whether American troops would themselves go to Ukraine's aid, Biden made it clear that that option was entirely off the table. That was the pathway, he feared, to World War III.

IN THE END, of course, nothing that the Biden administration did—not the direct diplomatic pressure, not the downgrading and sharing of intelligence, not the stark threats of the economic and political costs he would face—would keep Putin from invading Ukraine.

Sure, it had slowed him down, many Biden officials had argued, and forced him to reconfigure his plan. It had prevented him from seizing the narrative to demonize Ukraine: forcing him to deny what he ultimately did, which exposed him as a liar. And it had enabled the military forces of the Western allies to brace for the worst: to assemble sanctions packages, to prepare to ship arms, and, perhaps most transformatively, to work with Germany to reach an agreement to block Nord Stream 2 two days before the invasion started. As one of Biden's top aides later told me, even if the allies didn't believe the American intelligence that Russia would invade, "they humored us by getting prepared."

Ultimately, it was possible that nothing would have stopped Putin's expansionist campaign. While a handful of American scholars joined Putin's argument that the United States and NATO were to blame by creating an intolerable security environment for Putin, others argued that it was Putin's own ego that made the violence inevitable. "What I think occurred," one prominent Western security official said to me, "is that Putin's goal coming out of the pandemic was to cement his power and legacy and to reclaim the past for Russia. It's a tsarist mentality." Throughout January, the official said, even at the height of the diplomatic outreach efforts, no one thought the Russians were serious about negotiating. "Putin already knew what was going to happen," the official added, and eventually the rest of Russian leadership started to figure it out, too.

Then the official hesitated. During a private diplomatic session held in early 2022, a Russian official had spoken unusually candidly. Putin, that official said, had gathered the Russian Foreign Ministry together and said that there had to be a treaty on stopping the expansion of NATO. Or else. There was no alternative. The United States and NATO, the Russian official warned, were now seen as outright enemies. And for the first time, he didn't know if the world would get out of this without a war.

CHAPTER 11

A PARTNERSHIP
"WITHOUT LIMITS"?

The partnership is real. . . . I don't know if it's an alliance yet, but the world is in a very different place.

Wendy Sherman, deputy secretary of state, September 2022

I do not believe this is a "marriage of convenience." It's a coalition of the aggrieved . . . [and] a profound strategic step that poses a real risk to the West.

Kurt Campbell, National Security Council coordinator for the Indo-Pacific, May 2023

IT WASN'T JUST the Europeans who thought the United States was hyping the evidence that Russia was preparing to go to war. The Chinese thought so too, American intelligence agencies concluded. So when a mask-clad Xi Jinping strode into the Bird's Nest—the nickname for the Beijing National Stadium—to open the 2022 Winter Olympics, his primary concern was keeping the world calm for the duration of the games.

It was early February, and he began by offering the usual platitudes about peace, the spirit of the games, and fair competition. But just hours before the opening ceremony, he and Vladimir Putin met at the Diaoyutai State Guesthouse, the graceful diplomatic complex built on the site of a long-ago emperor's favorite fishing spot, to fire the starting gun for a far more consequential contest.

It had been more than two years since the two autocrats had last met, each isolated during the worst of the pandemic. Putin had not traveled outside the country. Now they saw a chance to come together, at least performatively, in what one of Biden's aides described to me as a demonstration of the power of the "Axis of Resistance."

Forgoing the usual handshake—a COVID precaution—the two men paused to pose for the cameras before disappearing into the back to hammer out the details of a new relationship between the two countries that seemed to have one driving motivation: standing up to the United States.

The two dictators said almost nothing in public. But later that night, they released a five-thousand-word document that suggested the two longtime rivals were forming a true alliance—overcoming years of mutual suspicion and, at moments, armed conflict.

This paragraph toward the end of the statement was striking:

> The sides call for the establishment of a new kind of relationships [*sic*] between world powers on the basis of mutual respect, peaceful coexistence and mutually beneficial cooperation. . . . *Friendship between the two States has no limits,* there are no "forbidden" areas of cooperation, strengthening of bilateral strategic cooperation is neither aimed against third countries nor affected by the changing international environment and circumstantial changes in third countries.

The declaration did not come out of nowhere. A 2001 treaty between Putin and Chinese leader Jiang Zemin had proclaimed their mutual "hope of promoting and establishing a just and fair new world order." A 2004 joint statement declared that "China-Russia relations have reached an unprecedented high level."

But this time, it was clear that this declaration was something more than diplomatic rhetoric as usual. The two men, from radically different backgrounds—one a spy, the other the son of a famous party cadre—had spent years investing in each other. In 2013, during a short visit to Moscow—his first as China's president—Xi had assured reporters that the two were "good friends." In 2014, after the annexation of Crimea, the Chinese had defied the call for sanctions and signed three dozen deals with Russia. (Xi did not, however, recognize the annexation.) And in

2015, during the seventieth-anniversary celebrations of the end of World War II, Xi was there in Moscow with a contingent of Chinese soldiers. By 2018, Xi was calling Putin his "best, most intimate friend." The two flipped Russian pancakes stuffed with caviar in front of the cameras. The next year, Putin threw Xi a birthday party, complete with a cake and champagne. Trade between the two countries jumped. And while China was making a point of refusing to become a party to any military bloc, the two signed dozens of bilateral agreements, and their militaries conducted joint exercises at a pace that picked up sharply after 2015.

In the United States and Europe, there was almost no public awareness of this burgeoning bromance. But intelligence officials had been picking it apart, trying to understand what was real and what was bravado in the nearly forty meetings between the two men.

This time, though, the "no limits" declaration—coming at the very moment that war seemed imminent—set off alarm bells: If Russia invaded Ukraine, would China back them with arms, ammunition, and political clout? White House officials feared that if China truly threw its weight into the war, it would be game over.

But there was also significant risk for Xi and China, particularly given their regular mantra upholding the importance of territorial integrity, which remains their core argument for why Taiwan belongs to them. Tellingly, while Russia had reiterated its support in the declaration for the One China policy and emphasized that Taiwan's government was illegitimate, China had said nothing about Ukraine in the joint statement.

As soon as the meeting ended, American intelligence officials went into overdrive to figure out what Putin had said to Xi about his plans to take Ukraine. For weeks, when I asked intelligence officials what they had concluded, I got a range of answers. Eventually, they converged on a single assessment: Putin had talked about it but not in any great detail. It appeared as if Putin had described his invasion plans to Xi vaguely, characterizing them as a limited operation that would be concluded quickly—an internal matter, nothing for Xi to trouble himself about. Perhaps that was what Putin believed. Xi had just one request: He asked Putin to hold off while the Olympics were still under way. The Olympics had been years in the planning, and the Chinese leader wanted no distractions from China's moment in the sun.

Yet that didn't answer the fundamental question, whether the five thousand words of anti-Western rhetoric presaged a new era. A new China-Russia condominium had the potential to be the most consequential change in the geopolitical landscape in decades. If it succeeded—even if it was only a partial success—it would create an alternative axis of power unlike any that existed in the Cold War. During those years, of course, China had been a bit player, with little choice but to bend to Moscow's wishes. Now, it would be the dominant power in the relationship, whatever form it took.

The predominant view in Washington in early 2022 was that at best it would be an uneasy partnership. "They have every reason to sleep together and none to move in together," one senior administration official told me. "The Russians," another noted, "have no interest in being subservient to the Chinese."

The leadership of the intelligence agencies seemed to take the risk more seriously. "It's a strong partnership," Bill Burns told me later, choosing his words carefully, "that is born of a shared interest in chipping away at an American-led international order. I think it's also born of a strong personal bond between President Putin and President Xi."

Yet over time, Burns predicted, the partnership would run into its own challenges, as the two countries' competing political and economic interests collided. "It's always good to start with history, and that we'd never underestimate the depths historically of mistrust between the Chinese and the Russians. That mistrust still hasn't gone away. . . . Russians are going to chafe at being China's junior partner."

Still, he warned, it would be dangerous to discount the relationship, which represented "an increasingly important partnership for both of them—a willingness to do things in terms of military cooperation that fifteen years ago they weren't willing to do."

WASHINGTON CAME SLOWLY to the idea that the Chinese and the Russians could form a true alliance—mostly because, for so many decades, they'd maneuvered against each other just as fiercely as they had against the West. Back in 2018, when I asked Secretary of State Mike Pompeo, who was fresh off a term as the CIA director, about this, he told me the two countries had such long-running enmity that they would never work together effectively. In fact, the history between the two countries wasn't so clear-cut: Like planets moving in and out of each other's orbits, there were moments when they moved closer and farther apart. But this history—when they worked together and when they blasted apart—illuminated what made their cooperation in 2022 so different.

In the summer of 1949, even before his forces successfully chased the Nationalist military of Chiang Kai-shek off the Chinese mainland, Mao Zedong was already busy outlining a public vision for a grand socialist alliance. China, he argued, must "lean to one side" in its foreign policy decision-making: to "ally ourselves with the Soviet Union, with the People's Democracies, and with the proletariat and the broad masses of the people in all other countries, and form an international united front."

Within weeks of establishing his new state, now called the People's Republic of China, he visited Stalin in Moscow with the aim of establishing a powerful new alliance to assure the spread of communist ideals. It was a heavier lift than Mao had anticipated, as Stalin was not particularly interested. But after two months, Mao returned to Beijing with a new "Treaty of Friendship, Alliance, and Mutual Assistance" (and a battered ego).

Within a matter of weeks they found themselves with a new joint project—the need to support a fellow socialist, North Korean leader Kim Il Sung, in his invasion of the South. It was a telling moment: The Chinese poured more than a quarter million soldiers into the initial fight in 1950 and suffered incredible losses—while the Soviets, relying on their superior technology, sent mainly pilots and air support. It did not escape Mao's notice that the two countries were not equally committed.

In fact, over the next two decades, the dream of a grand socialist alliance was slowly crushed, in part by the day-to-day grind of national interests but even more by clashes of personality. Mao and Stalin had gotten along enough: While Mao loathed how Stalin treated him, he refrained from publicly criticizing the Soviet leader. But his relationship with Nikita Khrushchev, who emerged on top following the power struggle that accompanied Stalin's 1953 death, was a disaster. Mao was rankled by Khrushchev's critique of Stalin's violent purges; for his part, Khrushchev concluded in his memoir that "Mao suffered from the same megalomania Stalin had all his life. He had the same diseased outlook on other people." Both claimed to speak for the "true" communism— and disagreed on how to best implement it. (Khrushchev watched some of Mao's more radical policies—like the "Great Leap Forward"—with barely disguised contempt.)

The greatest split developed as Mao accused Khrushchev of going soft on confronting the United States. Khrushchev recalled Mao saying in 1957 that he was willing to lose 300 million people in a war with the United States. "So what?" the Soviet leader recalled him saying. "War is war. The years will pass and we'll get to work producing more babies than ever before." (Khrushchev wrote that he was cleaning up Mao's language.) To Khrushchev's horror, Mao suggested that he could defeat the West with wave after wave of soldiers; he waved away Khrushchev's wariness about risking nuclear war. Khrushchev despaired that Mao "wouldn't even listen to my arguments and obviously regarded me as a coward."

Much of this was for show. While Mao lionized guerrilla warfare, the kind that propelled him to control of all of mainland China, he knew that the USSR's own arsenal gave it powers to confront the United States that China could only dream of. The Soviets not only had the Bomb; they also had ICBMs that could reach any American city. Yet Mao turned down Khrushchev's proposals to put Soviet submarine bases or even a radio station on the Chinese coast, to monitor American military activities. He feared that "with a few atomic bombs" Moscow would think it was "in a position to control us."

As that exchange makes clear, Mao was convinced that the Soviet leadership looked down on him, regarding him as just another republic that should follow directives from Moscow and do whatever it was asked when it came to supporting the Soviet effort to create a sphere of influence in the Pacific. It didn't help that the Soviets had just invaded Czechoslovakia. "Khrushchev and Mao had all the instincts and prejudices of nationalists, however much they might be communists," concluded the great Cold War historian John Lewis Gaddis.

For his part, Khrushchev thought Mao never missed an opportunity to humiliate him—or to provoke the United States. When, in 1958, it looked like the United States and China might go to war over Taiwan and the other offshore islands, Mao chose the moment to fight with

Khrushchev—even while requesting Russian military assistance against Chiang Kai-shek, the leader of the nationalists in Taiwan. "They asked for aircraft, long-range artillery and air force advisors," Khrushchev wrote, and the Soviets gave it to them "because we thought they were absolutely right in trying to unify all the territories of China." But their support was not absolute: In 1959, Khrushchev pulled back on five years of nuclear cooperation with China, reneging on the Soviet promise to send Beijing a model of an atomic bomb to study. So it was no surprise that Mao began seeking his own atomic bombs—aiming to make sure that he would never be dependent on the Soviet arsenal. Naturally, a nuclear-armed China posed a threat to America, but it also posed a threat to the Soviet Union. The Johnson administration thought about inviting the Soviets to jointly strike Lop Nor, the Chinese nuclear testing site. William C. Foster, the director of the Arms Control and Disarmament Agency, said in one recently declassified memo that "if we could get together with the USSR, the Chinese could be handled even if it required an accidental drop on their facilities." Wisely, the Johnson administration abandoned the idea, determining in April 1964 that the risk of a Chinese nuclear capability "is not such as to justify the undertaking of actions which would involve great political costs or high military risks."

But the split between the countries' leaders worsened. In the summer of 1964, Mao warned, "We cannot only pay attention to the East [the United States] and not to the North, only pay attention to imperialism and not revisionism, we must prepare for war on both sides." And by March 1969—twenty years after Mao's "lean" toward Moscow—the two countries were nearly at war, exchanging fire over the Ussuri River, part of a disputed border in northeastern China. There was talk of a nuclear exchange—but not one involving the West. For a time the discussion was about the Soviet Union and China facing off against each other. President Nixon told his national security aides that it would not be in American interests to see China destroyed by the more powerful Soviet force.

It was the beginning of an astounding diplomatic reversal that changed the world. After Nixon and Henry Kissinger, his national security advisor, dropped unsubtle hints to the Chinese through intermediaries, Kissinger received a formal invitation to take a secret trip to Beijing in 1971. (Kissinger, never known for an excess of modesty, pulled Nixon out of a White House dinner to declare, "This is the most important communication that has come to an American president since the end of World War II.")

The next year, Nixon, who had risen to the presidency railing about the threat of communism, was meeting Mao in Beijing, and the two men were finding common national interests. Both men had plenty of reason to worry about the Soviets. "History has brought us together," Nixon declared. The visit staggered the Soviets, the North Vietnamese, and the Democrats.

"That China and the United States would find a way to come together was inevitable given the necessities of the time," Kissinger later wrote in *On China,* referring to domestic strife in the two countries and a common interest in resisting Soviet advances. But he also insisted that he had not been seeking to isolate Russia as much as to conduct a grand experiment in balance-of-power politics with Moscow and Beijing. "Our view," he wrote, "was that the existence of the triangular relations was in itself a form of pressure on each of them." This was the start of the delicate dance of the "one-China policy," in which the United States recognized the government of the People's Republic of China as the true government of China, while at the same time asserting the need to peacefully solve the Taiwan question and refusing to acknowledge the mainland's control over it. This posture enabled the Chinese to begin to invest in relationships with key Americans, most notably George H. W. Bush, the second American representative in Beijing. (This was before there were formal diplomatic relations, and thus ambassadors.)

By the mid-1980s, China and the United States were collaborating, cautiously, to stymie the Soviets in Afghanistan and frustrate their efforts to gain a foothold in Southeast Asia. More intriguing was the burgeoning intelligence collaboration between Beijing and Washington, one that is hard to imagine in the current atmosphere. Following a 1979 conversation with Senator Joseph Biden on his first visit to China—he was thirty-six years old—Beijing agreed to install two listening posts loaded with American equipment to monitor Soviet nuclear tests across the border in Kazakhstan. Trucks loaded with classified tapes regularly trundled the approximately thirty hours from Xinjiang to the American embassy in Beijing—a partnership that endured for more than a decade. (The Americans believed they benefited more from the intelligence collection than the Chinese, but the Chinese derived their own value from the arrangement: U.S. human rights advocates alleged that George H. W. Bush tamped down condemnation of the killings in Tiananmen Square in 1989 in order to avoid angering the Chinese leadership and risking this key source of intelligence.)

The dissolution of the Soviet Union left Beijing somewhat stunned. Several weeks before the fall of the Berlin Wall, Deng Xiaoping had used the brutality of his military to massacre student activists in Tiananmen Square. Mikhail Gorbachev, having witnessed the gathering storm in Tiananmen Square from a dinner at the Great Hall of the People, took the opposite tack when his moment came, standing aside as the Soviet republics seceded one by one.

What followed was America's unipower moment. China used the coming years to lift more people out of poverty than any World Bank program ever could. For its part, Russia used it to create oligarchs and rearm but failed at the key task of diversifying its economy. And it barely noticed as a generation of innovators, starting with Sergey Brin, one of the founders of Google, took their talents to the United States.

Unsurprisingly, Russia and China spent the first decade of the 2000s maintaining a wary distance. Russia eyed China's increasing demand for energy as a potentially lucrative market, but it was obvious to everyone that Moscow was also nervous about China's rise—and far from eager to play the junior partner in the relationship. Beijing was hesitant to back some of Russia's expansionist ventures, most significantly the 2008 invasion of Georgia. China was largely silent when Putin annexed Crimea. And the next year both countries worked alongside each other, though not exactly together, in reaching a deal to delay the day when Iran would get a nuclear weapon.

But in the years that followed, something changed, first slowly and then suddenly. As China found itself increasingly at odds with Washington—over the South China Sea and computer chips, over Huawei and human rights, in space and cyberspace—the same national interests that drew Beijing and Moscow together, and then apart, once again became an attracting magnetic force. The two countries had become wildly different nations, of course: China's economy completely intertwined with the West, Russia still dependent on selling fossil fuels.

But Xi and Putin found common ground in their opposition to the American-led order, much as Mao and Stalin had. If there was ever a reason to haul out the well-worn notion that nations have no permanent allies or enemies—only permanent interests—the odd relationship between Moscow and Beijing became enduring evidence.

BY THE TIME the 2022 Olympics kicked off, the world was watching a strange split-screen moment. On one screen people could see the United States urgently warning about a countdown to a Ukraine invasion; on the other was Xi Jinping's proudest moment and his implicit declaration that by 2049, the hundredth anniversary of the creation of the People's Republic, China would be the world's dominant technological, economic, and military superpower.

Xi was intent on wowing the global audience. In the February 4 opening ceremony, some three thousand performers, most of them teenagers, danced in precisely choreographed moves. Artists and engineers made use of artificial intelligence and virtual reality to make sure that the games became a showcase for made-in-China technology routed over made-by-Huawei 5G networks. Supercomputers were used to model whether there would be enough wind to blow the massive Chinese national flag completely flat as it was raised. In a region that had virtually no ski slopes a decade earlier, a ski resort had been created by clearing a mountainside, with massive snowmaking equipment installed.

But the biggest triumph on display for China that day was that the games were happening at all. COVID had delayed Tokyo's summer 2020 games by a full year. Xi was determined to display not only China's athletic and artistic prowess but also the combined benefits of central planning, precise logistics, and social control. Even as the rest of the world was slowly opening up—due in large part to widely available mRNA vaccines that were proving more effective than China's—Beijing wanted to show that it could pull off the ultimate sports event without turning it into a super-spreader.

Ultimately the games had a COVID infection rate of .01 percent—or so the Chinese contended. Chinese officials boasted that China's strong centralized state and its ability to assert control made the games safe, suggesting that in the winter of 2022 no other country—no other system—could have pulled it off. (One Canadian athlete called the experience of constantly being tested, shuttled from place to place, and quarantined "kind of like sports prison.")

Xi's unsubtle message was that at a time of epic upheaval, China was a sea of stability. As he liked to say, in an era of "turbulence and transformation," China was prepared to be the rock. "The world is turning its eyes to China," he said the day before the Olympics began, "and China is ready."

American government officials weren't there, of course. Citing human rights abuses in Xinjiang and elsewhere, Biden had announced a diplomatic boycott of the games. But before the games began, Kurt Campbell and other American officials were dispatched to warn the Chinese of Putin's planned "special military operation."

"The president authorized us to brief the Chinese in an effort to prevent the Russian invasion," Campbell later told me. "We told them all the issues we were worried about." It was a version of the briefing that had been done for America's allies but with certain sensitive intelligence excised.

In response, Campbell recalled, "they promised to report back to the highest levels." But it was clear to him that the midlevel Chinese officials he was talking with "doubted the veracity of our case and thought this was another effort to split China and Russia." It was less obvious what top-level Chinese officials, most importantly Xi himself, might have known.

When I asked a senior intelligence official how it could be that a superpower as plugged into everything that was happening around the globe as China might have made such a fundamental mistake, the answer was enlightening. Part of the issue, the official said, was that the Chinese intelligence service is particularly strong in some areas—like technical collection—and particularly weak in others, including assessing the intent of foreign leadership. So they missed the signs. "They did not have a good picture of Putin's intent before the war. They had, I think, an inflated view of the capability of the Russian military and of Russian weapon systems." (They were hardly alone in making that mistake.) The United States may have shared a fair amount of information, continued the official, but "they didn't buy it. And to be fair, they were in good company. Because other than the Brits, most people didn't buy it either—including our closest European allies."

The second part, the official said, was that "there is also a tendency amongst the Chinese services to tell their leadership what they think they want to hear. So that was also evident in that period as well."

It was a sign of how close the relationship between China and Russia had become that, as American officials later learned, the Chinese just turned around and shared all of the intel with Moscow.

PART THREE

WARS, HOT AND COLD

CHAPTER 12

SHORT INVASION, LONG WAR

This will probably be much more difficult than we thought. But the war is on their territory, not ours. We are a big country and we have patience.

Vladimir Putin, in conversation with Naftali Bennett, prime minister of Israel, March 2022

IN THE FIRST week of December 2021, as Antony Blinken and Jake Sullivan were desperately trying to convince allies that Putin was preparing to invade, Marine Corps Major Sharon Rollins and a small team of digital-savvy service members from the United States' Cyber National Mission Force were on the move.

They flew from Maryland to western Ukraine on an urgent mission: Find the cyber vulnerabilities in Ukraine's government and critical infrastructure networks—things like power grids, transportation systems, and communications networks that Russia would likely attempt to exploit in the first days of an invasion—and advise the Ukrainians on the best ways to patch them. It's what the U.S. government calls a "hunt forward" operation—one of dozens conducted in recent years to help boost the cybersecurity of American partners and allies.

Over the previous few months, as the conversation in Washington turned from *whether* Russia would invade to *how* it would invade, most senior officials in the White House thought it would likely begin with a blitzkrieg cyberattack meant to blind and deafen the Ukrainian government in the critical opening days of the war. And as they played out the scenarios, they imagined what that would look like: panicked civilians who couldn't communicate with their families, access clean water, or withdraw money from ATMs. Escape methods out of the country, like bus systems and train routes, would become unreliable. So they set out to do something about it.

Like so many cyberwarriors, Major Rollins took a path to running a defensive cyber team that wasn't precisely traditional. She'd begun her career studying travel industry management before joining the Marines at age twenty-six—just as her husband was leaving the force. A bit older than most of the new recruits, she was soon slotted into a post as a communications officer and sent to Japan. Then, in 2018, just as General Nakasone was expanding the cyber mission forces—some offensively minded and dedicated to breaking into the networks of adversaries, others strictly defensive and designed to protect American networks—she took one of the first available cyber slots for Marine Corps officers.

"My first assignment was within Cyber Command," she recalled, "as a mission commander for a combat mission team"—one of the offensive cyber teams that break into many of the most heavily guarded networks around the world—"and it was a really exciting experience." But to round out her skills, she knew, "I should probably understand defense as well."

She quickly found that defending networks is an art form of its own kind, requiring an encyclopedic understanding of the most potent cyber threats and how they are hidden. It is deceptively difficult to do, because you always suspect you are missing something—and usually you are. But the point of these "hunt forward" teams was that cyberattacks that occur in one country don't usually stay in that country. So by helping other governments strengthen their own networks—teaching them new techniques that would increase their resilience to attacks—Americans would become safer by default.

The challenge was this: After decades of establishing itself as the world's most formidable cyber espionage force, the U.S. Cyber Command, with the help of the NSA, was now knocking on front doors around the world and asking governments to allow American soldiers to place sensors on their most sensitive networks. Rollins and her cyber operators would need physical, sustained access to networks in order to catch possible attack points. It was a tricky ask. "There's never any skepticism about having U.S. cyber operators on your network," William Hartman, the Cyber National Mission Force commander, said wryly, highlighting the difficulty of the task.

It helped, in part, that American service members weren't directly patching holes in Ukraine's systems. "We put our hands on our own keyboards. They put their hands on their keyboards," Hartman explained. But for the Ukrainians, it was a leap of faith.

In December 2021, as Rollins landed in Ukraine, she knew very little about what to anticipate from her first-ever trip to Ukraine. "We obviously planned and executed this mission very quickly," she recalled more than a year later. "And I didn't quite know what exactly we would see when we got there. I didn't know how the mission would end, if Russia would invade. . . . There were so many unknowns and a lot of uncertainties."

The day after landing, Rollins and her team met with about two dozen senior Ukrainian officials. "We just emphasized to them that we were here to support them, to provide as much cyber defense support as we could during this contentious situation that they were possibly going to be in with Russia," she said. The threat was so urgent that the Ukrainians agreed immediately—and started suggesting where to place their sensors on the networks.

Originally, Rollins's team planned to conduct a short site visit, go back home to design a plan of action, and then return to execute it. Within a week, Rollins realized that this wouldn't be nearly quick enough, given the geopolitical context. She called back to headquarters: We aren't leaving, she told them, and we need you to send more people.

Their main mission was to test the vulnerabilities of three major networks and offer security solutions. But as the Russians began "preparing the battlefield" in January and February—sending waves of cyberattacks—the cyber team found themselves advising the Ukrainians in real time as the attacks unfolded. "This was kind of the moment where it was like, 'Okay, you know, we're in it,'" Rollins said. "The cyberattacks are happening."

Ultimately, some four dozen American cyber operators worked side by side with their Ukrainian counterparts for more than two months.

They worked right through the Christmas holidays, a time when the Russians had, in past years, taken out parts of the Ukrainian power grid. They disbanded only when the invasion seemed imminent early in 2022—because Biden wanted all American troops in Ukraine out of harm's way. Just a few weeks later the Microsoft team outside Dulles airport saw the cyber evidence that the Russian tanks were about to roll.

BEFORE VOLODYMYR ZELENSKY became the world's most instantly recognizable communicator—before he'd rallied billions of dollars of military aid from Western allies, and before astounding the world by remaining in Kyiv in the midst of battle—he left many of his countrymen rather unimpressed with his governing skills.

In April 2019, Zelensky won election as president of Ukraine with a clear mandate: to fight corruption and wind down the slow, grinding war with Russia in the east without giving up an inch of Ukrainian territory. But by the first few weeks of 2022, he had made little to no progress. Negotiations with Moscow were sporadic at best. And his popularity as a real president—rather than just someone who played one on television—had taken a hit. While Zelensky remained more popular than other national politicians, polls showed a majority of Ukrainians saying they would rather he not run for the presidency again. Similar numbers said the country was headed in the wrong direction.

"The Comedian-Turned-President Is Seriously in Over His Head," ran an opinion piece written by Olga Rudenko, editor-in-chief of *The Kyiv Independent,* in *The New York Times* just days before the invasion. Zelensky, argued Rudenko, had struggled to govern: His reforms were lagging, his relationship with the press was contentious, and he surrounded himself with "yes men," which had made him "insular." Worse, she argued, when it came to preparing the nation for impending disaster, he was all over the place. She was right. When I saw him in Munich the Saturday before the Russians pulled the trigger, he took the position that talk of an impending disaster would merely stoke panic and trigger the flight of millions of Ukrainian refugees. At other moments he seemed to dismiss the fears of others with a laugh. Then, in private, he would demand to know what Europe and the United States would do to protect his nation.

Yet for all his strengths and weaknesses, in the early morning hours on February 24, Zelensky was the only leader Ukraine had. And he rose to the occasion—beginning by staunchly refusing to leave Kyiv.

As the battle for Kyiv raged, some of Zelensky's aides pleaded with him to leave the city, warning that an assassination plot had been launched against him. Others chimed in that there was a good chance the defenders couldn't hold the city. If he died, they reasoned, Ukraine would lose the only viable leader it had. Zelensky argued back that if he left, Ukraine would effectively not have a leader anyway. Eventually, *The Washington Post* reported, Zelensky bluntly told his aides to stop talking about abandoning the city. "This is the last time I am going to hear this," one advisor recalled him saying. "I don't want to hear it again."

When Western officials made the same argument, they got similar results. "The fight is here; I need ammunition, not a ride," Zelensky reportedly told them. (The quip has become urban legend—even printed on T-shirts—though no one can confirm he actually said it.)

Then Zelensky started talking—not just to Ukrainians but to the world. He recorded video messages to his fellow Ukrainians, urging them not to panic and reassuring them that their military was prepared to fight. He urged civilians to make Molotov cocktails and take up rifles themselves.

He and his aides called up presidents and prime ministers, parliamentarians and members of Congress, and explained in graphic detail the real-time events that were unfolding on the ground in Ukraine— and what types of weapons and international support he would need to keep fighting. The Ukrainians weren't just defending themselves, Zelensky said; they were defending all of Europe—at an unbelievable cost. Sometimes, his aides recalled, foreign leaders were reduced to tears.

Suddenly, the comedian—the one who understood the power of a narrative and knew how to deploy sweeping rhetoric to tell a clear story of good and evil—seemed to be exactly the right man for the job. His aides understood how it worked, too: Andriy Yermak, the film producer who had become the head of the presidential office, said that he regularly texted photos of destroyed Ukrainian homes and slaughtered children directly to decision-makers like Jake Sullivan and members of Congress.

As dusk fell on February 25, about thirty-six hours after the invasion began, the ability of Kyiv's defenders to hold the city was still in doubt.

Women and children were fleeing west, toward Poland and beyond. Missile strikes in the early hours had turned parts of the night sky orange. Russian jets zoomed overhead, as both sides battled for control of the country's airspace. Now there were reports of gunshots downtown—all the while a double column of Russian troops was marching steadily down toward Kyiv, along either side of the Dnieper River.

Later that night, Zelensky—wearing his trademark green shirt and military bomber jacket—filmed a shaky, self-recorded video from an unidentified street in Kyiv.

"We are all here," Zelensky said, individually introducing the four men around him—including his prime minister, who held up a phone screen to the camera, showing proof of date and time. "Our soldiers are here. The citizens of the country are here. We are all here, protecting our independence, our country, and we are going to continue to do so. Glory to the defenders of Ukraine. Glory to Ukraine."

But just as quickly, Zelensky also took several steps that were more controversial. He imposed martial law and banned all men between the ages of eighteen and sixty from leaving the country so that they could join the military defense. Then he began to consolidate media control under the state—ensuring, he argued, a single, reliable source of information. And as the war dragged on, Zelensky and his top officials began to crack down on the journalists covering the war, banning them from key areas, particularly when coverage was unfavorable.

THE OFFICIAL RUSSIAN line was that a full-scale invasion of Ukraine would be a cakewalk.

As the American ambassador at the time, John Sullivan, recalled of a fall 2021 conversation with the head of Russia's security council, Nikolai Patrushev, the Russians were supremely confident in their ability to crush Ukraine. "Patrushev didn't qualify it," he said. "He was saying, 'We can do this. We're back.' The way I would describe it was that this was already decided, and they were supremely confident. His message was, 'It's not going to be a problem for us to do what we want to do.'"

The Americans feared that Patrushev was right. For the previous several years, the formal Pentagon assessments of Russia's military modernization described a reinvigorated, precision force. Each year, Putin would boast about how he was supplementing Russia's traditional military forces with unstoppable hypersonic weapons designed to evade the West's most sophisticated defensive systems. So any inventory of Ukrainian capabilities and weapons compared to their Russian equivalents looked distinctly one-sided: The International Institute for Strategic Studies reported that in 2021, Ukraine spent just over a tenth of what Russia did on its defense. Russian personnel outnumbered Ukrainians five to one—and had a pool of reservists twice as large to draw upon. And when it came to hardware—bombers and jet fighters, nuclear and ballistic missiles, submarines and tanks—the numbers weren't even close.

But at least a few military leaders in Russia cut through the impressive statistics—and hubris—to sound the alarm. In late January, Leonid Ivashov, a retired Russian general and head of an association for retired officers, warned that an invasion of Ukraine would bring Russia nothing but pain. "The use of military force against Ukraine will, first of all, call into question Russia's very existence as a state," he wrote in Russian in an open letter published on the association's website that was later deleted. "Second, it will turn Russians and Ukrainians into mortal enemies. Third, thousands (tens of thousands) [sic] of young, healthy people will die on both sides."

The disaster wouldn't stop there, he believed. "In addition, there is no doubt that Russia will be added to the category of countries that pose a threat to peace and international security, subjected to the most severe sanctions, transformed into a pariah in the eyes of the international community and probably lose the status of an independent state. There is no way that the president, the government and the Defense Ministry do not understand these consequences."

TWO WEEKS BEFORE the war broke out, the prevailing wisdom in Washington—repeated endlessly on cable news shows—was that Kyiv would fall a few days after the Russians came over the border. Two weeks after the invasion, in true Washington fashion, all the conventional wisdom had been reversed.

Kyiv, astoundingly, remained standing—in Ukrainian hands. The Russian plan to decapitate and replace the government never got off the ground. Zelensky was broadcasting messages every day. The military was fighting back, learning its battle rhythms, innovating until Western weapons could arrive in large numbers. The West had agreed on a pre-negotiated sanctions package, and—because it had prepared in advance—they executed it within hours. Rather than fragmenting, Europe welcomed Ukrainian refugees with open arms—absorbing them into society with a generosity that didn't exist a few years earlier, when Syrians had poured into Europe.

Suddenly the question became how long Putin could afford to continue his costly battle for control of the capital: American intelligence officials were picking up intercepted voice conversations in which Russians talked about a strategic retreat to friendlier territory in Ukraine's south and east, the same territory that had been the site of a grinding war since 2014.

At the White House, Sullivan, his deputy Jon Finer, and Mark Milley gathered daily in the Situation Room, along with the heads of the intelligence agencies, to learn how everything they had been told about how the first days of the war would unfold turned out to be wrong.

The scope of Putin's miscalculations became clear—first in trickles, then in torrents. It started with the opening hours of the conflict. The satellite photographs projected on the big screens of the half-underground complex in the West Wing told the story of one inexplicable Russian mistake after another—some of which had been helped along by the White House.

In a secret trip to Kyiv in mid-January, Bill Burns had warned Zelensky and his top aides that the Russian offensive would start with an effort to take Hostomel Airport, about twenty miles from the heart of Kyiv. It was a crucial piece of intelligence, because the airport—used almost entirely for cargo—was Moscow's best air bridge to bring in the troops, vehicles, and weapons required to take Kyiv.

Forewarned but not entirely prepared, the Ukrainians put up an impressive early resistance. When the Russian choppers appeared that morning in neat columns bearing a landing team of a hundred or more troops, several were brought down, in crashes caught on cell-phone videos. Over the next few hours, by American estimates, upward of three hundred Russian paratroopers died as Ukrainians, some outside the airport fences, took down wave after wave of helicopters. Even the Russian mission commander suffered a hard landing after his chopper was hit.

The Americans, one senior military official told me, were astounded: "We watched it all unfold in real time, amazed that the Russians didn't gain early control of the airspace."

Ultimately, the Russians took the airfield the next day, and in the crossfire they destroyed the world's biggest aircraft: the Antonov An-225, called Mriya, which had been sitting at the airfield for engine maintenance on the day of the invasion. As it turned out, taking the airport and its runways was a Pyrrhic victory: The damage was so extensive that the airfield couldn't play the central role the Russians had in mind. "In retrospect," a senior military official told me months later, "this was an early indicator of what was to come."

There was plenty of other evidence about how unprepared the Russian troops were for the realities of modern warfare. The Russian troops who thought they were on "exercises" in Belarus and inside Russia were using their own cellphones—on Ukrainian networks—to call home to express their angst to family members and girlfriends that they had been deceived and were suddenly in a real battle. Others were posting on TikTok or Instagram. Again, the Ukrainians were in a position to exploit such amateurism: New recruits tucked away in hidden monitoring centers were busy geolocating the calls and social media phones and sharing that information with the military to launch precision attacks.

As Pentagon officials watched the invasions unfold, they were also struck by the evidence that Russian supply and logistics operations were hopelessly snarled and backlogged. Not only had the Russians failed to bring along enough food to sustain a battle of more than a few days, but the column of Russian troops marching down to Kyiv had stalled out entirely. The forty-mile-long traffic jam of Russian tanks, personnel carriers, and fuel tanks became the iconic image of early Russian blundering.

The incident also revealed something deeper, one senior military official who studied it told me. "The Russians clearly had not trained their unit commanders to think on their own and improvise," he said. "Our guys would have veered off into the woods and found another way." Instead, the Russians became sitting ducks, giving the Ukrainians the chance to target the fuel trucks caught in the backup. As they erupted in flames, Russian soldiers abandoned their vehicles, running into the woods for fear they were going to be next.

Mark Milley later diagnosed the problem as characteristic of "a top-down, very, very top-heavy directive in nature" military force, in which there are "settled orders coming from the top, which is not necessarily the best thing to do in a dynamic battlefield."

That was undoubtedly true. But the classified analysis went far deeper than what Milley was willing to say in an open congressional hearing. The Russian military, the Pentagon concluded in several studies, had invested in the kinds of hardware Putin could boast about. There were lots of new hypersonic missiles, run-silent submarines, new fighters, and a reinvigorated nuclear arsenal. But the Russian forces didn't make use of the basic equipment they had trained on for years. While they were expert in electronic warfare, they never closed down Ukrainian communications. They didn't make effective use of close air support for their troops—partly because the Ukrainians had better air defenses than the invading forces expected. From the earliest days of fighting, it became clear that rampant Russian corruption had led to the wrong tires being ordered for combat vehicles and shortages of spare parts for aging aircraft. The level of corruption, an official told me, was "well known." Still, he said, "because you never really see exactly how fragile it is until you engage in combat, it's hard to make accurate judgments."

The most damning conclusion among the Pentagon experts was that the Russians failed at what they thought they were best at, what the U.S. military calls "combined arms operations," the ability to integrate land, sea, and air power together in precisely coordinated battlefield operations. "We did not anticipate two things," one U.S. defense official told me. The first was "the degree to which the Russian military failed to follow its own doctrine with respect to combined arms," even though such operations were constantly emphasized in Russian military drills that the United States had monitored with care. In the American war-gaming of a Russian invasion, it was assumed that after practicing those operations so often and so vigorously, the Russians would know how to execute it on a real battlefield.

But that was not "what they actually did," the official told me. "And when a military doesn't follow the rules it sets for itself, that confuses the conscripts and confuses the midlevel leaders. This is already a military which is heavily top-down-directed. So lots of confusion on the battlefield early."

Yet Pentagon analysis missed something else that proved crucial—the American reaction. Maybe it was the legacy of Iraq and Afghanistan and the assumption that the United States would be deeply reluctant to get into the middle of another major foreign conflict—especially one with a nuclear-armed nation. Maybe it was the hangover from the Trump years. Maybe it was the series of threats from Putin, culminating with a vow on the morning of the invasion that Russia would respond to any interference by outside countries with "consequences . . . such as you have never seen in your entire history." But the war-game models, the official told me, "did not anticipate the extent to which the United States would be so active in supporting Ukraine in providing information and the extent to which that really enabled—especially in the early days—very effective Ukrainian counterattacks. So when we set up and run our war games, we see lots of examples of relatively small militaries on the border being dominated by the Russian military before the United States and NATO can come to help. That was not the case in Ukraine."

Russia made many other unforced errors. The brutality with which they prosecuted the war hardened the Ukrainians' resolve, even among those who previously had had some sympathy for Russia. There were hundreds of reports of Russian soldiers looting everything they could from Ukrainian homes: first food and phones, later jewelry, alcohol, and TVs. The stories that came out later were far worse: the gut-wrenching summary rapes and killings by Russian soldiers, the intentional missile strikes on apartment buildings and shelters. It was the forced deportation of children that led to Putin's indictment from the (largely powerless) International Criminal Court. Ultimately, the crimes against civilians were a sign of how undisciplined Putin's army actually was, as the "special military operation" spiraled out of their control.

The only military unit that actually seemed capable of fighting a war—in the most horrifically brutal way possible—was the Wagner Group: a shadowy band of mercenaries whose violent tactics Putin had relied on many times over the past several years. Putin had long denied that Wagner was an arm of the Russian state, even as it had a remarkable habit of showing up in troubled foreign countries—from Syria to Ukraine to the Central African Republic—propping up local autocrats there and then funneling billions in lucrative oil, gas, and mining concessions back to Moscow.

Yet it was only after the onset of war in Ukraine in 2022, after Wagner mercenaries quickly proved themselves some of Putin's most effective forces, that the man bankrolling the operation finally admitted to his role. It was Yevgeny Prigozhin, the man I had seen serve dinner to Putin and Bush as they floated down the Neva in 2002. In the twenty years since, he'd built up a multi-billion-dollar empire by helping Putin solve his thorniest geopolitical problems—most famously by setting up the so-called "troll farms" in 2016 to influence the American election. But it seemed he had quickly figured out that more money—and power—lay in prosecuting Putin's battles abroad.

DESPITE THEIR LITANY of mistakes on the ground, the Russians pulled off one operation—in cyberspace—that no country had ever pulled off in wartime. Just an hour before missiles began hitting Ukraine, Russia's military intelligence directorate, the GRU—which had successfully attacked Ukraine's power grid in the past—took out Viasat, a commercial satellite network that was serving as the communications backbone for much of the Ukrainian government and military.

At the time, the incident received little attention; the drama of knocking out a satellite network paled in comparison to rolling tanks through a neighboring country. And the attack itself, while notable, didn't require the Russians to knock out Viasat with anti-satellite weapons in low-earth orbit. Instead, the GRU achieved the same goal with a familiar technique: It used wiper malware to attack the modems and routers that enabled the satellites to connect to ground networks. It exposed a huge vulnerability for satellites of all kinds, proving that you don't need lasers and roaming spacemines to take out orbiting satellites. All you have to wipe out is their connection on the ground.

It wasn't, of course, just the Ukrainians who felt the loss of Viasat. Tens of thousands of customers around Europe and North Africa were disconnected too—everyone from broadband companies in the U.K. to utilities in Germany. But by disrupting key command and control for the Ukrainian forces in the opening hours of a major conflict, the stakes were radically higher: Without communications, the military couldn't direct its soldiers, share information, coordinate among different branches, or share warnings and updates. They likely had other, more limited means to talk to each other—but not on the scale that was needed to repel an invasion.

It might have worked, too. But early on the morning of February 26, Mykhailo Fedorov, Ukraine's deputy prime minister for digital transformation, sent a plea to the one person he was confident could get Ukraine back online: Elon Musk, for a time the world's richest man. Musk's company SpaceX had developed a constellation of low earth orbit satellites called Starlink that promised its users the ability to get online almost anywhere in the world. Armed with a Starlink terminal, users could tap into the network of thousands of tiny satellites operating high above.

"@elonmusk," he tweeted, "while you try to colonize Mars—Russia try to occupy Ukraine! While your rockets successfully land from space—Russian rockets attack Ukrainian civil people! We ask you to provide Ukraine with Starlink stations and to address sane Russians to stand [down]."

By that evening, Musk had replied publicly. "Starlink service is now active in Ukraine. More terminals en route," he tweeted.

Rushing in five hundred Starlink terminals, of course, had been in no one's military plan for Ukraine. The Ukrainians hadn't thought much about what would happen if they lost Viasat, and the United States hadn't either, several American officials conceded. Musk, who later incurred the wrath of millions as he hollowed out Twitter and appeared to endorse antisemitic posts on the site, was a hero of the early days of the invasion. But it was also a reminder that the owners of commercial technology platforms were going to be asked to pick a side in a war that was increasingly digital—and most of them swiftly sided with Ukraine. (Musk later had second thoughts and threatened to end Starlink services unless the Pentagon paid for the cost of keeping the Ukrainian government online; in fact, the Pentagon later contracted with SpaceX, at a price of hundreds of millions of dollars, to do exactly that.) "Had Starlink not stepped in, that Viasat hack would have had a real impact on the Ukrainian military's ability to communicate," Anne Neuberger emphasized to me several months later.

Despite the success of the Viasat hack, the role of cyber did not seem to be the defining factor that the Americans had anticipated. It was a reality that Neuberger attributed in part to the speed at which the Ukrainian cyber defenders learned their role—aided not only by Major

Rollins and her "hunt forward" team but by years of partnerships and relationship-building between the United States and Ukraine. Kyiv's own investments to strengthen its networks were also critical. "I think the Ukrainians were just really fast at recovery and then just kept pushing through" to bring their networks back online, she said.

American and international technology companies also jumped in to aid Ukraine. Microsoft and Amazon were pouring hundreds of millions of dollars' worth of services into securing Ukraine's networks and responding to attacks. Google was doing the same—at the start of the war it reconfigured Google Maps on the fly to show residents of Kyiv how to get out of the city, and out of the country—without tipping off the Russians as to where vulnerable refugees were convening.

There were two other factors that likely shaped how the cyber war played out. The first was that cyber has long been the right tool for "short-of-war" conflicts, when the objective is to undercut or influence an adversary without triggering a full-on war. But when the shooting starts, the utility of modern cyberweapons can wane. There is often not enough time, or enough access to networks, to use it effectively. Why spend months seeking the perfect entrée into the electric power grid, and figuring out what code might shut it down, when you can aim a missile directly at the power plant?

But there was, of course, one more key element, which a senior intelligence official pointed out to me: "Putin didn't tell his conventional forces that he was about to send them into war," he said. "So there's no reason to believe he told his cyber forces, either."

If there was one American soldier who personified the leap from the age of counterterrorism to the new era of superpower conflict, it may well have been (then) Major General Chris Donahue, the commander of the 82nd Airborne Division. Just six months after he stepped aboard a plane in Kabul to become the last American soldier to leave Afghanistan, Donahue was once again in the thick of the action, this time in southern Poland, right on the border of Ukraine, trying to prepare for another evacuation of noncombatants. This mission would focus on getting Americans and the citizens of allies out of the line of fire, should war break out between Russia and Ukraine.

It was hardly an unexpected assignment. If anything, the two weeks of sheer chaos he had managed at what was then still Hamid Karzai

International Airport had been an interregnum of sorts. He had been ordered into Kabul because the storied 82nd Airborne specialized in inserting itself quickly into crises, and it specialized in rapid, risky evacuations. Afghanistan turned out to be one of the hardest and, ultimately, among the deadliest. But after Donahue returned to Fort Bragg and saw his family again, his focus returned to the project that had consumed him for several years: preparing for the possibility of another devastating war in Europe.

Donahue wouldn't say as much in public, of course. And NATO allies were clearly not eager to embrace the possibility. But the 82nd's job is to prepare for contingencies. And managing a conflict with a nuclear-armed Russia involved a level of complexity that the U.S. military—after twenty years of hunting al-Qaeda and ISIS—was only beginning to understand.

"We got comfortable with our understanding of al-Qaeda, Iran, anything in the Middle East," Donahue told me. There was a huge difference, he said, between managing the kinds of counterterrorism operations he had come of age fighting and the conflict in Ukraine he was now dealing with each day.

In the counterterrorism operations, he said, "You could sit there, and no matter what you did . . . whatever lever you pulled, you knew exactly what would happen." He could predict how an adversary would respond or how an ally would respond. The missions were hard and dangerous. But there was a battle rhythm that the United States understood.

After the Russian annexation of Crimea in 2014, the U.S. military began focusing anew on Europe—its Cold War preoccupation. The battles with the Taliban and ISIS in Syria continued, of course. But now there was an added level of complexity, with a back-to-the-future feel. In response to the Crimea annexation, American troops began to be posted in Poland and down through the Baltics. Trucks, tanks, and weapons rolled though former Soviet states—a conspicuous effort to train allies, test American logistical prowess, and serve as both a deterrent and a red flag to Putin. NATO organized a new annual exercise: Swift Response, billed as the largest combined airborne training in Europe since the end of the Cold War. American troops, alongside forces from nearly a dozen allied partners, parachuted in full fatigues into forests and fields. They landed in Chinooks and marched through poppy fields.

Donahue spent a nine-month rotation in Eastern Europe in 2017, working on building up military capability to deter Russia—at the very moment President Trump was declaring that he believed Putin's denials that Russia had sought to influence the 2016 election. In May 2021, just after the Russian buildup on the Ukraine border, he returned for another year of Swift Response. This time, the planned exercise had a more urgent flavor—jumping brigades into Estonia and establishing military task forces in Romania, all ripe targets for the Russians.

The exercises revealed many vulnerabilities. Most of the NATO members had dragged their feet on meeting defense spending targets, and it showed. As they tested their communications capabilities, it became obvious that, in combat, Europe's military communications would be overwhelmed. These exercises were largely theoretical—until the Russian buildup resumed. In January 2022, he got instructions to pick up the 82nd Airborne command headquarters and head to Poland, where the refugee crisis was expected to be the most intense. His hosts were not thrilled. "The Poles were like, 'You're crazy. What are you doing here? Nothing's going to happen.'" The country that had been invaded so many times by the Russians and their predecessors couldn't believe that Russia's foreign policy was about to disrupt life again.

Over the next several weeks, the 82nd prepared themselves to deploy from Poland to Kyiv at a moment's notice in the event of a noncombatant evacuation. But when the time finally came—in the final days of February 2022—there was no need for an airlift. "One, the Russian plan sucked, so there was no reason to," Donahue told me. "Two, because the Poles—who don't get enough credit—absorbed all these people," he said, pointing to the massive number of refugees who streamed out of Ukraine's borders in the opening days of the war. And finally, he said, "The Ukrainians held, to a certain degree. Not 100 percent," but more than anticipated.

But Donahue put the lion's share of the blame on the Russian leadership who planned the war. "It was the worst plan on earth," he said, shaking his head as he referenced the original battle plans that deployed Russian troops entering Ukraine along five major lines of conflict. It spread forces too thin and lacked supply lines to back up the troops. "Anyone who knows anything about the military looked at it and said, 'That is an F in any war college.'"

The problem, Donahue argued, was that the Russians hadn't planned a combat operation. They'd planned for a fairly bloodless takeover, believing that most of Ukraine was on their side and that a quick move on the capital—a "decapitation strike"—could take out leadership. (Putin's lackeys, the British intelligence service reported a few months earlier, had already identified their would-be new president: Yevgeniy Murayev, a baby-faced forty-five-year-old pro-Russian Ukrainian politician who later claimed he knew nothing about it.) In short, it was an intelligence plan intended to maintain order and mop up after Ukraine fell into Russia's lap.

This was partly why, Donahue said, Russia performed with almost impossible incompetency at the beginning of the conflict. "The Russians didn't tell their military anything," he pointed out. "So whenever they crossed the border, they had police cars in the lead. They're like, 'We're here to help you. We're here to get rid of the Nazis.' It's insane, right? But they truly thought that."

It was also why, he warned, that didn't mean it was safe to underestimate the Russians. "People think the Russians aren't doing well," he told me, shaking his head to make a point. "And I'm like, the Russians are completely content. They think they're doing great. I mean, they wish they could have won faster in their eyes, but they're learning. I'm not saying they're going to win. But the Russians are doing business exactly the way the Russians want to do business. And they're quite content."

What was coming, it seemed clear to Donahue, was a long, grinding war.

ULTIMATELY, OF COURSE, there was one more factor that turned aside the invasion in February 2022: the full force of a furious, united Ukraine—one that had borne the brunt of Russian interference for decades and suffered through eight years of warfare in the Donbas. During this time, the Ukrainian military had created a more flexible hierarchy, one that empowered lower-level officers to make decisions in real time. They trained with NATO, drilling on logistics and prioritizing training forces on how to work together using fancy new hardware.

The Russian mistakes and Ukrainian strength added up: Early estimates suggested that the Russian Army was losing at least three hundred soldiers a day in the first week of the war, a daily casualty rate equivalent to the entire cost of the 2014 campaign to take Crimea. (Less conservative estimates from the Ukrainians ran more to a thousand a day—along with, they claimed, 30 Russian planes, 31 Russian helicopters, and 211 Russian tanks. Of course, the Ukrainians gave no account of their own losses.)

Suddenly, the White House was thinking about a possibility that had barely entered their heads a few months before: Zelensky might win—or eke out, at least, a partial victory. Intelligence agencies were digging as hard as they could for a sense of Putin's thinking, as a cakewalk turned into a morass.

Not only had the Russians failed to seize Kyiv in a lightning strike: In two short weeks, the West had been renewed, not just in some paper commitments but by the common necessity of getting Javelin anti-tank weapons and Stinger missiles into the hands of the Ukrainians. Putin, mired in a battle that looked much harder than he was told it would be, was stunned by the cost of the gambit. There was the shutdown of the Moscow stock market for fear of what would happen if it opened, the most far-reaching coordinated sanctions package ever attempted against an economy of Russia's size, the sudden inaccessibility of foreign currency reserves, the rapid departure of companies—even McDonalds, the first to open in the era of "glasnost" in the 1990s. The Germans—the Germans!—were committing to vastly higher defense spending, and Putin's own military was now a punchline.

"I think Putin has to adjust his aim to reality," Jake Sullivan said to me a few weeks into the war. "He's beginning to realize it will be hard to salvage an improved position for himself."

HISTORIANS WILL SPEND the next century arguing over whether the United States and allies pushed Putin to invade Ukraine in 2022 or whether, by pressing Russia's integration with Europe, they placed a big bet that just went bad.

But what seemed increasingly clear is that while Putin's core beliefs never changed—that he, and he alone, would assume the mantle of Peter the Great—his strategy did alter. After the Munich speech and Putin's brief war with Georgia, it should have been clear that Ukraine was in his sights. When the world underreacted to the annexation of Crimea in 2014, a drive to grab the whole country was, in retrospect, only a question of timing. He chose 2022.

In the end, the question of why Putin invaded may be less interesting than why so many in the West—from Washington to Berlin—missed the signals.

"All foreign policy discussions have a flavor of righteousness," the German ambassador to the United States, Emily Haber, told me one early winter afternoon from her northwest D.C. residence, a sprawling minimalist building with lots of right angles.

A lifelong diplomat, she had served for a time in Moscow. When we spoke, she was just a few months short of retirement, perhaps making her more willing than most serving diplomats to assess what she and her colleagues had missed. At its core, she concluded, diplomacy was premised on "a wager, a bet on a result, or a desire. We end up being right or wrong. And in the end"—on Putin, on Russia's direction for the future—"we got it wrong."

"But," she continued firmly, "was it wrong to attempt to make Putin a responsible stakeholder from the outset? With hindsight, we failed. But in the early years, and for some time, it would have seemed irresponsible to us to forgo, as a matter of principle, the option of 'responsible stakeholdership.'" For several years, she pointed out, there had been some signs of progress in the relationship, and episodic cooperation. And what was more, the Russians in 2022—for all their brutality in Ukraine—had pulled some punches, at least when it came to NATO. Putin didn't seem to be aiming for a broader war. He avoided escalation where he could—something that the West was trying to match in response while still enabling Kyiv to fight.

But how long could it last?

"I don't know," she admitted. "We are all doing bets on his red lines . . . and I doubt we'll get it right."

CHAPTER 13

BOILING THE FROG

Obviously we are in a position . . . where we are supporting Ukraine, but we also do not want to ultimately end up in World War III, and we do not want to have a situation in which actors are using nuclear weapons.

Avril Haines, director of national intelligence, at a Senate hearing, May 10, 2022

PRESIDENT BIDEN WAS on the phone to Bill Burns at the CIA, and he was livid.

Biden, at seventy-nine, retained his old habit of reading the print edition of *The New York Times.* That morning, on the right-hand side of the May 6, 2022, front page, was a two-column headline: "U.S. Intelligence Aided Ukraine in Its Strike on Russian Flagship." Beneath it, in stark detail, my *Times* colleagues laid out the degree to which the United States was increasingly engaged in guiding the Ukrainians as they navigated the war that had descended on them just two months before:

The United States provided intelligence that helped Ukrainian forces locate and strike the flagship of Russia's Black Sea fleet last month, another sign that the administration is easing its self-imposed limitations on how far it will go in helping Ukraine fight Russia, U.S. officials said.

The targeting help, which contributed to the eventual sinking of the flagship, the Moskva, is part of a continuing classified effort by the Biden administration to provide real-time battlefield intelligence to Ukraine. That intelligence also includes sharing anticipated Russian troop movements, gleaned from a recent American assessment of Moscow's battle plan for the fighting in the Donbas region of eastern Ukraine, the officials said.

The administration has sought to keep much of the battlefield and maritime intelligence it is sharing with the Ukrainians secret out of fear it will be seen as an escalation and provoke President Vladimir V. Putin of Russia into a wider war.

Biden's anger wasn't hard to understand. American presidents hate leaks—at least the ones they don't authorize. But Biden thought this leak was particularly invidious, because it drew a direct link between the provision of U.S. targeting data and the killing of Russians. That was exactly the kind of impression he was trying to keep out of the papers.

Biden's aides immediately argued that the story was overblown. Ukraine, they insisted, had enough quality intelligence of their own to sink the *Moskva,* the pride of the Russian fleet. They didn't need Washington's help. Others, in quiet "guidance" for reporters, said that the intel was more of a mix of information.

In fact, the Ukrainians had developed their own information about where the *Moskva* was located and where it was headed. But they weren't confident in it. So they reached out to their U.S. military liaison for a confirmation.

What happened next is still in some dispute. The Navy provided a general confirmation but no exact coordinates. That was for a reason: The rules that the United States established prohibited giving certain types of data that led to the deaths of Russian troops or sailors. Legally, that would have made the United States a more direct combatant. Still, the fact was that the United States was getting deeper and deeper into the conflict, walking right up to the line between combatant and noncombatant.

In the weeks since the conflict had begun, Biden's administration had teed up billions of dollars in aid for the Ukrainian armed forces, both for defensive weapons and, increasingly, powerful offensive ones. Far less visible, but perhaps more vital, was the sharing of intelligence about Russian whereabouts and intentions, picking apart their capabilities and weaknesses. Navigating the process of sharing potentially sensitive battlefield intelligence with a non-NATO ally made for a steep learning curve. In fact, as one military official recalled to me, the intelligence-sharing process in the early days of the war was "very, very slow, and cumbersome." But the cost of that slowness was obvious— Ukrainian soldiers were dying for lack of targeting information that Americans were sitting on, particularly counter-battery data—and the national security system quickly evolved. Within weeks, it was increasingly clear that American support was playing a decisive role in the Ukrainians' ability to kill their invaders—but the specifics of what the United States was providing were always classified, frequently complicated, and deeply shrouded in legalese.

The key, national security officials argued, was that the Ukrainians were the only ones making the final decision about whether, where, and when to shoot. Americans, the White House and Pentagon lawyers said, could collaborate on devising Ukrainian military strategy, arm Ukraine's soldiers, and tell them generally where the enemy would be and when they would be there—all while avoiding becoming a "co-combatant" in the conflict. It was a finely turned legal distinction, but one very important to Biden, Jake Sullivan, and Antony Blinken, who had to make the case that the United States was aiding Ukraine, not fighting Russia.

Just days before the *Moskva* story, the *Times* had revealed that the United States was helping Ukraine target "mobile command centers" that the Russians were using to prosecute the war. But while the United States could insist that it and other NATO members were merely helping Ukraine find critical command-and-control facilities—a legitimate wartime target—the Ukrainians were busy tracking which of these facilities were run by one-star Russian generals. The result, not unexpectedly, was a remarkable casualty rate among said Russian generals. By some reports upward of a dozen were killed in the opening months of the war.

The White House pushed back at these stories—but not very convincingly. We're not targeting individual officers, they insisted. (This was literally true, but the administration also knew that unless the generals were off on their lunch break, they would likely be hit.)

So when Biden chewed out Burns and also Avril Haines about the *Moskva* story, he had several complaints. First, that news about the intelligence sharing was getting out at all. "I think he was upset about a leak that demonstrated a lack of discipline," Haines later told me. Second, that they came across as boasting—particularly in an instance in which the Americans hadn't really intended to share the information in the first place. And third, the leaks risked reinforcing Putin's argument that he was really at war with NATO and the United States—which, he contended, were truly aiming to destroy the Russian state.

But the *Moskva* leak also demonstrated a widening rift between the Americans and the Ukrainians. That rift would play out repeatedly, as the Ukrainians pressed for more, and the United States attempted to police an ever-shifting line between protecting the country and entering the war. What Biden was focused on, Haines told me, was giving Ukraine information "that would allow them to protect themselves." While providing targeting information for the pride of the Russian fleet would clearly prevent the ship from attacking the Ukrainians at a later date, in the short term it looked like the Americans were helping Zelensky go on the offensive, killing Russians. Ultimately, Biden's underlying concern was that the revelations themselves would force Putin into a corner—and that he would lash out against the United States and NATO, exactly the escalation he was trying to avoid. "He is a very, very, very calculating man," Biden told a crowd at a Democratic fundraiser on the evening of May 9, just after the stories ran. "And the problem I worry about now is that he doesn't have a way out right now, and I'm trying to figure out what we do about that."

IN RETROSPECT, the fate of the *Moskva* was an early symbol of Putin's arrogance in the first year of the war, and his assumption that the Ukrainians would collapse in the face of Russia's onslaught.

The ship had already played a short-lived but memorable part in the early days of the conflict. On February 24, during the initial invasion, the crew of the *Moskva* famously demanded that a garrison of thirteen border guards on the Ukrainian-owned Snake Island—right at a crucial military and shipping access point to the Black Sea—lay down their arms and surrender. Their response, roughly translated as "Russian warship, go fuck yourself," went viral.

Barely six weeks later, the ship was aflame in the same sea it was protecting, hit by a pair of Ukrainian-made Neptune missiles. The photographs that followed were yet another embarrassment to Putin: There was the pride of Russia's Black Sea fleet, christened after its capital city, burning brightly. In state media, the Russian government claimed the ship had caught fire and sunk in bad weather—an excuse that even some of its own state TV hosts didn't buy. The death toll remained unknown.

The successful attack became the first of many stories about Ukrainian inventiveness and pluck. "People are using the MacGyver metaphor," observed Ben Hodges, the former United States Army commander for Europe, referring to the popular 1980s TV show in which the lead character constantly improvised to get out of impossible jams. "With the *Moskva,* they MacGyvered a very effective antiship system that they put on the back of a truck to make it mobile and move it around."

More importantly, the war's narrative was changing. The Russians had retreated from Kyiv. They had lost their warship. For the first time it looked like Ukraine might survive. There was even talk about Ukraine winning—if you defined winning as forcing Russia to retreat back to its own borders, the borders that existed prior to February 24, 2022.

But even if that happened, Jake Sullivan was quick to point out, Ukraine would be under constant threat for years, maybe decades—a threat so omnipresent that it would need to be able to deter Russia from another invasion, whenever Putin rebuilt his sorry force. Meeting that challenge would require an increase in aid and support on a scale that NATO, that Congress, and that even the Ukrainians had never thought about before. "When you think about what we provided in 2021, it was more than we had provided ever before," Sullivan pointed out much later, looking back at the early days of the war. "It was less than a billion dollars."

That amount was tiny compared to the kind of numbers now kicking around the Pentagon. For Ukraine to survive over the long term, its military would need to be completely overhauled. It needed to become like Israel, said one former military official who was now serving in the

Biden administration. It would have to go from a force that was dependent on decrepit Soviet-era leftovers to modern, Western arms—all while fighting a brutal war in real time on its own territory. It might not be a member of NATO for a long, long time. But it needed to be armed like one.

BY THE SUMMER of 2022, Jake Sullivan was telling people that he had become "Ukraine's quartermaster."

He meant it as an ironic aside that had the ring of truth: He had come to know, down to the range of different artillery shells and bullets, every major weapons system that the United States stockpiled. But a quartermaster usually focuses on allocating the weapons, not designing the strategy for when, where, and how to use them. Sullivan found himself doing both.

It was a role he hadn't anticipated. "I want to be clear," he told me at one point, "we didn't set out" to make Ukraine one of the most heavily armed countries in Europe. "We didn't set out to say, 'You know what we're going to do, here's the schedule for the weapons systems and supplies.'" At the beginning of the conflict, no one thought there was time for a schedule—Russia, with its overwhelming firepower, would win too quickly for airlifts of American weapons to make much of a difference. But after that turned out not to be the case, the plan had to change.

And so, just weeks into the war, Biden and Sullivan, along with a range of intelligence and military officials, began to confront a set of issues they would grapple with time and again.

What weapons should America send to Ukraine? What intelligence would they make available? What training?

How should the aid be paced, given the changing nature of the war and the limits on getting artillery shells into a long supply chain that stretched from the Army Ammunition Plant in Scranton, Pennsylvania—just three miles from Biden's childhood home—to the border towns of Poland and then into Ukraine?

How much risk were they willing to take when it came to taunting Vladimir Putin?

How much blame—and domestic public pressure—were they willing to take for refusing Zelensky's requests?

None of these were easy to answer in the fog of a fast-moving war. But over time, a strategy emerged that some in the administration began to call "boiling the frog." The phrase is based on the myth that a live frog, placed in a pot and slowly boiled, will not leap out if the temperature rises incrementally enough.

In the geopolitical analog, the question was whether it was possible to turn up the temperature on Putin slowly enough that he would adjust to a rising level of Western aid—longer-range weapons for the Ukrainians, better training, new capabilities to watch and listen in on Russian units—without striking out at NATO or reaching into his arsenal of tactical nuclear weapons.

The tactic started small, simmering the water rather than boiling it. Biden authorized Javelins and Stingers, the kind of weapons that Obama declined to give to the Ukrainians after the Crimea annexation in 2014, for fear they would be too provocative to Putin, and that Trump had nominally given but not allowed them to unbox. "Those are the kinds of systems that you'd provide sort of off the shelf," Sullivan said, making it clear that whatever Obama had been worried about, Biden wasn't.

Other requests were easy enough: ammunition for existing weapons systems, rifles, grenade launchers, radar and surveillance systems, patrol boats, secure communications systems, and medical supplies. The Pentagon itself worked on "scrounging up every Soviet legacy system," one senior Pentagon official recalled, and "especially the ammunition they needed," particularly 152-mm shells from the former countries of the Warsaw Pact.

Soon the conversation turned from what Washington would give Ukraine to how the Ukrainians would use it.

FOR MUCH OF 2022, Sullivan struggled with striking a delicate balance between arming Zelensky and taunting Putin.

A miscalculation in either direction would spell disaster. Too little support and Zelensky's forces might get rolled over, once the Russian military began to course-correct after their abysmal first showing. Too much too fast, Biden and Sullivan and Blinken worried, and a cornered Putin might decide he had no choice but to strike at the supply bases in Poland, where arms were being gathered and slipped into unmarked vans and railroad cars. Both were NATO nations, and an attack on either could, overnight, put the alliance into a general war with Russia. In fact, Biden and his aides feared that a Russian attack might be under way in November 2022, when a missile landed in Poland and killed two people. It turned out to be a false alarm—the strike originated from a Ukrainian antimissile system that had misfired.

There was another risk: that the Ukrainians, despite Zelensky's promises, would use the American-sourced weapons to strike directly at Russia, perhaps even taking a shot at Moscow. The more Biden and Sullivan and others examined the variables, the more difficult each decision looked.

Yet as time went on and they learned what Putin would tolerate—or not—new options seemed to open up. What this often meant, in practice, was that decisions that seemed bold or even risky at the time later seemed far too modest. The day after the war began, Biden signed off on a $350 million aid package that contained mostly short-range defensive weapons systems and ammunition, things like Javelins, Stingers, and rifles. At the time, it seemed like a huge risk. No one knew how Putin would respond.

One senior official recalled thinking, "If Russia moved 350 million dollars' worth of American-troop-killing equipment into Iraq or to the Taliban, would we just lie down and take it?"

The question was rhetorical. The answer was obvious. But as the war dragged on, the administration kept testing Putin at each turn, cranking up the heat and then checking in on the psychological state of the frog.

Biden often said—in public, and in private to his staff—that he had two goals: to liberate Ukraine and to avoid direct conflict between American and Russian forces. But increasingly, he was finding those goals to be in some tension, particularly as different theories emerged about what Ukraine most needed, and how fast.

Some requests were a quick yes. Sanctions targeted most—but not all—of Russia's financial institutions. Germany withdrew on Nord Stream 2's permission to operate. Even early on, the West moved to cut off some Russian banks from the SWIFT global banking system and freeze the foreign assets of the country's central bank. Travel bans prevented visits to foreign territories, and tourism restrictions went into effect—and Putin, Lavrov, and other government officials and oligarchs were singled out. A new task force hunted oligarchs, confiscating their superyachts and their country estates around the world, totaling billions. The United States also quickly banned the export of American computer chips to Russia, arguing that they could be used to make guided missiles.

Some requests from Zelensky drew a hard no and would stay that way. In a video appearance before Congress days after the war broke out, Zelensky had asked for the United States to enforce a "no-fly zone" over Ukraine. Biden rejected it: Enforcing the restricted airspace would inevitably pit American pilots against Russians. Then Poland offered to give Soviet-era MIGs, for which they had little use, directly to Ukraine. But the offer came with a hitch: They would only send them if American or NATO pilots flew the planes into Ukraine and replenished the Polish forces with modern American jets.

Blinken explained the administration's rejection of the request. "The prospect of fighter jets at the disposal of the United States government departing from a U.S. NATO base in Germany to fly into airspace contested with Russia over Ukraine raises some serious concerns for the entire NATO alliance," Blinken said. "Our goal is to end the war, not to expand it—including potentially expand it to NATO territory."

Other sensitivities kept the Americans and Europeans from giving Zelensky everything he wanted. Biden decided against designating Russia a state sponsor of terrorism, fearing it would be counterproductive, derailing any hope of keeping grain exports flowing or getting to a peace negotiation that could bring an end to the war. They froze, but didn't initially seize, central bank assets—worrying that other states around the world would not entrust their national deposits to the New York Federal Reserve out of concern that they too could be grabbed.

Some asks were beyond the control of Western governments: When Zelensky wanted the .ru domain taken down to cut Russia off from the world, the non-profit ICANN, tasked with keeping the global internet interoperable, refused, saying it would harm ordinary Russians and prevent them from learning the horrors of what Putin was doing in Ukraine. That was a relief to American intelligence agencies, who desperately needed the .ru domain to remain; it was a key window into Russia and often a pathway to hacking into Russian systems. And it was critical to recruiting, as the CIA tried to lure disaffected Russians, especially those around the Kremlin and the Russian military, to come over to their side. Within months, the agency began producing short videos, encouraging Russians with knowledge of the war to use a secure digital dead drop to get in touch.

IN PUBLIC, the White House support for Zelensky in the early months of the war seemed limitless. It was hard not to love his bravado: He routinely taunted Putin, once posting a photo of a missile fragment found near the Ukrainian leader's residence, with the dry caption "Missed." In his signature drab green T-shirt, Zelensky appeared in nightly videos, rallying the Ukrainian public. Speaking to Congress virtually in early March, he dipped into America's own experience of wartime tragedy and surprise attack: "Remember Pearl Harbor—terrible morning of December 7, 1941, when your sky was black from the planes attacking you. . . . Remember September the 11th, a terrible day in 2001. . . ."

Behind the scenes, the story was more complicated. Privately, tensions were building between the Ukrainian leader and his American backers. Every week—both in public and private—President Zelensky was pressing the West for more. While Biden wanted to gradually "boil the frog," Zelensky wanted to jack up the temperature as quickly as possible. As Biden confided to one aide, he feared that Zelensky was trying to "pull us into World War III."

In most conversations between the two men in the early days of the war, several officials told me, Zelensky related his "shopping list" to Biden. It didn't matter if he was told no. He just asked again.

Zelensky wanted—he *needed*—air defenses. F-16 fighter jets, to maintain air supremacy against the far larger Russian Air Force. A no-fly zone. Tanks. Advanced drones. Most important, long-range missile launchers. There was one in particular that the Pentagon, with its penchant for completely unintelligible acronyms, called the High Mobility Artillery Rocket System (HIMARS). Zelensky wanted to arm these launchers with one of the crown jewels of the U.S. Army, a missile known as ATACMS that could strike targets nearly two hundred miles away with precision accuracy. That, of course, would give him the capability to fire right into command-and-control centers deep inside Russian territory—exactly Biden's worst fear.

In time, Zelensky added to his list of requests another weapon that raised enormous moral issues: He sought "cluster munitions," a weapon many of the arms control advocates in the Biden administration had spent decades trying to limit or ban. Cluster bombs are devastating weapons that release scores of tiny bomblets, ripping apart people and personnel carriers and power lines and often mowing through civilians unlucky enough to be living in the area where they are dropped. Worse yet, unexploded bomblets can remain on the ground for years; from past American battlefields—from Vietnam to Afghanistan and Iraq—there were stories of children killed or maimed after picking one up years later. Blinken told colleagues he had spent much of his professional life getting weapons like this banned. Yet the Pentagon stored them across Europe because they were cruelly effective in wiping out an advancing army. And anyway, they said, the Russians were using cluster munitions in Ukraine.

With each proposal it was Biden who was most reluctant: F-16s were simply too provocative, he told his staff, because they could strike deep into Russia. The cluster munitions were simply too dangerous to civilians. Conversations with Zelensky were heated. "The first few calls they had turned pretty tense," one senior administration official told me. Part of the issue was style. Zelensky, in Biden's view, was simply not grateful for the aid he was getting—a cardinal sin in Biden's world. By mid-May 2022, his administration had poured nearly $4 billion to the Ukrainian defenses, including some fifty million rounds of small ammunition, tens of thousands of artillery rounds, major antiaircraft and anti-tank systems, intelligence, medical equipment, and more. Zelensky had offered at best perfunctory thanks before pushing for more.

To some degree, though, the tension was inevitable. Biden's national interests—and his global responsibilities—ran headlong into Zelensky's urgent need to survive another day, another month, another year. Biden feared feeding Putin's narrative—or his paranoia—but Zelensky saw it differently. As that shell fragment near Zelensky's residence made clear, Putin was out to kill him and eradicate his country. Zelensky was in a war for the survival of his nation, a war he would never win if Putin could fire on Ukraine from Russian territory and he could not fire back. Biden's preoccupation was avoiding escalation.

As the war's weeks turned to months, Biden developed another worry: The rate at which Ukraine was burning through ammunition was astounding everyone. Jake Sullivan began to order up quick studies of what it would take to vastly expand production of quantities of ammunition that few had contemplated the United States ever again needing for a hot war.

Soon, the problems of depleted stockpiles and slow production reached well beyond Ukraine. In the summer of 2022, the CIA was circulating an analysis that China could be moving up the target date for attacking Taiwan out of fear that the United States would move quickly to bolster its defenses. The reality was that the United States was so stressed keeping up with Ukraine's demands and commitments to other allies, like Saudi Arabia, that it couldn't supply Taiwan with everything it needed. And Biden knew that the American support for Ukraine could begin to erode. He was already facing a tricky political situation at home, with voters understandably more focused on gas prices and inflation.

So Biden had to pace himself. Zelensky, however, had to run as fast as he could. "If I was in his position," Blinken told me, "I'd be doing just what he is doing. Pressing for as much as I could get."

In an April 2022 interview with *The Atlantic,* Zelensky expressed his frustration with the whole dance. "When some leaders ask me what weapons I need, I need a moment to calm myself, because I already told them the week before. It's *Groundhog Day.* I feel like Bill Murray." Nor was Zelensky very patient with excuses about production rates. "Western countries have everything to make it happen," he said in a video posted to Twitter, and "the number of people saved depends on them."

Biden's aides knew that if they let this tension between Biden and Zelensky fester, the relationship could devolve into constant bickering. So they quietly began working on coaching Zelensky on how to deal with Biden. The new American ambassador to Ukraine, Bridget Brink, was dispatched to see Zelensky before each conversation with Biden in order to gently guide him about what a call between leaders sounds like. Stay at thirty thousand feet, she told him. Talk about big principles. Let someone else haggle over the shopping list.

It began to work—partly due to Brink's guidance, partly due to Zelensky's learning curve, and partly because, as the war dragged on, Biden's calculus increasingly seemed to align with Zelensky's.

Over the next year, a pattern emerged. Ukraine's request for a specific type of arms would at first get a frosty reception in Washington, perhaps an outright no, a one-word answer Biden delivered himself to reporters who asked about sending the F-16s, which could strike Moscow.

After saying absolutely not, the Biden White House would then say it was "studying" each request, trying to line up Ukraine's capabilities with weapons that could do the job. Situation Room meetings would be devoted to the question of whether a specific weapon was truly "escalatory." Leaks to the press assured that the debate played out in public, creating new pressures. And then, as Biden discovered that Russia's "red lines" were not as bright as first feared, he would relent, noting that Ukraine's defense demands had changed—from defending Kyiv to defending vast sections of Ukraine's industrial east. Eventually, a commitment to deliver weapons previously off-limits would follow.

At one point, Zelensky's representatives argued that the cycle from "no" to "studying it" to "yes" was so well trod that the United States could save itself a lot of time and money by just saying yes from the get-go—or at least begin training Ukrainians on how to fly an F-16 or drive an Abrams tank months before actually agreeing to send the weapons. It would save time, the advisor said to me, "and maybe scare the shit out of the Russians."

Over time, a divide began to open up between the State Department and the Pentagon. Secretary of Defense Lloyd Austin and Colin Kahl, Austin's undersecretary of defense for policy and a former national security advisor to Biden during his vice presidency, were focused on the here and now. Blinken, less engaged in the day-to-day war-fighting needs, worried that the administration wasn't thinking hard enough about what Ukraine would need over the long term to deter Putin from regrouping and trying to take the entire country again. Still, one official quietly told me, it was time to focus on the long run, or whatever gains Ukraine made to foil the initial invasion would eventually be reversed. At the end of the day, he said, Ukraine needed a force large enough, potent enough, and deadly enough that Putin would never think of taking Kyiv again.

THE FIRST FEW months of the war were all about urban warfare—battles for airports, bridges, and city centers. Anti-tank missiles and small arms were the right tool for the job.

But then the conflict moved to the broad plains of the south and east. Once the Russians gave up on taking the capital, they immediately began digging into the Donbas, carving trenches that stretched for miles, laying mines to stop an eventual Ukrainian counteroffensive. Different terrain called for different weapons. And so Zelensky's asks changed—and took on an increasingly urgent tone.

Suddenly the need for HIMARS—with its accuracy and ability to arc over those minefields and reach deep into Russian-held territory—became vital. And HIMARS was mobile, meaning that the Ukrainian troops, if properly trained, could fire and rapidly move to a different spot before the Russians could counterfire. To Zelensky, this weapon had the potential to be a game changer. "The core of the battle, right now, is on Ukrainian territory in the east," Colin Kahl told reporters. "The systems that we're providing" would "allow Ukraine to arrange any target they need for that fight inside Ukrainian territory."

The Russians had already told the United States that providing the Ukrainians with HIMARS was a "red line," arguing that because the system could reach deep into Russia, it posed an existential threat to the country. The argument was exaggerated: The missiles under discussion could not reach Moscow. But they could hit Crimea—and it was undeniable that HIMARS would give Ukraine a reach and accuracy sufficient to take out Russian command posts and launch areas like nothing else in their arsenal. By late May, Biden relented—Zelensky could get HIMARS, with limits.

There was no way to pretend that this wasn't a dramatic escalation. So on May 31, 2022, Biden published an op-ed in *The New York Times* that sought to explain his turnaround:

As President Volodymyr Zelensky of Ukraine has said, ultimately this war "will only definitively end through diplomacy." Every negotiation reflects the facts on the ground. We have moved quickly to send Ukraine a significant amount of weaponry and ammunition so it can fight on the battlefield and be in the strongest possible position at the negotiating table.

That's why I've decided that we will provide the Ukrainians with more advanced rocket systems and munitions that will enable them to more precisely strike key targets on the battlefield in Ukraine.

It turned out he wasn't giving them everything. Biden approved HIMARS but avoided sending the longest-range missile system (ATACMS) that could reach 190 miles, which would put many Russian cities into Ukraine's crosshairs. The missiles that the Americans sent topped out around fifty miles. And in order to receive them, Zelensky had to make a promise to the Americans: No matter what, he would not use them to take the fight into Russia.

Extracting that promise was clearly the only way to preempt Biden's "World War III" scenario. But it emphasized the obvious tension. "The unfortunate conclusion to draw is that we in the West are telling Russia, 'It's OK for you to shoot from Belarus into Ukraine. It's OK for you to shoot from Russia,'" General Philip Breedlove, the former Supreme Allied Commander for Europe, said shortly after. "'But it is not OK for Ukraine to shoot back into Russia.'"

Naturally, the Ukrainians found a quick workaround. They abided by Biden's restrictions with most American weapons and intelligence—with one exception that drew a rapid reprimand—but quickly figured out other ways of striking the Russians where it hurt most: at home. Ukrainian-made drones buzzed the Kremlin. Others, loaded with small explosives, struck Russian Navy ships around Crimea.

And there were a series of deniable operations: In September 2022, seismic instruments in the Baltic Sea picked up a series of explosions in international waters. Then the systems that monitored the Nord Stream pipelines—pipelines that hadn't operated since the invasion of Ukraine months earlier but that were still full of gas—detected a loss in pressure. For days gas bubbled to the surface, and the fingerpointing quickly began. Zelensky and his commanding general, Valerii Zaluzhny, denied responsibility. Why, they asked, would we blow up a pipeline that was not delivering gas? It took months to get to the truth. In March 2023, a *Times* team determined that former Ukrainian special forces operators were behind the explosion, and in summer 2023 *The Washington Post* broke a fuller story: Six covert Ukrainian operatives had rented a sailboat and placed the explosives, in a mission likely approved by Zaluzhny and hidden from Zelensky to give him room to deny Ukrainian involvement.

. . .

IN THE SUMMER OF 2022, a new map appeared on the wall in the seventh-floor office of CIA Director Bill Burns.

It was a vivid depiction of Putin's invasion plan from back in February 2022, in a simple frame over the stiff chair where Burns usually sat when visitors dropped by the director's office. Superimposed over the outline of Ukraine were thick, curved red arrows pointing in at Kyiv from multiple directions, indicating where the prewar intelligence warned that Russian troops would come from: south, from the border with Belarus; north, from the areas Russia had annexed back in 2014; and east, from the disputed eastern territories where the de facto civil war was raging.

There wasn't much mystery about why Burns posted this map so conspicuously. It was a satisfying illustration of Putin's frustrated ambitions, his hubris, and, ultimately, his miscalculation. It was also a quiet declaration by the consummate Russia hand inside the Biden administration—the man who had watched Putin assume power—that the Russian leader had not only overreached, he perhaps had made a grave mistake.

The map had another significance: It made a quiet statement about the effectiveness of the American-backed resistance, without which, Putin's forces, for all their many mistakes, might well have toppled the Zelensky government and taken over the entire country. It was too soon to know, Burns would tell visitors, but Putin had clearly set in motion a crisis he was having trouble managing.

"Putin was not banking on a long war," Burns told me one morning in the late summer of 2022. That was obvious. First, Russian special forces had been decimated in their failed attempt to take over Kyiv. Then their regular military had been forced to retreat to the south and the east. Now Putin was scrambling for troops—and trying to avoid conscripting middle-class kids from Moscow and Leningrad whose parents would not quietly allow their children to become cannon fodder.

What's more, Putin was having trouble explaining why Russian universities were getting cut off from Europe; why oligarchs were losing their yachts; why iPhones were getting increasingly difficult to replace as U.S. sanctions tightened and as other companies found moral or social reasons to disengage from the Russian market.

Of course, in Putin's telling, it was all part of a Western conspiracy to undermine Russian power. But from the beginning, there were cracks in this façade. Several hundred thousand young Russian professionals fled in the first few months of 2022 alone, moving their businesses to cafés in Europe and the Caucasus.

Of those who remained, polls and anecdotal reports initially indicated most were trying to ignore the war and get on with their lives, much as they did when Russia was in Afghanistan a generation earlier. Yet as the three-day "special operation" stretched into a half a year, Putin's hope that ordinary Russians would ignore the conflict as a small sideshow was beginning to wash away, especially as a large-scale mobilization was ordered. As Burns said that summer, even amid the relentless optimism of state-controlled TV and media, it is hard to hide that sons aren't coming home—even in a world of information control.

But in Russia, Putin wasn't giving an inch—at least publicly. The Americans and the British took every opportunity to offer up horrific estimates of Russian casualties. Twenty thousand Russians died in the first six months of fighting, British intelligence reported, nearly three times the number of Americans who died in Afghanistan and Iraq over the previous twenty years. Another sixty thousand were injured.

At the CIA, I was struck by the other new addition to Burns's wall: a wanted poster for Ayman al-Zawahiri, the leader of al-Qaeda. Just weeks before, Zawahiri had been killed by a missile launched from a CIA drone. But by the time Zawahiri was killed, most Americans barely knew of him: Even one of Biden's closest national security aides admitted to me he thought the killing of al-Qaeda's No. 2 "would be a blip." Putin, in contrast, was in the headlines every day. He had spent the summer fighting over inches and feet in the Donbas, and his plan to take the whole country—the plan on Burns's battle map—seemed like ancient history. But Burns did not believe that Putin thought he was losing. "It's his own cockiness," he said. "He is convinced that when winter comes and prices for energy rise, the Europeans will back off. And he thinks the Americans have attention-deficit when it comes to overseas wars." No matter what message Burns's battle map sent, six months into the war, Europe was a changed place. Save for Ukraine itself, its borders looked the same. Its psyche did not.

Gone forever was the certainty that a "Europe whole and free"—the mantra of George H. W. Bush when the Berlin War fell—meant very much. The assumption that the Russians would be a stable supplier of gas—because it was in their economic interest—not only looked outdated, it looked wildly naïve.

"There's a new sense of vulnerability everywhere," said one senior French diplomat to me during a visit to Washington. In some cities protesters took to the streets objecting to high energy prices, fearful of the worst when winter came. Seventy thousand took over Wenceslas Square in Prague, arguing for some kind of accord—anything, really—that would bring down prices. Estonians and Latvians, while celebrating that Putin had received a black eye after trying to take all of Ukraine in one gulp, harbored no illusions that Putin's humiliating retreat would change his ultimate goals.

"If you think the sanctions taught him a lesson," the senior French official told me, "think again." In fact, Washington and London were awash in intelligence reports, all highly classified, assessing where Putin might head next and how he would react if he feared an embarrassing retreat. The State Department turned out a list of nations that needed financial support to ward off any future Russian aggression: It had roughly two dozen countries on it, including Poland and other NATO nations.

"Putin hasn't changed his overall goals," warned John Kirby, the retired admiral who served as the Defense Department spokesman before Biden brought him to the White House. "His plan is to overthrow the current government in Ukraine and supplant it with one of his own. Beyond that, we just don't know."

But that goal appeared, for now, to be out of Putin's reach. Ukraine itself had morphed into two nations—one in the midst of a desperate war for survival, one in the cafés.

In the south and the east, the buildings were carcasses, the people were homeless, the shelling was senseless. Families were evaporated in a single strike. Nothing worked—not the electricity, not the gas. To those suffering the worst of it, in cities like Kherson, fate always seemed in someone else's hands—maybe Putin's, maybe Biden's, maybe those of some low-ranking soldier stuffing rounds into an artillery piece and firing blindly.

On August 24, 2022, Ukraine's Independence Day, which, by an accident of the calendar, coincided with the six-month anniversary of the war, Zelensky tried again to rally the country, though this time in a prerecorded video since it was clear Russia would target him at any live

274 WARS, HOT AND COLD

celebration. "It is important to never, not for a minute, relent to the enemy's pressure," he said. "Don't bend, don't show weakness."

Yet in the capital, residents of Kyiv had returned to something approaching normalcy. Coffee shops were filled; ordering an espresso was suddenly an act of defiance. While remnants of missile strikes from the late winter were everywhere, businesses began to return. Residents warily took the train back from Poland, though they always made sure they had a Plan B, a fast way out. Putin had been vanquished. But everyone understood that, in the new world, he had ways of wreaking new havoc.

They suspected the havoc was coming. They just didn't know how bad it would be.

ON AUGUST 30, Mikhail Gorbachev, the man who dissolved the Soviet Union, died in Moscow—and so did, for many, the last reminder of what could have been.

At ninety-one, Gorbachev had been sidelined for years, celebrated by a dwindling number of Russian reformists and reviled among millions of Russians who blamed him for the country's three decades of decline. In his later years, Gorbachev himself had come to accept, reluctantly, that his grand hopes of integrating Russia into Europe had collapsed; Putin had made sure of that. But in his final months, the brutality of the events running across his television screen left him truly confused. Those who knew him best and stuck with him said that he died "shocked and bewildered" by the invasion of Ukraine.

Pavel Palazhchenko, who had spent decades working with Gorbachev and was a player in the arms-control talks with the Reagan administration, told Reuters that it was not just the invasion that left Gorbachev so stunned. It was "the entire evolution of relations between Russia and Ukraine over the past years that was really, really a big blow to him. It really crushed him emotionally and psychologically." All of his work had been undone.

So it might have been some small solace to Gorbachev that, in death, he provided many Russians with something they desperately needed: a legal way to protest Putin's war.

By the thousands, Russians nostalgic for the era of glasnost poured into Moscow's famous "House of the Unions"—the domed palace where services had also been held for Lenin and Stalin—to pay their respects. As classical music wafted through the air, they arrived with flowers. They also came with a recognition that Gorbachev, for all his mistakes and limitations, for all the bungling of the dissolution of the state, had given them a glimpse of what freedom is like. But only briefly.

By the time Gorbachev died, the only truly lasting element of his legacy was that the Union of the Soviet Socialist Republics remained dissolved, with many of its former states now part of NATO. The free-spirited, sometimes freely critical press that had sprung up in the Gorbachev and Yeltsin eras had been gradually choked off during twenty years of Putin's rule. The students who had crowded into that university event featuring Putin and George W. Bush asking when they could get work permits or education visas to Europe and the United States were now middle-aged, despairing that the moment to consider themselves Europeans had passed for good. A student in the crowd told two of my *Times* colleagues that "for so many of us in Moscow, his death seems the death of democracy."

Putin, of course, had nothing but disdain for Gorbachev: Like many Russians, he associated the former leader with an era of chaos and humiliation. And as Masha Gessen wrote in *The New Yorker* shortly after Gorbachev's death, "He has never forgiven Gorbachev for abandoning KGB officers in Dresden, the satellite country itself, and the dream of a giant European empire."

Putin skipped the funeral, but his statement about Gorbachev's legacy was masterly. He called him "a politician and statesman who had a huge impact on the course of world history." It could not have been clearer: Putin regarded Gorbachev's "impact" as an unmitigated disaster—one that Putin had devoted the past thirty years of his life attempting to reverse. The Ukraine invasion was the most dramatic—and risky—step in that direction.

Yet he knew he had to tread lightly. Gorbachev's supporters knew it, too—Putin could not risk arresting Russians for coming out to celebrate Gorbachev's legacy. His exquisitely timed death was a one-time opportunity, a chance to legally gather in support of Russia's brief experiment with something approaching a free society. Once Gorbachev was in the ground, they all knew, any similar act of quiet dissent would result in arrest.

So for now, they sang and mourned. A few recalled Vitaly Mansky's *Gorbachev. Heaven,* one of the last documentaries that Gorbachev had appeared in, as he sang along to the Russian national anthem while ringing in the 2020 New Year. When the line "Be glorious, our free fatherland!" was sung, Gorbachev was shown smiling.

"And who brought the freedom?" he had asked.

CHAPTER 14

CROSSING THE LINE

Those who play with fire will perish by it. It is hoped that the U.S. will be clear-eyed about this.

Xi Jinping to Biden, July 28, 2022, days before Nancy Pelosi landed in Taiwan

O N A MIDSUMMER day in 2022, a U.S. Air Force Boeing jet flying under the call sign SPAR19 took an unusual route from Kuala Lumpur, the Malaysian capital, to Taipei, Taiwan. Even flying directly, this would be no short trip but a nearly three-thousand-kilometer slog northeast.

But this flight, on August 2, was anything but ordinary. As it headed to Taipei, the plane was being tracked live on CNN and carefully monitored in Beijing. It was also the subject of breathless news reports in Asia. As the plane took a broad C-shaped path, sweeping east across Indonesia and then back northwest through the Philippine Sea—nearly doubling the flight time—the question resonated around the world: How were the Chinese going to react once it lands?

The reason for the world's attention—and the circuitous routing—was the plane's cargo: Nancy Pelosi, the eighty-two-year-old speaker of the U.S. House of Representatives, who was determined that she was going to make an official visit to Taiwan before her tenure ended. As she headed to the island, one stop in a longer itinerary that hopscotched through southeast Asia, the Air Force jet's pilots were determined not to tempt fate by flying over Chinese airspace—or anywhere near it.

"It was very . . . long," recalled Andy Kim, the New Jersey Democrat who was one of several members of Congress on board that day. "I remember looking out the window at some point and I was like, 'I think we're flying over Borneo?'"

For Kim and the four other members of Congress accompanying Pelosi on the flight, this was more drama than they were used to. For the most part, official congressional visits abroad—known in Washington-speak as "CODELs"—never make the news. They usually fall on the spectrum somewhere between educational tourism and shopping-and-dining junkets. John McCain was never happier than when he was roaming through Baghdad in a flak jacket. But occasionally, one will hit a geopolitical nerve and land on the news. Two members of Congress were criticized for dropping in on Kabul in the middle of the evacuation of embassy personnel from Afghanistan. What made Pelosi's visit different was that she wasn't dropping into a war zone. The concern was that it was provoking the Chinese.

In fact, hitting a nerve is exactly what Pelosi had in mind. She had never been to Taiwan as Speaker, and she knew her time in leadership was nearing its end. To her mind, she had a long history of challenging Beijing on human rights issues. She had visited Tiananmen Square just two years after student protesters were killed in 1989, hand-delivered petitions to President Hu Jintao, and protested the first Olympics held on Chinese territory in the summer of 2008. This trip would be the capstone of a career-long effort to stand up to Beijing.

But when the rumors first surfaced that summer that Pelosi's routine Asia trip would feature a stop in Taiwan, Biden's team—particularly Campbell and Sullivan—grew uneasy. Xi was weeks away from being reaffirmed for a third term as president in the 20th Communist Party Congress and would face enormous pressure to make clear that Taiwan—what they called a "renegade province" that China had long regarded as its own—would be reunified with the mainland. U.S. intelligence officials thought Xi was more than likely to use Pelosi's visit as an excuse to change the status quo and step up military pressure against Taipei.

Still, it was evident that Biden—a man who had spent nearly four decades in the Senate—felt he had no business unilaterally telling the

Speaker of the House what she could or could not do. What Xi had to understand, the White House maintained, was that there were three coequal branches of government in the United States, and this was a routine congressional visit to a democratic partner. There was even precedent: Newt Gingrich had visited Taipei when he was Speaker.

So Biden refused to call Pelosi and ask her not to go, which she made clear was the only way she would back down. In public, the most President Biden would offer was a half-hearted warning: "The military," he said back in July, "thinks it's not a good idea right now."

Yet, as Pelosi and her staff planned their trip, Biden's top advisors went to considerable lengths to convince them to skip Taiwan—without ever directly telling her to back down. In multiple rounds of talks— many of which were held in a secure facility inside the Capitol Building— Sullivan, Campbell, and others briefed Pelosi and staff on the latest intelligence and their best guesses about how Xi would exploit the moment. Military exercises off Taiwan's coast were a given. Missile tests into the Taiwan Strait and surrounding waters were likely. Some officials thought that China might demonstrate its ability to establish a "quarantine" of the island—in the style of the Cuban Missile Crisis sixty years before—in a not-so-subtle demonstration of a potential disruption of the supply chain of computer chips that the West depended on for everything from iPhones to F-35s.

"It was never framed as, 'We urge you not to go on this trip' or something like that," recalled Congressman Kim, who attended several of the briefings. "And then usually, at the very end, Jake and/or Kurt would lay out just a little bit more directly that, you know, 'Maybe now's not the time' or 'Maybe this is too much on the plate.' But I never heard anyone directly say, 'The president doesn't want you to go on this trip.'"

Andy Kim was a member of a small cohort of former national security wonks who had made the leap to retail politics but maintained a strong interest in America's defenses and its approach to the world. A second-generation American—his parents immigrated from South Korea—he spent his early adulthood as a civilian advisor to the military and a midlevel official in the National Security Council, dealing with what seemed like the challenge of his generation: counterterrorism and the unraveling of America's once-great ambitions for Afghanistan and Iraq.

Now Kim, like many in that establishment, was boning up on a whole new era of conflict and competition for the United States. And he worried that Taiwan could be a flashpoint—a pawn caught between two powers whose rhetoric, he feared, could be driving toward war.

Kim admitted he had his own concerns about the wisdom of Pelosi's trip. But they did not stop him from signing up for the delegation. "Part of it was, I did want to go to Taiwan at some point," he told me. "If the United States is in a place where we even have to contemplate what to do next when it comes to Taiwan, I wanted to see with my own eyes. I wanted to go and engage and get a sense of the readiness of their military." Having served as a civilian advisor to the U.S. military in Afghanistan and Iraq, Kim had watched the fall of Kabul the previous year in horror. He needed to know if the United States was heading for anything like that in the case of a Chinese attack against Taiwan.

And so, on August 2, SPAR19 became a minor internet sensation: Nearly 3 million people checked into FlightRadar24's website, temporarily crashing the online service. Like moths to a flame, they wanted to know if Pelosi would bail out at the last minute and skip over Taiwan—or whether, as she herself had speculated with a considerable dose of drama, there was a chance that the "plane would get shot down or something like that by the Chinese."

Onboard the plane, Kim recalled, the atmosphere was relatively quiet. But as the craft headed into Taiwan's airspace, three capitals quietly went into crisis mode.

IN WASHINGTON, the Pelosi visit couldn't have come at a worse moment. For nearly six months, Biden and his national security team had been focused on keeping Ukraine from being cracked apart. Now they were bracing themselves for the very real possibility that, on the other side of the globe, a conflict requiring a major American military presence would escalate beyond control with very little warning.

The month of August 2022 was, Toria Nuland later recalled, "a bracing experience." The same small group of national security officials would move from a meeting on the Ukraine war directly to a meeting on avoiding a conflict over Taiwan. "There was no way of knowing— from the low end of public noise and a few more sorties to an actual physical effort to pressure Taiwan—how extreme the PRC reaction to Pelosi was going to be," she said, using a familiar acronym for the People's Republic of China. "So we had to plan for the whole spectrum."

The fear was that Xi, understanding Biden's preoccupation with Ukraine, might conclude that the moment had come to make his move on Taiwan. Pentagon planners always talked about whether the United States was prepared to fight two wars simultaneously, but here the question was different: Could it handle two crises with two very different nuclear-armed adversaries?

"In the worst case, could we handle both at once?" Nuland recalled wondering.

IN BEIJING, Pelosi's flight was seen as an opportunity, a chance to alter the status quo in the air and waters around Taiwan, by expressing outrage and then executing a carefully planned retaliation.

For months Beijing had been issuing a stream of warnings that the visit of any high-ranking American, especially the Speaker of the House, would prompt retaliation. It was clear that many of the warnings were designed for public consumption, and they grew sharper as the visit drew closer. It was grimly amusing that one of China's top diplomats, Liu Xiaoming, turned to Twitter—a platform banned in China, of course—to make his case. "We are closely following the itinerary of #Pelosi," he wrote. "A visit to #Taiwan by her would constitute a gross interference in #China's internal affairs, seriously undermine China's sovereignty and territorial integrity, wantonly trample on the #one-China principle."

A former editor for the *Global Times,* the Communist Party mouthpiece, was more succinct: "If she dares to stop in Taiwan, it will be the moment to ignite the powder keg of the situation in the Taiwan Straits."

The trip was important enough to merit a conversation at the highest levels of both governments. The week before Pelosi left, Xi and Biden spoke on the phone for over two hours in a wide-ranging conversation that featured an "in-depth discussion" on Taiwan.

While the United States was careful to share little about the call, the Chinese didn't hesitate to make their position clear: "China firmly opposes separatist moves toward 'Taiwan independence' and interference by external forces, and never allows any room for 'Taiwan independence' forces in whatever form. . . . Those who play with fire will perish by it. It is hoped that the U.S. will be clear-eyed about this." It wasn't the first time that Xi had used this kind of language. In the current moment, it seemed stark.

The White House insisted that the call had been in the works for some time. The Chinese emphasized that the conversation was at Biden's request. What was clear was that the call was an effort by the Biden administration to engage in a bit of personal diplomacy with Xi—to try to make sure that even if an international incident flared up, the two countries could continue to work together on unrelated topics such as climate and health security.

The chatter that American intelligence agencies were picking up made it evident: The Chinese military was ready for a show of force. It was the excuse they'd been waiting for, a chance to tighten the screws on Taiwan without looking like the instigator.

IN THE PRESIDENTIAL Palace in Taipei, no one was watching the Chinese reaction more closely than Alex Huang, one of President Tsai Ing-wen's most influential staffers. Rail-thin with a trimmed goatee, he was known for spending day and night at work.

"I was in the president's office all day," Huang said, referring to the ornate building in the heart of Taipei that once housed Japanese occupation forces but now hosts President Tsai's staff. "From the moment Pelosi took off to the moment she landed, we were watching carefully."

On the wall of Huang's office, a framed copy of the American Declaration of Independence made it plain, without quite saying it, where he stood on the question of Taiwan independence.

What worried Huang, he told me months later, was that even before Pelosi's trip, China had been steadily tightening the screws on Taipei. In June, it claimed "sovereignty, sovereign rights, and jurisdiction" over the Taiwan Strait—arguing, essentially, not only that did it not belong to Taiwan but that the rest of the world could not so much as traverse it without China's explicit permission. Then Huang had watched as Chinese military drills in the region stepped up dramatically—some of which had crossed into the first island chain, which runs from well north of Taiwan down to Malaysia and Vietnam.

Huang and his colleagues found themselves in a tricky spot. Beijing was no doubt going to take some form of escalatory action in response to Pelosi's visit. But Taiwan couldn't just roll over. There was a principle at stake: Beijing could not dictate with whom the Taiwanese president could meet. If the Taiwanese leadership bowed to the mainland on this, who knew what the next demand would be?

"It was a sensitive time" for China, too, Huang said, quite matter-of-factly. The 20th Party Congress, where Xi would be anointed as China's leader for another five years and perhaps for life, was just weeks away. Huang knew Xi would view Pelosi's trip as a test of his toughness. "So they had to overreact," he concluded.

The real trouble, he feared, would start not when Pelosi was on the island. It would come when she left again.

NO CRISIS HAPPENS in a vacuum. To some of the Chinese leaders, the latest Taiwan crisis was not so much about Pelosi getting on an airplane as it was about the recent pattern of the famously loose-lipped Joe Biden talking openly—and repeatedly—about how the United States would send forces to defend Taiwan in the event of an unprovoked invasion of the island. This was different from Ukraine, where he had banned sending forces, Biden kept telling interviewers. Taiwan, he noted, is an island democracy whose partnership with the United States stretches back decades that is also host to the most critical network of semiconductor manufacturing facilities in the world.

For decades, the United States has maintained a delicate balance of support for Taiwan under a policy known as "strategic ambiguity," refusing to clarify exactly how America would come to Taipei's defense in the event of a Chinese invasion. The idea was to leave both foreign governments guessing and, presumably, unwilling to take the risk of escalating a direct confrontation with the other. Strategic ambiguity had been more or less successful in keeping the peace for decades. It kept the Taiwanese from doing something stupid that would start a war, and it kept the Chinese from acting on their invasion plans.

In practice, strategic ambiguity meant that eight American presidents in a row had refused to enunciate how the United States would respond to an invasion of Taiwan. They would repeat, almost by rote, that there is only "One China" and that the dispute between Taiwan and the mainland would have to be resolved peacefully. Taiwan should not provoke a crisis by declaring independence. Beijing should not provoke a crisis by settling the issue by force.

The problem was that strategic ambiguity was not only difficult to decode—What constitutes a "provocation"? Is a cyberattack an "invasion"?—it was difficult to maintain. Remaining ambiguous requires constant adjustments to rhetoric and action and sometimes carefully calibrated demonstrations of force.

In his first few months in office Biden was clearly worried that strategic ambiguity had waned, and that the Chinese believed it was highly unlikely that the United States would deploy its military to come to the island's aid. The Trump years had made it clear to the Chinese that there was a significant constituency in the United States for pulling back America's expensive troop commitments in Asia. And while Biden was now saying he was investing in Asia, his decision to pull out from Afghanistan underscored the absence of American staying power. "He thought 'strategic ambiguity' had eroded over time," one of Biden's advisors told me in 2022. So over the course of thirteen months—from August of 2021 through September of 2022—Biden sought to sow seeds of fresh doubt in the minds of the Chinese leadership about how America would respond to aggression toward Taiwan.

He started with an interview right at the moment the United States was withdrawing from Afghanistan. When asked about Taiwan, he said that no one should doubt his willingness to defend treaty allies like Japan and South Korea—and Taiwan. To these allies, he added, the United States had a "sacred commitment." It was that line, perhaps more than any other, that struck such a chord in Beijing—it sounded different from the canned lines of past presidents.

Taiwan is not a treaty ally, like Japan or South Korea or the members of NATO. The details of the U.S. defense commitments have consistently remained unstated. So after the "sacred commitment" comment, White House press aides rushed to assure reporters that it represented no change in policy. They hinted, without saying so, that the president had just misspoken. It was just Biden being Biden, the spokesman suggested.

But then, in October 2021, Biden said it again. The United States had a "commitment" to come to the island's defense. This time it was a senior administration official who called to assure me that Biden wasn't changing American policy.

The next declaration came in May 2022, three months after the invasion of Ukraine, during a presidential visit to Tokyo. America's commitment to Taiwan, Biden insisted with the Japanese prime minister standing beside him, was "even stronger" after Ukraine, suggesting that he would send troops if needed to defend Taiwan from invasion. The senior official called again, conceding with an embarrassed chuckle that it was getting harder to assert that nothing had changed.

Finally, in a *60 Minutes* interview in the fall of 2022, Biden repeated that U.S. forces would defend Taiwan "if in fact, there was an unprecedented attack." The interviewer pressed him: Did that mean that—unlike in Ukraine—he would send American men and women to fight directly against a nuclear-armed superpower?

"Yes," he said.

This time, my source at the White House didn't even bother calling to clarify the comments.

Who knows what Biden, or a successor, would actually do in another Taiwan crisis? At a minimum, Biden was determined to make the Chinese leadership ask that very question—to make them hesitate before assuming that the United States no longer had the reach or the will to steam across the Pacific for a task as overwhelming as defending a small democracy a hundred miles off the Chinese coast.

BIDEN WAS HARDLY the first president to grapple with the problem of Taiwan. In point of fact, he was the fourteenth. But the options over the past seven decades hadn't really improved. What had changed were the stakes: The island's importance to the world—to the global economy—had grown exponentially compared to Truman and Eisenhower's time.

In the 1950s, Taiwan was a mountainous exile for Generalissimo Chiang Kai-shek, the nationalist leader of the Kuomintang (KMT) who had met with Roosevelt and Churchill at the end of the Pacific War to plan Japan's defeat, only to find himself in a desperate civil war back at home. He was a brutal authoritarian who kept the country under martial law—his forces killed tens of thousands of civilians and locked up tens of thousands more. There was no political freedom and no freedom of the press. But he ranked among America's favorite dictators because he stood up to the communists running the mainland. In an era governed by the domino theory, Taiwan was a key bulwark.

Initially, Harry Truman had little interest in Taiwan or its defense. When Chiang's forces retreated to the island, Truman said he would "not provide military aid or advice to Chinese forces on Formosa," which was the island's former name. In fact, Truman assumed that the communists, under Mao, would take the island back from Chiang in a matter of months. But after the Korean War broke out—and the United States found itself fighting the Soviets and the Chinese on the Korean Peninsula—Truman reversed course. He sent the Seventh Fleet into the Taiwan Strait and recognized Taiwan as the real China, making sure it, and not the People's Republic of China governed by Mao, held the single Chinese seat at the United Nations. Over the next decades, keeping the rest of Asia out of communist hands became the driving goal of American foreign policy.

In the 1960 presidential election, no one was more fixated on pushing the communists back from Taiwan than Richard Nixon. During his presidential debates with John F. Kennedy, he argued that the United States should have done more to defend two tiny islands belonging to Taiwan—Matsu and Quemoy—which had come under episodic shelling from the People's Liberation Army in the 1950s.

A dozen years later, the world looked different. When Nixon made his famous visit to China in 1972, it was motivated in large part by a fierce desire to keep China and the Soviet Union from joining forces against the United States. America formally recognized the People's Republic as the sole government of China in 1979, under Jimmy Carter's administration, and suddenly the United States had to redefine its relationship with Taiwan, which was no longer, in American eyes or American law, a real country. It was now an island, in every sense.

For the four decades since, Taiwan has lived in an uneasy netherworld; it has diplomats in the United States but cannot declare its presence in Washington an "embassy." It buys weapons from the United

States but has been warned not to provoke China by declaring independence. The goal, as described in the 1979 Taiwan Relations Act, is to "maintain the capacity of the United States to resist any resort to force or other forms of coercion that would jeopardize the security, or the social or economic system, of the people on Taiwan."

The vagueness of the commitment only adds to the awkwardness of American officials' discourse about the obligation. The act, for example, vows to defend "the people on Taiwan"—but not the island itself. American officials wove a series of understandings that they repeated, mantra-like, at every meeting with Chinese officials: There is only One China, and it is up to the mainland and Taiwan to sort it all out—peacefully. Then, by rote, they tick off the "six assurances" and the "three communiqués" that guide the relationship with the mainland. "I can do it in my sleep," one of Biden's advisors told me.

By the time I first traveled to Taipei in the late 1980s, it was clear that the Taiwanese were much more fixated on their own internal political battles—and the effort to move from authoritarian rule to democracy—than they were on the prospect of a forced reunification with the mainland. Martial law had been lifted. Younger generations had begun to identify themselves as Taiwanese, not Chinese—a national identity that only hardened over the years. And a genuine opposition party, the Democratic Progressive Party, had formed, and it was often unapologetic about its desire for an independent Taiwan.

Perhaps the biggest change on the island was not well understood at the time. A year after Chiang's death in 1975, his government convinced RCA, the American electronics giant, to begin teaching the Taiwanese how to make semiconductors. That move would turn out to become one of the primary reasons that Taiwan would matter so greatly to the rest of the world four decades later. If Taiwan ceased to exist—or smoldered under Chinese artillery barrages—the digital economy would crack apart.

As real politics began to emerge in the 1980s and 1990s, so did real conversation—and substantial trade—with the mainland. Semiofficial delegations began to meet; in Hong Kong in 1992, they worked out a tentative new political relationship—nothing approaching diplomatic recognition but rather the ambiguous framework that dictated relations for thirty years.

"I call it 'creative ambiguity,'" said Su Chi, the former KMT official who served first as the minister responsible for managing Taiwan's relationship with mainland China and then as the head of Taiwan's national security council. At the core of the ambiguity, according to Su, was that both sides agreed there was only One China, but each side could interpret for itself what that meant.

The agreement supercharged the burgeoning trade relationship. China became one of Taiwan's largest trading partners—no small feat considering that until 2003, direct flights between the two were still not permitted. (Everyone had to switch planes in places like Hong Kong.) Within a decade China had become Taiwan's largest export market. The key was preserving a "gray area," Su told me, for the political leaders in both Taipei and Beijing. It was "mysterious," he conceded, but "ambiguous enough for China to agree that 'okay, we [can] work on this basis.'"

Thinking back on the era, Su was struck by the absence of urgency on the part of China to move on its territorial claim on Taiwan. As long as everyone was making money, there was no rush. In turn, Taiwan had come to live with the fact that as long as it didn't declare independence, it could live between two worlds. And make a lot of money.

It was a wonderful non-compromise. Su told me that for a number of years he believed that Taiwan might truly be able to "float" in between the great powers, supplying both, siding with neither. As their relative power rose and fell, Taiwan could shift alliances and strategies accordingly—a sort of "strategic equilibrium" that others have attempted. It was very French.

Naturally, it couldn't last. Over the next few decades, the delicate political balance—held together chiefly by mutual economic benefit—began to fray at the edges. While trade increased, China used every bit of its economic leverage to force countries to abandon their diplomatic recognition of Taiwan and embrace the mainland as the only true China. Only Vatican City and about a dozen small powers recognized Taiwan, and Beijing was picking them off one by one.

The breaking point came as Xi Jinping consolidated power. Gradually, it became clear that all the American intelligence analysis stating that he would focus on the economy and avoid conflict was wrong. Xi was determined to control the outliers—starting with Tibet, Hong

Kong, and the Muslim-majority area of Xinjiang. When the last of Hong Kong's street protesters were finally crushed in 2020, it was clear that Taiwan could easily be next.

And Su argued to me that Taiwan overplayed its hand, too, moving too close to the United States too quickly. Dialogue with the mainland ceased when President Tsai, representing the Democratic Progressive Party, came in; it was instantly clear that whatever ambiguous consensus had been reached in 1992, she wasn't buying it. In Su's mind, that was a mistake. "You should always give China hope," he said, "Like, 'Yes, of course I'll marry you. But not yet.'" (Of course, Tsai's allies argue that the KMT is composed of China apologists who were trying to sell the country back to Beijing.)

But the larger problem, Su argued, was the rapid decline in the U.S.-China relationship, which, starting late in the Trump administration, had been in free fall. "You've got a lot of 'Young Turks' in your government," he said, indicating that they were a bunch of radicals committed to dramatically changing the status quo.

It was true that U.S. politicians were engaged in a contest to show which party could be more critical of China. But Beijing was also throwing its weight around, alienating regional allies and would-be partners with its predatory lending, its transparent manipulation of global standards, its crackdowns against its own people. And so as tensions worsened, the possibility of a forced reunification with Taiwan, even a full-scale invasion of the island, started to loom ever larger.

This was the turbulence that Nancy Pelosi was flying into.

AS HUANG WATCHED from his office in the presidential palace, Pelosi landed uneventfully at Taipei's Songshan Airport about an hour before midnight on August 2. The Chinese military steered clear of her plane, showing little desire to provoke an immediate crisis or risk direct engagement with the U.S. Air Force.

It had not been the easiest of days for Huang. Disinformation operations were running amok. At the national university, hacked screens proclaimed, "There is only One China in the world"; in 7-Eleven stores across the country, TV screens read, "Warmonger Pelosi get out of Taiwan." Cyberattacks—fairly unsophisticated ones, to be sure—targeted government computers in the Presidential Office and the Legislative Yuan, Taiwan's law-making body.

Rumors spread online that violence—or even outright war—was imminent. Chinese troops were firing live artillery, warned one report. Another claimed that the People's Liberation Army was deployed just across the Taiwan Strait—using a photograph of a North Korean drill from 2017. Some claimed that three U.S. warplanes had flown near the island. (They had not.) Then reports circulated that nearly two dozen Chinese warplanes had crossed into Taiwan's air defense identification zone that day. (This was true, but the region is so crowded that China, Taiwan, Korea, and Japan have overlapping claims.)

Pelosi showed no sign of being perturbed as she descended onto the tarmac, perfectly coiffed—as usual—in a powder-pink power suit, pearls, and pristine white pumps. Crowds with American flags and signs flooded around the airport, creating a parade-like atmosphere. There were also some protesters, whom Representative Kim noticed as he got off the plane. It was "actually kind of heartening," he said, a hallmark of authentic democracy.

The next day, Pelosi stood side by side with President Tsai in a high-ceilinged reception room down the hall from the Presidential Office. The comments were pro forma—the significance of the visit lay in the fact that she had come at all, not in anything she said.

Tsai quite consciously connected the lesson of the war in Ukraine and Taiwan's predicament. "Russia's invasion of Ukraine earlier this year has made security over the Taiwan Strait another focus of worldwide attention," she said. "Aggression against democratic Taiwan would have a tremendous impact on the security of the entire Indo-Pacific."

"Our solidarity with you is more important than ever, as you defend Taiwan and their freedom," Pelosi responded. She said she had come to highlight the "very strong contrast" between democracy in Taiwan and "what's happening on mainland China." There was "no more evidence needed than what happened in Hong Kong under 'one country, two systems.' That didn't happen."

Her comments amounted to something scores of American officials had said before. But because of where she was standing, they triggered a diplomatic nightmare.

. . .

AS PELOSI LANDED in Taiwan, R. Nicholas Burns, the veteran American diplomat serving as ambassador to Beijing, knew that he would be on the receiving end of the first blast from the Chinese government. Refreshingly, for him, it meant that for once he would get some high-level contact with the Foreign Ministry.

Since his arrival in Beijing in March 2022, Burns had lived in something of a gilded prison in the American ambassador's residence in Beijing, an aging but graceful residence that dates back to George H. W. Bush's days as the American representative to Beijing in the 1970s. The strange mix of COVID lockdowns and the Chinese desire to freeze out the Biden administration's top representative—much as they believed the Chinese ambassador was treated in Washington—meant that Burns had far less contact with the upper reaches of the Chinese leadership than he was accustomed to in previous ambassadorships.

Without question, Burns ranked among America's most experienced diplomats. He served as the American ambassador to NATO during the worst days of the Forever Wars, as he tried to convince European diplomats to help pacify and then rebuild Afghanistan. He designed the first efforts to isolate Iran, hoping that the right mix of deterrence, dissuasion, and economic incentives would draw it away from its nuclear ambitions. Now, after a thirteen-year hiatus teaching at Harvard, he was back in the diplomacy business, but this time in a country whose relationship with the United States was spiraling down as Chinese diplomats and military officials argued that America was in an irreversible decline. When his wife, Libby, asked him what would constitute success in this new diplomatic mission, Burns responded: "Avoiding war."

But fulfilling that mission required actually meeting and talking with Chinese officials, who, despite all the differences between the two countries, were among the "hardest-working, best prepared" diplomats in the world, according to Burns.

But those meetings were slow to happen.

"COVID dominated my first ten months here until the Chinese government did away with the zero-COVID protocols," he told me, referring to Beijing's "maximum suppression" strategy for combating the pandemic. Beyond his own embassy staff, he had few interactions with ordinary Chinese, so he came up with an innovative solution. Because Beijing required regular COVID testing, he would go outside the high walls of the embassy and line up with the locals in his neighborhood, chatting with diplomats and delivery people, students and office workers as they waited. Chinese social media noticed. While the Communist Party leadership was getting red-carpet treatment, Burns was standing in line like everyone else. "I thought that it was a really important thing to show the Chinese people that we were going to take whatever hardships they were," he said.

On the rare occasion he got in to see Chinese officials, it wasn't very productive. When he went to present his diplomatic credentials in March 2022 to the chief of protocol at the Chinese foreign ministry, he expected it to be routine: a handshake, maybe a brief sit-down over tea to trade pleasantries. To his surprise, the officer launched into a carefully scripted diatribe. "He was criticizing the United States and NATO up and down for having caused the war in Ukraine," Burns recalled. The officer's complaint echoed what was beginning to show up in the Chinese press: The United States and NATO had driven Putin to invade by expanding NATO nearly two decades earlier. "We had challenged Putin," Burns was told. "We had hurt his feelings, and we had caused the war . . . nearly twenty years later." Burns pushed back hard, drawing on his years as NATO ambassador, punching holes in the official Chinese history. But he knew China was settling in on its narrative of events—one that closely matched Putin's.

Five months later, with Pelosi landing in Taipei, Burns was awaiting the inevitable Chinese eruption—likely from a higher-ranking Chinese diplomat this time—another step down in what was now a plummeting relationship with Beijing. He had no way of knowing just how severe China's reaction would be, or whether Xi would exploit the moment to change the status quo in the Taiwan Strait.

Predictably, on the night of August 2, one of China's vice ministers for foreign affairs, Xie Feng, summoned Burns to the ministry at 10:45 P.M.—as Pelosi's plane was scheduled to land—to read him the riot act. Burns had been anticipating the call—in fact, he had left his summer vacation with his wife and grandchildren on the New England coast so that he would be back in Beijing—with the required ten days of quarantine in Shanghai behind him—before the Pelosi visit.

Burns knew that the summons from Xie was timed to be supremely inconvenient. But diplomatic convention dictated that when ambassadors are summoned for a démarche, they cheerfully head off for their ass-chewing. Once inside the office, Xie argued that the United States was paying lip service to its agreements with China while openly fomenting rebellion in Taiwan. "For quite some time, the United States has said one thing but done the opposite, constantly distorted, altered, obscured and hollowed out the one-China principle in an attempt to cross the red line," said Xie, clearly working from a carefully prepared script as he lectured Burns. "Those who play with fire will perish by it. Taiwan is China's Taiwan, and will eventually return to the embrace of the motherland."

The content of this conversation became immediately known to all interested parties because the Chinese government published it—their side of it, at least. No mention was made of Burns's response, of course. Burns told them that in American democracy, the executive branch doesn't control the legislative branch, so Pelosi was free to do what she viewed as fit. He refused Xie's demand for an apology and dismissed China's argument that the United States, and the United States alone, had escalated regional tensions. It was China that was bombarding Taiwan with cyberattacks and buzzing it with fighter jets. Beijing, he told Xie, never missed an opportunity to overreact.

But as Burns left the building, he shook his head, thinking back to the days when he, like most American diplomats, was strongly in the "engagement" camp. Burns had given up on that approach after a 2010 trip to China's Central Party School—the government-run think tank—led him to conclude that China had chosen a different path. Now, the best bet, in his mind, was to double down on alliances with like-minded nations—many of them nondemocracies or fragile democracies. Alliances were the only force multiplier that mattered. Burns was convinced that far more countries would be nervous in a world that used China's operating system rather than that developed by the United States.

PELOSI'S TRIP WOUND down with no sign of an imminent Chinese attack. Maybe, one leading Taiwanese legislator told me, "China is just a paper tiger."

The reprieve didn't last long. Just hours after Pelosi departed, Chinese naval and military aircraft began exercises in the South China Sea, encircling the island and preparing for what the Chinese state broadcaster described as practice sea assaults, land strikes, aerial combat, and "joint containment." They shot eleven ballistic missiles into the sea around Taiwan—something that had not occurred since 1996. They crossed the median line of the Taiwan Strait, an informal line of demarcation they had usually respected.

Taiwan did not announce any of these incursions. The Japanese, who couldn't help but notice that five of them had landed in its own exclusive economic zone, made the news public. "We didn't want to cause panic," Huang told me when I asked about Taiwan's restraint. Besides, he said, the military had told him that a missile launched that high into the atmosphere wasn't technically in Taiwanese airspace anyway.

Over the next week, more than fifty Chinese warships and more than two hundred combat planes launched a series of complex maneuvers down the middle of the Strait. The message was lost on no one: If China ever decided to take the island by force or to squeeze it, cutting off its undersea cables and connections to the broader world, here was a taste of what it would look like.

IN WASHINGTON, Pelosi's visit was largely forgotten by the next news cycle. Not so in the Pacific, where there would be no return to the status quo. Beijing stopped shooting missiles over Taiwan, but made it clear that the median line no longer existed. The move into Japan's "exclusive economic zone" sent the message that the zone was no longer so exclusive. By circling the island, they were saying that this was all Chinese waters.

Around that time, a new piece of intelligence began circulating in Washington: an analysis, generated largely by the CIA, suggesting that the Chinese leadership might have accelerated its timeline for taking Taiwan. Until then, Washington had been operating on the assumption that China's military would not be ready to take the island before 2027—the year that Xi had told his commanders they needed to be fully prepared.

Now, there was new thinking, the analysis said. China was likely spooked by all the talk of turning Taiwan into a "porcupine," bristling with antiship missiles and sea mines and hardened communications that could defy efforts to shut off the island. Xi had to assume that Taiwan's defenses would improve faster than China's offensive game could be put into play.

But the administration was developing another line of thinking. China's economic growth was slowing dramatically. Xi might want to make a show of being able to take Taiwan, but it was far from clear that he could risk doing it anytime soon, especially if the West reacted the way it did to the Ukraine invasion. Biden said later that fall that Xi had his hands full, privately noting that the Chinese leadership was more concerned that the United States keep the next Taiwanese government, taking power in 2024, from declaring independence—and forcing China's hand.

CHAPTER 15

THE NUCLEAR PARADOX

Above all, while defending our own vital interests, nuclear powers must avert those confrontations which bring an adversary to a choice of either a humiliating retreat or a nuclear war. To adopt that kind of course in the nuclear age would be evidence only of the bankruptcy of our policy—or of a collective death-wish for the world.

John F. Kennedy, speech at American University, June 10, 1963

JOE BIDEN WAS standing in the Upper East Side townhouse owned by James Murdoch, a son of Rupert Murdoch, the famed founder of the of Fox media empire, surrounded by liberal New York Democrats who had paid handsomely to come hear the president at a political fundraiser.

It might have seemed odd to cram that many Democrats into the home of a Murdoch, but James was the political black sheep of the family: He had donated heavily to Biden's campaign efforts in 2020, and his wife, Kathryn Hufschmid, was a longtime executive of the Clinton Climate Initiative—not exactly the favorite cause of Fox News and *The Wall Street Journal*.

Reporters who follow Biden around know that he speaks most candidly in situations like this—events where he is trying to create a sense of intimacy with an audience of wealthy donors. After all, that was what these New Yorkers had come for, eager for any pearl they could drop later in the week at a dinner party, "So Biden told me. . . ." But Biden's words on this night—October 6, 2022—as guests stood amid the art collection in the Murdoch living room and chatted about their fall travel plans, carried a disturbing message that sent a chill through the room.

For the "first time since the Cuban Missile Crisis, we have a direct threat of the use of the nuclear weapon if, in fact, things continue down the path they've been going," he told the crowd, many of whom—Murdoch included—were far too young to remember the 1962 missile showdown, arguably the closest the United States and the Soviet Union ever came to an all-out nuclear war.

It began to dawn on the attendees that the president of the United States was talking about the prospect of the first wartime use of a nuclear weapon since Hiroshima and Nagasaki. And not at some vague moment in the future. He meant the next few weeks.

Biden then started talking about Putin and his episodic threats—always a bit elliptical but nonetheless clear—to reach into his nuclear arsenal to resolve the Ukraine issue. "We've got a guy I know fairly well," said Biden. "He is not joking when he talks about the potential use of tactical and nuclear weapons, or biological or chemical weapons because his military is, you might say, significantly underperforming."

In this case, the nuclear weapons Putin was considering were not aimed at Miami or New York, the way many had feared in the Cuban Missile Crisis. Instead, they were so-called battlefield nukes: tactical weapons small enough to be loaded into an artillery shell and designed to eviscerate a military unit or a few city blocks. At least initially, their use would look nothing like an exchange of intercontinental ballistic missiles, the great fear of the Cold War. The effects would be horrific but limited to a relatively small geography—perhaps detonated over the Black Sea, or blasted into a Ukrainian military base.

Yet Biden's point that night was that once the post–World War II taboo on nuclear use was shattered, there was no way of knowing how it might spread. What happened in Ukraine might not stay in Ukraine. "I don't think there's any such thing as an ability to easily [use] a tactical nuclear weapon and not end up with Armageddon," he said.

The room went silent. Until then, most Americans had thought of the Ukraine war as a faraway conflict, not one that could threaten their own well-being. But Biden's message that night was that no one—not even rich New Yorkers—could afford to think they were immune once nuclear weapons started to be exchanged.

These musings were classic Biden. He was, seemingly impulsively, declaring out loud what he and his aides had been secretly discussing for weeks. (One of those aides later dubbed it, dryly, the "Armageddon Speech.")

Biden knew he was speaking on the record—reporters routinely cover his comments at campaign fundraisers, and he knew there is no way for a president to talk to that large a group and not have his comments spill out into the wider world.

One explanation was that Biden was being Biden: His willingness to blurt a truth out loud was legendary. He was probably tired. Just a few days before the fundraiser, Putin himself had once again raised the prospect of nuclear use, declaring he would use "all available means" to defend Russian territory—which he had just declared included four provinces of eastern Ukraine. Putin had pointedly reminded his audience that day that it was Harry Truman who first made use of the Bomb, arguing that it was the Americans who had created the precedent.

But something else was lurking beneath the surface of Biden's comments. Before and after the fundraiser, a series of highly classified signals intercepts circulated through the White House, the intelligence agencies, and the Pentagon. For the first time since the war had broken out, Russian officials were conducting frequent conversations about reaching into the nuclear arsenal. Some were just "various forms of chatter," one official told me. But others involved the units that would be responsible for moving or deploying the weapons. The most alarming of the intercepted conversations revealed that one of the most senior Russian military commanders was explicitly discussing the logistics of detonating a weapon on the battlefield. Putin's public bluster was bad enough; this sounded closer to an operational plan.

Fortunately, there was no evidence of weapons being moved. But soon the CIA was warning that, under a singular scenario in which Ukrainian forces decimated Russian defensive lines and looked about to retake Crimea, the possibility of nuclear use might rise to 50 percent or even higher. That "got everyone's attention fast," said an official involved in the discussions. No one knew how to assess the accuracy of that estimate. But it wasn't the kind of warning any American president can dismiss.

From his first days in the Senate, Biden had spent a lot of time thinking about how the United States could wind up in a nuclear conflict. But when the Berlin Wall fell, the whole concept of a nuclear exchange with Moscow receded. As vice president, Biden had helped cut the deal for what became the New START nuclear treaty. With that issue out of the way, Biden immersed himself in the problem of "rogue" nuclear states like North Korea. He had been deeply involved in the planning, in 2009 and 2010, to sabotage Iran's nuclear program and the 2015 nuclear deal with Tehran that followed.

But the case of Ukraine posed new complications. Russia held thousands of tactical weapons, and they were not restricted by treaties, including New START. None had ever been used before in conflict. But if Putin felt his territory or regime threatened, he might very well reach for one. And it was deeply unclear how the world would respond.

In background conversations, the administration had already told me and a small group of other national security reporters that if Putin used a small atomic weapon on a non-NATO ally—read Ukraine— the United States' response would have to be non-nuclear. But they quickly added there would have to be *some* kind of dramatic response— perhaps even a conventional attack on the units that launched the nuclear weapons—or they would risk emboldening not only Putin but every other authoritarian with a nuclear arsenal, large or small. Yet as the "Armageddon speech" made clear, no one knew what kind of nuclear demonstration Putin had in mind. The war-gaming at the Pentagon and at think tanks around Washington imagined that Putin's use of a tactical weapon—perhaps followed by a threat to detonate more— could come in a variety of circumstances. One simulation that I sat through envisioned a successful Ukrainian counteroffensive that sent Russian troops fleeing, imperiling Putin's hold on Crimea. In this scenario Putin ordered the detonation of a single tactical weapon in a remote area of Ukraine—unlikely to cause many casualties—with the threat of more unless Kyiv backed off from an offensive. That was followed by a demand from Moscow that the West halt all military support for the Ukrainians: no more tanks, no more missiles, no more ammunition.

The aim would be to split NATO; in the simulation I observed, the detonation served that purpose. While the United States and Britain held firm and began discussing sanctions and non-nuclear strikes, several Western European members of NATO turned wobbly. Biden's efforts to buck them up failed; several of the traditional NATO states, including Germany and France, argued for agreeing to a cease-fire that allowed Russian forces to stay in disputed territory.

As reports of the results made their way to Biden's senior national security team, the discussion inside the White House about the risk of the Ukraine war going nuclear became quite vivid—far more vivid than officials had been willing to let on.

In fact, Putin had tried this before, but it was barely noticed at the time. Back in 2014, when he moved to annex Crimea, Putin warned that he was prepared to consider using nuclear weapons if it was the only way to keep Ukraine and the West from fighting for control of Crimea. But his annexation never faced any military challenge, so his words weren't put to the test.

Eight years later, in February 2022, when he announced the "special military operation" against Ukraine, Putin ran essentially the same playbook. His most explicit warning came just three days after the invasion began, on the first Sunday of the war. With television cameras rolling in a staged meeting with his military and intelligence aides, he declared that Russia's strategic forces—in charge of Russia's long-range nuclear weapons—would be placed into "special combat readiness." But there was no evidence that he ever carried through on that threat. "We looked for any sign," one senior American intelligence official told me, "and found none."

In those early days, Putin carefully avoided direct use of the word "nuclear." He didn't have to say anything: Everyone understood that he was signaling that the West should stay out of the war or face extraordinary peril.

In the shock of the invasion, it was a bit lost on the world what a remarkable, dangerous change was under way. Not only was the leader of one of the original nuclear powers threatening to use his arsenal, he was threatening to use it against a non-nuclear state. In fact, he was threatening to use it against a state that had given up the nuclear weapons on its territory nearly thirty years before and turned the missiles over to Moscow in accordance with the 1994 Budapest Memorandum. Ukraine thought that in return, it was receiving an assurance of protection. Instead, it got a threat of annihilation.

Putin didn't *want* to violate the nuclear taboo and catalyze a potential World War III, argued Kremlin spokesman Dmitry Peskov that March. But the West might force his hand. Peskov, who was so close to Putin that they used similar terminology, adopted the Russian tale of victimhood. "We have a concept of domestic security, and it's public," he argued, defending the saber-rattling as in accordance with Russia's military doctrine. "You can read all the reasons for nuclear arms to be used. So if it is an existential threat for our country, then it can be used in accordance with our concept."

It wasn't clear, of course, whether Putin defined "existential" threats only as threats to the integrity of the Russian state or as threats to himself. As the war went on, he blended the two. The state was Putin; Putin was the state.

What Biden didn't say during that October fundraiser in New York was that the chances of Putin using a nuclear weapon were still considered relatively low—but substantially higher than they had been just a few months ago. Before the Ukraine war broke out, one senior administration official told me, he would have put the chances under 1 percent—vanishingly remote. They edged up a bit higher when Putin made his first nuclear threats in the opening weeks of the war. Now, with Putin losing ground and running low on ammunition, White House officials worried that the chances had dramatically increased.

Of course, no one could quantify those probabilities with any accuracy: the factors that played into decisions to use nuclear weapons, or even to threaten their use, were too abstract, too dependent on human emotion and accident, to measure with any precision. But over the previous few months, the Ukraine conflict had changed the world's calculus of nuclear risk on at least three fronts:

For the first time ever, commercial nuclear power plants had become pawns for the major powers. In Ukraine's southeast, a war was raging on the perimeter of a giant nuclear power plant, where six nuclear reactors were essentially being held hostage to gain battlefield advantage by occupying Russian troops.

For the first time since the end of the Cold War, the leader of one of the established nuclear states was threatening to use a nuclear weapon to resolve a conventional fight. And, as Biden had warned in the Murdoch living room, it might not stop there.

After a thirty-year hiatus, the risk of nuclear proliferation seemed on the rise again. It had been a little more than thirteen years since Barack Obama had stood in the central square in Prague and declared a goal to eliminate all nuclear weapons from the earth—and committed to putting the world on that path. "I'm not naïve," he said that day. "This goal will not be reached quickly. Perhaps not in my lifetime." But, he made clear, it was the arc of history that America, Russia, China, and others would follow.

Now, that arc had been inverted. You could see it on the satellite photographs of China's new fields of missile silos and of Iran's new nuclear centrifuge operations. You could see it in North Korea's expanding arsenal. Anyone who hoped the age of nuclear gamesmanship had ended with the collapse of the Berlin Wall discovered that the holiday from history was over.

RAFAEL GROSSI, the usually impeccably dressed Argentinian chief of the International Atomic Energy Agency, stepped out of his armored car at a Ukrainian checkpoint wearing a UN bulletproof vest over a blue IAEA T-shirt. He was on a mission to prevent the world's biggest dirty bomb from going off. And he was running into roadblocks.

It was September 1, about a month before Biden's fundraiser, and Grossi, an intense sixty-one-year-old with decades of experience in the tough art of nuclear diplomacy, had spent weeks negotiating to get into the Zaporizhzhya Nuclear Power Plant in southeast Ukraine.

Zaporizhzhya was Europe's largest nuclear power plant, by far. And since the start of the war it had been on the brink, with Russian troops occupying its control rooms, artillery fire episodically cutting off the vital power to the plant that keeps the nuclear material cool, and the threat of destruction—and with it the risk of meltdown—looming larger every day.

By early August, the workers at the plant were raw. Reports of a fire within yards of one of the reactors made headlines, as did repeated power outages to various parts of the complex. Nearby residents stocked up on potassium iodide pills in the hope that they would help protect their thyroids from the effects of radiation if the worst happened.

The nuclear complex was "a disaster waiting to happen," Grossi had told me earlier in the summer. "It sits on the front line. Not near, or in the vicinity," he emphasized. "*On* the front line." For months he had worried that the Zaporizhzhya plant was, essentially, a giant "dirty bomb"—a conventional weapon with a small bit of radioactive material mixed in designed as a weapon of terror, to take out a few city blocks and spread fear.

Naturally, the Ukrainians accused the Russians of shelling the plant. The Russians said they had no reason to shell a facility that their own troops were occupying. But they were using the plant as a shield: If the Ukrainians tried to fire on the forces holed up there and triggered an accident, they could easily blame Ukraine. Getting at the truth of what was happening was nearly impossible in those conditions, and Grossi told me he didn't care who was doing the shooting. It just had to stop.

"The idea that a nuclear power plant would be caught in a conflict is something we have thought about a lot before, and it's why the plants were designed to withstand attack," said Gary Samore, who was the lead nuclear advisor on the National Security Council to Presidents Clinton and Obama. "But," he told me, "the idea that a plant would be used as a shield for forces occupying a plant or that someone like Putin would use the risk of attacks or accident as a form of intimidation—I don't think that was something we fully contemplated."

THE INTERNATIONAL ATOMIC Energy Agency was never really designed to deal with a problem like Zaporizhzhya. The agency was a product of President Dwight Eisenhower's "Atoms for Peace" program. Eisenhower knew that nuclear energy would spread around the world. But with each new plant came the risk that the uranium fuel—and plutonium byproducts—might be spirited away to build nuclear weapons.

So "Atoms for Peace" was based on an explicit deal: Countries that forswore nuclear weapons would get help from the United States and the other nuclear powers to build commercial nuclear power plants. The lure of seemingly limitless sources of electricity, the United States was betting, would outweigh the desire for a nuclear weapons option.

It was the job of the IAEA, created in 1957, to make sure that the plants were safe and that no nuclear fuel was surreptitiously diverted. Its mandate is deliberately narrow: Contrary to popular belief, IAEA inspectors don't search for weapons, just the fuel that powers them. In fact, there are only a handful of true weapons experts in the tall towers in Vienna overlooking the Danube River.

Grossi was born four years after the agency was created. After starting in the Argentine foreign service, he followed his passion for documenting and limiting weapons around the world, working on the staff of the IAEA and helping develop guidance for who gets nuclear technology and how it can be transferred without being stolen.

But his real ambition was to run the IAEA, with its vast network of highly trained inspectors, and assume responsibility for nuclear safety around the globe. "I feel like I prepared for this my whole life," he told me over drinks one night in 2020, soon after he was elected the group's head.

Grossi initially believed that Iran, along with North Korea, would dominate his next few years. Donald Trump's decision in 2018 to pull out of the Obama-era agreement that sharply constrained Iran's nuclear fuel production was coming around to bite the rest of the world: Iran was resuming production and limiting inspections, despite the best efforts of the Europeans to keep the deal alive.

Then the Ukraine war broke out. Grossi's first trip to the country, just a month later, was a visit to the South Ukraine Nuclear Power Plant, one of the country's four operating nuclear facilities, which had just been defended against a Russian onslaught. A few weeks later he went to Chernobyl to make sure that the plant, which had been shuttered for decades, still had emergency personnel monitoring the vast facility. He marveled that the Russians had sent their troops through the Chernobyl Exclusion Zone—where the soil was still radioactive—without protective gear. Many slept in the forest.

With Chernobyl secure, Grossi was desperate to get inside the Zaporizhzhya plant and assess its condition. His biggest concern was whether the reactor buildings had been breached by random fire. But he also needed to evaluate the reliability of the electricity supply to run the cooling systems that keep the fuel from melting down, as well as the working conditions of the exhausted plant operators, some of whom were now essentially prisoners of war. They were almost all Ukrainians; there were reports that early in the Russian occupation of the plant, some were held at gunpoint.

Grossi knew there was little he could do to improve the conditions at Zaporizhzhya. He could not order the creation of a demilitarized zone—at best he could negotiate an agreement not to target areas close to the plant. He could not order the Russian troops to leave the premises. He had no power to stop the shelling. "Even demanding that we keep inspectors at the major plants, that was probably beyond my authority," he told me. The IAEA possessed only one power: to raise the alarm if it saw that nuclear fuel was being diverted to weapons use or if it detected a risk to safety. No one else had the mandate, the prestige, and the expertise to do that except the IAEA.

So, Grossi argued, the only way to get the job done at Zaporizhzhya was to lead a group of inspectors into the plant and look for themselves. And on that morning of September 1, he was only a few dozen miles away, trying to figure out how to make the final run to the front gates.

A Ukrainian military force had escorted him from Kyiv, where he had met President Zelensky, to the edge of the "gray zone": the no-man's-land surrounding the plant where Ukrainian control of the territory ended and Russia's control had not quite begun. The road through it was littered with mines and the carcasses of destroyed vehicles; the booming of heavy artillery resonated constantly, with menacing thumps from firing just a few miles away.

But now, an officious Ukrainian soldier who identified himself as a colonel was telling Grossi that it was simply too dangerous to proceed. "He said the situation was very 'complicated.'" Grossi recalled, and he couldn't guarantee the inspectors' safety.

Grossi, frustrated after days of overland travel across the battle-strewn landscape of post-invasion Ukraine, told the colonel that he had just been in Kyiv visiting President Zelensky. The president himself had given him permission to cross into the plant to do what nuclear inspectors are supposed to do—inspect for damage. Zelensky was, of course, self-interested: Not only was he worried about the potential for the plant to become a dirty bomb, he also needed the imprimatur of ongoing collaboration with the UN to win the propaganda battle the Russians were playing—and to prove to the Russians that the world still considered the territory to be Ukrainian.

But little of that had filtered down to the troops, and now Grossi found himself arguing with the colonel. "At some point I said if I don't move within the next ten minutes," Grossi would return back to safe ground and call a press conference. At that moment, he warned the colonel, "I will identify you as the one responsible for holding the head of the International Atomic Energy Agency here, against the instructions of your president."

The colonel finally relented. Grossi could go, he said, but if he got blown up along the way—by an errant Russian shell or a trigger-happy Ukrainian soldier with an automatic weapon—that wouldn't be the colonel's problem.

And so they pulled out into the gray zone, into the oncoming sound of guns and artillery. It wasn't clear if they were the target or not, Grossi said, but there was "sustained fire." "We were not hit," he said, "but it was quite a couple of minutes. The drivers were cursing and saying, 'Speed up! Speed up!' so it was quite dramatic."

Once they came within sight of the huge plant, they were greeted by a clutch of Russian officials, who exclaimed, "Welcome to Russia!" The message was clear: In entering the plant, Grossi was entering Russian territory.

Inside the plant, Grossi spent the afternoon inspecting the reactors and cooling ponds and making plans to shut down much of the energy production in order to make disaster less likely. When he departed six hours later, he left several of the agency's inspectors behind, a permanent, independent presence capable of raising the alarm. He didn't care if it was beyond his authority, and he didn't bother to ask permission.

The next month, in late October, Grossi traveled to St. Petersburg to meet with Putin, planning to make his case that if the shelling took out key facilities inside the gates, Zaporizhzhya would forever be remembered as the Putin-triggered Chernobyl. To drive home the point, he wanted to remind Putin that, given the prevailing winds, if the plant did melt down there was a good chance that the radioactive cloud would spread over parts of Russia.

They met at a palace near the city, part of the complex George W. Bush had visited in sunnier times with Putin. Putin treated Grossi graciously; he clearly did not want to be seen as obsessed by the war—or even bothered by it. If anything, he wanted to be seen as the sober, responsible one. (In early August, just weeks before, he'd claimed in a letter to a nonproliferation conference that "there can be no winners in a nuclear war and it should never be unleashed"—just adding to the nuclear ambiguity that he so often used to his benefit.)

Once they dispensed with pleasantries, Grossi tried to persuade him to come to an agreement not to fire on the plant. "He didn't disagree," Grossi told me a few days later. But he also made no promises.

Putin, he recalled, didn't seem confused or angry about what had happened to his humiliated forces or that his plan to take the whole country had collapsed. Instead, the IAEA chief noted, the Russian leader was focused on the plant. He knew how many reactors there were, Grossi told me, and he knew where the backup power supplies were. It was as if he had prepared for the meeting by memorizing a map of the facilities. "He knew every detail," Grossi said. "It was sort of remarkable."

It wasn't all that remarkable if one thought about why Putin put his forces into the plant to begin with. For Putin, Zaporizhzhya was not a war trophy; it was a key part of his plan for how he would exercise control over all of Ukraine—and help intimidate or blackmail much of Europe.

According to a study conducted by the Royal United Services Institute, the British think tank that published many of the most compelling analyses of the war, Russia had big plans for Zaporizhzhya and the rest of the country's nuclear infrastructure. The most obvious was to have a protected place for Putin's troops, equipment, and ammunition. Equally important, the think tank said, was Russia's determination to make sure it could control—or, if need be, cut off—Ukraine's access to electric power. For that purpose, Zaporizhzhya was the single most important facility: It provided some 20 percent of Ukraine's electricity in 2021.

But perhaps what Putin sought the most, Grossi thought, was the psychological advantage of controlling Zaporizhzhya. If Putin's plan was frustrated, he had the option of threatening to shell the plant—introducing the prospect of radioactive clouds floating toward Kyiv and on to the rest of Europe.

There was a potential disinformation element as well. Russian television and websites wove constant conspiracy theories—which stuck, several studies showed—of American bioweapons labs secreted away in Ukraine. Putin himself pushed another theory in February, that Zelensky's government was secretly developing its own nuclear weapons program. The only place it could get the fuel, of course, was from its nuclear power infrastructure. "If Ukraine acquires weapons of mass destruction," Putin had warned just days before the invasion began, as he was fabricating a justification for moving against Kyiv, "the situation in the world and in Europe will drastically change, especially for us, for Russia," he said. "We cannot but react to this real danger, all the more so since, let me repeat, Ukraine's Western patrons may help it acquire these weapons to create yet another threat to our country."

Grossi left the meeting with the sense that Putin knew—and perhaps enjoyed—that he was blurring the once-sharp distinction between nuclear weapons and civilian nuclear facilities. If there were heightened risks of nuclear disaster, he seemed to suggest, that was the fault of the Ukrainians for resisting Russia's efforts to "reabsorb" the territory. Grossi feared that as the war dragged into the fall, Putin would be tempted to rely on the threat of using real nuclear weapons—not just the endangered power plant—to avoid a humiliating defeat.

That was exactly what was about to happen.

A WEEK LATER, in early September, Tony Blinken and his entourage of aides boarded a train from eastern Poland into Kyiv on a not-so-secret mission to see Volodymyr Zelensky.

Getting to Kyiv was no easy task, even for a secretary of state. His security personnel would not let him fly in: It was simply too dangerous. So instead he spent hours rattling along a bumpy, noisy track, with Ukrainian and old Soviet-style treats on the train's café menu. This must be what Elihu Root did, one of his aides noted later, shaking his head, referring to Teddy Roosevelt's secretary of state, who had, in 1917, traveled to Russia in an effort to open up relations with the Bolsheviks.

There was a particular urgency to Blinken's trip. As he rumbled across western Ukraine, he and his aides were struggling to understand the early progress Ukrainian forces were making in their freshly launched counteroffensive: a bold new effort to regain the initiative in the war.

In secret meetings over the summer, Pentagon planners and their

British counterparts had helped Zelensky, General Zaluzhny, and his lieutenants plan strategies to take back some of the territory that the Russians had claimed early in the war. If the Ukrainians could suddenly break out of the grinding war of attrition and seize back territory, it would be a big boost to national morale and the effort to keep Western arms and money flowing. The question was how to do it.

Senior U.S. and Ukrainian generals warned that Ukraine's initial plan—a sweeping attack across the South—was likely doomed. Casualties would run high, and the territorial gains would be minimal. After blunt phone calls between Jake Sullivan and his Ukrainian counterpart, and General Milley and his equivalent in the Ukrainian armed forces, the Ukrainians went back to the drawing board. This was a major evolution in the partnership, one that was barely recognized at the time. For the first six months of the war, the United States and its NATO allies were, as Sullivan had put it, essentially quartermasters, giving the Ukrainians what they needed to stay alive. Now the American and British were acting more like coaches, modeling plays that they thought would exploit Russia's weakest points. Those included its miserable command-and-control, its dwindling supply of precision weapons, and its shortage of troops—particularly as Putin held off in ordering a general mobilization to shore up the number available.

What emerged was a two-part play—one obvious, the other designed to take the Russians by surprise in a part of the country they weren't paying much attention to defending. The first part was a well-telegraphed attack on Russian-occupied Kherson, a territory just north of Crimea, and the only regional capital that Russia had claimed since the war's beginning: one that they hoped would further pave the way to the "land bridge" that the Russians were using to pour troops, supplies and ammunition into the war zone.

The Russians, seeing what was coming, dug in throughout the Donbas: bolstering supply lines, moving divisions into place, and drawing up plans to push another sham "referendum" throughout the territory—an effort to give a semblance of legal cover to their claim that this was truly Russian land unjustly taken from them in the Soviet breakup.

But their bluster was better than their defenses. As Ukrainian troops bombarded Russian positions and supply lines with Western-provided weapons, the Russians began to pull back. "Run away, go home," Zelensky had warned Russian soldiers in his evening address at the start of the offensive. They would, he vowed, "chase them to the border." Slowly, the counteroffensive in Kherson started to gain ground. Village by village, Russian flags were lowered, and the Ukrainian flag was raised.

The daily cost for the Ukrainians was horrific—though Ukraine's own propaganda machine often hid the true casualty numbers. Every once in a while, a glimpse of the truth emerged. Ukrainian forces were outmanned and outgunned: "We lost five people for every one they did," a wounded soldier named Ihor told *The Washington Post* as the battle raged on. "If we fire three mortars, they fire 20 in return," a soldier named Oleksandr agreed.

Yet what the Ukrainians lacked in numbers and firepower, they made up for in ingenuity. For months, as all eyes turned to Kherson, a few Ukrainian military leaders, led by Colonel General Oleksandr Syrsky, had been trying to focus their colleagues on how thin Russia's defenses were getting in the north, around Kharkiv—a city of 1.4 million people located about twenty-five miles from the Russian border. Now satellite photographs showed a significant movement of Russian troops to the south, to join the fight in Kherson. Their lines were clearly overextended.

"We saw the fact that the Russians actually relocated a lot of their best forces down to the south in preparation for the other counteroffensive that the Ukrainians kicked off," said Colin Kahl, then the Pentagon's policy chief. "So we had reason to believe that because of the persistent morale challenges, and the pressure of the Ukrainians, that there might be pockets of the Russian military that are a little more brittle than they appear on paper."

It was still a risky gambit. Ukrainian planners estimated that a successful offensive might take far more ammunition than they had on hand. They began pulling some howitzers in from the east to bolster their own forces. The biggest danger, Syrsky knew, would come if the Ukrainians didn't make progress quickly enough. In that scenario, planners warned, the Russians could regroup and counterattack.

Just before Blinken's train trundled into Kyiv, Syrsky launched his offensive in Kharkiv. It worked better than even the Ukrainians' most optimistic predictions. At the beginning, Russian forces simply melted away, leaving mountains of heavy weaponry and ammunition behind. Russian resolve was stiffer in some areas, but within days, Ukrainian forces had driven them back to the fringes of the province. Victory in Kherson took longer, but it followed as well. In September and October, Zelensky reported on a string of surrounding towns and villages that had been liberated. Officially, Kherson was retaken on November 11, 2022.

The startling success of the Ukrainian forces in Kharkiv and Kherson was electrifying. Images raced around the world of citizens freely emerging from their homes for the first time in nine months, unfurling Ukrainian flags in town squares, celebrating amid the rubble. It looked a bit like World War II pictures of the liberation of Paris—this scrappy little nation, which was supposed to get rolled over, had sent the Russian Army fleeing.

By the time Blinken arrived in Kyiv and made a show of walking around the downtown with Zelensky, victory was in the air. "We know this is a pivotal moment, more than six months into Russia's war of aggression against Ukraine, as your counteroffensive is now under way and proving effective," Blinken said. He brought stuffed animals to wounded children and toured scenes of devastation in towns around Kyiv.

But behind the public celebration, Blinken and his aides were more cautious. The victory was great, but it didn't mean much unless the Ukrainian forces could maintain momentum. "They caught a break in Kharkiv," a top American official told me later, matter-of-factly. The Russian lines "were long and very thin. And Ukraine pressed. Kharkiv was a morale booster, but they fell into it."

Biden's national security team knew, however, that the victory wasn't big enough to pressure Putin to the negotiating table. Ukraine was still missing 20 percent of its territory and something like 30 percent of its industrial and agricultural capacity. And the Ukrainians were going to need help getting through the winter without freezing. There was no doubt that Putin would do everything he could to knock out the electricity and the ability to produce heat in his effort to break the Ukrainians' will.

In fact, days after Blinken left, Putin's forces blasted the power plants around Kharkiv and turned off the heat—and the lights. If his troops couldn't occupy the city, he seemed to be saying, his missiles could make it uninhabitable. In response, Zelensky went to great lengths to make the case—poetically—that Putin would fail. "Do you still think that we are 'one nation'?" he taunted Putin. "Read my lips:

Without gas or without you? Without you. Without light or without you? Without you. . . . Cold, hunger, darkness, and thirst are not as scary and deadly for us as your 'friendship and brotherhood.' But history will put everything in its place. And we will be with gas, light, water, and food . . . and WITHOUT you!"

MORE THAN SIX months into the war, the Russians were still unable to get their act together. But back in Biden's White House, the celebrations were tempered by a lurking unease. Putin was dangerous enough when he was trying to become Peter the Great. He might be even more dangerous, Biden was told, if he was being frustrated in his efforts to become Peter the Great.

After the Ukrainians' success in Kherson and Kharkiv, Washington was swept by a haunting fear, that the Ukrainians were so successful in pushing Russian forces out of Ukraine that Putin would conclude he had only one real option left to avoid the humiliation Kennedy had warned of nearly sixty years before: to reach for its nuclear arsenal.

"It's the nuclear paradox," Mark Milley, chairman of the Joint Chiefs of Staff, would tell visitors to his office and policymakers in the Situation Room. "The more successful the Ukrainians are at ousting the Russian invasion, the more likely Putin is to threaten to use a bomb—or reach for it."

By the time Milley spoke about the paradox, he was spending almost every day consumed by it. Every decision that confronted the administration eventually boiled down to a question of where Putin's limits really were. Would he use the latest shipment of arms to Zelensky and his forces as an excuse to roll out his nuclear weapons? Would the loss of more territory inside Ukraine prompt him to threaten the ultimate response? "He's on a downward slope," Milley said of Putin, "and that makes him more dangerous."

It all raised the bigger issue of whether Biden's careful calculations about avoiding escalation even mattered. If there was a lesson over the past twenty-five years of dealing with Putin, it was that Washington's ability to influence his next moves was limited. Were we falling back into the same trap that we had for decades, convincing ourselves that if we just pulled the right levers, we could control Putin's plans?

Of course, Biden could hardly tell the Ukrainians they couldn't push the Russians out of their country—that was, after all, the goal of the whole operation. The United States was committed to doing everything it could to keep Ukraine independent; as the nature of the battle changed from the defense of Kyiv to an artillery battle in the South and East, Biden gradually decided to provide the Ukrainians with increasingly sophisticated arms. His critics—even some in the administration—worried he was always running behind events. But there was also a growing sense that Putin was less reactive to what types of weapons the United States sent than Biden had feared early in the war.

Meanwhile, the Ukrainians were trying to seize the moment to emphasize how much more they could do against the Russians, if only the West would lift some of its weapons restrictions. "After eight years of ongoing Russian aggression, and nearly seven months of overt escalation, Ukrainian Armed Forces have proved that we are capable to win," Hanna Hopko—a former Ukrainian MP who reportedly was hesitant about Zelensky's candidacy on the grounds that he would be too friendly with Russia—told a group of journalists in Washington, D.C., that September. Hopko and her peers were starting to make a habit of transatlantic trips to lobby Washington for more: more weapons, more support, more aid, and more training.

The faster Washington moved, she said, the faster victory would come. Yet as the fruits of the counteroffensive were starting to become clear, the Ukrainians grew concerned about war fatigue on the part of their allies. "We're worried about the Europeans," Hopko said bluntly. "The ones who want to give Putin an off-ramp. Those who want to help him save face." The French. The Italians. Even some of the Germans, she said, who had come a long way but clearly would prefer a quick territorial compromise to a long, drawn-out war. A weakened Russia was still dangerous, she warned, and now was not the time to let up the pressure on Putin—no matter what devastation he threatened. And after seeing the destruction and Russian savagery at Bucha and Mariupol, there was no way, she argued, that the Ukrainians or the world could accept any outcome that allowed the Russians to keep any inch of Ukrainian territory.

The Ukrainians' increasingly hard-line attitude worried the Biden administration. On the one hand, they acknowledged, the Ukrainians were engaged in a bloody, deadly fight for their survival—when that is the case, only total victory seems like the sensible path. But the fear in Washington was that America's ratcheting up of support for the Ukrainians, combined with their gains, was backing Putin into a corner—making a negotiation more difficult and potentially risking nuclear disaster.

Suddenly, Putin, whose implicit bargain with the Russian people had been that they shouldn't worry about his limited "special operation" in Ukraine—that he'd take care of it with dispatch—changed his tone. On September 21 he announced that he was drafting three hundred thousand more men to throw into the fight. Suddenly the educated middle class could no longer ignore Putin's aggressive folly. Within days, tens of thousands of military-eligible men began to flee for Turkey, Georgia, and Kazakhstan.

The effect on Russian society was profound. My colleague Valerie Hopkins—the only *New York Times* correspondent who was back reporting from the ground in Russia during this time—said she saw a huge change.

Throughout the summer of 2022, daily life looked normal, at least on the surface. But mobilization significantly changed the politics of the war in Russia. It was no accident that in the early days of the conflict the invading troops were drawn from the countryside; these were not the sons of Moscow and St. Petersburg. Putin had been denying that he would issue a draft—right up until the moment that he did, of course. That announcement stunned the Russians. The invasion was no longer a television event. Cars backed up for hours at border crossings. Men avoided the Metro stations of Moscow and St. Petersburg, fearing that they'd be served with conscription papers while on the train. Others set up camps in the forest—some staying for months, even through the winter. The cityscape changed: Billboards were erected glorifying soldiers and the army. Antimissile defenses were added to the roofs of government buildings.

Clearly, for Putin, the war was creeping closer to becoming a threat to his rule. And his language reflected his concern. He cast the war as a battle not just with Ukrainians but with Americans and NATO. The West's goal, Putin railed, was "to weaken, divide and ultimately destroy our country." And then he doubled down: "If the territorial integrity of our country is threatened, we will without a doubt use all available means to protect Russia and our people," he vowed. "This is not a bluff."

In case anyone missed the nuance of "all available means," his apparatchik, Dmitry Medvedev, piled on: "Russia has the right to use nuclear weapons if necessary," he asserted. "The demagogues across the ocean and in Europe are not going to die in a nuclear apocalypse." Translation: With just the suggestion that nuclear weapons would be used, Biden and his allies would back away.

By Western estimates, Russian casualties were already at one hundred thousand dead or injured and spiking toward double that. And in the war-game scenarios run quietly at the Pentagon and think tanks around Washington, it was usually humiliation or the potential loss of Crimea that led to the brandishing of a nuclear weapon. Even if Putin didn't intend to use it, the threat of doing so might look like the least bad option.

The Ukrainian leadership all but dismissed the nuclear threat. In their view, Putin would threaten repeatedly but never press the button. Even if he did, some told me, how could it be worse than his leveling of whole cities? Their bigger fear was that Putin's bluff would work and lead the West to back off. This was the unspoken follow-on to Milley's nuclear paradox: The more the Ukrainians were successful and Putin blustered, the more tempted the West would be to warn the Ukrainians against taking back too much of their own territory.

BY ONE OF those odd coincidences of history, the renewed fears of nuclear confrontation came exactly fifty years to the week after history's greatest nuclear brinkmanship moment: the Cuban Missile Crisis. On October 16, 1962, President John F. Kennedy's aides came to him with aerial images from U-2 spy planes that showed the Soviets secretly shipping nuclear weapons into Cuba. The question was how to get them off the island without triggering an escalation into full-fledged nuclear conflict.

What happened over the next thirteen days remains the most studied, dissected, and debated scare of the Cold War. Members of Kennedy's hastily convened nuclear crisis committee initially leaned toward more aggressive recommendations and briefly even debated a preemptive nuclear strike. Fortunately, Kennedy rejected that advice and let a delicate exchange of messages with Nikita Khrushchev, the Soviet premier, play out. In the end, the two men defused the crisis, striking a secret deal that resulted in the Soviets backing off and the United States, months later, taking Jupiter nuclear-armed missiles out of Turkey.

Not surprisingly, in the Biden White House there was a lot of time spent in the fall of 2022 studying the lessons of the Cuban Missile Crisis, in case they found themselves in a similar situation. The first big lesson was one Kennedy himself described: that the United States had to avoid putting Khrushchev in the position of choosing between "humiliating defeat or a nuclear war."

But there were other lessons, and they were equally worrisome. The first of these was that in 1962, the public spotlight was not as bright. JFK's administration had time, space, and secrecy in which to maneuver. Kennedy didn't have to worry about critics on social media or far-right Republicans egging him on in public to attack the Soviet Union or risk looking weak. Similarly, no one was going on Soviet television urging nuclear war, as they were in 2022. Another difference was that Khrushchev was not a lone decision-maker—he had to worry about the views of a collective Soviet leadership. Putin did not.

There was another worry inside the White House and the Pentagon in the fall of 2022—that if Putin wanted to convince the world he was serious, he might conduct an aboveground test, "perhaps detonating one someplace unpopulated to make a point," as one American military official told me at the height of Washington's nuclear angst. Even the mere threat of moving weapons around seemed ominous: When weapons move, accidents become more likely. The history of the Cold War was filled with tales of near disaster, usually from human error.

There was the moment, in 1979, when an American nuclear watch officer reported that sensors were warning of a massive, incoming Soviet strike. It turned out that someone had loaded a training tape into the real warning system. In September 1983, a Soviet lieutenant colonel saw a warning flashing that five American intercontinental ballistic missiles were coming straight for the Soviet Union. Trusting his gut, he called the Soviet army headquarters to report a system malfunction. Just months later, nuclear calamity nearly struck again when a 1983 NATO training exercise designed to culminate in a simulated nuclear attack got a little too real—and the Soviets began to prepare for war.

So if the first lesson of 1962 had been that it was the height of folly to make an adversary choose between humiliation and the nuclear option, the lessons that followed were that human error, digital malfunction, miscommunication, or sheer inattention to detail could be equally deadly.

So as the nuclear crisis of 2022 played out, Biden's aides spent several days sorting through their options and trying to settle on a strategy for how much to tell Putin about what they suspected. They agreed they needed to warn Putin about how severely the West would respond to any use of a nuclear weapon. But they didn't want to burn their sources, and they feared that going public with the information could trigger panic. In the end, Biden decided that the best course was to send Putin a series of reinforcing warnings about what would happen if he went the nuclear route. So the White House choreographed a series of messages— first from Washington, then from other leaders around the world.

They started with a call from Jake Sullivan to his counterpart, Nikolai Patrushev. Then Lloyd Austin called up Russia's defense minister, Sergei Shoigu, twice. The Pentagon's announcement of both calls and the very fact that the two men spoke twice in three days after months of no communication made it clear that something was up. Austin's message was simple: If Russia set off a nuclear weapon, all the restraints that Biden had enforced to avoid direct American involvement in the war would come off. Americans would, under that circumstance, take on Russians directly. "His message was essentially, 'We will destroy what is left of your military in Ukraine,' " one official told me.

Shoigu reached for a familiar talking point: Ukraine, he said, was getting ready to set off a "dirty bomb" against Russian forces. If they did that, he told Austin, Russia would have no choice but to use a nuclear weapon in response.

That's bullshit, Austin said. Everyone knew that Russia's favorite tactic was to create a threat and then stage it as a false-flag attack.

I don't take well to being threatened, Shoigu retorted.

General Shoigu, Austin responded, I run the most powerful military in the world. I don't make threats.

The call ended inconclusively. It was impossible to know whether Putin believed the threat. Would Biden, always so cautious about escalation, take the risk of striking directly at Russian troops? Even some of his own aides said they didn't know. But they did note that Putin was pretty concerned about keeping NATO out of the war. "Putin knows where every base is in Poland where we are dropping off the weapons" for transfer into Ukraine, said one of Biden's aides. "He hasn't attacked a single one, even once." His conclusion: "Putin can be deterred."

Then Biden sent a direct, confidential missive to Putin with a simple message: We need a meeting.

Not face-to-face, of course. They had not met since Geneva just before the war broke out, and in the interim Putin had invaded a sovereign state and Biden had called him a war criminal. Nothing productive would come from getting in the same room. Instead, a meeting of intermediaries was arranged on neutral-ish ground: Ankara, Turkey, where the discussion would be hosted by the Turkish security service. Turkey was a NATO member, but its leader, Recep Tayyip Erdoğan, was deeply enamored of Putin and frequently took his side.

Putin sent Sergei Naryshkin, head of the SVR, the Russian foreign intelligence service. It was Naryshkin's spies who had pulled off Solar-Winds, the digital supply chain hack of the U.S. government that Biden found so damaging during the transition. Again, Biden chose Bill Burns.

They saw each other on a mid-November day in 2022, with the nuclear threats still ringing in Burns's ears. Naryshkin came into the meeting with high hopes: For reasons that no one on the American side quite understood, he expected that Burns had been dispatched by Biden with the authority to negotiate an armistice agreement that would end the war. He told Burns that any such negotiation had to begin with an understanding that Russia would get to keep any land that was currently under their control.

It took some time for Burns to disabuse Naryshkin of the idea that the United States was ready to trade away Ukrainian territory for peace. I can't negotiate on Ukraine's behalf, he warned, and Biden was not about to try to force Zelensky to give up any part of his country.

They went several rounds on this, back and forth. Finally, they turned to the topic Burns had traveled around the world to discuss: Putin's nuclear threats—and what the United States and its allies were prepared to do to Russia if Putin made good on them. "I made it clear," Burns later recalled from his seventh-floor office, "there would be clear consequences for Russia."

Just how specific Burns was about the nature of the American response was left murky by American officials. He wanted to be detailed enough to deter a Russian attack but without telegraphing Biden's precise reaction. But he told Naryshkin that Russia doesn't have many friends and allies around the world. If Russia reached for a nuclear bomb, China and India might distance themselves entirely. In a war in which Putin had already made many mistakes, this would be the biggest one.

"Naryshkin swore that he understood and that Putin did not intend to use a nuclear weapon," Burns told me.

Unsure of what effect Burns's warning would have, the White House also launched a backup plan: a dual-track effort, led by Antony Blinken at the State Department, to get China and India—the two most powerful nations that had stuck close to Moscow after the invasion—to declare that nuclear weapons could never be used in Ukraine. "Some of the diplomacy that we did with allies and partners was very important in dealing with that moment," Blinken said later.

When the new German chancellor, Olaf Scholz, was on his way to Beijing to meet Xi Jinping, one of his aides told me, a condition of the meeting was a public statement from the Chinese leader that there was no role for nuclear weapons in the Ukraine war. On November 4, with Scholz by his side, Xi "reaffirmed" that he was in favor of a negotiated settlement to the crisis. It was critical, state media wrote—quoting their leader—that everyone involved in the crisis "oppose the use of or the threat to use nuclear weapons, advocate that nuclear weapons cannot be used and that nuclear wars must not be fought."

To Biden's mind, those statements made a difference. Once Putin's most important protector said nuclear use had to be off the table, the Russian leader backed off, if grudgingly. At a meeting of Russia's Human Rights Council at the Kremlin on December 7, he repeated his familiar line that Russia would use "all available means at our disposal" to defend itself. But then he went on, in a statement that seemed directed at Xi and others who thought he had pushed too far. "We have not gone crazy. . . . We are not going to brandish these weapons like a razor, running around the world."

Yet as 2022 came to a close, the fear resonating in the White House was that the nuclear threat was not over; it was simply in abeyance.

CHAPTER 16

A HIGH FENCE FOR
A SMALL YARD

Finally, we are protecting our foundational technologies with a small yard and high fence. As I've argued before, our charge is to usher in a new wave of the digital revolution—one that ensures that next-generation technologies work for, not against, our democracies and our security.

Jake Sullivan, national security advisor, April 2023

JUST OVER AN hour's drive southwest from Taipei, on former farmland that over the centuries was populated by aboriginal tribes, Spanish missionaries, Dutch explorers, and Japanese occupiers, lies Taiwan's greatest commercial treasure. Today it is known as the Hsinchu Science Park, built around the most valuable firm in Asia: Taiwan Semiconductor Manufacturing Company, known universally as TSMC.

TSMC only makes one thing: computer chips. While it produces all varieties of high-quality semiconductors—from memory and graphics chips to the kind of advanced, custom-designed microprocessors that power Apple's iPhone—it made its name by focusing purely on precision, low-cost manufacturing in the fabrication plants (or "fabs") it built in the Science Park and then scattered across the island. It doesn't design chips. It takes other company's designs and churns out the chips the world relies on, for everything from F-35s and HIMARS artillery systems to Android cellphones and smart TVs. Today politicians regularly call chips "the new oil"—the analogy is flawed, but it does capture their centrality to the global economy.

Chip manufacturing is the technology America let get away. Silicon Valley's early pioneers at Fairchild Semiconductor and Texas Instruments, Intel and Motorola had pioneered chip technology and changed the world. But over the decades, those companies and others, in a series of separate profit-driven decisions, gradually moved production overseas without much thought about the national security implications of becoming so dependent on the supply of chips from a single vulnerable island off the coast of China. It was assumed that, like oil through the Strait of Hormuz, the chips would just keep flowing across continents and borders.

Ultimately, America's dependence on a complex, easily severed supply chain for chips became even more acute than our dependence on the Persian Gulf for oil. Many of the "legacy" chips that the world used to power the most basic products—dishwashers and the dashboards of gas-powered cars and industrial equipment—either came from China or were "finished" there, meaning that the chips were put in the packaging that plugs into circuit boards.* This gave the Chinese tremendous leverage. But the American overreliance on vulnerable Taiwan—where the most advanced chips come from—is the central issue. By the time Biden's team settled into office, the figure being thrown around in Washington was that Taiwan produced nearly 90 percent of the most modern, advanced chips used around the world—though everyone defines "advanced chips" differently.

Definitional debates aside, one thing is clear: If TSMC's plants at the Hsinchu Science Park shut down, it will be bad news for anyone who drops an iPhone. Replacements will dry up. The A-17 "bionic" Apple chip in the iPhone 15 is stuffed with 19 billion transistors, and for now Apple depends almost exclusively on TSMC to churn them out. Tim Cook, Apple's chief executive, spends an inordinate amount of his time trying to diversify the sources of his supply, moving a bit of production to India and elsewhere. But Apple will be overwhelmingly dependent on

---

* Roughly, there are three steps involved in semiconductor production. The first is design of chips and chipmaking equipment (dominated by the West and Western allies); the second is manufacturing (dominated by TSMC); the third is packaging and assembling (dominated by China).

Taiwan for years, if not decades, to come, as will Nvidia—the chip-design company that has come to play a central role in designing generative artificial intelligence programs, including ChatGPT.

TSMC's dominance in the global chip race has brought the entire island of Taiwan wealth and importance beyond anything imaginable when Chiang Kai-shek retreated there under fire. But that success has also changed every calculation of what would happen if Taiwan were to be invaded by China, quarantined, or forcibly reunited with the mainland—a set of risks that the rest of the world has only recently begun to understand.

When TSMC was founded, the biggest risk seemed to be earthquakes, which is why the company put its fabs all around the island. But as Xi's threats to take Taiwan became more ominous, economists and war-planners alike began running simulations that included the damage that would be done to the world economy if the company's facilities were disrupted or destroyed, or if Chinese action cut it off from its just-in-time suppliers around the world. The projected hit to the global economy ran into the billions—and that was just in the first few days.

"No one wanted to think about this, so they didn't," one chief executive with major investments in China and Taiwan told me, shortly after sitting through a tabletop simulation of the economic impacts of a war for Taiwan's territory. When he raised the issue to other top executives, though, "people waved it away."

Partly, this was willful ignorance. But business executives had good reason to be skeptical about worst-case scenarios: China could not live without TSMC any more than the United States or Europe could. Many of its own products rely on TSMC chips, as do Beijing's (and everyone else's) elaborate plans to take the lead in space and artificial intelligence. The result of this mutual dependency, some have argued, is what has come to be called the "Silicon Shield," the notion that TSMC is too critical a supplier to China itself for Xi to risk it getting destroyed in the violence of forced unification with Taiwan. After all, what leader in his right mind would knowingly bomb his own supply chain?

At least that was the theory. In practice, no one knew if it would really hold up. Xi's hesitation to harm China's own economy might delay military action for years, but from the executive suites at TSMC to the Presidential Palace in Taipei to the Pentagon, I had yet to find someone who thought it possible to hold off an invasion forever.

In the long term, the Shield seemed bound to erode, as China slowly learned to replicate much of the work that could be done on Taiwan. And even in the short term, the long-held assumption that Xi and his inner circle are made up of rational economic actors—and that his emphasis on "security first" would be tempered by the huge economic and political risks—was no longer a safe bet. Just look, the hawks said, at how Xi squashed Hong Kong—China's profitable capitalist outpost—as soon as he perceived that it was a dangerous node of dissent. Or how decisively he used the power of the state to bring powerful billionaire tech entrepreneurs like Jack Ma, the founder of Alibaba, to heel. If Xi was willing to risk Jack Ma's empire—which brought billions of dollars and critical technology to China—would he be willing to gamble with TSMC as well?

Naturally, no one at TSMC wanted to talk, at least on the record, about that possibility. I asked Mark Liu, the sophisticated, Berkeley-educated chairman of TSMC, how he viewed the risk. "I don't spend a second contemplating invasion," he said calmly. "Because that is unimaginable." In fact, it wasn't unimaginable: It was the doomsday scenario that military planners in Taipei and Washington were thinking about every day.

TAIWAN'S EMERGENCE AS the critical hub of the most important supply chain in the world was the result of a remarkable confluence of events: unusually skillful and well-timed state-planning by Taiwan at a moment when it was barely emerging as a democracy; remarkable vision by a single brilliant engineer, Morris Chang, a Harvard-and-MIT-educated U.S. immigrant who left Texas Instruments in disgust when he felt underappreciated; and a series of astoundingly bad business judgments made in the United States.

The deciding factor was Chang himself. A Chinese-born, American-educated engineer and entrepreneur, Chang had barely visited the island of Taiwan until he was invited by the government's minister for technology development, K. T. Li, to come for a visit—and a little arm-twisting. Among Taiwan's leaders, Li best understood that the island was stuck at the low-profit end of the semiconductor supply chain—mostly packaging chips or integrating them into cheap electronics. If it wanted to move up the ladder, to prosper like Japan, it needed a new business plan that would put it at the heart of the manufacturing process.

That was where Chang entered the picture. For years he had been mulling the concept of developing a semiconductor "foundry," a company that could cast chips to fit the custom designs of scores of different customers from the world over. The foundry could focus entirely on the magic of making cutting-edge semiconductors. It was an unconventional plan: Companies like Intel or Texas Instruments that designed chips also manufactured them. The key to success, Chang argued, was to leave the design to others and focus on becoming the custom tailors of the industry.

Li was impressed. "Tell me how much money you need," he asked. He didn't blink when he heard the numbers.

Chang's vision proved to be just the right move at the right moment. As semiconductors grew dense with more circuits and drastically more complex, they became far more expensive to produce. New fabs capable of stuffing more and more transistors on a chip, using narrower and narrower circuitry cut by the world's most advanced lasers, were beginning to cost more than a billion dollars to set up. A few years later a billion-dollar fab would look like a bargain. As Chang had anticipated, companies began looking to farm out the manufacturing. Those who continued to try to make their own encountered a shortage of trained American engineers.

Washington was accustomed to reviewing Chinese investments in American tech firms and stopping them whenever they detected a threat to national security. There was no equivalent process to stopping companies from moving their production overseas—that was purely a business decision. So over the years, American tech firms decided to focus on designing their own chips and leave the manufacturing to the true experts like TSMC. It was a strategy reinforced by the reassuring myth that in a globalized world, it didn't really make any difference *where* you produced the semiconductors that fuel the information age. Sure, there might be temporary disruptions, but in a region where making money was the supreme goal, keeping supply chains flowing seemed in everyone's economic interest—especially China's.

That was the prevailing public wisdom for decades. Then COVID hit, and with it came the dawning realization that when the supply chain gets interrupted, crises multiply fast. As most chip fabrication plants shut down and cargo flights were canceled, newly made cars and trucks began to stack up at factory lots, awaiting a single delayed chip for navigation systems or antiskid brakes. BMW began to fret about its new flagship all-electric car—the i7—which took thousands of chips to manufacture.

The economic snarl wasn't easy to understand—or to remediate. Policymakers who barely grasped the process of making chips got a crash course in the hard realities of why America could not simply turn this manufacturing process back on at home. There were still several dozen fabs in the United States, in plants that appeared in clusters from Burlington, Vermont, to Bloomington, Minnesota, to Hillsboro, Oregon. But chips are hardly interchangeable: what fits in the dashboard of a Ford F-150 is not usable in a Whirlpool washing machine. The time, cost, and complexity of building new facilities was staggering. And while TSMC's fabs kept running during the pandemic, it didn't require much imagination to envision what would have happened to the world economy if they hadn't.

The pandemic woke policymakers up to scenarios that a small cadre of national security aides and Pentagon officials had been gaming out for years. By the time Biden took office, the oft-cited statistic was that the share of semiconductors manufactured in America had fallen from 37 percent in 1990 to around 12 percent in 2020, and the biggest danger to TSMC was coming clearly into view. China's reaction to the Pelosi visit led even the most Panglossian executives and investors to think seriously about the implications of an invasion—or even just an extended blockade if China decided to make good on its vow to reunify the mainland with its rebellious "province." In the ensuing disruption, it would be almost impossible to keep the carefully calibrated fabs running. If the undersea cables surrounding the island were cut, they would lose their connections to chip designers in the West. If a naval quarantine were imposed, they would quickly run out of chemicals and silicon—and their engineers would likely flee with their families to San Jose and Tokyo and cities across Europe.

.   .   .

IN THE SPRING of 2023, TSMC head Mark Liu was in his late sixties, with the quiet demeanor of an engineer who spent his life designing ever-faster chips. He had only recently turned his mind toward the risk of escalating superpower conflict. For the majority of his career, he told me, "my focus was speed": the speed at which electrons moved through ever-more-compact transistors. But now, a few years past the age when most Taiwanese retire, he found himself attempting to stay ahead of the competition while navigating the speculation that an aggressive, risk-taking Chinese leadership could destroy his company.

All of this was unimaginable when Liu was growing up in an authoritarian Taiwan still reeling from Chiang Kai-shek's retreat. His parents, both of whom had fled from the mainland as members of Chiang's defeated army, met in Taiwan and found jobs as high school teachers. "We lived in a pretty shabby place," Liu recalled, until his father, launching a second career, became the lieutenant governor of Taiwan, building many of the roads that now connect the country's technology hubs to Taipei. Liu attended Taiwan's most prestigious university before moving to the United States to get his PhD from Berkeley: a recognition that the key innovations in technology were still largely American. In 1983, he landed his first job in the United States at Intel—at the time the most storied company in Silicon Valley.

Intel had been founded in 1968 by two engineers who came to define American innovation: Robert Noyce—who once told me his career was the culmination of "a bunch of dissatisfactions" and who had been awarded a patent in the late 1950s for putting interconnecting transistors on a single silicon chip—and Gordon Moore.

Liu arrived just as the processing power packed into Intel's chips was beginning to give IBM personal computers a capability that most computer executives could scarcely imagine. He soon fell under the wing of another key Intel partner: Andrew Grove, an intense immigrant from Hungary whose family had escaped both the Nazis and a Soviet invasion. Grove had become a driving force within the company. Around Intel, he became known for his catchphrase "Only the paranoid survive."

Grove's focus at the time was the production of Intel's most crucial product—the 386 microprocessor: the computer-on-a-chip that put the company on the map. He pushed his staff, Liu included, to take the 386 into the stratosphere; it was widely understood that its brilliant design changed the world's perception of what a small computer could do.

But design was only part of the game. Success and profitability lay in producing it, jamming 275,000 transistors onto microscopically thin layers on each tiny chip—a staggering figure at the time. To add to the manufacturing challenge, scores of chips were produced at a time, fitted onto a round six-inch "wafer" of silicon. Liu's challenge was to increase the yield of good chips that could be harvested from each wafer.

Pressed by stiff Japanese competition in innovation and for market share, Grove eventually pulled the company out of the memory-chip business and bet the future of the firm on designing and producing microprocessors—the logic chips at the core of the personal computer revolution. Liu became a bridge between two groups of Intel employees who rarely talked to each other: the chip designers and the production engineers. "They didn't understand the technology," Liu said of the production engineers. With his calm demeanor, he was tasked with taming the chaos, taking up residence in the Intel fabs to help them smooth out differences—a task that was, he said, "a hell of a challenge." He would on occasion be visited by the famously impatient Grove. "Why can't you go faster?" Liu recalled him asking. "Motorola is ahead of us!"

In the next two decades, especially after Grove's retirement as chief executive, Intel's focus on manufacturing waned—one of many reasons that production of the most vital chips moved overseas. After a six-year stint in the late 1980s as a researcher at Bell Laboratories—then considered among the most innovative corporate labs in the world—Liu got an offer he could not refuse: Return to Taiwan and help TSMC make the island a manufacturing powerhouse competitive with the United States and Japan. He packed up the family and headed home to a country that was still shockingly undeveloped; when he couldn't find a coffee shop to feed his American-nurtured caffeine habit, he wound up at McDonalds.

At TSMC, Liu acted as the bridge between the designers and the manufacturers. The company attracted huge customers: Intel, AMD, Nvidia, Qualcomm, Broadcom, MediaTek, Sony, Apple, China's Huawei, and carmakers around the world. They all counted on the same thing: Through political tensions and global disruptions, Apple could still design what it needed in Cupertino, transmit the data-packed designs over undersea cables to the Hsinchu Science Park, where they would be etched on Japanese-provided silicon wafers by a Netherlands-made lithography machine produced by a company known as ASML, whose equipment carved the tiniest circuit lines on earth. The resulting chip would then make its way to Foxconn in China for final assembly. And that list leaves out hundreds of interim steps conducted by smaller suppliers. It seemed obvious that in a peaceful, "flat" world, one with seamless supply chains, it was almost beside the point where the chips were made.

Over time, TSMC became the coordinator as well as the hub for this. It was the biggest place in the world where the tools and the know-how coincided. And TSMC took off: Its revenues and profit margins soared. It was uniquely situated to export semiconductors to both the United States and China. By the time Liu and I talked in his headquarters, TSMC's market capitalization was on par with that of ExxonMobil. But its public name recognition was virtually nil, even though it made the beating heart of every iPhone. The low profile was fine by Liu. "We don't have to be up front," he told me.

But TSMC's technological dominance was making its customers nervous. After COVID hit, fear of overdependence drove many countries to start seeking a more diverse supply chain. Xi's vow to solve the Taiwan problem only accelerated the angst.

Liu understood the first concern: What country didn't want to make its own chips? But he had come to a simple conclusion: "It's impossible for one country to make all these things" that go into the production of a chip. Leaders in Beijing and politicians in Washington might talk about becoming self-sufficient in chipmaking, but it was a fantasy. "It's a nationalist's ambition," Liu said to me. Anyone who has made semiconductors knows that it simply won't happen.

He didn't have an easy answer for the question so many asked him: What would happen to the world's most important chipmaker if China invaded? Over time Liu grew practiced at stepping around the question, falling back on describing his company as a boat in the tossing waters of geopolitical power plays beyond his control. TSMC was doing what it could, he said, to mitigate various national security concerns by building new fabs in the United States, Japan, and, if it worked out, Germany.

But Liu knew these investments were no real protection if Taiwan came under attack. The core of the company, its thousands of engineers, is in Taiwan, and without them there is no way to produce the most intricate chips, the kind American and Chinese officials care about the most. As Liu told two of my *Times* colleagues in mid-2023, "China will not invade Taiwan because of semiconductors. China will not *not* invade Taiwan because of semiconductors. It is really up to the U.S. and China: How do they maintain the status quo, which both sides want?"

It was a convenient deflection but not an especially helpful one. TSMC would inevitably be at the center of whatever struggle was to come. The threat of invasion or turmoil around the Taiwan Strait hung over every major business decision Liu and his investors made. It was the impetus behind the recent effort to build new TSMC plants abroad. It preoccupied investors like Warren Buffett, who sank $4 billion into a stake in TSMC in 2022, only to sell most of that stake a few months later, giving the blunt explanation that he didn't care for the location.

The Pentagon shared the concern. Quietly, its analysts tried to quantify just how dependent American defense contractors were on Taiwanese-manufactured chips for its leading weapons systems, fighter jets, satellites, drones, and communications systems. It was not encouraging. "No one could give a real answer," one senior official told me, because it was unclear where subcontractors were sourcing their chips. So defense planners worked out a rough estimate. The resulting number was immediately classified.

"All I can tell you," the official added, "is that no one in their right mind would make themselves that dependent on a single source that could be wiped out in a day by your most powerful adversary."

FIVE DAYS AFTER the Russian invasion of Ukraine, Biden stood before a joint session of Congress for his first official State of the Union Address. After celebrating the country's extraordinary progress to get beyond the pandemic and decrying Putin's violent land grab, he turned to the centerpiece of his message: To create a manufacturing renaissance in America, the country had to make its own computer chips again.

"If you travel twenty miles east of Columbus, Ohio, you'll find a thousand empty acres of land," Biden said, spinning a vision that was as much about politics as economics. "It won't look like much. But if you stop and look closely, you'll see a 'field of dreams'—the ground on which

America's future will be built." That was where Intel, Biden explained, was going to build a semiconductor "megasite." "Up to eight state-of-the-art factories in one place," said Biden. "Ten thousand new jobs."

In fact, Intel had committed to only two fabs; the other six were an aspiration. Even so, getting the company to construct its first new manufacturing site on American soil in forty years had been a major coup for the administration—especially in Ohio, a swing state Biden lost in 2020 by eight points. The politics were so attractive that Biden's aides even toyed with the idea of moving the entire State of the Union Address to the empty field.

Yet by early summer 2022, it looked like the field of dreams might remain an empty lot. Intel's chief executive, Pat Gelsinger, had been warning the White House for months that he wouldn't move forward with the groundbreaking ceremony until the federal government guaranteed that it would pick up part of the cost of building the $20 billion dollar facility. The Biden administration was trying; they'd been championing a legislative package that included a $52 billion pot of money and incentives specifically designated to help companies like Intel bolster their domestic chip-manufacturing capacity. But the bill—known as the CHIPS Act—had already been stuck in Congress for a year.

Gelsinger decided to play political hardball: He warned Biden that if the logjam that had held up the bill was not broken soon, there would be no groundbreaking and no photo op for the president in Ohio. Left unsaid was that Biden would have to explain to the voters what had happened to the field of dreams—and why a $100 billion investment had vanished into the air.

A series of heated conversations followed, including direct exchanges between Gelsinger and Biden. "We are doing our part," Gelsinger declared in public, "but we can't do it alone." What he didn't say in public was that the future of Intel was at stake: His charge as CEO was to reverse Intel's recent long slump, and that meant fundamentally changing the company's business model so that it could compete with TSMC—a company that made some of Intel's microprocessors but also produced chips designed by others. "We're becoming a foundry," he told his board when he took the role. "We're going to manufacture at scale." The key to having that happen on U.S. soil, he said, was to have the federal government help offset the 30 to 50 percent higher cost of building at home.

Privately, Biden told Gelsinger holding the project hostage would be unproductive. The Intel CEO might understand how to make chips, Biden told him, but he knew a thing or two about how to get a bill through Congress. It was Biden's view, recalled one of his top economic aides, "that momentum begets momentum."

In fact, Biden's team was as frustrated as Gelsinger. Based on an early meeting with a bipartisan group of senators in the Oval Office, they thought the CHIPS Act would be a straightforward win. Eighteen months later, it remained caught in the maw of Capitol Hill. Democrats had other priorities—their signature infrastructure bill, "Build Back Better"; voting rights; and fulfilling Biden's promises on social safety net issues like childcare. Progressives like Bernie Sanders, the Vermont independent, argued that chip manufacturers had themselves caused the problem by moving plants and jobs overseas; now, he argued, they were demanding a "bribe" to return production to American soil.

Republicans had their own complaints, some rooted in raw politics and others reasonably substantive: How would Biden prevent American taxpayer funds from benefiting Chinese firms? And wasn't this a textbook case of industrial policy? The phrase alone triggered hives among Republicans. The bill's supporters emphasized that this was "seed money" designed to unlock private capital—not to fund the projects single-handedly—and that the remaining funds would flow up and down the supply chain to facilitate everything from raw inputs to the facilities needed to package and finalize the chips. Skeptics of industrial policy recalled the lessons of SEMATECH, a 1980s government-funded chip-producing consortium that had failed.

Despite lawmakers' concerns, the fact remained that if the United States was going to reduce its dependency on Taiwan and compete with China, it was going to have to write a big check. "Around the globe, authoritarian governments smell blood in the water," the Senate majority leader, Chuck Schumer, had said in 2021. "They believe that squabbling democracies like ours can't come together and invest in national priorities the way a top-down, centralized, and authoritarian government can. They are rooting for us to fail so they can grab the mantle of global economic leadership and own the innovations."

But at Intel, no one was going to take a gamble on an investment this big without government backing. "We were very worried they would never get it done," recalled Bruce Andrews, who emerged from the Obama administration to become Intel's chief government affairs officer, putting him on the receiving end of a strategy for which he had helped lay the early groundwork.

If Gelsinger's delay of the groundbreaking looked a bit like corporate coercion, well, it was. Gelsinger and Andrews believed that if the CHIPS Act didn't pass over the summer, it would get lost amid congressional recesses and the sure-to-be-contentious 2022 midterm election. Whatever momentum had built up might never be recaptured.

LATE ON A Wednesday afternoon in mid-July of 2022, Gina Raimondo— the fifty-two-year-old powerhouse former governor of Rhode Island whom Biden had chosen to be his commerce secretary—made the short trek from her office to a secure hearing room on Capitol Hill. Her sole focus was to convince skeptical senators to push the CHIPS Act across the finish line. She had decided the only path to success was reframing the discussion to focus on the risk to the United States if it remained highly dependent on chips produced in Taiwan.

"I never used 'industrial policy,'" she told me later, describing the rhetorical hoops the administration was jumping through to avoid describing this effort for what it was. "I was like, 'This is a presidential priority. This is national security.'" Her challenge was to convince senators that a technology many of them struggled to understand was as critical to the United States as the number of missiles the United States kept in its stockpiles. She wanted to "paint a picture to them of how vulnerable we were . . . what would happen to our economy and our national security apparatus if we couldn't access those chips." The choke point to just about everything, she said, was Taiwan. It wouldn't take a full-blown war over the island to endanger the United States; a Chinese-imposed quarantine on the island's imports and exports—a scenario the Pentagon had gamed out many times—would shut down every major American manufacturer.

Just ahead of the hearing, she had set her aides on a task: Go find out for me, she said, how many chips are in a Javelin anti-tank missile. That was, of course, a weapon America was shipping to Ukraine—and one that was central to the Pentagon's own arsenal. "That became a constant talking point of mine," she told me, because it "made it real for people."

Raimondo was no stranger to the ugly realities of the legislative process—she had been immersed in it, on a far smaller scale, as governor of Rhode Island. Her political savvy and working-class roots were a large part of the reason Biden was so eager to persuade her to become commerce secretary, overcoming her original hesitance by promising, "We're going to rebuild American manufacturing together." The opportunity fit with the origin story of her political rise: as a sixth-grader, she'd seen her father lose his job of twenty-seven years at the Bulova watch factory, one of the casualties as the jewelry industry shifted overseas to Asia. "It was a horrible time," she recalled. "My dad would come home and tell my mom, 'I can see the writing on the wall. They're just dismantling this place.'"

That visceral sense of helplessness shaped the direction of her career. After earning degrees from Harvard, Yale, and Oxford, she returned to Rhode Island and co-founded a venture capital firm, then launched her political career as a moderate, get-stuff-done governor. She poured state dollars into attracting corporate investment and economic development and leveraging what she learned in the venture capital world. Just a few years into her term, unemployment had plummeted, and the state coffers were filling. Her critics called her a "corporatist Democrat"; her own venture capital firm, others noted, had fled to Boston. But it was obvious to friends and detractors alike that Raimondo had both political ambitions and enormous charisma—and the cabinet position Biden was dangling was a next natural step.

When she settled into the vast secretary's office in the nearly century-old Commerce Department building in March 2021, it was evident that one of her biggest tasks was going to be to bring back the semiconductor industry, which had gone the way of Bulova watches. But as she dug in, she was somewhat surprised to discover that her team would not be starting from scratch. "All the mapping around diagnosing the problem had been done" by predecessors in the Obama and Trump administrations, she recalled. "You've got to give credit where credit's due," she said, rattling off a list of Trump-era national security officials who had left her some tools, including her predecessor, Wilbur Ross, alongside Mike Pompeo and Keith Krach.

One tool that her Commerce Department was eager to build on was a Trump-era executive order that gave them the power to block financial transactions involving communications technologies run at the direction of "a foreign adversary"—language so broad that it could be directed at Huawei or TikTok or China Telecom. China's Semiconductor Manufacturing International Corporation, known as SMIC, had been added to a sanctions list, restricting its access to advanced chipmaking tools. TSMC had already committed to building a semiconductor plant in Arizona, largely because its biggest customers, Apple included, had insisted on it. Mark Liu knew the U.S. outposts would never be economically competitive compared to his fabs in Taiwan, but this was about politics and secure supply chains, not profits.

So when Raimondo met the senators in closed session in July 2022, she enlisted the help of the two most powerful women leading Joe Biden's national security apparatus: Avril Haines and Kathleen Hicks, the deputy secretary of defense who was driving the effort to bring twenty-first-century technology to a Pentagon still far too reliant on Vietnam-era weapons. "What I spent time talking about was how technology was really at the heart of President Xi Jinping's strategy for making China a global power, and how semiconductors are a 'Rosetta Stone' for technologies across the board," Haines told me later, emphasizing the enormous effort that China was undertaking to create its own indigenous semiconductor industry. But, she recalled, it was Hicks who delivered some of the most telling statistics: The vast majority of chips used by Pentagon contractors come from overseas. Many of the "legacy" chips in older weapons systems are only produced in China. And 98 percent of all the chips used in Pentagon systems are finished in Asia. If that supply were ever to get choked off, it would be game over.

For nearly two hours, the senators peppered the three officials with questions. Just how vulnerable was Taiwan, really? Why couldn't America stockpile chips? Weren't there any back-up suppliers? And why, exactly, was it necessary to funnel more than $50 *billion* into building U.S. fabs—surely they couldn't be that expensive?

Indeed they could. "You have to think of each one of those fabs as an aircraft carrier," explained James Lewis at the Center for Strategic and International Studies. The last aircraft carrier built by the United States—the USS *Gerald R. Ford*—clocked in at $13 billion, roughly the price of each of TSMC's next-generation fabs, give or take a billion dollars. When I mentioned the comparison in early 2023 to a senator responsible for defense spending, he told me he thought his colleagues would have no problem voting for ten new aircraft carriers, even if they were sitting ducks. Ten new semiconductor fabs, he said, would be a problem.

It seemed like a remarkable oversight: Texas Instruments brought out the first single-chip microcontroller in 1971, more than a half century ago. "I know it doesn't seem that hard to figure out," Chris Coons, the Delaware senator, said to me. "But for many of my colleagues, this seems to be a tough leap."

Two weeks after Raimondo's trip to the Hill, the bill finally passed in the Senate 64–33, establishing the precedent that the United States was willing to underwrite technological "national champions," just as the Chinese, the Taiwanese, and the Europeans do. Other proposed legislation directed money to many of the same kinds of projects that Beijing identified in its "Made in China 2025" strategy: batteries for electric cars, biotechnology, and artificial intelligence. As Schumer said in the weeks before the bill passed, the days had ended when "the government could afford to sit on the sidelines."

But viewed another way, the effort had come late, and it was far too small for the job at hand. "Our Congress is working at political speed," Eric Schmidt, the former Google CEO who had gone on to lead the National Security Commission on Artificial Intelligence, complained to me. "The Chinese government is working at commercial speed."

Raimondo knew that if the United States was truly intent on reducing its dependence on long and tenuous overseas supply chains for the most important hardware of the twenty-first century, it would need steady infusions of government cash, spurring even larger private investment. And that combination would have to deliver, again and again, as the technology evolved.

Biden had put the United States on the right track—but America was moving far too slowly. It was 2015 when Xi announced the "Made in China 2025" program. It was 2019 before Congress began to take the issue seriously—while committing no money to the effort. It was 2022 before the CHIPS funding passed. And Raimondo's team began committing it to projects only toward the end of 2023.

. . .

ON OCTOBER 7, 2022, Biden's Commerce Department turned out a pair of rules that profoundly rewired the global chip supply chain. They were effective immediately. And they were so technical that you had to parse them with care to understand that they represented a cruise missile headed right for the hull of China's most innovative scientific and military projects.

One rule blocked the sale to China of the most advanced chips— particularly those suited for artificial intelligence applications—and the U.S.-built chipmaking manufacturing equipment, materials, and software that China would need to try to make its own alternatives. The second made it simpler for the Commerce Department to ban trade with specific companies or individuals.

As Biden's national security team settled into the West Wing a year and a half earlier, they quickly realized that the semiconductor supply chain shortage that was spiking the price of cars, refrigerators, and printers was only the immediate challenge. A steady stream of classified reports issued in the early months of 2021 by the CIA's new China center and other intelligence agencies warned that the technology race for advanced chips and the arms race with China had essentially merged. All of the innovations that Beijing was trying to develop—surveillance satellites and killer satellites, hypersonic missiles and quantum computers intended to break even the most heavily encrypted communications, "swarms" of sea and air drones that used artificial intelligence to work together—required ever more advanced semiconductors. So Beijing was scouring markets around the world for the West's most sophisticated chips. Essentially, the Chinese were relying on American innovation— and the openness of the Western system—to build the tools intended to defeat its creators.

If America wanted to hold its own, the Biden administration was going to have to find a way to cut off Beijing's access to Western chips and the sophisticated manufacturing equipment used to make them. It wasn't part of the original plan, Brian Deese, the head of Biden's national economic council, told me. "The strategy to build domestic semiconductor capability was the first and primary focus," he said, "but then over time, it became clearer" that it would only work when combined with a strategy of denial. So part of the time, Deese was convening chipmakers on video calls, trying to break through the choke points. The rest of the time, he and Jake Sullivan, with teams from the intelligence agencies, the Pentagon, and the Commerce Department, contemplated new rules that would cut the Chinese off from the most advanced Western-made chips.

It wasn't a totally novel problem for the United States. During the Cold War, the Americans had gone to great lengths to block Soviet access to raw materials and chemical data. The Trump administration, just a few years before, had started the ball rolling against China with somewhat clunky efforts to cut off chips to Huawei and block the Chinese from acquiring some chip-making equipment. But the Biden team knew that if they wanted to have any hope at truly keeping their edge against China, such ad-hoc measures wouldn't suffice. They needed a larger, comprehensive, export-focused, and legally sustainable program against the world's second-largest economy and a technological power in its own right. And for that there was no real playbook. "It took a year of consuming the intelligence information, assessing the landscape, and more deeply understanding the actual technology pathways to get to a view of how it is that we could effectively put together an export control regime," Deese told me.

In the fall of 2022, Sullivan began laying out the strategy in a series of public speeches. The concept, he said, was to erect a "high fence" around "a small yard," cutting China off from a handful of carefully selected technologies that were critical to fulfilling its military ambitions. "Choke points for foundational technologies have to be inside that yard," he said, "and the fence has to be high because these competitors should not be able to exploit American and allied technologies to undermine American and allied security." What the Biden administration wasn't trying to do, he contended, was contain China's competitiveness or decouple the two economies.

To American ears, it sounded eminently reasonable. But it was one thing to enunciate a policy and quite another to make it work as stated. Because chips are such a multipurpose technology—"dual use" technology, in Washington's lingo—there was no way to cut off the Chinese military without also cutting off Chinese commercial and research applications. "Because everything is dual use, it's impossible to be perfect,"

Raimondo admitted to me. "It is very difficult to draw the cut line in such a precise way that you don't have some denial to the commercial application."

Translation: No matter what the administration did, this would look like an effort to contain Beijing's military *and* commercial power. Worse yet, when members of Congress talked about the issue, they made clear they hoped to cut off both the People's Liberation Army and Chinese industry.

China's immediate response was sharp and predictable outrage. Xi himself declared, "Western countries led by the United States have implemented all-around containment, encirclement and suppression of China," he said, "which has brought unprecedented severe challenges to our country's development."

American companies were not exactly thrilled, either. As much as they wanted Biden's administration to safeguard their intellectual property and subsidize new manufacturing sites, they did not want to be cut off from lucrative revenue streams in China. Chief among them was Nvidia, the onetime game maker whose A100 chips had emerged as the fastest processors for assembling the "large language models" needed for artificial intelligence systems. The company was quickly realizing these export controls could cost it billions in lost sales. For Nvidia there was one obvious solution—it immediately designed two "China market" chips that fell just below the speed limits established by the Commerce Department. Fairly quickly, White House officials were calling Situation Room meetings on how to crack down on the chipmaker, tightening the rules so that Chinese users couldn't string several Nvidia chips together. It was clear that with every new rule there would be new workarounds.

MOST FOREIGN LEADERS visiting Washington, D.C., are eager to be seen chatting with the American president. But in January 2023, it was the greatest wish of Mark Rutte—the longest-serving prime minister of the Netherlands—to slip in and out of the White House as unobtrusively as any high-level leader can. Pressed back in the Netherlands about his Oval Office meeting, he refused to discuss it. "We don't communicate about this," he said.

His reluctance was understandable. In the visits and in back-channel communications with Biden and Sullivan, Rutte found himself perhaps the most important single player in the escalating American-led effort to choke off China's access to the most advanced chips. The administration wanted his help to prevent Beijing from obtaining the massive lithography machines at the heart of every advanced chip fab.

The very best of these machines—each of which comes with a price tag of $150 million and is so large that it takes forty cargo containers and three cargo planes to move it—come from a company called ASML, which operates out of the quiet Dutch suburb of Veldhoven. The most advanced of ASML's machines use "extreme ultraviolet" light waves to print transistors onto silicon wafers. The physics problem of using light at such short wavelengths is incredibly complex, and no other company in the world has matched ASML's success.

The overriding challenge in chipmaking has always been to pack more and more tiny transistors on each successive generation of semiconductors. More circuits translated into more and faster computing power. For decades, there was a rough rule for the pace of innovation in the industry: every two years, the number of transistors on a chip roughly doubled—that was the essence of Moore's law, named for the same Intel co-founder who coined the easy metric of progress.

But eventually, the laws of physics began to intervene. The cost of shrinking the circuitry skyrocketed, and miniaturization slowed. Making breakthroughs became a multi-billion-dollar enterprise, requiring ever thinner beams of light, moving in smaller and smaller wavelengths, to produce ever smaller circuits. And ASML's machines, with their special lens coatings and innovative light sources, became the only ones that could effectively produce these types of chips at scale. By the time Rutte came to the White House to see Biden, the firm's machines could produce chips with circuits that are only three nanometers wide: roughly thirty thousand times thinner than a human hair.

Veldhoven had become the central cog that made Silicon Valley and TSMC work. Beijing could not seem to replicate its technology—despite throwing billions of dollars and scores of spies and engineers at the problem. "Everyone understood from the start of the administration that this is China's vulnerability," one of Biden's senior advisors told me soon after the president took office. "The question is how long a lead we have and whether we can extend it."

Biden's argument to Rutte was that keeping ASML's machines out of the hands of Beijing's chip engineers was perhaps the single most important step in the West's military competition with China. These machines comprised the critical Western advantage—just as it once held the lead in building radar, the atomic bomb, satellites, and supercomputers. An American intelligence community estimate in Biden's first year concluded that when it came to the most advanced chips, it might take China ten years to catch up.

The Dutch government was key to the effort. It controlled the export licenses that ASML needs to ship their machines abroad. This was not Rutte's first Washington visit on the subject. Back in 2018, in quiet meetings with Trump's national security officials, he had agreed to refrain from shipping ASML's most sophisticated machines to China. It was partly a self-interested decision: ASML knew that as soon as the technology was on the mainland, it would become another victim of Beijing's drive to vacuum up Western intellectual property.

In 2022 and 2023, the Biden team was focused on "the next set of tools down," as one official put it. Intelligence reports suggested the Chinese government and manufacturers were scouring Southeast Asia and other locales to get their hands on slightly older ASML machines that could be pressed to the limit. Biden wanted those older machines cut off from China, too.

But he had to tread gently, Raimondo told me. "It was really important to the Dutch to come to their own independent conclusion," she said. "Not to be told what to do by the United States but to do their own policy homework, to get comfortable that this was the right thing to do."

Rutte did come to that conclusion on his own time. As promised, he did not advertise it.

But the chief executive of ASML, Peter Wennink, likened the effort to the Dutch story about the boy who put his fingers in a dike to hold back the water. "If they cannot get those machines, they will develop them themselves."

There were already hints that the Chinese were cracking the code. In the weeks just before the CHIPS Act passed, SMIC produced a seven-nanometer chip that was used in a Chinese system for mining cryptocurrency. It was a surprise: As recently as 2020, amid the pandemic, China had appeared stuck at forty nanometers. The CIA spent weeks examining the chip and concluded it was based on, or perhaps stolen from, TSMC's own designs. A year later, in the late summer of 2023, Huawei brought out a new cellphone using a chip with the same circuit dimensions.

The message seemed clear: The United States could deprive Beijing of the tools, and impose embargo after embargo. But China was determined to find its own way to the goal.

CHAPTER 17

"DON'T MAKE US CHOOSE"

Everywhere I go I would be asked, "Are you trying to force us to choose between you and China?" That's not our game. We don't want you to choose, we want you to have choices. We want you to be able to make your own decisions, and free from coercion.

Daniel Kritenbrink, U.S. assistant secretary of state for East Asian and Pacific Affairs, January 2023

IT WAS BLISTERING hot in Jeddah, the ancient port city on the Red Sea, on the mid-July day in 2022 when Joe Biden grudgingly exited his hotel for his first meeting as president with Saudi Arabia's de facto leader, Crown Prince Mohammed bin Salman al-Saud, or MBS, as he was universally called.

Biden clearly did not want to be there. His aides had been sharply divided on the wisdom of the trip. Many of them, especially those at the State Department, told him it would be a terrible mistake to show up on Saudi territory, paying tribute to a country he had vowed during the campaign to turn into a "pariah." They warned that every news story about the trip would remind readers of that promise in the first paragraph (they were right). And it would be even worse if there were images and photos of him being greeted by MBS, whom Biden had vowed he would make "pay the price" for the brutal killing and dismemberment of the Saudi dissident turned *Washington Post* columnist Jamal Khashoggi in 2018. Sure, MBS was implementing impressive reforms that were bringing the Kingdom out of the nineteenth century—women finally permitted to drive, the Wahhabis purged—but he was still jailing activists who pressed for change, to say nothing of opponents he identified as a threat.

The counterargument came from the advisors in the West Wing—notably Sullivan and Brett McGurk, his Middle East strategist—who argued that if Biden was going to push Saudi Arabia toward full recognition of Israel, steer it away from letting Huawei wire up the Kingdom for 5G, and persuade it to pump enough oil to make up for the shortages of Russian exports, then some serious, Kissinger-like realpolitik was going to be in order.

There was another reason as well, and it hung over the trip as Air Force One banked over the Red Sea into lands the United States had been protecting since the Saudi royal family met with Standard Oil of California executives in the desert nine decades earlier. In recent years the Saudis were flirting hard with China, which imported 18 percent of the Kingdom's oil. China had already displaced the United States as the Saudis' biggest trading partner.

When Biden cast Saudi Arabia as a "pariah," Xi saw his opportunity. He didn't need to remind MBS and other Saudi officials that Beijing wasn't going to lecture the Saudis about human rights. Xi wasn't going to embarrass them by releasing intelligence assessments, as Biden had done in the first weeks of his presidency, describing in detail how it had dismembered its most prominent critic in the Saudi consulate in Istanbul.

Simply put, Biden was in Jeddah because he felt boxed in. He had largely built that box himself, with his early talk of a clean divide between democracies and autocracies. He knew better than anyone that the world didn't break down quite that easily—as he had seen, time and again, in his years dealing with some of the world's worst dictators. The explanation his aides offered me for why Biden had settled on the democracy-vs.-autocracy framing was to emphasize the difference with Trump, who had never met a dictator he disliked. But as his administration wore on, the compromises were inevitable.

So now, here was Biden, fist-bumping one of the world's more vicious autocrats. The photo raced across the internet, making some of Biden's aides grimace. The moment was not scripted, one of the advisors told me later in the trip. But the effort to explain away the optics seemed strained.

By the next day, though, Biden found his footing—and explained his rationale. "We will not walk away and leave a vacuum to be filled by China, Russia, or Iran," Biden told a group of nine Arab leaders who had flown to Jeddah to see him. In fact, Biden knew that the vacuum was already being filled. China was negotiating several dozen new energy and investment deals, and soon after Biden left the Kingdom, Xi swept in for his own visit.

Of course, countries are more complicated than the tally of trade and investment deals, and the Saudis made the point that they could cut their deals with Beijing and still stay under the security umbrella of Washington. That was the argument that the Saudi ambassador to the United States, Princess Reema bint Bandar al-Saud, made when I asked her about the Biden administration announcement that the United States and Saudi Arabia would conduct a joint experiment in new 5G technologies, a clear effort to muscle Huawei, the Chinese giant, out of Saudi networks. She looked at me as if I had just asked her to choose between her two favorite children.

The announcement, she said, was like having "a Starbucks and a Coffee Bean" or "a McDonalds and a Burger King." Her message was clear: The Saudis didn't think that they had to choose. Why should they, when they could have both?

She wasn't the only one to ask the question. Just a few months before, an Arab diplomat in Washington had noted to me that when Biden came into office, he made little secret of his desire to extract the United States from the dead-end wars and initiatives in the Middle East and pivot to Asia. "So first you tell us you're leaving," the diplomat said, "And then you complain that we are talking to the Chinese. . . ."

AS BIDEN AND his national security team settled into the White House, what struck them most was the breadth and scope of Beijing's new strategy—and how sophisticated the country had become in seeking to mold events at home and around the world.

In the four years since many of Biden's aides had last been in the White House, China had made great strides in making full use of what

Pentagon strategists call "all elements of national power." It reinvigorated the BRICS grouping, which pulled together Brazil, Russia, India, and South Africa in an economic partnership that, very much by design, excluded the United States and other Western powers. It was gradually turning into a loosely aligned bloc with growing political power and a healthy dose of resentment toward the American-led system.

China deployed its white-hulled Coast Guard ships into disputed sea lanes, making the case that it was "protecting" commerce—while at the same time staking a territorial claim. It had persuaded American allies like Poland and the Philippines to join the Asia Infrastructure Investment Bank, backed by the Chinese government as an alternative to the World Bank and the International Monetary Fund. Often, China Telecom and Huawei were brought in to wire up those countries—assuring that the data could flow back to Beijing.

In cyberspace, China operated with more sophistication and subtlety. For the first time Chinese bloggers and cyber operators were running covert influence operations, some modeled on Russia's past successes. One of them, wonderfully dubbed "Spamouflage," was identified by Meta as "the largest known cross-platform covert influence operation in the world." Asking the Chinese to call in Chinese law enforcement to deal with the problem seemed beyond futile: Meta's investigators determined that Spamouflague was *run* by Chinese law enforcement.

By themselves, none of these actions seemed out of the ordinary for a rising superpower. When the United States was on the rise, Radio Free Asia, Radio Free Europe, and Radio Liberty were regarded as influence operations of another kind. So was the Peace Corps. To this day, the fact of the global economy being run in dollars gives America leverage—and the ability to make financial sanctions stick. Tens of thousands of troops are still based in Japan and South Korea, and the Pentagon regularly runs naval patrols through contested waters in the South Pacific to make the point that the United States does not recognize China's claims. America's ability to airlift food and medical supplies to disaster sites is the ultimate use of hard power for a soft-power purpose.

So it was hard for Biden's incoming team to make a credible case that sovereign countries shouldn't contract with Chinese firms or take advantage of Chinese government subsidies to buy 5G networks or build the new highways that they desperately needed. The problem, according to Kevin Rudd, the former Australian prime minister, a fluent Mandarin speaker, who later became the country's ambassador to the United States, had to do with China's intentions. Increasingly, the contest between Washington and Beijing was turning into a zero-sum game, driven by a growing sense that the United States "will either have to submit to Chinese interests, accommodate them, or actively seek to resist and, if possible, defeat them."

"The U.S. sees Xi as determined to alter the strategic and territorial status quo in the western Pacific and establish a Chinese sphere of influence across the Eastern Hemisphere," Rudd wrote in 2022, just before moving into the ambassador's residence.

In order to counteract China's long-term plans, Biden's aides found themselves in a country-by-country, island-by-island struggle for influence. In practice, that meant turbocharging the American presence with the goal of making it visible again. The United States dispatched diplomats to places they had rarely been seen in decades and invited leaders of tiny nations to the White House for regional summits, where they were suddenly showered with speeches about their exceeding importance. Modest new funding flowed, and embassies in long-abandoned capitals were reopened. But in much of the rest of America, where controlling the country's southern border seemed the more important priority, the need to counter China—arguing over spits of sand in the Pacific or telecommunications systems in Ecuador—seemed inexplicable. But rightly or wrongly, it had become an article of faith among internationalists in Washington that whatever the cost, the United States could not allow China to pick off countries that once were firmly, or even loosely, in the American camp.

The Biden approach to counter the Chinese island by island and technology by technology gave rise to some criticism—including from Washington insiders who served under President Biden. Jessica Chen Weiss, an American academic who had served in the State Department's policy planning staff for the first year of the administration, warned that China's capabilities were being overestimated and were feeding the cycle of fear that was making confrontation more likely. She argued that in this reaction-counterreaction cycle, the United States was losing sight of fundamental American strengths and values.

"Competition with China has begun to consume U.S. foreign policy," she wrote in an essay in the fall of 2022. "The instinct to counter every Chinese initiative, project, and provocation remains predominant, crowding out efforts to revitalize an inclusive international system that would protect U.S. interests and values even as global power shifts and evolves." Her warning was astute: While the attitude in Washington wasn't yet quite as bad as the worst days of the "Red Scare"—when Senator Joseph McCarthy demanded to know "Who lost China?" in the wake of Chiang Kai-shek's defeat at the hands of the communists—it often seemed as if Republicans and Democrats agreed that the answer to any Chinese challenge was to strike back harder.

American diplomats and Biden officials, of course, insisted they were not requiring countries to sign up for an American-led or Chinese-led bloc. Instead, they were offering them alternatives to overdependence on China's technology, security, or aid. Even so, Biden's approach made some American allies nervous that they would be swept into a direct confrontation with Beijing. Biden officials maintained that this wasn't just about Beijing; they were focused on the need to create what they called "purpose built" groupings, not true alliances, through the region. By this formulation, countries wouldn't have to be in complete lockstep to work together productively on particular issues. That was the idea behind elevating the Quad and convincing India's reluctant prime minister, Narendra Modi, to become a central player. India and the United States were at odds on many things, later including India's refusal to actively condemn the invasion of Ukraine. Yet New Delhi, perpetually at odds with Beijing over border conflicts high in the Himalayan Mountains, was a natural partner for the United States when it came to countering Chinese expansionism. This was the epitome of Biden's new geopolitical geometry: Modi and Biden could disagree on Russia and align on China. In other cases, making progress meant trying to mediate between regional allies. The hardest case was Japan and South Korea, whose relationship had been haunted for decades by the Japanese occupation of the Korean Peninsula in the first half of the twentieth century. World War II ended nearly eight decades ago, but there were continuing disputes over territory and Japan's brutality to Korean women who had been forced into sexual servitude. Yet in 2023, both leaders came to Camp David and announced strategies to counter

China, the common adversary that was never explicitly named, and to plan out joint military exercises and responses to North Korean provocations.

Like all such diplomatic initiatives, this one had an element of smoke and mirrors to it. The White House announced in 2023 that South Korea—but not Japan—would participate in "nuclear consultations" with the United States, giving the impression, if not actually promising, that its leaders would be central to decisions about when nuclear weapons might be deployed to defend the country. It was fairly transparently designed to counter those who had been arguing for the South to have its own nuclear force to counter the North's.

Even AUKUS had an element of hype. By the end of 2023 the Australians were still uncertain how they were going to foot the bill for their jointly designed submarine fleet—or where, exactly, the fleet would be produced. The first christening of a new submarine would not come until the 2030s; until then, Britain and the United States would rotate older submarines through Australian ports. For its part, China maintained that no one was being forced to take Beijing's loans, buy its telecommunications systems, or grant port rights to Chinese ships. Nations were able to make their own free choice—and, Chinese diplomats insisted as an aside, many were tired of America's insufferable assumption that the only form of governance worth replicating was Jeffersonian-style democracy. They were happy to remind the world that it was the United States that declared the Philippines a colony in 1898, that had captured Guam the same year and now used it as a critical base.

So while both capitals insisted that they were not requiring countries to pick a side, it increasingly appeared that is exactly what they were seeking. But the battle was not being fought to secure broad declarations of loyalty. Instead, the goal was to be the preference in dozens of small, seemingly technical decisions. Which countries would join the ban on selling the most advanced chips to China? Which would buy Huawei equipment or pay more for the Western alternative? Which would declare that if Taiwan was attacked they would come to its aid—or take the French position and define it as not their fight? Which would help Ukraine, overtly or covertly? Which would continue to operate in China, even if that meant observing Beijing's new rules about keeping all their data on servers inside Chinese territory, where they could be accessed by Chinese intelligence agencies?

"Don't force us to choose," one of Singapore's former ambassadors to the United States said to me in 2023. Increasingly, countries and companies felt they were being compelled to do exactly that.

WHEN KURT CAMPBELL, President Biden's Asia coordinator, touched down in the Solomon Islands in April 2022, he was determined to prove that, under a new administration, Washington was back. But he quickly realized he was already too late.

Just before Campbell arrived, Prime Minister Manasseh Sogavare announced that he'd signed a new security pact with Beijing, the contents of which were being kept secret. But there were hints: Leaked documents suggested that in exchange for showering Sogavare's government with economic aid, China would be empowered to bring in its armed forces and military police to protect its own interests—or Sogavare's political survival. The bottom line was that Beijing gained another military foothold in the region, within 1,200 miles of Australia.

The geopolitical power play was obvious. It was why Campbell had arrived that April—to, as he put it, "basically draw a line" for Sogavare. "You get to choose your friends," he told me, describing his conversation with the prime minister. If the Solomons wanted to work with China on health and human welfare issues or construction, "we have no problem with that. But once you start moving down the line towards creating a capacity that can be used for forward deployment for the Chinese military, you'll have a problem with us."

Sogavare argued that there was nothing for the West to worry about. The pact, he maintained, wouldn't allow permanent Chinese bases in the Solomons, even though the United States keeps bases in South Korea and Japan and Australia. In any case, he said, this wasn't anyone else's business. The Solomons was a sovereign nation. It could choose its own allies and partners.

He knew just what he was doing: challenging Biden's new Indo-Pacific strategy, much of it Campbell's brainchild. The plan was designed to leverage America's greatest asset in creating a bulwark against increased Chinese expansion in the region—its brand and its long history, with a heavy dose of World War II nostalgia. That would be updated with new investment, bolstered trade, and a renewed diplomatic presence. But the Chinese security pact threatened to flip the Solomons from the Western camp to the Chinese camp entirely.

It was a realignment long in the making. The last time the United States had paid sustained attention to the Solomon Islands was 1942, when American soldiers were sent into the main island of Guadalcanal to roll back the Japanese empire in some of the most desperate and deadly fighting of the Pacific War. Guadalcanal loomed large in the American consciousness, not only because it claimed the lives of at least five thousand Americans and twenty-one thousand Japanese but because of the battle's most famous survivor, Navy Lieutenant John F. Kennedy, whose PT-109 boat collided with a Japanese destroyer and sank. Eighteen years later, the legend of Kennedy and his role in rescuing his crew became a major part of his political narrative, as his fellow Navy survivors campaigned with him. For millions of Americans, that was the last time they gave the Solomon Islands a thought.

"We simply left," recalled Bill Farrand, the career Foreign Service officer who was serving simultaneously as the island-hopping ambassador to the Solomons, Papua New Guinea, and Vanuatu in the early 1990s. "We left the consulate, we left the airstrip, we left anything else we had built—and destroyed." It was the wrong move, he argued at length in an oral history. "I believe that small nations like the three to which I was ambassador—all of them democracies struggling, weak, but struggling democracies—need support," he said. People had a bad habit of thinking that "little governments" could "be ignored."

It was a noble diplomatic ideal, but it didn't carry much weight in Washington. A year after the fiftieth anniversary commemoration of the battle of Guadalcanal—a days-long celebration in which American veterans returned to the beaches and told stories of a desperate battle—the State Department closed the embassy on the Solomons, hoping to save, as Farrand recounted, $387,000 a year. Over the following decades, the United States constantly made promises—to reopen the embassy, to send in the Peace Corps, and to invest in a deepwater port. But there was no follow-through. Aid dribbled in—for disaster relief, to remove mines, to gain United States access to fisheries—but the Solomons were not an American priority. Few were more bitter about that absence than Sogavare, who began his fourth term as the country's prime minister in 2019. He had gradually come to the conclusion that the Americans talked a big game, but the Chinese signed big checks. And as the paranoid, corrupt, and increasingly autocratic leader of a perpetually broke country, Sogavare considered those checks very important.

Between 2013 and 2018, China's investments in the Pacific skyrocketed from $900 million to $4.5 billion. Xi himself crisscrossed the region, showing up in Papua New Guinea and Fiji; meanwhile, as of 2023, no sitting U.S. president has ever visited the region. Beijing showered particular largesse on the Solomons, donating seven sports facilities, repairing the country's largest gold mine, and financing a new wing of the National Referral Hospital.

There was a cost, of course. In 2019, Beijing made it clear that it had one non-negotiable demand: The Solomons had to cut all diplomatic ties with Taiwan and recognize the mainland. Sogavare acquiesced, despite the riots that followed. (Taiwan had long offered free healthcare to islanders as well as substantial development and educational funding; there were suspicions of bribery surrounding the diplomatic shift.) It turned out that the quid pro quo for abandoning recognition of Taiwan was $730 million in Chinese aid.

As Campbell arrived in April 2022, he was struck by how drastically the American imprint on the island had withered. The embassy had been gone for so long that no one under forty remembered it. There was a shoestring consular office in the capital staffed by a single, intrepid U.S. diplomat, who lived alone in a hotel room with his dog. Meanwhile, a new Chinese embassy loomed, a modern building that screamed China's newfound willingness to invest in the relationship.

Washington made a show of trying to compete. A few months after Campbell's trip, Vice President Kamala Harris announced a flurry of new American plans for the region. Aid would triple, embassies would be established in Tonga and in Kiribati, an island chain so long—2,400 miles—that it is a key to controlling sea lanes. The Peace Corps would return across the region, and a USAID mission would reopen in Fiji. "I don't think I've ever seen a more substantial turnaround in American policy, in a shorter period of time, than what we've done in the Pacific," Campbell told me.

It certainly was a turnaround—and the Chinese immediately pounced on the moves as opportunistic. After decades of "prolonged neglect by the West," an April 2022 article by the *Global Times* railed, the Solomon Islands "has suddenly become a 'favorite.'" But it wouldn't work out well for the Americans, the article claimed, citing anonymous business representatives who expressed confidence that "locals and officials have learned to discern the difference between an empty promise and substantial cooperation."

China's investment in the South Pacific was long in the making. Back in 2013, when Xi announced his signature development and trade undertaking, the Belt and Road Initiative, the Chinese said the loosely centralized program was a source of "win/win cooperation." Recipient states would get quick and easy funding for new, often sorely needed infrastructure projects—bridges, hospitals, roads, ports—without having to comply with the onerous requirements that Western-led institutions often demanded.

Yet when American diplomats saw the deals, they winced at how efficiently Beijing was leveraging its coffers to gain profit and influence. The funding might have been easy, but it was structured in a way that saddled countries with debt they would struggle to pay back: Interest rates from Chinese creditors were often four times higher than the Western equivalents, researchers found, and had to be repaid in a third of the time, on average. Frequently written into the contract was a stipulation that if the country fell behind on debt repayment, the project—typically, domestic infrastructure in strategic locations—or other key concessions would transfer to China. Beijing dismissed these fears as no more than a Western "smear campaign."

In Chinese propaganda films, the Belt and Road projects glistened, bringing impoverished families in remote corners of the developing world access to previously unavailable farm goods or medical care. The reality was more complicated—for both sides. Chinese-backed projects were more likely to run into problems of corruption or environmental or safety-related delays. They took longer to complete. Meanwhile, government debts soared: In 2021, eight countries had a debt exposure to Beijing equivalent to more than 25 percent of their annual GDP, and nearly forty owed at least 10 percent. By 2023, reports were spreading of crumbling Belt and Road projects around the globe: a tunnel in Pakistan, a hydroelectric plant in Ecuador, a housing project in Angola.

The most worrisome moment of all for Western officials came in 2017, when a key Sri Lankan port was handed over to a Chinese company with a ninety-nine-year lease. The simple explanation was that an unprofitable port had been leased out to a foreign company for a profit. The more pernicious alternative was that Beijing, using a tactic known as "debt-trap diplomacy," was putting itself in a position around the world to take over strategic infrastructure. Many in the United States seized upon the Sri Lanka incident—and a 2018 episode in which Malaysia was bombarded with Chinese state-backed cyberattacks until it agreed not to cancel two Chinese projects—as evidence of the Communist Party malice that they'd so long warned about. But many others pointed out that China was going through the same learning curve that the United States had gone through in the twentieth century—in which some of its aid initiatives were successful and some sparked debt crises. By 2021, Xi's government had introduced the Global Development Initiative, a new effort to invest in smaller and more environmentally and fiscally sustainable projects around the world.

Regardless of the geopolitical goals, it was clear that Washington was running well behind Beijing in terms of old-style dollar diplomacy. But Wendy Sherman, Biden's first deputy secretary of state, argued that success for the United States did not require matching every Chinese investment. "We have very different strategies," she told me in her office on the seventh floor of the State Department's Harry S. Truman Building shortly before leaving the administration. "China focuses on infrastructure, but often with high-interest loans" and without transferring any technology or knowledge to the country where the facilities are being built. "The U.S. invests in people and development, such as meeting basic needs, energy independence, transferring skills, and democratic freedoms. Democracy matters."

In August 2022, Sherman took her own trip to the region, stopping in Samoa, Tonga, and the Solomons. Sherman's visit to the Solomons was timed to coincide with the eightieth anniversary of the Battle of Guadalcanal, where her own father had fought and been wounded. She was joined by Caroline Kennedy, now the ambassador to Australia and the former president's only surviving child. The symbolism wasn't exactly subtle.

But Sogavare stayed in his office, refusing to participate in any of the ceremonies. Sherman confronted him later. "I'm sorry your schedule didn't allow you to go and to see the coastwatchers that defended your freedoms," she said, letting the sarcasm hang in the air.

Sogavare did come to Washington later that month to attend Biden's first Pacific Islands summit. But nearly a year later, when the White House held a follow-on event, it appeared that the United States was losing its effort to win over the Solomons. Sogavare skipped the meeting, citing the parliamentary calendar at home and commenting that "nothing came out of" the previous year's summit and that he was not interested in another "lecture . . . about how good they are."

The population of the Solomons is about equivalent to the population of North Dakota; that the Chinese prevailed is unlikely to be more than a footnote in the jockeying for control in the Pacific.

Biden did far better elsewhere. He concluded a security accord with Papua New Guinea—even though a budget negotiation forced him to cancel at the very last minute on a highly touted historical first visit for any American president. He also won over Fiji, with an economy several times larger than the Solomons.

But in this tug-of-war between East and West, every investment, every modest agreement, every diplomatic snub prompts a running reassessment of who's winning. It's the wrong question, of course—national power can't be reduced to a scorecard. Moreover, it misstates the reality of the new cold wars. Countries are increasingly deciding that they don't have to make a single "choice"; they can make as many choices as they want. In certain areas they might align with one power; in others, another—and neither the United States nor China, each focused on its long-term goals, can afford to freeze them out entirely. In this new world, the great powers continually have to court the smaller ones.

IN THE LATE fall of 2022, Biden and Xi finally met face to face, spending hours together on Bali, the Indonesian resort island where the annual G20 summit was under way. In private Xi, who was worrying about his country's slumping economy, which was still fettered by his zero-COVID policies, complained bitterly about American export controls and sanctions. Biden criticized China's export of influence operations and the technology of repression. Yet both men emerged saying all the right things about stemming the downward spiral in the relationship. There were common areas in which they could work together, they insisted. They would have follow-up meetings and reciprocal visits of the kind American and Chinese diplomats got used to, and got tired of, in previous administrations. When pressed, American officials insisted that "engagement" was still dead—there would be no meetings for the sake of simulating action—but diplomacy to avert crises was being given new life. There was a difference, they claimed: You *engage* willing partners; you use *diplomacy* to manage difficult relationships, to keep small problems from spinning into large confrontations.

"I absolutely believe there need not be a new Cold War," Biden told reporters before he left the island. Indeed, it sounded as though after two years in which the relationship had deteriorated, both leaders were looking to call a time-out.

Over the next few months, two surprises that neither leader saw coming would scuttle that plan and suggest that the Chinese government wasn't the all-seeing, all-knowing, forever-in-control force that Washington thought it was.

The first came almost immediately. On December 7, 2022, weeks after he left Bali, Xi and his top leadership reversed course, ending the zero-COVID restrictions that had kept the Chinese people locked in their homes for months at a time, or forcibly evacuated from them if they tested positive. The reason for the abrupt change of course, which was announced with almost no warning, still isn't totally clear: Perhaps Xi and his inner circle were unnerved by the growing public outrage against the more inhumane elements of the policy: There were food shortages, gas shortages, widespread reports of the sick and elderly being unable to get to doctors. In Shanghai and Chengdu, tens of millions were locked down for months, unable to leave their homes. Suddenly, there were spontaneous antigovernment protests, some of the largest since Xi had come into power a decade before. Undoubtedly, the policy saved lives during the pandemic, but when Chinese watched the World Cup in Qatar—broadcast across a country that was, as in all other things, striving to become a soccer powerhouse—it was evident that the rest of the world was moving on. When Xi met Biden in Bali, neither leader was wearing a mask.

So when the order came to lift the restrictions, people poured into the streets, and, for a bit, the economy boomed just as anticipated. But unlike the experience in America and Europe, it then crashed back to earth. The long-awaited real estate crisis had finally arrived, bringing with it bankruptcies. Consumers pulled back, fearful that they would be unable to meet their monthly housing payments. Youth unemployment began to soar. Foreign firms froze new investments, then started looking elsewhere.

For years, the question of when China's underlying economic weaknesses would erupt had been a constant subject of debate. Until now the country had always seemed to evade the giant boulders in the river, magically shooting beyond them. Now, it looked like "Peak China" might have actually arrived. The question was whether this was a brief interruption in the 7- or 8-percent growth to which a generation of Chinese had grown accustomed or, rather, something calamitous was happening, akin to Japan's decades-long stagnation that began in the 1990s.

The second surprise came when someone in eastern Montana looked up in the sky and saw a giant balloon.

The word *balloon* does not quite capture what Montanans, and soon the rest of the country, were peering at. It was more like a surveillance dirigible, a large white ball floating in the air, carrying a container underneath it the size of a school bus. When government officials began to describe it as a "spy balloon" of Chinese origin, the whole notion seemed ridiculous: Who spied with balloons anymore? Hadn't the world given that up sometime around World War I, with the invention of the airplane?

In fact, balloons were back—as low-cost alternatives to launching satellites. But not many people knew about them. The Biden administration learned of the program in its first year, when the White House received briefings about apparent balloons sighted off Hawaii, Florida, and Texas. Size and flight path information made it plain that these giant, zeppelinlike craft were not there to gather weather data, although that was a reasonable cover story. From the indications that could be plucked out of the ether or gathered from military jets flying nearby, China appeared to be testing out an alternative means of sweeping up data from America's key military sites, lingering over them from an altitude of sixty thousand feet.

In a classified report to Congress distributed in late 2022, a month before the sighting over Montana, American intelligence officials reported that the People's Liberation Army balloon program was based on Hainan Island, an oasis off the Chinese coast known for its warm beaches and huge Chinese military bases. The U.S. military knew all about it: Early in the George W. Bush administration, an American spy plane and a Chinese fighter jet had collided nearby, triggering a small crisis for the new president.

The report noted that it had taken a while for American officials to understand a series of mysterious balloon sightings off the Hawaiian island of Kauai, near where antimissile lasers are tested, and around Pearl Harbor. Once Space Command and intelligence agencies began playing back the tapes of other unexplained aerial sightings, it became clear that these were no anomalies.

"This was a pretty good-sized program," one senior military official told me, and its roots went back decades. Biden asked if the United States was running any similar programs, and the answer was underwhelming. There were a few small surveillance-balloon research programs, but nothing that matched the size and sophistication of what the Chinese were experimenting with. It was a deficiency that some wags in the Pentagon, with a nod to the old Sputnik days, jokingly called "the balloon gap."

So the United States was watching in January 2023 when another balloon lifted off from the Hainan base. Then it began to head toward Alaska and dip down toward the American West. Intelligence officials picked up a bit of panic among the Chinese—and a certain amount of surprise. From everything they could see and hear, the Chinese operators had not deliberately set the balloon on a course toward Montana or anyplace else in the continental United States. But once it headed that way, they did not try very hard to redirect it.

"I think the truth sometimes is always more banal than people would like to think," Bill Burns told me several months later. "I do think the winds affected its course," he said, speculating about how a routine launch had made headlines.

American intelligence concluded Xi was not told about the balloon's course for several days, until it was already over North America. Biden later told reporters that he thought Xi was not in the loop until it was too late. "I think there was a fair amount of confusion among the Chinese leadership about whose bright idea this was," one senior official told me. Blinken canceled his planned trip to Beijing, which was intended to be the first one in years by an American secretary of state.

With the benefit of hindsight, the picture that emerged was one of Chinese leaders in a moderate amount of disarray, much as they had been during the crash of the fighter jet and the American surveillance plane in 2001. Miscommunication and chaos ruled the day. At a loss about what to do, Chinese officials dismissed the whole thing as American disinformation or repeated the weather balloon explanation.

The balloon incident was a reminder that the Chinese military and intelligence community is capable of its share of mistakes, misjudgments, and mismanagement. Still, for pure gall, the whole episode was in a category of its own. It was the in-your-face quality that landed the balloon's progress across the country into the front-page headlines. The airwaves were filled with China experts expounding on the scope of Beijing's surveillance state, as retired Air Force generals demanded that Biden shoot the invader out of the sky. That seemed more justified after orders went out from the White House and the Pentagon to "harden" military facilities in the balloon's path against stray transmissions.

Finally the balloon was shot down—on Biden's orders—with a Sidewinder missile over the shallow waters off South Carolina, where its shards could do little damage. The Coast Guard and the Navy recovered whatever they could, and the FBI was eager to reverse-engineer it. The FBI refused to reveal what it found.

IN THE DAYS before the 2022 invasion of Ukraine, China's top foreign policy official Wang Yi was asked what he thought about the impending Russian military action. His response, while indirect, had been impossible to misunderstand: "The sovereignty, independence, and territorial integrity of any country should be respected and safe-guarded because this is a basic norm of international relations . . . Ukraine is no exception."

A year later, as Western and Chinese officials met once again in Munich, Wang's message was different—a product, perhaps, of China's realization that the war—and Russia's mistakes—offered it a new chance to become a kingmaker. Now, he insisted, all sides in the Ukraine war needed to back off and reach a compromise, alluding darkly to "some forces" that did "not want to see peace talks materialize" because of "strategic goals larger than Ukraine itself."

But Ukraine was not Wang's main issue. He was still fuming about the destruction of the spy balloon, a reaction that he characterized as "absurd and hysterical." America, he said, had it out for China, for absolutely no reason. "The United States is using all of its means to clamp down and smear China and is co-opting other countries to do the same," he said. He railed at America's blatant protectionism, citing the CHIPS Act while ignoring Beijing's own subsidies of the microchip industry.

For all the bluster, though, American officials sensed that Wang—and China—were on the defensive. The balloon incident was a huge embarrassment. So when Wang slipped into a Munich hotel suite to meet Blinken on a Saturday night in mid-February 2023 for the first time since Blinken's canceled trip to Beijing, the handful of Americans in the room thought that he might show a little contrition.

Blinken tried to give him a way out. We're all adults here, he told Wang. We all spy on each other. But we don't fly balloons over other nations' territory. Had an American craft lingered over sensitive military locations on mainland China, Blinken said, the Chinese would have almost certainly reacted the same way.

But rather than look for a way out, Wang doubled down. The "balloon incident," as he called it, was yet another expression of American aggression—America's first instinct, he claimed, was to shoot something down just because it looked Chinese. Sending a jet up to destroy the airborne vehicle was an act of obvious overreaction that revealed American weakness. He told Blinken that it was the Americans who needed to apologize. The few aides in the room stared at him with a mix of admiration and wonderment. "It took a lot of nerve," one of them said later.

To the Americans, it sounded ludicrous. But the Chinese officials, U.S. intelligence concluded, believed that the international reaction to the balloon had been mostly "impartial," portraying the issue as a symbol not of Chinese espionage overreach but of a downturn in the relationship.

From there the conversation went downhill. Wang, fully aware that China's spying equipment was now spread out in an FBI laboratory in Virginia, said that he was sure the United States would put out more fake news about what it found. The United States, he said, was making a fuss about the incident simply to divert attention from its domestic problems.

Maybe this was just China's way of clearing the air, Blinken thought. Wang had to report back that he had issued a stiff protest. So Blinken changed the subject to the conflict in Ukraine and issued a warning.

For weeks, officials in Washington had been fixated on new intelligence that had begun to circulate over the winter. It seemed that the relationship between Russia and China was getting stronger, quickly, as the two countries realized they could band together as a bulwark against the United States. Since the war's beginning, they knew, Putin, in particular need of drones and ammunition and missiles, had been overtly pressing Beijing to help supply his battlefield needs. Sure, Putin might be able to rely on bullets from the North Koreans and drones from the Iranians in the short term, but over the long term Chinese military aid was the only viable option.

Yet for just about a year now, China had hesitated. Its reasoning wasn't precisely clear. On the one hand, the United States believed, on the Ukraine issue China was caught in a place it never wanted to be: allied with a country that was systematically undercutting China's own professed commitment to territorial integrity. On the other hand, American intelligence officials believed that China was open to providing the weapons; it just didn't want to do so overtly and risk another round of American-led sanctions.

Now, intelligence officials warned, it appeared that Xi's calculus had changed. In mid-February, according to a top-secret report that was later leaked, American intelligence found that Chinese military officials had signed off on the "incremental provision of lethal aid" to support the Russian war. It would be, the report warned, disguised as civilian equipment and sent out on planes, trains, and ships. It was not stated where the information had come from, but it had clearly come from tapping into Russian communications.

"What we were learning from the intelligence community was that the relationship was really about to take a turn," one administration official later told me. "And if the Chinese came in hard on Russia's side in the war, it would have a dramatic effect. A really dramatic effect."

So in early February, the United States began quietly briefing its allies about the back-channel activity between Xi's aides and Putin's aides. They were describing a new world to the Europeans, one in which the dreaded scenario of the original Cold War—a Beijing-Moscow partnership—was coming to pass in the New Cold War.

The first fruits of the relationship might well be the military aid and support that Putin had long desired. But over the long term, what Putin really needed was a big, powerful ally with the money and influence to face down the increasingly aggressive West. China was the only answer; he would just have to get accustomed to being the weaker partner in the relationship.

It was in China's interest, too, to make sure that Washington pay a stiff price for supporting Ukraine, in both dollars and ammunition. The more that Washington's gaze was drawn away from the Pacific, the more room China had to maneuver. It viewed the problem much the way it had regarded the American interventions in Afghanistan and Iraq: The United States just couldn't help itself from intervening in distant wars with supposedly righteous causes. And China might as well take advantage of its distraction.

In that Bavarian hotel suite, Blinken reminded Wang in no uncertain terms that if it emerged that China was giving military aid to Russian forces, there would be a huge economic price to pay. According to one participant, Wang's response was just to "deny, deny, deny."

The two sides left the session as far apart—and as distrustful—as ever.

PART FOUR

FIGHTING FOR CONTROL

CHAPTER 18

SEARCHING FOR ENDGAMES

Go back to Kennan's long cable. It's all there. In fact, if you read . . . passages from that cable today from 1947 . . . you could literally insert Russia and Putin for what he says about the then Soviet Union.

Antony J. Blinken, secretary of state, on the first anniversary of the Ukraine invasion

GERMAN CHANCELLOR OLAF SCHOLZ was on the phone to Tony Blinken, and he was forcefully making the case that the last thing anyone wanted to see was German tanks rolling across Europe.

This wasn't precisely true, Blinken argued. With the Russians digging in across the Donbas for an offensive in the early months of 2023, the top weapon on the Ukrainians' wish list was clear: tanks. Old-fashioned, World War II–style tanks, updated with modern targeting capability. In an era of drone strikes and satellite-based surveillance, it was hard to imagine. But piercing Russian defenses and traversing trenches and other obstacles required real armored vehicles, preferably the kind that could roar across rough terrain, maneuver, and shoot at the same time.

Russia had already lost more than half the tanks it had deployed against Ukraine, many of them to land mines or to long-range strikes from precision-guided missile systems, like HIMARS. But the Russian numbers still far outstripped what Ukraine could muster. To gain the advantage, Zelensky wanted German-made Leopard 2 tanks and the far larger, gas-guzzling American M1 Abrams tanks.

But Germany—and Scholz himself—remained deeply reluctant to send in the Leopards, and Blinken was becoming exasperated. He told Scholz that if he was bothered by the imagery of German tanks rolling eastward toward the capital cities they'd crushed some eighty years before, he might be the only one in Europe even thinking about it—because this time, their purpose would be purely defensive. (Of course, for antiwar elements in Germany, tanks did touch a particular nerve.)

Fine, countered Scholz. If the United States was so eager, it should be willing to contribute, too, and send the Abrams tanks to Ukraine first. Then the Germans would follow with the Leopards—a move that meant sending its own tanks as well as authorizing the re-export of Leopards that were in use by other NATO allies. It wasn't exactly a bluff, but Scholz knew what Blinken knew, that the Pentagon didn't think the Abrams was the right weapon for the job. "The Abrams tank," said Colin Kahl, "is a very complicated piece of equipment." And so, he added, "we should not be providing the Ukrainians systems they can't repair, they can't sustain, and that they, over the long term, can't afford, because it's not helpful."

The lighter Leopard tanks, in contrast, seemed ideal for the Ukrainian soldiers in frontline positions: troops who, despite all the talk of high-powered arms being shipped by the West, often remained dependent on their Soviet-era weapons systems, insufficient ammunition stores, and outdated firearms. The Leopards had been manufactured for years, were widely used across Europe, and could be delivered to the battlefields of Ukraine in a matter of weeks.

But Scholz held firm. He had already moved Germany further into the anti-Russia camp than anyone a year earlier would have thought possible—especially by cutting off Nord Stream 2. After being mocked for offering few truly offensive arms to Ukraine, Scholz had given in and sent anti-tank and anti-aircraft weapons, shattering another of Germany's long-standing taboos. There were protesters showing up on weekends, especially in the cities of the former East Germany, insisting that the country should be getting along with Russia, not sanctioning it.

Scholz's message to Blinken was clear: Other countries in Europe needed Germany's permission to export their tanks, and Germany needed American political cover before it could give that permission. After weeks of haggling, President Biden in late January issued a grudging statement: The United States would send thirty-one Abrams tanks. Never mind that with the need to retrofit existing Abrams tanks and ship them to the battlefield, they wouldn't arrive for eight more months at the earliest. It was a triumph of political calculation over logistical concerns—and it unlocked the Leopards.

"What is stunning about it," noted Evelyn Farkas, the Pentagon's senior official for Ukraine in the Obama administration, "is how afraid our allies are about facing Russia without the United States."

The struggle over sending tanks was just one example of how, one year into the war, America and its allies were sending more support to Ukraine than anyone could have imagined. Yet they were increasingly divided over what should be sent, when, and how much. Those divisions turned on differing assessments of what might be escalatory, what was politically viable, what was symbolic, and what would really make a difference on the battlefield.

The situation also turned on how well the Ukrainians were performing. Already there was talk of a spring counteroffensive that, to hear the country's most ardent Eastern European supporters describe it, would be enough to force Putin to the negotiating table. The expectations of American and British officials were more restrained—but even they were saying that the key to continued support was Ukraine putting some points on the board.

WHEN SECRETARY OF DEFENSE Lloyd Austin stepped from his motorcade onto the muddy fields of Grafenwoehr Training Area in Bavaria, Germany, in mid-February, he was met by half a dozen Ukrainian officers standing smartly at attention in the misting rain. As the secretary greeted each of them, relentless reports from a machine gun echoed from a training range somewhere beyond the woods.

For nearly a century, Grafenwoehr has been where Europe's soldiers learned to fight. German Emperor Wilhelm II's soldiers trained there in the years before the First World War. Hitler himself visited the camp, reviewing the troops from his open Mercedes touring car to assess their readiness to roll across Eastern Europe. After Germany's defeat, the site became the place where American troops prepared for the day when the Cold War might turn hot.

Now it was Ukraine's turn to train amid the remains of seventeenth-century churches crumbling in the forests and World War II–era bunkers that Hitler's forces had tested on the site. Hundreds, eventually thousands, of Ukrainian troops were being pulled from the cities or the front lines, sent by train across Ukraine and Poland, through Czechia, and southwest into Germany for a five-week crash course in the newest weapons that the West was sending their way.

On that chilly February morning, Austin watched as the Ukrainians, guided by their Western counterparts, practiced shooting off rounds from howitzers, learned how to drive and maintain vehicles, drilled marksmanship and combat medicine, and, most important, worked to coordinate different types of units during a battle—the "combined arms" approach to warfare that the Russians had so conspicuously failed to master.

If, as the U.S. Army believed, the Ukrainians could learn to integrate different types of weapons and operations—utilizing infantry and armored units together or complementing on-the-ground warfare with air support—they might be able to drive the Russians from their trenches in the increasingly grinding war in the East.

But for the most part, the Ukrainians were starting from scratch. Some 60 to 70 percent, the trainers estimated, had never been around artillery before. Some had never held a weapon before; some said they'd joined up mere days after the start of the conflict the previous February.

Austin watched, his face hard to read, as Ukrainian units worked together to enact medical rescues from a mock battlefield and to shoot howitzers into the far distance in a burst of smoke. A former commander in Iraq and Afghanistan, he spent much of his time watching to see how quickly the Ukrainians picked up the quirks of Bradley Fighting Vehicles—a lightweight, armored technology from the Vietnam era that the United States had only begun delivering to the Ukrainians a few weeks before. At the time, Austin and the teams of American trainers thought the Bradleys would be critical to the counteroffensive—a way to get soldiers past the minefields they knew the Russians were laying.

Many of the Ukrainian soldiers were in the fourth week of their five-week training program. Within days, they would leave the training grounds of Grafenwoehr and return to the front lines and into a very uncertain future. For all their show of enthusiasm—one soldier ripped a patch off his uniform sleeve and pressed it into the secretary's palm; others sent up a Ukrainian victory chant when he passed by—the news from the battlefield was discouraging. It had been the better part of three months since the Ukrainians had achieved a major military victory. They were deeply bogged down in Bakhmut, a city just under a hundred miles to the west of Luhansk. The Americans believed the city had little strategic value, but it held outsized symbolic importance to Zelensky, who had brought a trophy from the battle—a signed flag—to the U.S. Congress when he made his surprise visit to Capitol Hill in late 2022.

No one knew whether all this training on the fields of Bavaria would make a difference when the counteroffensive began. Ultimately, the question was whether the Ukrainians, their dedication not in doubt, could learn in a few short weeks what it took American units many months to perfect. Nor did they have any idea whether, even if they could become masters of combined arms, it would force Vladimir Putin to back off.

"EVERY WAR HAS two endgames," Dmytro Kuleba, Ukraine's urbane foreign minister, told a packed lunchtime crowd in Munich days before the first anniversary of the invasion. "The first one is when the guns are silent, and the enemy leaves your territory. . . . It's the full liberation of Ukrainian territory. . . . There will be no concessions on territory." There was no room for negotiation with Putin, he continued, over giving up any of Ukraine's land. He and others in the room that day had nothing but contempt for anyone who even raised that possibility.

"Then," Kuleba said, "there comes the long endgame. . . . But most importantly, it will be a question of, how do we make sure that Russia is not capable of repeating it?"

To the audience that weekend in Munich, this was exactly what they wanted to hear, even if it seemed disconnected from the reality of the battlefield. The message carried even more impact coming from Kuleba, who, in his sports coat and tie, appeared to be the personality opposite of his boss, Zelensky. But just because he eschewed the green T-shirt did not mean he was more soft-spoken. By calling for dismantling Russia's military capability, he was amplifying a line Lloyd Austin had made in a rare unguarded moment a few months into the war, that the goal of the West was "to see Russia weakened to the degree that it can't do the kinds of things that it has done in invading Ukraine." Inside the White House, officials had shaken their heads when Austin spoke, because they knew that Putin would seize on the line as evidence that the true American goal was to hobble Russia. But he had accurately described the administration's goal. As one official said, "His only offense was uttering the quiet part out loud."

One year earlier, the Europeans who had gathered at the Munich Security Conference had dismissed the overwhelming evidence that Russia was preparing to invade. Now they displayed the passion of the converted. On the eve of the first anniversary of the invasion, several Eastern European leaders were pushing even beyond Austin's goal, claiming that there was no viable endgame without the complete collapse of Russia.

"For me, the end of the war will be," Kuleba told the crowd, "when the Russian president—whatever his name will be—will pay a visit to Ukraine, will stand on his knees in front of the monument to the victims of the Russian aggression, and will beg for an apology." The room burst into fervent applause.

When Kuleba talked of making Russia into a pariah state or dismantling Putin's regime, no one dared question him. Not on the record, at least. Putin, they nodded in agreement in Munich, would have to pay for his naked aggression. The only question was how. In the hallways, there was discussion of future war-crimes trials, and Vice President Harris showed up at the conference to declare that the United States had now formally concluded that Russia had conducted "crimes against humanity," a term meant to evoke memories of the Holocaust and the trials in Nuremberg that followed.

For the allies meeting in Munich that weekend, this talk of dissolving the Russian state and the vague vision of Putin in the dock of the International Criminal Court was something of a balm, a show that unity went beyond shipping Stingers and Leopard tanks over the border from Poland. Most said they wanted a permanent solution to the Putin problem, arguing that if Russia remained as it was, it would continue to be a threat not only to Ukraine but to the world. And they were emboldened by the fact that some of their biggest fears about the first year of the war had not come to pass.

There was much to celebrate, they agreed. Putin had failed at freezing Europe in the first winter of the war. Somehow, Germany and its neighbors, assisted by a mild winter, managed to wean themselves off Russian energy faster than anyone had thought possible. China, for all its claims of a "relationship with no limits" with Russia, was mostly acting with caution. It was buying Russia's oil but, at least for the moment, not selling it weapons. And, as Tony Blinken liked to point out, Putin's hopes of widening the long-standing fractures among the Western allies had come to nothing. "Vladimir Putin has done more than anyone on earth to strengthen the NATO alliance," Blinken said that weekend.

But privately, many of the leaders in Munich worried that all the talk of making Putin pay was bravado. The realities on the battlefield were clear: The Russians were making precious little progress, but they weren't leaving either. Moreover, there was no evidence, despite the horrific cost of the war, that Putin's grip on power was in jeopardy. He had suffered huge losses—two hundred thousand casualties, as many as sixty thousand dead in the first year of the war—more deaths than the United States suffered during the entirety of the Vietnam War. Yet public opposition to Putin had not materialized; protests were brutally put down, and somehow the mothers and fathers of those sent off to the carnage had been silenced.

What remained were signs of stalemate, a long, bitter slog that would cost thousands, or tens of thousands, more lives, for modest territorial reclamation.

The Ukrainian military victories in the fall of 2022 were proving hard to reproduce. The Russians were beginning to learn from their mistakes. And Ukrainian forces were rapidly depleting Western stocks of bullets and missiles, triggering angst among the NATO allies that they could no longer funnel much-needed ammunition to Ukraine without leaving their own military forces vulnerable.

This was a legitimate worry. In barely a year, Ukraine had used up the equivalent of six production years' worth of Raytheon's shoulder-fired Stinger missiles and nearly as many Javelins. The long-awaited Leopard tanks had yet to arrive; after European governments agreed to transfer them to Ukraine, they suddenly learned that it wasn't as easy as driving them off the used-tank lot. After decades in storage, the older tanks were largely not battle-worthy. Of course, the Russians were dealing with the same problem.

The Europeans pledged that they would do anything for the Ukrainians, but their definition of "anything" seemed limited. There was no appetite to let the country into NATO, as that would commit European and American troops to open combat. More tellingly, there was little progress in admitting Kyiv to the European Union; when asked, European officials said that while sympathy for Ukraine was enormous, the country fell well short of meeting requirements for membership. "Now there's more sympathy and the feeling that Ukraine is a part of Europe, but that's sentimental and not hard-core," Anna Wieslander, a Swede who directs northern Europe for the Atlantic Council, told my *Times* colleague Steve Erlanger.

The reality was that outside of Europe and a few of America's allies in the Pacific—notably Japan and South Korea—support for Ukraine was spotty at best. When the invasion first took place, Israeli leaders refused to sanction either Putin or Russia: The country was simply too important to Israeli interests in Syria, they said. One Israeli diplomat in Washington contended that Israel never took sides in outside territorial disputes, despite the obvious disconnect between this position and Israel's insistence that its own borders be recognized around the world. While Kyiv's supporters liked to point to a pair of United Nations General Assembly votes that roundly criticized Moscow for invading its neighbor and demanded its retreat, nearly three dozen countries had abstained. They represented a huge percentage of the world's population, including China, India, Pakistan, South Africa, and Ethiopia.

India, which also gets touchy about its borders, was particularly adamant that the West's problems were not New Delhi's concern. "I am not sitting on the fence," India's foreign affairs minister Subrahmanyam Jaishankar said in the summer of 2022, responding to criticism, "I am sitting on my ground." Europe's belief in its own centrality, he argued, was not only flawed, it was the product of an outdated view of the world, one that considered the borders of Europe more sacrosanct than those of, say, Kashmir. Getting to a global consensus, it was clear, was harder than ever.

Back in Munich, fears of a coming stalemate, the reality of dwindling arms supplies, and ambivalence about whether to let Ukraine into the European club were combining to create a noticeable split in strategy about what Year Two of the war should look like.

In the first camp were the frontline states that shared a border with Russia and feared that they might be next: Estonia, Latvia, Lithuania, and Poland. Having been on the receiving end of Russian and Soviet expansionism over the previous decades, they all believed that Putin could under no circumstances be rewarded for his aggression. To allow him to gain one inch of Ukrainian territory, they argued, would be an inducement for him to keep going.

The second camp, composed mostly of the Western European nations and led by France and Germany, believed in the Ukrainian cause but saw a negotiated settlement as the only plausible pathway to end hostilities. While there were high hopes at the beginning of the war that Putin would run into unexpected opposition at home, that had not happened. In some quarters in Russia, he was more popular than ever. And though the Russian economy was slowed by sanctions, Biden's claim that the West could reduce the ruble to "rubble" had also not come to pass. The only way out, the Western European countries contended, was an unhappy compromise—not unlike the compromises that resolved past conflicts with Russia.

The Americans neatly straddled both positions. Publicly, they often sounded more like the hawks—declaring that Russia had "lost" and that its military was "shattered." But in private, American and British officials told me they were having a hard time envisioning an endgame. In Washington, the chairman of the Joint Chiefs of Staff, General Mark Milley, told anyone who would listen that neither side was in a position to emerge victorious—all the talk of total victory was utterly disconnected from reality. "Zelensky has publicly stated many times that the Ukrainian objective is to kick every Russian out of Russian-occupied Ukraine," he said in an interview with *Defense One*. "And that is a significant military task. Very, very difficult military task. You're looking at a couple hundred thousand Russians who are still in Russian-occupied Ukraine."

The most likely outcome, he and others contended, was a cease-fire or armistice that would cement Russian control of parts of the south and east without any concession of territory by the Ukrainian government. America's role was to put the Ukrainians "in the best possible position" in the event that the two sides finally entered into negotiations. Some American officials believed that the territorial issues would remain indefinitely unresolved and a topic for negotiation down the line.

This huge gap between the total-victory soundbites and the let's-settle-this-thing reality had a simple explanation. Yes, Ukraine could fight to the last man, as one of Biden's top aides put it to me. But that would involve killing off a generation of young Ukrainians to defend a couple hundred miles of industrial flatlands in the Donbas, largely in towns where both Ukrainian and Russian are spoken. It would be a waste of human lives. It would be a drain on Western money. It would be of little strategic value for the Ukraine of the future, the one built on the country's considerable technological skills. Even as it brought the world nearer to World War III, it would seem more and more like an echo of World War I.

Yet to Putin, these dueling Western strategies offered a distinction without a difference, because to him it was all existential. While the tactics of NATO nations might differ, he said, their objective was the same. "They have one goal: to disband the former Soviet Union and its fundamental part—the Russian Federation," Putin said in an interview with Russian state television. He quickly made the turn that he knew would resonate with his supporters: What the West really wanted, he warned, was Russia's cultural erasure. "I do not even know if such an ethnic group as the Russian people will be able to survive in the form in which it exists today."

To make up for his outsize mistakes, to justify a war going bad, Putin was trying to turn his land grab into a grand existential struggle. To hear him tell it, it was about more than territory. It was about Russia's survival. Of course, it was about his survival too.

A year before, Biden's ad-libbed line at the end of a speech in Poland that Putin "cannot remain in power" had gotten him into trouble, leading the White House to declare that it was not America's goal to bring about regime change. But even so, as the war continued, that was increasingly the message the Russians were hearing—from Ukraine and from some American allies. And that message worried political leaders and military officials who pointed out the obvious: Political settlements are how wars come to an end. As one top-ranking military leader from a Nordic country warned, "This puts all the ammo in the hands of Putin, that it's a 'Western plot to destroy Russia.'"

ON FEBRUARY 20, 2023, with the first anniversary of the war's outbreak looming, Air Force One touched down in Poland. The next day Biden was scheduled to hold meetings and give speeches to mark a year of sacrifice—for the Ukrainians, for the Poles, for everyone whose lives had been upended. And, of course, for the tens of thousands who had died in a war of expansion few had thought possible in modern times.

But Biden's return from Poland wasn't planned until Wednesday afternoon—and there was a stretch of time earlier in the day that was unaccounted for.

Suspicious by nature and after many years of experience, the reporters heading out to cover the trip began to speculate that Wednesday morning would be the perfect time to sneak the president over the border and into Ukraine. From Warsaw, it was a very short flight to the city of Przemyśl in southern Poland. Biden could then be driven a few miles into Ukraine, returning to a country he had last visited in January 2017, as vice president. He would be close enough to be whisked back into NATO territory at the slightest hint of trouble. There was a widespread assumption that this would be the way for an octogenarian president to say he went to Ukraine—and witnessed its grit—without exposing himself to serious danger.

Naturally, everyone got it all wrong. For months the White House had been working on a secret plan to get Biden to Kyiv *ahead* of the Poland trip. A small group reporting to Sullivan had looked at flying Biden in and dismissed it as too risky, given all the missiles flying around. They settled on sending him in by the same method used by Blinken and other dignitaries—on a train that was redolent of a 1940s movie, down to the tufted leather seats and wood-paneled dining car.

Around 3:30 A.M. Eastern time on Sunday, Biden was sped through the streets of Washington and put on a small version of Air Force One, a plane seldom used for international travel. It was not likely to attract attention. Landing in Poland after dark, Biden boarded an unmarked train—jokingly dubbed "Rail Force One"—to begin the ten-hour journey into Kyiv.

Even in the pantheon of presidential visits to war zones—President-elect Eisenhower to Korea, Johnson to Vietnam, George W. Bush to Iraq mere months after the invasion—nothing about this trip was ordinary. In those cases the United States had thousands of troops on the ground, and the military could escort the president every step of the way. Biden himself had traveled to Iraq in 2016, so he knew what that felt like.

This was different. By Biden's own order, there were no American troops on the ground. He would have to travel with a skeleton staff. If he needed rescue, it would have to come from a Special Forces team just over the border.

But Biden wanted to send Putin a signal. Just as President John F. Kennedy, standing in West Berlin in 1963, had declared, "Ich bin ein Berliner," and President Ronald Reagan had urged Soviet leader Mikhail Gorbachev to "tear down this wall," Biden was seeking to cast the moment as part of this generation's struggle against Moscow—even if the line between the West and Moscow had moved a few hundred miles to the east.

The secrecy held. And by the time images of Biden stepping off the train at the Kyiv-Pasazhyrsky railway station arrived back in the United States, he had already moved on to Mariinsky Palace to see Zelensky and his wife, Olena Zelenska. Biden looked like he had just come off his old Amtrak commute to Delaware.

Zelensky, in his signature fatigues, thanked Biden for coming "at a huge moment for Ukraine." Biden's own remarks were brief. "I thought it was critical," he said firmly, "that there not be any doubt, none whatsoever, about U.S. support for Ukraine in the war." He also announced the release of another half billion dollars' worth of assistance to Ukraine, including more weapons and ammunition.

As he and Zelensky walked around some cordoned-off sections of downtown Kyiv, air raid sirens wailed. But behind the scenes Jake Sullivan had already informed the Russians that Biden would be making the unannounced trip. No one expected the Russians to target Biden, and it was in everyone's interest to avoid a disastrous accident.

The Russians, Sullivan reported back, acknowledged receipt—and said not another word. They did not attempt to interfere, and after about five hours, including a closed-door strategy session with Zelensky about the coming spring offensive, Biden boarded his train and returned to the Polish border without incident.

Once the surprise of Biden's trip wore off in Washington, the grand-standing began. Democrats cheered the trip. He may be eighty, they said, but he still gets around. Even Lindsey Graham, the Republican senator from South Carolina, called Biden's move "the right signal to send at the right time." But the more MAGA members of the Republican Party, in a precursor of what was to come, accused Biden of thinking more about Ukrainians than Americans. "The president's now spent more time in Kyiv than he has at our southern border," said Kevin Hern, a House Republican from Oklahoma. To the surprise of no one, Trump told a group of supporters that "Putin never, ever would have gone into Ukraine if I were president."

WHAT UNFOLDED TWENTY-FOUR hours after Biden's trip to Kyiv was a split-screen glimpse of two radically opposing worldviews—a head-to-head comparison, even if the White House insisted it wasn't intended that way.

In Warsaw to mark the first year of the war, Biden decided to return to the gardens of the Royal Castle, a sixteenth-century palace that has repeatedly been destroyed and rebuilt as waves of European violence swept through Poland. Putin also decided to speak that day—in front of the Russian Federal Assembly, for his equivalent of the U.S. president's annual State of the Union Address, a forum that would assure him unanimous applause. Unsurprisingly, these two leaders, now in something that increasingly looked like a survivalist contest, delivered variations on a common message: *I'm not backing down.*

Putin went first, for nearly two hours. He doubled down on the war and the narrative that it had been started by the West—which, he said, had deployed biological weapons and was busy training the Ukrainian population to attack Russian citizens. The West had "tricked" everyone, even those living within its own borders, "with tall stories about the search for peace." He added that "the Western elites have become a symbol of total, unprincipled lies."

In Putin's version of events, Russia was as strong as ever. The economy had held up in the face of vicious sanctions, he argued, and Russians had learned to adapt. Moreover, the country remained a bastion of defense against the moral decadence of the West, with its casual embrace of LGBTQ+ rights and its adoption of other affronts to conservative orthodox values. (He ignored the inconvenient fact that certain European leaders who were virulently opposed to LGBTQ+ rights, like Andrzej Duda of Poland, had joined Ukraine's cause.)

But, he said ominously, the situation could turn against Russia. Those in the West "plan to finish us once and for all," he warned. In the last moments of the speech, he delivered the coup de grâce: an announcement that he was "compelled to announce today that Russia is suspending its membership in the New START Treaty." With that, the last remaining nuclear arms treaty—the one that Obama had fought to negotiate, that Biden had renewed within weeks of taking office—was suddenly in limbo. No one knew exactly what "suspending" meant, but it was clear the Russians were not going to restart the verification procedures that had already been suspended—first because of COVID lockdowns and then because of the invasion.

Biden was scheduled to follow eight hours later, in Warsaw. By the afternoon, lines were forming to get onto the castle grounds. Despite sporadic sleet, the whole scene had the feel of a rock concert, with speakers blaring 1980s hits like "Danger Zone" and "We're Not Gonna Take It." Blue lights streamed into the sky, visible through the mist from a smoke machine. Red, white, blue, and yellow bunting lined the railings, and Polish girl scouts handed out small Ukrainian, American, and Polish flags to the attendees, who jostled to get the best view of the podium where Biden would soon speak from behind bulletproof glass.

It was a self-selected crowd, displaying more enthusiasm than Biden sometimes got at home. The Poles knew they had done something remarkable: In a year's time, they had welcomed millions of refugees and set up a complex—if shadowy—network to slip a vast supply of arms over the border to the Ukrainians. As people waited, they told stories of how they self-organized in the opening days of the war, collecting clothes and food and driving south in their own vehicles to see it delivered to the border. The Poles were, in part, reflecting their own legacy of having their borders redrawn by force, most memorably on September 1, 1939, when Hitler's troops rolled across Poland. And two weeks later, when the Soviets, having signed a secret pact with Germany to divide up the country, mounted their own invasion to take the eastern half of the country.

As the sun began to set, Biden took the podium. "One year ago," he proclaimed, "the world was bracing for the fall of Kyiv. Well, I have just come from a visit to Kyiv, and I can report: Kyiv stands strong! Kyiv stands proud. It stands tall. And most important, it stands free."

And as usual, he extended an olive branch to the Russian population. "The United States and the nations of Europe do not seek to control or destroy Russia. The West was not plotting to attack Russia, as Putin said today," Biden said, responding directly to the Russian's speech. "And millions of Russian citizens who only want to live in peace with their neighbors are not the enemy."

The next day Biden met the Eastern European leaders who had the most reason to worry that the war would spread beyond Ukraine's borders.

And as for that Wednesday morning gap in Biden's public schedule? The famously devout Catholic president used it to have a priest conduct an Ash Wednesday service in his hotel room.

A YEAR TO the day after Russia's invasion of Ukraine, President Sauli Niinistö of Finland was working from Mäntyniemi, the newest of the country's three presidential residences. Custom-designed by a pair of married Finnish architects in 1989, Mäntyniemi is a low building designed to blend in with the trees and hills. Made of natural materials, it sits on a spit of land overlooking the Baltic Sea.

Seated in a small reception room just off the main lobby, Niinistö gestured at a large window with a sweeping view of the icy water. "Estonia is out that way," he said. "And so is Russia."

Niinistö personified old-school Finnish politics: He had risen from the city council of Salo, in the country's southwest, in the mid-1970s, and was elected to Parliament in the last days of the Cold War. After the Berlin Wall fell, he became finance minister, justice minister, and speaker of the Parliament, and dealt often with the Russians—mostly on prosaic, apolitical projects like assembling the financing for a wastewater project in St. Petersburg. In 2012 he became Finland's president, a job that gives him final say on the country's foreign policy. Once he settled into office, Niinistö began edging closer to NATO. He stepped up joint training exercises with NATO forces, who needed Finnish intelligence about what was traversing the Baltic Sea as much as Finland needed NATO's defensive expertise.

But at the same time, Niinistö was also meeting regularly with Putin, taking his measure. It didn't take long for Putin to make it clear that in his view what was his was his—and what used to be Finland's was also his. "In our first meeting—that was 2012—he suddenly said to me, 'Why are you heading for NATO? You can't get Karelia back,'" said Niinistö, referring to territory that the Soviets took from Finland in the last days of World War II. (The Karelian region has changed hands many times over the centuries; today it is divided between Finland and Russia.)

Niinistö reacted with astonishment. Reclaiming a sliver of territory that had been Russian since before he was born was not high on his list. "I said that every independent nation maximizes its security. And that was the end of it. We never came back to this issue."

During the Cold War, this careful wending between Moscow and the West came to be known as "Finlandization," a somewhat pejorative shorthand for the deal with the devil that the country struck to avoid Russia's wrath and retain its own independence. By steering clear of formal alliances—and not allowing NATO forces to sit on its unfenced eight-hundred-mile border with Russia—Finland could avoid contributing to Putin's paranoia that the Western alliance was creeping east and surrounding him. Although the need for Finlandization ended with the Cold War, and the country later joined the European Union, it steadfastly refrained from joining NATO—largely for reasons of regional stability, it argued, and always retaining the right to join if the situation changed. While Finland didn't have the formal protection of NATO membership, it also had no obligation to go to war with Russia if any NATO member suddenly found itself the victim of a Russian onslaught. Or at least, that is what Niinistö could say to Putin. Whether Putin believed it was another matter.

As the invasion of Ukraine looked increasingly inevitable in the fall of 2021, the question in Niinistö's mind was whether the era of straddling the line had come to an end. Quietly, his government had begun to prepare for the worst. "The ultimatums Russia gave to the United States and NATO in December concern Europe," he said in his New Year's Day speech to the Finnish people. "They are in conflict with the European security order. . . . Finland's room to maneuver and freedom of choice also include the possibility of military alignment and of applying for NATO membership, should we ourselves so decide," he said. It's not clear if anyone was listening, but he had planted the seed.

Niinistö told me later that his convictions only hardened with time. A week before the invasion—when it was clear the Russians would attack—he told the Swedish defense minister that if Russia invaded Ukraine, both Sweden and Finland would have to start discussing in earnest how to join NATO. This was a monumental proposition. Both countries would be acting directly contrary to Putin's effort to force the West back from Russia's borders. At the very moment Putin was demanding that NATO shrink, it would be expanding, adding its thirty-first and thirty-second members. And there would be eight hundred additional miles of borders between NATO and Russia, worsening Putin's paranoia about the West's intentions.

Eventually, that seemed like the lesser evil. "I was shocked that the attack was so massive," Niinistö recalled of the invasion, but most particularly "that they were after Kyiv. Because that meant that they were going to try to take the whole country."

In the year since the invasion, working the phones and traveling to Washington every few months, Niinistö moved his country firmly into the Western camp. He applied for full NATO membership, along with Sweden, a fact that Biden mentioned time and again, always to twist the knife that Putin had accomplished "exactly what he had tried to avoid": an expansion of NATO. What Biden blew past, of course, was how hard that path had been. Even in the urgency of the war, NATO hadn't been able to get out of its own way. What seemed like a clean vote to admit two qualified members—Finland and Sweden—got hung up, as Turkey spent the last several months withholding its vote in an effort to leverage political concessions from the Swedish government.

Yet as he reflected on the anniversary of the war from the presidential residence in Helsinki just days after Putin's and Biden's speeches, Niinistö knew that he had basically, finally, accomplished his goal.

Within six weeks, Finland was going to become a NATO ally—and the Baltic Sea harbor just outside his window would become NATO territory. Without question, it would add to Putin's sense of encirclement.

I asked Niinistö what drove Finland to make a decision it had ostentatiously avoided for decades. He didn't hesitate. "Putin did that," Niinistö told me. Just as the Russian dictator managed to drive just about all of the Ukrainian population—even millions who had been sympathetic to Russia—to defend their homeland, his brazenness and his lies about his intentions had turned the Finnish public solidly against him.

Yet as Niinistö spoke that morning, with the Baltic churning just behind him, he noted that Europe was also to blame—for its conviction that it had emerged from the Cold War as a permanent winner.

He told his own story about that European overconfidence, dating from twenty years earlier. It was March 2000, more than a decade before he became president, when he was representing Finland at that year's meeting of the European Council in Lisbon, Portugal.

"I was a bit amazed," he said. "It was a Saturday, and we talked for two to three hours about how good Europe is and how Europe will be the best continent in the world in ten years' time," he recalled. In his memory, it was as if they had ended the meeting by saying, "We are the best. It's done. Let's go."

It was perhaps the culmination of a pan-European certainty that the continent could bring the rest of the world around to its way of thinking, its systems, its model, its orbit. And Russia would play along, because it had no other choice—with the Soviet Union dissolved, it had no place to go but to join its European neighbors.

Fast-forward twenty years. Today, he acknowledged, there was "nothing left from that." Europe now realized it had painted an "unrealistic picture" of its own strength and security. That picture was ripped away by pandemic and war. No one knew, Niinistö said, if the war would last a year more, or five years more, or a generation. And no one had a realistic plan for how to deal with Russia beyond sanctions, heightened defenses, and isolation.

Moreover, the blocs he saw forming around the world—the West tightening its alliances, and Russia and China doubling down on their own uneasy partnerships—imperiled Finland's magic formula. The country had prospered on its smarts and its flexibility, its ability to weave between spheres of influence.

"I think it's not in anybody's interest that the world will be divided deeply into different camps," he warned. And if the world was divided that way, he said, the problem was that the "West"—even if that term included Japan, South Korea, Australia, and New Zealand—would be far outnumbered by the rest of the world.

"How I started to think about this," he said, was that "we have approximately eight billion people in the world." Yet how many of these, he wondered, could be said to belong to some type of liberal, democratic tradition? "Do we get two billion?" he asked. "Well, there are another six" left to join Russia and China's camp or to try to float on their own, betting on a multipolar world.

"I think we get into a certain miscalculation of ourselves," he warned.

FOR ALL OF Europe's posturing and confidence, there was evidence one year in that its hard-fought unity was cracking—and that countries were beginning to fray internally over the question of whether this should really be the West's war.

An iconic illustration of this fracturing appeared in the heart of Berlin, just a few blocks from the Brandenburg Gate, the powerful symbol of German reunification after the fall of the Wall in 1989. When the war broke out, the Gate was regularly lit up in blue and yellow, in solidarity with Ukraine. But on the one-year anniversary of the war, a rusty T-72 Russian tank recovered off the battlefield in Ukraine sat incongruously parked with its turret pointed directly at the Russian embassy in Berlin.

On February 24, thousands gathered around the tank to show their support for Ukraine. The very next day, German socialist and antiwar politicians held a counterprotest around this same tank. Their target was not Putin but the German government, for becoming party to the conflict by delivering arms—including tanks—and by training Ukrainians on German territory.

"We call on the German chancellor to stop the escalation of arms deliveries. Now! . . . Because every day lost costs up to 1,000 more lives—and brings us closer to a 3rd world war," warned one of the organizers, a leader of Germany's far-left movement, Sahra Wagenknecht. Wagenknecht insisted that the protest wasn't about Ukraine; it was about Germany—for sending weapons to fuel the crisis and failing to learn the proper lessons of World War II. But the group's goals aligned with two other groups: far-right forces and pro-Putin sympathizers.

So it was no surprise that the Russian tank itself became ground zero: a standoff in the heart of Berlin between the pro-Russian protesters, who placed thousands of red roses on the rusty hull of the tank, and those who trampled the flowers and replaced them with photographs of Ukrainians who had been killed in the previous year.

There, on the streets of Berlin, a year to the day after the invasion, the predictably messy next phase of the war was beginning to come into view.

CHAPTER 19

THE DIGITAL WAR— AND ITS LIMITS

At the end of the day, this became our laboratory. The worst thing that ever happened to China is Ukraine.

Lieutenant General Chris Donahue, now commander of the XVIII Airborne Corps, March 2023

MORE THAN A thousand miles west of Ukraine, deep inside an American base in the heart of Europe, an intelligence-gathering center unlike any seen in past wars operated around the clock. American officials almost never discussed its existence, chiefly because it raised all the fundamental questions about Western involvement in Ukraine: specifically, how deeply involved the United States was in the day-to-day management of the battle against Russian forces.

Its operators called the center "the Pit," and it was the place where U.S. and British military officers, a handful of Ukrainian soldiers and civilians, and some of the most innovative Silicon Valley defense contractors worked side by side to collect and filter battlefield intelligence—and to help decide which portions should go to the Ukrainian commanders.

What made the Pit so different from similar intelligence centers set up to fight recent wars was the particular content of the large display screen that dominated the room. The outlines were familiar. It showed Ukraine's borders and the positions of Ukrainian and Russian forces across the battlefield. But touch any of the icons on this screen and it all popped to life: Unclassified images from commercial satellite companies like Maxar and Planet Labs. Data scraped from Twitter or shared on Telegram channels or encrypted communications apps like Signal. YouTube videos of recent events. Instagram shots that might reveal dug-in positions or camouflaged rocket launchers. Radio transmissions, broadcast out in the open. Facial-recognition images of soldiers and civilians passing checkpoints. Geolocational data from Russian soldiers who lacked the discipline to turn off their cellphones—which use Ukraine's own telecommunications infrastructure—or to flip off their location indicators before tweeting out photos. Mixed in, selectively, were inputs from some of Washington's most classified spy satellites and the NSA's communications intercepts, for the eyes of the Americans and the British. It was all merged into a near real-time, constantly updated map of the war on the ground.

In the strange jargon of the Pentagon and the contractors who assemble and digest all these streams of data, this big display screen is called "the single pane of glass." It is part management console, part social media digest, and part spymaster's dream, a vision of the battlefield fed by a revolution in digital technologies—much of it collected from unclassified commercial sources.

Each day, the operators in the Pit walked the ever-familiar line between helping Ukraine defend itself and actively providing the data to hit specific targets. The information on display could easily have been pipelined right to Kyiv. But instead, with delicate technological footwork overseen by a clutch of military lawyers, the American officials and contractors guided the Ukrainians without pointing them to specific targets.

Sullivan offered a clear delineation between actually selecting the targets and helping the Ukrainians understand the threats that surrounded them. "Ukraine is not fighting on behalf of the United States of America to further our objectives," he told Susan Glasser of *The New Yorker*. "The analogy to me is much closer to the way the United States supported the U.K. in the early years of World War Two."

Yet even when offered anonymity, the people inside the system wrapped themselves into a pretzel trying to explain how it actually worked.

"Ukraine comes and says 'We are looking for command, artillery, where drones are,'" one senior military official told me. "We hand them a flashlight and say 'Look here'—then they turn their stuff on. We don't answer every question. We spend a lot of time debating."

Or as a top official of a government contractor put it to me with an obliqueness that in any other situation might be comical, "The U.S. hypothetically has a process and a mechanism by which they take the situational awareness that they've generated through all the means and capabilities America has and figure out an unclassified version of it. Then something happens"—note the studied refusal to be specific—"and people in Ukraine are able to take the situational awareness that the U.S. provides."

But if no one wanted to speak openly about the sensitivities of what the Ukrainians were learning from the Americans, they were much happier to explain what the Pentagon was learning from Ukraine—what Lieutenant General Chris Donahue, who was experimenting with the technology before and after his role in the Afghanistan withdrawal, termed a "laboratory" to test how the technologies and tactics developed over the past decade performed in a real-life conflict with one of America's largest and ostensibly most skilled adversaries. "We learned more from the first eighteen months of this war than from the past thirty years," another Pentagon leader told me.

THE SINGLE PANE of glass was an American innovation, twenty years in the making, driven by a U.S.-led revolution in software and the digital might of Silicon Valley. But it quickly merged with an impressive list of Ukrainian innovations, many of which were just weeks or months in the making, produced on the fly and dirt cheap. It quickly became clear that the same tasks that got bogged down in the Pentagon—where every program had to accord with government specifications set years before—the Ukrainians prided themselves in doing overnight. "Ukraine is the best test ground, as we have the opportunity to test all hypotheses in battle and introduce revolutionary change in military tech and modern warfare," said Mykhailo Fedorov, Ukraine's deputy prime minister of digital transformation, in October 2022.

On a trip to Ukraine in the beginning of 2023, a group of White House and State Department officials were shown how Ukrainian soldiers brought a 3D printer to the rear lines of the battlefield to replace worn-out parts for an artillery battery, rather than send the whole battery back to Poland for repair. The Ukrainians designed a tank-killing drone that cost roughly five thousand dollars each and then worked on swarms of far cheaper ones meant to overwhelm Russian air defenses. "Ukraine is, in a very rapid environment, in two to three years, inventing stuff that will take thirty years to be worked out by everybody else," one senior tech sector executive told me.

In the first year or so of the conflict, it seemed like this technological edge over the plodding, unimaginative Russian forces was making all the difference—and might even help Ukraine eke out a victory over its invader. Innovation and creativity, bolstered by some unintentionally provided intelligence from the United States, explained the sinking of the *Moskva*. The precision intelligence played out in the targeting of Russian command posts and the retaking of Kharkiv and Kherson. The American and European officials who made eager pilgrimages to Kyiv came away visibly impressed. "I don't think the Pentagon ever considered making parts on the battlefield," one administration official told me after returning from a tour. In fact, they had. The idea had kicked around places like the Defense Innovation Unit for years. It's just that the Ukrainians accomplished in a few months what the Pentagon couldn't execute over a stretch of a few years.

But, as happens in all conflicts, the Ukrainians' best new weapons begat countermoves. The drones used to target ships in the Crimean fleet that had proven so effective in the spring of 2022 began to fall into the sea as the Russians learned how to shoot them down with machine guns and helicopter fire. The U.S.-provided HIMARS artillery system, a game changer across the wide plains of the battlefield in the fall of 2022, was episodically jammed by high-intensity Russian electronic warfare operations.

Not surprisingly, the battle for Ukraine soon began to hinge on the question of which country could dominate the electromagnetic spectrum over the battlefield. The Russians had a long history in electronic warfare going back to Cold War days, when they learned how to counter American fighter jets and disrupt communications links among the

NATO allies. Now they were racing to produce "antidrone guns" that would swamp tiny receivers on Ukraine's most effective weapons or spoof them into hitting the wrong target. "The Russians have been more nimble at responding than we would have expected from their ground behavior," James Lewis told some of my *Times* colleagues.

Meanwhile, the Russians were refining their own strategy for using unmanned vehicles. They began flying them over Odessa and other cities in an effort to force the Ukrainians to fire million-dollar missiles at swarming $20,000 Iranian Shahed drones. "There are only so many missiles," one official told me. "There will be more and more Iranian-made drones."

When the long-delayed "spring offensive" began in the early summer of 2023, the limits of new technology became more apparent. The Ukrainians knew exactly where the Russians troops were. But, as the battle moved from open plains into a bloody slog through seven lines of Russian trenches and minefields, the Ukrainians' technological edge became increasingly blunted. Ukrainian tanks, armored-personnel vehicles, and soldiers had to navigate through a mine-studded section of forest just to get within fighting range. By the end of 2023, the sheer weight of the dug-in Russian Army was apparent, and the talk of a quick Ukrainian win was giving way to a word no American official wanted to utter in public: stalemate. In a stalemate, data is still vital—especially to prevent surprise attacks—but it doesn't necessarily move the needle.

THE REMARKABLE SUCCESS of the huge flow of intelligence funneled to the Ukrainians prompted a moment of reflection by General Paul Nakasone in the months before he was set to retire as the director of the NSA and commanding general of United States Cyber Command.

"Let me give you a story," he told me as we sat in the new command center he had built on the campus of the National Security Agency, the largest of America's eighteen intelligence agencies. "I spent twenty years of my life doing the following things: going into and out of countries like Iraq and Afghanistan and other countries in the Middle East. And it was almost always the same M.O. I put my boots on the ground, we'd put out ground sensors, we would do our collection, we would deploy our tools forward, and then we would fly our airborne intelligence surveillance reconnaissance up and down the country. Collect everything.

"And we thought we had the cat's meow. We had all that collection. It was fantastic, great signals intelligence. Fast-forward to February 24, 2022. I have no boots on the ground in Ukraine. I have no airborne ISR," he said, referring to intelligence, surveillance, and reconnaissance. "I have no networks in-country, yet I have intelligence that I've never seen before, in thirty-seven years in the United States Army. Eye-watering."

Nakasone began his career in the waning years of the Cold War. A Minnesota native, father of four, and son of a Japanese American Army interpreter who decoded intercepted messages in World War II, Nakasone recalled joining the American military at a time when few understood how harnessing information would change everything about the modern battlefield.

"Looking back on it now," he told me, as he tried to trace the huge increase in data available to the American military, "we had really no appreciation, or a limited appreciation, for how much information and intelligence would drive future operations—until Desert Shield/Desert Storm. That was a big change. That's the first time we start to see the power of the nation being able to bring together intelligence—and this is pretty rudimentary intelligence, if you think about it, at the time."

Nakasone laid out for me the major inflection points, as he saw them, over the next three decades, as the NSA found itself at the heart of an information and intelligence revolution that was rapidly transforming warfare. There was the conflict in Yugoslavia, he said, where for the first time you saw people indicted for war crimes being chased down by precision intelligence—things like signals intercepts and geolocation data collected by the NSA. Then came 9/11 ("Holy shit! How the hell did we ever get into this? How did we get caught so flat-footed?") and two decades of warfare in Iraq and Afghanistan—where, in the face of vast amounts of data, the NSA and later Cyber Command learned how to find the "needle in the haystack" and direct that intelligence to the operators on the battlefield when they needed it. That, reflected Nakasone, was "the agency at its finest: bringing its technology, its tradecraft, and its talent forward to places like Iraq and Afghanistan."

The technology was evolving, but the American mindset wasn't keeping pace. In the mid-2000s, when the Army transferred Nakasone, still a colonel, to NSA headquarters at Fort Meade, he figured it meant that his military career was winding down. "Why would they send me to a place like Fort Meade if I was going to be a future leader in our Army? I needed to go to places like Central Command or other places that were doing the really cool stuff." But Nakasone said he quickly learned that "the really cool stuff *was* being done here, little did I know it."

Back in 2007, his unit was tasked with getting information from the NSA into battlefields in the Middle East. The problem was that the NSA was hoovering up terabytes of data about terrorist movements and activities, but they weren't synthesizing it, narrowing it down, and getting it to the soldiers on the ground who needed it the most. The NSA estimated, according to journalist Garrett Graff in an article for *Wired*, that it was "delivering roughly 10 percent of what it knew, 18 hours after the fact." That meant that the United States was losing where it didn't need to be.

Putting cutting-edge technology and up-to-the-moment data in the hands of operators required a steep learning curve, but it turned out to be an arena in which Nakasone excelled. The world had changed, too. Now there were smartphones in the hands of nearly every combatant, high-resolution satellites above every potential nuclear testing site, and networked weapons platforms dotting every battlefield. All of that was fair game to Nakasone's hackers. They also began to learn how urgently the government and the private sector needed to exchange information: everyone from banks under cyberattack to companies like Mandiant and Microsoft, which monitored networks around the world and were currently sitting on mountains of data entirely off-limits to the NSA.

Meanwhile, of course, the United States' relationships with Russia and China were spiraling down, prompting the Trump administration's 2017 national security strategy to proclaim a new era of great power competition. But it took, in Nakasone's estimation, another couple of years for that reality to sink in and to galvanize the bureaucracy, and for the NSA to shift its focus from counterterrorism toward competition with near-peer competitors.

Then came the Russian invasion of Ukraine. Suddenly, the lessons learned from counterterrorism and tracking down war criminals—and twenty-plus years of building intelligence operations and partnerships with allies during the Global War on Terror—needed to scale up. And they did, in a way that went far beyond what most people understood.

The lessons that evolved from tracking and tapping terrorists in the wars in Iraq and Afghanistan, confirming their location, and killing or disabling them—what the Pentagon called "find, fix and finish"—had established the groundwork for a new era of conflict. Ukraine represented the first time these expanded capabilities were deployed at scale against a superpower adversary. "We have space, and we have the ability to do computer network exploitation," said Nakasone. "We hack better than anyone in the world."

But it wasn't enough. While the United States was awash in information, it still didn't know how to make use of all of it—and increasingly, this kind of data was available to everyone, not just spy agencies with billion-dollar budgets. We were living, said Sue Gordon, the longtime CIA officer then serving as deputy director of national intelligence, "in a world where, now, every technology is available to everyone. But we still think of technology itself as a strategic advantage, when it's much more of a commodity than that, making clever, fast use the source of strength."

FOUR YEARS BEFORE the screen in the Pit offered an unprecedented real-time view of the battlefield, the Pentagon program underpinning part of it triggered a full-scale revolt on the Google campus in Silicon Valley.

In March 2018, news leaked out that Google had entered into a modest $9 million contract to help the Pentagon develop artificial intelligence tools to process drone footage and label suspicious features. The counterterrorism wars were still dominating the Pentagon's thinking, and the goal was to take the reams of data sent back by multi-million-dollar Reaper and Predator drones and learn to tell the difference between a militant holding an AK-47 and a farmer holding a rake.

The contract was a small part of a larger Department of Defense initiative called "Project Maven" that would grow into an ambitious experiment to make sense of those massive flows of information that Gordon was discussing. But the project went further. It developed algorithms that would synthesize the data and begin to predict where troops, equipment, and attacks might happen, thus edging the Pentagon into the arena of artificial intelligence.

"In those early days, it was pretty simple," said Lieutenant General Jack Shanahan, the first director of the Pentagon's Joint Artificial Intelligence Center, which was tasked with overseeing the military's stutter-step experiments in merging existing weapons with new techniques in machine learning. "It was as basic as you could get," he told me. "Identifying vehicles, people, buildings, and then trying to work our way to something more sophisticated."

Google, with its skill at developing "computer vision"—basically, the ability of computers to read images and understand what they're seeing—was the natural choice for this part of the Maven contract. Inside the company's offices, executives convinced themselves that by using computer vision to help drone operators improve their identification of legitimate targets, they would also be reducing civilian casualties. It didn't hurt that their biggest competitors, Amazon and Microsoft, were already vying for multi-billion-dollar government contracts.

But explaining this military project on a campus full of left-leaning employees was not going to be easy. Emails that leaked out later from Dr. Fei-Fei Li, then the head of Stanford's artificial intelligence lab, who was taking a sabbatical year at Google Cloud as chief scientist of artificial intelligence and machine learning, warned company executives that when talking publicly they must "avoid at ALL COSTS any mention or implication of AI" and especially the nexus between AI and weapons.

As word spread through Google about the project, stickers popped up in its offices reading, "Do the right thing." A dozen engineers resigned, and dozens more were threatening to follow suit, just as soon as they could line up new jobs. "Google should not be in the business of war," read the first line of an open letter to the company's chief executive, Sundar Pichai. It was signed by thousands of employees.

Ultimately, Google backed down, dropping out of Maven when its contract lapsed. But Maven didn't die; the Pentagon just turned to other contractors. And it expanded exponentially, from a simple computer vision program to what the Pentagon now called "algorithmic warfare." "I'm not saying there was no interruption—there was," Shanahan recalled. "But it wasn't as dramatic as sometimes it gets portrayed by people who are presenting one side or the other. So we just kept going."

By the time the Ukraine war was brewing, elements of Maven had been designed and built by nearly five dozen firms stretching from Virginia to California. Yet there was one commercial company—equally skilled at integrating data and spinning a story about itself in Washington—that proved most successful at integrating the information sources into a big, user-friendly picture on that "single pane of glass": Palantir, a company co-founded in 2003 by Peter Thiel that focused on organizing, and visualizing, masses of data. Thiel is one of Silicon Valley's oddest billionaires, a man who has embraced right-wing causes, founded PayPal, promoted the concept of "floating cities" in the ocean, and backed a lawsuit against the news media site *Gawker* that bankrupted its parent firm.

Early versions of Maven, relying on Palantir's technology, had been deployed by the U.S. government during the COVID-19 pandemic to aggregate state data and track the vaccine rollouts; in the Kabul noncombatant evacuation operation, it was used to coordinate resources and track readiness. (More controversially, the company had contracted separately with Trump's Immigration and Customs Enforcement office to profile and track undocumented immigrants.) It was a powerful new tool—and the right people in the U.S. military were paying attention. They were beginning to see the future, a set of technologies useful not only for intelligence gathering but also for conducting combat operations.

Project Maven had been created mostly for intelligence purposes, Shanahan recalled. "We had this torrent of data, but humans couldn't process it all," he said. "I call it a 'success catastrophe': more collection from more sources than any time in history." Maven might have remained an intelligence tool had it not been for a handful of senior military officers—including General Donahue and his former boss Erik Kurilla, later the top commander for the Middle East—who realized that its revolutionary potential could apply to staging and moving weapons and soldiers on the battlefield, providing "situational awareness" or a "common operating picture."

"What Kurilla and Donahue both realized is that on the operational side, Maven could be equally valuable but used a little bit differently," Shanahan said. "It was combining the best of both worlds: intelligence data and operational context." When capabilities like Palantir's and others were added into the battlefield environment, it suddenly became possible to learn far more about potential targets—and to prepare an offensive operation. Maven's growing capabilities meant that commanders could ask to see a car and its occupants and then roll back the tape and see where that same car was an hour before—and ten hours before. They could chart numbers of enemy forces and vehicles over time, providing up-to-date context for the assessments provided by intelligence experts. And they could see what other commanders were doing—providing a bigger picture to help reduce confusion on the battlefield.

For the Pentagon, grasping the program's potential was anything but easy. For decades, getting the military to think differently—to embrace new technology and to break out of an acquisitions system that everyone agreed was broken and that most major defense contractors were desperately seeking to preserve—was a problem that had defeated one defense secretary after another. Obama's final defense secretary, Ash Carter, pushed the hardest to move the Pentagon toward rapid, data-driven decision-making and even tried to bring Silicon Valley engineers into the Pentagon to change the culture. He traveled to Silicon Valley, highlighting technologies that could revolutionize the Pentagon. In 2015, he established a new organization to tap into commercial technologies to make a difference on the battlefield. Initially it was called DIUx for "Defense Innovation Unit, experimental"; the "x" was dropped two years later to indicate its more permanent role. In 2020 the Pentagon announced that the organization had initiated six dozen programs and had concluded about half of them. Carter, who died in 2022, knew that many of these experiments would fail. He often said to me, "That's a badge of honor in Silicon Valley." In Washington failure is just regarded as a waste of money—and a political vulnerability for someone to exploit.

Maven quickly became the standout success among the Pentagon's many efforts to tiptoe into algorithmic warfare. As the project grew, it became the umbrella for many other new technologies, most of them in search of stable government funding. By the time the single pane of glass dominated the Pit, it was incorporating feeds from Maven, nearly two dozen other Defense Department programs, and commercial sources into an unprecedented common operating picture for the U.S. military.

"There's just not much else out there that's done the level, the depth, of what Maven did and the scale of things," Shanahan said. But Shanahan's pride in the accomplishment only underscored how far behind the technological curve the Pentagon remained in so many other arenas. "There are individual little projects that people will be very proud of and rightfully proud of. But if you were to ask me, am I happy where things are? . . . I don't think the level of investment is where it needs to be."

ONE MORNING EARLY in the war, a top American military official and one of Ukraine's senior generals met on the Polish border to talk about a new technology that might help the Ukrainians repel the Russians.

In his car, the American had a computer tablet, operating Maven through Palantir's software and connected to a Starlink terminal. I have something you need to see, he said. His tablet's display showed many of the same intelligence feeds that the operators in the Pit were seeing—the movement of Russian armored units, the chatter among the Russian forces as they fumbled their way to Kyiv—but at a lower classification level.

As the two men talked, it quickly became evident that the Americans knew more about what was happening on the battlefield that day than the Ukrainian general did. The Ukrainian was quite certain his troops had taken a city back from the Russians; the American intelligence suggested otherwise. Call your commander, the American suggested. The Ukrainian general placed the call and quickly discovered that the American had been right.

The Ukrainian was impressed—and angry. You Americans, he said, should be fighting the Russians alongside us. We can't do that, the American responded—President Biden forbade that. What we can provide, he said, are elements of this evolving picture of the battlefield.

At the outbreak of the war, the Ukrainian military leadership might have been taken aback by the American capabilities. But their surprise didn't last long. Even before the invasion, Ukraine was known as one of the most tech-savvy nations in Eastern Europe. The Ukrainians knew how to take a concept, technology, or piece of code and run with it—often beyond the Americans' imaginings. So while they often relied on information received from places like the Pit, they were already building their own systems and sourcing. They quickly revived their home-grown battle-management system called Delta—one that had been designed in collaboration with NATO advisors in previous years—to create their own version of situational awareness software. They turbo-boosted their intelligence-gathering capabilities, learning to extract what they needed from commercial satellite imagery and its growing fleet of surveillance drones as well as jury-rigging a signals intelligence collection system to hoover up geolocational data from cellphones around Ukraine—tracking Russians who were, by necessity, using the Ukrainian telephone network. And, of course, they drew on their remarkable collaboration with the CIA, which, for years before the invasion, had been training Ukrainian operatives, including in the United States, in tradecraft and providing them with equipment. That investment proved critical once the war began, although the United States steered clear of the targeted killings of Russians that Ukraine was carrying out.

Then Ukrainian government officials looked beyond their borders, leaning heavily on governments and commercial companies to do what they could not. "Fedorov called every week with, like, five things he wanted us to be doing," recalled one U.S. defense official, referring to Ukraine's young digital minister. Some were things the United States could deliver, such as helping with intelligence collection or working with U.S. companies to pull down malicious Russian apps. Others were impossible—like getting the Defense Department to modify the back-end code of a third-party app to make it more useful to their missions.

Pretty quickly, the Ukrainians were using this rich supply of data to target their artillery, gauge the accuracy and impact of an artillery strike, and incorporate that information into their next shot. Some of the targeting programs ran directly from the software, enabling Ukrainian soldiers to select a missile, drone, or artillery piece, fire it, and evaluate the damage with subsequent drone footage. In a December 2022 column for *The Washington Post,* David Ignatius described this as the "wizard war," suggesting it was "a big reason David is beating Goliath" on the eastern plains of Ukraine.

It was hardly a seamless process—the Ukrainian system was nothing like the homogenized command and control, centralized decision-making, and well-honed intelligence collection processes relied on by the United States. Some commanders used Delta, others the Palantir system, and some a combination of the two. But many relied on drone, radar, and satellite feeds from localized remote command centers—meaning they saw their own area but not the larger picture.

Still, the only way the Wizard War could work was if the digital devices on the battlefield could connect online—and for that, Starlink was the lifeline.

That was a lesson the Ukrainians learned early on, when Russia brought down the ViaSat system that Kyiv had depended on for its internal communications and for many of its military communications. "This was the satellite communications capability that spans the country," Nakasone told me, recalling how that event could have frozen the country on the eve of the invasion. "I mean there is no Zelensky, the master communicator, without Starlink. And that's something the Russians never planned for."

As Fedorov put it, "Starlink is indeed the blood of our entire communication infrastructure now." Starlink's satellite constellation was usually the only thing connecting soldiers to headquarters or to each other. This fact reinforced what was becoming blindingly obvious: Starlink's network of some five thousand satellites proved "nearly as good as—and sometimes better than—our billion-dollar systems," as one White House official described it to me.

So it was no coincidence that about eighteen months into the war, the Pentagon announced a collaboration with SpaceX to develop a new military system called "Starshield." The Army started testing it in weeks, not years. It was a stark example, American officials told me, of what the Pentagon was learning from this war: A private company had deployed a mesh of inexpensive satellites that was more reliable, more capable of fixing itself, than the billion-dollar models on which the military had depended for years.

But relying on a single company for their communications in this dire situation was teaching the Ukrainians—and by extension the Americans—a darker lesson. It turned out that depending on a foreign company, especially one run by a man who once described himself as a narcissist, albeit "a useful one," was a double-edged sword. Musk saved Ukraine, but a few months after the war started, he demonstrated just how much the Ukrainian generals would have to cater to his whims. He refused an emergency request from Fedorov to enable Starlink systems over Crimea so that Ukraine could conduct a drone-submarine strike on the Russian naval fleet off the coast of the peninsula. Musk had decided, after an earlier conversation with Russian officials, that an attack on Crimea might start a nuclear war. So he decided to step in and prevent it, using the singular powers that come with control over the world's most powerful satellite network.

Musk made no apologies. Ukraine "is now going too far and inviting strategic defeat," he said later. "If the Ukrainian attacks had succeeded in sinking the Russian fleet, it would have been like a mini Pearl Harbor and led to a major escalation. We did not want to be a part of that."

American officials told me privately that they understood where Musk was coming from. "It's his own asset," one of them said. But to other officials, it underscored the risk of having a single company in control of a technology central to accomplishing key military objectives—especially communications and targeting. When Musk decided to step in to halt a Ukrainian attack around Crimea based on his own calculation of what might happen next, he was, in effect, appointing himself national security advisor.

IN A SUBURB of Kyiv, Ukrainian high school students spent the summer of 2023 working in a long-neglected factory, soldering together Chinese-supplied components. Amid the broken-out windows, they were custom-making drones for the Ukrainian military. The teenagers, said Wayne Pak, a former Army Blackhawk helicopter pilot turned entrepreneur who had lent his talents to the effort that summer, had been selected for their "steady hands for the soldering."

When the high schoolers finished assembling their electronic parts, another team mounted them on carbon-fiber airframes—light, stiff, and cheap. Each contraption cost about $350. Soldiers would then strap a two-to-three-pound explosive charge to each one that was designed to immobilize an armored vehicle or kill the operators of a Russian artillery brigade. The drones were designed for what amounted to unmanned kamikaze missions.

"A good pilot would need four to six of them to destroy their target," Pak told me, describing the miniature drones coming out of the Kyiv factory. "A bad one would take eight or ten." Those numbers were not big enough to create a swarm. But the chances were that a few of them would get through to their targets. The factory was churning out twenty drones a day that summer, Pak said, "when they had all their components." They aspired to double or triple that output, but often they ran short of parts. "We had the manpower," he told me. "A soldering iron and computer is all you need. But the hard part is getting the Chinese components—motors, plastic propellers, a basic camera, the chips. The Chinese parts are the cheapest, but they are also what the Russians are massively buying up." Fortunately for Ukraine, the Chinese appeared happy to keep supplying both sides and keep the war going. As one senior military official said to me, there was more in this for the Chinese than just war profiteering. "They get an inside view," he said, "on what works for both sides."

The broken-down factory near Kyiv encapsulated all the complications and contradictions of the Ukraine war. From the start, the Ukrainians understood that to win, or even to stay in the game, they had to reinvent drone warfare—a remarkable insight for a country suddenly fighting for its life. There were some early victories, including buzzing the Kremlin—a stunt intended to remind Putin that his capital was not invulnerable, even if it didn't make much of a dent in the buildings themselves.

All this entrepreneurial fervor amazed Eric Schmidt, who spent over a dozen years as the legendary chief executive of Google before turning his mind and foundations to issues of national security. "For a country that really didn't understand drones very well at all as of February 24, they have made remarkable progress," Schmidt said in October 2023. But what really struck him was the relentless focus on driving down the cost of production. "What's interesting is, they do it at a price point that is inconceivable in America." So too was the speed, which was the opposite of the Pentagon's plodding approach: the exquisitely engineered Predator drone, with its fifty-five-foot wingspan, which had its first test flights in 1994, had taken more than a decade to design, build, and test and cost tens of millions each.

Brought on to Google at its inception by co-founders Larry Page and Sergey Brin in an effort to commercialize their fledgling startup, Schmidt was the rare engineer with an acute business sense. He was known for his practicality, his air of quiet self-confidence, and his occasional flashes of bluntness that would have gotten him in more trouble if he wasn't running one of the most powerful tech companies in the world. It had been Schmidt who had backed bringing Maven to Google, putting him at odds with many of his own employees, some of whom complained about his prominent role advising the Defense Department. After he departed Google in late 2017, he founded a series of technology and philanthropic initiatives and wrote books and articles with Henry Kissinger about the future, and dangers, of artificial intelligence.

Schmidt is a complex personality—great curiosity mixed with great caution and a quiet self-assurance born of experience and wealth. His last years at Google were riddled with conflicts, some born of the objections to Maven that he thought were a manifestation of antigovernment fever gone wild. He was drawn to Ukraine, he told me, out of a combination of patriotism and the certainty that he was the best man to help the Ukrainians figure out which innovations would enable them to defeat a far larger and wealthier enemy. He began visiting the front lines, a billionaire swathed in Kevlar, and then the startups popping up around the country that aimed to help the Ukrainian war effort by upping the country's software skills in everything from designing next-generation drones to demining the country's battle-scarred forests.

"Ukraine," Schmidt said, "has become the best laboratory in the world on drones." He described the sudden appearance of several hundred drone startups in Ukraine of "every conceivable kind." Some were designing cheap quadcopters that were specially designed to take out tanks. (The key was to aim for the treads.) Others focused on submarine drones: drone torpedoes that run underwater and motorized paddleboards that skimmed the surface, both designed to operate under Russian radar. Explosives were strapped to both and aimed at the hulls of Russian ships—which appeared to force the Russians to pull back their fleets. Of course, when the Russians woke up to the kinds of losses they were taking from bomb-laden quadcopters, they brought in their electronic warfare units to disorient the small drones and bring them crashing down before they could do any damage. The Ukrainians had a similar program, wonderfully named SkyWiper. The drone wars were fully under way.

Still, by the fall of 2023 Schmidt was worrying that Ukraine's innovative edge alone would not be enough. Russia's population was too big and too willing to sacrifice; oil prices remained high; China was still supplying Russia with key technologies and parts; and Russian tank production had sped up—and the country possessed a nearly infinite supply of artillery shells. More than eighteen months into the conflict, the Ukrainian front lines were at a virtual standstill. Despite the ferocity of the Ukrainians' spring counteroffensive—with its fleet of NATO-provided tanks and access to American, British, and French artillery—the Ukrainian military had barely moved the battle lines. In some places, it had even lost ground. Just a year before, administration officials had talked to me about the possibility of "catastrophic success"—the idea that the Ukrainians, invigorated by victories at Kharkiv and Kherson, were barreling toward victory. Now that looked like wishful thinking.

Even as Ukrainian pop-up factories churned out increasingly cheap drones, Schmidt feared they would quickly be outmatched. While the Chinese had rejected Putin's appeals for fully built, inexpensive, high-quality drones, the Iranians had gladly signed on. A year into the supply effort they began construction on an Iranian drone factory inside Russia. As Russia ramped up, the Ukrainians calculated they would have to churn out upward of ten thousand drones a month just to keep pace, a huge challenge. Washington tried to help, sanctioning Chinese and other suppliers of critical components. But the results seemed unimpressive. As the Iranians ramped up, Russia matched, then exceeded, the Ukrainian drone production.

As Schmidt saw all this unfold in his visits to Ukraine's factories, he began to worry that for all the innovation, time was not on Zelensky's side. In an extended, slow war of attrition, he feared that Russia would win.

There wasn't much he could do to reverse events in the ground war: He was an engineer and an entrepreneur, not a military strategist. But he was convinced he could help the Ukrainians take the drones and many other wartime innovations to the next level by focusing on software, not hardware.

Not surprisingly, the pop-up factories were focused on finding durable parts and extending the range of the kamikaze flights. Like the drones anyone could purchase on Amazon, they were guided by some combination of GPS software and drone operators twitching joysticks.

That worked well enough for guiding individual drones. But Schmidt had a different vision. He wanted to take the leap toward more autonomous drones operating in small groups or swarms and running on cloud-based software. These drones would be able to "talk" to each other. What this would create was a new generation of smart, self-protecting weapons that could evade Russian air defenses and keep going after their targets. By attacking in large numbers, they could make up for the fact that the explosive charges they carried were small.

But most important, Schmidt envisioned drones that could be pro-grammed and reprogrammed in batches, even redirected in midair, by relying on algorithms rather than human decision-making. Schmidt's vision of the future of warfare was one in which swarms of drones could recognize enemies and friends and then act accordingly, even if the drone had lost its connection to its human operators.

This was hardly a new insight. The United States, China, and others have been experimenting with the concept for years. But pulling off such a technological leap in the middle of a war would be quite a feat. It also crept toward the type of AI-based warfare that activist groups had long been working to ban. The Pentagon had been wrestling with this issue for a decade, establishing rules stating that any system that could kill humans had to be guided by "appropriate levels of human judgment over the use of force." But those rules—always evolving—applied to American weapons, not Ukrainian weapons.

"There's an awful lot of moral issues here," Schmidt readily admit-ted, "but what I want you to think about is, as a technological matter, can I do this? The answer is yes."

He also came to a harsh conclusion. Whatever this new version of warfare looked like, it would likely be awful. The vision of warfare that had been prevalent even a few years ago—of drones fighting drones in high-stakes but bloodless battles—was wrongheaded.

"Conventional wisdom might posit the widespread use of drones would sanitize warfare," he and Will Roper wrote in mid-2023, "but the in-the-mud reality we witnessed debunks this. Ground troops, with drones circling overhead, know they're constantly under the watchful eyes of unseen pilots a few kilometers away. And those pilots know they are potentially in opposing crosshairs watching back. . . . This feeling of exposure and lethal voyeurism is everywhere in Ukraine."

. . .

IN AUGUST 2023, Kathleen Hicks, the deputy secretary of defense, announced "Replicator," a new Pentagon initiative whose goal was to get cheap, plentiful AI-powered military systems into the field in less than two years. At its core, Replicator wasn't unlike what Schmidt was advocating for the battlefields of Ukraine. It was just a whole lot bigger—and, essentially, flipped the Pentagon's acquisition system on its head. "America still benefits from platforms that are large, exquisite, expensive, and few," she said. "But Replicator will galvanize progress in the too-slow shift of U.S. military innovation to leverage platforms that are small, smart, cheap, and many"—what are called, in Pentagon parlance, "attritable, autonomous systems."

With the Replicator announcement, Hicks joined the long line of defense officials who swore, over the last two decades, they could make the Pentagon think differently about the future of battle. And she knew many elements of Replicator were so experimental that some would fail. But she also sensed the world had changed. Ukraine had fundamentally altered how everyone thought about taking on a superpower. China's own preparations—their dominance of the commercial drone industry, their hypersonics, their nuclear advances—made it easy to make the case for urgency. And the Chinese, she noted, had spent the last twenty years building "a modern military" that was carefully crafted "to blunt the operational advantages we've enjoyed for decades."

She readily admitted that her goals were sky-high for a Pentagon that moved dead-slow. "I'm deeply, personally familiar with almost every maddening flaw in our system," she said. "But I also know that when the time is right, and when we apply enough leadership, energy, urgency, and depth of focus, we can get it done." It helped, she argued, that the new initiative wasn't structured as a new weapons program that Congress would have to vote on. That would only take more time and give traditional contractors an opportunity to slow everything down. "We're not creating a new bureaucracy. And we will not be asking for new money" in the immediate term, she said in September.

But Hicks wasn't especially specific about what Replicator would look like, offering instead a gauzy image of the future, somewhere between *Star Wars* and *The Terminator*. "Imagine distributed pods of self-propelled . . . systems afloat, powered by the sun and other virtually-limitless resources, packed with sensors aplenty, enough to give us new, reliable sources of information in near-real-time," she said. Or imagine, she continued, them "flung into space scores at a time, numbering so many that it becomes impossible to eliminate or degrade them all," or "flying at all sorts of altitudes, doing a range of missions, building on what we've seen in Ukraine. They could be deployed by larger aircraft, launched by troops on land or sea, or take off themselves."

The possibilities were limitless. The challenge was whether America, finally, could make them happen fast enough.

CHAPTER 20

THE DOWNWARD SPIRAL

Planet Earth is big enough for the two countries to succeed.

Xi Jinping to Biden, at a summit meeting in California, November 15, 2023

He's a dictator.

Biden the same day, when asked by a reporter whether his view of the
Chinese leader had changed

ON SATURDAY, JUNE 24, 2023, Biden and his aides gathered in the
West Wing's Ward Room to watch as the unthinkable unfolded.
In the middle of an all-out war between Russia and Ukraine, a mercenary warlord was marching on Moscow. As Biden's aides jammed into
the basement room, Yevgeny Prigozhin was a few hundred miles from
the capital, and, to everyone's amazement, there was virtually nothing in
his way.

For weeks now, U.S. intelligence agencies had been picking up signals that the brutal chief of the Wagner Group was seriously considering
open rebellion against the defense establishment in Moscow, which he
had grown to hate over the past year. At first, the hints were vague and
mostly open-source—chiefly Telegram diatribes posted by Prigozhin.
But then American intelligence agencies began detecting more indicators that Prigozhin was serious and had a plan. No one dared call it a
coup attempt—yet. But by June 21, the likelihood of an uprising looked

real enough that emergency briefings were held for administration and Pentagon officials and then top congressional leaders.

Still, the timing and nature of Prigozhin's actions appeared uncertain—and there wasn't much that the administration could do about it. The United States could hardly be seen as encouraging an uprising to take out the leadership of a nuclear-armed nation, yet Biden was also not about to pick up the phone and warn Putin of a threat lurking within his own forces.

But by early Friday morning, Bill Burns, the CIA chief, was struck by a video that Prigozhin had uploaded. "That video was the most scathing indictment of Putin's rationale for war, of the conduct of the war, of the corruption at the core of Putin's regime, that I've heard from a Russian or a non-Russian," Burns recalled several weeks later. No one could say the things Prigozhin had—on a channel watched by perhaps one-third of Russia's population, Burns stressed—and expect to get away with it.

Within hours of the posting of the video, Prigozhin recalled tanks and troops from the battlefields of Ukraine to take over the Russian southern regional military headquarters of Rostov-on-Don. Later, Prigozhin was shown sitting on the front porch of the command headquarters, sipping tea with the local commanders, a clear sign their loyalties, at least for the moment, were to him.

By midday Saturday, his march on Moscow was well under way. Trucks, troops, and even an air defense system rolled north toward the Kremlin—shooting down Russian attack helicopters and a giant Ilyushin Il-18 turboprop airliner being used as a Russian military command center, killing fifteen. But what truly stunned the Americans, as the mercenary leader inched closer to the capital, was that Putin's forces hadn't committed more aircraft to the fight. They had not strafed Wagner or obliterated Prigozhin's troops on the highway.

Where was Putin's vaunted military, Biden asked as he and the staff watched the slow-motion move toward Moscow? The television images, supplemented by feeds from spy satellites and intercepts from Prigozhin's forces, were painting a clear picture of *what* was happening but not *why*.

"For a while we wondered whether Putin's shield of invulnerability had cracked," one of the national security aides in the room that Saturday told me later. Another participant told me that "Prigozhin was betting on some level that the Russian people were going to be very supportive of this. And then, what of the rest of the Russian security establishment?"

On the edges of the Ward Room, amid its pictures of past naval battles, a discussion broke out about whether Putin or Prigozhin would be the more brutal leader of Russia—or a bigger threat to the United States. "I'm not sure we had a clear view," one participant told me later. "And we never would have articulated a preference," because the United States wanted to avoid the slightest impression that it was acting as puppet master in a coup.

And then, almost as abruptly as the march started, it ended. Just 125 miles outside of Moscow, Prigozhin gave up—ostensibly after the intervention of the president of Belarus, Aleksandr Lukashenko—and agreed to self-imposed exile in Belarus. He claimed that his mutiny had not been against Putin himself but had been intended to challenge the incompetent generals leading the Russian Army to slaughter on the plains of the Donbas. "We went to demonstrate our protest, and not to overthrow the government in the country," Prigozhin claimed days later.

Regardless of his intent, Prigozhin's uprising was the first concrete piece of evidence that Putin's control over Russia and particularly over the Russian military was weaker than the United States had assumed. For Putin, the catastrophe had been building for a long time.

Over the previous sixteen months, it had been Prigozhin—certain that he had special privileges because Putin needed him more than he needed Putin—who had taken on the role of a vociferous critic of the conduct of the war, even as his private army was actively fighting it. His complaints about the Russian military carried an authority that no retired Russian general sitting in an air-conditioned television studio could boast. In Telegram posts and videos uploaded from muddy redoubts in Ukraine, Prigozhin had long argued that his troops, essentially a mercenary force recruited largely from Russian prisons and other down-and-out corners of the country, were being deprived of the resources they needed to win. He portrayed Putin's defense minister, Sergei Shoigu, as a pampered armchair commander. "Shoigu! Gerasimov! Where is the . . . ammunition?" he railed in a May 2023 interview. Wagner, he added, "came here as volunteers and die for you to fatten yourselves in your mahogany offices." If battlefield conditions didn't improve, he threatened, Russia might see an armed revolution "just like in 1917." Still, Prigozhin was careful never to take on Putin himself—only his underlings—and so he seemed to have not just license to kill but license to criticize.

Yet by the time he conducted that interview, Prigozhin's power was not as unconstrained as he liked to portray it. His forces were deeply bogged down around the city of Bakhmut, and Putin, apparently tired of Prigozhin's tirades, had stopped talking to him. By June, the Russian leader had given Shoigu permission to counterpunch, establishing a requirement that all private military companies operating in Ukraine—Wagner included—sign contracts that would bring them under the complete control of the Ministry of Defense. Prigozhin would have to report to the man he had described as an idiot. He flat-out refused to comply. He would be loyal to one man, he insisted: Putin himself. "Wagner is absolutely completely subordinate to the interests of the Russian Federation and the supreme commander in chief," he wrote on Telegram a day later, on Sunday, June 11. Not even two weeks later, his troops were marching on Moscow.

"It was remarkable to watch as the attempted coup was unfolding," Avril Haines told me several months later, recalling how the intelligence community worked in real time to piece together the motivations and likely next steps of the major players in the unfolding drama. "For example, what's in the mind of Prigozhin? And one of the questions, at least for me, was . . . if he hadn't blinked, how far would he have been able to go?"

Many questions remained unanswered—particularly after Prigozhin resurfaced from his exile, showing up in late July at a summit meeting of African leaders in Moscow, and visiting Wagner troops abroad. But one part wasn't in question at all. "Putin is someone who generally thinks that revenge is a dish best served cold," said Bill Burns. "So he's going to try to settle the situation to the extent he can. But, again, in my experience, Putin is the ultimate apostle of payback."

He paused. "If I were Prigozhin, I wouldn't fire my food taster."

The only thing Burns got wrong was the means of Prigozhin's demise. Just over a month later, on a clear summer day in late August, there was an explosion onboard an Embraer Legacy 600 business jet that

Wagner Group often used, just thirty-three minutes after it took off from an airstrip outside Moscow. With one wing blown off, the aircraft headed straight to earth, its descent captured on video. Though the jet was registered in Prigozhin's name and the Russian authorities claimed that DNA results matched Prigozhin's, Western media outlets were so skeptical of all information coming out of Moscow that they initially hesitated to declare that Russia's most flamboyant warlord was dead. But Putin had little doubt. Prigozhin, he said in a half-eulogy, was "a talented man" who had "made serious mistakes in life."

If the first hours of the Prigozhin rebellion seemed to call into question Putin's grip on power, the aftermath clearly demonstrated his ability to reassert control. Just a few months after the mutiny—what Burns called "the most direct assault on the Russian state in Vladimir Putin's twenty-three years in power"—it was already being treated in Russia not as a mortal wound for the president but as an embarrassing sidenote to an ill-conceived war. When it was over, Putin had locked down power; his onetime chef had served his last meal; Wagner fighters were working for the Russian military; and Russian forces were digging in for the long haul.

As the summer of 2023 faded, it seemed that Prigozhin was not the only one who had miscalculated. All three superpowers—Russia, China, and the United States—appeared less focused on competing with each other than on managing fractures within. Putin might have vanquished his biggest challenger, but he couldn't hide the substantial casualty count—estimated by U.S. intelligence at over 300,000, including 120,000 deaths—in a war that was supposed to last a matter of days. The Chinese were in a deep malaise, having emerged from the darkest days of COVID only to discover that the days of hypergrowth appeared to be over—and that Xi's focus on security had come at a considerable economic cost. The United States found itself more divided than ever, with more than a quarter of voters telling pollsters that they thought political violence might be the best way to save what they cherished most about the country. And even the Ukrainians, while happy to have survived a near-death experience, were coming to realize that the West was not rushing to let them into NATO—and that the possibility of abandonment might be real.

The overarching lesson, perhaps, was that none of the three major powers had as much influence and control—over their own populations, their neighbors, or the world order—as they thought. At moments, it seemed like superpower competition intersected with superpower unraveling.

ON THE AFTERNOON of Tuesday, July 11, Jake Sullivan and his aides were in the back room at a NATO summit in Vilnius, Lithuania, staring at a phone bearing an angry tweet just posted by Volodymyr Zelensky. For months, Biden had been telling Zelensky that when the members of NATO gathered in Lithuania's capital, just under two hundred miles from the Russian border, they would celebrate Ukraine's survival and offer plans for its reconstruction. But Biden always stopped short of saying he would back a timeline for Ukraine's desperately desired membership in NATO. "Ukraine isn't ready for NATO membership," he told reporters just days before the summit.

Instead, he and Sullivan had been floating an alternative idea, an "Israel model" defense pact between Ukraine and the United States: an arrangement in which the United States would commit to a decade-long plan to give Ukraine what the Pentagon calls a "qualitative military edge." In Biden's mind, this was as valuable as—maybe more valuable than—full membership in NATO. What could be a surer sign of American support? As the idea evolved, American officials envisioned that other countries in America's network of alliances—even Japan and South Korea—would enter into similar arrangements, giving the Ukrainians what they needed most: a steady flow of money and arms.

Zelensky was less enthused. "Zelensky just never bought it," one member of the administration who joined in many of the sessions with the Ukrainian president told me. As he pushed back on Biden, he argued that if Ukraine had entered NATO years before, Putin might not have dared to invade at all. There was a reason, he told Biden, that the war had not expanded beyond Ukraine's borders: Putin was simply afraid to take on NATO forces. So if Ukraine was on a clear pathway to NATO membership, Putin would get the message—and withdraw his troops. But this was the one issue on which Biden dug in.

It all came to a head in the runup to the long-scheduled Vilnius summit. In the weeks before the meeting, several NATO allies—led by the former states of the Soviet bloc, from the Baltics to Poland—began to circulate drafts with wording that would essentially commit the alliance to a loose timeline for letting Ukraine join. Secretary of State Blinken, realizing that the clear majority of NATO nations were moving toward faster admission of Ukraine, warned Biden that he was losing the argument. The Eastern European members, Blinken said, "did not want to continue the status quo." Worse, he told Biden, Zelensky was threatening to bail on the summit if some kind of clear commitment was not forthcoming. All the pressure was now on the only two major countries standing in Ukraine's way: the United States and Germany. Only Scholz seemed to share Biden's fear that once Ukraine was in NATO, its membership would put the alliance on an unavoidable path to conflict with Moscow.

When the NATO leadership finally met in Vilnius, Biden and Scholz insisted on watering down the wording of the declaration. Ultimately, just a day before the summit officially began, they settled on the vague proposition that "Ukraine's future is in NATO"—without saying how or when.

Zelensky, hearing about the result on his way to Vilnius, flew into a rage. "It's unprecedented and absurd when time frame is not set neither for the invitation nor for Ukraine's membership," he wrote on Twitter.

What Zelensky was doing, of course, was threatening to shatter the public façade of unity around the summit. Sullivan told his aides this was pure Zelensky, complete with the dramatic outrage. A full-court press began to persuade him to keep his grievances private and make his gratitude public. By the next day, somewhat unhappily, Zelensky was back on message, repeating the usual platitudes about the support of the Western democracies. He had little choice.

In retrospect, though, Vilnius turned out to be a turning point—and not the one Biden and Zelensky had in mind. Throughout that summer and into the fall, a new narrative began to take hold in Washington and throughout Europe. It was a fear that while neither side could win, neither side had motivation to move to a negotiated settlement.

Zelensky's predicament was increasingly evident. The feat he accomplished starting in the late spring of 2022 through the end of the year, sending the Russians fleeing and reclaiming hundreds of square miles of Ukraine each week, had ground to a halt. While his troops trained at Grafenwoehr and learned how to use new NATO weapons, the Russians used that time to dig in, calculating that they could stop the tanks with trenches stretching hundreds of miles, interlaced with layer after layer of minefields.

Prigozhin's complaints notwithstanding, the Russian generals had learned from their serial mistakes, improved their tactics, and found more recruits by emptying Russian prisons and luring the poorest from their provinces. Russian forces figured out how to fly Iranian drones and jam the Ukrainian models. They fired incompetent field commanders. Most important, the Russians honed their skill at evading sanctions. In the fall of 2023, the International Monetary Fund raised its estimate for the country's economic growth to 2.2 percent for the year. Hardly spectacular, but also not exactly a sign that the West's aggressive sanctions package had its desired effect. As one Pentagon official told me, "It took a long while, but eventually they got their shit together."

While Zelensky's government kept issuing enthusiastic nightly pronouncements from Kyiv intended to bolster spirits at home and rally the allies to keep contributing money and arms, the raw statistics looked pretty bleak. Since the launch of Ukraine's much-advertised counteroffensive in the south and the east in June 2023, it had lost about the same amount of land it had gained along the front lines. Moreover, the Ukrainian forces had failed to accomplish their primary military objective: to cut off Russia's land bridge to Crimea. Exhaustion had set in. In Kyiv, there were the first organized protests by family members of the troops, calling for an eighteen-month cap on frontline military service. To Zelensky's generals, that demand was simply impossible to meet: It would deprive them of their most experienced troops.

The economic outlook was similarly bleak. One of the remarkable diplomatic accomplishments during the first year of the war was that Ukraine was still able to export grain—with Russia's reluctant acquiescence—under the Black Sea Grain Initiative. That arrangement, brokered by Turkey and the United Nations in the early days of the war, assured that wheat shipments from both Russia and Ukraine—two of the world's largest exporters—could continue. Cities and military sites might be bombed, military ships might be taken out, but the giant grain carriers would be allowed through—preventing a catastrophic rise in wheat prices for the world's most impoverished countries. The deal worked—for a while. But then Russia refused to renew unless Western economic sanctions on Moscow were lifted. When the arrangement collapsed, Ukrainian grain exports—the country's greatest source of hard currency—fell dramatically. The Russians mined several key ports, and efforts to find alternative routes largely failed.

While Biden's advisors kept up a good front in public, they feared that Putin's plan was to hold out until the next American election, in the hope that Donald Trump, or someone Trump-like, would win. The administration began telling members of Congress and foreign visitors that there were three ways Putin could prevail. One was if the Ukrainians ran out of ammunition. The second was if the United States lost its passion for the cause—in which case Europe would certainly follow suit. And even if the American devotion to Ukraine held, the third risk was that European unity might begin to fracture—especially if Germany lost its nerve. "Putin thought time was on his side," Avril Haines told me in the fall of 2023, looking back on nearly two years of war. "And he continues to believe that."

Zelensky got a dose of the changing political dynamic when he came to Washington in September 2023 to make the case for billions more in aid and arms. On his first wartime visit to Capitol Hill just nine months before, he had received multiple standing ovations. But now the Republicans controlled the House, and many on the right flank openly opposed a repeat performance. Somewhat embarrassed, Speaker Kevin McCarthy arranged to move Zelensky's speech to the National Archives, where the Ukrainian president could speak in the shadow of the Declaration of Independence. But the waning enthusiasm was unmistakable— and so were the warning signs. The grand alliance propping up Ukraine's government was tiring of spending tens of billions of dollars annually.

"Ukraine has one single point of failure, and it's the United States," Paul Kolbe, the former CIA station chief in Moscow, told me. "The message to Zelensky is that he was going to have to conduct the war on a budget."

During that September visit, Biden quietly delivered one piece of good news to the Ukrainian president: The powerful weapons system the Ukrainian leader had demanded for more than a year—the long-range ATACMS—would soon be on the way. Biden cautioned him to keep it quiet, warning that the Russians had every reason to attack the shipments on their way into Ukraine. And there was value, he told Zelensky, in taking Russian forces by surprise.

In the long list of turnarounds for Biden in the course of the war—from HIMARS to tanks, to F-16s, to cluster munitions—this was among the most remarkable. The Russian Foreign Ministry had previously said that the ATACMS was one of President Putin's red lines, and Biden took that seriously; when asked by reporters in 2022, he had categorically and repeatedly ruled out sending the weapon.

But as Sullivan returned from Vilnius, he was increasingly convinced that ATACMS might now play a critical role in helping Ukrainian defenders at an increasingly dire moment. Zelensky's forces needed a way to destroy the fleets of helicopters and other aircraft that the Russians were flying, with startling effectiveness, over the frozen battle lines of southern and eastern Ukraine. The ATACMS, especially the versions loaded with cluster bomblets, could do maximum damage to unprotected targets like aircraft sitting on the tarmac.

When Sullivan and his deputy, Jon Finer, went to Biden, they argued that Putin's red lines weren't as definitive as they had once appeared. After all, they pointed out, in May the British had sent their rough equivalent of the ATACMS to Ukraine—a weapon called the "Storm Shadow"—and permitted their use against the Russian fleet around Crimea. And Putin had not done much.

When Biden finally approved the ATACMS in the late summer of 2023, some of his critics argued that he had just repeated the same mistake: He had waited too long to give the Ukrainians what they needed. Sullivan and other aides insisted that was not the case. The president, they contended, was running a rigorous process, balancing the risks of escalation against the benefits on the battlefield. And the battlefield had changed.

The first use of ATACMS on the field in Ukraine in mid-October was indeed a surprise, just as Biden had hoped. The attack destroyed nine helicopters on Russian-controlled territory, a major success, and forced the Russians to move their aircraft beyond the weapon's reach, more than a hundred miles behind the front lines. Yet there was no magic bullet, no weapon in NATO's arsenal that would turn the course of the conflict.

This was going to be a long war, and the only thing that mattered was to signal to Putin that American support would not evaporate.

That was the public line. In private, officials across Washington seethed that Zelensky and his generals had dismissed American military advice. They had spread their forces too thin, American military commanders told me, to support simultaneous attacks in three different areas, rather than concentrating their firepower on a single set of Russian defenses. After retaking about half of the territory that Russia had seized in 2022, the Ukrainians "wasted their best shot in 2023," one official said to me.

The Ukrainians had other explanations, of course, and rounds of finger-pointing ensued. But as the year ended, one conclusion was inescapable. The United States and its allies were giving Ukraine enough to survive, Ukrainians said, but not enough to win. The problem was that winning—even modestly defined as restoring Ukraine's borders to where they were on February 23, 2022—was still the strategic objective. "There is a mismatch between our stated ends and the resources to accomplish our goals," said Douglas Lute, a retired Army general who had run the Afghan war operations for both Bush and Obama. "And that never ends well."

No one captured the Ukrainian dilemma more starkly than General Zaluzhny himself. As the counteroffensive petered out late in 2023, the top Ukrainian general uttered the one word that everyone had been trying to avoid in public. "Just like in the First World War we have reached the level of technology that puts us into stalemate," he told *The Economist.* "There will most likely be no deep and beautiful breakthrough." He then wrote his own five-thousand-word essay for the magazine, describing how drone reconnaissance made it impossible for either side to surprise the other.

Zelensky was outraged, and his rebuke of Zaluzhny's public conclusions revealed the depth of the rift in Ukraine's own war council. The general's conclusions, Zelensky's office told Ukraine's citizenry in early November 2023, "eases the work of the aggressor" and stirred "panic" among the allies.

"Time has passed, people are tired," Zelensky himself noted. "But this is not a stalemate." He sounded like he was trying to convince himself.

Zaluzhny, though, did not let up. A few days after the *Economist* interview appeared, the Ukrainian commander met Secretary of Defense Lloyd Austin and General Christopher Cavoli, the Supreme Allied Commander Europe, in Kyiv. To the astonishment of everyone in the room, he told the Americans that to win the war, Ukraine would need a trillion dollars, 17 million artillery rounds, and a million drones. The wish list seemed so fanciful that even other Ukrainian officials in the room rolled their eyes. The gap between Ukraine's needs and what the West could provide had never seemed wider.

IN LATE AUGUST 2023, Gina Raimondo touched down in Beijing to an improbably warm welcome by the very officials in China who had every reason to see the U.S. commerce secretary as a key source of their growing economic woes.

After all, it had been Raimondo who served as the architect of the U.S. export restrictions on sophisticated semiconductors and the equipment needed to make them. The Chinese officials knew she was central to the accelerating effort to cut Huawei out of the telecommunications networks of America's Western allies, and that now the Biden administration was gunning for TikTok, which it increasingly saw as a national security threat—even as its users soaked up the platform's addictive videos.

But what struck Raimondo the most, she told me shortly after the trip, was that "I got no speeches . . . zero rhetoric, zero mention of Xi Jinping Thought." Nor was there any discussion of Taiwan or any lecture about how it was time for Americans to learn to live with Chinese-developed rules rather than the other way around.

Perhaps the tone reflected how sharply economic fortunes had turned against Beijing. With economic growth slowing sharply, some Chinese economic officials—in sharp opposition to China's defense and intelligence establishment—clearly believed they needed the Americans more than the Americans needed them. Gone was the certainty that China's leadership had cracked the code of limitless growth or that Xi could move ahead with his obsession with control—of businesses, of the nation's political discourse, of the military—without exacting a severe economic cost. COVID restrictions had finally lifted, but the expected economic revival had failed to materialize. Banks were in trouble; property companies were going bust. The birthrate was plummeting. The cost of living continued to be sky-high, even as a collapse in property values loomed.

Years ago, Chinese leaders had told American officials that their most important task was keeping a young, restless population fully employed: Millions of unmarried, unemployed males wandering the coastal cities, Hu Jintao once told George W. Bush, would be a recipe for trouble. Now youth unemployment had surged to a record 21 percent—at least officially—before party officials stopped reporting the statistics. And the employed didn't seem much happier. A disillusioned former factory worker had popularized the phrase "lying flat"—describing a generation less interested in boosting productivity than in having a simpler, slower life untethered to finely calibrated measures of achievement. Emigration was jumping, with the richest Chinese buying second homes in Canada and the Caribbean in the hopes of evading Xi's iron control. Evan Osnos, the *New Yorker* correspondent who lived in China during its boom years, noted that the number of rich emigrants from China exceeded the number of wealthy Russians fleeing the country to avoid the draft.

"My impression," Raimondo told me, "was that the economic team—like [Commerce] Minister Wang [Wentao]—wants to do more business with America. They're asking for more American foreign direct investment. They use words like, 'Let's have our commercial relationship be a ballast for the rest of the relationship.'" But when Raimondo spoke in public during her trip, she avoided all of the traditional incantations about how the world's two largest economies, forever entangled, couldn't live without each other. "Increasingly I hear from American business that China is uninvestable because it's become too risky," she told reporters traveling with her, a line that rocketed around China. She didn't hesitate to cite the reasons: partly because of China's economic slowdown, partly because of continued intellectual property theft, and increasingly because Chinese security personnel were raiding U.S. offices and arresting their workers on vague national security concerns. American chief executives, she told me, wanted to do business in China but were "scared to death" of the new counterespionage laws.

Raimondo, in short, had flipped the switch, ending the kind of happy talk that had marked the past four decades of economic exchanges. To much of America, China still looked ten feet tall, the job-killing economic giant. But for the first time in years it wasn't hard to sense China's insecurities. Raimondo's chip restrictions had fueled China's fears that despite its billions in investments, the country was running behind in developing the most sophisticated artificial intelligence systems, because the most leading-edge programs required huge amounts of computing power. With their banks and property markets in crisis, infusions of Western capital seemed critical. When Raimondo was escorted into the Great Hall of the People for a half-hour meeting with China's premier, it stretched to an hour and a half.

Raimondo told me later she assured her counterparts that the United States was not looking to decouple its economy from China's and was not looking to contain its power. All of this was exactly what China's beleaguered economic team wanted to hear—but had good reason to disbelieve, because Raimondo's other message was that the "high wall around a small yard" was about to get higher and the yard a bit bigger. While the export controls Biden had published the year before had slowed China's chip and artificial intelligence industries, they weren't slowing it enough. Chinese companies were successfully scouring the world for black-market chips or looking for legal loopholes like renting the chips' computing power from third parties. China's intelligence agencies had so stepped up their efforts to steal industrial secrets—especially the "large language models" at the core of generative AI technology—that federal officials began issuing specific warnings to companies and universities to lock down their work. For this reason, Raimondo told me in September, her team was about to expand its year-old restrictions, with an update that would further limit China's access to leading-edge technologies.

Yet when the protests against the new regulations began, they came from the very American companies that Biden thought he was protecting—companies like Nvidia, Qualcomm, and Intel. Each warned that if they were blocked from exporting to China they would lose billions. "We have become unable to sell more advanced semiconductor chips to one of our largest markets," Nvidia's chief executive, Jensen Huang, complained over the summer of 2023. At Intel, Pat Gelsinger, who had lobbied so hard for the CHIPS and Science Act as a counter to Chinese advances, was similarly concerned: "China is one of the largest markets in the world and one of Intel's most important markets," he said.

Raimondo said she had some sympathy for this position. But the economic plight of an individual company wasn't her top priority. "If we decide that it's in our national security interest to change the goalposts," she told me in September, "I'm changing the goalposts."

THAT RAIMONDO WAS in Beijing at all, let alone engaging in real conversation, was somewhat remarkable, given the downward spiral in the U.S.-China relationship. For all of Biden's talk at a summit with Xi in late 2022 in Bali about setting a "floor" under the relationship, it clearly kept plummeting. The spy balloon incident of the first weeks of 2023 had forced Blinken to postpone the first trip by a secretary of state to China in years; the Chinese military cut off communications because their defense minister had been placed on an American sanctions list. With Chinese fighters coming within feet of American surveillance planes off the coast of China, Biden and his aides feared a catastrophic mishap. But Biden was determined to move on. At the G-7 meeting in Hiroshima in the early summer of 2023, he brushed aside the rupture between the two countries by referring to "this silly balloon that was carrying two freight cars' worth of spying equipment" and predicted that "a thaw" would begin quickly.

In fact, that was already happening—underpinned by secret meetings in the spring between China's intelligence chiefs and Bill Burns and between Sullivan and Wang Yi, a reflection of China's preference to talk directly to White House officials. In June, Blinken finally got to Beijing and spent time with Xi himself, assuring that Biden's messages got to him directly. He was followed by a series of officials that Biden thought the Chinese had every reason to engage: Treasury Secretary Janet Yellen, climate envoy John Kerry, and, ultimately, Raimondo.

The whole idea was to set up what Sullivan called "guardrails" in the relationship: "Just as the use of seat belts cuts traffic fatalities in half, so do communication and basic safety measures reduce the risk of geopolitical accidents," he wrote later that fall. But the risk was that these meetings could become talk for talk's sake, the sort of empty diplomacy that the Biden team had described as the failure of past administrations.

Privately, Sullivan explained his view of the difference between "engage-ment" and "diplomacy": "Engagement is premised on the theory that deeper interdependence with China, and working groups with China to resolve issues, would produce changes in Chinese behavior," he said to me. That, he said, was the mistake that this White House would not make. Diplomacy, he said, is about managing conflict.

Much of that responsibility fell to Nick Burns, the American ambas-sador in Beijing, who had been warning since the spring of 2023 that after the balloon incident, the relationship with Beijing had become far too unstable. There were, he said, "too few reliable channels" of com-munication. The governments had to find a way to reconnect—even if just to reach a modicum of stability. He saw an opening, if a narrow one, in the spring of 2023. Soon after he formally presented his credentials to Xi Jinping, he discovered that officials were eager to meet to set up the cabinet-level visits, and when the Senate Majority Leader, Chuck Schumer of New York, arrived with a bipartisan delegation of senators, Xi himself welcomed them for an eighty-minute discussion. When the subject turned to stopping the sale of precursor chemicals for fentanyl, which had emerged as the top killer of Americans age eighteen to forty-five, Xi said, "We don't want Americans to die. We want to help."

"Clearly, something had changed," Burns later told me. It may have been that the downturn in the Chinese economy finally spooked Xi and his inner circle; for the first time in a quarter century, investors were leaving China in significant numbers, and every American and Japanese company that was still there was thinking about a Plan B to get out if they needed to. All of a sudden, China was interested in scheduling another meeting with Biden—this time in California, if it could be ar-ranged, during the next Asia Pacific Economic Cooperation summit. Burns didn't think this marked a fundamental change in China's view of the United States. It was a completely tactical move, he concluded, but he urged his colleagues to play it out and see where it led.

DESPITE THE SUDDEN outreach, though, the potential for conflict be-tween the two countries still looked all too real. Just as the FBI was exam-ining the shot-down remnants of the spy balloon, American intelligence agencies had detected a more worrisome intruder: mysterious computer code that was showing up in telecommunications systems near the giant U.S. military base in Guam and then around the United States, including at other military facilities. Apparently the Chinese, with more stealth and skill than the Russians, were dropping code into electric grids, gas and water pipelines, and other critical infrastructure. A series of secret meetings at the White House followed, concluding with a lengthy public advisory, published jointly with English-speaking allies, that described the code and warned of a "recently discovered cluster of activity" from China.

The question was why. "We think it's about Taiwan," one national security official told me. Beijing had calculated that if a conflict ever erupted over the island the key would be slowing down an American response. What better way to do so than by freezing up the American bases that would have to send aid?

The discovery added to an increasingly murky picture of China's intentions toward Taiwan. From his earliest days in office, Xi had vowed to bring about the "great rejuvenation of the Chinese nation." Many in Washington fixated on 2027, the year by which Xi had commanded that the People's Liberation Army must be ready to coerce a unification, by military means if necessary. And the continuing flights and naval activity around the island—more than seventeen hundred flight incursions into Taiwanese airspace in 2022 and even more in 2023—suggested that the pressure might just accelerate.

But in the summer of 2023, intelligence analysis coming out of the CIA's new China center and other corners of the government prompted a rethinking: With China's economic growth slowed, an invasion of Taiwan would be far riskier for Xi than it would have been two years before. Economic sanctions, if they came, could do far more damage to an economy growing at 2 or 3 percent a year than to an economy growing at 8 percent. Xi himself, the thinking went, must be wondering if his generals were overestimating the skills of the People's Liberation Army, just as Putin's generals had predicted a short war in Ukraine. "There may be more time on the clock than we think," one of Biden's top Asia aides told me. Others noted that in private meetings, away from the cameras, the Chinese made no threats and seemed worried about whether Taiwan would elect leaders who moved toward declaring independence—a move that would force Beijing's hand and possibly even trigger a conflict they wanted to avoid.

One other feature of China's military buildup worried Washington: its rapid buildup of nuclear weapons. In the fall of 2023, the Pentagon assessed that China already had deployed five hundred nuclear weapons—roughly twice as many as in recent years—and was "on track to exceed previous projections."

Inside the White House, those figures drove an effort to draw China into arms control negotiation, a process it had long refused. When Sullivan had pitched the idea to a senior Chinese official in 2022, he'd been flat out rejected; when Beijing was finished with its nuclear buildup and had roughly matched the size of the American and Russian deployed arsenals, he was told, China might be interested in talking.

Yet by the fall of 2023, China's position appeared to be softening. Suddenly the Chinese seemed, vaguely, to be interested in some kind of dialogue—perhaps because they didn't want to get into an expensive arms race, perhaps because the tightened military alliance between Washington and Tokyo gave the United States new counterstrike capabilities into China—with conventional weapons—that Beijing wanted moved away from its shores. Even if China didn't want to talk about nuclear weapons, it was interested in putting some limits on artificial intelligence systems. Some in the White House and the Pentagon saw that as an opening: An agreement not to let nuclear decision-making out of the hands of human beings seemed a good way to show that China and the United States were looking for ways to avoid blowing each other up. It wouldn't be the grand arms control deals of the Cold War, but it would be better than nothing.

In the meantime, though, something truly strange was happening in Beijing. Top leaders in the Chinese government were vanishing, one by one, like characters in an Agatha Christie novel. The first to go was the wolf warrior that Xi had sent to Washington: Qin Gang, who had seemed to be on the rise when he was brought back to Beijing and promoted to foreign minister. Then, one day in June after he appeared with the foreign minister of Sri Lanka, he simply vanished. Rumors appeared in the Chinese and American press that while he was ambassador to the United States, he had had an affair with a Chinese broadcaster, but in the Chinese hierarchy that hardly seemed like a career-ending move. His dismissal was followed, in short order, by the removal of two of the generals in charge of the country's nuclear arsenal as well as of the defense minister. There were vague rumors that some of the officials had been compromised by American intelligence. The inner machinations seemed almost impossible to decode, but clearly Xi had lost confidence in members of the team he had personally assembled.

The national malaise, the mysterious dismissals, the constant war between Xi's economic team and the hawks pursuing a strategy of internal suppression and external aggression all conjured something the United States had not contemplated for twenty years: the risks of dealing with a weak China. This was the question I had raised with Bush at his ranch in January 2001, nearly a quarter century ago: Was the United States better off with a strong, confident China or an economically struggling, insecure one?

"We expect China to remain a major player on the world stage for the foreseeable future," wrote Jake Sullivan in an article for *Foreign Affairs* in the fall of 2023. "We do not expect a transformative end state like the one that resulted from the collapse of the Soviet Union." Still, he wrote, "the past two and a half years have upended assumptions on the relative trajectories of the United States and China." It was an oblique reference to all of those straight-line projections in which China overtook the United States in all spheres—military, economic, technological—which suddenly weren't looking all that straight anymore.

JUST A WEEK before the outbreak of a new war that no one saw coming—least of all its target, the Israelis—Biden and his aides were beginning to celebrate some modest successes in refocusing the country on new challenges and setting aside America's old and expensive preoccupations.

At a conference in late September, Jake Sullivan ticked off a long list of diplomatic accomplishments that he thought were allowing the country to focus its energies on taking on Beijing and putting the squeeze on Russia. American manufacturing was back, including new semiconductor fabs sprouting in the desert Southwest. Iran's ambitions seemed contained: While its nuclear program had made great progress after Trump pulled out of the nuclear deal, enrichment had slowed—the result, though Sullivan didn't say so, of a quiet understanding with the United States that relieved a bit of sanctions pressure. Attacks on U.S. forces in Syria and Iraq had abated. There was a brittle truce in Yemen, which Biden's team had helped forge, and the Iraqi government was stable, which was the best one could hope for. And while he was circumspect about the details, Sullivan hinted at an ambitious diplomatic project to redesign the Middle East for a new era.

At the core of the new deal would be Saudi recognition of Israel—based on the Trump-era Abraham Accords, but, given the Saudi role at the heart of the Muslim world, the stakes would be far bigger—in return for a new defense pact and an agreement that the Saudis, like the Iranians, could enrich their own nuclear fuel. While many central concessions had yet to be nailed down—starting with the hardest, Israel committing to a two-state solution—the contemplated grand bargain would mark a huge turning point for the Middle East, ending the battle that dated back seventy-five years about Arab challenges to Israel's right to exist.

The plan was a sign that slow, patient, behind-the-scenes diplomacy could pay off. "The Middle East region is quieter today," Sullivan said with some pride that September day, "than it has been in two decades." He had spent less time on the region, he said, than any of his predecessors, even as he cautioned that could change at any moment.

At the White House that week, Sullivan had been putting the final touches on a detailed explanation of how the Biden administration had brought this shift about. In a lengthy essay for *Foreign Affairs*—entitled "The Sources of American Power," an echo of George F. Kennan's "The Sources of Soviet Conduct"—he argued that Biden had spent three years focusing the country on the right battles. In the post–Cold War era, he argued, the country had forgotten what it did best from the 1950s to the 1970s: build its international influence around its own technological and industrial strength. Yet once the Soviet Union collapsed, there was "little perceived need" for such investment, because the United States had no "peer competitor."

Now, he wrote, the United States needs to steel itself for a "new period of competition in an age of interdependence and transnational challenges." He defended the decision to get out of Afghanistan as crucial to that effort. "If the United States were still fighting in Afghanistan, it is highly likely that Russia would be doing everything it could right now to help the Taliban pin Washington down there, preventing it from focusing its attention on helping Ukraine." Now, the United States needed to complete the turn, by helping the Middle East enter a new era.

"This disciplined approach frees up resources for other global priorities, reduces the risk of new Middle Eastern conflicts, and ensures that U.S. interests are protected on a far more sustainable basis," he wrote. He acknowledged that the "Israeli-Palestinian situation is tense, particularly in the West Bank, but in the face of serious frictions, we have de-escalated crises in Gaza and restored direct diplomacy between the parties after years of its absence."

His point focusing on vital American national interests was hard to dispute. His timing couldn't have been worse.

Even as Sullivan's essay was coming off the printing presses, thousands of militants from the Iran-backed terror group Hamas broke out from the Gaza Strip—the tiny, impoverished, occupied Palestinian enclave on the southern coast of Israel—in a long-planned attack that resulted in the bloodiest day for the world's Jews since the Holocaust. Suddenly, the old Middle East—the one of violence and bitterness, territorial claims and slogans about taking back Palestine "from the river to the sea"—was back, imperiling the vision of something entirely new.

Indeed, Hamas's vengeance may have been intended to accomplish just that. A permanent peace between the Israelis and the Saudis—custodians of the two holy mosques and protectors of the holy cities—would undercut the terror group's reason for existing. Whatever the motives, the scenes the world woke up to that Saturday morning were beyond gruesome: Gunmen on motorbikes broke through Israel's high-tech border walls; disabled cameras and sensors; rampaged through local military headquarters, killing the few on duty; massacred young concertgoers at an open-air music festival; and besieged local kibbutzim. They shot parents in front of their children, and raped, tortured, and killed many others, videoing their own savagery. Roughly 240 captives were dragged back to Gaza, screaming. By noon, over 1,200 Israeli and foreign citizens were dead. Israel was stunned, much as Americans had been one sunny September morning twenty-two years before.

In an instant, almost everything the world had come to take for granted about the omnipotence and competence of Israel's security institutions seemed wrong. Its intelligence services had failed to recognize the significance of the months or years of planning and the deliberate dismantling of the digital surveillance infrastructure around Gaza. The barriers that protected Israelis from underground tunneling were useless against terrorists using gliders to fly over them and bulldozers to knock down fences. The Israel Defense Force was pitifully slow to respond. "On that fateful day, the country's long-standing security doctrine crumbled in the face of a perfect storm," wrote Amos Yadlin, the country's former military intelligence chief, and Udi Evental, a retired colonel in the Israel Defense Force. Yadlin was a legend in the country: As a young fighter pilot he had flown covertly into Iraq and destroyed a nuclear reactor that Saddam Hussein had been building. Now he was declaring that Israel's government had failed at its most basic task because "its intelligence and military institutions were unable to keep citizens safe."

But this was more than a case of early-warning systems being shut off. Though they declined to say so in public, Biden and many of his aides were convinced it was also the result of the hubris of Prime Minister Benjamin Netanyahu and the extremism of the right-wing coalition that he had assembled to cling to power. For months, over Biden's public and private objections, Netanyahu had poured his energies into passing legislation that would have undercut the authority of Israel's courts to challenge the government's mandates. Many suspected the effort was designed to protect Netanyahu himself, who was facing criminal charges from a long-running criminal investigation. Now the price of that distraction was clear to all. The man who had defeated virtually all opponents over the years by campaigning as the one leader who kept Israelis safe had clearly misread the threat gathering on Israel's southern border. Netanyahu had operated in the apparent belief—bolstered by faulty intelligence—that Hamas had been tamed, that it had put aside its goal of wiping Israel off the map in favor of profiting from its corrupt rule over Gaza. He and his inner council also appeared to believe that Hamas could not conduct an attack on this scale—and that the Israeli government's policy of indefinitely trapping 2.3 million Palestinians behind the high fences of Gaza, with nearly half the population lacking employment, was a sustainable status quo.

Now, enraged by the bloodshed and no doubt sensing that the inevitable investigations into why Israel slept would mark the end of his political career, Netanyahu set two strategic goals: dismantling Hamas and winning the release of the hostages. Biden, an instinctual backer of Israel even when he clashed with Netanyahu over the years, pledged unfailing support—a surge in weaponry, military advice, and some $14 billion in American military aid, more than triple what Israel receives in a typical year.

"Let there be no doubt: The United States has Israel's back," he said. "We're with Israel." Yet by the time he landed at Ben Gurion Airport days after the attack, in a whirlwind trip to embrace the prime minister and honor the families of the dead and the captured, Biden already seemed to sense that the ferocious retribution Netanyahu was planning posed its own distinct threat to the Israeli state.

"Justice must be done," Biden said in a speech before he left the country. "But I caution this: While you feel that rage, don't be consumed by it. After 9/11, we were enraged in the United States. And while we sought justice and got justice, we also made mistakes."

Israel's first response in the days after the attack was to cut off food, water, medicine, fuel, and at times the internet to Gaza—a move it said was aimed at flushing Hamas out of its tunnels under Gaza City and beyond but that ended up punishing millions of Palestinians and foreign civilians, who soon faced desperate conditions. Then, day after day and night after night, hospitals, schools, and homes were bombed. Gazan children were killed in proportions rarely seen in modern wars; their houses collapsed in air strikes that used thousand- and two-thousand-pound bombs few had ever envisioned being used on cities. Among Israel's targets were hospitals, which the country contended, with some evidence, were being used by Hamas to shield their fighters and hide the entrances to the vast underground tunnel system built beneath Gaza City. The result was a horror that resembled Kherson in 2022 or Dresden in 1945. The few hospitals that remained open ran out of disinfectants and operated without anesthetics. In just two months, the Palestinian death toll rose to over twenty thousand, or sixteen times more than those killed in the original attack, by the estimates of the Gaza Health Ministry, an arm of Hamas. American officials in the region said the true toll was likely higher. Israeli officials maintained that thousands of those killed in the opening two months were Hamas members, but that didn't address the central question: whether civilians were being killed "indiscriminately," a word Biden himself used at one point.

In his increasingly tense conversations with Netanyahu, conducted every few days, it became clear to Biden and his aides that Netanyahu regarded the daily bloodshed in Gaza as an acceptable price for a necessary military campaign. His arguments with Biden, played out in secure calls that the United States said little about, grew more and more vivid. Hadn't the United States firebombed Tokyo during World War II? Netanyahu demanded. Hadn't it unleashed two atom bombs? What about the thousands who died in Mosul, as the United States sought to wipe out ISIS?

It is hard to know how much Biden pushed back. While Blinken and others were declaring that "far too many Palestinians have been killed," Biden was struck by Israel's argument that Hamas had declared it was looking for another opportunity to attack.

While Biden's calls for restraint grew somewhat sharper, Netanyahu veered between ignoring him and contradicting him. This was Israel's existential fight—and while it needed America's help, it was not about to be driven by American sensibilities. "There is a long history of U.S. presidents realizing they don't have as much leverage over Israel as they thought," Representative Seth Moulton, a Massachusetts Democrat and former Marine who served four tours in Iraq, told me.

As the carnage grew, hundreds of thousands began to protest on behalf of the Palestinians caught in the horrific bombing. "Anywhere else, attacking civilian infrastructure and deliberately starving an entire population of food, water, basic necessities would be condemned, accountability would be enforced," said King Abdullah II of Jordan, one of America's staunchest regional allies. In the "Global South," the vast swath of the world that the United States was working to win over, more and more leaders pointed out the double standard: The United States would condemn indiscriminate Russian missile attacks on Odessa but not the use of thousand-pound, American-produced bombs on Gaza City.

It was an imperfect analogy—Russia had begun an unprovoked war, while Israel was responding to an attack that killed a staggering number of its citizenry in the most brutal way possible. But Biden, as Israel's protector and arms supplier, had the legal authority to place strict limits on how American weapons could be used against civilian targets, much as he kept Zelensky from using American weapons on Russian territory.

Biden's careful walk on the tightrope looked and felt like a failure of clear leadership. He had come to office declaring that the defining conflict of the age was democracy versus autocracy. But in Saudi Arabia, he soon had to embrace the worst form of autocrat in order to push back on Iran and China. And now he was in a bear hug with an Israeli democracy that was bombing Palestinian children to pursue what Netanyahu was calling "mighty vengeance." Biden's most critical initial comment was that he was "heartbroken by the tragic loss of Palestinian life." When Biden and Blinken declined to call for a cease-fire, blocking U.N. Security Council resolutions that demanded an end to the hostilities, Blinken's own State Department became the site of a minor uprising. Hundreds of career diplomats and civil servants used the "dissent channel" to argue that American policy had gone off the rails.

As the horrifying numbers of civilian deaths in Gaza kept rising, Biden was far too reluctant, for too long, to publicly call out Netanyahu and the far-right members of his coalition. His own deputy national security advisor, Jon Finer, admitted in February 2024 that the administration had made "missteps," failing to acknowledge "how much the president, the administration" values Palestinian lives. Yet even so, Biden refused to impose conditions on how Israel could use American weaponry.

Beyond the human tragedy, Israel's reaction threatened to trigger the kind of regional conflagration in the Middle East that Biden had been trying to avoid. Complicating matters, Iran was at the center of the disruption. Its proxies launched Iranian-made drones and missiles to attack Americans in Syria, Iraq, and Jordan, killing some and injuring many. In the Red Sea, the Houthis used Iranian weaponry and intelligence to target shipping, forcing interruptions in international commerce. And meanwhile, the Iranian nuclear program edged closer and closer to the Bomb—without quite going over the red line that would invite attack. Understandably, Biden did not want to strike Tehran directly and risk rekindling a full-scale Mideast war. But that caution opened him up to the predictable election-year critique that he was projecting American weakness. And in an election year, such slogans have a way of sticking.

.   .   .

IN MID-NOVEMBER, nearly six weeks into the Middle East's new war, Xi Jinping's giant presidential limousine—Chinese-made, of course, and designed to replicate the American president's, only larger—pulled into an estate on the edges of Silicon Valley for the first meeting between the leaders of the world's largest powers in a year.

Biden's expectations were low. After three years of sparring over technology theft and Taiwan, territorial claims and balloon flights, both sides knew the other's talking points by heart. But Biden considered it essential that he remain able to talk directly to Xi, especially if the moment came to avoid a crisis—or a war. He knew that the dream of more than a decade earlier, when the two men had traveled together and talked about whether the influence, power, and wealth of the world's largest economies could be combined to make progress on climate or nuclear proliferation, had long ago been tossed aside. Now Biden would settle for the bare minimum: competitive coexistence.

When they settled into the ballroom of an old California gold baron's estate, now used for weddings of the Valley's tech elite, the sheer formality of the setting suggested this would not be one of those summits where the leaders would wander off together on a path in the woods seeking deep understanding. The conversation was stilted: fifteen-minute presentations by each side, laboriously translated. All the diplomatic niceties were there, but neither side wanted to walk out having appeared to give any ground.

Arrayed along one side of a long boardroom-style table was Xi and his national security inner circle, an all-male group of intense party loyalists, the expressions on their faces suggesting that what they wanted most was to get the whole thing over with. Biden brought the cabinet members he had dispatched to Beijing in recent months: He was flanked by Blinken and Yellen. Raimondo was a few seats down. Sullivan and Wang Yi, who had spent hours together on everything from avoiding clashes at sea to setting some common rules on artificial intelligence, were each parked at his boss's elbow.

Xi opened with a greeting mixed with a warning. "For two large countries like China and the United States, turning their back on each other is not an option," he told Biden. Conflict and confrontation, he added, have "unbearable consequences for both sides." But he went on to say that America and China had to disabuse each other of the thought that one was going to change the other. It was an interesting and unusual line for the brief, public part of the session. Xi was essentially telling the Americans what they already knew: The grand experiment of creating a different China had been tried for thirty years, and it had failed. The tension between the two systems was a permanent feature of the relationship, not a passing fad.

But what was most striking over the next two days, as Xi made his way from event to event in San Francisco, where the annual Asia-Pacific Economic Cooperation summit was under way, was the subtle but noticeable shift in the power dynamic.

For the first time in years, a Chinese leader desperately needed a few things from the United States. After reporters were ushered out of the room, Xi complained bitterly about the chip and chipmaking export bans that had, at least temporarily, crimped Beijing's ability to make the most advanced semiconductors and the artificial intelligence breakthroughs they enable. He repeated his usual talking points about Taiwan but added a worry that the next president elected on the island could press for independence and force Beijing's hand. "You could see what worried him," one of the Americans in the room told me the next day. "He is all about control, but he made no effort to hide it."

There was another interesting moment when it came to discussing election interference. Biden told Xi that the United States would be looking for any signs that Beijing was interfering in the Taiwan elections, an exchange the United States told reporters about when the meeting was over. But the conversation continued with an exchange that they did not mention: Biden warned as well against interfering in the coming 2024 presidential election. "It was a marker," one of the participants said. "Nothing more." Xi kept his silence. But he must have concluded that this ranked among Biden's biggest worries.

The formal agreements announced that day were modest. Military-to-military communications would resume, Xi promised, and several times he told Biden that if there was ever a problem he should just pick up the phone. ("As if it happens that way," one of Biden's top aides said, rolling his eyes.) There was an agreement on cracking down on fentanyl precursors, as Xi had discussed with Chuck Schumer and his Senate delegation. A working group was set up to discuss the dangers of AI—everything from the risk that it could be used to create biological weapons to the need to make sure that humans, not machines, make the decisions about when to launch nuclear weapons.

There was no talk of America's inevitable decline or China's unstoppable rise. When Xi headed into San Francisco for a reception and dinner with the likes of Tim Cook and Elon Musk, there were no lectures about the superiority of the Chinese system or how American firms would have to adapt themselves to capitalism with Chinese characteristics. Xi found himself in the odd position of needing to sell China as a good place to do business—something no Chinese leader for the previous thirty years had had to do. He was, in essence, asking American business to come back, to invest and build factories and hire Chinese workers. But he did so without promising an end to the arbitrary arrests of their Chinese corporate leadership for ill-defined violations of the national security laws. There was no promise to end the harassment and technology theft making U.S. businesses flee. He avoided talking about property-value collapses or bankruptcies or the coming labor shortages. Or the new national security law, which any company could potentially violate by gathering ordinary economic data.

"Over the next decades we're going to put points on the board, and the Chinese are, too," Jake Sullivan said as he was preparing for the meeting. His message was clear: Americans were going to have to learn how to handle it when the Chinese surge ahead and not conclude that every minor loss is an existential defeat. That would become the new reality.

EPILOGUE

This is not the world we wanted, or were trying to shape, after the
Cold War.

Secretary of State Antony J. Blinken, February 2023

THERE IS RARELY a clean start to a new geopolitical era.
The transition under way today, messy to its core, is no exception. For the past fifteen years, the leaders of the world's greatest powers repeatedly warned of the perils of slipping back into Cold War habits. The post–Cold War era, named for what it wasn't, was marked by such exponential wealth production and technological progress that no one could imagine reverting to a pre-networked, preglobalized age. The key to keeping it going was cooperation among the major nations that benefited most. So whenever they seemed to row in the same direction—agreeing to slow climate change or limit the spread of nuclear weapons or contain viruses—each stroke was celebrated.

Yet instead of becoming more frequent, these bursts of collaboration grew increasingly fleeting. And it took longer than it should have for Washington to realize what that decline portended. Trump's 2017 national security strategy was a first attempt to refocus the nation on great power competition; Biden's conclusion in 2022 that "the post–Cold War era is definitively over" was an effort to thrust the country into the new reality. Yet he stopped short of offering a vision of what this new era might look like. Perhaps that was wise: It was *terra nova,* akin to what faced European mapmakers of the seventeenth century, who resorted to drawing pictures of familiar animals in the interior of the "New World" because they didn't know what was there but couldn't quite admit it.

The outlines of this new era are slowly beginning to take shape. Globalization is out; self-reliance and control of a nation's own supply chains are in. Nationalism is back in vogue, and so are the strongmen who preach it. North Korea and Iran are now military suppliers to Russia and increasingly in alignment with China. The partnership that Xi and Putin celebrated at the opening of the Olympics is stronger than at any point since the Korean War. Putin's threat to deploy battlefield nuclear weapons to deter other countries from aiding Ukraine risks inspiring other nuclear-armed autocrats. Trench warfare is back in Europe—though soldiers now command drones and conduct cyberattacks from their foxholes. Acts of mass terror never truly ceased, but today they are staged in part to create viral, gruesome images in hopes that the attacks—and the retaliation sure to follow—will shape the sympathies of a global audience. Iran's many proxies—Hezbollah and the Houthis, among a long list—have discovered that the way to seize the world's attention, and establish credibility, is to threaten the West's supply lines of oil and goods, and draw it into a conflict with the "Axis of Resistance."

These are the contours of the new cold wars: a combustible mix of simultaneous, high-stakes conflicts nested inside each other. They form the foundations of an era that will almost certainly outlive the current septuagenarian and octogenarian leaders of China, Russia, and the United States—and may indeed prove a near-permanent condition for the next several decades.

Yet it would be a grave mistake to think that we are simply replaying the confrontations of the twentieth century, or that the restraints that worked in the 1960s and 1970s will apply in the 2020s and 2030s. As that *s* in *New Cold Wars* suggests, the addition of new players, acting sometimes independently and sometimes in tandem, makes the current era far more complex to manage than the old one. While history offers some guidance, anyone who is looking to solve the current geopolitical conundrum by trying to force new puzzle pieces into a seemingly familiar picture will be frustrated.

The original Cold War, for all its nuclear terrors, followed some predictable cadences. After a series of horrifying close calls, the major states converged on a vague set of red lines and largely hewed to them—patting themselves on the back for avoiding Armageddon even as millions were wounded or perished in proxy wars around the globe. And that Cold War famously ended with one of the contestants collapsing of its own dysfunction. Today, China does not appear at risk of that fate—quite the contrary. And for all of Putin's troubles at home, his decision to bind Russia more closely to China and Iran has given him both access to technology he badly needs and a degree of staying power. After two years of sanctions, and despite the cracks in his regime made evident by the Prigozhin uprising, there are few signs that he is truly imperiled.

Technology has both complicated and accelerated the struggle on all sides. The rapid integration of artificial intelligence into battlefield operations and decision-making could easily accelerate minor conflicts into larger conflagrations before humans have a chance to reconsider. Yet there may be no turning back: As military leaders assess Russia's and China's experiments with autonomous weapons, it is becoming an article of faith in the Pentagon that anyone who insists on human decision-making risks losing the next conflict in its opening moments.

There are dangers beyond combat operations: AI is making it even easier for determined adversaries to spread disinformation and undermine elections in one another's societies. It can facilitate Chinese-style mass surveillance, enabling autocrats to track and hunt down dissidents. It is already speeding ransomware attacks of the kind that brought down Colonial Pipeline, as well as helping defenders identify vulnerabilities and patch their networks. But, mostly, it will act as an accelerant.

Robert Gates, the former CIA director and the defense secretary under presidents Bush and Obama, captured this moment in stark terms: "The United States now confronts graver threats to its security than it has in decades," he wrote in the fall of 2023. "Never before has it faced four allied antagonists at the same time—Russia, China, North Korea, and Iran—whose collective nuclear arsenal could within a few years be nearly double the size of its own. Not since the Korean War has the United States had to contend with powerful military rivals in both Europe and Asia. And no one alive can remember a time when an adversary had as much economic, scientific, technological, and military power as China has today."

With luck, Gates's sense of imminent threat will prove exaggerated; Washington's rivals have their own vulnerabilities, and they deeply distrust one another. Each confronts tremendous, if quite different, economic troubles at home, exacerbated by American-led sanctions and export controls.

Yet from the Ukraine invasion to the serial confrontations in the Pacific to the outbreak of new conflicts in the Middle East, America is confronting an era of frequent, barely managed flashpoints. And each incident is made more fraught by the realization that direct superpower conflict is just one miscalculation, one missile strike, or one devastating cyberattack away.

DURING THE COLD WAR, it was an article of faith that America would lead the Western bloc. The political debates circled around the question of how to best fulfill that role.

From Truman to Eisenhower, Kennedy to Johnson, Nixon, Ford, Carter, Reagan, and George H. W. Bush, Washington believed that Americans were better off with the United States in an active international role: setting the rules, promoting democracy, and keeping the peace.

Yet in the Cold War's wake, that fundamental bipartisan consensus, once so central to America's long-term strategy, was incrementally eroded. Today it has been shredded: Donald Trump's presidency was both a symptom of the xenophobic, isolationist instinct that episodically surfaces in the American national psyche and a catalyst to drive it forward. Of course, America's inward turn isn't limited to Republicans, or even the fringes of the political spectrum. Progressives have long made the case that the American Century has been far from an unalloyed good for humanity, starting with the wreckage U.S. forces left in their wake from Vietnam to Iraq. Selfish economic or political interests have frequently been sold as public goods. The rule of international law and the importance of global norms have been invoked selectively, justifying the overthrow of democratically elected leaders, the use of torture in the name of preventing another 9/11, and the launch of kinetic and cyber operations that, if directed at the United States, would have been described as acts of war.

That tainted history helps explain why Obama was so reluctant to intervene, even for the most humanitarian causes. "We dropped more ordnance on Cambodia and Laos [during the Vietnam War] than on Europe in World War II," he told Jeffrey Goldberg of *The Atlantic* in 2016, adding that "all we left behind was chaos, slaughter, and authoritarian governments that finally, over time, have emerged from that hell." By 2020, just about the only thing that Donald Trump and Joe Biden agreed on was the need to get out of Afghanistan, even if they claimed very different motivations: Trump to focus on building walls at home, Biden to focus on China.

Months later, the Russian invasion of Ukraine posed the ultimate test of Biden's instinct that if the United States did not intervene, no one would. He had no treaty obligation to come to Ukraine's defense. Yet the invasion offended his faith in one of the greatest principles of the post–World War II order: that the world should not tolerate, or recognize, the use of force to redraw borders. Biden declared adamantly that the United States would give Ukraine everything it needed—except for American troops. And he created a new playbook for how to support a threatened democracy that was not a NATO ally.

But the results were mixed, at best. For roughly 6 percent of the American defense budget, the United States exposed the rot at the core of the Russian military and learned—on the battlefield and in cyberspace—how to exploit the vulnerabilities of one of its chief adversaries. U.S. intelligence estimates reported that Putin's forces had been battered by more than three hundred thousand casualties. More important, Ukraine had held its own. Yet for all its successes, it appeared to have little prospect of driving Russia completely out of its territory any time soon. After two years of war, Putin's military was finally beginning to make good use of technologies it had invested in for years, starting with electronic warfare. More strikingly, he turned sanctions evasion into an art form, and then into a profitable enterprise, by seizing the assets of fleeing Western companies and generating over a billion dollars to finance the war by taxing the firms as they left. He used the money to pour fresh troops, swarms of drones, and new missile batteries into the fight. Stalemate, it was clear, favored the Russians, and so, at least publicly, Putin expressed no rush to head to the negotiating table. "Peace will come when we achieve our goals," he proclaimed in late 2023. Privately, he was sending signals that he was open to discussing a cease-fire, but only if it froze existing battle lines—meaning Ukraine would have to cede, at least for now, control over roughly 20 percent of its territory.

For the time being, Putin's overture was being rebuffed—not least because Western officials feared it was a feint and he was looking for a pause that would enable him to rebuild a shattered military. But it was becoming increasingly apparent that a negotiated solution was all but inevitable, not only because of the stalemate but because cracks were appearing in America's commitment. As so often happens in wars that open with bursts of remarkable heroism followed by calls for total victory, the grim realities of prosecuting a long war were setting in. As 2023 drew to a close, the argument that Biden had deployed so effectively in early 2022—"If Putin takes Ukraine he won't stop there"—was losing its punch. Republicans in Congress were refusing to authorize new spending for Kyiv, vowing not to relent until the White House cracked down on immigration.*

And so, when Zelensky returned to Washington two weeks before Christmas 2023 to plead for more aid, he found that even his biggest supporters now feared a harsh moment of truth was approaching for Ukraine. Zelensky could try to stick to his political goal—winning back all of Ukraine's occupied lands, Crimea included—or he could look for a negotiated settlement. Both options seemed too painful to contemplate. The first guaranteed more bloodshed, at a moment when Biden's promise of "whatever it takes" had quietly transformed into "as long as we can." The second option, which Zelensky dismissed as "insane," meant rewarding Putin for his aggression. As the Russians stepped up their missile and drone attacks on Kyiv and other key Ukrainian cities in the last days of 2023, Zelensky had increasingly sharp words for the Westerners who, he thought, were deluded if they believed that Europe's future wasn't tied to Ukraine's. "Putin feels weakness like an animal, because he is an animal," he said at year's end. "He senses blood, he

---

* There were, of course, reasonable questions about Ukraine's strategy, Zelensky's reliance on martial law, and even whether the administration was overstating its case when it argued that if Putin was victorious in Ukraine, it would inspire Xi to move against Taiwan. But those questions were not what Congress was discussing.

senses his strength. And he will eat you for dinner with all your EU, NATO, freedom, and democracy."

Biden and his team were sympathetic; it was, after all, their own argument being broadcast back to Washington, with all its echoes of the domino theory that had been used to justify America's involvement in Vietnam. But they found themselves confronted with accusations that America's role in the conflict—one that it had entered into for the clearest of moral imperatives—looked increasingly like it was drawn from one of the worst traditions of the old Cold War: a classic proxy war. "Ukraine has become a battlefield now for America and America's own future," warned the Russia scholar Fiona Hill at the end of 2023. "For Putin, Ukraine is a proxy war against the United States, to remove the United States from the world stage."

Biden's aides made a good case for why this war was more analogous to America's support for Britain before World War II than it was to a Cold War maneuver. Indeed, all the alternatives if Washington and its allies stood aside appeared far worse. The United States' goal, they insisted, was simply to contain the war, to help Ukraine remain independent, and to ensure Putin's "strategic defeat."

The dispute among the allies is how to accomplish that objective. Ukraine's future will only be cemented when it enters the European Union and when the United States and Germany, among other members of the alliance, drop their objections to full NATO membership. The model here—of a viable democracy protected by its alliances—is clear. It is the Korean peninsula, where an armistice has kept an imperfect peace for decades, long enough for the South to overcome a history of corruption and authoritarianism and to emerge as one of the world's largest economies, a technological powerhouse, and a true democracy. And that would require setting up a reliable system to provide Ukraine with a stable supply of aid and arms to keep it independent for years or decades to come. The harder part could be letting Putin keep what he's already taken in Ukraine. As in Korea, the price is high: rewarding aggression and condemning a portion of the population to live under despotic rule.

Yet joining the Western alliance—somehow, sometime—is not enough to assure Ukraine's future if that alliance is no longer credible. And as I moved between Washington and Europe in early 2024, there was a palpable fear among American allies. Several senior leaders of

NATO countries admitted that they were already beginning to think about how they might respond in a world in which Ukraine lost and Putin, after resetting his forces for several years, attempted to pick off a NATO member. If the U.S. ever pulled out of NATO—or even signaled that it might—"Putin would test the system," one senior European official told me, "and I'm not sure we would be up to the test." It was a chilling thought. This would be the ultimate challenge to the alliance created after 1945. European nations would suddenly question whether they were still protected by America's nuclear deterrent.

Yet Europe's leaders were doing little to prepare their population for this new reality. "Our public grew up hearing that security would come from our collaboration with Russia," one said to me. "Now it will come from our ability to contain Russian power and adventurism." He paused. "And I'm not sure how we do that without the Americans."

AMERICA HAS NEVER faced a competitor like China before, and it shows: Despite a decade of rising fears about Beijing's intentions, the United States is only now seriously reorganizing itself to meet the military, economic, structural, and political challenges posed by the direction Xi Jinping has taken the country. And Biden deserves considerable credit for creating a credible game plan, one that starts by rebuilding American competitiveness at home.

But the rationale for that strategy has been poorly communicated. Biden's own cabinet members do not share a common understanding of what "engagement" with China means. While much of the strategy focuses on America's national security interests, the Trump-era tariffs and some investment bans ooze pure economic protectionism. And while Biden has said repeatedly that the United States will defend Taiwan—including the possibility of sending American troops—there are few ongoing efforts to convey to the American people the catastrophic loss of life that conflict would likely entail.

In the next few years, three immediate risks seem likely to dominate America's dealings with Xi's government. The first is that a future U.S. administration will abandon our current technology strategy, despite early signs that it is beginning to work. So far, the aggressive mix of investment in developing key technologies at home with increasing control of sensitive exports to Chinese firms has prompted Xi Jinping's strongest protests. The danger is not simply a reversal of the strategy, but a failure to drive it further forward.

America's effort to reclaim a slice of chip manufacturing offers the starkest example. Passing the CHIPS act was an important first step. But many in Congress viewed the $52 billion in taxpayer spending on new production as a one-time fix, rather than as a down payment on a long-term investment in national security. As the 2024 campaign heated up, some politicians returned to the old caricature of the government "picking winners" rather than letting the free market generate innovation. This is a false choice: When it comes to critical technology that has extraordinary national security implications, government investment is hardly new. The U.S. government spent billions of dollars to learn how to get satellites aloft—and that investment not only helped send astronauts to the moon in the 1960s, it paved the way for Starlink half a century later. Along the way, the country blew up a lot of missiles and rockets, and several manned space missions ended in tragedy. There will be failures in chipmaking as well—less dramatic, but very possibly more expensive.

The second risk is that Washington could go too far with its sanctions and tariffs, and thereby play right into Xi's argument that America's real goal is "containment, encirclement, and suppression." Not every Chinese advance is a Sputnik moment. When China masters the technology to manufacture chips with three-nanometer circuits or celebrates a leap in artificial intelligence or space launches, there will be calls to react and, most likely, overreact. The better approach, striking a balance, requires understanding which technological advantages Americans need to protect and which are less critical to our safety. Much of the money America once spent on missiles and fighter aircraft may well be better directed now to working on artificial intelligence techniques that help preserve the independence of our elections or halt crippling cyberattacks on our infrastructure. Protecting the information space at home may be more important than protecting the airspace around Mischief Reef.

The third risk is that, through some combination of America's overheated rhetoric and its enthusiasm for new sanctions, America and its allies unintentionally drive Russia and China closer together. Washington already has a severe case of anti-China animus, bordering on unchecked xenophobia. As elections approach, there is no easier political target than the Chinese Communist Party. At the end of 2023, there was talk among some in Congress that the combination of Russia and China, along with Iran, constituted an "axis of evil" that America needed to "deal with." (It was never made clear what "deal with" meant, exactly.) What's missing in that overheated debate is discussion of a real strategy for driving a wedge in the emerging partnership between Beijing and Moscow. That will require a combination of cunning and diplomatic nuance: an updated and improved version of what Kissinger and Nixon pulled off half a century ago by focusing American diplomatic efforts to exploit existing differences and natural tensions between the two nations.

AS BIDEN ENTERED the last year of his term, he and his aides expressed some hope that China's economic troubles—its debt overhang and the stagnation of its growth—would buy some time to stabilize the relationship and delay any Chinese plans to act against Taiwan. Xi's decision during the San Francisco summit to drop the wolf-warrior show and cajole American investors into returning to China marked the first time in decades that a Chinese leader had entered a summit meeting knowing that he was playing a weak hand. He seemed increasingly desperate for American help.

But to Biden's team, this seemed more of a tactical shift than any fundamental rewriting of Xi's goals. Once China got past its economic downturn, Xi would focus once again on pushing the United States out of the region. "Xi has told us his view of what China needs to do in the next twenty-five years," one of those senior officials told me. "We should, at a minimum, listen to him."

For the next decade, the competition for supremacy will take place in many arenas, but three interlocking arms races will command the most attention: nuclear weapons, space, and artificial intelligence. All rely, at their core, on who can produce the most potent next-generation chips, which explains the struggle for semiconductor supremacy under way. But each race requires a different strategy, a different mindset, and different kinds of investment.

The revived nuclear arms race is Xi's personal project; no Chinese leader since Mao has invested so heavily in the country's arsenal. He has more than doubled China's stock of weapons, to five hundred warheads, and Chinese officials have told their American counterparts they have no interest in seriously discussing arms control until China reaches rough parity with the United States and Russia. While Xi's nuclear strategy is wrapped in secrecy, there seems little doubt that he wants a nuclear arsenal large enough to assure he can keep the United States at bay while simultaneously intimidating Taiwan. It is a lesson, American and Asian intelligence officials suspect, driven home by Putin's nuclear threats to Ukraine.

Predictably, there are already calls in Washington to match China's buildup, in hopes of keeping Beijing from ever reaching parity. That seems like a waste of scarce resources. One lasting lesson of the Cold War is that such buildups rarely make us safer. Even if China ends up with 1,500 weapons in a decade—the Pentagon's current estimate—Washington's capability to deter a strike would not be impaired. It seems far more sensible to launch swarms of communications and surveillance satellites to assure that the U.S. cannot be blinded in space. That would provide more confidence that the American nuclear arsenal could not be destroyed by an adversary's first strike. Resiliency is more important than sheer numbers.

Assuring the survivability of America's nuclear force will also require leaning into two other races—space and cyberspace—where America no longer enjoys a long lead. Our vulnerabilities in both are profound.

One of the most vivid lessons of the war in Ukraine is that moving the country's government operations to the cloud was worthless without a hard-to-jam communications network that kept the country running; that was Starlink, with its network of nearly five thousand satellites. China's plan for a future conflict with the United States, if it comes to that, is to blind American forces, from our aircraft carrier groups to our nuclear submarines. Even now, China is inserting code into American power and water supply systems, presumably to slow a response if a Taiwan crisis erupts.

Perhaps in no technology will the competition be fiercer—or more worrisome—than artificial intelligence. For years, the United States feared that billions of dollars in Chinese investment were putting Beijing ahead, and that it would use its advantages in quantum computing to decrypt American secrets and run circles around slower-moving American defenses, in both the military and corporate spheres. The ascent of programs like ChatGPT and other examples of generative artificial intelligence gives the U.S. opportunity to win back lost ground.

Unlike in the early days of the nuclear age, today almost all the talent needed to maintain the United States' edge is in the private sector. Marshaling that talent—and focusing companies on the national security implications of their work—will not be easy. And the combined public and private investments required will be on a scale not seen since the U.S. government spurred the creation of highways across the country or launched the space program. Biden made some headway by laying out a first, tentative plan to regulate the technology, recognizing early on that there are huge risks for abuse. For the next president, confronting the risks of AI will not be an episodic problem; it will almost certainly be the subject matter of every President's Daily Brief.

WHEN HENRY KISSINGER, in his last years, was asked about the U.S.-China relationship, he compared it to an alpine military campaign. "We are still in the foothills of a Cold War," he said in a Bloomberg Forum.

Kissinger viewed himself as the last guardian of Washington's relationship with Beijing, and he meant the analogy as a hopeful statement. There was still time, he suggested, for the United States and China to learn to listen to each other, understand the other's interests, and avoid a disaster. But he grew steadily more pessimistic with the years. By 2020, he claimed the world was in "the mountain passes" of the new cold war. By 2021, it was "through the mountain pass, on a precipice." Still, months before he died, as Xi celebrated Kissinger's hundredth birthday, the American diplomat remained insistent there were plenty of off-ramps and that conflict could be avoided.

It could be a decade, maybe more, before we know if he was right. But even Kissinger, the man who thought it was the destiny of the United States to shape the world order, conceded by the end of his life that the era in which the United States unilaterally set the rules and laid the foundation for the global order had come to an end.

In fact, that era had been winding down for more than twenty years. The bitter American experience in Afghanistan and Iraq seemed to underscore the dangers of imperial overreach. When Washington set out to

build democracies or shape the world to suit its interests, it rarely succeeded. Yet the alternatives all seemed worse. China, for all its power
and progress, has proven itself ill-suited: It has few natural allies, and its
efforts to buy the loyalties of nations around the world have been too
heavy-handed, too openly exploitative. Russia has proven itself an angry
disruptor, seemingly barely capable of reestablishing its long-ago empire, much less expanding its influence.

Although it is seldom heard in domestic arguments about what ails
the country, the United States enters this next era—the struggle to define
"what comes next"—with more advantages than any other single player.
First and foremost is the multiplying force of America's vast network of
allies, a lesson the world learned as the West came together to rally behind Ukraine. That was a reminder that the arc of American power bends
toward collaboration with allies, the ultimate force multiplier ever since
Lafayette came to help fight off the British. That list of partners has
grown in recent years. Today it includes nations seeking refuge from
China's wrath or wary of Russia's threats. In contrast, China and Russia
have few real allies, just partners of convenience, starting with each other.

America remains a super-magnet among nations. There is a reason
that the world's brightest minds still desperately want to come to
American campuses, to Silicon Valley, to the country known for a
startup culture. Though the inflow was temporarily halted by the pandemic, students around the world—aspiring Chinese scientists, Russians escaping draft notices for a pointless war, aspiring business leaders
from India and Africa—are still drawn to the United States, despite its
well-advertised troubles. The combined lure of an open society, the rule
of law, technological prowess, and the opportunity to innovate remains
the core of what Joseph Nye called American "soft power."

Yet as the economic and technological gap between the United States
and its chief competitors—especially China—diminishes, our political
system has not kept up. Worried about yet another argument over immigration, the United States passed up the chance to deliver a truly devastating blow to Putin by inviting a young generation of Russia's most
promising entrepreneurs and brightest minds to emigrate to our shores
and build the next Google. It was an example of how the bitter, winner-
take-all turn in domestic political dialogue has, more than at any other
time in recent history, taken a toll on America's luster and its standing.

We are losing our reputation as a generous nation: The images of desperate Afghans clinging to the wheel wells of the last American planes out of Kabul or of migrant children being separated from their parents at the southern border have done lasting damage. And America's unwillingness to put explicit conditions on how Israel uses American-made weapons to kill Palestinian civilians—in what President Biden himself called "indiscriminate bombing"—made stark, for so many in the Global South, the hypocrisy of an America that often seems to care more about the fate of white Europeans. The point was not lost on even the closest of American allies in the Arab world.

The choices Americans make in the next few years will determine if we are willing to engage in reinvigorating an international order that will, by necessity, be far less Washington-centric than the one that took shape after 1945. There has always been a part of the population that just wants to pretend that what happens beyond our borders can be walled off, physically or metaphorically. Much of the Republican Party, in Trump's thrall, has plunged into the 2024 election cycle as if history mattered little, or not at all. "Trump whiplashes between a wish to project U.S. power abroad and isolationism," Kori Schake, a former Republican defense official, wrote as the campaign got under way. "Recently, he has vowed to withdraw from NATO, end imports of Chinese goods, deploy the U.S. military onto American streets to fight crime and deport immigrants, and drive out 'warmongers' and 'globalists' from the U.S. government."

At the same time, Trump and his adherents still express the belief that America's military might and financial influence give it the power to force nations—even close allies—to bend to Washington's will whenever it suits the president's needs. It is a certainty grounded in raw power, not the power of alliances. Getting past both fantasies will require political and generational change, but it seems worth the try—especially since the only looming alternative to the existing global order is a far more repressive system being designed largely to serve China's interests, and Russia's.

A good start is to recognize that nations around the world are not going to simply follow signals from Washington, Moscow, or Beijing. "The weight of the hedging middle is growing economically, politically, and militarily," Bill Burns noted in the summer of 2023. From the Solomon Islands to India, from South Africa to Brazil, countries are more open about their plans to play off larger powers against each other and navigate a middle pathway. They see no need to sign up with one super-power or another, insisting on a greater say in how the world runs: an echo, though far more powerful today, of the Non-Aligned Movement's contention that it would not be forced into choosing between two spheres of influence during the old Cold War. These voices are amplified by the ubiquity of cellphone videos that can reveal a massacre in Bucha, slaughtered teenagers in southern Israel, or a grieving family in Gaza, all the while connecting like-minded activists with a tap on a screen. In so many corners of the world, people are ignoring the daily scorecard of the new cold wars—whether China is developing the fastest chip, whether Russia is diverting more resources to its battered military, whether the U.S. is engaging allies or shunning them—in favor of their own local interests.

"Superimposed on great power competition are a series of intercon-nected transnational challenges that are on steroids," Blinken said to me in early 2023, ticking off a familiar list. For all the wealth that was built over the past decade, the number of refugees and internally dis-placed people soared. Famine was on the rise, exacerbated by the war in Ukraine and by renewed conflict in the Middle East that targeted major shipping channels. The pace of environmental devastation was picking up—reinforcing the sense that the effects of climate change had arrived faster than most scientists had predicted. The first casualty of the new cold wars is the hope that once-fierce rivals would make good on their promises to tackle these challenges together, out of na-tional self-interest.

NAVIGATING THIS NEW period will be especially fraught. Three major powers—and dozens of smaller ones—maneuvering for simultaneous advantage create far more potential for conflict, both accidental and deliberate, than the world has confronted before. Ours is an era that has echoes of the early days of the Cold War—and of the period of open great power competition that preceded the First World War—and car-ries with it all the fears of escalation that underpinned that age and the devastation that followed.

For all the present risks, it is worth remembering that one of the most remarkable and little-discussed accomplishments of the old Cold War was that the great powers never escalated their differences into a direct conflict. That is an eight-decade-long streak we cannot afford to break.

ACKNOWLEDGMENTS

NEW COLD WARS reflects years of reporting, some dating back to American engagements with Russia and China that I covered as a young foreign correspondent, and much of it drawn from my thirty years in the Washington bureau of *The New York Times.* Yet this book includes events that few could have imagined when I started planning its contours during the 2020 election season—long before it seemed possible that Russia would seek to take all of Ukraine, or that relations with China would deteriorate so quickly that avoiding a conflict between the world's most powerful nations seemed the most urgent item on the American national security agenda. As the concepts behind *New Cold Wars* hardened, the book grew in scope, ambition, and complexity. So too has my indebtedness to many colleagues, family, friends, assistants, and sources for their help and insights.

I begin my thanks with the remarkable Mary K. Brooks, who brought her creativity, insights, reporting skills, and graceful writing to every part of this project. When she was still a student at Harvard, Mary signed on to work on *The Perfect Weapon* and threw herself into some of the hardest questions about the role of cyber in modern competition between states. She went on to become the associate producer of the HBO version of that book, and then another documentary, *Year One,* examining President Biden's first year in office. She is a natural reporter and an incisive analyst, and as we traveled the world trying to understand the new shape of superpower competition, she contributed wisdom beyond her years. Her expert touch is on every page.

Michelle Kurilla joined our project in 2022 and devoted endless hours to research, fact-checking, and rewriting. We benefited greatly from her talents and her good judgment as she sorted fact from spin. Chris Li almost single-handedly navigated us through Taiwan—lending us his impeccable translation skills but also his remarkable familiarity with the island's politics, institutions, and leadership. Stephen Stamas, who joined as our summer intern and stayed on, delved into the hardest research questions with skill and enthusiasm.

Sophie Faaborg-Anderson, a graduate student at the Harvard Kennedy School, delved into hypersonics and supported research on other critical technologies. Ariel S. contributed valuable research as well.

The Crown division of Penguin Random House has published all of my books, and I am lucky to have Kevin Doughten as a brilliant editor, a dear friend, and a solver of every publishing challenge. Kevin edited *The Perfect Weapon,* and there is no better editor in the country at the intersection of technology and national security. He was in on this book's conception, helped define the historical era it would cover, and constantly pressed me for deeper reporting, all while staying focused on telling the stories at the center of some of the hardest issues in American national security. His questions and insights never stopped, even while we paddled kayaks in Vermont.

Gillian Blake, Crown's publisher, grabbed hold of this project and has nurtured it with her infectious enthusiasm and careful eye. David Drake, Crown's president, has backed every one of my books, along with Annsley Rosner. My thanks to Amy Li, Evan Camfield, Martin Schneider, Sally Franklin, Elizabeth Rendfleisch, Christopher Brand, Stacey Stein, Dyana Messina, and Julie Cepler, who made the magic of publishing come together.

Michael Carlisle of Inkwell Management has been my agent, consigliere, and wise friend for three decades, and he made this book happen. Jon Liebman, of Brillstein Entertainment Partners, helped turn our first thinking about this book into *Year One,* with its foundational interviews across the Biden administration. And my partner in that documentary, John Maggio, who directed that film and *The Perfect Weapon,* showed me you could cover the hardest stories in the world, tell vivid stories, and still keep laughing.

The reporting in this book would not have been possible without the backing of *The New York Times*, an institution with a role at the core of American democracy that is more vital today, I believe, than at any point since its founding in 1851. Beginning with my grandparents, Elliott and Eleanor Sanger, members of the Sanger family have worked at the *Times,* in different capacities, for nearly eighty years. I joined just a few months after graduating from college in 1982, and in the forty-one years since I have been fortunate to hold a press pass to the world, with the freedom to cover political convulsions, technological revolutions, and global realignments. Few other news organizations in the world could make that possible, and I am deeply grateful to A. G. Sulzberger—the *Times*'s innovative publisher—and acutely aware of the responsibility for independent reporting that he has championed.

Joe Kahn, an extraordinary foreign and Washington correspondent and now our executive editor, and his predecessor, Dean Baquet, gave me the leave to complete this book. I thank them for their patience and their friendship. Elisabeth Bumiller, our stellar Washington bureau chief and a colleague from my Tokyo days, gave me time and space—but never hesitated to call when she knew that book work needed to be set aside to focus on the crisis of the day. Dick Stevenson, a colleague of nearly forty years, has a depth of understanding of how the world operates that few other editors can match and helped hone my reporting. Our two managing editors, Marc Lacey and Carolyn Ryan, were always sources of encouragement, while Michael Slackman and Phil Pan provided excellent insight in this strange post-post–Cold War moment. And Matt Purdy, who oversees our most ambitious journalism, helped me refine my thinking about how to tell the geopolitical story of our times.

There is nothing like our White House team—brilliant reporters, witty, collegial, and generous. My colleagues Peter Baker, Michael Shear, Zolan Kanno-Youngs, Erica Green, and Katie Rogers are also the best traveling companions one could find. They helped me think through the puzzles of this era while we covered the president's trips to Jerusalem and Jeddah, Warsaw and Hiroshima, Vilnius and San Francisco. The patient, insightful editing of Elizabeth Kennedy, a foreign correspondent to her core, extracts the best from her reporters, pushing for more and deeper reporting. I thank them all for their friendship.

The *Times*'s national security team is the best in the business, and the list of colleagues who aided me is too long to print. But Eric Schmitt,

Julian Barnes, Edward Wong, Michael Crowley, Eric Lipton, Mark Mazzetti, and Helene Cooper were always generous with insights and sources. The *Times*'s foreign desk, of which I am an alumnus, is unparalleled, and Steve Erlanger, Anton Troianovski, Andrew Kramer, Valerie Hopkins, Greg Winter, Adrienne Carter, and Doug Schorzman were among many who offered advice and reporting. Bill Broad, my partner in so many endeavors for forty years, and Chris Buckley, one of our premier China correspondents, helped me delve into the new nuclear age.

My other professional home is Harvard, at the Kennedy School of Government's Belfer Center for Science and International Affairs, where I have served as an adjunct lecturer and senior fellow for many years. My thanks to Graham Allison and Derek Reveron, my co-teachers in "Central Challenges in American National Security, Strategy, and the Press," the case-study course that has produced many American leaders in the national security arena. Our students challenged my preconceptions and helped me see the world anew. We all miss the late Ashton Carter, a former defense secretary and director of the center, as well as an inspiration. Meghan O'Sullivan, Belfer's current director, was a font of insight and encouragement. Joe Nye, who along with Graham trained me decades ago in this subject matter, challenged some of my thinking about cold wars, often while we pulled trout and salmon out of rivers across North America. They did a better job teaching me how to think about national security than how to cast. The dean of the Kennedy School, Douglas Elmendorf, would stop by and engage on the issues of the book and the school. My thanks also go to the staff of Belfer—especially Simone O'Hanlon, Arissa Shang, and Mike Miner.

This book would not have been completed save for the Woodrow Wilson International Center for Scholars, which offered Mary Brooks and me a place to get this work done. No one was more central to this effort than Robert Litwak, who directs the international studies program and stopped by daily to discuss what we were learning and helped capture it on the page. My thanks to him and to Mark Green, the president of the center.

Needless to say, none of my books would have been possible without the love and remarkable editing eye of my wife, Sherill, who throws herself 100 percent into everything she does—and, in her warm and wonderful way, makes everyone in the book process part of the family. I am even more astounded by her now than I was when I first met her in 1978, during our freshman year at Harvard. Our sons, Andrew and Ned, now launched on their own careers, are not only sources of love and inspiration; they asked the questions at the core of the book. And we held together through a lot of loss as this book was being written. Each day we feel the absence of my mother and father, Joan and Kenneth Sanger, my sister Ellin, and her husband Mort. Their memory is a blessing.

This is a work of current history, meaning that parts will be lasting and parts will be overtaken by events, and judgments made along the way will be, by necessity, temporary and unsettled. It would be a lot easier to write long-ago history. But the benefit of trying to capture the precariousness of today's conflicts is that we still have a chance to shape these events and to keep the new Cold Wars from devolving into something far worse. Nonetheless, errors of fact and interpretation are, needless to say, mine.

A NOTE ON SOURCES

NEW COLD WARS is based on reporting about America's role in the world that dates back to my years as a *New York Times* foreign correspondent and bureau chief in Asia more than thirty years ago. But it relies primarily on reporting conducted since I arrived in Washington in 1994 and focuses intensively on the first three years of the Biden administration. As the endnotes indicate, I drew heavily on my reporting as a *Times* White House correspondent, including many stories written with *Times* colleagues. I also made selective use of internal cables and memoranda that have leaked out of the government during that time.

The bulk of the most recent reporting in this book was gathered through interviews with senior administration officials in the Obama, Trump, and Biden White Houses and dozens of their deputies and assistants. Almost every senior member of President Biden's national security team sat down to talk about their experiences, several of them repeatedly. Most insisted on speaking on background, meaning that they could not be quoted by name unless they specifically approved. But most did ultimately place many of those comments on the record. In other cases, I have relied on on-the-record statements and interviews, including for the HBO documentary *Year One,* broadcast in 2022, an account of President Biden's first year in national security decision-making.

Naturally, the level of their candor in these conversations varied, as it always does in reporting exercises like this, when interviewees are mindful that the president is still in office and up for reelection.

Readers are rightly suspicious of anonymous sources. So am I. But decades of reporting have driven home to me that in discussions of sensitive intelligence operations, defense matters, or diplomatic negotiations, there often is no other way to conduct a useful conversation. Using the standards employed at the *Times* and in consultation with editors, I withheld a handful of details that government officials were concerned could jeopardize ongoing intelligence or defense operations.

Endnotes are reserved for quotations, specific numbers, original reporting, and information that is non-obvious.

NOTES

ix   **"There are changes happening":** As quoted in Alexander Gabuev, "What's Really Going on Between Russia and China," *Foreign Affairs,* April 12, 2023, www.foreignaffairs.com /united-states/whats-really-going-between-russia-and-china.

PROLOGUE

3   **"The great democracies":** Winston Churchill, *Triumph and Tragedy* (Boston: Houghton Mifflin, 1953).

8   **"partners and friends":** Steven Erlanger and Andrew E. Kramer, "President Zelensky Asks the West to Make No Deals 'Behind Our Back' as the Threat to Ukraine Grows," *The New York Times,* February 19, 2022, www.nytimes.com/2022/02/19/world/europe/russia -backed-rebels-in-ukraine-call-for-taking-up-arms.html.

11   **Burt's team responded quickly:** Tom Burt, "Malware Attacks Targeting Ukraine Government," *Microsoft on the Issues,* January 15, 2022, blogs.microsoft.com/on-the-issues/2022 /01/15/mstic-malware-cyberattacks-ukraine-government/.

17   **"What we may be witnessing":** Francis Fukuyama, "The End of History?" *The National Interest* 16 (Summer 1989).

21   **"This is a battle":** President Joseph R. Biden Jr., "Remarks by President Biden in Press Conference," The White House, March 25, 2021, www.whitehouse.gov/briefing-room /speeches-remarks/2021/03/25/remarks-by-president-biden-in-press-conference/.

22   **"We'll cooperate wherever":** Secretary Antony J. Blinken, "The Administration's Approach to the People's Republic of China," U.S. Department of State, May 26, 2022, www .state.gov/the-administrations-approach-to-the-peoples-republic-of-china/.

22   **"We are trying":** Meet the Press, Sept. 3, 2023, www.nbcnews.com/meet-the-press/meet -press-september-3-2023-n1307124.

26   **"post–Cold War era":** "Biden-Harris Administration's National Security Strategy," The White House, October 12, 2022, www.whitehouse.gov/wp-content/uploads/2022/10 /Biden-Harris-Administrations-National-Security-Strategy-10.2022.pdf.

1. FLOATING PAST THE HERMITAGE

29   **"Who lost Russia?":** William J. Burns, "How the U.S.-Russian Relationship Went Bad," Carnegie Endowment for International Peace, March 8, 2019, carnegieendowment.org /2019/03/08/how-u.s.-russian-relationship-went-bad-pub-78543.

31   **stage-managed signal:** Gerhard Peters and John T. Woolley, "Remarks and a Question-and-Answer Session with Students at St. Petersburg State University in St. Petersburg," The American Presidency Project, UC Santa Barbara, retrieved September 1, 2023, www .presidency.ucsb.edu/documents/remarks-and-question-and-answer-session-with-students -st-petersburg-state-university-st.

32   **"For five centuries"**: Michael Wines, "In Czar Peter's Capital, Putin Is Not as Great," *The New York Times*, May 20, 2002, www.nytimes.com/2002/05/20/world/in-czar-peter-s-capital-putin-is-not-as-great.html.

33   **gas deployed by the police**: Steven Lee Myers, "Hostage Drama in Moscow: Russia Responds; Putin Vows Hunt for Terrorist Cells Around the World," *The New York Times*, October 29, 2002, www.nytimes.com/2002/10/29/world/hostage-drama-moscow-russia-responds-putin-vows-hunt-for-terror-cells-around.html.

33   **"The common enemy"**: Angela Stent and Lilia Shevtsova, "America, Russia, and Europe: A Realignment?" *Survival*, no. 44 (2002), doi.org/10.1080/00396330212331343532.

34   **avoid blaming Bush directly**: Rebecca Leung, "60 Minutes Transcript: Vladimir Putin," CBS News, May 8, 2005, www.cbsnews.com/news/transcript-vladimir-putin/.

34   **disapproved of the Chechen conflict**: Russia Matters, "Did the US Government Support Chechen Separatism?" Harvard Kennedy School Belfer Center for Science and International Affairs, www.russiamatters.org/node/20317.

37   **Americans realized they could reunite Germany:** M. E. Sarotte, *Not One Inch: America, Russia, and the Making of Post–Cold War Stalemate* (New Haven, Conn.: Yale University Press, 2021).

37   **"[It] would be the most"**: George F. Kennan, "A Fateful Error," *The New York Times*, February 5, 1997, www.nytimes.com/1997/02/05/opinion/a-fateful-error.html.

38   **flexed its muscles**: David E. Sanger, "The Nation: Agony of Victory; America Finds It's Lonely at the Top," *The New York Times*, July 18, 1999, www.nytimes.com/1999/07/18/weekinreview/the-nation-agony-of-victory-america-finds-it-s-lonely-at-the-top.html.

39   **the West was making a dangerous mistake:** Steven Lee Myers, "As NATO Finally Arrives on Its Border, Russia Grumbles," *The New York Times*, April 3, 2004, www.nytimes.com/2004/04/03/world/as-nato-finally-arrives-on-its-border-russia-grumbles.html.

39   **"Russia has no concerns"**: "Russia Has No Concerns About the Expansion of NATO from the Standpoint of Ensuring Security, But Russia Will Organize Its Military Policies Accordingly in Connection with NATO Nearing Its Borders, President Vladimir Putin Announced After Talks With the Federal Chancellor of Germany Gerhard Schroeder," President of Russia, April 2, 2004, en.kremlin.ru/events/president/news/30679.

39   **"You Americans"**: William J. Burns, "How the U.S.-Russian Relationship Went Bad," Carnegie Endowment for International Peace, March 8, 2019, carnegieendowment.org/2019/03/08/how-u.s.-russian-relationship-went-bad-pub-78543.

40   **"the wave of so-called"**: Darya Korsunskaya, "Putin Says Russia Must Prevent 'Color Revolution,'" Reuters, November 20, 2014, www.reuters.com/article/us-russia-putin-security/putin-says-russia-must-prevent-color-revolution-idUSKCN0J41J620141120.

41   **"tightly fused"**: Fiona Hill and Clifford G. Gaddy, *Mr. Putin: Operative in the Kremlin*, paperback ed. (Washington, D.C.: Brookings Institution Press, 2015), 389.

41   **Putin called Lenin's dream**: Doug Stanglin, "Vladimir Putin Blames Lenin for Soviet Collapse," *USA Today*, January 21, 2016, www.usatoday.com/story/news/2016/01/21/vladimir-putin-blames-lenin-soviet-collapse/79116132/.

42   **"night and day"**: as quoted in M. E. Sarotte, *Not One Inch* (New Haven, Conn.: Yale University Press, 2021), 20.

42   **"I think Putin is not"**: Peter Baker, "The Seduction of George W. Bush," *Foreign Policy*, November 6, 2013, foreignpolicy.com/2013/11/06/the-seduction-of-george-w-bush/.

44   **"Putin's Russia seemed"**: David Ignatius, "Putin Warned the West 15 Years Ago. Now in Ukraine, He's Poised to Wage War," *The Washington Post*, February 20, 2022, www.washingtonpost.com/opinions/2022/02/20/putin-ukraine-nato-2007-munich-conference/.

44   **"One Cold War was"**: Thom Shanker, "Gates Counters Putin's Words on U.S. Power," *The New York Times*, February 11, 2007, www.nytimes.com/2007/02/11/us/11cnd-gates.html.

46   **"We didn't give them MAPs"**: George W. Bush, *Decision Points* (New York: Penguin Random House, 2011), 431.

46   **"Ukraine is not even"**: Olga Allenova, Elena Geda, and Vladimir Kommersant-Novikov, "NATO Bloc Divided into Blocking Packages," *Kommersant*, April 7, 2008, www.kommersant.ru/doc/877224.

46   **twenty-year lease:** Serhii Plokhy, *The Russo-Ukrainian War* (New York: W. W. Norton & Company, 2023).

46   **option off the table:** Ben Smith, "U.S. Pondered Military Use in Georgia," *Politico,* February 3, 2010, www.politico.com/story/2010/02/us-pondered-military-use-in-georgia -032487.

47   **American imports of Russian oil:** "U.S. Imports from Russia of Crude Oil and Petroleum Products," U.S. Energy Information Administration, retrieved July 31, 2023, www.eia.gov /dnav/pet/hist/LeafHandler.ashx?n=PET&s=MTTIM_NUS-NRS_1&f=M.

47   **"Russia attempts to challenge":** Stephen J. Hadley, Peter D. Feaver, William C. Inboden, and Meghan L. O'Sullivan, eds., *Hand-Off: The Foreign Policy George W. Bush Passed to Barack Obama* (Lanham, Md.: Rowman & Littlefield, 2023), 403–4; Peter Baker, "From George to Barack: A Look at Secret Bush Memos to the Obama Team," *The New York Times,* February 14, 2023, www.nytimes.com/2023/02/14/us/politics/bush-obama-memos.html.

48   **"I'm aware of not only":** Josh Gerstein, "Obama Meets with Vladimir Putin," *Politico,* June 7, 2009, www.politico.com/story/2009/07/obama-meets-with-vladimir-putin-024621.

50   **It was published in mid-2009:** "An Open Letter to the Obama Administration from Central and Eastern European Leaders," as published in Radio Free Europe/Radio Liberty, July 16, 2009, www.rferl.org/a/An_Open_Letter_To_The_Obama_Administration_From _Central_And_Eastern_Europe/1778449.html.

50   **getting to yes:** Peter Baker, "U.S.-Russian Ties Still Fall Short of 'Reset' Goal," *The New York Times,* September 2, 2013, www.nytimes.com/2013/09/03/world/europe/us-russian -ties-still-fall-short-of-reset-goal.html.

51   **"We will have to think":** Miriam Elder, "Vladimir Putin Accuses Hillary Clinton of En- couraging Russian Protests," *The Guardian,* December 8, 2011, www.theguardian.com /world/2011/dec/08/vladimir-putin-hillary-clinton-russia.

51   **won the presidential vote:** David M. Herszenhorn, "Putin Wins, but Opposition Keeps Pressing," *The New York Times,* March 4, 2012, www.nytimes.com/2012/03/05/world /europe/russia-votes-in-presidential-election.html.

2. THE LOST DECADES

53   **"By joining the WTO":** "Full Text of Clinton's Speech on China Trade Bill," March 9, 2000, archive.nytimes.com/www.nytimes.com/library/world/asia/030900clinton-china-text .html.

53   **"Americans have often thought":** Aaron Friedberg, Wang Jisi, J. Stapleton Roy, Thomas Christensen, Patricia Kim, Joseph S. Nye Jr., Eric Li, Kurt M. Campbell, Ely Ratner, "Did America Get China Wrong?" *Foreign Affairs,* June 14, 2018, www.foreignaffairs.com /articles/china/2018-06-14/did-america-get-china-wrong.

53   **"When I was at Goldman":** David E. Sanger, "Mr. Rubin's Long March to China," *The New York Times,* September 28, 1997, www.nytimes.com/1997/09/28/business/mr-rubin -s-long-march-to-china.html.

54   **putting China very much:** "World Bank GDP Data," The World Bank, data.worldbank .org/indicator/NY.GDP.MKTP.CD?locations=CN.

54   **how fast China was growing:** "China's Economic Rise: History, Trends, Challenges, and Implications for the United States," Congressional Research Service, June 25, 2019, sgp.fas .org/crs/row/RL33534.pdf.

58   **"I'm China's Zhu Rongji":** Steven Mufson, "Economic Pragmatist to Be China Premier," *The Washington Post,* March 5, 1998, www.washingtonpost.com/wp-srv/inatl/longterm /china/stories/zhu030598.htm.

59   **"Zhu basically went":** David E. Sanger, "How Push by China and U.S. Business Won Over Clinton," *The New York Times,* April 15, 1999, www.nytimes.com/1999/04/15/world /how-push-by-china-and-us-business-won-over-clinton.html.

60   **by 2017, it had tripled again, to $8,817:** "GDP per capita (current US$)—China," *The World Bank,* retrieved November 18, 2023, data.worldbank.org/indicator/NY.GDP.PCAP .CD?locations=CN.

61 **"strategic competitor":** Thomas W. Lippman, "Bush Makes Clinton's China Policy an Issue," *The Washington Post,* August 20, 1999, www.washingtonpost.com/wp-srv/politics/campaigns/wh2000/stories/chiwan082099.htm.

62 **"China . . . is on a rising path":** "President Bush Speaks at Tsinghua University," The White House Archives, February 22, 2002, georgewbush-whitehouse.archives.gov/news/releases/2002/02/20020222.html.

62 **curb the piracy of movies:** David E. Sanger and Joseph Kahn, "Chinese Leader Gives Bush a Mixed Message," *The New York Times,* November 21, 2005, www.nytimes.com/2005/11/21/world/asia/chinese-leader-givesbush-a-mixed-message.html.

64 **"You were my teacher":** Paul Blustein, "The Untold Story of How George W. Bush Lost China," *Foreign Policy,* October 2, 2019, foreignpolicy.com/2019/10/04/the-untold-story-of-how-george-w-bush-lost-china/.

65 **"The debate over whether China":** Stephen J. Hadley, Peter D. Feaver, William Inboden, and Meghan L. O'Sullivan, eds., *Hand-Off: The Foreign Policy George W. Bush Passed to Barack Obama* (Washington, D.C.: Brookings Institution Press, 2023), 424.

65 **personalities and motivations:** Edward Wong, "Chinese Vice President Ends U.S. Tour on Friendly Note," *The New York Times,* February 17, 2012, www.nytimes.com/2012/02/18/world/asia/chinese-vice-president-xi-jinping-tours-los-angeles-port.html.

66 **"You were the first group":** Chris Steinbach, "To Me, You Are America," *Muscatine Journal,* February 15, 2012, muscatinejournal.com/news/local/to-me-you-are-america/article_f72a4782-584c-11e1-98b4-0019bb2963f4.html.

66 **some twenty hours:** Joseph R. Biden Jr., "Remarks by Vice President Biden at Lunch in Honor of Vice President Xi of the People's Republic of China," The White House, February 17, 2012, obamawhitehouse.archives.gov/the-press-office/2012/02/17/remarks-vice-president-biden-lunch-honor-vice-president-xi-peoples-repub.

67 **"Really, the big trouble":** "Mixed Chinese Reaction to VP Biden's Visit," *VOA News,* August 21, 2011, www.voanews.com/a/mixed-chinese-reaction-to-vp-bidens-visit-128172073/144148.html.

67 **"unswervingly pursue":** "Dai Bingguo Publishes Signed Articles in French and British Media Elaborating China's Peaceful Development," Ministry of Foreign Affairs, People's Republic of China, September 25, 2011, www.fmprc.gov.cn/mfa_eng/gjhdq_665435/3265_665445/3291_664540/3293_664544/201109/t20110928_574401.html.

68 **"shot in front of his colleagues":** Mark Mazzetti, Adam Goldman, Michael S. Schmidt, and Matt Apuzzo, "Killing C.I.A. Informants, China Crippled U.S. Spying Operations," *The New York Times,* May 20, 2017, www.nytimes.com/2017/05/20/world/asia/china-cia-spies-espionage.html.

70 **were indicted:** See my book *The Perfect Weapon: War, Sabotage, and Fear in the Cyber Age* (New York: Crown, 2018).

71 **aircraft hangars appeared:** David E. Sanger and Rick Gladstone, "New Photos Cast Doubt on China's Vow Not to Militarize Disputed Islands," *The New York Times,* August 8, 2016, www.nytimes.com/2016/08/09/world/asia/china-spratly-islands-south-china-sea.html.

71 **"fair and competitive market environment":** "Notice of the State Council on the Publication of Made in China 2025," Center for Security and Emerging Technology, March 8, 2022, cset.georgetown.edu/wp-content/uploads/t0432_made_in_china_2025_EN.pdf.

74 **instructed officials to stop using that language:** David B. Larter, "White House Tells the Pentagon to Quit Talking About 'Competition' with China," *Navy Times,* September 26, 2016, www.navytimes.com/news/your-navy/2016/09/26/white-house-tells-the-pentagon-to-quit-talking-about-competition-with-china/.

75 **"Since the end of the Cold War":** See, for example, Rush Doshi, *The Long Game: China's Grand Strategy to Displace American Order* (New York: Oxford University Press, 2023).

75 **"There is no such thing as the so-called Thucydides Trap":** Graham Allison, "The Thucydides Trap: Are the U.S. and China Headed for War?" *The Atlantic,* September 24, 2015, www.theatlantic.com/international/archive/2015/09/united-states-china-war-thucydides-trap/406756/.

3. PUTIN'S SEVEN-YEAR ITCH

77   **"Hello! My congratulations":** *Servant of the People,* directed by Volodymyr Zelensky, aired 2017, Kvartal 95 Studio.

78   **get a laugh:** Sonya Bilocerkowycz, "Rewatching Zelensky's *Servant of the People* as Russia Wages War on Ukraine," *Literary Hub,* April 12, 2022, lithub.com/rewatching-zelenskys -servant-of-the-people-as-russia-wages-war-on-ukraine/.

78   **"dangerously pro-Russian":** Alexander J. Motyl, "Ukraine's TV President Is Dangerously Pro-Russian," *Foreign Policy,* April 1, 2019, foreignpolicy.com/2019/04/01/ukraines-tv -president-is-dangerously-pro-russian/.

79   **"high energy prices and wounded pride":** William J. Burns, *The Back Channel* (New York: Penguin Random House, 2020), 413.

80   **"China. China. China. Russia.":** Katrina Manson, Aime Williams, and Michael Peel, "What Does a Biden Presidency Mean for the World?" *Financial Times,* January 19, 2021, www.ft.com/content/75592d75-61ec-43f2-b435-c760db86394a.

80   **other end of the secure line:** Glenn Thrush and Kenneth P. Vogel, "What Joe Biden Actually Did in Ukraine," *The New York Times,* November 10, 2019, www.nytimes.com/2019 /11/10/us/politics/joe-biden-ukraine.html.

80   **just under $1 billion:** Elizabeth Piper, "Why Ukraine Spurned the EU and Embraced Russia," Reuters, December 19, 2013, www.reuters.com/article/us-ukraine-russia-deal -special-report/special-report-why-ukraine-spurned-the-eu-and-embraced-russia -idUSBRE9BI0DZ20131219.

81   **undercut his lavish lifestyle:** Katya Gorchinskaya, "A Brief History of Corruption in Ukraine: The Yanukovych Era," *eurasianet,* June 3, 2020, eurasianet.org/a-brief-history-of -corruption-in-ukraine-the-yanukovych-era.

81   **"You Americans don't understand":** William J. Burns, *The Back Channel* (New York: Penguin Random House, 2020), 290.

82   **the country was split:** Interfax-Ukraine, "Poll: More Ukrainians Disapprove of Euro-Maidan Protests than Approve of It," *Kyiv Post,* February 7, 2014, www.kyivpost.com/post /7158.

82   **at least nine times:** Julie Pace, "Biden at Center of US Diplomacy with Ukraine," Associated Press, February 25, 2014, apnews.com/general-news-f35db960879645a4b77ba601ea 4daa86.

83   **what Yanukovich would do:** Julie Pace, "Biden at Center of U.S. Diplomacy with Ukraine," Associated Press, February 25, 2014, apnews.com/general-news-f35db9608796 45a4b77ba601ea4daa86.

83   **"sphere of influence":** Gabriela Baczynska and Alexandra Hudson, "Russia Accuses EU of Seeking Ukraine 'Sphere of Influence,'" Reuters, February 14, 2014, www.reuters.com /article/uk-ukraine-russia-eu/russia-accuses-eu-of-seeking-ukraine-sphere-of-influence -idUKBREA1D0PM20140214.

83   **viewed with suspicion and outright hostility:** David Remnick, "Watching the Eclipse," *The New Yorker,* August 2, 2014, www.newyorker.com/magazine/2014/08/11/watching -eclipse.

83   **"pay in blood and money":** Glenn Thrush and Kenneth P. Vogel, "What Joe Biden Actually Did in Ukraine," *The New York Times,* November 10, 2019, www.nytimes.com/2019 /11/10/us/politics/joe-biden-ukraine.html.

84   **"The fact is":** Jeffrey Goldberg, "The Obama Doctrine," *The Atlantic,* April 2016, www .theatlantic.com/magazine/archive/2016/04/the-obama-doctrine/471525/.

84   **"This is not another":** President Barack Obama, "Remarks by the President in Address to European Youth," Office of the Press Secretary, March 26, 2014, obamawhitehouse .archives.gov/the-press-office/2014/03/26/remarks-president-address-European-youth.

84   **"You just don't":** Reid Epstein, "Kerry: Russia Behaving Like It's the 19th Century," *Politico,* March 2, 2014, www.politico.com/blogs/politico-now/2014/03/kerry-russia -behaving-like-its-the-19th-century-184280.

85 **"shambolic":** Catherine Ashton, *And Then What?* (London: Elliott & Thompson, 2023), 200.

85 **weapons transfer to the rebels:** Mike Corder, "MH17 Inquiry: 'Strong Indications' Putin OK'd Missile Supply," Associated Press, February 8, 2023, apnews.com/article/politics -russia-government-donetsk-netherlands-business-443d74853abceb3c9eab7770c7a1a6d2.

87 **Obama aides broached the potential conflict of interest:** Glenn Thrush and Kenneth P. Vogel, "What Joe Biden Actually Did in Ukraine," *The New York Times,* November 10, 2019, www.nytimes.com/2019/11/10/us/politics/joe-biden-ukraine.html.

87 **"Merkel's Moscow stuff":** Julian Reichelt, "What U.S. Politicians Really Think About the Germans in the Ukraine Crisis," *Bild,* February 8, 2015, www.bild.de/politik/inland /muenchner-sicherheitskonferenz/was-us-politiker-ueber-deutschland-denken-39678276 .bild.html.

89 **"Putin captured us":** Roger Cohen, "The Making of Vladimir Putin," *The New York Times,* March 26, 2022, www.nytimes.com/2022/03/26/world/europe/vladimir-putin -russia.html.

89 **more than 50 percent:** Philip Oltermann, "How Reliant Is Germany—and the Rest of Europe—on Russian Gas?" *The Guardian,* July 21, 2022, www.theguardian.com/world /2022/jul/21/how-reliant-is-germany-and-europe-russian-gas-nord-stream.

89 **deprive Ukraine:** Anders Åslund, "What Will the Impact Be If Nord Stream 2 Is Completed?" Atlantic Council, April 27, 2021, www.atlanticcouncil.org/in-depth-research -reports/issue-brief/what-will-the-impact-be-if-nord-stream-2-is-completed/.

89 **"Nord Stream 2 is a political bribe":** "President of Ukraine Proposes Germany to Modernize Ukrainian GTS," *UA Post,* April 9, 2018, uapost.us/en/news/president-of-ukraine -proposes-germany-to-modernize-ukrainian-gts/.

90 **"Why should we have been":** Katrin Bennhold, "The Former Chancellor Who Became Putin's Man in Germany," *The New York Times,* April 23, 2022, www.nytimes.com/2022 /04/23/world/europe/schroder-germany-russia-gas-ukraine-war-energy.html.

90 **kept the gas flowing:** Per Högselius, *Red Gas* (London: Palgrave Macmillan, 2013), 3.

4. AMERICA FIRST

95 **"A revisionist Russia":** Peter L. Jones, Ricky Waddell, Wilson C. Blythe Jr., and Thomas Pappas, "Unclassified Summary of the U.S. Army Training and Doctrine Command Russian New Generation Warfare Study," U.S. Army Training and Doctrine Command, www .armyupress.army.mil/Portals/7/online-publications/documents/RNGW-Unclassified -Summary-Report.pdf.

95 **"beer salesman":** Peter Baker and Susan Glasser, *The Divider: Trump in the White House, 2017–2021* (New York: Doubleday, 2022), 65–66.

96 **"America first":** Erica R. Hendry, "Read Trump's Full Speech Outlining His National Security Strategy," *PBS NewsHour,* Public Broadcasting Service, December 18, 2017, www .pbs.org/newshour/politics/read-trumps-full-speech-outlining-his-national-security -strategy.

97 **"NATO," he told Maggie Haberman and me:** "Transcript: Donald Trump Expounds on His Foreign Policy Views," *The New York Times,* March 26, 2016, www.nytimes.com/2016 /03/27/us/politics/donald-trump-transcript.html.

97 **"strategic deterrent":** Karen DeYoung, "The U.S. Has Been Rushing to Arm Ukraine, But for Years It Stalled on Providing Weapons," *The Washington Post,* February 27, 2022, www .washingtonpost.com/national-security/2022/02/27/ukraine-us-arms-supply/.

98 **"Look at this guy":** "H. R. McMaster: Why Did Trump Dump National Security Adviser?" BBC, March 22, 2018, www.bbc.com/news/world-europe-39033934.

98 **lose ten stories:** Bret Stephens, "John Bolton Is Right About the U.N.," *The New York Times,* March 23, 2018, www.nytimes.com/2018/03/23/opinion/john-bolton-un-united -nations.html.

99 **"was like an archipelago":** John Bolton, *The Room Where It Happened,* Simon & Schuster, 2020.

101 **China didn't buy any:** Ana Swanson, "China Fell Far Short of Promises It Made to Pur-

chase American Goods," *The New York Times,* February 8, 2022, www.nytimes.com/2022 /02/08/business/china-us-trade.html.

102 **never to militarize:** Morgan Ortagus, "China's Empty Promises in the South China Sea," U.S. Department of State, September 27, 2020, https://2017-2021.state.gov/chinas -empty-promises-in-the-south-china-sea/.

102 **Tipped off by suspicions:** Rebecca Smith, "U.S. Seizure of Chinese-Built Transformer Raises Specter of Closer Scrutiny," *The Wall Street Journal,* May 27, 2020, www.wsj.com /articles/u-s-seizure-of-chinese-built-transformer-raises-specter-of-closer-scrutiny -11590598710.

104 **"inevitable that the superiority":** Tanner Greer, "Xi Jinping in Translation: China's Guid- ing Ideology," *Palladium,* May 31, 2019, www.palladiummag.com/2019/05/31/xi-jinping -in-translation-chinas-guiding-ideology/.

104 **"swallowing sawdust by the bucketful":** Simon Leys, "The Art of Interpreting Nonexistent Inscriptions Written in Invisible Ink on a Blank Page," *The New York Review of Books,* Octo- ber 11, 1990, www.nybooks.com/articles/1990/10/11/the-art-of-interpreting-nonexistent -inscriptions-w/.

105 **"China sought to 'blunt' American":** Rushabh Doshi, "The Long Game: Chinese Grand Strategy After the Cold War," doctoral dissertation, Graduate School of Arts and Sciences, Harvard University, 2018, dash.harvard.edu/handle/1/41121327.

110 **effort to block:** "The Clean Network," U.S. Embassy and Consulates in the United King- dom, retrieved August 15, 2023, uk.usembassy.gov/our-relationship/policy-history/policy /the-clean-network/.

110 **cutoff of U.S. intelligence:** For more information, read my book *The Perfect Weapon.*

110 **it devastated Huawei's revenues:** Ellen Nakashima and Jeanne Whalen, "U.S. Threatens Use of Novel Export Control to Damage Russia's Strategic Industries If Moscow Invades Ukraine," *The Washington Post,* January 23, 2022, www.washingtonpost.com/national -security/2022/01/23/russia-ukraine-sanctions-export-controls/.

111 **The initiatives Krach:** Keith Krach and Kurt Campbell, "Building Trust with Allies Through Tech Diplomacy," Atlantic Council, streamed live on April 6, 2022, www.youtube .com/watch?v=tchgqomHthw.

112 **"Love it or hate it":** Thomas L. Friedman, "China and America Are Heading Toward Di- vorce," *The New York Times,* June 23, 2020, www.nytimes.com/2020/06/23/opinion/china -united-states-trump.html.

112 **promised Zelensky:** Philip Bump, "Trump Promised Zelensky a White House Meeting. More Than a Dozen Other Leaders Got One Instead," *The Washington Post,* Decem- ber 13, 2019, www.washingtonpost.com/politics/2019/12/13/trump-promised-zelensky -white-house-meeting-more-than-dozen-other-leaders-got-one-instead/.

113 **was a conspiracy theory:** "The Trump-Ukraine Impeachment Inquiry Report," House Permanent Select Committee on Intelligence, December 11, 2019, p. 16, www.congress .gov/116/crpt/hrpt335/CRPT-116hrpt335.pdf.

113 **traced it back to Russian actors:** "CrowdStrike's Work with the Democratic National Committee: Setting the Record Straight," *CrowdStrike Blog,* June 5, 2020, www.crowdstrike .com/blog/bears-midst-intrusion-democratic-national-committee/.

113 **"a terrible place":** "The Trump-Ukraine Impeachment Inquiry Report," House Perma- nent Select Committee on Intelligence, December 11, 2019, p. 38, www.congress.gov/116 /crpt/hrpt335/CRPT-116hrpt335.pdf.

114 **demand that Zelensky help him:** "The Trump-Ukraine Impeachment Inquiry Report," House Permanent Select Committee on Intelligence, December 11, 2019, p. 83, www .congress.gov/116/crpt/hrpt335/CRPT-116hrpt335.pdf.

114 **launch an investigation:** "The Trump-Ukraine Impeachment Inquiry Report," House Permanent Select Committee on Intelligence, December 11, 2019, p. 89, www.congress .gov/116/crpt/hrpt335/CRPT-116hrpt335.pdf.

114 **withhold hundreds of millions of dollars:** Caitlin Emma and Connor O'Brien, "Trump Holds Up Ukraine Military Aid Meant to Confront Russia," *Politico,* August 28, 2019, www.politico.com/story/2019/08/28/trump-ukraine-military-aid-russia-1689531.

5. INHERITING THE WRECKAGE

121 **"It just said 'security brief'":** The Cipher Brief, "2021 Cybersecurity Summit Day 1 Mandia Petraeus," March 23, 2019, www.youtube.com/watch?v=fdofqh4z-TM.

122 **"We were still sitting":** The Cipher Brief, "2021 Cybersecurity Summit Day 1 Mandia Petraeus," March 23, 2019, www.youtube.com/watch?v=fdofqh4z-TM.

122 **from the Treasury Department and Cisco Systems:** Dina Temple-Raston, "A 'Worst Nightmare' Cyberattack: The Untold Story of the SolarWinds Hack," National Public Radio, April 16, 2021, www.npr.org/2021/04/16/985439655/a-worst-nightmare-cyberattack-the -untold-story-of-the-solarwinds-hack.

123 **the company's exceptionally poor level of cybersecurity:** Civil Action No. 23-cv-9518, "SolarWinds Corporation and Timothy G. Brown," brought by the Securities and Exchange Commission in the United States District Court Southern District of New York, October 30, 2023, www.sec.gov/files/litigation/complaints/2023/comp-pr2023-227.pdf

124 **"Of course I can't":** David E. Sanger, "Biden Assails Trump over Handling of Russia Hacking," *The New York Times,* December 22, 2020, www.nytimes.com/2020/12/22/us /politics/biden-trump-russia-hack.html.

125 **"The Cyber Hack is far":** Donald J. Trump (@realDonaldTrump), Twitter, December 19, 2020, twitter.com/realDonaldTrump/status/1340333618691002368.

126 **"the holiday of democracy is over":** "Putin Silent on Washington Unrest as Russian Foreign Ministry Calls U.S. Electoral System Archaic," *The Moscow Times,* January 7, 2021, www.themoscowtimes.com/2021/01/07/putin-silent-on-washington-unrest-as-russian -foreign-ministry-calls-us-electoral-system-archaic-a72549.

128 **"He's yesterday":** Bob Woodward and Robert Costa, *Peril,* online version (New York: Simon & Schuster, 2021), 403.

132 **killed more Americans:** Sergio Peçanha and Yan Wu, "One Million of Us," *The Washington Post,* May 18, 2022, www.washingtonpost.com/opinions/interactive/2022/how-many -people-died-covid-united-states-1-million-graphic/.

133 **fear of a new nuclear arms race:** President John F. Kennedy's Inaugural Address, 1961, National Archives, accessed September 1, 2023, www.archives.gov/milestone-documents /president-john-f-kennedys-inaugural-address.

6. THE END OF THE FEVER DREAM

134 **"The United States is in the midst":** Kurt Campbell and Jake Sullivan, "Competition Without Catastrophe," *Foreign Affairs,* August 1, 2019, www.foreignaffairs.com/articles /china/competition-with-china-without-catastrophe.

138 **"welcomes the continuing rise":** Barack Obama, "Remarks by President Obama at the University of Queensland," Office of the Press Secretary, November 15, 2014, obamawhite house.archives.gov/the-press-office/2014/11/15/remarks-president-obama-university -queensland.

140 **"In the last fifteen or so years":** USC U.S.-China Institute, "Conversation with Kurt Campbell: The U.S. and Asia—A Status Report," September 28, 2012, www.youtube.com /watch?v=dzGoSoLrcRc.

140 **"The greatest challenge":** Democratic National Convention, "DemPlatform Hearing Day 2 Honorable Kurt Campbell," June 9, 2016, www.youtube.com/watch?app=desktop&v =vmjm3FylWcA.

142 **"no prospect for a pro-China administration":** "ODNI's Declassified Intelligence Community Assessment of Foreign Threats to the 2020 U.S. Federal Elections," CNN, March 16, 2021, www.cnn.com/2021/03/16/politics/read-odni-foreign-threats-2020/index.html.

145 **"the biggest threat":** Chris Buckley, " 'The East Is Rising': Xi Maps Out China's Post-Covid Ascent," *The New York Times,* March 3, 2021, www.nytimes.com/2021/03/03 /world/asia/xi-china-congress.html.

146 **"Some Washington politicians":** "Xinhua Commentary: Xi-Biden Telephone Call Sends Positive Signals to World," *Xinhua,* February 12, 2021, www.xinhuanet.com/english/2021 -02/12/c_139738046.htm.

148   **"containment, encirclement, and suppression":** John Ruwitch, "China Accuses U.S. of Containment and Warns of Potential Conflict," National Public Radio, March 7, 2023, www.npr.org/2023/03/07/1161570798/china-accuses-u-s-of-containment-warns-of -potential-conflict.

149   **"whole-process democracy":** "Xi's U.S. Envoy Invokes Lincoln in Declaring China a Democracy," Bloomberg, September 23, 2021, www.bloomberg.com/news/articles/2021-09 -23/xi-s-u-s-envoy-invokes-lincoln-in-declaring-china-a-democracy#xj4y7vzkg.

7. A DANGEROUS DANCE

151   **"The Biden administration":** "Fact Sheet: Imposing Costs for Harmful Foreign Activities by the Russian Government," The White House, April 15, 2021, www.whitehouse.gov /briefing-room/statements-releases/2021/04/15/fact-sheet-imposing-costs-for-harmful -foreign-activities-by-the-russian-government/.

151   **Biden's approval rating still hovered:** "Biden Approval Polling Tracker," Reuters, July 12, 2023, www.reuters.com/graphics/USA-BIDEN/POLL/nmopagnqapa/.

152   **launched by cyber criminals:** Maggie Miller, "Biden Says Colonial Pipeline Hackers Based in Russia, But Not Government-Backed," The Hill, May 13, 2021, thehill.com /policy/cybersecurity/553386-biden-says-colonial-pipeline-hackers-based-in-russia-but -not-government/.

153   **the confidential assessment:** David E. Sanger and Nicole Perlroth, "Pipeline Attack Yields Urgent Lessons About U.S. Cybersecurity," The New York Times, May 14, 2021, www .nytimes.com/2021/05/14/us/politics/pipeline-hack.html.

153   **worked too slowly:** William Turton, Michael Riley, and Jennifer Jacobs, "Colonial Pipeline Paid Hackers Nearly $5 Million in Ransom," Bloomberg, May 13, 2021, www.bloomberg .com/news/articles/2021-05-13/colonial-pipeline-paid-hackers-nearly-5-million-in -ransom#xj4y7vzkg; Committee on Homeland Security and Governmental Affairs United States Senate, "Threats to Critical Infrastructure: Examining the Colonial Pipeline Cyberattack," U.S. Government Publishing Office, June 8, 2021, www.govinfo.gov/content/pkg /CHRG-117shrg46569/pdf/CHRG-117shrg46569.pdf.

153   **"I will admit":** Collin Eaton and Dustin Volz, "Colonial Pipeline CEO Tells Why He Paid Hackers a $4.4 Million Ransom," The Wall Street Journal, May 19, 2021, www.wsj.com /articles/colonial-pipeline-ceo-tells-why-he-paid-hackers-a-4-4-million-ransom -11621435636.

154   **"This has been a wakeup call":** Emma Newburger, "Colonial Pipeline Hack Was 'Wakeup Call' on U.S. Cyber Vulnerability, Buttigieg Says," CNBC, May 13, 2021, www.cnbc.com /2021/05/13/colonial-pipeline-hack-wakeup-call-on-us-cyber-vulnerability-buttigieg .html.

154   **"It's all fun and games":** David E. Sanger and Nicole Perlroth, "Pipeline Attack Yields Urgent Lessons About U.S. Cybersecurity," The New York Times, May 14, 2021, www .nytimes.com/2021/05/14/us/politics/pipeline-hack.html.

157   **"The Kremlin has fears":** Amanda Macias, "Secretary of State Warns Moscow of Consequences as Russian Troops Amass Near Ukraine," CNBC, April 11, 2021, www.cnbc.com /2021/04/11/blinken-warns-moscow-of-consequences-amid-troop-buildup-near-ukraine .html.

157   **"a new war":** Yevgeny Matyushenko, "Ukraine Could Be 'Destroyed' in Case of Donbas Escalation, Russia's Lavrov Threatens," Ukrainian Independent Information Agency, April 1, 2021, www.unian.info/politics/donbas-ukraine-could-be-destroyed-in-case-of -escalation-lavrov-claims-11374168.html.

157   **force readiness:** Amanda Macias, "Secretary of State Warns Moscow of Consequences as Russian Troops Amass Near Ukraine," CNBC, April 11, 2021. www.cnbc.com/2021/04 /11/blinken-warns-moscow-of-consequences-amid-troop-buildup-near-ukraine.html.

157   **Blinken assured Ukraine's foreign minister:** Ned Price, "Secretary Blinken's Call with Ukrainian Foreign Minister Kuleba," U.S. Department of State, March 31, 2021, www .state.gov/secretary-blinkens-call-with-ukrainian-foreign-minister-kuleba/.

157 **a $125 million defensive package:** "Readout of Secretary of Defense Lloyd J. Austin III's Call With Ukrainian Minister of Defence Andrii Taran," U.S. Department of Defense, April 1, 2021, www.defense.gov/News/Releases/Release/Article/2558616/readout -of-secretary-of-defense-lloyd-j-austin-iiis-call-with-ukrainian-ministe; "Defense Department Announces $125M for Ukraine," U.S. Department of Defense, March 1, 2021, www .defense.gov/News/Releases/Release/Article/2519445/defense-department-announces -125m-for-ukraine/.

158 **he had promised to end the war:** "Ukraine Conflict: Anger as Zelensky Agrees Vote Deal in East," BBC, October 2, 2019, www.bbc.com/news/world-europe-49903996; Christopher Miller, "Zelensky's First Year: He Promised Sweeping Changes. How's He Doing?" Radio Free Europe Radio Liberty, April 25, 2020, www.rferl.org/a/zelenskiys-first-year-he -promised-sweeping-changes-how-s-he-doing-/30576329.html.

158 **biography published in 2022:** Serhii Rudenko, "New Zelensky Biography Reveals First Meeting with Putin: 'Bundle of Nerves,' " *Newsweek,* June 30, 2022, www.newsweek.com /new-zelensky-biography-reveals-first-meeting-putin-bundle-nerves-1720370.

158 **success for a political neophyte:** Andrew Higgins, "In First Meeting with Putin, Zelensky Plays to a Draw Despite a Bad Hand," *The New York Times,* December 9, 2019, www .nytimes.com/2019/12/09/world/europe/putin-zelensky-paris-ukraine.html.

158 **"Ukraine will definitely not":** "Juncker Says Ukraine Not Likely to Join EU, NATO for 20–25 Years," Radio Free Europe Radio Liberty, March 4, 2016, www.rferl.org/a/juncker -says-ukraine-not-likely-join-eu-nato-for-20-25-years/27588682.html.

159 **held only about 7 percent:** Peter S. Goodman, Jack Ewing, and Matt Phillips, "Sanctions on Russian Debt are Called a 'First Salvo' That Sends a Message," *The New York Times,* citing Oxford Economics in London, April 15, 2021, www.nytimes.com/2021/04/15 /business/biden-russia-sanctions-debt.html.

160 **"The organizers of any provocations":** Andrew E. Kramer, Ivan Nechepurenko, Anton Troianovski, and Katie Rogers, "Putin Says Nations That Threaten Russia's Security Will 'Regret Their Deeds,' " *The New York Times,* April 21, 2021, www.nytimes.com/2021/04 /21/world/europe/putin-russia-threats.html.

160 **"I think this was a dress rehearsal":** "Fareed Zakaria GPS: Putin's Power Plays at Home and Abroad," CNN, April 25, 2021, transcripts.cnn.com/show/fzgps/date/2021-04-25 /segment/01.

161 **Biden was already being criticized:** Michael Crowley, "Republicans Call Biden 'Soft' on Russia, Leaving Out Trump's Defense of Putin," *The New York Times,* June 15, 2021, www .nytimes.com/2021/06/15/us/politics/republicans-biden-russia.html.

163 **a major movie studio:** David E. Sanger and Nicole Perlroth, "U.S. Said to Find North Korea Ordered Cyberattack on Sony," *The New York Times,* December 17, 2014, www .nytimes.com/2014/12/18/world/asia/us-links-north-korea-to-sony-hacking.html.

163 **biggest cyber threat:** Dave Lawler and Zachary Basu, "Putin Calls Biden Summit 'Constructive,' but Blames U.S. for Tensions," *Axios,* June 16, 2021, www.axios.com/2021/06 /16/vladimir-putin-press-conference-biden-summit.

163 **"We're holding these exercises":** "Transcript of Putin's Press Conference in Geneva," *Kyiv Post,* June 17, 2021, www.kyivpost.com/post/7469.

164 **get hold of a decryption key:** "Ransomware Key to Unlock Customer Data from REvil Attack," BBC, July 23, 2021, www.bbc.com/news/technology-57946117.

164 **REvil was clearly emboldened:** David E. Sanger, "Russia's Most Aggressive Ransomware Group Disappeared. It's Unclear Who Made That Happen," *The New York Times,* July 13, 2021, www.nytimes.com/2021/07/13/us/politics/russia-hacking-ransomware-revil.html.

164 **Biden wanted to try:** Michael D. Shear, "Biden Urges Putin to 'Take Action to Disrupt' Russia-Based Hackers Behind Ransomware Attacks," *The New York Times,* July 9, 2021, www.nytimes.com/2021/07/09/us/politics/putin-biden-ransomware-hackers.html.

164 **The cause was unknown:** David E. Sanger, "Russia's Most Aggressive Ransomware Group Disappeared. It's Unclear Who Made That Happen," *The New York Times,* July 13, 2021, www.nytimes.com/2021/07/13/us/politics/russia-hacking-ransomware-revil.html.

165   **promptly shut back down:** Lily Hay Newman, "Security News This Week: An International Operation Knocked a Notorious Ransomware Group Offline," *Wired*, October 23, 2021, www.wired.com/story/revil-ransomware-hack-sinclair-group-argentina-data-breach-security-news/.

165   **Later, aides reported:** Garrett M. Graff, " 'Something Was Badly Wrong': When Washington Realized Russia Was Actually Invading Ukraine," *Politico*, February 24, 2023, www.politico.com/news/magazine/2023/02/24/russia-ukraine-war-oral-history-00083757.

8. THE MELTDOWN

167   **"Whatever happens in Afghanistan":** Glenn Kessler, "Biden, Trump, and Afghanistan: Statements That Haven't Aged Well," *The Washington Post*, August 17, 2021, www.washingtonpost.com/politics/2021/08/17/biden-trump-afghanistan-statements-that-havent-aged-well/.

168   **assembling a retribution list:** Carlotta Gall, "As the Taliban Tighten Their Grip, Fears of Retribution Grow," *The New York Times*, August 29, 2021, www.nytimes.com/2021/08/29/world/asia/afghanistan-taliban-revenge.html.

168   **project an aura of confidence:** Zolan Kanno-Youngs, Eric Schmitt, and Thomas Gibbons-Neff, "Biden Says Afghans Must 'Decide Their Future' as U.S. Troops Withdraw," *The New York Times*, June 25, 2021, www.nytimes.com/2021/06/25/us/politics/biden-afghanistan-withdrawal.html.

168   **they came to the White House:** Lara Seligman, "Top Generals Contradict Biden, Say They Urged Him Not to Withdraw from Afghanistan," *Politico*, September 28, 2021, www.politico.com/news/2021/09/28/top-generals-afghanistan-withdrawal-congress-hearing-514491.

168   **maybe eighteen months:** Lara Seligman, "Top General on Afghanistan: 'I Don't Think the End Game Is Yet Written,' " *Politico*, July 21, 2021, www.politico.com/news/2021/07/21/mark-milley-top-general-afghanistan-taliban-500445.

169   **"We've seen this movie before":** Helene Cooper, Eric Schmitt, and David E. Sanger, "Debating Exit from Afghanistan, Biden Rejected Generals' Views," *The New York Times*, April 17, 2021, www.nytimes.com/2021/04/17/us/politics/biden-afghanistan-withdrawal.html.

169   **same litany of arguments:** Michael Hirsh, "From Moral Responsibility to Magical Thinking: How Biden Changed His Mind on Afghanistan," *Foreign Policy*, April 6, 2021, foreignpolicy.com/2021/04/16/from-moral-responsibility-to-magical-thinking-how-biden-changed-his-mind-on-afghanistan/.

169   **"Our true strategic competitors":** President Joseph R. Biden Jr., "Remarks by President Biden on Afghanistan," The White House, August 16, 2021, www.whitehouse.gov/briefing-room/speeches-remarks/2021/08/16/remarks-by-president-biden-on-afghanistan/.

170   **a hasty, deadly retreat:** Michael D. Shear, "Biden Faces a Tragedy He Pledged to Avoid," *The New York Times*, August 26, 2021, www.nytimes.com/2021/08/26/us/politics/biden-afghanistan-attack.html.

170   **Not surprisingly, adversaries abroad:** For example, see the DoD's finding that "P.R.C. officials and state media outlets also repeatedly condemned the U.S. withdrawal from Afghanistan and cited the withdrawal as evidence that the U.S. is an unreliable partner and declining power." "Military and Security Developments Involving the People's Republic of China 2022," U.S. Department of Defense, 2022, media.defense.gov/2022/Nov/29/2003122279/-1/-1/1/2022-MILITARY-AND-SECURITY-DEVELOPMENTS-INVOLVING-THE-PEOPLES-REPUBLIC-OF-CHINA.PDF.

170   **"the top priority":** Paul D. Miller, "Setting the Record Straight on Obama's Afghanistan Promises," *Foreign Policy*, March 29, 2016, foreignpolicy.com/2016/03/29/setting-the-record-straight-on-obamas-afghanistan-promises/.

170   **long soured on the war:** Joe Biden and Katie Couric, "A Conversation with Senator Joseph R. Biden, Jr. (Video Highlight)," Council on Foreign Relations, February 25, 2008, www.cfr.org/event/conversation-senator-joseph-r-biden-jr-video-highlight.

170 **he had voted:** Helene Cooper, Eric Schmitt, and David E. Sanger, "Debating Exit from Afghanistan, Biden Rejected Generals' Views," *The New York Times,* April 17, 2021, www .nytimes.com/2021/04/17/us/politics/biden-afghanistan-withdrawal.html.

170 **Obama's bottom-up review:** Greg Jaffe, "The War in Afghanistan Shattered Joe Biden's Faith in American Military Power," *The Washington Post,* February 18, 2020, www .washingtonpost.com/politics/2020/02/18/biden-afghanistan-military-power/.

171 **" 'Don't let them jam you' ":** Helene Cooper, Eric Schmitt, and David E. Sanger, "Debating Exit from Afghanistan, Biden Rejected Generals' Views," www.nytimes.com/2021/04 /17/us/politics/biden-afghanistan-withdrawal.html.

171 **"We overestimate the ability":** Eric Schmitt, "U.S. Envoy's Cables Show Worries on Afghan Plans," *The New York Times,* January 25, 2010, www.nytimes.com/2010/01/26/world /asia/26strategy.html.

171 **disparaging Obama's team:** Michael Hastings, "The Runaway General: The Profile That Brought Down McChrystal," *Rolling Stone,* June 22, 2010, www.rollingstone.com/politics /politics-news/the-runaway-general-the-profile-that-brought-down-mcchrystal-192609/.

171 **"Why are we continuing":** Twitter, August 21, 2012, twitter.com/realDonaldTrump /status/237913235045638144.

172 **"solution" might look like:** "What to Know About the Afghan Peace Negotiations," Council on Foreign Relations, September 11, 2020, www.cfr.org/article/what-know-about -afghan-peace-negotiations.

172 **Mike Pompeo, Trump's secretary of state:** Matthew Lee, "U.S., Taliban Set Peace Signing for America's Longest War," Associated Press, February 28, 2020, apnews.com/article/706 26747d0b9ee4dec98042119efff98.

172 **Ghani publicly criticized that:** "Afghan President Casts Doubt on Key Aspect of U.S.-Taliban Peace Deal," Radio Free Europe Radio Liberty, March 1, 2020, www.rferl.org/a /trump-us-troops-to-begin-leaving-afghanistan-immediately/30462190.html.

173 **Taliban was the strongest:** Zachary Laub and Lindsay Maizland, "Timeline: The U.S. War in Afghanistan," Council on Foreign Relations, September 27, 2022, www.cfr.org/timeline /us-war-afghanistan.

173 **congressionally mandated working group:** "Afghanistan Study Group Final Report: A Pathway for Peace in Afghanistan," United States Institute of Peace, February 3, 2021, www.usip.org/publications/2021/02/afghanistan-study-group-final-report-pathway-peace -afghanistan.

174 **"commandos":** Tom Bowman and Monika Evstatieva, "The Afghan Army Collapsed in Days. Here Are the Reasons Why," National Public Radio, August 20, 2021, www.npr .org/2021/08/20/1029451594/the-afghan-army-collapsed-in-days-here-are-the-reasons -why.

174 **keep a small contingent:** Barbara Sprunt, "Generals Say They Recommended Keeping U.S. Troops in Afghanistan," National Public Radio, September 28, 2021, www.npr.org /2021/09/28/1040877300/austin-milley-mckenzie-senate-hearing-afghanistan.

174 **There was no sense from the intelligence briefings:** Michael D. Shear, David E. Sanger, Helene Cooper, Eric Schmitt, Julian E. Barnes, and Lara Jakes, "Miscue After Miscue, U.S. Exit Plan Unravels," *The New York Times,* August 21, 2021, www.nytimes.com/2021/08 /21/us/politics/biden-taliban-afghanistan-kabul.html.

174 **launched a new offensive:** Michael D. Shear, David E. Sanger, Helene Cooper, Eric Schmitt, Julian E. Barnes, and Lara Jakes, "Miscue After Miscue, U.S. Exit Plan Unravels," *The New York Times,* August 21, 2021, www.nytimes.com/2021/08/21/us/politics/biden -taliban-afghanistan-kabul.html.

175 **That would send a signal:** Nomaan Merchant and Zeke Miller, "Misread Warnings Helped Lead to Chaotic Afghan Evacuation," Associated Press, August 18, 2021, apnews .com/article/joe-biden-evacuations-32bb6a22846f649b626a3130f8c5dffb.

175 **"speed equals safety":** Lara Seligman, " 'Speed Equals Safety': Inside the Pentagon's Controversial Decision to Leave Bagram Early," *Politico,* September 28, 2021, www.politico .com/news/2021/09/28/pentagon-decision-leave-bagram-514456.

175 **Afghan commander of Bagram:** Kathy Gannon, "U.S. Left Afghan Airfield at Night, Didn't Tell New Commander," Associated Press, July 6, 2021, apnews.com/article/bagram -afghanistan-airfield-us-troops-f3614828364f567593251aaaa167e623.

175 **"In one night":** Kathy Gannon, "U.S. Left Afghan Airfield at Night, Didn't Tell New Commander," Associated Press, July 6, 2021, apnews.com/article/bagram-afghanistan -airfield-us-troops-f3614828364f567593251aaaa167e623.

176 **secret diplomatic cable:** "2022 Awards for Constructive Dissent," American Foreign Service Association, December 2022, afsa.org/2022-awards-constructive-dissent.

176 **possibility of an imminent evacuation:** Joshua Kaplan, Joaquin Sapien, Brian J. Conley, Mohammad J. Alizada, Samira Nuhzat, Mirzahussain Sadid, and Abdul Ahad Poya, "Hell at Abbey Gate: Chaos, Confusion, and Death in the Final Days of the War in Afghanistan," *ProPublica,* April 2, 2022, www.propublica.org/article/hell-at-abbey-gate-chaos-confusion -and-death-in-the-final-days-of-the-war-in-afghanistan.

177 **"days or weeks":** Michael D. Shear, David E. Sanger, Helene Cooper, Eric Schmitt, Julian E. Barnes, and Lara Jakes, "Miscue After Miscue, U.S. Exit Plan Unravels," *The New York Times,* August 21, 2021, www.nytimes.com/2021/08/21/us/politics/biden -taliban-afghanistan-kabul.html.

179 **"We do not heavy-breathe":** Joe Buccino and General Chris Donahue, "Episode 37: We Do Not 'Heavy Breathe' in the 82nd Airborne Division: A Discussion with General Chris Donahue," *The 18th Airborne Corps Podcast,* June 7, 2021, thedoomsdayclock.podbean .com/e/episode-37-we-do-not-heavy-breathe-in-this-division-a-discussion-with-maj-gen -chris-donahue/.

179 **forced to play God:** Helene Cooper and Eric Schmitt, "Witnesses to the End," *The New York Times,* November 7, 2021, www.nytimes.com/2021/11/07/us/politics/afghanistan -war-marines.html.

179 **micromanaged the military:** "Why the Afghan Security Forces Collapsed," Special Inspector General for Afghan Reconstruction (SIGAR), February 2023, www.sigar.mil/pdf /evaluations/SIGAR-23-16-IP.pdf.

180 **refused to negotiate:** Ayaz Gul, "Taliban Rejects Afghan Team for Peace Talks," *Voice of America News,* March 28, 2020, www.voanews.com/a/south-central-asia_taliban-rejects -afghan-team-peace-talks/6186552.html.

180 **Ghani was sidelined:** "Afghan President Ashraf Ghani Blames U.S. Troop Pullout for Worsening Violence Amid Taliban Gains," CBS News, August 2, 2021, www.cbsnews.com /news/afghanistan-ashraf-ghani-blames-us-troop-pullout-for-worsening-violence-taliban -gains/.

182 **entire southern half of the airfield:** General Kenneth F. McKenzie Jr., "General Kenneth F. McKenzie Jr., Commander, U.S. Central Command, Holds a Press Briefing," U.S. Department of Defense, February 4, 2022, www.defense.gov/News/Transcripts/Transcript /Article/2924617/general-kenneth-f-mckenzie-jr-commander-us-central-command-holds -a-press-briefi/.

182 **dispatched to talk to the Taliban leadership:** John Hudson, "CIA Director William Burns Held Secret Meeting in Kabul with Taliban Leader Abdul Ghani Baradar," *The Washington Post,* August 24, 2021, www.washingtonpost.com/national-security/burns -afghanistan-baradar-biden/2021/08/24/c96bee5c-04ba-11ec-ba15-9c4f59a60478_ story.html.

184 **"It is a pretty good encapsulation":** Katie Bo Lillis, Zachary Cohen, and Natasha Bertrand, "CIA Warned Children Were Possibly Present Seconds Before U.S. Missile Killed 10," CNN, September 18, 2021, www.cnn.com/2021/09/18/politics/united-states -military-drone-strike-kabul-civilians/index.html.

184 **visual investigations unit:** Christoph Koettl, Evan Hill, Matthieu Aikins, Eric Schmitt, Ainara Tiefenthäler, and Drew Jordan, "How a U.S. Drone Strike Killed the Wrong Person," *The New York Times,* September 10, 2021, www.nytimes.com/video/world/asia /100000007963596/us-drone-attack-kabul-investigation.html.

185 **force appeared unwilling:** President Joseph R. Biden Jr., "Remarks by President Biden on

Afghanistan," The White House, August 16, 2021, www.whitehouse.gov/briefing-room /speeches-remarks/2021/08/16/remarks-by-president-biden-on-afghanistan/.

185 **"Taliban advances would accelerate":** "U.S. Withdrawal from Afghanistan," The White House, April 6, 2023, www.whitehouse.gov/wp-content/uploads/2023/04/US-Withdrawal -from-Afghanistan.pdf.

9. A "SPUTNIK" MOMENT

188 **"The relationship between China":** "ONLY ON AP UN Chief: We Must Avoid US/China 'Cold War,' " Associated Press, September 25, 2021, www.youtube.com/watch?v =gBJ_tyeH_Us.

189 **track and intercept missiles:** Jaganath Sankaran and Steve Fetter, "Defending the United States: Revisiting National Missile Defense Against North Korea," *International Security* 46, no. 3 (2022): 51–86, doi.org/10.1162/isec_a_00426.

190 **Hyten had testified before Congress:** Rebecca Kheel, "Russia, China Eclipse U.S. in Hypersonic Missiles, Prompting Fears," *The Hill,* March 27, 2018, thehill.com/policy/defense /380364-china-russia-eclipse-us-in-hypersonic-missiles-prompting-fears/.

190 **first to break the news:** Demetri Sevastopulo and Kathrin Hille, "China Tests New Space Capability with Hypersonic Missile," *Financial Times,* October 16, 2021, www.ft.com /content/ba0a3cde-719b-4040-93cb-a486e1f843fb.

190 **"close enough":** David Martin, "Exclusive: No. 2 in U.S. Military Reveals New Details About China's Hypersonic Weapons Test," CBS News, November 16, 2021, www.cbsnews .com/news/china-hypersonic-weapons-test-details-united-states-military/.

190 **fallen behind in the space race:** Sara Sorcher and Karoun Demirjian, "Top U.S. General Calls China's Hypersonic Weapon Test Very Close to a 'Sputnik Moment,' " *The Washington Post,* October 27, 2021, www.washingtonpost.com/nation/2021/10/27/mark-milley -china-hypersonic-weapon-sputnik/.

191 **"The significance":** Senator Angus S. King Jr., "Senator King Discusses the Threat of Hypersonic Weapons," July 15, 2022, www.youtube.com/watch?v=dZVNIB2dTaE.

191 **"intelligence base":** Warren P. Strobel and Gordon Lubold, "Cuba to Host Secret Chinese Spy Base Focusing on U.S.," *The Wall Street Journal,* June 8, 2023, www.wsj.com/articles /cuba-to-host-secret-chinese-spy-base-focusing-on-u-s-b2fed0e0.

191 **move an entire satellite:** Laura Dobberstein, "China Has a Satellite with an Arm—and America Worries It Could Be Used to Snatch Other Spacecraft," *The Register,* April 21, 2021, www.theregister.com/2021/04/21/the_legit_real_star_wars/.

192 **$70 billion:** "Current U.S. Missile Defense Programs at a Glance," *Arms Control Association,* updated August 2019, www.armscontrol.org/factsheets/usmissiledefense.

192 **front page of the Soviet daily:** James J. Harford, "Korolev's Triple Play: Sputniks 1, 2, and 3," adapted from James J. Harford, *Korolev: How One Man Masterminded the Soviet Drive to Beat America to the Moon* (New York: John Wiley, 1997).

192 **"losing the satellite-missile race":** "50th Anniversary of the Missile Gap Controversy," John F. Kennedy Presidential Library and Museum, 2011, www.jfklibrary.org/events -and-awards/forums/past-forums/transcripts/50th-anniversary-of-the-missile-gap -controversy.

193 **"Launched on the same night":** Asif A. Siddiqi, *The Red Rocket's Glare* (Cambridge, U.K.: Cambridge University Press, 2010).

194 **physical challenges:** Tom Karako and Masao Dahlgren, "Complex Air Defense: Countering the Hypersonic Missile Threat," Center for Strategic and International Studies, February 7, 2022, csis-website-prod.s3.amazonaws.com/s3fs-public/publication/220207 _Karako_Complex_AirDefense.pdf?VersionId=SmaHq1sva9Sk.TSlzpXqWY72fg8 PdLvA.

194 **"hundreds":** Colin Clark, " 'Hundreds' of China Hypersonic Tests Vs. 9 US; Hyten Says U.S. Moves Too Slowly," *Breaking Defense,* October 28, 2021, breakingdefense.com/2021 /10/hundreds-of-china-hypersonic-tests-vs-9-us-hyten-says-us-moves-too-slowly/.

194   **Also debuting in 2019:** David Hambling, "These Are the Hypersonic Missiles That Terrify the U.S. Military," *Popular Mechanics,* January 9, 2023, www.popularmechanics.com /military/a42386379/hypersonic-missiles-arms-race/.

194   **"superweapons":** Vladimir Isachenkov, "Putin Shows New Russian Nuclear Weapons: 'It Isn't a Bluff,'" Associated Press, March 1, 2018, apnews.com/article/de8fb0159f314a849e 1c36ff975c4637.

194   **"Avangard":** Samuel Bendett, Mathieu Boulègue, Dr. Richard Connolly, Dr. Margarita Konaev, Dr. Pavel Podvig, and Dr. Katarzyna Zysk, "Advanced Military Technology in Russia: Capabilities, Limitations, and Challenges," Chatham House, September 23, 2021, www.chathamhouse.org/2021/09/advanced-military-technology-russia/03-putins-super -weapons.

195   **$4.7 billion in 2023:** "Hypersonic Weapons: Background and Issues for Congress," Congressional Research Service, February 13, 2023, sgp.fas.org/crs/weapons/R45811.pdf.

197   **significantly ahead of the West:** Dr. Jamie Gaida, Dr. Jennifer Wong Leung, Stephan Robin, Danielle Cave, and Dannielle Pilgrim, "ASPI's Critical Technology Tracker— Sensors & Biotech Updates," Australian Strategic Policy Institute, retrieved October 2, 2023, www.aspi.org.au/report/critical-technology-tracker.

197   **a "knife in the back":** David E. Sanger, "Secret Talks and a Hidden Agenda: Behind the U.S. Defense Deal That France Called a 'Betrayal,'" *The New York Times,* September 17, 2021, www.nytimes.com/2021/09/17/us/politics/us-france-australia-betrayal.html.

198   **Bush used it in a 2002 conversation:** September 12, 2002, meeting in the Oval Office with President Bush and other reporters.

199   **largest supplier of goods:** Anshu Siripurapu and Noah Berman, "The Contentious U.S.-China Trade Relationship," Council on Foreign Relations, December 2, 2022, www.cfr.org /backgrounder/contentious-us-china-trade-relationship.

199   **"it's no longer debatable":** Hal Brands and John Lewis Gaddis, "The New Cold War: America, China, and the Echoes of History," *Foreign Affairs,* October 19, 2021, www .foreignaffairs.com/articles/united-states/2021-10-19/new-cold-war.

199   **"The fact that the Cold War":** David E. Sanger, "Washington Hears Echoes of the '50s and Worries: Is This a Cold War with China?" *The New York Times,* October 17, 2021, www.nytimes.com/2021/10/17/us/politics/china-new-cold-war.html.

199   **new nuclear missile silos:** William J. Broad and David E. Sanger, "A 2nd New Nuclear Missile Base for China, and Many Questions About Strategy," *The New York Times,* July 26, 2021, www.nytimes.com/2021/07/26/us/politics/china-nuclear-weapons.html.

200   **deter an attack from larger powers:** David E. Sanger, William J. Broad, and Chris Buckley, "3 Nuclear Superpowers, Rather Than 2, Usher in a New Strategic Era," *The New York Times,* April 19, 2023, www.nytimes.com/2023/04/19/us/politics/china-nuclear-weapons -russia-arms-treaties.html.

200   **live with the Chinese Bomb:** Jim Mann, "U.S. Considered '64 Bombing to Keep China Nuclear-Free," *Los Angeles Times,* September 27, 1998, www.latimes.com/archives/la-xpm -1998-sep-27-mn-26986-story.html.

200   **maintained deployed arsenals five times larger:** "Fact Sheet: China's Nuclear Inventory," Center for Arms Control and Non-Proliferation, January 25, 2023, armscontrolcenter.org /fact-sheet-chinas-nuclear-arsenal/.

200   **"establish a strong system":** Amber Wang, "Analysts Seize on Xi's Mention of Strong 'Strategic Deterrence' as Sign of China's Nuclear Build-Up," *South China Morning Post,* October 18, 2022, www.scmp.com/news/china/military/article/3196408/analysts-seize -xis-mention-strong-strategic-deterrence-sign-chinas-nuclear-build.

200   **just a start:** Mike Yeo and Robert Burns, "Pentagon Warns of China's Progress Toward Nuclear Triad," *Military Times,* November 3, 2021, www.militarytimes.com/news /pentagon-congress/2021/11/03/pentagon-chinese-nuke-force-growing-faster-than -predicted/.

201   **much of the earlier silo construction:** Matt Korda and Hans Kristensen, "China Is Build-

ing a Second Nuclear Missile Silo Field," Federation of American Scientists, July 26, 2021, fas.org/publication/china-is-building-a-second-nuclear-missile-silo-field/.

201   **"Just because you build":** William J. Broad and David E. Sanger, "A 2nd New Nuclear Missile Base for China, and Many Questions About Strategy," *The New York Times,* July 26, 2021, www.nytimes.com/2021/07/26/us/politics/china-nuclear-weapons.html.

202   **"We are probably not":** David E. Sanger, William J. Broad, and Chris Buckley, "3 Nuclear Superpowers, Rather Than 2, Usher in a New Strategic Era," *The New York Times,* April 19, 2023, www.nytimes.com/2023/04/19/us/politics/china-nuclear-weapons-russia -arms-treaties.html.

10. BLOWING SMOKE

203   **he enjoyed embarrassing her:** This incident is reported in detail in my book *The Perfect Weapon* (page 177), in which I called Nuland "Patient Zero" in what became Putin's efforts to interfere in the 2016 election.

205   **established a predicate:** Vladimir Putin, "On the Historical Unity of Russians and Ukrainians," President of Russia, July 12, 2021, en.kremlin.ru/events/president/news/66181.

205   **road map for Putin's eventual move:** Anders Åslund, "Putin's Dangerous Ukraine Narrative," Project Syndicate, July 14, 2021, www.project-syndicate.org/commentary/putin -denial-of-ukrainian-independence-could-lead-to-war-by-anders-aslund-2021-07.

206   **"It has been said":** Condoleezza Rice, *No Higher Honor* (New York: Penguin Random House, 2012), 357.

207   **at least, a close partnership:** Ashley Parker and Anne Gearan, "Biden Backs Lasting Support for Ukraine as Both Nations Move On from the Trump-Era Obsession with Kyiv," *The Washington Post,* September 1, 2021, www.washingtonpost.com/politics/biden-ukraine /2021/09/01/e67bdd62-0b32-11ec-9781-07796fffb56fe_story.html.

207   **"a very big agenda":** Maegan Vazquez and Kevin Liptak, "Ukrainian President Accomplishes Years-Long Quest for a White House Visit with Biden Meeting," CNN, September 1, 2021, www.cnn.com/2021/09/01/politics/ukraine-volodymyr-zelensky-biden-white -house/index.html.

207   **"All-out war":** Oliver Carroll, "Russia May Launch All-Out War with Ukraine, Says President Zelensky," *The Independent,* September 10, 2021, www.independent.co.uk/news /world/europe/russia-ukraine-border-conflict-zelensky-b1917799.html.

208   **Milley had publicly apologized:** Ryan Browne, Barbara Starr, and Zachary Cohen, "Top General Apologizes for Appearing in Photo-Op with Trump After Forceful Removal of Protesters," CNN, June 11, 2020, www.cnn.com/2020/06/11/politics/milley-trump -appearance-mistake/index.html.

208   **trying to calm them down:** Bob Woodward and Robert Costa, *Peril* (New York: Simon & Schuster, 2021), 13, 14.

209   **Occupying the country would be a nightmare:** Erin Banco, Garrett M. Graff, Lara Seligman, Nahal Toosi, and Alexander Ward, " 'Something Was Badly Wrong': When Washington Realized Russia Was Actually Invading Ukraine," *Politico,* February 24, 2023, www .politico.com/news/magazine/2023/02/24/russia-ukraine-war-oral-history-00083757.

213   **lay out the details:** Erin Banco, Garrett M. Graff, Lara Seligman, Nahal Toosi, and Alexander Ward, " 'Something Was Badly Wrong': When Washington Realized Russia Was Actually Invading Ukraine," *Politico,* February 24, 2023, www.politico.com/news/magazine/2023 /02/24/russia-ukraine-war-oral-history-00083757.

213   **engaged in a bluff:** Shane Harris, Karen DeYoung, Isabelle Khurshudyan, Ashley Parker, and Liz Sly, "Road to War: U.S. Struggled to Convince Allies, and Zelensky, of Risk of Invasion," *The Washington Post,* August 16, 2022, www.washingtonpost.com/national-security /interactive/2022/ukraine-road-to-war/.

215   **design offensive cyberweapons:** Scott Shane, Nicole Perlroth, and David E. Sanger, "Security Breach and Spilled Secrets Have Shaken the NSA to Its Core," *The New York Times,* November 12, 2017, www.nytimes.com/2017/11/12/us/nsa-shadow-brokers.html.

216   **trying to lock down America's secrets:** "Spy World Wary as Biden Team Keeps Leaking

Russia Intel," *Politico,* February 8, 2022, www.politico.com/news/2022/02/08/spy-world
-biden-leaking-russia-intel-00006956.

217   **authorized leaking goes back:** Amy Zegart, "George Washington Was a Master of Decep-
tion," *The Atlantic,* November 25, 2018, www.theatlantic.com/ideas/archive/2018/11
/george-washington-was-master-deception/576565/.

218   **planning to surround Ukraine on three sides:** Shane Harris and Paul Sonne, "Russia
Planning Massive Military Offensive Against Ukraine Involving 175,000 Troops, U.S. Intelligence Warns," *The Washington Post,* December 3, 2021, www.washingtonpost.com
/national-security/russia-ukraine-invasion/2021/12/03/98a3760e-546b-11ec-8769
-2f4ecdf7a2ad_story.html.

218   **warned of a false flag attack:** Natasha Bertrand and Jeremy Herb, "U.S. Intelligence Indi-
cates Russia Preparing Operation to Justify Invasion of Ukraine," CNN, January 14, 2022,
www.cnn.com/2022/01/14/politics/us-intelligence-russia-false-flag/index.html.

219   **stage a video displaying corpses:** Ellen Nakashima, Shane Harris, Ashley Parker, John
Hudson, and Paul Sonne, "U.S. Accuses Russia of Planning to Film False Attack as Pretext
for Ukraine Invasion," *The Washington Post,* February 3, 2022, www.washingtonpost.com
/national-security/2022/02/03/russia-ukraine-staged-attack/.

219   **told the Americans to stop fomenting panic:** Liz Sly, "Zelensky Faces Outpouring of
Criticism over Failure to Warn of War," *The Washington Post,* August 19, 2022, www
.washingtonpost.com/world/2022/08/18/zelensky-ukraine-wapo-interview-warn-of-war/.

220   **sphere of influence:** David E. Sanger, "In U.S.-Russia Talks, How Far Can Putin Turn
Back the Clock?" *The New York Times,* January 10, 2022, www.nytimes.com/2022/01/10
/world/europe/us-russia-cold-war-ukraine.html.

220   **did not agree to the whole list:** Mary Ilyushina, "Putin Threatens 'Retaliatory Military-
Technical' Measures as Standoff with U.S. and NATO over Ukraine Escalates," CBS News,
December 22, 2021, www.cbsnews.com/news/russia-ukraine-war-news-putin-retaliatory
-military-technical-measures/.

220   **"It was the United States":** Anton Troianovski, Andrew E. Kramer, and David E. Sanger,
"Putin Mixes Positive Note with Threats, Keeping West on Edge," *The New York Times,*
December 23, 2021, www.nytimes.com/2021/12/23/world/europe/russia-putin-ukraine
.html.

221   **"a minor incursion":** Asma Khalid, "How Biden Is Trying to Clean Up His Comments
About Russia and Ukraine," National Public Radio, January 20, 2022, www.npr.org/2022
/01/20/1074466148/biden-russia-ukraine-minor-incursion.

221   **option was entirely off the table:** Zachary B. Wolf, "Here's What Biden Has Said About
Sending U.S. Troops to Ukraine," CNN, February 24, 2022, www.cnn.com/2022/02/24
/politics/us-troops-ukraine-russia-nato/index.html.

222   **agreement to block Nord Stream 2:** Paul Belkin, Michael Ratner, and Cory Welt, "Russia's Nord Stream 2 Natural Gas Pipeline to Germany Halted," Congressional Research
Service, March 10, 2022, crsreports.congress.gov/product/pdf/IF/IF11138.

222   **intolerable security environment:** See, e.g., Isaac Chotiner, "Why John Mearsheimer
Blames the U.S. for the Crisis in Ukraine," *The New Yorker,* March 1, 2022, www.new
yorker.com/news/q-and-a/why-john-mearsheimer-blames-the-us-for-the-crisis-in-ukraine;
Ken Moskowitz, "Did NATO Expansion Really Cause Putin's Invasion?" *The Foreign Service Journal,* October 2022, afsa.org/did-nato-expansion-really-cause-putins-invasion.

11. A PARTNERSHIP "WITHOUT LIMITS"?

224   **lengthy essay:** Eva Dou, "What Is—and Isn't—in the Joint Statement from Putin and Xi,"
The Washington Post, February 4, 2022, www.washingtonpost.com/world/2022/02/04
/russia-china-xi-putin-summit-statement-beijing/; "Joint Statement of the Russian Federation and the People's Republic of China on the International Relations Entering a New
Era and the Global Sustainable Development," President of Russia, February 4, 2022,
en.kremlin.ru/supplement/5770, emphasis added.

224   **"good friends":** Alexei Anishchuk and Timothy Heritage, "China's New Leader
Welcomes Russia's Putin as a Friend," Reuters, March 22, 2013, www.reuters.com

/article/us-china-russia/chinas-new-leader-welcomes-russias-putin-as-a-friend
-idUSBRE92L0KE20130322.

225   **"best, most intimate friend":** Jason Lemon, "Vladimir Putin 'Is My Best, Most Intimate
Friend,' Chinese President Xi Jinping Says," *Newsweek,* June 8, 2018, www.newsweek.com
/putin-my-best-most-intimate-friend-chinese-president-xi-says-967531.

225   **flipped Russian pancakes:** "Putin and Xi Make Pancakes," Voice of America, September 11, 2018, www.youtube.com/watch?v=r5qZoT6bbJo.

225   **Putin threw Xi a birthday party:** "Ice Cream and Cake: Vladimir Putin Hosts Birthday
Party for Xi Jinping—Video," *The Guardian,* June 15, 2019, www.theguardian.com/world
/video/2019/jun/15/ice-cream-and-cake-vladimir-putin-hosts-birthday-party-for-xi
-jinping-video.

225   **nearly forty meetings:** Anton Troianovski and Steven Lee Myers, "Putin and Xi Show
United Front Amid Rising Tensions with U.S.," *The New York Times,* December 15, 2021,
www.nytimes.com/2021/12/15/world/asia/china-russia-summit-xi-putin.html.

225   **importance of territorial integrity:** "China Says It Respects Ukraine's Sovereignty and
Russia's Security Concerns," *Reuters,* February 25, 2022, www.reuters.com/world/europe
/china-says-it-respects-ukraines-sovereignty-russias-security-concerns-2022-02-25/.

227   **"lean to one side":** Mao Zedong, "On the People's Democratic Dictatorship: In Commemoration of the Twenty-eighth Anniversary of the Communist Party of China," The
Wilson Center Digital Archive, June 30, 1949, digitalarchive.wilsoncenter.org/document
/mao-zedong-peoples-democratic-dictatorship-commemoration-twenty-eighth
-anniversary.

227   **a heavier lift:** Odd Arne Westad, *Restless Empire: China and the World Since 1750* (New
York: Basic Books, 2014), 292–93.

227   **sent mainly pilots and air support**: Zhang Xiaoming, "China, the Soviet Union, and the
Korean War: From an Abortive Air War Plan to a Wartime Relationship," *Journal of Conflict Studies* 22, no. 1 (Spring 2002).

227   **refrained from publicly criticizing:** Tim Weiner, "Stalin-Mao Alliance Was Uneasy, Newly
Released Papers Show," *The New York Times,* December 10, 1995, www.nytimes.com/1995
/12/10/world/stalin-mao-alliance-was-uneasy-newly-released-papers-show.html.

227   **"Mao suffered from the same megalomania":** Nikita Khrushchev, *Khrushchev Remembers: The Last Testament,* translated and edited by Strobe Talbott (Boston: Little, Brown,
1974), 252.

228   **"War is war":** Nikita Khrushchev, *Khrushchev Remembers: The Last Testament,* translated
and edited by Strobe Talbott (Boston: Little, Brown, 1974), 255.

228   **"wouldn't even listen":** John Lewis Gaddis, *The Cold War: A New History* (London: The
Penguin Press, 2005), 142.

228   **"with a few atomic bombs":** John Lewis Gaddis, *The Cold War: A New History* (London:
The Penguin Press, 2005), 141.

229   **"They asked for aircraft":** Nikita Khrushchev, *Khrushchev Remembers: The Last Testament,*
translated and edited by Strobe Talbott (Boston: Little, Brown, 1974), 261–62.

229   **"is not such as to justify":** David E. Sanger and William J. Broad, "A New Superpower
Competition Between Beijing and Washington: China's Nuclear Buildup," *The New York
Times,* June 30, 2020, www.nytimes.com/2020/06/30/us/politics/trump-russia-china
-nuclear.html.

229   **"We cannot only pay attention":** Odd Arne Westad, *Restless Empire: China and the World
Since 1750* (New York: Basic Books, 2014), 345.

230   **"This is the most important communication":** Francis P. Sempa, "Nixon and China: 50
Years Later," *The Diplomat,* February 21, 2022, thediplomat.com/2022/02/nixon-and
-china-50-years-later/.

230   **"History has brought us together":** "Mao Zedong Meets Richard Nixon, February 21,
1972," USC US-China Institute, retrieved September 1, 2023, china.usc.edu/mao-zedong
-meets-richard-nixon-february-21-1972.

230   **China and the United States were collaborating:** Don Oberdorfer, "U.S. and China
Agree to Try to Counter Afghanistan Invasion," *The Washington Post,* March 21, 1980,

www.washingtonpost.com/archive/politics/1980/03/21/us-and-china-agree-to-try-to
-counter-afghanistan-invasion/7ca0028c-b50f-4aa5-be62-e0d8ad968093/.

230 **Following a 1979 conversation:** Michael Schuman, "When Biden Went to China," *The Atlantic,* August 11, 2022, www.theatlantic.com/international/archive/2022/08/joe-biden
-china-cold-war-1979-visit/671053/.

231 **Americans believed they benefited:** George Lardner Jr. and R. Jeffrey Smith, "Intelligence Ties Endure Despite U.S.-China Strain," *The Washington Post,* June 25, 1989, www
.washingtonpost.com/archive/politics/1989/06/25/intelligence-ties-endure-despite-us
-china-strain/f8b2789d-0f0c-4ea7-932b-9f4267a994a3/.

232 **some three thousand performers:** Jaclyn Diaz and Marco Storel, "The Winter Games Have Begun. See Photos and Highlights from the Opening Ceremony," National Public Radio, February 4, 2022, www.npr.org/sections/pictureshow/2022/02/04/1078160616
/the-2022-winter-olympics-open-with-a-colorful-but-subdued-ceremony-in-beijing.

232 **artificial intelligence and virtual reality:** Wang Yiming, "Technology Amazes the World at Beijing 2022 Opening Ceremony," China.org, February 9, 2022, www.china.org.cn/sports
/2022-02/09/content_78037680.htm.

233 **"kind of like sports prison":** Adam Kilgore, "The Closed Loop Eliminated Covid, and Joy, from the Olympics," *The Washington Post,* February 18, 2022, www.washingtonpost
.com/sports/olympics/2022/02/18/beijing-olympics-closed-loop/#.

12. SHORT INVASION, LONG WAR

237 **"This will probably be":** "Putin's War," *The New York Times,* August 21, 2023, www
.nytimes.com/interactive/2022/12/16/world/europe/russia-putin-war-failures-ukraine
.html.

240 **headed in the wrong direction:** "Political Attitudes of the Population of Ukraine: The Elections of the President of Ukraine and the Verkhovna Rada of Ukraine According to the Results of a Telephone Survey Conducted on January 20–21, 2022," Kyiv International Institute of Sociology, January 24, 2022, www.kiis.com.ua/?lang=ukr&cat=reports&id
=1090&page=1.

240 **"The Comedian-Turned-President":** Olga Rudenko, "The Comedian-Turned-President Is Seriously in Over His Head," *The New York Times,* February 21, 2022, www.nytimes
.com/2022/02/21/opinion/ukraine-russia-zelensky-putin.html.

241 **"This is the last time":** Paul Sonne, Isabelle Khurshudyan, Serhiy Morgunov, and Kosti-antyn Khudov, "Battle for Kyiv: Ukrainian Valor, Russian Blunders Combined to Save the Capital," *The Washington Post,* August 24, 2022, www.washingtonpost.com/national
-security/interactive/2022/kyiv-battle-ukraine-survival/.

241 **urban legend:** Glenn Kessler, "Zelensky's Famous Quote of 'Need Ammo, Not a Ride' Not Easily Confirmed," *The Washington Post,* March 6, 2022, www.washingtonpost.com
/politics/2022/03/06/zelenskys-famous-quote-need-ammo-not-ride-not-easily
-confirmed/.

241 **reduced to tears:** Paul Sonne, Isabelle Khurshudyan, Serhiy Morgunov, and Kostiantyn Khudov, "Battle for Kyiv: Ukrainian Valor, Russian Blunders Combined to Save the Capi-tal," *The Washington Post,* August 24, 2022, www.washingtonpost.com/national-security
/interactive/2022/kyiv-battle-ukraine-survival/.

241 **texted photos of destroyed Ukrainian homes:** Paul Sonne, Isabelle Khurshudyan, Serhiy Morgunov, and Kostiantyn Khudov, "Battle for Kyiv: Ukrainian Valor, Russian Blunders Combined to Save the Capital," *The Washington Post,* August 24, 2022, www.washington post.com/national-security/interactive/2022/kyiv-battle-ukraine-survival/.

242 **showing proof of date and time:** Valerie Hopkins, "In Video, a Defiant Zelensky Says, 'We Are Here,'" *The New York Times,* February 25, 2022, www.nytimes.com/2022/02/25
/world/europe/zelensky-speech-video.html.

242 **crack down on the journalists**: Alice Speri, "Ukraine Blocks Journalists from Front Lines with Escalating Censorship," *The Intercept,* June 22, 2023, theintercept.com/2023/06/22
/ukraine-war-journalists-press-credentials/.

242 **"Patrushev didn't qualify it":** "Putin's War," *The New York Times,* August 21, 2023, www

.nytimes.com/interactive/2022/12/16/world/europe/russia-putin-war-failures-ukraine
.html.

242   **reinvigorated, precision force:** See, e.g., "Russia Military Power Building a Military to
Support Great Power Aspirations," Defense Intelligence Agency, November 15, 2017,
www.dia.mil/Portals/110/Images/News/Military_Powers_Publications/Russia_Military
_Power_Report_2017.pdf.

243   **Ukraine spent just over a tenth:** "Ukraine and Russia's Militaries Are David and Goliath.
Here's How They Compare," CNN, February 25, 2022, www.cnn.com/2022/02/25
/europe/russia-ukraine-military-comparison-intl/index.html, citing "The Military Balance
2021," International Institute for Strategic Studies, February 2021, www.iiss.org
/publications/the-military-balance/the-military-balance-2021.

243   **"The use of military force against Ukraine":** Leonid Ivashov, "Address of the All-Russian
Officers' Assembly to the President and Citizens of the Russian Federation," January 31,
2021, available via the Wayback Machine at web.archive.org/web/20220305010813/https://
ooc.su/news/obrashhenie_obshherossijskogo_oficerskogo_sobranija_k_prezidentu_i
_grazhdanam_rossijskoj_federacii/2022-01-31-79.

244   **a generosity that didn't exist:** Deena Zaru, "Europe's Unified Welcome of Ukrainian Refugees Exposes 'Double Standard' for Nonwhite Asylum Seekers: Experts," ABC News,
March 8, 2022, abcnews.go.com/International/europes-unified-ukrainian-refugees-exposes
-double-standard-nonwhite/story?id=83251970.

244   **Bill Burns had warned Zelensky:** John Hudson, "CIA Director Holds Secret Meeting
with Zelensky on Russia's Next Steps," *The Washington Post,* January 19, 2023, www
.washingtonpost.com/national-security/2023/01/19/cia-william-burns-zelensky-ukraine
-russia/.

245   **using their own cellphones:** " 'Putin Is a Fool': Intercepted Calls Reveal Russian Army in
Disarray," *The New York Times,* September 28, 2022, www.nytimes.com/interactive/2022
/09/28/world/europe/russian-soldiers-phone-calls-ukraine.html.

246   **Russians failed at what:** Tara Copp, " 'The Convoy Is Stalled': Logistics Failures Slow Russian Advance, Pentagon Says," *Defense One,* March 2, 2022, www.defenseone.com/threats
/2022/03/convoy-stalled-logistics-failures-slow-russian-advance-pentagon-says/362666/.

247   **"consequences . . . such as you have never seen":** Address by the President of the Russian Federation, The Kremlin, February 24, 2022, en.kremlin.ru/events/president/news
/67843.

247   **looting everything they could:** Shaun Walker and Andrew Roth, " 'They Took Our
Clothes': Ukrainians Returning to Looted Homes," *The Guardian,* April 11, 2022, www
.theguardian.com/world/2022/apr/11/ukrainian-homes-looted-by-russian-soldiers; Shan-
non Vavra, "Russian Troops' Embarrassing Drunkfest in Ukraine Prompts Alcohol Bans,"
The Daily Beast, July 6, 2022, www.thedailybeast.com/russian-troops-are-getting-so-drunk
-in-ukraine-theyre-banned-from-buying-alcohol.

248   **with a familiar technique:** Patrick Howell O'Neill, "Russia Hacked an American Satellite
Company One Hour Before the Ukraine Invasion," *MIT Technology Review,* May 10, 2022,
www.technologyreview.com/2022/05/10/1051973/russia-hack-viasat-satellite-ukraine
-invasion/.

249   **"@elonmusk":** Mykhailo Fedorov (@FedorovMykhailo), Twitter, February 26, 2022,
twitter.com/FedorovMykhailo/status/1497543633293266944.

249   **hundreds of millions of dollars:** Dan Lamothe, "Pentagon Discloses It's Paying for Elon
Musk's Starlink Internet in Ukraine," *The Washington Post,* June 1, 2023, www.washington
post.com/national-security/2023/06/01/starlink-ukraine-pentagon-elon-musk/.

250   **utility of modern cyberweapons:** For more, see my book *The Perfect Weapon.*

250   **this time in southern Poland:** Eric Schmitt, "U.S. Army Troops Arrive in Poland to Reas-
sure Allies," *The New York Times,* February 17, 2022, www.nytimes.com/2022/02/17/us
/politics/us-troops-ukraine-russia.html.

251   **largest combined airborne training:** "Swift Response to Exercise NATO Airborne Forces
in Europe," U.S. Army Europe Public Affairs, August 21, 2015, www.army.mil/article
/153395/swift_response_to_exercise_nato_airborne_forces_in_europe.

253 **their would-be new president:** Michael Schwirtz, David E. Sanger, and Mark Landler, "Britain Says Moscow Is Plotting to Install a Pro-Russian Leader in Ukraine," *The New York Times*, January 24, 2022, www.nytimes.com/2022/01/22/world/europe/ukraine-russia-coup-britain.html.

253 **a more flexible hierarchy:** See, e.g., Jim Garamone, "NCOs Key to Ukrainian Military Successes Against Russia," U.S. Department of Defense, February 28, 2023, www.defense.gov/News/News-Stories/Article/Article/3313982/ncos-key-to-ukrainian-military-successes-against-russia/.

254 **equivalent to the entire cost:** Helene Cooper and Eric Schmitt, "Russian Troop Deaths Expose a Potential Weakness of Putin's Strategy," *The New York Times*, March 1, 2022, www.nytimes.com/2022/03/01/us/politics/russia-ukraine-war-deaths.html.

254 **30 Russian planes:** Sinéad Baker, "Ukraine Says Almost 6,000 Russians Have Been Killed in the First 6 Days of Their Invasion," *Business Insider*, March 2, 2022, www.businessinsider.com/ukraine-says-almost-6000-russians-killed-first-6-days-invasion-2022-3.

13. BOILING THE FROG

257 **"Obviously we are in a position":** "Hearing to Receive Testimony on Worldwide Threats," U.S. Senate Committee on Armed Services, May 10, 2022, www.armed-services.senate.gov/imo/media/doc/22-40_05-10-2022.pdf.

257 **"The United States provided intelligence":** Helene Cooper, Eric Schmitt, and Julian E. Barnes, "U.S. Intelligence Helped Ukraine Strike Russian Flagship, Officials Say," *The New York Times*, May 5, 2022, www.nytimes.com/2022/05/05/us/politics/moskva-russia-ship-ukraine-us.html.

258 **provision of U.S. targeting data:** Julian E. Barnes, Helene Cooper, and Eric Schmitt, "U.S. Intelligence Is Helping Ukraine Kill Russian Generals, Officials Say," *The New York Times*, May 4, 2022, www.nytimes.com/2022/05/04/us/politics/russia-generals-killed-ukraine.html.

259 **"He is a very, very, very calculating man":** "Remarks by President Biden at a Democratic National Committee Fundraiser," The White House, May 9, 2022, www.whitehouse.gov/briefing-room/speeches-remarks/2022/05/10/remarks-by-president-biden-at-a-democratic-national-committee-fundraiser-4/.

259 **crew of the *Moskva* famously demanded:** " 'Go Fuck Yourself,' Ukrainian Soldiers on Snake Island Tell Russian Ship—Audio," *The Guardian*, February 25, 2022, www.theguardian.com/world/video/2022/feb/25/go-fuck-yourself-ukrainian-soldiers-snake-island-russian-ship-before-being-killed-audio.

260 **"People are using the MacGyver metaphor":** Helene Cooper and Eric Schmitt, "The 'MacGyvered' Weapons in Ukraine's Arsenal," *The New York Times*, August 28, 2022, www.nytimes.com/2022/08/28/us/politics/ukraine-weapons-russia.html.

263 **turned out to be a false alarm:** Phil Mattingly, Kevin Liptak, Radina Gigova, Jim Sciutto, and Sophie Tanno, "Poland, NATO Say Missile that Killed Two Likely Fired by Ukraine Defending Against Russian Attack," CNN, November 16, 2022, www.cnn.com/2022/11/16/europe/poland-missile-russia-ukraine-investigation-wednesday-intl-hnk/index.html.

264 **state sponsor of terrorism:** Trevor Hunnicutt and Jarrett Renshaw, "Biden Will Not Declare Russia a State Sponsor of Terrorism—White House," Reuters, September 6, 2022, www.reuters.com/world/biden-will-not-declare-russia-state-sponsor-terrorism-white-house-2022-09-06/.

266 **Russians were using cluster munitions:** "Under Secretary of Defense for Policy Dr. Colin Kahl Holds Press Briefing," U.S. Department of Defense, July 7, 2023, www.defense.gov/News/Transcripts/Transcript/Article/3452000/under-secretary-of-defense-for-policy-dr-colin-kahl-holds-press-briefing/.

267 **target date for attacking Taiwan:** Edward Wong, David E. Sanger, and Amy Qin, "U.S. Officials Grow More Concerned About Potential Action by China on Taiwan," *The New York Times*, July 25, 2022, www.nytimes.com/2022/07/25/us/politics/china-taiwan-biden-pelosi.html.

267 **"It's *Groundhog Day*":** Anne Applebaum and Jeffrey Goldberg, "Liberation Without Vic-

tory," *The Atlantic,* April 15, 2022, www.theatlantic.com/international/archive/2022/04 /zelensky-kyiv-russia-war-ukrainian-survival-interview/629570/.

269 **"The core of the battle":** David E. Sanger, Eric Schmitt, and Julian E. Barnes, "The U.S. Is Sending Advanced Weapons to Ukraine. But Conditions Apply," *The New York Times,* June 1, 2022, www.nytimes.com/2022/06/01/us/politics/the-us-is-sending-advanced -weapons-to-ukraine-but-conditions-apply.html.

270 **avoided sending the longest-range missile:** Michael R. Gordon, "U.S. Altered Himars Rocket Launchers to Keep Ukraine from Firing Missiles into Russia," *The Wall Street Journal,* December 5, 2022, www.wsj.com/articles/u-s-altered-himars-rocket-launchers-to-keep -ukraine-from-firing-missiles-into-russia-11670214338.

270 **"The unfortunate conclusion":** David E. Sanger, Eric Schmitt, and Julian E. Barnes, "The U.S. Is Sending Advanced Weapons to Ukraine. But Conditions Apply," *The New York Times,* June 1, 2022, www.nytimes.com/2022/06/01/us/politics/the-us-is-sending-advanced -weapons-to-ukraine-but-conditions-apply.html.

270 **Six covert Ukrainian operatives had rented a sailboat:** Shane Harris and Souad Mekhennet, "U.S. Had Intelligence of Detailed Ukrainian Plan to Attack Nord Stream Pipeline," *The Washington Post,* June 6, 2023, www.washingtonpost.com/national-security/2023/06 /06/nord-stream-pipeline-explosion-ukraine-russia/.

274 **"It is important":** Anton Troianovski, Andrew E. Kramer, and Steven Erlanger, "6 Months into War, Ukraine and Russia Are Both Reshaped," *The New York Times,* August 24, 2022, www.nytimes.com/2022/08/24/world/europe/ukraine-russia-six-months.html.

274 **"shocked and bewildered":** "Russia Bids Farewell to Gorbachev in Low-Key Funeral Snubbed by Putin," *France 24,* September 3, 2022, www.france24.com/en/europe /20220903-russia-to-bid-farewell-to-gorbachev-in-low-key-funeral-snubbed-by-putin.

275 **"for so many":** Valerie Hopkins and Ivan Nechepurenko, "Russians Mourn Gorbachev in Silent Protest Against an Absent Putin," *The New York Times,* September 3, 2022, www .nytimes.com/2022/09/03/world/europe/mikhail-gorbachev-russia-funeral.html.

275 **"abandoning KGB officers":** Masha Gessen, "Mikhail Gorbachev, the Fundamentally Soviet Man," *The New Yorker,* August 31, 2022, www.newyorker.com/news/postscript /mikhail-gorbachev-the-fundamentally-soviet-man.

275 **"a politician and statesman":** "The Death of Mikhail Gorbachev: Putin Issues Brief Condolences as World Reacts to Gorbachev's Death," *The New York Times,* August 30, 2022, www.nytimes.com/live/2022/08/30/world/gorbachev-dead.

276 **"And who brought the freedom?":** Valerie Hopkins and Ivan Nechepurenko, "Russians Mourn Gorbachev in Silent Protest Against an Absent Putin," *The New York Times,* September 3, 2022, www.nytimes.com/2022/09/03/world/europe/mikhail-gorbachev-russia -funeral.html.

14. CROSSING THE LINE

277 **"Those who play with fire":** "President Xi Jinping Speaks with U.S. President Joe Biden on the Phone," Ministry of Foreign Affairs, People's Republic of China, July 28, 2022, www.fmprc.gov.cn/eng/zxxx_662805/202207/t20220729_10729593.html.

278 **roaming through Baghdad in a flak jacket:** "McCain Visits Iraq—His Eighth Trip There," NBC News, March 16, 2008, www.nbcnews.com/id/wbna23658239.

279 **There was even precedent:** Wenxin Fan, "China Tolerated Visit to Taiwan 25 Years Ago. It Now Sees That as Mistake," *The Wall Street Journal,* August 2, 2022, www.wsj.com /livecoverage/nancy-pelosi-taiwan-visit-china-us-tensions/card/china-tolerated-a-visit-to -taiwan-25-years-ago-it-now-sees-that-as-a-mistake—VNK7ekOOP0Coch9JrB03.

279 **"The military":** "Biden Says U.S. Military Thinks It's 'Not a Good Idea' for Pelosi to Visit Taiwan Now," CBS News, July 21, 2022, www.cbsnews.com/news/biden-us-military-not -a-good-idea-pelosi-visit-taiwan-now/.

280 **minor internet sensation:** Jackie Wattles, "Pelosi's Flight to Taiwan Was the Most-Tracked of All Time, Flightradar24 Says," *CNN,* August 3, 2022, www.cnn.com/2022/08/03/tech /pelosi-taiwan-flight-tracker/index.html.

280 **"plane would get shot down":** Thomas Maresca, "Pelosi: Pentagon Worried China Would

Shoot Down Her Plane if She Visits Taiwan," United Press International, July 22, 2022, www.upi.com/Top_News/World-News/2022/07/22/Nancy-Pelosi-Taiwan-warplane-shoot-down-visit/9431658470639/.

281   **"We are closely":** Liu Xiaoming (@AmbLiuXiaoMing), Twitter, August 1, 2022, twitter.com/AmbLiuXiaoMing/status/1554257955289268224.

281   **"If she dares":** "As Pelosi Starts Asia Tour, China Warns of Military Action If She Visits Taiwan," CBS News, August 1, 2022, www.cbsnews.com/news/pelosi-taiwan-asia-tour-china-warnings-military-action/.

281   **Xi and Biden spoke on the phone:** "Background Press Call on President Biden's Call with President Xi Jinping of the People's Republic of China," The White House, July 28, 2022, www.whitehouse.gov/briefing-room/press-briefings/2022/07/28/background-press-call-on-president-bidens-call-with-president-xi-jinping-of-the-peoples-republic-of-china/.

281   **"China firmly opposes":** Steven Nelson and Mark Moore, "China's Xi Warns Biden over Pelosi Taiwan Trip: 'Those Who Play with Fire Will Perish,'" *New York Post,* July 28, 2022, nypost.com/2022/07/28/chinas-xi-jinping-warns-biden-over-pelosi-taiwan-trip-those-who-play-with-fire-will-perish/.

282   **conversation was at Biden's request:** "President Xi Jinping Speaks with US President Joe Biden on the Phone," Ministry of Foreign Affairs, People's Republic of China, July 28, 2022, www.fmprc.gov.cn/eng/zxxx_662805/202207/t20220729_10729593.html.

283   **unprovoked invasion of the island:** Conor Finnegan, "Biden Claims No Change in Policy, but His Taiwan 'Gaffe' May Be No Accident: Analysis," ABC News, May 24, 2022, abcnews.go.com/Politics/biden-claims-change-policy-taiwan-gaffe-accident-analysis/story?id=84937418.

283   **Biden kept telling interviewers:** David Brunnstrom and Trevor Hunnicutt, "Biden Says U.S. Forces Would Defend Taiwan in the Event of a Chinese Invasion," Reuters, September 19, 2022, www.reuters.com/world/biden-says-us-forces-would-defend-taiwan-event-chinese-invasion-2022-09-18/.

284   **"sacred commitment":** "Full Transcript of ABC News' George Stephanopoulos' Interview with President Joe Biden," ABC News, August 19, 2021, abcnews.go.com/Politics/full-transcript-abc-news-george-stephanopoulos-interview-president/story?id=79535643.

284   **White House press aides:** "U.S. Position on Taiwan Remains Unchanged Despite Biden Comment, Official Says," CNBC, August 20, 2021, www.cnbc.com/2021/08/20/us-position-on-taiwan-unchanged-despite-biden-comment-official-says.html.

285   **"commitment":** Kevin Liptak, "Biden Vows to Protect Taiwan in Event of Chinese Attack," CNN, October 22, 2021, www.cnn.com/2021/10/21/politics/taiwan-china-biden-town-hall/index.html.

285   **would send troops:** Seung Min Kim, Michelle Ye Hee Lee, and Cleve R. Wootson Jr., "Biden Takes Aggressive Posture Toward China on Asia Trip," *The Washington Post,* May 23, 2022, www.washingtonpost.com/politics/2022/05/23/biden-japan-taiwan-china/.

285   **"if in fact":** "Biden Tells 60 Minutes U.S. Troops Would Defend Taiwan, but White House Says This Is Not Official U.S. Policy," CBS News, September 18, 2022, www.cbsnews.com/news/president-joe-biden-taiwan-60-minutes-2022-09-18/.

286   **"not provide military aid or advice":** "The President's News Conference," Harry S. Truman Presidential Library and Museum, Independence, Missouri, January 5, 1950, www.trumanlibrary.gov/library/public-papers/3/presidents-news-conference.

287   **teaching the Taiwanese:** Zen Soo, Li Tao, and Chua Kong Ho, "Taiwan Became Top Chip Manufacturer with U.S. Help. Can It Stay There?" *South China Morning Post,* September 11, 2019, www.scmp.com/tech/tech-leaders-and-founders/article/3026766/taiwan-became-top-chip-manufacturer-us-help-can-it.

289   **"Warmonger Pelosi get out of Taiwan":** Hui-An Ho and Summer Chen, "Nancy Pelosi's Visit Sparks New Wave of Misinformation in Taiwan," Taiwan FactCheck Center, August 13, 2022, tfc-taiwan.org.tw/articles/8018; Sarah Wu and Eduardo Baptista, "From 7-11s to Train Stations, Cyber Attacks Plague Taiwan over Pelosi Visit," Reuters, August 4, 2022, www.reuters.com/technology/7-11s-train-stations-cyber-attacks-plague-taiwan-over-pelosi-visit-2022-08-04/.

290   **Some claimed:** "Clip of Military Aircraft Flying at Sea Dates to at Least April 2021,"
      Reuters, August 2, 2022, www.reuters.com/article/factcheck-pelosi-taiwan/fact-check-clip
      -of-military-aircraft-flying-at-sea-dates-to-at-least-april-2021-idUSL1N2ZE1J6.

290   **air defense identification zone:** Abbie Shull, "21 Chinese Warplanes, Including More
      Than a Dozen Fighter Aircraft, Flew Through Taiwan's Air Defense Zone on the Day of
      Pelosi's Visit," *Business Insider,* August 2, 2022, www.businessinsider.com/chinese-warplanes
      -enter-taiwan-air-defense-zone-pelosi-visit-2022-8.

290   **parade-like atmosphere:** Jason Pan, "Pelosi's Visit: Groups Hold Rival Rallies Outside
      Legislature," *Taipei Times,* August 4, 2022, www.taipeitimes.com/News/taiwan/archives
      /2022/08/04/2003782957.

290   **"Russia's invasion of Ukraine":** "President Tsai Meets U.S. Delegation Led by House of
      Representatives Speaker Nancy Pelosi," Office of the President, Republic of China (Tai-
      wan), August 3, 2022, english.president.gov.tw/NEWS/6292.

290   **"Our solidarity with you":** "Transcript of Pelosi Remarks at Press Event Following Bilat-
      eral Meeting with President Tsai Ing-wen of Taiwan," Press Office of Nancy Pelosi 11th
      District, pelosi.house.gov/news/press-releases/transcript-of-pelosi-remarks-at-press-event
      -following-bilateral-meeting-with.

292   **summoned Burns:** John Feng, "China Summons U.S. Ambassador amid Backlash over
      Pelosi's Taiwan Visit," *Newsweek,* August 3, 2022, www.newsweek.com/china-summons
      -american-ambassador-nicholas-burns-nancy-pelosi-taiwan-visit-1730456.

293   **"For quite some time":** "The Ministry of Foreign Affairs Summons U.S. Ambassador to
      China to Lodge Stern Representations and Strong Protests Against Nancy Pelosi's Visit to
      China's Taiwan," Ministry of Foreign Affairs, People's Republic of China, August 3, 2022,
      www.fmprc.gov.cn/eng/wjbxw/202208/t20220803_10733167.html.

15. THE NUCLEAR PARADOX

296   **"Above all, while defending":** "Commencement Address at American University, Wash-
      ington, D.C., June 10, 1963," John F. Kennedy Presidential Library and Museum, Boston,
      Massachusetts, June 10, 1963, www.jfklibrary.org/archives/other-resources/john-f-kennedy
      -speeches/american-university-19630610.

297   **"first time since the Cuban Missile Crisis":** "Remarks by President Biden at Democratic
      Senatorial Campaign Committee Reception," The White House, October 6, 2022, www.
      whitehouse.gov/briefing-room/speeches-remarks/2022/10/06/remarks-by-president-biden
      -at-democratic-senatorial-campaign-committee-reception/.

298   **Americans who had created:** "Putin Vows to Defend Illegally Seized Regions in Ukraine
      by 'All Available Means,'" *PBS NewsHour,* September 30, 2022, www.pbs.org/newshour
      /show/putin-vows-to-defend-illegally-seized-regions-in-ukraine-by-all-available-means.

301   **"We have a concept":** "Russia Would Only Use Nuclear Weapons Faced with 'Existential
      Threat': Kremlin," France 24, March 22, 2022, www.france24.com/en/live-news/20220322
      -russia-would-only-use-nuclear-weapons-faced-with-existential-threat-kremlin.

302   **"I'm not naïve":** "Remarks by President Barack Obama in Prague as Delivered," The White
      House, April 5, 2009, obamawhitehouse.archives.gov/the-press-office/remarks-president
      -barack-obama-prague-delivered.

303   **protect their thyroids:** Josh Lederman, "Radiation Tablets Are Handed Out near Ukrai-
      nian Nuclear Plant as Fears of a Leak Mount," CNBC, August 26, 2022, www.nbcnews
      .com/news/world/russia-ukraine-war-zaporizhzhia-nuclear-plant-radiation-fears-iodine
      -rcna45041.

303   **"The idea that a nuclear power plant":** David E. Sanger, "Russia's Occupation of Nuclear
      Plant Gives Moscow a New Way to Intimidate," *The New York Times,* August 30, 2022,
      www.nytimes.com/2022/08/30/us/politics/russia-ukraine-nuclear-plant.html.

307   **"there can be no winners":** Pavel Byrkin, "Putin Says 'There Can Be No Winners in a
      Nuclear War and It Should Never Be Unleashed,'" NBC News, August 1, 2022, www
      .nbcnews.com/news/world/putin-says-can-no-winners-nuclear-war-never-unleashed
      -rcna40964.

307   **According to a study:** Mykhaylo Zabrodskyi, Jack Watling, Oleksandr V. Danylyuk, and Nick Reynolds, "Preliminary Lessons in Conventional Warfighting from Russia's Invasion of Ukraine: February–July 2022," Royal United Services Institute for Defence and Security Studies, November 30, 2022, p. 11, www.rusi.org/explore-our-research/publications /special-resources/preliminary-lessons-conventional-warfighting-russias-invasion-ukraine -february-july-2022.

307   **single most important facility:** Andrian Prokip, "Why the Zaporizhzhia Nuclear Power Plant Matters . . . for the Whole World," Woodrow Wilson International Center for Scholars, Washington, D.C., September 19, 2022, www.wilsoncenter.org/blog-post/why -zaporizhzhia-nuclear-power-plant-mattersfor-whole-world.

308   **"If Ukraine acquires weapons":** David E. Sanger, "Putin Spins a Conspiracy Theory That Ukraine Is on a Path to Nuclear Weapons," *The New York Times,* February 23, 2022, www .nytimes.com/2022/02/23/us/politics/putin-ukraine-nuclear-weapons.html.

308   **not-so-secret mission:** John Hudson and Missy Ryan, "Blinken, in Kyiv, Pledges to Support Ukraine 'for as Long as It Takes,'" *The Washington Post,* September 8, 2022, www .washingtonpost.com/national-security/2022/09/08/blinken-visit-kyiv-security-aid/.

309   **held off in ordering a general mobilization:** Charles Maynes, "Putin Is Mobilizing Hundreds of Thousands of Russian Reservists to Fight in Ukraine," National Public Radio, September 21, 2022, www.npr.org/2022/09/21/1124215514/putin-announces-a-partial -military-mobilization-for-russian-citizens.

309   **"Run away, go home":** Olga Voitovych, Jo Shelley, Tara John, Olha Konovalova, and Rebecca Wright, "Ukraine Claims Early Success in Counteroffensive as Zelensky Vows to 'Chase' Russians to the Border," CNN, August 30, 2022, edition.cnn.com/2022/08/30 /europe/ukraine-kherson-counteroffensive-intl/index.html.

310   **"We lost five people":** John Hudson, "Wounded Ukrainian Soldiers Reveal Steep Toll of Kherson Offensive," *The Washington Post,* September 7, 2022, www.washingtonpost.com /world/2022/09/07/ukraine-kherson-offensive-casualties-ammunition/.

310   **made up for in ingenuity:** Isabelle Khurshudyan, Paul Sonne, Serhiy Morgunov, and Kamila Hrabchuk, "Inside the Ukrainian Counteroffensive That Shocked Putin and Reshaped the War," *The Washington Post,* www.washingtonpost.com/world/2022/12/29 /ukraine-offensive-kharkiv-kherson-donetsk/.

310   **"We saw the fact":** Julian E. Barnes, Eric Schmitt, and Helene Cooper, "The Critical Moment Behind Ukraine's Rapid Advance," *The New York Times,* September 13, 2022, www .nytimes.com/2022/09/13/us/politics/ukraine-russia-pentagon.html.

310   **Ukrainian planners estimated:** Isabelle Khurshudyan, Paul Sonne, Serhiy Morgunov, and Kamila Hrabchuk, "Inside the Ukrainian Counteroffensive That Shocked Putin and Reshaped the War," *The Washington Post,* www.washingtonpost.com/world/2022/12/29 /ukraine-offensive-kharkiv-kherson-donetsk/.

311   **"We know this is a pivotal moment":** John Hudson and Missy Ryan, "Blinken, in Kyiv, Pledges to Support Ukraine 'for as Long as It Takes,'" *The Washington Post,* September 8, 2022, www.washingtonpost.com/national-security/2022/09/08/blinken-visit-kyiv-security -aid/.

311   **Ukraine was still missing:** Barbara Plett Usher, "Blinken Flies In to Rally Western Support for Ukraine War," BBC, September 8, 2022, www.bbc.com/news/world-europe-62841392.

311   **"Do you still think":** Sana Noor Haq, Kostan Nechyporenko, and Anna Chernova, "'Without Gas or Without You? Without You': Zelensky's Words for Russia as Ukraine Sweeps Through Northeast," CNN, September 12, 2022, www.cnn.com/2022/09/12 /europe/zelensky-message-kharkiv-russia-ukraine-intl/index.html.

314   **thousands of military-eligible men:** Kareem Fahim, Zeynep Karatas, and Robyn Dixon, "The Russian Men Fleeing Mobilization, and Leaving Everything Behind," *The Washington Post,* September 28, 2022, www.washingtonpost.com/world/2022/09/28/russia-turkey -partial-mobilization-ukraine/.

314   **"to weaken":** "Read Putin's National Address on a Partial Military Mobilization," *The Washington Post,* September 21, 2022, www.washingtonpost.com/world/2022/09/21 /putin-speech-russia-ukraine-war-mobilization/.

314   **"If the territorial integrity":** W. J. Hennigan, " 'This Is Not a Bluff.' Putin Raises Specter of Nuclear Weapons Following Battlefield Losses," *Time,* September 21, 2022, time.com /6215610/putin-nuclear-weapons-threat/.

315   **"The demagogues across":** "Medvedev Raises Spectre of Russian Nuclear Strike on Ukraine," *U.S. News,* September 27, 2022, www.usnews.com/news/world/articles/2022 -09-27/russias-medvedev-warns-west-that-nuclear-threat-is-not-a-bluff.

316   **"humiliating defeat":** Daryl G. Kimball, "JFK's American University Speech Echoes Through Time," Arms Control Association, www.armscontrol.org/act/2013-06/jfk%E2 %80%99s-american-university-speech-echoes-through-time.

319   **"oppose the use":** "Update: Xi Meets German Chancellor Olaf Scholz," Xinhua, November 5, 2022, english.news.cn/20221105/bdffa606c7924d1aa9134c7dc700cfca/c.html.

319   **"all available means":** Jessie Yeung and Katharina Krebs, "Ukraine War Is Going to 'Take a While,' Putin Says as He Warns Nuclear Risk Is Increasing," CNN, December 8, 2022, www.cnn.com/2022/12/07/europe/putin-ukraine-russia-nuclear-intl-hnk/index.html.

16. A HIGH FENCE FOR A SMALL YARD

320   **"Finally, we are protecting":** "Remarks by National Security Advisor Jake Sullivan on Renewing American Economic Leadership at the Brookings Institution," The White House, April 27, 2023, www.whitehouse.gov/briefing-room/speeches-remarks/2023/04 /27/remarks-by-national-security-advisor-jake-sullivan-on-renewing-american-economic -leadership-at-the-brookings-institution/.

321   **nearly 90 percent:** David Sacks and Chris Miller, "The War Over the World's Most Critical Technology: A Conversation with Chris Miller," Council of Foreign Relations, January 3, 2023, www.cfr.org/blog/war-over-worlds-most-critical-technology-conversation-chris-miller.

321   **stuffed with 19 billion transistors:** Tae Kim, "Apple Unveils 'Fastest' iPhone Chip Ever: A17 Pro," *Barron's,* September 12, 2023, www.barrons.com/livecoverage/apple-iphone -15-event-today/card/apple-unveils-fastest-iphone-chip-ever-a17-pro-V3tciSdIDnh0 ABqlC7Nn.

324   **"Tell me":** Chris Miller, *Chip War: The Fight for the World's Most Critical Technology* (New York: Scribner, 2022). Miller's history of the Taiwanese chip industry includes a compelling, deep account of TSMC's origins.

325   **America had fallen from 37 percent:** "Fact Sheet: Biden-Harris Administration Bringing Semiconductor Manufacturing Back to America," The White House, January 21, 2022, www.whitehouse.gov/briefing-room/statements-releases/2022/01/21/fact-sheet-biden -harris-administration-bringing-semiconductor-manufacturing-back-to-america-2/.

326   **"Only the paranoid survive":** Andrew S. Grove, *Only the Paranoid Survive* (New York: Penguin Random House, 1999).

328   **Its revenues and profit margins:** "Annual Net Revenue of Taiwan Semiconductor Manufacturing Company from 2015 and 2022," *Statista,* accessed October 1, 2023, www .statista.com/statistics/1177807/taiwan-semiconductor-manufacturing-company-net -revenue/.

328   **TSMC's market capitalization:** As of 2023: "The 100 Largest Companies in the World by Market Capitalization in 2023," *Statista,* August 30, 2023, www.statista.com/statistics /263264/top-companies-in-the-world-by-market-capitalization/.

329   **"China will not invade Taiwan":** John Liu and Paul Mozur, "Why TSMC Will Keep Its Roots in Taiwan, Even as It Goes Global," *The New York Times,* August 4, 2023, www .nytimes.com/2023/08/04/technology/tsmc-mark-liu.html.

329   **he didn't care for the location:** Jim Geraghty, "Why Warren Buffett's Taiwan Pullout Has Unsettling Implications," *The Washington Post,* May 24, 2023, www.washingtonpost.com /opinions/2023/05/24/warren-buffett-taiwan-exit-china/.

330   **would be no groundbreaking:** Ken Thomas and Asa Fitch, "Intel Delays Groundbreaking Ceremony for Ohio Plant amid Uncertainty over Chips Legislation," *The Wall Street Journal,* June 23, 2022, www.wsj.com/articles/intel-delays-groundbreaking-ceremony-for-ohio -plant-amid-uncertainty-over-chips-legislation-11656004874.

330   **"We are doing our part":** "President Biden Delivers Remarks on Semiconductor Manu-facturing in the United States," The White House, January 21, 2022, YouTube video, www.youtube.com/watch?v=qRUtepiZRK4&t=2079s.

331   **"bribe":** "Sanders Opposes All Blank Checks to Chip Companies," U.S. Senator for Ver-mont Bernie Sanders, July 15, 2022, www.sanders.senate.gov/press-releases/news-sanders-opposes-all-blank-checks-to-chip-companies/.

331   **"Around the globe":** David E. Sanger, Catie Edmondson, David McCabe, and Thomas Kaplan, "Senate Poised to Pass Huge Industrial Policy Bill to Counter China," The New York Times, June 7, 2021, www.nytimes.com/2021/06/07/us/politics/senate-china-semiconductors.html.

333   **unemployment had plummeted:** Katharine Q. Seelye, "After Long Economic Slide, Rhode Island Lures New Business," The New York Times, March 13, 2017, www.nytimes.com/2017/03/13/us/raimondo-rhode-island-economy-new-business.html.

333   **"corporatist Democrat":** Dylan Scott, "The Rhode Island Governor's Race, the Left's Next Chance for an Upset, Explained," Vox, September 12, 2018, www.vox.com/policy-and-politics/2018/9/11/17832502/rhode-island-primary-elections-2018-gina-raimondo-matt-brown; Katharine Q. Seelye, "After Long Economic Slide, Rhode Island Lures New Business," The New York Times, March 13, 2017, www.nytimes.com/2017/03/13/us/raimondo-rhode-island-economy-new-business.html.

334   **could be directed at Huawei:** "Securing the Information and Communications Technol-ogy and Services Supply Chain," Executive Office of the President, May 17, 2019, www.federalregister.gov/documents/2019/05/17/2019-10538/securing-the-information-and-communications-technology-and-services-supply-chain.

334   **added to a sanctions list:** Jill Disis, "U.S. Bans China's Top Chipmaker from Using Amer-ican Technology," CNN, December 18, 2020, www.cnn.com/2020/12/18/tech/smic-us-sanctions-intl-hnk/index.html.

334   **supply were ever to get choked off:** Nik Popli, "How a Closed-Door National Security Briefing Convinced Senators to Pass the Chips Bill," Time, July 28, 2022, time.com/6201675/chips-bill-national-security/.

335   **"Made in China 2025" strategy:** "Made in China 2025," Institute for Security and Development Policy, June 2018, isdp.eu/content/uploads/2018/06/Made-in-China-Backgrounder.pdf.

335   **"the government could afford":** David E. Sanger, "China Has Leapfrogged the U.S. in Key Technologies. Can a New Law Help?" The New York Times, July 28, 2022, www.nytimes.com/2022/07/28/us/politics/us-china-semiconductors.html.

335   **"The Chinese government":** David E. Sanger, "China Has Leapfrogged the U.S. in Key Technologies. Can a New Law Help?" The New York Times, July 28, 2022, www.nytimes.com/2022/07/28/us/politics/us-china-semiconductors.html.

336   **the West's most sophisticated chips:** Ana Swanson and Edward Wong, "With New Crackdown, Biden Wages Global Campaign on Chinese Technology," The New York Times, October 13, 2022, www.nytimes.com/2022/10/13/us/politics/biden-china-technology-semiconductors.html.

337   **During the Cold War:** "Evolution: 1913–1995," U.S. Department of Commerce, re-trieved September 26, 2023, www.commerce.gov/about/history/evolution.

338   **"Western countries led by":** Keith Bradsher, "China's Leader, with Rare Bluntness, Blames U.S. Containment for Troubles," The New York Times, March 7, 2023, www.nytimes.com/2023/03/07/world/asia/china-us-xi-jinping.html.

338   **"We don't communicate about this":** Cagan Koc and Jenny Leonard, "Biden Wins Deal with Netherlands, Japan on China Chip Export Limit," Bloomberg, January 27, 2023, www.bloomberg.com/news/articles/2023-01-27/biden-wins-deal-with-dutch-japan-on-china-chip-export-controls#xj4y7vzkg.

340   **quiet meetings:** Alexandra Alper, Toby Sterling, and Stephen Nellis, "Trump Adminis-tration Pressed Dutch Hard to Cancel China Chip-Equipment Sale: Sources," Reu-ters, January 6, 2020, www.reuters.com/article/us-asml-holding-usa-china-insight/trump

-administration-pressed-dutch-hard-to-cancel-china-chip-equipment-sale-sources
-idUSKBN1Z50HN.

340   **"If they cannot get":** Cagan Koc, "ASML Says Chip Controls Will Push China to Create
Own Technology," *Bloomberg,* January 25, 2023, www.bloomberg.com/news/articles/2023
-01-25/asml-says-chip-controls-will-push-china-to-create-own-technology#xj4y7vzkg.

341   **a seven-nanometer chip:** David E. Sanger, "China Has Leapfrogged the U.S. in Key Technologies. Can a New Law Help?" *The New York Times,* July 28, 2022, www.nytimes.com
/2022/07/28/us/politics/us-china-semiconductors.html.

341   **same circuit dimensions:** Aimee Picchi, "Huawei Is Releasing a Faster Phone to Compete
with Apple. Here's Why the U.S. Is Worried," CBS News, September 8, 2023, www
.cbsnews.com/news/huawei-new-phone-mate-60-pro-apple-stock/.

17. "DON'T MAKE US CHOOSE"

342   **"Everywhere I go":** "US Will Not Make Philippines Choose Sides over China Rivalry,"
Radio Free Asia, January 20, 2023, www.rfa.org/english/news/china/usphilippines-0120
2023145200.html.

344   **Xi swept in:** Kawala Xie, "During Xi's Visit to Middle East, China and Saudi Arabia Sign
34 Energy and Investment Deals," *South China Morning Post,* December 8, 2022, www
.scmp.com/news/china/diplomacy/article/3202503/during-xis-visit-middle-east-china
-and-saudi-arabia-sign-34-energy-and-investment-deals.

344   **"a Starbucks and a Coffee Bean":** David E. Sanger and Peter Baker, "As Biden Reaches
Out to Mideast Dictators, His Eyes Are on China and Russia," *The New York Times,*
July 16, 2022, www.nytimes.com/2022/07/16/world/middleeast/biden-saudi-arabia-china
-russia.html.

345   *run* **by Chinese law enforcement:** Guy Rosen, "Raising Online Defenses Through Transparency and Collaboration," Meta, August 29, 2023, about.fb.com/news/2023/08/raising
-online-defenses/.

346   **"The U.S. sees Xi":** Kevin Rudd, *The Avoidable War: The Danger of a Catastrophic Conflict
Between the U.S. and Xi Jinping's China* (New York: Public Affairs, 2022).

347   **"The instinct to counter every Chinese initiative":** Jessica Chen Weiss, "The China
Trap," *Foreign Affairs,* August 18, 2022, www.foreignaffairs.com/china/china-trap-us
-foreign-policy-zero-sum-competition.

349   **Sogavare argued:** Daniel Hurst, "Solomon Islands PM Suggests Australia's Reaction to
China Security Deal Is Hysterical and Hypocritical," *The Guardian,* April 29, 2022, www
.theguardian.com/world/2022/apr/29/solomon-islands-pm-suggests-australias-reaction-to
-china-security-deal-is-hysterical-and-hypocritical.

350   **"We simply left":** Charles Stuart Kennedy and Ambassador Robert William Farrand,
"Foreign Affairs Oral History Project," Association for Diplomatic Studies and Training,
2005, www.adst.org/OH%20TOCs/Farrand,%20Robert%20W.toc.pdf.

351   **investments in the Pacific:** Zongyuan Zoe Liu, "What the China–Solomon Islands Pact
Means for the U.S. and South Pacific," Council on Foreign Relations, May 4, 2022, www
.cfr.org/in-brief/china-solomon-islands-security-pact-us-south-pacific.

351   **seven sports facilities:** Sydney Bauer, "The 2023 Pacific Games Wrap Small Countries in
Big Power Struggles," *Foreign Policy,* February 3, 2023, foreignpolicy.com/2023/02/03
/solomon-islands-pacific-games-china-united-states-australia/.

351   **$730 million in Chinese aid:** Zongyuan Zoe Liu, "What the China–Solomon Islands
Pact Means for the U.S. and South Pacific," Council on Foreign Relations, May 4, 2022,
www.cfr.org/in-brief/china-solomon-islands-security-pact-us-south-pacific.

352   **April 2022 article:** "BRI Projects Being Carried Out as Usual in Pacific Island Nations
Despite Western Smear Campaign," *The Global Times,* April 27, 2022, www.globaltimes.cn
/page/202204/1260552.shtml.

352   **"win/win cooperation":** "China President Xi Says Goal of Belt and Road Is Advance
'Win-Win Cooperation,' " Reuters, April 25, 2019, www.reuters.com/article/china-silkroad
-xi/china-president-xi-says-goal-of-belt-and-road-is-advance-win-win-cooperation
-idUKB9N21901J.

352 **researchers found:** Rob Garver, "China's Belt and Road Initiative Is About Profit, not Development, Study Finds," Voice of America News, October 1, 2021, www.voanews.com /a/china-s-belt-and-road-initiative-is-about-profit-not-development-study-finds/6252992 .html.

352 **longer to complete:** Rob Garver, "China's Belt and Road Initiative Is About Profit, Not Development, Study Finds," *Voice of America News,* October 1, 2021, www.voanews.com /a/china-s-belt-and-road-initiative-is-about-profit-not-development-study-finds/6252992 .html.

352 **government debts soared:** Ammar A. Malik, Bradley Parks, Brooke Russell, Joyce Jiahui Lin, Katherine Walsh, Kyra Solomon, Sheng Zhang, Thai-Binh Elston, and Seth Goodman, "Banking on the Belt and Road: Insights from a New Global Dataset of 13,427 Chinese Development Projects," AidData, College of William and Mary, September 2021, pp 51–52.

352 **reports were spreading:** Ryan Dube and Gabriele Steinhauser, "China's Global Mega-Projects Are Falling Apart," *The Wall Street Journal,* January 20, 2023, www.wsj.com /articles/china-global-mega-projects-infrastructure-falling-apart-11674166180.

353 **unprofitable port was leased:** Deborah Brautigam and Meg Rithmire, "The Chinese 'Debt Trap' Is a Myth," *The Atlantic,* February 6, 2021, www.theatlantic.com/international /archive/2021/02/china-debt-trap-diplomacy/617953/.

354 **"nothing came out of":** "Solomon Islands Leader Says He Skipped Biden Summit to Avoid 'Lecture,'" *Reuters,* September 27, 2023, www.reuters.com/world/solomon-islands -leader-says-he-skipped-biden-summit-avoid-lecture-2023-09-27/.

355 **"I absolutely believe":** Katie Rogers and Chris Buckley, "With Tensions Mounting, Biden and Xi Try a Warmer Tone," *The New York Times,* November 14, 2022, www.nytimes.com /2022/11/14/world/asia/biden-xi-bali-g20.html.

358 **"The sovereignty, independence":** Munich Security Conference (@MunSecConf), Twitter, February 23, 2022, twitter.com/MunSecConf/status/1496482251826245126.

359 **Wang's message was different:** "MSC 2023: Chinese Top Diplomat Wang Yi Announces Peace Initiative for Ukraine," BR24, via YouTube, February 18, 2023, www.youtube.com /watch?v=OrunZDxYDzo.

18. SEARCHING FOR ENDGAMES

365 **"Go back to Kennan's long cable":** "Secretary Antony J. Blinken Virtual Conversation on 'Russia's War on Ukraine: One Year Later' with Jeffrey Goldberg of *The Atlantic,*" U.S. Department of State, February 23, 2023, www.state.gov/secretary-antony-j-blinken-virtual -conversation-on-russias-war-on-ukraine-one-year-later-with-jeffrey-goldberg-of-the -atlantic/.

366 **"we should not be providing the Ukrainians systems":** David E. Sanger, Eric Schmitt, and Helene Cooper, "How Biden Reluctantly Agreed to Send Tanks to Ukraine," *The New York Times,* January 25, 2023, www.nytimes.com/2023/01/25/us/politics/biden-abrams -tanks-ukraine-russia.html.

367 **"What is stunning":** David E. Sanger, Eric Schmitt, and Helene Cooper, "How Biden Reluctantly Agreed to Send Tanks to Ukraine," *The New York Times,* January 25, 2023, www.nytimes.com/2023/01/25/us/politics/biden-abrams-tanks-ukraine-russia.html.

369 **brought a trophy from the battle:** "Zelensky Presents Ukraine Battle Flag to U.S. Congress," BBC, December 22, 2022, www.bbc.com/news/av/world-us-canada-64061196.

369 **"Every war has two end games":** Victor Pinchuk Foundation, "6th Ukrainian Lunch on the Margins of the Munich Security Conference," February 18, 2023, www.youtube.com /watch?v=k19IZm3yhCo.

370 **"to see Russia weakened":** Missy Ryan and Annabelle Timsit, "U.S. Wants Russian Military 'Weakened' from Ukraine Invasion, Austin Says," *The Washington Post,* April 25, 2022, www.washingtonpost.com/world/2022/04/25/russia-weakened-lloyd-austin-ukraine-visit/.

370 **"crimes against humanity":** Edward Helmore and Reuters, "Russia Has Committed Crimes Against Humanity, Says Kamala Harris," *The Guardian,* February 18, 2023, www .theguardian.com/world/2023/feb/18/us-accuses-russia-crimes-against-humanity-kamala -harris-ukraine.

371   **assisted by a mild winter:** Aura Sabadus, "Putin Failed to Freeze Europe but Russia's Energy War Will Continue," Atlantic Council, March 14, 2023, www.atlanticcouncil.org /blogs/ukrainealert/putin-failed-to-freeze-europe-but-russias-energy-war-will-continue/.

371   **not selling it weapons:** Vivian Salama, William Mauldin, and Nancy A. Youssef, "U.S. Considers Release of Intelligence on China's Potential Arms Transfer to Russia," *The Wall Street Journal,* February 23, 2023, www.wsj.com/articles/u-s-considers-release-of-intelligence -on-chinas-potential-arms-transfer-to-russia-8e353933.

371   **"Vladimir Putin has done more":** "Secretary Antony J. Blinken with German Foreign Minister Annalena Baerbock and Ukrainian Foreign Minister Dmytro Kuleba at the Munich Security Conference," U.S. Department of State, February 18, 2023, www.state.gov /secretary-antony-j-blinken-with-german-foreign-minister-annalena-baerbock-and -ukrainian-foreign-minister-dmytro-kuleba-at-the-munich-security-conference/.

371   **in jeopardy:** Helene Cooper, Eric Schmitt, and Thomas Gibbons-Neff, "Soaring Death Toll Gives Grim Insight into Russian Tactics," *The New York Times,* February 2, 2023, www .nytimes.com/2023/02/02/us/politics/ukraine-russia-casualties.html.

371   **two hundred thousand casualties:** Ann M. Simmons and Nancy A. Youssef, "Russia's Casualties in Ukraine Near 200,000," *The Wall Street Journal,* February 4, 2023, www.wsj .com/articles/russias-casualties-in-ukraine-near-200-000-11675509981.

371   **Raytheon's shoulder-fired Stinger missiles:** Eric Lipton, Michael Crowley, and John Ismay, "Military Spending Surges, Creating New Boom for Arms Makers," *The New York Times,* December 18, 2022, www.nytimes.com/2022/12/18/us/politics/defense-contractors -ukraine-russia.html.

372   **largely not battle-worthy:** Erika Solomon, Steven Erlanger, and Christopher F. Schuetze, "Scrounging for Tanks for Ukraine, Europe's Armies Come Up Short," *The New York Times,* February 28, 2023, www.nytimes.com/2023/02/28/world/europe/ukraine-tanks .html.

372   **commit European and American troops:** Edward Wong and Lara Jakes, "NATO Won't Let Ukraine Join Soon. Here's Why." *The New York Times,* January 13, 2022, www.nytimes .com/2022/01/13/us/politics/nato-ukraine.html.

372   **"there's more sympathy":** Steven Erlanger, "The E.U. Offered to Embrace Ukraine, but Now What?" *The New York Times,* March 3, 2023, www.nytimes.com/2023/03/03/world /europe/ukraine-eu-nato.html.

373   **that had not happened:** Denis Volkov and Andrei Kolesnikov, "My Country, Right or Wrong: Russian Public Opinion on Ukraine," Carnegie Endowment for International Peace, September 7, 2022, carnegieendowment.org/2022/09/07/my-country-right-or -wrong-russian-public-opinion-on-ukraine-pub-87803.

373   **the ruble to "rubble":** Kate Davidson, "Biden Turned the Ruble into Rubble. Then It Quickly Came Back." *Politico,* March 31, 2022, www.politico.com/news/2022/03/31 /ruble-recovery-russia-biden-sanctions-00021850.

373   **"Zelensky has publicly stated":** Kevin Baron, "Ukraine Victory Unlikely This Year, Milley Says," *Defense One,* March 31, 2023, www.defenseone.com/threats/2023/03/ukraine -victory-unlikely-year-milley-says/384681/.

374   **"in the best possible position":** "Administrator Samantha Power and NSA Jake Sullivan on CNN Town Hall—Russia's Invasion of Ukraine: One Year Later," USAID, February 23, 2023, www.usaid.gov/news-information/speeches/feb-23-2023-administrator-samantha -power-and-nsa-jake-sullivan-cnn-town-hall-russias-invasion-ukraine-one-year-later.

374   **"They have one goal":** Guy Faulconbridge, "Putin Casts War as a Battle for Russia's Survival," Reuters, February 26, 2023, www.reuters.com/world/europe/putin-russia-must -take-into-account-nato-nuclear-capability-state-tv-2023-02-26/.

376   **journey into Kyiv:** Peter Baker and Michael D. Shear, "Biden's Surreal and Secretive Journey into a War Zone," *The New York Times,* February 20, 2023, www.nytimes.com/2023 /02/20/us/politics/biden-kyiv-ukraine.html.

376   **"at a huge moment":** Details provided per the February 20, 2023, White House Pool Report, written by *Wall Street Journal* reporter Sabrina Siddiqui.

377   **"the right signal"**: Stephen Neukam, "Graham: Biden Visit to Ukraine Sends 'Right Signal' at 'Right Time,'" *The Hill,* February 20, 2023, thehill.com/policy/international/3866695-graham-biden-visit-to-ukraine-sends-right-signal-at-right-time/.

377   **"The president's now spent"**: Chris Stein, "Republicans Criticize Biden's Trip to Kyiv as Putin Withdraws from Nuclear Treaty," *The Guardian,* February 21, 2023, www.theguardian.com/us-news/2023/feb/21/republicans-reaction-biden-trip-kyiv-ukraine-putin.

377   **"Putin never, ever"**: Asawin Suebsaeng, "Trump Defends Putin as Biden Visits War-Torn Ukraine," *Rolling Stone,* February 20, 2023, www.rollingstone.com/politics/politics-news/trump-putin-biden-ukraine-russia-1234683165/.

377   **"tricked"**: "Putin's Address to Russia's Parliament," February 21, 2023, en.kremlin.ru/events/president/news/70565.

378   **other affronts to conservative orthodox values:** "Putin's Address to Russia's Parliament," February 21, 2023, en.kremlin.ru/events/president/news/70565.

379   **"One year ago"**: "Remarks by President Biden Ahead of the One-Year Anniversary of Russia's Brutal and Unprovoked Invasion of Ukraine," The White House, February 21, 2023, www.whitehouse.gov/briefing-room/speeches-remarks/2023/02/21/remarks-by-president-biden-ahead-of-the-one-year-anniversary-of-russias-brutal-and-unprovoked-invasion-of-ukraine/.

380   **deal with the devil:** Cora Engelbrecht, "'Finlandization' of Ukraine Is Part of the Diplomatic Discourse. But What Does That Mean?" *The New York Times,* February 8, 2022, www.nytimes.com/2022/02/08/world/europe/ukraine-russia-finlandization.html.

381   **"room to maneuver and freedom of choice"**: "President of the Republic of Finland Sauli Niinistö's New Year's Speech on 1 January 2022," President of the Republic of Finland, January 1, 2022, www.presidentti.fi/en/speeches/president-of-the-republic-of-finland-sauli-niinistos-new-years-speech-on-1-january-2022/.

383   **Russian embassy in Berlin:** "Destroyed Russian T-72 Placed near the Russian Embassy in Berlin," *Militarnyi,* accessed October 1, 2023, mil.in.ua/en/news/destroyed-russian-t-72-placed-near-the-russian-embassy-in-berlin/.

383   **politicians held a counterprotest:** Kate Connolly, "Thousands Protest in Berlin Against Giving Weapons to Ukraine," *The Guardian,* February 25, 2023, www.theguardian.com/world/2023/feb/25/thousands-protest-in-berlin-against-giving-weapons-to-ukraine.

384   **Germany's far-left movement:** "Protest in Berlin over Arming Ukraine Against Russia Draws Thousands," Reuters, February 25, 2023, www.reuters.com/world/europe/protest-berlin-over-arming-ukraine-against-russia-draws-thousands-2023-02-25/.

384   **standoff in the heart of Berlin:** "German Peace Activists Park Rusty Tank Outside Russian Embassy," Reuters, February 24, 2023, www.reuters.com/world/europe/german-activists-park-destroyed-rusting-tank-outside-russian-embassy-2023-02-24/; Yuras Karmanau, Liudas Dapkus, and Vanessa Gera, "Russians Place Flowers at Burnt Out Tanks in Baltic Cities," Associated Press, March 1, 2023, apnews.com/article/russia-ukraine-war-tanks-baltics-5dec53101f37366a49cbb1e1f816405f.

19. THE DIGITAL WAR—AND ITS LIMITS

386   **"Ukraine is not fighting on behalf"**: Susan B. Glasser, "Jake Sullivan's Trial by Combat," *The New Yorker,* October 9, 2023, www.newyorker.com/magazine/2023/10/16/trial-by-combat.

387   **"Ukraine is the best"**: Lara Jakes, "For Western Weapons, the Ukraine War Is a Beta Test," *The New York Times,* November 15, 2022, www.nytimes.com/2022/11/15/world/europe/ukraine-weapons.html.

388   **Russian electronic warfare operations:** Alex Marquardt, Natasha Bertrand, and Zachary Cohen, "Russia's Jamming of U.S.-Provided Rocket Systems Complicates Ukraine's War Effort," CNN, May 6, 2023, www.cnn.com/2023/05/05/politics/russia-jamming-himars-rockets-ukraine/index.html.

389   **"The Russians have been more nimble"**: Paul Mozur and Aaron Krolik, "The Invisible War in Ukraine Being Fought Over Radio Waves," *The New York Times,* November 19,

2023, www.nytimes.com/2023/11/19/technology/russia-ukraine-electronic-warfare-drone
-signals.html.

391   **"delivering roughly 10 percent":** Garrett M. Graff, "The Man Who Speaks Softly—and
Commands a Big Cyber Army," October 13, 2020, www.wired.com/story/general-paul
-nakasone-cyber-command-nsa/.

392   **Google had entered into:** Kate Conger and Dell Cameron, "Google Is Helping the Pentagon Build AI for Drones," *Gizmodo,* March 6, 2018, gizmodo.com/google-is-helping-the
-pentagon-build-ai-for-drones-1823464533.

393   **"avoid at ALL COSTS":** Scott Shane, Cade Metz, and Daisuke Wakabayashi, "How a
Pentagon Contract Became an Identity Crisis for Google," *The New York Times,* May 30,
2018, www.nytimes.com/2018/05/30/technology/google-project-maven-pentagon.html.

394   **bankrupted its parent firm:** Davey Alba, "Peter Thiel Just Got His Wish: Gawker Is Shutting Down," *Wired,* August 18, 2016, www.wired.com/2016/08/peter-thiel-just-got-wish
-gawker-shutting/.

395   **bring Silicon Valley engineers:** Jessi Hempel, "DOD Head Ashton Carter Enlists Silicon
Valley to Transform the Military," *Wired,* November 18, 2015, www.wired.com/2015/11
/secretary-of-defense-ashton-carter/.

395   **organization had initiated six dozen programs:** "DIU Making Transformative Impact
Five Years In," *DOD News,* August 27, 2020, www.defense.gov/News/News-Stories/Article
/Article/2327021/diu-making-transformative-impact-five-years-in/.

397   **situational awareness software:** Sam Schechner and Daniel Michaels, "Ukraine Has Dig-
itized Its Fighting Forces on a Shoestring," *The Wall Street Journal,* January 3, 2023, www
.wsj.com/articles/ukraine-has-digitized-its-fighting-forces-on-a-shoestring-11672741405
?ns=prod/accounts-wsj.

397   **investment proved critical:** Greg Miller and Isabelle Khurshudyan, "Ukrainian Spies with
Deep Ties to CIA Wage Shadow War Against Russia," *The Washington Post,* October 23,
2023, www.washingtonpost.com/world/2023/10/23/ukraine-cia-shadow-war-russia/.

397   **"wizard war":** David Ignatius, "How the Algorithm Tipped the Balance in Ukraine," *The
Washington Post,* December 19, 2022, www.washingtonpost.com/opinions/2022/12/19
/palantir-algorithm-data-ukraine-war/.

398   **"Starlink is indeed the blood":** Adam Satariano, Scott Reinhard, Cade Metz, Sheera
Frenkel, and Malika Khurana, "Elon Musk's Unmatched Power in the Stars," *The New York
Times,* July 28, 2023, www.nytimes.com/interactive/2023/07/28/business/starlink.html.

398   **new military system:** Jeff Schogol, "Army Combat Advisors Testing Military Version of
Elon Musk's Starlink," *Task and Purpose,* October 9, 2023, taskandpurpose.com/news
/army-sfab-starshield-spacex-elon-musk/.

398   **"a useful one":** Elon Musk (@elonmusk), Twitter, July 8, 2018, twitter.com/elonmusk
/status/1016005381686943744.

399   **world's most powerful satellite network:** Walter Isaacson, "'How Am I in This War?': The
Untold Story of Elon Musk's Support for Ukraine," *The Washington Post,* September 7,
2023, www.washingtonpost.com/opinions/2023/09/07/elon-musk-starlink-ukraine-russia
-invasion.

400   **"For a country that":** "Our AI Future: Hopes and Hurdles Ahead," Harvard Kennedy
School: Institute of Politics, October 11, 2023, iop.harvard.edu/events/our-ai-future
-hopes-and-hurdles-ahead

403   **"Conventional wisdom might posit":** Eric Schmidt and Will Roper, "Ukraine Shows
How Drones Are Changing Warfare," *Time,* September 28, 2023, time.com/collection
/time100-voices/6317661/eric-schmidt-drones-warfare-voices/.

404   **"America still benefits":** "Deputy Secretary of Defense Kathleen Hicks Keynote Address:
'The Urgency to Innovate' (As Delivered)," U.S. Department of Defense, August 28, 2023,
www.defense.gov/News/Speeches/Speech/Article/3507156/deputy-secretary-of-defense
-kathleen-hicks-keynote-address-the-urgency-to-innov/.

404   **"We're not creating":** "Deputy Secretary of Defense Kathleen Hicks' Remarks: 'Unpack-
ing the Replicator Initiative' at the Defense News Conference (As Delivered)," U.S. De-

partment of Defense, September 6, 2023, www.defense.gov/News/Speeches/Speech/Article
/3517213/deputy-secretary-of-defense-kathleen-hicks-remarks-unpacking-the-replicator
-ini/.

20. THE DOWNWARD SPIRAL

406 **"Planet Earth is big":** Amy Hawkins, " 'Planet Earth Is Big Enough for Two': Biden and
     Xi Meet for First Time in a Year," *The Guardian,* November 15, 2023, www.theguardian
     .com/us-news/2023/nov/15/joe-biden-xi-jinping-san-francisco-china-apec.

407 **"That video":** "DCIA Fireside Chat with William Burns," Aspen Security Forum, July 20,
     2023, www.cia.gov/static/598a62b34629a8120fb16d68e440aa15/Director_Burns_Aspen
     _Security_Forum_Transcript_07202023.pdf

408 **"We went to demonstrate":** Valerie Hopkins, "In His First Remarks Since His Revolt,
     Prigozhin Claims He Wasn't Trying to Overthrow Putin," *New York Times,* June 26, 2022,
     www.nytimes.com/live/2023/06/26/world/russia-ukraine-news.

408 **"Where is the . . . ammunition?":** Paul Kirby, "Yevgeny Prigozhin: Wagner Group Boss
     Says He Will Pull Fighters out of Bakhmut," BBC, May 5, 2023, www.bbc.com/news
     /world-europe-65493008.

409 **"just like in 1917":** Rob Picheta and Mariya Knight, "Wagner Chief Warns Russians
     Could Revolt If Invasion Continues to Struggle," CNN, May 25, 2023, www.cnn.com
     /2023/05/24/europe/wagner-prigozhin-russia-manpower-ukraine-intl/index.html.

409 **had stopped talking to him:** Matthew Loh, "Wagner Boss Says the Kremlin Won't Talk to
     Him Anymore After He Complained That Russia Isn't Giving His Troops Enough Ammo,"
     Business Insider, March 10, 2023, www.businessinsider.com/wagner-boss-yevgeny-prigozhin
     -vladimir-putin-cut-him-off-2023-3.

409 **"Wagner is absolutely completely subordinate":** Paul Sonne, "Wagner Founder Rebuffs
     Order Over Fighter Contracts with Russian Military," *The New York Times,* June 11, 2023,
     www.nytimes.com/2023/06/11/world/europe/wagner-russia-defense-ministry-contract
     .html.

409 **"If I were Prigozhin":** "DCIA Fireside Chat with William Burns," Aspen Security Forum
     2023, July 20, 2023, www.cia.gov/static/598a62b34629a8120fb16d68e440aa15/Director
     _Burns_Aspen_Security_Forum_Transcript_07202023.pdf.

410 **"a talented man":** Anna Chernova, Rob Picheta, and Tara John, "Putin Says Prigozhin
     Was 'Talented Man' Who 'Made Serious Mistakes' in First Comments Since Plane Crash,"
     CNN, August 24, 2023, www.cnn.com/2023/08/24/europe/putin-prigozhin-comments
     -intl/index.html.

411 **"Ukraine isn't ready":** Steven Erlanger, "What NATO Said About Ukraine: Highlights of
     the Alliance's Communiqué," *The New York Times,* July 11, 2023, www.nytimes.com/2023
     /07/12/world/europe/nato-ukraine-membership.html.

412 **"It's unprecedented and absurd":** Volodymyr Zelenskyy / Володимир Зеленський
     (@ZelenskyyUa), Twitter, July 11, 2023, twitter.com/ZelenskyyUa/status/16787076748
     11187200.

413 **2.2 percent:** "IMF Raises Russia's 2023 GDP Growth Outlook to 2.2% from 1.5%," *In-
     terfax,* October 10, 2023, interfax.com/newsroom/top-stories/95277/.

415 **"red lines":** "Russia Says Longer-Range U.S. Missiles for Kyiv Would Cross Red Line,"
     Reuters, September 15, 2022,www.reuters.com/world/europe/russia-says-longer-range-us
     -missiles-kyiv-would-cross-red-line-2022-09-15/.

418 **number of rich emigrants:** Evan Osnos, "China's Age of Malaise," October 23, 2023,
     www.newyorker.com/magazine/2023/10/30/chinas-age-of-malaise.

419 **renting the chips' computing power:** William Alan Reinsch, Matthew Schleich, and
     Thibault Denamiel, "Insight into the U.S. Semiconductor Export Controls Update," Cen-
     ter for Strategic and International Studies, October 20, 2023, www.csis.org/analysis/insight
     -us-semiconductor-export-controls-update.

419 **Nvidia, Qualcomm, and Intel:** Tripp Mickle, David McCabe, and Ana Swanson, "How
     the Big Chip Makers Are Pushing Back on Biden's China Agenda," *The New York Times,*

October 5, 2023, www.nytimes.com/2023/10/05/technology/chip-makers-china-lobbying
.html.

419   **"We have become unable to sell":** Yoon Young-sil, "U.S. Semiconductor Firms Concerned
over Additional Possible Export Controls against China," *Business Korea,* July 19, 2023,
www.businesskorea.co.kr/news/articleView.html?idxno=118640#google_vignette.

420   **"this silly balloon":** "Remarks by President Biden in a Press Conference," The White
House, May 21, 2023, www.whitehouse.gov/briefing-room/speeches-remarks/2023/05/21
/remarks-by-president-biden-in-a-press-conference/.

420   **"guardrails":** "The Sources of American Power: A Foreign Policy for a Changed World,"
Foreign Affairs, October 24, 2023, www.foreignaffairs.com/united-states/sources-american
-power-biden-jake-sullivan.

422   **lengthy public advisory:** "People's Republic of China State Sponsored Cyber Actor Living Off the Land to Evade Detection," CISA, May 24, 2023, www.cisa.gov/news-events
/cybersecurity-advisories/aa23-144a.

422   **more than seventeen hundred flight incursions:** Robert A. Manning, "Is a Chinese Invasion of Taiwan the Most Likely Scenario?" The Stimson Center, October 27, 2023, www
.stimson.org/2023/is-a-chinese-invasion-of-taiwan-the-most-likely-scenario/.

424   **"We expect China":** "The Sources of American Power: A Foreign Policy for a Changed
World," *Foreign Affairs,* October 24, 2023, www.foreignaffairs.com/united-states/sources
-american-power-biden-jake-sullivan.

EPILOGUE

437   **"The United States now confronts graver threats":** Robert M. Gates, "The Dysfunctional
Superpower," *Foreign Affairs,* September 29, 2023, www.foreignaffairs.com/united-states
/robert-gates-america-china-russia-dysfunctional-superpower.

439   **he turned sanctions evasion into an art form:** Paul Sonne and Rebecca R. Ruiz, "How
Putin Turned a Western Boycott into a Bonanza," *The New York Times,* December 17,
2023.

439   **Privately, he was sending signals:** Anton Troianovski, Adam Entous, and Julian E. Barnes,
"Putin Quietly Signals He Is Open to a Ceasefire in Ukraine," *The New York Times,*
December 23, 2023, www.nytimes.com/2023/12/23/world/europe/putin-russia-ukraine
-war-cease-fire.html.

440   **"as long as we can":** Biden's shift of language came in a press conference with Zelensky.
www.whitehouse.gov/briefing-room/speeches-remarks/2023/12/13/remarks-by-president
-biden-and-president-zelenskyy-of-ukraine-in-joint-press-conference-2/. See also: Susan B.
Glasser, "A Congressional Christmas Gift to Putin," *The New Yorker,* December 14, 2023.

441   **Biden's aides made a good case:** Susan Glasser, Jake Sullivan's Trial By Combat," *The New
Yorker,* October 16, 2023, www.newyorker.com/magazine/2023/10/16/trial-by-combat.

443   **"dealt with":** Danielle Wallace, "McConnell Calls China, Russia, Iran New 'Axis of Evil'
That U.S. Must Deal With: 'This Is an Emergency,'" Fox News, October 22, 2023, www
.foxnews.com/politics/mcconnell-calls-china-russia-iran-new-axis-evil-us-must-deal
-emergency.

446   **"through the mountain pass":** Andrew Browne, "Kissinger Warns U.S. and China Are on
the 'Precipice,'" *Bloomberg,* November 17, 2021, www.bloomberg.com/news/newsletters
/2021-11-17/what-s-happening-in-the-world-economy-u-s-and-china-on-precipice.

448   **"Anywhere else, attacking civilian infrastructure":** Neil MacFarquhar, "Developing
World Sees Double Standard in West's Actions in Gaza and Ukraine," *The New York Times,*
October 23, 2022, www.nytimes.com/2023/10/23/us/ukraine-gaza-global-south-hypocrisy
.html.

448   **"Trump whiplashes":** Kori Schake, "The Case for Conservative Internationalism," *Foreign
Affairs,* January/February 2024, www.foreignaffairs.com/united-states/case-conservative
-internationalism.

INDEX

About the Authors

David E. Sanger is the White House and National Security Correspondent for *The New York Times.* In more than four decades at the *Times,* he was a member of three teams that won the Pulitzer Prize. He has served as Tokyo bureau chief, chief economic correspondent, and chief Washington correspondent for the *Times.* He teaches national security at the Kennedy School of Government and is a contributor to CNN. A graduate of Harvard College, he lives in Washington, D.C.

Mary K. Brooks is a Public Policy Fellow at the Woodrow Wilson International Center for Scholars. Previously, she was a fellow for cybersecurity and emerging threats at the R Street Institute, a researcher on *The Perfect Weapon* (2018), and an associate producer for the HBO documentary of the same name. She was an Aspen Strategy Group Rising Leader in 2022 and is a graduate of Harvard College.